Life of Her Most Gracious Majesty Queen Victoria: All Volumes
By Sarah Tytler

PREFACE.

I have been asked to write a few words of preface to this work.

If the life-long friendship of my mother with her Majesty, which gained for me the honour of often seeing the Queen, or a deep feeling of loyalty and affection for our sovereign, which is shared by all her subjects, be accepted as a qualification, I gratefully respond to the call, but I feel that no written words of mine can add value to the following pages.

Looking over some papers lately, I found the following note on a sketch which I had accidentally met with in Windsor Castle—a coloured chalk drawing, a mere study of one of the Queen's hands, by Sir David Wilkie, probably made for his picture now in the corridor of the Castle, representing the first council of Victoria. Of this sketch I wrote as follows:—

"I was looking in one of the private rooms at Windsor Castle at a chalk sketch, by Sir David Wilkie, of a fair, soft, long-fingered, dimpled hand, with a graceful wrist attached to a rounded arm. 'Only a woman's hand,' might Swift, had he seen that sketch, have written below. Only a sketch of a woman's hand; but what memories that sketch recalls! How many years ago Wilkie drew it I know not: that great artist died in the month of June, 1841, so that more than forty years have passed, at least, since he made that drawing. The hand that limned this work has long ago suffered 'a sea change.' And the hand which he portrayed? That is still among the living—still occupied with dispensing aid and comfort to the suffering and the afflicted, for the original is that of a Queen, beloved as widely as her realms extend—the best of sovereigns, the kindest-hearted of women."

To write the life of Queen Victoria is a task which many authors might well have felt incompetent to undertake. To succeed in writing it is an honour of which any author may well be proud. This honour I humbly think has been realised in the work of which these poor lines may form the preface.

RONALD GOWER.

CHAPTER I. SIXTY-THREE YEARS SINCE.

The 24th of May, 1819, was a memorable and happy day for England, though like many such days, it was little noticed at the time. Sixty-three years since! Do many of us quite realise what England was like then; how much it differed from the England of to-day, even though some of us have lived as many years? It is worth while devoting a chapter to an attempt to recall that England.

A famous novel had for its second heading, "'Tis sixty years since." That novel—"Waverley"—was published anonymously just five years before 1819, and, we need not say, proved an era in literature. The sixty years behind him to which Walter Scott—a man of forty-three—looked over his shoulder, carried him as far back as the landing of Prince Charlie in Moidart, and the brief romantic campaign of the '45, with the Jacobite songs which embalmed it and kept it fresh in Scotch memories.

The wounds dealt at Waterloo still throbbed and burnt on occasions in 1819. Many a scarred veteran and limping subaltern continued the heroes of remote towns and villages, or starred it at Bath or Tunbridge. The warlike fever, which had so long raged in the country, even when ruined manufacturers and starving mechanics were praying for peace or leading bread-riots, had but partially abated; because whatever wrong to trade, and misery to the poor, closed ports and war prices might have meant, the people still depended upon their armed defenders, and in the hardest adversity found the heart to share their triumphs, to illuminate cities, light bonfires, cheer lustily, and not grudge parliamentary grants to the country's protectors. The "Eagle" was caged on his rock in the ocean, to eat his heart out in less than half-a-dozen years. Still there was no saying what might happen, and the sight of a red coat and a sword remained cheering—especially to soft hearts.

The commercial world was slowly recovering from its dire distress, but its weavers and mechanics were blazing up into fierce, futile struggle with the powers by which masses of the people believed themselves oppressed. If the men of war had no longer anything to do abroad, there was great fear that work might be found for them at home. All Europe was looking on in the expectation that England was about to follow the example of France, and indulge in a revolution on its own account—not bloodless this time.

Rarely since the wars of the Commonwealth had high treason been so much in men's mouths as it was in Great Britain during this and the following year. Sedition smouldered and burst into flame—not in one place alone, but at every point of the compass. The mischief was not confined to a single class; it prevailed mostly among the starving operatives, but it also fired minds of quite another calibre. Rash, generous spirits in every rank became affected, especially after an encounter between the blinded, maddened mobs and the military, when dragoons and yeomanry charged with drawn swords, and women and children went down under the horses' hoofs. Great riotous meetings were dispersed by force at Manchester, Birmingham, Paisley. Political trials went on at every assize. Bands of men lay in York, Lancaster, and Warwick gaols. At Stockport Sir Charles Wolseley told a crowd armed with bludgeons that he had been in Paris at the beginning of the French Revolution, that he was the first man who made a kick at the Bastille, and that he hoped he should be present at the demolition of another Bastille.

On the 22nd of August, 1819, Sir Francis Burdett wrote to his electors at Westminster: "....It seems our fathers were not such fools as some would make us believe in opposing the establishment of a standing army and sending King William's Dutch guards out of the country. Yet would to heaven they had been Dutchmen, or Switzers, or Russians, or Hanoverians, or anything rather than Englishmen who have done such deeds. What! kill men unarmed, unresisting; and, gracious God! women too, disfigured, maimed, cut down, and trampled on by dragoons! Is this England? This a Christian land—a land of freedom?"

For this, and a great deal more, Sir Francis, after a protracted trial, was sentenced to pay a fine of two thousand pounds and to be imprisoned for three months in the Marshalsea of the Court. In the Cato Street conspiracy the notorious Arthur Thistlewood and his fellow-conspirators planned to assassinate the whole of the Cabinet Ministers when they were dining at Lord Harrowby's house, in Grosvenor Square. Forgery and sheep-stealing were still punishable by death. Truly these were times of trouble in England.

In London a serious difficulty presented itself when Queen Charlotte grew old and ailing, and there was no royal lady, not merely to hold a Drawing-room, but to lend the necessary touch of dignity and decorum to the gaieties of the season. The exigency lent a new impetus to the famous balls at Almack's. An anonymous novel of the day, full of society scandal and satire, described the despotic sway of the lady patronesses, the struggles and intrigues for vouchers, and the distinguished crowd when the object was obtained. The earlier hours, alas! only gave longer time for the drinking habits of the Regency.

It is a little difficult to understand what young people did with themselves in the country when lawn-tennis and croquet were not. There was archery for the few, and a good deal more amateur gardening and walking, with field-sports, of course, for the lads.

The theatre in 1819 was more popular than it showed itself twenty years later. Every country town of any pretensions, in addition to its assembly rooms had its theatre, which reared good actors, to which provincial tours brought London stars. Genteel comedy was not past its perfection. Adaptations of the Waverley novels, with musical dramas and melodramas, drew great houses. Miss O'Neill had just retired, but Ellen Tree was making a success, and Macready was already distinguished in his profession. Still the excellence and prestige of the stage had declined incontestably since the days of Mrs. Siddons and John Kemble. Edmund Kean, though he did much for tragedy, had a short time to do it in, and was not equal in his passion of genius to the sustained majesty of the sister and brother.

In the same way, the painters' art hovered on the borders of a brilliant epoch. For Lawrence, with his courtly brush, which preferred flattery to truth and cloying suavity to noble simplicity, was not worthy to be named in the same breath with Reynolds. Raeburn came nearer, but his reputation was Scotch. Blake in his inspiration was regarded, not without reason, as a madman. Flaxman called for classic taste to appreciate him; and the fame of English art would have suffered both at home and abroad if a simple, manly lad had not quitted a Scotch manse and sailed from Leith to London, bringing with him indelible memories of the humour and the pathos of peasant life, and reproducing them with such graphic fidelity, power, and tenderness that the whole world has heard of David Wilkie.

The pause between sunset and sunrise, the interregnum which signifies that a phase in some department of the world's history has passed away as a day is done, and a new development of human experience is about to present itself, was over in literature. The romantic period had succeeded the classic. Scott, Coleridge, Southey (Wordsworth stands alone), Byron, Shelley, Keats, Campbell, Moore, were all in the field as poets, carrying the young world with them, and replacing their immediate predecessors, Cowper, Thompson, Young, Beattie, and others of less note.

Sir Walter Scott had also risen high above the horizon as a poet, and still higher as a novelist. A great start in periodical literature was made in 1802 by the establishment of The Edinburgh

Review, under Jeffrey and Sydney Smith, and again in 1817 by the publication of Blackmoods Magazine, with Christopher North for its editor, and Lockhart, De Quincey, Hogg, and Delta among its earlier contributors. The people's friend, Charles Knight, was still editing The Windsor and Eton Express.

In 1819 Sir Humphry Davy was the most popular exponent of science, Sir James Mackintosh of philosophy. In politics, above the thunderstorm of discontent, there was again the pause which anticipates a fresh advance. The great Whig and Tory statesmen, Charles James Fox and William Pitt, were dead in 1806, and their mantles did not fall immediately on fit successors. The abolition of the slave-trade, for which Wilberforce, Zachary Macaulay, and Clarkson had fought gallantly and devotedly, was accomplished. But the Catholic Emancipation Bill was still to work its way in the teeth of bitter "No Popery" traditions, and Earl Grey's Reform Bill had not yet seen the light.

George III.'s long reign was drawing to a close. What changes it had seen from the War of American Independence to Waterloo! What woeful personal contrasts since the honest, kindly, comely lad, in his simple kingliness, rode out in the summer sunshine past Holland House, where lady Sarah Lennox was making hay on the lawn, to the days when the blind, mad old king sat in bodily and mental darkness, isolated from the wife and children he had loved so well, immured in his distant palace-rooms in royal Windsor.

His silver beard o'er a bosom spread
  Unvexed by life's commotion,
Like a yearly lengthening snow-drift shed
  On the calm of a frozen ocean:
Still o'er him oblivion's waters lay,
  Though the stream of time kept flowing
When they spoke of our King, 'twas but to say
  That the old man's strength was going.
At intervals thus the waves disgorge,
  By weakness rent asunder,
A piece of the wreck of the Royal George
  For the people's pity and wonder.

Lady Sarah, too, became blind in her age, and, alas! she had trodden darker paths than any prepared for her feet by the visitation of God.

Queen Charlotte had come with her sense and spirit, and ruled for more than fifty years over a pure Court in England. The German princess of sixteen, with her spare little person and large mouth which prevented her from being comely, and her solitary accomplishment of playing on the harpsichord with as much correctness and taste as if she had been taught by Mr. Handel himself, had identified herself with the nation, so that no suspicion of foreign proclivities ever attached to her. Queen Charlotte bore her trials gravely; while those who came nearest to her could tell that she was not only a fierce little dragon of virtue, as she has been described, but a loving woman, full of love's wounds and scars.

The family of George III. and Queen Charlotte consisted of seven sons and his daughters, besides two sons who died in infancy.

George, Prince of Wales, married, 1795, his cousin, Princess Caroline of Brunswick, daughter of the reigning Duke and of Princess Augusta, sister of George III. The Prince and Princess of Wales separated soon after their marriage. Their only child was Princess Charlotte of Wales.

Frederick, Duke of York, married, 1791, Princess Frederica, daughter of the reigning King of Prussia. The couple were childless.

William, Duke of Clarence, married, 1818, Princess Adelaide, of Saxe-Meiningen. Two daughters were born to them, but both died in infancy.

Edward, Duke of Kent, married, 1818, Princess Victoria of Saxe-Coburg, widow of the Prince of Leiningen. Their only child is QUEEN VICTORIA.

Ernest, Duke of Cumberland, married, 1815, Princess Frederica of Mecklenburg-Strelitz, widow, first of Prince Frederick Louis of Prussia, and second, of the Prince of Saliris-Braunfels. Their only child was George V., King of Hanover.

Augustus, Duke of Sussex, married morganatically.

Adolphus, Duke of Cambridge, married, 1818, Princess Augusta of Hesse-Cassel, daughter of the Landgrave of Hesse-Cassel. They had three children—George, Duke of Cambridge; Princess Augusta, Duchess of Mecklenburg-Strelitz; and Princess Mary, Duchess of Teck.

The daughters of King George and Queen Charlotte were:—

The Princess Royal, married, 1797, the Prince, afterwards King, of Wurtemberg. Childless.

Princess Augusta, unmarried.

Princess Elizabeth, married, 1818, the Landgrave of Hesse-Homburg. Childless.

Princess Mary, married, 1816, her cousin, William, Duke of Gloucester. Childless.

Princess Sophia, unmarried.

Princess Amelia, unmarried.

In 1817 the pathetic idyl, wrought out amidst harsh discord, had found its earthly close in the family vault at Windsor, amidst the lamentations of the whole nation. Princess Charlotte, the candid, fearless, affectionate girl, whose youth had been clouded by the sins and follies of others, but to whom the country had turned as to a stay for the future—fragile, indeed, yet still full of hope—had wedded well, known a year of blissful companionship, and then died in giving birth to a dead heir. It is sixty-five years since that November day, when the bonfires, ready to be lit at every town "cross," on every hill-side, remained dark and cold. Men looked at each other in blank dismay; women wept for the blushing, smiling bride, who had driven with her grandmother through the park on her way to be married not so many months before. There are comparatively few people alive who had come to man's or woman's estate when the shock was experienced; but we have all heard from our predecessors the story which has lent to Claremont a tender, pensive grace, especially for royal young pairs.

Old Queen Charlotte nerved herself to make a last public appearance on the 11th of July, 1818, four months before her death. It was in her presence, at Kew, that a royal marriage and re-marriage were celebrated that day. The Duke of Clarence was married to Princess Adelaide of Saxe-Meiningen, and the Duke of Kent was re-married, in strict accordance with the English Royal Marriage Act, to Princess Victoria of Saxe-Coburg, the widowed Princess of Leiningen. The last couple had been already united at Coburg in the month of May. The Archbishop of Canterbury and the Bishop of London officiated at the double ceremony. The brides were given away by the Prince Regent. The Queen retired immediately afterwards. But a grand banquet, at which the Prince Regent presided, was given at six o'clock in the evening. An hour later the

Duke and Duchess of Kent drove off in her brother, Prince Leopold's, carriage to Claremont. Of the two bridegrooms we have glimpses from Baron Stockmar, a shrewd observer, who was no flatterer.

The Duke of Clarence, at fifty-three years of age, was the "smallest and least good-looking of the brothers, decidedly like his mother, as talkative as the rest;" and we may add that he was also endowed with a sailor-like frankness, cordiality, and good humour, which did not, however, prevent stormy ebullitions of temper, that recommended him to the nation of that day as a specimen of a princely blue-jacket. Since the navy was not considered a school of manners, he was excused for the absence of much culture or refinement.

The Duke of Kent, at fifty-one, was a tall, stately man, of soldierlike bearing, already inclined to great corpulence.... He had seen much of the world, and of men. His manner in society was pleasant and easy. He was not without ability and culture, and he possessed great activity. His dependents complained of his strictness and pedantic love of order.... The Duke was well aware that his influence was but small, but this did not prevent him from forwarding the petitions he received whenever it was possible, with his own recommendation, to the public departments.... Liberal political principles were at that time in the minority in England, and as the Duke professed them, it can be imagined how he was hated by the powerful party then dominant. He was on most unfriendly terms with his brothers.... The Duke proved an amiable and courteous, even chivalrous, husband."

Judiciously, in the circumstances, neither of the brides was in her first youth, the future Queen Adelaide having been, at twenty-six, the younger of the two. The Duchess of Kent, a little over thirty, had been already married, in 1803, when she was seventeen, to Prince Emich Charles of Leiningen. Eleven years afterwards, in 1814, she was left a widow with a son and daughter. Four years later she married the Duke of Kent. The brides were very different in looks and outward attractions. The Duchess of Clarence, with hair of a peculiar colour approaching to a lemon tint, weak eyes, and a bad complexion, was plain. She was also quiet, reserved, and a little stiff, while she appears to have had no special accomplishments, beyond a great capacity for carpet-work. The Duchess of Kent, with a fine figure, good features, brown hair and eyes, a pretty pink colour, winning manners, and graceful accomplishments—particularly music, formed a handsome, agreeable woman, "altogether most charming and attractive."

But both Duchesses were possessed of qualities in comparison with which beauty is deceitful and favour is vain—qualities which are calculated to wear well. Queen Adelaide's goodness and kindness, her unselfish, unassuming womanliness and devout resignation to sorrow and suffering, did more than gain and keep the heart of her bluff, eccentric sailor-prince. They secured for her the respectful regard of the nation among whom she dwelt, whether as Queen or Queen-dowager. The Archbishop of Canterbury could say of her, after her husband's death, "For three weeks prior to his (King William's) dissolution, the Queen sat by his bedside, performing for him every office which a sick man could require, and depriving herself of all manner of rest and refection. She underwent labours which I thought no ordinary woman could endure. No language can do justice to the meekness and to the calmness of mind which she sought to keep up before the King, while sorrow was pressing on her heart. Such constancy of affection, I think, was one of the most interesting spectacles that could be presented to a mind desirous of being gratified with the sight of human excellence." [Footnote: Dr. Doran] Such graces, great enough to resist the temptations of the highest rank, might well be singled out as worthy of all imitation. The Duchess of Kent proved herself the best of mothers—as she was the best of wives, during her short time of wedlock—in the self-renunciation and self-devotion with which, through all difficulties, and in spite of every opposition and misconception, she pursued the even tenor of her way. Not for two or ten, but for well-nigh twenty years, she gave herself up unreservedly, turning her back on her country with all its strong early ties, to rearing a good queen, worthy of her high destiny. England owes much to the memories of Queen Adelaide and the Duchess of Kent, who succeeded Queen Charlotte, the one as Queen Consort, the other as mother of the future sovereign, and not only served as the salt to savour their royal circles, but kept up nobly the tradition of honourable women among the queens and princesses of England, handing down the high obligation to younger generations.

The Duke and Duchess of Kent withdrew to Germany after their re-marriage, and resided at the castle of Amorbach, in Bavaria, part of the inheritance of her young son. The couple returned to England that their child might be born there. The Duke had a strong impression that, notwithstanding his three elder brothers, the Crown would come to him and his children. The persuasion, if they knew it, was not likely to be acceptable to the other Princes. Certainly, in the face of the Duke's money embarrassments, his kinsmen granted no assistance to enable the future Queen of England to be born in her own dominions. It was by the help of private friends that the Duke gratified his natural and wise wish.

Apartments in Kensington Palace were assigned to the couple. The old queen had died at Kew, surrounded by such of her daughters as were in the country, and by several of her sons, in the month of November, 1818. George III. was dragging out his days at Windsor. The Prince Regent occupied Carlton House.

The Kensington of 1819 was not the Kensington of today. In spite of the palace and gardens, which are comparatively little altered, the great crowded quarter, with its Museum and Albert Hall, is as unlike as possible to the courtly village to which the Duke and Duchess of Kent came, and where the Queen spent her youth. That Kensington consisted mainly of a fine old square, built in the time of James II., in which the foreign ambassadors and the bishops in attendance at Court congregated in the days of William and Mary, and Anne, and of a few terraces and blocks of buildings scattered along the Great Western Road, where coaches passed several times a day. Other centres round which smaller buildings clustered were Kensington House—which had lately been a school for the sons of French emigres of rank—the old church, and Holland House, the fine seat of the Riches and the Foxes. The High Street extended a very little way on each side of the church and was best known by its Charity School, and its pastrycook's shop, at the sign of the "Pineapple," to which Queen Caroline had graciously given her own recipe for royal Dutch gingerbread. David Wilkie's apartments represented the solitary studio. Nightingales sang in Holland Lane; blackbirds and thrushes haunted the nurseries and orchards. Great vegetable-gardens met the fields. Here and there stood an old country house in its own grounds. Green lanes led but to more rural villages, farms and manor-houses. Notting Barns was a farmhouse on the site of Notting Hill. In the tea-gardens at Bayswater Sir John Hill cultivated medicinal plants, and prepared his "water-dock essence" and "balm of honey." Invalids frequented Kensington Gravel pits for the benefit of "the sweet country air."

Kensington Palace had been bought by William III. from Daniel Finch, second Earl of Nottingham. His father, the first Earl, had built and named the pile of brick-building Nottingham House. It was comparatively a new, trim house, though Evelyn called it "patched up" when it passed into the hands of King William, and as such might please his Dutch taste better than the beautiful Elizabethan Holland House—in spite of the name, at which he is said to have looked, with the intention of making it his residence.

The Duke of Sussex, as well as the Duke and Duchess of Kent, had apartments in the palace. He dwelt in the portion of the southern front understood to belong to the original building. His brother and sister-in-law were lodged not far off, but their apartments formed part of an addition made by King William, who employed Sir Christopher Wren as his architect.

The clumsy, homely structure, with its three courts—the Clock Court, the Princes' Court, and the Princesses' Court—had many interesting associations in addition to its air of venerable respectability. William and Mary resided frequently in the palace which they had chosen; and both died under its roof. Mary sat up in one of these rooms, on a dreary December night in 1694, after she felt herself stricken with small-pox, seeking out and burning all the papers in her possession which might compromise others. The silent, asthmatic, indomitable little man was carried back here after his fall from his horse eight years later, to draw his last breath where Mary had laid down her crown. Here Anne sat, with her fan in her mouth, speaking in monosyllables to her circle. George I.'s chief connection with Kensington Palace was building the cupola and the great staircase. But his successors, George II. and Queen Caroline, atoned for the deficiency. They gave much of their time to the palace so identified with the Protestant and Hanoverian line of succession. Queen Caroline especially showed her regard for the spot by exercising her taste in beautifying it according to the notions of the period. It was she who caused the string of ponds to be united so as to form the Serpentine; and he modified the Dutch style of the gardens, abolishing the clipped monsters in yew and box, and introducing wildernesses and groves to relieve the stiffness and monotony of straight walks and hedges. The shades of her beautiful maids of honour, "sweet Molly Lepell," Mary Bellenden, and Sophy Howe, still haunt the Broad Walk. Molly Lepell's husband, Lord Hervey (the "Lord Fanny" of lampoons and songs), composed and read in these rooms, for the diversion of his royal mistress and the princesses, with their ladies and gentlemen, the false account of his own death, caused by an encounter with footpads on the dangerous road between London and the country palace. He added an audacious description of the manner in which the news was received at Court, and of the behaviour of the principal persons in the circle.

With George II. and Queen Caroline the first glory of the palace departed, for the early Court of George III. and Queen Charlotte took its country pleasures at Kew. Then followed the selection of Windsor for the chief residence of the sovereigns. The promenades in the gardens, to which the great world of London flocked, remained for a season as a vestige of former grandeur. In George II.'s time the gardens were only thrown open on Saturdays, when the Court went to Richmond. Afterwards the public were admitted every day, under certain restrictions. So late as 1820 these promenades were still a feature on Sunday mornings.

Kensington Palace has not yet changed its outward aspect. It still stands, with its forcing-houses, and Queen Anne's banqueting-room— converted into an orangery—in its small private grounds, fenced off by a slight railing and an occasional hedge from the public gardens. The principal entrance, under the clock-tower, leads to a plain, square, red courtyard, which has a curious foreign aspect in its quiet simplicity, as if the Brunswick princes had brought a bit of Germany along with them when they came to reign here; and there are other red courtyards, equally unpretentious, with more or less old-fashioned doors and windows. Within, the building has sustained many alterations. Since it ceased to be a seat of the Court, the palace has furnished residences for various members of the royal family, and for different officials. Accordingly, the interior has been divided and partitioned off to suit the requirements of separate households. But the great staircase, imposing in its broad, shallow steps of black marble and its faded frescoes, still conducts to a succession of dismantled Presence-chambers and State-rooms. The pictures and tapestry have been taken from the walls, the old panelling is bare. The distinctions which remain are the fine proportions of the apartments— the marble pillars and niches of one; the remains of a richly-carved chimneypiece in another; the highly-wrought ceilings, to which ancient history and allegory have supplied grandiose figures—their deep colours unfaded, the ruddy burnish of their gilding as splendid as ever. Here and there great black-and-gold court-stools, raised at the sides, and finished off with bullet heads of dogs, arouse a recollection of Versailles or Fontainebleau, and look as if they had offered seats to Court ladies in hoops and brocades, and gentlemen-in-waiting in velvet coats and breeches and lace cravats. One seat is more capacious than the others, with a round back, and in its heavy black-and-gold has the look of an informal throne. It might easily have borne the gallant William, or even the extensive proportions of Anne.

There is a word dropped of "old kings" having died in the closed rooms behind these doors. George II., in his old age? or William, worn out in his prime? or it may be heavy, pacific George of Denmark, raised to the kingly rank by the courtesy of vague tradition? The old chapel was in this part of the house. Leigh Hunt tells us it was in this chapel George I. asked the bishops to have good short sermons, because he was an old man, and when he was kept long, he fell asleep and caught cold. It must have been a curious old chapel, with a round window admitting scanty light. The household and servants sat below, while a winding staircase led round and up to a closed gallery in near proximity to the pulpit. It was only a man's conscience, or a sense of what was due to his physical well-being, which could convict him of slumbering in such a peaceful retreat. It is said that her late Royal Highness the Duchess of Kent objected to the obscurity of this place of worship, and, to meet her objections, the present little chapel was fitted up.

The Duchess of Kent's rooms were in an adjacent wing; spacious rooms enough, and only looking the more habitable and comfortable for the moderate height of the ceilings. In a room with three windows on one side, looking out on the private grounds, the Queen was born. It was thinking of it and its occupants that the warm-hearted, quick-witted Duchess-mother, in Coburg, wrote: "I cannot express how happy I am to know you, dearest, dearest Vickel, safe in your bed, with a little one…. Again a Charlotte—destined, perhaps, to play a great part one day, if a brother is not born to take it out of her hands. The English like queens; and the niece (by marriage) of the ever-lamented, beloved Charlotte, will be most dear to them."

In another wide, low room, with white pillars, some eighteen years later, the baby Princess, become a maiden Queen, held her first Council, surrounded by kindred who had stood at her font—hoary heads wise in statecraft, great prelates, great lawyers, a great soldier, and she an innocent girl at their head. No relic could leave such an impression as this room, with its wonderfully pathetic scene. But, indeed, there are few other traces of the life that budded into dawning womanhood here, which will be always linked with the memories of Kensington Palace. An upper room, sunny and cheerful, even on a winter's day, having a pleasant view out on the open gardens, with their straight walks and great pond, where a child might forget sometimes that she had lessons to learn, was a princess's school-room. Here the good Baroness who played the part of governess so sagaciously and faithfully may have slipped into the book of history the genealogical table which was to tell so startling a tale. In another room is a quaint little doll's-house, with the different rooms, which an active-minded child loved to arrange. The small frying-pans and plates still hang above the kitchen dresser; the cook stands unwearied by the range; the chairs are placed round the tables; the tiny tea-service, which tiny fingers delighted to handle, is set out ready for company. But the owner has long done with make-believes, has worked in earnest, discharged great tasks, and borne the burden and heat of the day, in reigning over a great empire.

CHAPTER II CHILDHOOD.

In the months of March and May, 1819, the following announcements of royal births appeared in succession in the newspapers of the day, no doubt to the satisfaction alike of anxious statesmen and village politicians beginning to grow anxious over the chances of the succession:—

"At Hanover, March 26, her Royal Highness the Duchess of Cambridge, of a son; and on March 27, her Royal Highness the Duchess of Clarence, of a daughter, the latter only surviving a few hours."

"24th May, at Kensington Palace, her Royal Highness the Duchess of Kent, of a daughter."

"27th May, at her hotel in Berlin, her Royal Highness the Duchess of Cumberland, of a son."

Thus her Gracious Majesty Queen Victoria first saw the light in Kensington Palace on the 24th of May, 1819, one in a group of cousins, all, save herself, born out of England.

The Duke of Sussex, the Duke of Wellington, and other officers of State were in attendance on the occasion, though the probability of her succession to the throne was then very doubtful. The Prince Regent had already made overtures towards procuring a divorce from the Princess of Wales. If he were to revive them, and prove successful, he might marry again and have heirs. The Duchess of Clarence, who had just given birth to an infant that had only survived a few hours, might yet be the joyful mother of living children. The little Princess herself might be the predecessor of a troop of princes of the Kent branch. Still, both at Kensington and in the depths of rural Coburg, there was a little flutter, not only of gladness, but of subdued expectation. The Duke of Kent, on showing his baby to his friends, was wont to say, "Look at her well, for she will be Queen of England." Her christening was therefore an event of more than ordinary importance in the household. The ceremony took place a month afterwards, on the 24th of June, and doubtless the good German nurse, Madame Siebold, who was about to return to the Duchess of Kent's old home to officiate on an equally interesting occasion in the family of the Duchess's brother, the reigning Duke of Saxe-Coburg-Saalfeld, carried with her flaming accounts of the splendour of the ceremonial, as well as pretty tales of the "dear little love" destined to mate with the coming baby, whose big blue eyes were soon looking about in the lovely little hunting-seat of Rosenau. The gold font was brought down from the Tower, where for some time it had been out of request. The Archbishop of Canterbury and the Bishop of London officiated, as they had done the year before at the re-marriage of the Duke and Duchess. The godfathers were the Prince Regent, present in person, and Alexander, Emperor of Russia, then at the height of his popularity in England, represented by the Duke of York. The godmothers were the Queen-dowager of Wurtemberg (the Princess Royal), represented by Princess Augusta, and the Duchess-dowager of Coburg (mother of the Duchess of Kent, and grandmother of both the Queen and the Prince Consort), represented by the Duchess of Gloucester (Princess Mary).

It is said there had been a proposal to name the little princess Georgiana also, after her grandfather and uncle, George III. and George, Prince Regent; but the idea was dropped because the latter would not permit his name to stand second on the list.

Among the other privileged guests at the christening was Prince Leopold, destined to be the child's second father, one of her kindest and wisest friends. It is not difficult to comprehend what the scene must have been to the young man whose cup had been so full two years before, who was now a widower and childless. We have his own reference to his feelings in a letter to one of the late Princess Charlotte's friends. It had been hard for him to be present, but he had felt it to be his duty, and he had made the effort. This was a man who was always facing what was hard, always struggling and overcoming in the name of right. The consequence was that, even in his youth, all connected with him turned to him as to a natural stay. We have a still better idea of what the victory cost him when we read, in the "Life of the Prince Consort," it was not till a great misfortune happened to her that Prince Leopold "had the courage to look into the blooming face of his infant niece." With what manly pity and tenderness he overcame his reluctance, and how he was rewarded, we all know.

In December, 1819, the Duke and Duchess of Kent went for sea-air to Woolbrook Cottage, Sidmouth, Devonshire.

The first baby is always of consequence in a household, but of how much consequence this baby was may be gleaned by the circumstance that a startling little incident concerning the child made sufficient mark to survive and be registered by a future chronicler. A boy shooting sparrows fired unwittingly so near the house that the shot shattered one of the windows of the nursery, and passed close to the head of the child in the nurse's arms. Precious baby-head, that was one day to wear, with honour, a venerable crown, to be thus lightly threatened at the very outset! One can fancy the terror of the nurse, the distress of the Duchess, the fright and ire of the Duke, the horror and humiliation of the unhappy offender, with the gradual cooling down into magnanimous amnesty—or at most dignified rebuke, mollified by penitent tears into reassuring kindness, and just a little quiver of half-affronted, half-nervous laughter.

But there was no more room for laughter at false alarms at Woolbrook Cottage. Within a month the Duke was seized with the illness which ended his life in a few days. The particulars are simple and touching. He had taken a long walk with his equerry and great friend, Captain Conroy, and came in heated, tired, and with his feet so wet that his companion suggested the propriety of immediately changing his boots. But the baby of whom he was so fond and proud came in his way. She was eight months old, able to stretch out her little arms and laugh back to him. He stayed to play with her. In the evening it was evident he had caught a chill; he was hoarse, and showed symptoms of fever. The complaint settled at once on his lungs, and ran its course with great rapidity. We hardly need to be told that the Duchess was his devoted nurse, concealing her anxiety and grief to minister to him in everything.

There is a pathetic little reference to the last illness of the Duke of Kent in one of the Princess Hohenlohe's letters to the Queen. This elder sister (Princess Feodora of Leiningen) was then a little girl of nine or ten years of age, residing with her mother and stepfather. "Indeed, I well remember that dreadful time at Sidmouth. I recollect praying on my knees that God would not let your dear father die. I loved him dearly; he always was so kind to me."

On the afternoon of the 22nd his case was hopeless, and it became a question whether he had sufficient consciousness to sign his will. His old friend, General Wetherall, was brought up to the bed. At the sound of the familiar voice which had always been welcome to him, the sick man, drifting away from all familiar sounds, raised himself, collected his thoughts for the last time, and mentioned several places and people intelligently. The poor Duke had never been negligent in doing what he saw to be his duty. He had been forward in helping others, even when they were not of his flesh and blood. He heard the will read over, and with a great effort wrote the word "Edward," looking at every letter after he wrote it, and asking anxiously if the signature was legible.

In this will, which left the Duchess guardian to the child, and appointed General Wetherall and Captain Conroy trustees of his estate for the benefit of his widow and daughter, it is noticeable that the name in each case is given in the French version, "Victoire." Indeed so rare was the term in England at this date, that it is probable the English equivalent had scarcely been used before the christening of the Queen.

The Duke died on the following day, the 23rd of January, 1820. Only six days later, on the 29th, good old King George expired at Windsor. The son was cut down by violent disease while yet a man in middle life, just after he had become the head of a little household full of domestic promise, and with what might still have been a great public career opening out before him. The father sank in what was, in his case, the merciful decay of age, after he had been unable for ten years to fulfil the duties and charities of life, and after surviving his faithful Queen a year. The language of the official announcement of the physicians was unusually appropriate: "It has pleased the Almighty to release his Majesty from all further suffering." To complete the disasters of the royal family this month, the new King, George IV., who had been labouring under a cold when his father died, was seized immediately after his proclamation with dangerous inflammation of the lungs, the illness that had proved fatal to the Duke of Kent, and could not be present at his brother's or father's funerals; in fact, he was in a precarious state for some days. The Duke of Kent was buried, according to the custom of the time, by torchlight, on the night of the 12th of February, at Windsor. As an example of the difference which distance made then, it took nearly a week's dreary travelling to convey the Duke's body from Woolbrook Cottage, where it lay in State for some days, to Cumberland Lodge, from which the funeral train walked to Windsor. The procession of mourning-coaches, hearse, and carriages set out from Sidmouth on Monday morning, halting on successive nights at Bridport, Blandford, Salisbury, and Basingstoke, the coffin being deposited in the principal church of each town, under a military guard, till on Friday night Cumberland Lodge was reached. The same night a detachment of the Royal Horse Guards, every third man bearing a flambeau, escorted a carriage containing the urn with the heart to St. George's Chapel, where in the presence of the Dean, the officers of the chapel, and several gentlemen appointed for the duty, urn and heart were deposited in the niche in which the coffin was afterwards to be placed. The body lay in State on the following day, that it might be seen by the inhabitants of Windsor, his old military friends, and the multitude who came down from London for the two mournful ceremonies. At eight o'clock at night the final procession was formed, consisting of Poor Knights, pages, pursuivants, heralds, the coronet on a black velvet cushion, the body under pall and canopy, the supporters of the pall and canopy field-marshals and generals, the chief mourner the Duke of York, the Dukes of Clarence, Sussex, Gloucester, and Prince Leopold in long black cloaks, their trains borne by gentlemen in attendance.

These torchlight funeral processions formed a singular remnant of mediaeval pageantry. How the natural solemnity of night in itself increased the awe and sadness of the scene to all simple minds, we can well understand. Children far away from Windsor remembered after they were grown men and women the vague terror with which they had listened in the dim lamplight of their nurseries to the dismal tolling of the bell out in the invisible church tower, which proclaimed that a royal duke was being carried to his last resting-place. We can easily believe that thousands would flock to look and listen, and be thrilled by the imposing spectacle. The show must have been weirdly picturesque when wild wintry weather, as in this case, added to the effect, "viewed for the distance of three miles, through the spacious Long Walk, amidst a double row of lofty trees, whilst at intervals the glittering of the flambeaux and the sound of martial music were distinctly seen and heard."

The Duke's funeral only anticipated by a few days the still more magnificent ceremonial with which a king was laid in the tomb.

But the real mourning was down in Devonshire, in the Sidmouth cottage. It would be difficult to conceive more trying circumstances for a woman in her station than those in which the young Duchess—she was but little over thirty—found herself left. She had lost a kind husband, her child would miss a doting father. She was a foreigner in a strange country. She had entered into a divided family, with which her connection was in a measure broken by the death of the Duke, while the bond that remained, however precious to all, was too likely to prove a bone of contention. The Duke had died poor. The Duchess had previously relinquished her German jointure, and the English settlement on her was inadequate, especially if it were to be cumbered with the discharge of any of her husband's personal debts. It was not realised then that the Duchess of Kent, in marrying the Duke and becoming his widow and the guardian of their child, had given up not only independence, but what was affluence in her own country, with its modest ways of living—even where princes were concerned—for the mortification and worry of narrow means, the strain of a heavy responsibility, the pain of much unjustifiable and undeserved interference, misconception, and censure, until she lived to vindicate the good sense, good feeling, and good taste with which she had always acted.

But the Duchess was not altogether desolate. Prince Leopold hurried to her and supported her then, and on many another hard day, by brotherly kindness, sympathy, and generous help. It was in his company that she came back with her child to Kensington.

One element of the Coburg character has been described as the sound judgment and quiet reasonableness associated with the temperate blood of the race. Accordingly, we find the Duchess not only submitting with gentle resignation to misfortune, but rousing herself, as her brother might have done in her circumstances—as doubtless he urged her to do—to the active discharge of the duties of her position. On the 23rd of February, before the first month of her widowhood was well by, she received Viscount Morpeth and Viscount Clive, the deputation bearing to her the address of condolence from the House of Commons. She met them with the infant Princess in her arms. The child was not only the sign that she fully appreciated and acknowledged the nature of the tie which united her to the country, it was the intimation of the close inseparable union with her daughter which continued through all the years of the Queen's childhood and youth, till the office of sovereign forced its holder into a separate existence; till she found another fitting protector, when the generous, ungrudging mother gave way to the worthy husband, who became the dutiful, affectionate son of the Duchess's declining years.

Five months after these events the Duchess, at her own request, had an interview with William Wilberforce, then living in the house at Kensington Gore which was occupied later by the Countess of Blessington and Count D'Orsay. "She received me," the good man wrote to Hannah More, "with her fine, animated child on the floor by her side, with its playthings, of which I soon became one. She was very civil, but, as she did not sit down, I did not think it right to stop above a quarter of an hour; and there being but a female attendant and a footman present, I could not well get up any topic so as to carry on a continual discourse. She apologised for not speaking English well enough to talk it; intimated a hope that she might talk it better and longer with me at some future time. She spoke of her situation, and her manner was quite delightful."

The sentence in italics opens our eyes to one of the difficulties of the Duchess to which we might not otherwise have given much consideration. We are apt to take it for granted that, though there is no royal road to mathematics, the power of speaking foreign languages comes to royal personages, if not by nature, at least by inheritance and by force of circumstances. There is some truth in this when there is a foreign father or mother; when royal babies are brought up, like Queen Victoria, to speak several languages from infancy, and when constant contact with foreigners confirms and maintains the useful faculty. Even when a prince or a princess is destined from his or her early youth to share a foreign throne, and is brought up with that end, a provision may be made for an adopted tongue to become second nature. But the Duchess of Kent was not brought up with any such prospect, and during her eleven years of married life in Germany she must have had comparatively little occasion to practise what English she knew; while, at the date of her coming to England, she was beyond the age when one learns a new language with facility. Any one of us who has experienced the fettered, perturbed, bewildered condition which results from being reduced to express ourselves at an important crisis in our history through a medium of speech with which we are but imperfectly acquainted, will know how to estimate this unthought-of obstacle in the Duchess of Kent's path, at the beginning of her widowhood.

This was the year (1820) of the greatest eclipse of the sun which had been seen for more than a century, when Venus and Mars were both visible, with the naked eye, for a few minutes in the middle of the day. Whatever the portents in the sky might mean, the signs on the earth were not reassuring. When the Bourbon monarchy had seemed fairly restored in France, all the world was shocked by the assassination of the Duc de Berri at the door of the Opera-house in Paris. Three kingdoms which had but recently been delivered from the clutch of the usurper were in revolt against the constituted authorities—Portugal, Spain, and Naples. Of these, the two former were on the brink of wars of succession, when the royal uncles, Don Miguel and Don Carlos, fought against their royal nieces, Donna Maria and Donna Isabella. At home the summer had been a sad one to the royal family and the country. The ferment of discontent was kept up by the very measures—executions and imprisonments—taken to repress anarchy, and by the continuance of crushed trade, want of work, and high prices. The Duchess of York died, making the third member of the royal family dead since the new year; yet she, poor lady, was but a unit in the sum, a single foreign princess who, however, kind she might have been to the few who came near her, was nothing to the mass of the people.

The name of another foreign princess was in every man's mind and on every man's tongue. However, there were many reasons for the anomaly. Caroline of Brunswick was the Queen until she should be proved unworthy to bear the title. Her quarrel with the King had long made her notorious. Though the story reflected little credit on her, it was so utterly discreditable to him that it raised up friends for her where they might have been least expected. His unpopularity rendered her popular. Her name became the rallying-cry for a great political faction. The mob, with its usual headlong, unreasoning appropriation of a cause and a person, elevated her into a heroine, cheered frantically, and was ready to commit any outbreak in her honour.

After six years' absence from England Queen Caroline had come back on the death of George III. to demand her rights. She had landed at Dover and been welcomed by applauding crowds. She had been escorted through Kent by uproarious partisans, who removed the horses from her carriage and dragged her in triumph through the towns. London, in its middle and lower classes, had poured out to meet her and come back in her train, till she was safely lodged in South Audley Street, in the house of her champion, Alderman Wood.

The King had instructed his ministers to lay before the House of Lords a bill of Pains and Penalties against the Queen which, if sustained, would deprive her of every claim to share his rank and would annul the marriage. The Queen was prepared with her defence, and furnished with two of the ablest advocates in the kingdom, Mr. Brougham and Mr. Denman. In the earlier stages of the proceedings she was present almost every day in the House of Lords. She entered in her puce or black sarcenet pelisse and black velvet hat, a large, not uncomely woman, a little over fifty, and took the chair of State provided for her, the House rising to receive the Queen whom it was trying. The trial, in its miserable details of gross folly well-nigh incredible, lasted from July to November—four months of burning excitement—when it collapsed from the smallness of the majority (nine) that voted for the second reading of the bill. The animus of the prosecution and the unworthy means taken to accomplish its purpose, defeated the end in view. It is said that had it been otherwise the country would have broken out into widespread insurrection.

The Queen's supporters, of all classes, sects, and shades, indulged in a perfect frenzy of rejoicing. Festivals, illuminations, every token of triumph for her and condemnation for him accompanied what was equivalent to her acquittal. She went in something like State, with her queer, motley household—Bohemian, English and Italians—and her great ally, Alderman Wood, to offer up thanksgiving in St. Paul's, where, at the same time, she found her name omitted from the Church service. She wore white velvet and ermine, and was surrounded by thousands of shouting followers, as if she had been the most discreet of queens and best of women. The poor passionate, wayward nature, which after all had been cruelly dealt with, was touched as well as elated.

On the very day after Queen Caroline's arrival in London in June, she had dispatched Alderman Wood to Kensington, to condole with the Duchess of Kent on her recent widowhood, and inquire after the health of the infant princess. The message was innocent in itself, but alarming by implication; for Queen Caroline was not a woman to be kept at a distance, or to hesitate in expressing her sentiments if she fancied her overtures slighted by the embarrassed Duchess. In the month of August Queen Caroline had established herself at Brandenburg House—the Margravine of Anspach's house, by the river at Hammersmith—near enough to Kensington Palace, to judge from human nature, to disconcert and provoke a smile against the smiler's will—for Caroline's extravagances would have disturbed the gravity of a judge—in the womanly Princess at the head of the little household soberly settled there. Never were princesses and women more unlike than Caroline of Brunswick and Victoria of Coburg; But poor Queen Caroline was not destined to remain long an awkward enigma—a queen and yet no queen, an aunt and yet no aunt, a scandal and a torment in everybody's path.

In the summer of the following year, when the country was drawn away and dazzled by the magnificent ceremonial of the coronation of George IV., she exercised her last disturbing influence. She demanded to be crowned along with her husband; but her demand was refused by the Privy Council. She appeared at the door of Westminster Abbey, but the way was barred to her. A fortnight afterwards, when King George had gone to Ireland to arouse the nation's loyalty, his wife had passed where Privy Council ushers and yeomen of the guard were powerless, where the enmity of man had no voice in the judgment of God. She had been attacked by severe illness, and in the course of five days she died, in the middle of a wild storm of thunder, wind, and rain. The night before, a boatful of Methodists had rowed up the Thames, within sound of the open windows of her sick-room, and sung hymns to comfort her in her extremity. The heart of a large part of the nation still clung to her because of her misfortunes and the insults heaped upon her. The late Queen's body was conveyed back to Brunswick. The funeral passed through Kensington, escorted by a mighty mob, in addition to companies of soldiers. The last were instructed to conduct the cortege by the outskirts of London to Harwich, where a frigate and two sloops of war were waiting for the coffin. The mob were resolute that their Queen's funeral should pass through the city. The first struggle between the crowd and the military took place at the corner of Church Street, Kensington. The strange, unseemly, contention was renewed farther on more than once; but as bloodshed had been forbidden, the people had their way, and the swaying mass surged in grim determination straight towards the Strand and Temple Bar. The captain of the frigate into whose keeping the coffin was committed in order to be conveyed back to Brunswick had been, by a curious, sorrowful coincidence, the midshipman who, "more than a quarter of a century before, handed the rope to the royal bride whereby to help her on board the Jupiter," which was to bring her to England.

One can fancy that, when that sorry tragedy was ended, and its perpetual noisy ebullitions had sunk into silence, a sense of relief stole over the palace-home at Kensington.

Round the childhood and youth of sovereigns, especially popular sovereigns, a growth of stories will gather like the myths which attend on the infancy of a nation. Such stories or myths are chiefly valuable as showing the later tendency of the individual or people, the character and history of the monarch or of the subjects, in accordance with which, in reversal of the adage that makes the child father to the man, the man is, in a new sense, father to the child, by stamping on his infancy and nonage traits borrowed from his mature years. Mingled with the species of legendary lore attaching to every generation, there is a foundation more or less of authentic annals. It is as affording an example of this human patchwork of fancy and fact, and as illustrating the impression deeply engraved on the popular mind, that the following incidents of the Queen's childhood and youth are given.

First, the people have loved to dwell on the close union between mother and child. The Duchess nursed her baby—would see it washed and dressed. As soon as the little creature could sit alone, her small table was placed by her mother's at meals, though the child was only allowed the food fit for her years. The Princess slept in her mother's room all through her childhood and girlhood. In the entries in the Queen's diary at the time of the Duchess of Kent's death, her Majesty refers to an old repeater striking every quarter of an hour in the sick-room on the last night of the Duchess's life—"a large watch in a tortoiseshell case, which had belonged to my poor father, the sound of which brought back to me all the recollections of my childhood, for I had always used to hear it at night, but had not heard it for now twenty-three years."

When the Princess was a little older, and lessons and play alternated with each other, she was taught to attend to the thing in hand, and finish what she had begun, both in her studies and games. One day she was amusing herself making a little haycock when some other mimic occupation caught her volatile fancy, and she flung down her small rake ready to rush off to the fresh attraction. "No, no, Princess; you must always complete what you have commenced," said her governess, and the small haymaker had to conclude her haymaking before she was at liberty to follow another pursuit.

From the Princess's fifth year Dr. Davys, afterwards Bishop of Peterborough, was her tutor. When it became clear that the little girl would, if she lived, be Queen of England, a prelate high in the Church was proposed to the Duchess of Kent as the successor of Dr. Davys in his office. But the Duchess, with the mild firmness and conscientious fidelity which ruled her conduct, declared that as she was perfectly satisfied with the tutor who had originally been appointed (when the appointment was less calculated to offer temptations to personal ambition and political intrigue), she did not see that any change was advisable. If a clergyman of higher rank was necessary, there was room for the promotion of Dr. Davys. Accordingly he was named Dean of Chester.

The Baroness Lehzen was another of the Queen's earliest guardians who remained at her post throughout her Majesty's youth. Louise Lehzen, daughter of a Hanoverian clergyman, came to England as governess to Princess Feodora Leiningen and remained as governess to Princess Victoria, entering on her duties in 1824. In 1827 she was raised to the rank of a Hanoverian Baroness, by George IV., at the request of Princess Sophia. From that time Baroness Lehzen acted also as lady in attendance. On her death, so late as 1870, her old pupil recorded of her, in a passage in the Queen's journal, which is given in the "Life of the Prince Consort," "My dearest, kindest friend, old Lehzen, expired on the 9th quite gently and peaceably…. She knew me from six months old, and from my fifth to my eighteenth year devoted all her care and energies to me with the most wonderful abnegation of self, never even taking one day's holiday. I adored, though I was greatly in awe of her. She really seemed to have no thought but for me…. She was in her eighty-seventh year." This constancy and permanency in the family relations were in themselves inestimable boons to the child, who thus grew up in an atmosphere of familiar affection and unshaken trust, for the absence of which nothing in the world could have compensated. Another lady of higher rank was of necessity appointed governess to the Queen in 1831, when she became next heir to the throne. This lady, the Dowager Duchess of Northumberland, appears also as the Queen's friend in after life.

The late Bishop Wilberforce was told by Dr. Davys an interesting anecdote of his former pupil. "The Queen always had from my first knowing her a most striking regard to truth. I remember when I had been teaching her one day, she was very impatient for the lesson to be over—once or twice rather refractory. The Duchess of Kent came in, and asked how she had behaved. Lehzen said, 'Oh, once she was rather troublesome.' The Princess touched her and said, 'No, Lehzen, twice, don't you remember?' The Duchess of Kent, too, was a woman of great truth."

It had been judged meet that the future Queen should not be made aware of her coming greatness, which, for that matter, continued doubtful in her earlier years. She was to grow up free from the impending care and responsibility, happy and healthful in her unconscious girlhood—above all, unassailed by the pernicious attempts to bespeak her favour, the crafty flattery, the undermining insinuations which have proved the bane of the youth of so many sovereigns. In order to preserve this reticence, unslumbering care and many precautions were absolutely necessary. It is said the Princess was constantly under the eye either of the Duchess of Kent or the Baroness Lehzen. The guard proved sufficient; yet it was difficult to evade the lively intelligence of an observant sensible child.

"Why do all the gentlemen take off their hats to me and not to my sister Feodora?" the little girl is said to have asked wonderingly on her return from a drive in the park, referring to her elder half-sister, who became Princess of Hohenlohe, between whom and the questioner there always existed the strong sweet affection of true sisters. Perhaps the little lady felt indignant as well as mystified at the strange preference thus given to her, in spite of her sister's superiority in age and wisdom. We do not know what reply was made to this puzzling inquiry, though it would have been easy enough to say that the little Princess was the daughter of an English royal Duke, therefore an English Princess, and the big Princess was German on both sides of the house, while these were English gentlemen who had saluted their young countrywoman. We all know from the best authority that Sir Walter Scott was wrong when he fancied some bird of the air must have conveyed the important secret to the little fair-haired maiden to whom he was presented in 1828. The mystery was not disclosed for years to come.

The child, though brought up in retirement, was by no means secluded from observation, or deprived of the change and variety so advantageous to human growth and development. From her babyhood in the sad visit to Sidmouth in 1820, and from 1821, when she was at that pretentious combination of fantasticalness and gorgeousness, the Pavilion, Brighton, she was carried every year, like any other well-cared-for child, either to the seaside or to some other invigorating region, so that she became betimes acquainted with different aspects of sea and shore in her island. Ramsgate was a favourite resort of the Duchess's. The little Thanet watering-place, with its white chalk cliffs, its inland basin of a harbour, its upper and lower town, connected by "Jacob's Ladder," its pure air and sparkling water, with only a tiny fringe of bathing-machines, was in its blooming time of fresh rural peace and beauty when it was the cradle by the sea of the little Princess.

When she was five she was at Claremont, making music and motion in the quiet house with her gleeful laughter and pattering feet, so happy in being with her uncle that she could look back on this visit as the brightest of her early holidays. "This place," the Queen wrote to the King of the Belgians long afterwards, "has a peculiar charm for us both, and to me it brings back recollections of the happiest days of my otherwise dull childhood,—when I experienced such kindness from you, dearest uncle, kindness which has ever since continued…. Victoria plays with my old bricks, and I see her running and jumping in the flower-garden, as old, though I feel still little, Victoria of former days used to do." In the autumn of 1825 the Queen's grandmother, the Dowager Duchess of Coburg, visited England, and the whole family were together at Claremont.

In 1826, "the warm summer," when the Princess was seven years of age, she was invited to Windsor to see another uncle, George IV. That was a more formidable ordeal, but her innocent frank brightness carried her through it successfully. It is not easy for many men to contemplate with satisfaction their heirs, when those heirs are no offspring of theirs. It must have been doubly difficult for the King to welcome the little girl who had replaced his daughter, the child of his wronged brother and of a Princess whom King George persistently slighted and deprived of her due. But we are told his Majesty was delighted with his little niece's liveliness and intelligence. In the following year, 1827, the Duke of York died, and the Princess, was a step nearer to the throne, but she did not know it. So far from being reared in an atmosphere of self-indulgence, the invaluable lesson was early taught to her that if she were to be honourable and independent in any rank, she must not buy what she could not pay for; if she were to be a good woman she must learn to deny herself. An incident in illustration, which made a small stir in its locality at the time, is often quoted. The Duchess and her daughter were at Tunbridge Wells, dwelling in the neighbourhood of Sir Philip Sidney's Penshurst, retracing the vanished glories of the Pantiles, and conferring on the old pump-woman the never-to-be-forgotten honour of being permitted to present a glass of water from the marble basin to the Princess. The little girl made purchases at the bazaar, buying presents, like any other young visitor, for her absent friends, when she found her money all spent, and at the same time saw a box which would suit an absent cousin. "The shop-people of course placed the box with the other purchases, but the little lady's governess admonished them by saying, 'No. You see the Princess has not got the money; therefore, of course, she cannot buy the box.'" This being perceived, the next offer was to lay by the box till it could be purchased, and the answer was, "Oh, well, if you will be so good as to do that." On quarter-day, before seven in the morning, the Princess appeared on her donkey to claim her purchase.

In the reverence, peace, and love of her pure, refined, if saddened home, everything went well with Princess Victoria, of whom we can only tell that we know the old brick palace where she dwelt, the playground that was hers, the walks she must have taken. We have sat in the later chapel where she said her prayers, a little consecrated room with high pews shutting in the worshippers, a royal gallery, open this time, and an elderly gentleman speaking with a measured, melodious voice. We can guess with tolerable certainty what was the Princess's child-world of books, though from the circumstance that in the light of the future she was made to learn more than was usual then for English girls of the highest rank, she had less time than her companions for reading books which were not study, but the most charming blending of instruction and amusement. That was still the age of Mrs. Barbauld and Miss Edgeworth. "Evenings at Home," "Harry and Lucy," and "Frank and Rosamond," were in every well-conducted school-room. All little girls read with prickings of tender consciences about the lady with the bent bonnet and the scar on her hand, and came under the fascination of the "Purple Jar." A few years later, Harriet Martineau's bristling independence did not prevent her from feeling gratified by the persuasion that the young Princess was reading through her tales on political economy, and that Princess Victoria's favourite character was Ella of the far north.

In the Princess's Roman history one day she came to the passage where the noble matron, Cornelia, in answer to a question as to her precious things, pointed to her sons, and declared, "These are my jewels." "Why," cried the ready-witted little pupil, with a twinkle in her blue eyes, "they must have been cornelians."

When the Princess's lessons took the form of later English history, she was on the very spot for the study. Did her teacher tell her, we wonder, the pretty story of "Bucky," who interrupted grave, saturnine King William at his statescraft in one of yonder rooms? How the small dauntless applicant wiled his father's master, great Louis's rival, into playing at horses in the corridor? Or that sadder story of another less fortunate boy, poor heavy-headed William of Gloucester? Tutors crammed and doctors shook him up, with the best intentions, in vain. In his happier moments he drilled his regiment of little soldiers on that Palace Green before his uncle, King William.

Was the childish passion for exploring old garrets and lumber-rooms excited in this royal little woman by the narrative of the wonderful discovery which Queen Caroline had made in a forgotten bureau in this very palace? Did the little Princess roam about too, in her privileged moments, with a grand vision of finding more and greater art-treasures, other drawings by Holbein or Vandyke, fresh cartoons by Raphael?

All the more valuable paintings had been removed long ago to Windsor, but many curious pictures still remained on the walls of presence chambers and galleries, kings' and queens' great dining-rooms and drawing-rooms, staircases and closets. Did the pictures serve as illustrations to the history lessons? Was the inspection made the recreation of rainy days, when the great suites of State-rooms in which Courts were no longer held or banquets celebrated, but which still echoed with the remembered tread of kings' and courtiers' feet, must have appeared doubly deserted and forlorn?

What was known as the King's Great Drawing-room was not far from the Duchess of Kent's rooms, and was, in fact, put at her disposal in its dismantled, ghostly condition. Among its pictures—freely attributed to many schools and masters—including several battle-pieces and many portraits, there were three representations of English palaces: old Greenwich, where Elizabeth was born; old Hampton, dear to William and Mary; and Windsor, the Windsor of George III. and Queen Charlotte, the Princess's grandfather and grandmother. In the next room, amidst classic and scriptural subjects, and endless examples of "ladies with ruffs," "heads in turbans," &c., there were occasionally family portraits—the old King and Queen more than once; William, Duke of Gloucester; the Queen of Wurtemberg as the girl-Princess Royal, with a dog. (She died in Wurtemberg about this time, 1828. She had quitted England on her marriage in 1797, and in the thirty-one years of her married life only once came back, as an aging and ailing woman. She proved a good wife and stepmother.) A youthful family group of an earlier generation was sure to attract a child—George III. and his brother, Edward, Duke of York, when young, shooting at a target, the Duke of Gloucester in petticoats, Princess Augusta (Duchess of Brunswick, and mother of Caroline, Princess of Wales) nursing the Duke of Cumberland, and Princess Louisa sitting in a chaise drawn by a favourite dog, the scene in Kew Gardens, painted in 1746. Queen Elizabeth was there as a child aged seven, A.D. 1540—three-quarters, with a feather-fan in her hand. Did the guide of the little unconscious Princess pause inadvertently, with a little catch of the breath, by words arrested on the tip of the tongue, before that picture? And was he or she inevitably arrested again before another picture of Queen Elizabeth in her prime, returning from her palace, wearing her crown and holding the sceptre and the globe; Juno, Pallas, and Venus flying before her, Juno dropping her sceptre, Venus her roses, and the little boy Cupid flinging away his bow and arrows, and clinging in discomfiture to his mother because good Queen Bess had conquered all the three in power, wisdom, and beauty? We know the Princess must have loved to look at the pictures. More curious than beautiful as they were, they may have been sufficient to foster in her that love of art which has been the delight of the Queen's maturer years.

English princesses, even though they were not queens in perspective, were not so plentiful in Queen Victoria's young days as to leave any doubt of their hands and hearts proving in great request when the proper time came. Therefore there was no necessity to hold before the little girl, as an incentive to good penmanship, the example of her excellent grandmother, Queen Charlotte, who wrote so fair a letter, expressed with such correctness and judiciousness, at the early age of fifteen, that when the said letter fell, by an extraordinary train of circumstances, into the hands of young King George, he determined there and then to make that painstaking and sensible Princess, and no other, a happy wife and great Queen. There was no strict need for the story, and yet as a gentle stimulant it may have been administered.

Queen Victoria was educated, as far as possible, in the simple habits and familiarity with nature which belongs to the best and happiest training of any child, whatever her rank. There is a pleasant picture in Knight's "Passages of a Working Life": "I delighted to walk in Kensington Gardens in the early summer, on my way to town.... In such a season, when the sun was scarcely high enough to have dried up the dews of Kensington's green alleys, as I passed along the broad central walk I saw a group on the lawn before the palace, which, to my mind, was a vision of exquisite loveliness. The Duchess of Kent and her daughter, whose years then numbered nine, are breakfasting in the open air, a single page attending on them at a respectful distance, the mother looking on with eyes of love, while the fair, soft, English face is bright with smiles. The world of fashion is not yet astir. Clerks and mechanics passing onwards to their occupations are few, and they exhibit nothing of vulgar curiosity."

We have another charming description, by Leigh Hunt, of a glimpse which he had of Princess Victoria in these gardens: "We remember well the peculiar kind of personal pleasure which it gave us to see the future Queen, the first time we ever did see her, coming up a cross-path from the Bayswater Gate, with a girl of her own age by her side, whose hand she was holding as if she loved her. It brought to our minds the warmth of our own juvenile friendships, and made us fancy that she loved everything else that we had loved in like measure—books, trees, verses, Arabian tales, and the good mother who had helped to make her so affectionate. A magnificent footman in scarlet came behind her, with the splendidest pair of calves, in white stockings, that we ever beheld. He looked somehow like a gigantic fairy, personating for his little lady's sake the grandest kind of footman he could think of; and his calves he seemed to have made out of a couple of the biggest chaise-lamps in the possession of the godmother of Cinderella. With or without her big footman, the little Princess could have rambled safely in the grounds which her predecessors had made for her, could have fed the ducks which swam in the round pond before her palace windows, could have drunk from the curious little mineral well, where, in Miss Thackeray's 'Old Kensington,' Frank Raban met Dolly Vanburgh, or peeped out of the little side gate where the same Dolly came face to face with the culprits George and Rhoda. The future owner of all could have easily strayed down the alleys among the Dutch elms which King William brought, perhaps saplings, from the Boomjees, as far as the oak that tradition says King Charles set in the form of an acorn taken from his leafy refuge at Boscobel."

The Duke of Kent had brought an old soldier-servant, called Stillman, and established him, with his wife and family, in a cottage in one of the Kensington lanes. It is said the Duke had recommended this former retainer to the care of the Duchess, and that she and her daughter were in the habit of visiting and caring for the family, in which there were a sickly little boy and girl. An event happened in 1828 to the household in Kensington Palace which was of importance to all. It was a joyful event, and the preparations for the royal wedding, with the gala in which the preliminaries culminated, must have formed an era in the quiet young life into which a startling announcement and its fulfilment had broken, filling the hours of the short winter days with wonder, admiration, and interest.

Yet all the pleasant stir and excitement; the new member of the family prominent for a brief space; the gifts, the trousseau, the wedding-cake, the wedding guests, were but the deceptive herald of change and loss to the family, whose members were so few that each became deeply precious. The closely united circle was to be broken, and a dear face permanently withdrawn from the group. The Duchess of Kent's elder daughter, Princess Victoria's only sister, was about to marry. It was the most natural and the happiest course, above all when the Princess Feodora wedded worthily—how worthily let the subsequent testimony of the Queen and the Prince Consort prove. It was given at the time of the Prince of Hohenlohe's death, thirty-two years afterwards, in 1860.

The Queen wrote to her own and her sister's uncle, the King of the Belgians, in reference to the Prince of Hohenlohe: "A better, more thoroughly straightforward, upright, and excellent man, with a more unblemished character, or a more really devoted and faithful husband, never existed."

The Prince Consort's opinion of his brother-in-law is to be found in a letter to the Princess William of Prussia: "Poor Ernest Hohenlohe is a great loss. Though he was not a man of great powers of mind, capable of taking comprehensive views of the world, still he was a great character —that is to say, a thoroughly good, noble, spotless, and honourable man, which in these days forms a better title to be recognised as great than do craftiness, Machiavellism, and grasping ambition."

At the time of his marriage the Prince of Hohenlohe was in the prime of manhood, thirty-two years of age.

But the marriage meant the Princess Feodora's return to Germany and her separation from the other members of her family, with the exception of her brother, brought up in his own country. The bride, whom we hear of afterwards as a true and tender woman, was then a sweet maiden of twenty, whose absence must have made a great blank to her mother and sister. Happily for the latter, she was too young to realise in the agreeable excitement of the moment what a deprivation remained in store for her. There were eleven years between the sisters. This was enough difference to mingle a motherly, protecting element with the elder sister's pride and fondness, and to lead the younger, whose fortunes were so much higher, but who was unaware of the fact, to look up with affectionate faith and trust to the grown-up companion, in one sense on a level with the child, in another with so much more knowledge and independence.

It was a German marriage, both bride and bridegroom being German, though the bride had been nine years—the difference between a child and a woman—in England, and though the event occurred in an English household. Whether the myrtle was worn for the orange-blossoms, or any of the other pretty German wedding customs imported, we cannot tell. Anyhow, the ordinary peaceful simplicity of the palace was replaced by much bustle and grandeur on that February morning, the modest forerunner of another February morning in another palace, when a young Queen plighted her troth.

The royal family in England, with two exceptions, were at Kensington Palace to do honour to the marriage. The absent members were the King and Princess Augusta—the latter of whom was at Brighton. The company arrived soon after two o'clock, and consisted of the Duke and Duchess of Clarence, the Duke of Sussex, the Duke and Duchess of Gloucester, the Princess Sophia, the Princess Sophia Matilda of Gloucester, and Prince Leopold.

At three o'clock the party walked in procession to the great saloon adjoining the vestibule, in which a temporary altar had been fitted up. The bride was given away by the Duke of Clarence. The ceremony was performed in the simple Lutheran fashion by a simple Lutheran pastor, Dr. Kuper, "the chaplain of the Royal German Chapel."

Then came the parting, and the quiet palace-home was stiller and shadier than ever, when the gracious maidenly presence had gone, when the opening rose was plucked from the parent stem, and only the bud left.

In 1830 George IV. died, and William, Duke of Clarence, succeeded to the throne as King William IV. That summer was the last of the Princess's ignorance of her prospects; until then not even the shadow of a throne had been projected across the sunshiny path of the happy girl of eleven. She was with her mother in one of the fairest scenes in England—Malvern. The little town with its old Priory among the Worcester hills, looks down on the plain of Worcester, the field of a great English battle.

A dim recollection of the Duchess and the Princess is still preserved at Malvern—how pleasant and kind they were to all, how good to the poor; how the future Queen rode on a donkey like any other young girl at Malvern—like poor Marie Antoinette in the forest glades of Compiegne and Fontainebleau half a century earlier, when she was only four years older, although already Dauphiness of France. The shadowy records do not tell us much more; we are left to form our own conclusions whether the Queen anticipated her later ascents of Scotch and Swiss mountains by juvenile scrambles amongst the Worcester hills; whether she stood on the top of the Worcester or Hereford Beacon; or whether these were considered too dangerous and masculine exploits for a princess of tender years, growing up to inherit a throne? She could hardly fail to enter the Wytche, the strange natural gap between Worcestershire and Herefordshire, by which, at one step, the wayfarer leaves wooded England behind, and stands face to face with a pastoral corner of Wales; or to drive along the mile-long common of Barnard's Green, with the geese, and the hay-stacks, and the little cottages on either side, and always in front the steep ridge of hills with the grey Priory where Piers Plowman saw his vision, nestling at their feet; or to pull the heather and the wild strawberries in Cowleigh Park, from which every vestige of its great house has departed. She might have been a privileged visitor at Madresfield, where some say Charles II. slept the night before the battle of Worcester, and where there is a relic that would better become Kensington, in a quilt which Queen Anne and Duchess Sarah embroidered together in silks in the days of their fast friendship.

As it was part of the Princess's good education to be enlightened, as far as possible, with regard to the how and why of arts and manufactures, we make no question she was carried to Worcester, not only to see the cathedral, but to have the potteries exhibited to her. There was a great deal for the ingenuous mind of a royal pupil to see, learn, and enjoy in Worcester and

Warwickshire—for she was also at Guy's Cliff and Kenilworth.

It had become clear to the world without that the succession rested with the Duke of Kent's daughter. Long before, the Duchess of Clarence had written to her sister-in-law in a tender, generous struggle with her sorrow: "My children are dead, but yours lives, and she is mine too." As the direct heir to the crown, the Princess Victoria became a person of great importance, a source of serious consideration alike to the Government and to her future subjects. The result, in 1830, was a well-deserved if somewhat long-delayed testimony to the merits of the Duchess of Kent, which must have given honest satisfaction not only at Kensington, but at Claremont—to whose master the Belgian Revolution was opening up the prospect of a kingdom more stable than that of Greece, for which Prince Leopold had been mentioned. Away in the Duchess's native Coburg, too, the congratulations were sincere and hearty.

The English Parliament had not only formally recognised the Princess as the next heir and increased the Duchess's income to ten thousand a year, so relieving her from some of her difficulties; it had, with express and flattering reference to the admirable manner in which she had until then discharged the trust that her husband had confided to her, appointed her Regent in the event of King William's death while the Princess was still a minor. In this appointment the Duchess was preferred to the Duke of Cumberland. He had become the next royal Duke in the order of descent, but had failed to inspire confidence in his countrymen. In fact he was in England the most uniformly and universally unpopular of all George III.'s sons. There was even a wild rumour that he was seeking, against right and reason, to form a party which should attempt to revive the Salic law and aim at setting aside the Princess and placing Prince George of Cumberland on the throne of England as well as on that of Hanover.

The Princess had reached the age of twelve, and it was judged advisable, after her position had been thus acknowledged, that she herself should be made acquainted with it. The story—the authenticity of which is established beyond question—is preserved in a letter from the Queen's former governess, Baroness Lehzen, which her Majesty has, given to the world.

"I ask your Majesty's leave to cite some remarkable words of your Majesty when only twelve years old, while the Regency Bill was in progress. I then said to the Duchess of Kent, that now, for the first time, your Majesty ought to know your place in the succession. Her Royal Highness agreed with me, and I put the genealogical table into the historical book. When Mr. Davys (the Queen's instructor, afterwards Bishop of Peterborough) was gone, the Princess Victoria opened the book again, as usual, and seeing the additional paper, said, 'I never saw that before.' 'It was not thought necessary you should, Princess,' I answered. 'I see I am nearer the throne than I thought.' 'So it is, madam,' I said. After some moments the Princess answered, 'Now, many a child would boast, but they don't know the difficulty. There is much splendour, but there is more responsibility.' The Princess having lifted up the forefinger of her right hand while she spoke, gave me that little hand, saying, 'I will be good. I understand now why you urged me so much to learn even Latin. My aunts Augusta and Mary never did; but you told me Latin is the foundation of English grammar and of all the elegant expressions, and I learned it as you wished it, but I understand all better now;' and the Princess gave me her hand, repeating, 'I will be good.' I then said, 'But your aunt Adelaide is still young, and may have children, and of course they would ascend the throne after their father, William IV., and not you, Princess.' The Princess answered, 'And if it was so, I should never feel disappointed, for I know by the love aunt Adelaide bears me how fond she is of children.'"

No words can illustrate better what is striking and touching in this episode than those with which Mrs. Oliphant refers to it in her sketch of the Queen. "It is seldom that an early scene like this stands out so distinctly in the early story even of a life destined to greatness. The hush of awe upon the child; the childish application of this great secret to the abstruse study of Latin, which was not required from the others; the immediate resolution, so simple, yet containing all the wisest sage could have counselled, or the greatest hero vowed,' I will be good,' makes a perfect little picture. It is the clearest appearance of the future Queen in her own person that we get through the soft obscurity of those childish years." The Duchess of Kent remained far from a rich woman for her station, and the young Princess had been sooner told of her mother's straitened income than of the great inheritance in store for herself. She continued to be brought up in unassuming, inexpensive habits.

In February, 1831, when Princess Victoria was twelve, she made her first appearance in state at "the most magnificent Drawing-room which, had been seen since that which had taken place on the presentation of Princess Charlotte of Wales upon the occasion of her marriage." The Drawing-room was held by Queen Adelaide, and it was to do honour to the new Queen no less than to commemorate the approaching completion of the Princess's twelfth year that the heiress to the throne was present in a prominent position, an object of the greatest interest to the splendid company. She came along with the Duchess her mother, attended by an appropriate suite, including the Duchess of Northumberland, Lady Charlotte St. Maur, Lady Catherine Parkinson, the Hon. Mrs. Cust, the Baroness Lehzen, and the Princess's father's old friends, General Wetherall and Captain (now Sir John) Conroy, with his wife, Lady Conroy. The Princess's dress was made, as the Queen's often was afterwards, entirely of articles manufactured in the United Kingdom. She wore a frock of English blonde, "simple, modest, and becoming." She stood on the left of her Majesty on the throne, and "contemplated all that passed with much dignity, but with evident interest." We are further told, what we can well believe, that she excited general admiration as well as interest. We can without difficulty call up before us the girlish figure in its pure, white dress, the soft, open face, the fair hair, the candid blue eyes, the frank lips slightly apart, showing the white pearly teeth. The intelligent observation, the remarkable absence of self-consciousness and consequent power of self-control and of thought for others, which struck all who approached her in the great crisis of her history six years afterwards, were already conspicuous in the young girl. No doubt it was for her advantage, in consideration of what lay before her, that while brought up in wholesome privacy, she was at the same time inured, so far, to appear in public, to bear the brunt of many eyes—some critical, though for the most part kind—touched by her youth and innocence, by the circumstance that she was fatherless, and by the crown she must one day wear. She had to learn to conduct herself with the mingled self-respect and ease which became her station. Impulsiveness, shyness, nervousness, are more serious defects in kings and queens than in ordinary mortals. To use a homely phrase, "to have all their wits about them" is very necessary in their case. If in addition they can have all their hearts—hearts warm and considerate, nobly mindful of their own obligations and of the claims of others—so much the better for the sovereigns and for all who come under their influence. A certain amount of familiarity with being the observed of all observers, with treading alone a conspicuous path demanding great circumspection, was wanted beforehand, in order that the young head might remain steady in the time of sudden, tremendous elevation.

Nevertheless, the Princess was not present at the coronation of King William and Queen Adelaide, and her absence, as the heir-presumptive to the throne, caused much remark and speculation, and gave rise to not a few newspaper paragraphs. Various causes were assigned for the singular omission. The Times openly accused the Duchess of Kent of proving the obstacle. Other newspapers followed suit, asserting that the grounds for the Duchess's refusal were to be found in the circumstance that in the coronation procession, marshalled by Lord A. Fitzclarence, the place appointed for the Princess Victoria, instead of being next to the King and Queen, according to her right, was after the remaining members of the royal family. Conflicting authorities declared that the Prime Minister, Earl Grey, for some occult reason, opposed the Princess's receiving an invitation to be present at a ceremony which had so much interest for her; or that the Duchess of Northumberland, the governess of the Princess, took the same extraordinary course from political motives. Finally, The Globe gave, on authority, an explanation that had been offered all along in the midst of more sensational rumours. The Princess's health was rather delicate, and the Duchess of Kent had, on that account, got the King's sanction to her daughter's not being exposed to unusual excitement and fatigue. The statement on authority was unanswerable, but while it stilled one cause of apprehension it awakened another. After the untimely death of Princess Charlotte, the nation was particularly sensitive with regard to the health of the heir to the crown. Whispers began to spread abroad, happily without much foundation, of pale cheeks, and a constitution unfit for the burden which was to be laid upon it.

CHAPTER III. YOUTH.

In the month of August, 1831, the Princess went with her mother to profit by the soft, sweet breezes of the Isle of Wight. The Duchess and her daughter occupied Norris Castle for three months, and the ladies of the family were often on the shore watching the white sails and chatting with the sailors. Carisbrooke and King Charles the Martyr were brought more vividly home to his descendant, with the pathetic little tale of the girl-Princess Elizabeth. We do not know whether the Queen then learnt to feel a special love for the fair little island with which she has long been familiar, but of this we are certain, that she could then have had little idea that her chief home would be within its bounds. Even in 1831 transport and communication by land and water continued a tedious and troublesome business. However, the visit to the Isle of Wight was repeated in 1833. Perhaps to dissipate the gossip and calm the little irritation which had been created by the Princess's absence from the coronation, she made her appearance twice in public, on the completion of her thirteenth year, in 1832. That was a year in which there was much call for oil to be cast on the troubled waters: never since 1819, the date of the Queen's birth had there been greater restlessness and turmoil throughout the country. For some time public feeling had been kept at the boiling-point by the question of the Reform Bill—groaned over by some as the first step to democracy and destruction; eagerly hailed by others as a new dawn of freedom, peace, and prosperity. The delay in passing the Bill had rendered the King unpopular, and brought unmerited blame on Queen Adelaide, for having gone beyond her prerogative in lending herself to overthrow the King's Whig principles. The ferment had converted the old enthusiastic homage to the Iron Duke as a soldier into fierce detestation of him as a statesman. The carrying of the measure on which the people had set their hearts did not immediately allay the tempest—a disappointing result, which was inevitable when the universal panacea failed to work at once like a charm in relieving all the woes in the kingdom. Men were not only rude, and spoke their minds, the ringleaders broke out again into riots, the most formidable and alarming of which were those in Bristol, that left a deep impression on more than one chance spectator who witnessed them. But the girl Princess—praised for her proficiency in Horace and Virgil, and her progress in mathematics—could only hear far off the mutterings of the storm that was passing; and King William and Queen Adelaide sought to put aside what was perplexing and harassing them; and tried to forget that when they had shown themselves to their people lately they had been met—here with indifference—and there with hootings. The times were waxing more and more evil, as it seemed, to uneasy, vexed wearers of crowns, unlike those in which old King George and Queen Charlotte had been received with fervent acclamation wherever they went, whatever wars were being waged or taxes imposed. The manners of the Commons were not improving with the extension of their rights. But the King and Queen would do their duty, which was far from disagreeable to them, in paying proper respect to their niece and successor. Accordingly their Majesties gave a ball on the Princess's thirteenth birthday, 24th May, 1832, at which the heroine of the day figured; and four days later, on the 28th of May, she was present for the second time at a Drawing-room.

All the same, it is an open secret that William, living, for the most part, in that noblest palace of Windsor, considered the Princess led too retired a life, so far as not appearing often enough at his Court was concerned, and that he complained of her absence and resented it as a slight to himself. It is an equally well-established fact that, in spite of the King's kindness of heart and Queen Adelaide's goodness, King William's Court was not in all respects a desirable place for a Princess to grow up in, in addition to the objection that any Court in itself formed an unsuitable schoolroom for a young girl.

It is doubtful, since even the most magnanimous men have jealous instincts, whether the King's displeasure on one point would be appeased by what was otherwise a very natural and judicious step taken by the Duchess of Kent this year. She made an autumn tour with her daughter through several counties of England and Wales, in the course of which the royal mother and daughter paid a succession of visits to seats of different noblemen, taking Oxford on the way. If there was a place in England which deserved the notice of its future Queen, it was one of the two great universities—the cradles of learning, and, in the case of "the most loyal city of Oxford," the bulwark of the throne. The party proceeded early in October through the beautiful scenery of North Wales—the Princess's first experience of mountains—to Eaton Hall, the home of the Grosvenor family. From Eaton the travellers drove to the ancient city of Chester, with its quaint arcades and double streets, its God's Providence House and its cathedral. At Chester the Princess named the new bridge which was opened on the occasion. By the wise moderation and self-repression of those around her, the name bestowed was not the "Victoria," but simply the "Grosvenor Bridge."

From Eaton the Princess was taken to Chatsworth, the magnificent seat of the Cavendishes. She stayed long enough to see and hear something of romantic Derbyshire. She visited Hardwick, associated with Building Bess, whose granddaughter, the unfortunate "Lady Arbell," had been a remote cousin of this happy young Princess, and she went, like everybody else, to Matlock. At Belper the party, in diligent search after all legitimate knowledge, examined the great cotton-mills of the Messrs. Strutt, and the senior partner had the honour of showing to her Royal Highness, by means of a model, how cotton was spun.

From Chatsworth the Duchess and her daughter repaired to Alton Abbey, where the "Talbot tykes" still kept watch and ward; thence to Shugborough, the seat of the Earl of Lichfield, which enabled the visitors to see another fine cathedral and to breathe the air which is full of "the great Dr. Johnson."

At each of the towns the strangers were met by addresses—of course made to the Duchess and replied to by her. How original these formal compliments must have sounded to Princess Victoria! On the 27th of October their Royal Highnesses were at Pitchford Hall, the residence of the Earl of Liverpool, from which they visited Shrewsbury—another Chester—with a word of its own for the old fateful battle in which "Percy was slain and Douglas taken prisoner," and the

Welsh power broken in Owen Glendower. After getting a glimpse of the most picturesque portion of Shropshire, halting at more noble seats, and passing through a succession of Worcester towns, the royal party reached Woodstock on the 7th of November, and the same evening rested at Wytham House, belonging to the Earl of Abingdon. There was hardly time to realise that the memories of Alice Lee, the old knight Sir Henry, and the faithful dog Bevis, rivalled successfully the grisly story of Queen Eleanor and Fair Rosamond. Nay, the magician was still dogging the travellers' steps; for had he not made the little town of Abingdon his own by choosing it for the meeting-place of Mike Lambourne and Tressillian, and rebuilding in its neighbourhood the ruins of Cumnor Hall, on which the dews fell softly? Alas! the wizard would weave no more spells. A month before that princely "progress" Sir Walter Scott, after Herculean labours to pay his debts like an honest man had wrecked even his robust frame and healthful genius, lay dead at Abbotsford.

On the 8th of November the future Queen entered Oxford with something like State, in proper form escorted by a detachment of Yeomanry. There is no need to tell that she was received by the Vice-Chancellor of the University, and the dons and doctors of the various colleges, in full array. And she was told of former royal visitors: of Charles in his tribulation; of her grandfather and grandmother, King George and Queen Charlotte, when little Miss Barney was there to describe the festivities. The Princess went the usual round: to superb Christ Church, at which her sons were to graduate; to the Bodleian and Radclyffe libraries; to All Souls, New College, &c. She proceeded to view other buildings, which, unless in a local guide-book, are not usually included among the lions of Oxford. But this young lady of the land was bound to encourage town as well as gown; therefore she visited duly the Town Hall and Council Chamber. From Oxford the tourists returned to Kensington.

There are no greater contrasts than those which are to be found in royal lives. When the Princess Victoria was about to set out on her pleasant journey in peace and prosperity, the news came of the arrest of the Duchesse de Berri, at Nantes. It was the sequel to her gallant but unsuccessful attempt to raise La Vendee in the name of her young son, Henri de Bordeaux, and the end to the months in which she had lain in hiding. She was discovered in the chimney of a house in the Rue Haute-du-Chateau, where she was concealed with three other conspirators against the Government of her cousin, Louis Philippe. The search had lasted for several hours, during which these unfortunate persons were penned in a small space and exposed to almost intolerable heat. A mantelpiece had been contrived so as to turn on a swivel and form an opening into a suffocating recess. When the Duchesse and her companions were found their hands were scorched and part of their clothes burnt. She was taken to the fortress of Nantes, and thence transferred to the Castle of Blaze, where she suffered a term of imprisonment. She had acted entirely on her own responsibility, her wild enterprise having being disapproved alike by her father-in-law, Charles X., and her brother and sister-in-law, the Duc and Duchesse d'Angouleme.

In 1833, we are told, the Duchess of Kent and the fourteen years old Princess stopped on their way to Weymouth—the old favourite watering-place of King George and Queen Charlotte—and visited the young Queen of Portugal, at Portsmouth. Donna Maria da Gloria had been sent from Brazil to England by her father, Don Pedro, partly for her safety, partly under the impression, which proved false, that the English Government would take an active part in her cause against the usurpation of her uncle, Don Miguel. The Government did nothing. The royal family paid the stranger some courtly and kindly attentions. One of the least exceptional passages in the late Charles Greville's Memoirs is the description of the ball given by the King, at which the two young queens—to be—were present. The chronicle describes the girls, who were of an age—

having been born in the same year: the sensible face of the fair-haired English Princess, and the extreme dignity—especially after she had sustained an accidental fall—of the Portuguese royal maiden, inured to the hot sun of the tropics. Don Miguel was routed in the course of the following year (1834), and his niece was established in her kingdom. Within the same twelve months she lost a father and gained and lost a husband; for among the first news that reached her English acquaintances was her marriage, before she was sixteen, and her widowhood within three months. She had married, in January, the Duc de Leuchtenberg, a brother of her stepmother and a son of Eugene Beauharnais. He died, after a short illness, in the following March. She married again in the next year, her re-marriage having been earnestly desired by her subjects. The second husband was Prince Ferdinand of Coburg, belonging to the Roman Catholic branch of the Coburgs, and cousin both to the Queen and the Prince Consort. He was a worthy and, ultimately, a popular prince. Donna Maria was grand-niece to Queen Amelie of France, and showed much attachment to the house of Orleans. There is said to have been a project formed by Louis Philippe, which was frustrated by the English Government, that she should marry one of his sons, the Duc de Nemours.

In addition to the English tours which the Princess Victoria made with her mother, the Duchess of Kent was careful that as soon as her daughter had grown old enough to profit by the association, she should meet the most distinguished men of the day—whether statesmen, travellers, men of science, letters, or art. Kensington had one well-known intellectual centre in Holland House, presided over by the famous Lady Holland, and was soon to have another in Gore House, occupied by Lady Blessington and Count D'Orsay; but even if the fourteen years old Princess had been of sufficient age and had gone into society, such salons were not for her. The Duchess must "entertain" for her daughter. In 1833 Lord Campbell mentions dining at Kensington Palace. The company found the Princess in the drawing-room on their arrival, and again on their return from the dining-room. He records her bright, pleasant intelligence, perfect manners, and happy liveliness.

In July, 1834, when the Princess was fifteen, she was confirmed in the Chapel Royal, St. James's, by the Archbishop of Canterbury, in the presence of the King and Queen and the Duchess of Kent. She was advancing with rapid steps to the point at which the girl leaves the child for ever behind her, and stretches forward to her crown of young womanhood. She had in her own name confirmed the baptismal vow which consecrated her as a responsible being to the service of the King of kings. Still she was a young creature, suffered to grow up according to a gracious natural growth, not forced into premature expansion, permitted to preserve to the last the sweet girlish trust and confidence, the mingled coyness and fearlessness, pensive dreams and merry laughter, which constitute the ineffable freshness and tender grace of youth.

If the earlier story of the purchase, or non-purchase, of the box at Tunbridge Wells reads "like an incident out of 'Sandford and Merton,'" there is another anecdote fitting into this time which has still more of the good-fairy ring in it, while it sounds like a general endorsement of youthful wisdom. Yet it may have had its origin in some eager, youthful fancy of astonishing another girl, and giving her "the very thing she wanted" as a reward for her exemplary behaviour. The Princess was visiting a jeweller's shop incognito (a little in the fashion of Haroun-al-Raschid) when she saw another young lady hang long over some gold chains, lay down reluctantly the one which she evidently preferred, and at last content herself with buying a cheaper chain. The interested on-looker waited till the purchaser was gone, made some inquiries, directed that both chains should be tied up and sent together, along with the Princess Victoria's card, on which a few words were pencilled to the effect that the Princess had been pleased to see prudence prevail, while she desired the young lady to accept her original choice, in the hope that she would always persevere in her laudable self-denial.

In the autumn of 1835 the Duchess of Kent and the Princess went as far north as York, visiting the Archbishop at Bishopsthorpe, studying the minster—second only to Westminster among English abbeys—and gracing with the presence of royalty the great York Musical Festival. On the travellers' homeward route they were the guests of the Earl of Harewood, at Harewood House, Earl Fitzwilliam at Wentworth, and the Duke of Rutland at Belvoir. At Burghley House the Duchess and the Princess visited the Marquis of Exeter. The late Charles Greville met them there, and gives a few particulars of their visit. "They arrived from Belvoir at three o'clock, in a heavy rain, the civic authorities having turned out at Stamford to escort them and a procession of different people, all very loyal. When they had lunched, and the Mayor and his brethren had got dry, the Duchess received the Address, which was read by Lord Exeter, as Recorder. It talked of the Princess as 'destined to mount the throne of these realms.' Conroy handed the answer just as the Prime Minister does to the King. They are splendidly lodged, and great preparations have been made for their reception. The dinner at Burghley was very handsome; hall well lit, and all went off well, except that a pail of ice was landed in the Duchess's lap, which made a great bustle. Three hundred people at the ball, which was opened by Lord Exeter and the Princess, who, after dancing one dance, went to bed. They appeared at breakfast next morning at nine o'clock, and at ten set off to Holkham."

Romance was not much in Mr. Greville's way, but Burghley, apart from the statesman Cecil and his weighty nod, had been the scene of such a romance as might well have captivated the imagination of a young princess, though its heroine was but a village maiden—she who married the landscape-painter, and was brought by him to Burghley, bidden look around at its splendour, and told

"All of this is thine and mine."

Tennyson has sung it—how she grew a noble lady, and yet died of the honour to which she was not born, and how the Lord of Burghley, deeply mourning, bid her attendants

"Bring the dress and put it on her
Which she wore when we were wed."

In one of those autumns which the Duchess of Kent and her daughter spent at Ramsgate—not so rural as it had been a dozen years before, but still a quiet enough retreat—they received a visit from the King and Queen of the Belgians. Prince Leopold was securely established on the throne which he filled so well and so long, keeping it when many other European sovereigns were unseated. He was accompanied by his second wife, Princess Louise of France, daughter of Louis Philippe. She was a good woman, like all the daughters of Queen Amelie, while Princess Marie, in addition to goodness, had the perilous gift of genius. The following is Baron Stockmar's opinion of the Queen of the Belgians. "From the moment that the (Queen Louise) entered that circle in which I for so many years have had a place, I have revered her as a pattern of her sex. We say and believe that men can be noble and good; of her we know with certainty that she was so. We saw in her daily a truthfulness, a faithful fulfilment of duty, which makes us believe in the possible though but seldom evident nobleness of the human heart. In characters such as the Queen's, I see a guarantee of the perfection of the Being who has created human nature." We ought to add that Stockmar had not only the highest opinion of the character of Queen Louise, but also of her insight and judgment, and he often expressed his opinion that if anything were to happen to King Leopold the Regency might be entrusted to the Queen with perfect confidence. How much the Queen valued Queen Louise, how she became Queen Victoria's dearest friend, is fully shown at a later date by the extracts from the Queen's journal, and letters in the "Life of the Prince Consort"

About this time the Duchess of Kent and Princess Victoria paid a visit to the Duke of Wellington at Walmer Castle—the old tower with fruit-trees growing in the dry moat, and a slip from the weeping-willow which hung over the grave in St. Helena flourishing in its garden, where the Warden of the Cinque Ports could look across the roadstead of the Downs and count the ships' masts like trees in a forest, and watch the waves breaking twenty feet high on the Goodwin Sands. "The cut-throat town of Deal" which poor Lucy Hutchinson so abhorred, pranked its quaint red houses for so illustrious and dainty a visitor. The Duke had stood by her font, and if he had "no small talk," he was a courteous gentleman and gentle warrior when he fought his battles over again for the benefit of the young Princess.

A winter was spent by the Duchess and the Princess at St. Leonard's, not far from Battle Abbey, where the last Saxon king of England bit the dust, and William of Normandy fought and won the great battle which rendered his invasion a conquest.

1836 was an eventful year in the Queen's life. We read that the Duchess of Kent and her daughter remained at Kensington till the month of September. There was a good reason for staying at home in the early summer. The family entertained friends: not merely valued, kinsfolk, but visitors who might change the whole current of a life's history and deeply influence a destiny on which the hopes of many hearts were fixed, that concerned the well-being of millions of the human race. Princess Victoria had not grown up solitary in her high estate. It has been already pointed out that she was one in a group of cousins with whom she had cordial relations. But the time was drawing near when nature and policy alike pointed to the advisability of forming a closer tie, which would provide the Princess with companionship and support stretching beyond those of her mother, and, if it were well and wisely chosen, afford the people further assurance that the first household in the kingdom should be such as they could revere. The royal maiden who had been educated so wisely and grown up so simply and healthfully, was approaching her seventeenth birthday. Already there were suitors in store for her hand; as many as six had been seriously thought of—among them, Prince Alexander of the Netherlands, whose suit was greatly favoured by King William; Duke Ernest of Wurtemberg; Prince Adalbert of Prussia; and Prince George of Cambridge. Prince George of Cumberland was hors de combat, apart from the Duke of Cumberland's pretensions and the alienation caused by them. Prince George, when a baby, had lost the sight of one eye, a misfortune which his father shared. A few years later in the son's boyhood, as he was at play in the gardens of Windsor Castle, he began to amuse himself with flinging into the air and catching a long silk purse with heavy gold tassels, when the purse fell on the seeing eye, inflicting such an injury as to threaten him with total blindness. The last catastrophe was brought about by the blunder of a famous German oculist after Prince George had become Crown Prince of Hanover.

How much the Princess knew or guessed of those matrimonial prospects, how far they fluttered her innocent heart, we cannot tell; but as of all the candidates mentioned there was only one with whom she had any acquaintance to speak of, it may be supposed that the generality of the proposed wooers passed like vague shadows before her imagination.

In the meantime the devoted friends of her whole life had naturally not left this question—the most important of all—entirely unapproached. Her English cousins stood to her somewhat in the room of contemporary brothers and sisters; for her own brother and sister, however united to her in affection, were removed from her by age, by other ties, and by residence in a foreign country, to which in 1833 there was still no highway well trodden by the feet of kings and queens and their heirs-presumptive, as well as by meaner people, such as we find to-day. But there were other cousins of whom much had been said and heard, though they had remained unseen and personally unknown. For that very reason they were more capable of being idealised and surrounded by a halo of romance.

At the little ducal Court of Coburg there was the perfect young prince of all knightly legends and lays, whom fate seemed to have mated with his English cousin from their births within a few months of each other. When he was a charming baby of three years the common nurse of the pair would talk to him of his little far-away royal bride. The common grandmother of the two, a wise and witty old lady, dwelt fondly on the future union of her youngest charge with the "Mayflower" across the seas.

In all human probability these grandmotherly predictions would have come to nothing had it not been for a more potent arbiter of the fortunes of his family. King Leopold had once filled the very post which was now vacant, for which there were so many eager aspirants. None could know as he knew the manifold and difficult requirements for the office; none could care as he cared that it should be worthily filled. His interest in England had never wavered, though he had renounced his English annuity of fifty thousand a year on his accession to the throne of Belgium. He was deeply attached to the niece who stood nearly in the same position which Princess Charlotte had occupied twenty years before. Away in Coburg there was a princely lad whom he loved as a son, and who held the precise relation to the ducal house which he himself had once filled. What was there to hinder King Leopold from following out the comparison? Who could blame him for seeking to rebuild, in the interest of all, the fair edifice of love and happiness and loyal service which had been shattered before the dawn of those lives—that were like the lives of his children—had arisen? Besides, look where he might, and study character and chances with whatever forethought, he could not find such another promising bridegroom for the future Queen of England. Young, handsome, clever, good, endowed with all winning attributes; with wise, well-balanced judgment in advance of his years; with earnest, steadfast purpose, gentle, sympathetic temper, and merry humour.

King Leopold's instinct was not at fault, as the result proved; but it was not without the most careful consideration and many anxious consultations, especially with his trusty old friend, Baron Stockmar, that the King allowed himself to take the initiatory step in the matter. If the young couple were to love and wed it was certainly necessary that they should meet, that "the favourable impression" might be made, as the two honourable conspirators put it delicately. For this there was no more time to be lost, when so many suitors had already entered the lists, and the maiden only wanted a year of the time fixed for her majority. But with conscientious heedfulness for the feelings of the youthful pair, and for their power of forming separately an unbiassed opinion, it was settled that when an opportunity of becoming acquainted should be given them, the underlying motive must be kept secret from the Princess as well as the Prince, that they might be "perfectly at their ease with each other." This secrecy could not, however, extinguish the previous knowledge which the Prince at least possessed, that a marriage between the cousins had been mooted by some of those most interested in their welfare.

In spite of the obstacles which King William raised, an invitation was sent by the Duchess of Kent to her brother, the reigning Duke of Saxe-Coburg, to pay her a visit, accompanied by his two sons, in the spring of 1836. Accordingly, in the month which is the sweetest of the year, in spite of inconstant skies and chill east winds, when Kensington Gardens were bowery and fair with the tender green foliage—the chestnut and hawthorn blossoms—the lilac and laburnum plumes of early summer, the goodly company arrived, and made the old brick palace gay with the fresh and fitting gaiety of youth.

We may never know how the royal cousins met—whether the frank, kind, unconscious Princess came down under the wing of the Duchess as far as their entrance into the Clock Court; whether there was a little dimness of agitation and laughing confusion, in spite of the partial secrecy, in two pairs of blue eyes which then encountered each other for the first time; whether the courtly company ascended in well-arranged file, or in a little friendly disorder. It was fortunate that there were more doors and halls and staircases than one, for it goes without saying that nobody could have had time and attention to spare for the wonderfully elaborate staircase, the representation in chiaroscuro of horses and warlike weapons, the frieze with heads of unicorns and masks of lions. It must have been on another day that young heads looked up in jest or earnest at Hercules, Diana, Apollo, and Minerva, and stopped to pick out the heterogeneous figures in the colonnade—"ladies, yeomen of the guard, pages, a quaker, two Turks, a Highlander, and Peter the Wild Boy," which testified to the liberal imagination of Kent, who executed not only the architecture, but the painting, in the reign of George I.

The guests remained at Kensington for a month, the only drawback to their pleasure being a little attack of bilious fever, from which Prince Albert suffered for a few days. There is a published letter to his stepmother in which the Prince tells his doings in the most unaffected, kindly fashion. There were the King's levee, "long and fatiguing, but very interesting;" the dinner at Court, and the "beautiful concert" which followed, at which the guests had to stand till two o'clock; the King's birthday, with the Drawing-room at St. James's Palace, where three thousand eight hundred people passed before the King and Queen, and another great dinner and concert in the evening. There was also the "brilliant ball" at Kensington Palace, at which the gentlemen were in uniform and the ladies in fancy dresses. Duke William of Brunswick, the Prince of Orange and his sons, and the Duke of Wellington, were among the guests, and the Princes of Coburg helped to keep up the ball till four o'clock. They spent a day with the Duke of Northumberland at Sion House, they went to Claremont, and they were so constantly engaged that they had to make the most of their time in order to see at least some of the sights of London. To one of the sights the Queen referred afterwards. The Duke of Coburg and the two Princes accompanied the Duchess of Kent and the Princess to the wonderful gathering of the children of the different charity schools in St. Paul's Cathedral, where Prince Albert listened intently to the sermon. We hardly need to be told that he was full of interest in everything, paid the greatest attention to all he saw, and was constantly occupied. Among his pleasant occupations were the two favourite pursuits—which the cousins shared—music and drawing. He accompanied the Princess on the piano, and he drew with and for her. It was a happy, busy time, though some of the late dinners, at which, the Prince drank only water, were doubtless dull enough of the young people, and Prince Albert, accustomed to the early hours and simple habits of Germany, felt the change trying. He confessed that it was sometimes with the greatest difficulty he could keep awake. The Princess's birthday came round during her kinsman's visit. The Prince alluded to the event and to his stay at Kensington in writing to the Duchess of Kent three years later, when he was the proud and happy bridegroom of his cousin. He made no note of the date as having had an effect on their relations to each other, neither did he dwell on any good wish or gift [Footnote: Lady Bloomfield mentions among the Queen's rings "a small enamel with a tiny diamond in the centre, the Prince's gift when he first came to England, a lad of seventeen."] on his part; but in compliance with a motherly request from his aunt, the Duchess, that he would send her something he had worn, he returned to her a ring that she had given him on that May morning. The ring had never left his finger since then. The very shape proclaimed that it had been squeezed in the grasp of many a manly hand. The ring had her name upon it, but the name was "Victoria" too, and he begged her to wear it in remembrance of his bride and himself.

The favourable impression had been made in spite of the perversity of fortune and the vagaries of human hearts, which, amidst other casualties, might have led the Princess to accord her preference to the elder brother, Prince Ernest, who was also "a fine young fellow," though not so well suited to become prince-consort to the Queen of England. But for once destiny was propitious, and neither that nor any other mischance befell the bright prospects of the principal actors in the scene. When the King of the Belgians could no longer refrain from expressing his hopes, he had the most satisfactory answer from his royal niece.

"I have only now to beg you, my dearest uncle," she wrote, "to take care of the health of one now so dear to me, and to take him under your special protection. I hope and trust that all will now go on prosperously and well on this subject, now of so much importance to me."

At the same time, though an affectionate correspondence was started and maintained for a year, no further communication passed which could tend to enlighten the Prince as to the feelings he had excited. He went away to complete his education, to study diligently, along with his brother, at Brussels and Bonn; to feel in full the gladness of opening life and opening powers of no ordinary description; to rejoice, as few young men have the same warrant to rejoice, in the days of his unstained, noble youth.

On the King's birthday, the 21st August, the Duchess of Kent and Princess Victoria were at Windsor Castle on a visit. In spite of some soreness over the old grievance, the King proposed the Princess Victoria's health very kindly at the dinner. After he had drunk the Princess Augusta's health he said, "And now, having given the health of the oldest I will give that of the youngest member of the royal family. I know the interest which the public feel about her, and although I have not seen so much of her as I could have wished, I take no less interest in her, and the more I do see of her, both in public and private, the greater pleasure it will give me." The whole thing was so civil and gracious that it could hardly be taken ill, but, says Greville, "the young Princess sat opposite and hung her head with not unnatural modesty at being thus talked of in so large a company."

In the September of that year the Duchess and the Princess went again to Ramsgate, and stayed there till December. It was their last visit to the quiet little resort within a short pilgrimage of Canterbury—the great English shrine, not so much of Thomas a Becket, slain before the altar, as of Edward the Black Prince, with his sword and gauntlets hung up for ever, and the inscription round the effigy which does not speak of Cressy and Poictiers, but of the vanity of human pride and ambition. It was the last seaside holiday which the mother and daughter spent together untrammelled by State obligations and momentous duties, with none to come between the two who had been all in all with each other. In their absence a storm of wind passed over London, and wrought great damage in Kensington Gardens. About a hundred and thirty of the larger trees were destroyed. In the forenoon of the 29th of November "a tremendous crash was heard in one of the plantations near the Black Pond, between Kensington Palace and the Mount Gate, and on several persons running to the spot twenty-five limes were found tumbled to the earth by a single blast, their roots reaching high into the air, with a great quantity of earth and turf adhering, while deep chasms of several yards in diameter showed the force with which they had been torn up.... On the Palace Green, Kensington, near the forcing-garden, two large elms and a very fine sycamore were also laid prostrate."

In the following summer (1837) the Princess came of age, as princesses do, at eighteen, and it was meet that the day should be celebrated with all honour and gladness. But the rejoicings were damped by the manifestly failing health of the aged King, then seventy-one years of age. He had been attacked by hay fever—to which he had been liable every spring at an earlier period of his life, but the complaint was more formidable in the case of an old and infirm man, while he still struggled manfully to transact business and discharge the duties of his position. At the Levee and Drawing-room of the 21st May he sat while receiving the company. By the 24th he was confined to his rooms, and the Queen did not leave him.

At six o'clock in the morning the Union Jack was hoisted on the summit of the old church, Kensington, and on the flagstaff at Palace Green. In the last instance the national ensign was surmounted by a white silk flag on which was inscribed in sky-blue letters "Victoria." The little town adorned itself to the best of its ability. "From the houses of the principal inhabitants of the High Street were also displayed the Royal Standard, Union Jack, and other flags and colours, some of them of extraordinary dimensions." Soon after six o'clock the gates of Kensington Gardens were thrown open for the admission of the public to be present at the serenade which was to be performed at seven o'clock under the Palace windows, with the double purpose of awaking the Princess in the most agreeable manner, and of reminding her that at the same place and hour, eighteen years ago, she had opened her eyes on the May world. The sleep of youth is light as well as sound, and it may well be that the Princess, knowing all that was in store for her on the happy day that could not be too long, the many goodly tokens of her friends' love and gladness—not the least precious those from Germany awaiting her acceptance—the innumerable congratulations to be offered to her, was wide awake before the first violin or voice led the choir. The bells rang out merry peals, carriages dashed by full of fine company. Kensington Square must have thought it was the old days of William and Mary, and Anne, or of George II and Queen Caroline at the latest, come back again. The last French dwellers in Edwardes Square must have talked volubly of what their predecessors had told them of Paris before the flood, Paris before the Orleanists, and the Bonapartists, and the Republic—Paris when the high-walled, green-gardened hotels of the Faubourg St. Germain were full of their ancient occupants; when Marie Antoinette was the daughter of the Caesars at the Tuileries, and the bergere Queen at le Petit Trianon. Before the sun went down many a bumper was drunk in honour of Kensington's own Princess, who should that day leave her girlhood all too soon behind her.

But London as well as Kensington rejoiced, and the festivities were wound up with a ball given at St. James's Palace by order of the poor King and Queen, over whose heads the cloud of sorrow and parting was hanging heavily. We are told that the ball opened with a quadrille, the Princess being "led off" by Lord Fitzalan, eldest son of the Earl of Surrey and grandson of the Duke of Norfolk, Premier Duke and Earl, Hereditary Earl Marshal and Chief Butler of England. Her Royal Highness danced afterwards with Prince Nicholas Esterhazy, son of the Austrian Ambassador. Prince Nicholas made a brilliant figure in contemporary annals—not because of his own merits, not because he married one of the fairest of England's noble daughters, whose gracious English hospitalities were long remembered in Vienna, but because of the lustre of the diamonds in his Court suit. He was said to sparkle from head to heel. There was a legend that he could not wear this splendid costume without a hundred pounds' worth of diamonds dropping from him, whether he would or not, in minor gems, just as jewels fell at every word from the mouth of the enchanted Princess. We have heard of men and women behind whose steps flowers sprang into birth, but Prince Nicholas left a more glittering, if a colder, harder track.

CHAPTER IV. THE ACCESSION.

On the day after that on which Princess Victoria celebrated her majority. Baron Stockmar arrived at Kensington. He came from the King of the Belgians to assist King Leopold's niece in what was likely to be the great crisis of her life. During Baron Stockmar's former stay in England he had been in the character first of Physician in Ordinary to Prince Leopold, and afterwards of Private Secretary and Comptroller of his household. In those offices he had spent the greater part of his time in this country from 1816 to 1834. He had accompanied his master on his ascending the Belgian throne, but had returned to England in a few years in order to serve him better there. Baron Stockmar was thus an old and early friend of the Princess's. In addition he had a large acquaintance with the English political world, and was therefore well qualified to advise her with the force of a disinterested adviser in her difficult position. In the view of her becoming Queen, although her three predecessors, including George III after he became blind, had appointed and retained private secretaries, the office was not popular in the eyes of the Government and country, and it was not considered advisable that the future Queen should possess such a servant, notwithstanding the weight of business—enormous in the matter of signatures alone—which would fall on the Sovereign. Without any recognised position, Stockmar was destined to share with the Prime Minister one portion of the duties which ought to have devolved on a private secretary. He was also to act as confidential adviser.

Baron Stockmar, [Footnote: "An active, decided, slender, rather little man, with a compact head, brown hair streaked with grey, a bold, short nose, firm yet full mouth, and what gave a peculiar air of animation to his face, with two youthful, flashing brown eyes, full of roguish intelligence and fiery provocation. With this exterior, the style of his demeanour and conversation corresponded; bold, bright, pungent, eager, full of thought, so that amid all the bubbling copiousness and easy vivacity of his talk, a certain purpose was never lost sight of in his remarks and illustrations."—Friedrich Carl Meyer.] who was at this time a man of fifty, was no ordinary character. He was sagacious, warm-hearted, honest, straightforward to bluntness, painstaking, just, benevolent to a remarkable degree; the friend of princes, without forfeiting his independence, he won and kept their perfect confidence to the end. He loved them heartily in return, without seeking anything from them; on the contrary, he showed himself reluctant to accept tokens of their favour. While lavishing his services on others, and readily lending his help to those who needed it, he would seem to have wanted comfort himself. An affectionate family man, he consented to constantly recurring separation from his wife and children in order to discharge the peculiar functions which were entrusted to him. For he played in the background—contented, nay, resolute to remain there—by the lawful exercise of influence alone, no small part in the destinies of several of the reigning houses in Europe, and through them, of their kingdoms. Like Carlyle, he suffered during his whole life from dyspepsia; like Carlyle, too, he was a victim to hypochondria, the result of his physical state. To these two last causes may be attributed some whimsicalities and eccentricities which were readily forgiven in the excellent Baron.

Baron Stockmar did not come too soon; in less than a month, on the 20th of
June, 1837, after an illness which he had borne, patiently and reverently,
King William died peacefully, his hand resting where it had lain for hours,
on the shoulder of his faithful Queen.

The death took place at Windsor, at a little after two o'clock in the morning. Immediately afterwards the Archbishop of Canterbury, Dr. Howley, and the Lord Chamberlain, the Marquis of Conyngham, together with the Earl of Albemarle, the Master of the Horse, and Sir Henry Halford, the late King's physician, started from Windsor for Kensington. All through the rest of the summer night these solemn and stately gentlemen drove, nodding with fatigue, hailing the early dawn, speaking at intervals to pronounce sentence on the past reign and utter prognostications, of the reign which was to come. Shortly before five, when the birds were already in full chorus in Kensington Gardens, the party stood at the main door, demanding admission. This was another and ruder summons than the musical serenade which had been planned to wile the gentle sleeper sweetly from her slumbers and to hail her natal day not a month before. That had been a graceful, sentimental recognition of a glad event; this was an unvarnished, well-nigh stern arousal to the world of grave business and anxious care, following the mournful announcement of a death—not a birth. From this day the Queen's heavy responsibilities and stringent obligations were to begin. That untimely, peremptory challenge sounded the first knell to the light heart and careless freedom of youth.

Though it had been well known that the King lay on his death-bed, and Kensington without, as well as Kensington within, must have been in a high state of expectation, it does not appear that there were any watchers on the alert to rush together at the roll of the three royal carriages. Instead of the eager, respectful crowd, hurrying into the early-opened gates of the park to secure good places for all that was to be seen and heard on the day of the Princess's coming of age, Palace Green seems to have been a solitude on this momentous June morning, and the individual the most interested in the event, after the new-made Queen, instead of being there to pay his homage first, as he had offered his congratulations on the birthday a year before, was far away, quietly studying at the little university town on the Rhine.

"They knocked, they rang, they thumped for a considerable time before they could rouse the porter at the gate," says Miss Wynn, in the "Diary of a Lady of Quality," of these importunate new-comers. "They were again kept waiting in the courtyard, then turned into one of the lower rooms, where they seemed forgotten by everybody. They rang the bell and desired that the attendant of the Princess Victoria might be sent to inform Her Royal Highness that they requested an audience on business of importance. After another delay and another ringing to inquire the cause, the attendant was summoned, who stated that the Princess was in such a sweet sleep that she could not venture to disturb her. Then they said, 'We are come on business of State to the QUEEN, and even her sleep must give way to that.' It did; and, to prove that she did not keep them waiting, in a few minutes she came into the room in a loose white nightgown and shawl, her nightcap thrown off, and her hair falling upon her shoulders, her feet in slippers, tears in her eyes, but perfectly collected and dignified."

In those days, when news did not travel very fast, and was not always delivered with strict accuracy, a rumour got abroad that the Queen was walking in the Palace Garden when the messengers came to tell her she had succeeded to the Crown. A great deal was made of the poetic simplicity of the surroundings of the interesting central figure—the girl in her tender bloom among the lilies and roses, which she resembled. We can remember a brilliant novel of the time which had a famous chapter beginning with an impassioned apostrophe to the maiden who met her high destiny "in a palace, in a garden." Another account asserted that the Queen saw the Archbishop of Canterbury alone in her ante-room, and that her first request was for his prayers.

The Marquis of Conyngham was the bearer to the Queen of a request from the Queen-dowager that she might be permitted to remain at Windsor till after the funeral. In reply, her Majesty wrote an affectionate letter of condolence to her aunt, begging her to consult nothing but her own health and convenience, and to stay at Windsor just as long as she pleased. The writer was observed to address this as usual "To the Queen of England." A bystander interposed, "Your Majesty, you are Queen of England." "Yes," answered the unelated, considerate girl-Queen, "but the widowed Queen is not to be reminded of the fact first by me."

Their message delivered, the messengers returned to London, and the next arrival was that of the Prime Minister, Lord Melbourne, who appeared at nine o'clock, had an interview with the Queen, which lasted for half an hour, when he also took his leave to issue summonses for a Privy Council, to he held in the course of the next two hours at Kensington Palace, and not at St. James's, as had been anticipated.

The little town of Kensington must now have been up and about, for, perhaps, never had there been such a day in its annals, as far transcending the birthday celebration as a great reality surpasses the brightest promise; and Kensington might hug the day with all its might, for it was to be nearly the last of its kingly, queenly experience. The temporary Court was to pass away presently, never to come back. No more kings and queens were likely to be born or to die at the quiet spot, soon to become a great noisy suburb of great London. No later Sovereign would quit the red-brick palace of Mary and Anne, and the First George, to reign at Buckingham or Windsor; no other Council be held in the low-browed, white-pillared room to dispute the interests of the unique Council which was to be held there this day.

The first Council of any Sovereign must awaken many speculations, while the bearing of the principal figure in the assumption of new powers and duties is sure to be watched with critical curiosity; but in the case of Queen Victoria the natural interest reached its utmost bounds. The public imagination was impressed in the most lively manner by the strong contrast between the tender youth and utter inexperience of the maiden Queen and the weighty and serious functions she was about to assume—an anomaly best indicated by the characteristic speech of Carlyle, that a girl at an age when, in ordinary circumstances, she would hardly be trusted to choose a bonnet for herself, was called upon to undertake responsibilities from which an archangel might have shrunk. More than this, the retirement in which the young Queen had grown up left her nature a hidden secret to those well-trained, grey-bearded men in authority, who now came to bid her rule over them. Thus, in addition to every other doubt to be solved, there was the pressing question as to how a girl would behave under such a tremendous test; for, although there had been queens-regnant, popular and unpopular before, Mary and Elizabeth had been full-grown women, and Anne had attained still more mature years, before the crown and sceptre were committed to the safe keeping of each in turn. Above all, how would this royal girl, on whose conduct so much depended, demean herself on this crucial occasion? Surely if she were overcome by timidity and apprehension, if she were goaded into some foolish demonstration of pride or levity, allowance must be made, and a good deal forgiven, because of the cruel strain to which she was subjected.

Shortly after eleven o'clock, the royal Dukes and a great number of Privy Councillors, amongst whom were all the Cabinet Ministers and the great officers of State and the Household, arrived at Kensington Palace, and were ushered into the State apartments. A later arrival consisted of the Lord Mayor, attended by the City Marshals in full uniform, on horseback, with crape on their left arms; the Chamberlain, Sword-bearer, Comptroller, Town Clerk, and Deputy Town Clerk, &c., accompanied by six aldermen. These City magnates appeared at the Palace to pay their homage to her Majesty. The Lord Mayor attended the Council.

We have various accounts—one from an eye-witness wont to be cool and critical enough—of what passed. "The first thing to be done," writes Greville, "was to teach her her lesson, which, for this purpose, Melbourne had himself to learn. I gave him the Council papers and explained all that was to be done, and he went and explained all this to her. He asked her if she would enter the room accompanied by the great officers of State, but she said she would come in alone. When the Lords were assembled, the Lord President (Lord Lansdowne) informed them of the King's death, and suggested, as they were so numerous, that a few of them should repair to the presence of the Queen, and inform her of the event, and that their lordships were assembled in consequence; and accordingly the two royal Dukes (the Duke of Cumberland, by the death of William, King of Hanover, and the Duke of Sussex—the Duke of Cambridge was absent in Hanover), the two Archbishops, the Chancellor, and Melbourne went with him. The Queen received them in the adjoining room alone."

It was the first time she had to act for herself. Until then she had been well supported by her mother, and by the precedence which the Duchess of Kent took as her Majesty's guardian. But the guardianship was over and the reign begun. There could be no more sheltering from responsibility, or becoming deference to, and reliance on, the wisdom of another and a much older person. In one sense the stay was of necessity removed. The Duchess of Kent, from this day "treated her daughter with respectful observance as well as affection." The time was past for advice, instruction, or suggestion, unless in private, and even then it would be charily and warily given by the sensible, modest mother of a Queen. Well for her Majesty that there was no more than truth in what one of the historians of the reign has said, in just and temperate language, of her character: "She was well brought up. Both as regards her intellect and her character her training was excellent. She was taught to be self-reliant, brave, and systematical."

As soon as the deputation had returned, the proclamation was read; "Whereas it has pleased Almighty God to call to His mercy our late Sovereign Lord, King William the Fourth, of blessed and glorious memory, by whose decease the imperial Crown of the United Kingdom of Great Britain and Ireland is solely and rightfully come to the high and mighty Princess Alexandrina Victoria, saving the rights of any issue of his late majesty, King William the Fourth, which may be born of his late Majesty's consort; we, therefore, the lords spiritual and temporal of this realm, being here assisted with these of his late Majesty's Privy Council, with numbers of others, principal gentlemen of quality, with the Lord Mayor, aldermen and citizens of London, do now hereby, with one voice and consent of tongue and heart, publish and proclaim that the high and mighty Princess Alexandrina Victoria is now, by the death of our late Sovereign, of happy memory, become our only lawful and rightful liege Lady, Victoria, by the grace of God Queen of the United Kingdom of Great Britain and Ireland, Defender of the Faith, saving, as aforesaid: To whom, saving as aforesaid, we do acknowledge all faith and constant obedience, with all hearty and humble affection, beseeching God, by whom kings and queens do reign, to bless the royal Princess Victoria with long and happy years to reign over us.

"Given at the Court of Kensington this 20th day of June, 1837. (Signed by all the Lords of the Privy Council present). God Save the Queen."

"Then," resuming Mr. Greville's narrative, "the doors were thrown open, and the Queen entered, accompanied by her two uncles, who advanced to meet her. She bowed to the Lords, took her seat (an arm-chair improvised into a throne, with a footstool), and then read her speech in a clear, distinct, and audible voice, and without any appearance of fear or embarrassment:—

"'The severe and afflicting loss which the nation has sustained by the death of his Majesty, my beloved uncle, has devolved upon me the duty of administering the Government of this empire. This awful responsibility is imposed upon me so suddenly, and at so early a period of my life, that I should feel myself utterly oppressed by the burden were I not sustained by the hope that Divine Providence, which has called me to this work, will give me strength for the performance of it, and that I shall find in the purity of my intentions, and in my zeal for the public welfare, that support and those resources which usually belong to a more mature age and to longer experience.

"'I place my firm reliance upon the wisdom of Parliament and upon the loyalty and affection of my people. I esteem it also a peculiar advantage that I succeed to a Sovereign whose constant regard for the rights and liberties of his subjects, and whose desire to promote the amelioration of the laws and institutions of the country, have rendered his name the object of general attachment and veneration.

"'Educated in England, under the tender and enlightened care of a most affectionate mother, I have learned from my infancy to respect and love the Constitution of my native country.

"'It will be my unceasing study to maintain the reformed religion as by law established, securing at the same time to all the full enjoyment of religious liberty; and I shall steadily protect the rights and promote, to the utmost of my power, the happiness and welfare of all classes of my subjects.'"

Her Majesty's speech was after the model of English royal speeches; but one can feel at this day it was spoken in all ingenuousness and sincerity, and that the utterance—remarkable already for clearness and distinctness—for the first time, of the set words, ending in the solemn promise to do a Sovereign's duty, must have thrilled the hearts both of speaker and hearers.

A critical listener was not wanting, according to the testimony of the witness who, on his own account, certainly did not object to chronicle detraction of every kind. "The speech was admired, except by Brougham, who appeared in a considerable state of excitement. He said to Peel (whom he was standing near, and with whom he was not in the habit of communicating),

"'amelioration;' that is not English. You might perhaps say "melioration," but "improvement" is the proper word.'

"'Oh!' said Peel, 'I see no harm in the word; it is generally used.'

"'You object,' said Brougham, 'to the sentiment; I object to the grammar.'

"'No,' said Peel, 'I don't object to the sentiment.'

"'Well, then, she pledges herself to the policy of our Government,' said Brougham.

"She was quite plainly dressed, and in mourning. After she had read her speech, and taken and signed the oath (administered by the Archbishop of Canterbury) for the security of the Church of Scotland, the Privy Councillors were sworn, the two royal Dukes first by themselves."

The days of violence were ended, and whatever private, hopes he might once have entertained, Ernest, Duke of Cumberland, was the first to hail his niece as the high and mighty Princess Alexandrina Victoria, to whom the imperial Crown of Great Britain and Ireland had solely and rightfully come—the first to proclaim her, with one voice and consent of tongue and heart, on the part of himself and his peers, his only lawful and rightful liege Lady Victoria, to whom he acknowledged all faith and rightful obedience, with all hearty and humble affection. It may be, the fact that he had succeeded to the throne of Hanover rendered the step less difficult. His name was also the first in the signatures of princes, Privy Councillors, peers, and gentlemen affixed in the next room to the proclamation. His brother, the Duke of Sussex, followed. They were both elderly men, with the younger older in infirmities than in years. The King of Hanover was sixty-six, the Duke of Sussex sixty-four years of age.

"And as these two old men, her uncles, knelt before her, swearing allegiance and kissing her hand," Greville went on, with a sense of pathos, curious for him, in the scene, "I saw her blush up to the eyes, as if she felt the contrast between their civil and their natural relations, and this was the only sign of emotion which she evinced. Her manner to them was very graceful and engaging; she kissed them both, and rose from her chair and moved towards the Duke of Sussex, who was farthest from her, and too infirm to reach her. She seemed rather bewildered at the multitude of men who were sworn, and who came one after another to kiss her hand, but she did not speak to anybody, nor did she make the slightest difference in her manner, or show any in her countenance, to any individual of any rank, station, or party. I particularly watched her when Melbourne and the Ministers, and the Duke of Wellington and Peel approached her. She went through the whole ceremony, occasionally looking at Melbourne for instruction when she had any doubt what to do, which hardly ever occurred, and with perfect coolness and self-possession, but at the same time with a graceful modesty and propriety particularly interesting and ingratiating. When the business was done she retired as she had entered, and I could see that nobody was in the adjoining room."

Mr. Greville's comment on the scene was singularly enthusiastic from such a man. "Never was anything like the first impression she produced, or the chorus of praise and admiration which is raised about her manner and behaviour, and certainly not without justice. It was something very extraordinary, and something far beyond what was looked for." He quoted Sir Robert Peel's and the Duke of Wellington's opinions in accordance with his own. "He (Sir Robert) likewise said how amazed he was at the manner and behaviour, at her apparent deep sense of her situation, her modesty, and at the same time her firmness. She appeared, in fact, to be awed, but not daunted; and afterwards, the Duke of Wellington told me the same thing, and added, that if she had been his own daughter he could not have desired to see her perform her part better."

We can understand the fatherly reference of the Duke, and the sort of personal pride he took in his young Queen. He had been present at her birth in this very Palace of Kensington; he had known her at every stage of her life hitherto. She was doing credit not only to herself and her mother, but to every friend she had, by her perfect fulfilment of what was required of her. Lord Campbell was equally eulogistic. "As soon as I heard that King William had expired I hurried to Kensington, to be present at the first Council of the new Sovereign. This, I think, was the most interesting scene I have ever witnessed.... I am quite in raptures with the deportment of the young Queen. Nothing could be more exquisitely proper. She looked modest, sorrowful, dejected, diffident, but at the same time she was quite cool and collected, and composed and firm. Her childish appearance was gone. She was an intelligent and graceful young woman, capable of acting and thinking for herself. Considering that she was the only female in the room, and that she had no one about her with whom she was familiar, no human being was ever placed in a more trying situation."

What was most conspicuous in the Queen had been already remarked upon and admired in the young girl at Queen Adelaide's Drawing-room. Here were the same entire simplicity, with its innate dignity only further developed; the power of being herself and no other, which left her thoughtful of what she ought to do—not of how she should look and strike others—and rendered her free to consider her neighbours; the docility to fit guidance, and yet the ability to judge for herself; the quick sense all the time of her high calling.

That first Council at Kensington has become an episode in history—a very significant one. It has been painted, engraved, written about many a time, without losing its fascination. Sir David Wilkie made a famous picture of it, which hangs in a corridor at Windsor In this picture the artist used certain artistic liberties, such as representing the Queen in a white muslin robe instead of a black gown, and the Privy Councillors in the various costumes of their different callings—uniforms with stars and ribands, lawyers' gowns and full-bottomed wigs, bishops' lawn, instead of the ordinary morning dress of the gentlemen of their generation. It must have tickled Wilkie as he worked to come to an old acquaintance of his boyhood and youth in John, Lord Campbell, and to recognise how bewilderingly far removed from the bleak little parish of Cults and the quiet little town of Cupar was the coincidence which summoned him, the distinguished painter, in the execution of a royal commission, to draw the familiar features of his early playmate in those of the Attorney-General, who appeared as a privileged member of the illustrious throng. We still turn back wistfully to that bright dawn of a beneficent reign. We see the slight girlish figure in her simple mourning filling her place sedately at the head of the Council table. At the foot, facing her Majesty, sits the Duke of Sussex, almost venerable in his stiffness and lameness, wearing the black velvet skull-cap by which he was distinguished in those days. We look at the well-known faces, and think of the famous names among the crowd of mature men, each of whom was hanging on the words and looks of his mistress. There is Copley the painter's son, sagacious Lyndhurst, who lived to be the Nestor of the bench and the peerage; there is his great opponent, Robertson the historian's grand-nephew, Brougham, a tyrant of freedom, an illustrious Jack-of-all-trades, the most impassioned, most public-spirited, most egotistical of men. He was a contradiction to himself as well as to his neighbours. His strongly-marked face, with its shaggy brows, high cheek-bones, aggressive nose, mouth drooping at the corners, had not lost its mobility. He was restless and fault-finding in this presence as in any other. The Duke of Wellington's Roman nose lent something of the eagle to his aspect. It was a more patrician attribute than Sir Robert Peel's long upper lip, with its shy, nervous compression, which men mistook for impassive coldness, just as the wits blundered in calling his strong, serviceable capacity, noble uprightness, and patient labour "sublime mediocrity." William Lamb, Viscount Melbourne, was the type of an aristocrat, with brains and heart. He was still a very handsome man at fifty-eight, as he was also "perhaps the most graceful and agreeable gentleman of the generation." His colleague—destined to marry Lord Melbourne's sister, the most charming woman who ever presided in turn over two Ministerial salons, Lord Palmerston, in spite of his early achievements in waltzing at Almack's, was less personally and mentally gifted. He had rather an indiarubber-like elasticity and jauntiness than stateliness, or dignity, or grace. His irregular-featured face was comical, but he bore the bell in exhaustless spirits, which won him, late in life, the reputation of perennial juvenility, and the enviable if not altogether respectful sobriquet of "the evergreen Palm." Lord John Russell, with his large head and little body, of which Punch made stock, with his friendship for Moore and his literary turn, as well as his ambition to serve his country like a true Russell, was at this date wooing and wedding the fair young widow, Lady Ribblesdale, his devotion to whom had drawn from the wags a profane pun. They called the gifted little lord "the widow's mite." When the marriage ceremony was being performed between him and Lady Ribblesdale the wedding-ring fell from the bride's finger—an evil omen soon fulfilled for the marriage tie was speedily broken by her early death. "Plain John Campbell" was a very different man. The son of a minister of the Church of Scotland, in a presbytery which included among its members the father of Sir David Wilkie, his Scotch tongue, Scotch shrewdness, healthy appetite for work, and invulnerable satisfaction with himself and his surroundings, caused themselves to be felt in another sphere than that to which he was born. "The Cabinet Ministers tendered to the Queen the seals of their respective offices, which her Majesty was most graciously pleased to return, and they severally kissed hands on their reappointment." The last business done was to arrange for the public proclamation of the Queen, and to take her pleasure with regard to the time, which she fixed for the day following, Wednesday, the 21st of June, at ten o'clock. When Lord Albemarle, for whom she had sent, went to her and told her he was come to take her orders, she said, "I have no orders to give. You must know this so much better than I do, that I leave it all to you. I am to be at St. James's at ten to-morrow, and must beg you to find me a conveyance proper for the occasion." We are further informed that the Queen, in the course of the morning, received a great many noble and distinguished personages. So finished a busy and exciting day; the herald of many other days crowded with engagements and excitement.

The Palace of St. James's, where the proclamation was to take place, had been for a long time the theatre of all the principal events in the lives of the kings and queens of England. Even the young Queen already viewed it in this light, for though she had been baptized at Kensington, she had been confirmed at St. James's. She had attended her first Drawing-rooms, and celebrated her coming-of-age ball there. St. James's is a brick building, like Kensington Palace, but is far older, and full of more stirring and tragic associations. It has an air of antiquity about it, if it has few architectural claims on the world's interest; but at least one front, that which includes the turreted gateway into St. James's Street, is not without picturesque beauty. The situation of the palace, considering that it is in the middle of a great city, is agreeable. It has its park, with a stretch of pleasant water on one side, and commands the leafy avenue of the Mall and the sweep of Constitution Hill. As a royal residence it dates as far back as Henry VIII., whose daughter Mary ended her sad life here. Both of the sons of James I. received it as a dwelling, and were connected with it in troubled days. Prince Henry fell into his pining sickness and died here. Charles, after bringing Henrietta Maria under its roof, and owning its shelter till three of his children were born, was carried to St. James's as a prisoner. He was taken from it in a sedan-chair to undergo his trial at his new palace of Whitehall. He was conveyed back under sentence of death. Here Bishop Juxon preached the last sermon to which the King listened, and administered to him the Sacrament; and here Charles took leave of his children—the little Duke of Gloucester and the girl-Princess Elizabeth. From St. James's the King went to the scaffold on the bitter January morning, followed by the snowy night in which "the white King" was borne to his dishonoured burial. Other and less tragic scenes were enacted within its bounds. A familiar figure in connection with Kensington Palace—Caroline of Anspach, wife of George II.—died like herself here. Her King had fallen into a stupor of sorrow across the bed where she lay in her last agony, and she forbade his being disturbed. She told those who were praying to pray aloud, that she might hear them; then raising herself up and uttering the single German word of acquiescence, "So," her brave spirit passed away.

When the Queen arrived, accompanied by her mother and her ladies, and attended by an escort, on the June morning of her proclamation, she was received by the other members of the royal family, the Household, and the Cabinet Ministers. Already every avenue to the Palace and every balcony and window within sight were crowded to excess. In the quadrangle opposite the window where her Majesty was to appear a mass of loyal ladies and gentlemen was tightly wedged. The parapets above were filled with people, conspicuous among them the big figure of Daniel O'Connell, the agitator, waving his hat and cheering with Irish effusion.

"At ten o'clock," says the Annual Register, "the guns in the park fired a salute, and immediately afterwards the Queen made her appearance at the window of the tapestried ante-room adjoining the ante-chamber, and was received with deafening cheers. She stood between Lords Melbourne and Lansdowne, in their State dresses and their ribands, who were also cheered, as was likewise her Royal Highness the Duchess of Kent. At this and the two other windows we recognised the King of Hanover, the Dukes of Sussex, Wellington, and Argyle; Lords Hill, Combermere, Denbigh, Duncannon, Albemarle, and Winchester; Sir E. Codrington, Sir William Houston, and a number of other lords and gentlemen, with several ladies.

"Her Majesty looked extremely fatigued and pale, but returned the repeated cheers with which she was greeted with remarkable ease and dignity. She was dressed in deep mourning, with a white tippet, white cuffs, and a border of white lace under a small black bonnet, which was placed far back on her head, exhibiting her light hair in front simply parted over the forehead. Her Majesty seemed to view the proceedings with considerable interest. Her Royal Highness the Duchess of Kent was similarly dressed to the Queen."

"In the courtyard were Garter-King-at-Arms with heralds and pursuivants in their robes of office, and eight officers of arms on horseback bearing massive silver maces; sergeants-at-arms with their maces and collars; the sergeant-trumpeter with his mace and collar; the trumpets, drum-major and drums, and knights'-marshal and men."

"On Her Majesty showing herself at the Presence Chamber window, Garter-Principal-King-at-Arms having taken his station in the courtyard under the window, accompanied by the Duke of Norfolk as Earl-Marshal of England, read the proclamation containing the formal and official announcement of the demise of King William IV., and of the consequent accession of Queen Alexandrina Victoria to the throne of these realms … 'to whom we acknowledge all faith and constant obedience, with all humble and hearty affection, beseeching God, by whom kings and queens do reign, to bless the Royal Princess Alexandrina Victoria with long and happy years to reign. God save the Queen.' At the termination of this proclamation the band struck up the National Anthem, and a signal was given for the Park and Tower guns to fire in order to announce the fact of the proclamation being made. During the reading of the proclamation her Majesty stood at the Presence Chamber window, and immediately upon its conclusion the air was rent with the loudest acclamations by those within the area, which were responded to by the thousands without."

The scene drew from Elizabeth Barrett Browning the following popular verses:—

O, maiden, heir of kings,
  A king has left his place;
The majesty of death has swept
  All other from his face;
And thou upon thy mother's breast
  No longer lean adown,
But take the glory for the rest,
And rule the land that loves thee best.
  The maiden wept,
  She wept to wear a crown.

* * * * *

God bless thee, weeping Queen,
  With blessings more divine,
And fill with better love than earth
  That tender heart of thine;
That when the thrones of earth shall be
  As low as graves brought down,
A pierced hand may give to thee
The crown which angels shout to see.
  Thou wilt not weep
  To wear that heavenly crown.

A maiden Queen in her first youth, wearing the crown and wielding the sceptre, had become un fait accompli and the news spread over the length and breadth of the land. We have seen how it touched the oldest statesmen, to whom State ceremonials had become hackneyed—who were perhaps a little sceptical of virtue in high places. It may be imagined, then, how the knowledge, with each striking and picturesque detail, thrilled and engrossed all the sensitive, romantic young hearts in the Queen's dominions. It seemed as if womanhood and girlhood were exalted in one woman and girl's person—as if a new era must be inaugurated with such a reign, and every man worthy of the name would rally round this Una on the throne.

The prosaic side of the question was that the country was torn by the factions of Whig and Tory, which were then in the full bloom of party spirit and narrow rancorous animosity. The close of the life of William IV. had presented the singular and disastrous contradiction of a King in something like open opposition to his Ministers. William had begun by being a liberal in politics, but alarmed by the progress of reform, he had hung back resisted, and ended by being dragged along an unwilling tolerator of a Whig regime. The Duke of Kent had been liberal in his opinions when liberality was not the fashion. The Duchess was understood to be on the same side; her brother and counsellor, the King of the Belgians, was decidedly so. Accordingly, the Whigs hailed the accession of Queen Victoria as their triumph, likely to secure and prolong their tenure of office. They claimed her as their Queen, with a boasting exultation calculated to wound and exasperate every Tory in the kingdom. Lord Campbell, who, though a zealous Whig, was comparatively cool and cautious, wrote in his journal, after the Queen's first Council, "We basked in the full glare of royal sunshine;" and this tone was generally adopted by his party. They met with some amount of success in their loud assertion, and the consequence was a strain of indignant bitterness in the Tory rejoinder. A clever partisan inscribed on the window-pane of an inn at Huddersfield:

"The Queen is with us," Whigs insulting say,
"For when she found us in, she let us stay."
It may be so; but give me leave to doubt
How long she'll keep you when she finds you out.

There was even some cooling of Tory loyalty to the new Queen. Chroniclers tell us of the ostentatious difference in enthusiasm with which, at Tory dinners, the toasts of the Queen, and the Queen-dowager were received.

As a matter of course, Lord Melbourne became the Queen's instructor in the duties of her position, and as she had no private secretary, he had to be in constant attendance upon her—to see her, not only daily, but sometimes three or four times a day. The Queen has given her testimony to the unwearied kindness and pleasantness, the disinterested regard for her welfare, even the generous fairness to political opponents, with which her Prime Minister discharged his task. It seems as if the great trust imposed on him drew out all that was most manly and chivalrous in a character which, along with much that was fine and attractive, that won to him all who came in close contact with him, was not without the faults of the typical aristocrat, correctly or incorrectly defined by the popular imagination. Lord Melbourne, with his sense and spirit, honesty and good-nature, could be haughtily, indifferent, lazily self-indulgent, scornfully careless even to affectation, of the opinions of his social inferiors, as when he appeared to amuse himself with "idly blowing a feather or nursing a sofa-cushion while receiving an important and perhaps highly sensitive deputation from this or that commercial interest." The time has come when it is fully recognised that whatever might have been Lord Melbourne's defects, he never brought them into his relations with the Queen. To her he was the frank, sincere, devoted adviser of all that it was wisest and best for her to do. "He does not appear to have been greedy of power, or to have used any unfair means of getting or keeping it. The character of the young Sovereign seems to have impressed him deeply. His real or affected levity gave way to a genuine and lasting desire to make her life as happy and her reign as successful as he could. The Queen always felt the warmest affection and gratitude for him, and showed it long after the public had given up the suspicion that she could be a puppet in the hands of a Minister. "But men—especially Lord Melbourne's political adversaries—were not sufficiently large-minded and large-hearted to put this confidence in him beforehand. They remembered with wrath and disgust that, even in the language of men of the world, "his morals were not supposed to be very strict." He had been unhappy in his family life. The eccentricities and follies of Lady Caroline Lamb had formed the gossip of several London seasons long years before. Other scandals had gathered round his name, and though they had been to some extent disproven, it was indignantly asked, could there be a more unsuitable and undesirable guide for an innocent royal girl of eighteen than this accomplished, bland roue of threescore? Should he be permitted to soil—were it but in thought—the lily of whose stainlessness the nation was so proud? The result proved that Lord Melbourne could be a blameless, worthy servant to his Sovereign.

In the meantime the great news of Queen Victoria's accession had travelled to the princely student at Bonn, who responded to it in a manly, modest letter, in which he made no claim to share the greatness, while he referred to its noble, solemn side. Prince Albert wrote on the 26th of June: "Now you are Queen of the mightiest land of Europe; in your hand lies the happiness of millions. May Heaven assist you and strengthen you with its strength in that high but difficult task. I hope that your reign may be long, happy, and glorious, and that your efforts may be rewarded by the thankfulness and love of your subjects." To others he expressed his satisfaction at what he heard of his cousin's astonishing self-possession, and of the high praise bestowed on her by all parties, "which seemed to promise so auspiciously for her reign." But so far from putting himself forward or being thrust forward by their common friends as an aspirant for her hand, while she was yet only on the edge of that strong tide and giddy whirl of imposing power and dazzling adulation which was too likely to sweep her beyond his grasp, it was resolved by King Leopold and the kindred who were most concerned in the relations of the couple, that, to give time for matters to settle down, for the young Queen to know her own mind—above all, to dissipate the premature rumour of a formal engagement between the cousins which had taken persistent hold of the public mind ever since the visit of the Saxe-Coburg princes to Kensington Palace in the previous year, Prince Albert should travel for several months. Accordingly, he set out, in company with his brother, to make an enjoyable tour, on foot, through Switzerland and the north of Italy. To a nature like his, such an experience was full of keen delight; but in the midst of his intoxication he never forgot his cousin. The correspondence between them had been suffered to drop, but that she continued present to his thoughts was sufficiently indicated by the souvenirs he collected specially for her: the views of the scenes he visited, the Alpenrosen he gathered for her in its native home, Voltaire's autograph.

The Queen left Kensington, within a month of her uncle's death, we do not need to be told "greatly to the regret of the inhabitants." She went on the 13th of July to take up her residence at Buckingham Palace. "Shortly after one o'clock an escort of Lancers took up a position on the Palace Green, long previous to which an immense concourse of respectable persons had thronged the avenue and every open space near the Palace." About half-past one an open carriage drawn by four greys, preceded by two outriders, and followed by an open barouche, drawn by four bays, drove up from her Majesty's mews, Pimlico, and stopped before the grand entrance to the Duchess of Kent's apartments. The Queen, accompanied by the Duchess of Kent and Baroness Lehzen, almost immediately got into the first carriage. There was a tumult of cheering, frankly acknowledged. It is said the young Queen looked "pale and a little sad" at the parting moment. Then with a dash the carriages vanished in a cloud of July dust, and the familiar Palace Green, with its spreading trees and the red chimneys beyond—the High Street—Kensington Gore, were left behind. Kensington's last brief dream of a Court was brought to an abrupt conclusion. What was worse, Kensington's Princess was gone, never to return to the changed scene save for the most fleeting of visits.

We should like to give here one more story of her Majesty's stay at Kensington—a story that refers to these last days. We have already spoken of an old soldier-servant of the Duke of Kent's, said to have been named Stillman, who was quartered with his family—two of them sickly—in a Kensington cottage of the period, visited by the Duchess of Kent and the Princess Victoria. The little boy had died; the ailing girl still lived. The girl's clergyman, a gentleman named Vaughan, went to see her some days after the Queen had quitted the Palace, and found the invalid looking unusually bright. He inquired the reason. "Look there!", said the girl, and drew a book of Psalms from under her pillow, "look what the new Queen has sent me to-day by one of her ladies, with the message that, though now, as Queen of England, she had to leave Kensington, she did not forget me." The lady who had brought the book had said the lines and figures in the margin were the dates of the days on which the Queen herself had been accustomed to read the Psalms, and that the marker, with the little peacock on it, was worked by the Princess's own hand. The sick girl cried, and asked if this act was not beautiful?

CHAPTER V. THE PROROGUING OF PARLIAMENT, THE VISIT TO GUILDHALL, AND THE CORONATION.

Buckingham Palace had been a seat of the Duke of Buckingham's, which was bought by George II., and in the next reign was settled on Queen Charlotte instead of Somerset House, and called the "Queen's House." It was rebuilt by George IV. but not occupied by him, and had been rarely used by King William. Besides its gardens, which are of some extent, it shares with St. James's, which it is near, the advantage of St. James's Park, one of the most agreeable in London, and full of historic memories. Though it, too, was modernised by George IV., its features have still much interest. It was by its canal, which has been twisted into the Serpentine, that the Merry Monarch strolled alone, lazily playing with his dogs, feeding his ducks, and by his easy confidence flattering and touching his good citizens of London. On the same water his gay courtiers practised their foreign accomplishment of skating, which they had brought back with them from the Low Countries. In the Mall both Charles and his brother, the Duke of York, joined in the Court game of Palle Malle, when a ball was struck with a mallet through an iron ring down a walk strewn with powdered cockle-shells. At a later period the Mall was the most fashionable promenade in London. While dinners were still early on Sunday afternoons, the fashionable world walked for an hour or two after dinner in the Mall. An eyewitness declared that he had seen "in one moving mass, extending the whole length of the Mall, five thousand of the most lovely women in this country of female beauty, all splendidly attired, and accompanied by as many well-dressed men." For, as Mr. Hare, in his "Walks in London," points out, the frequenters of the Mall were very different in one respect from the company in the Row: "The ladies were in full dress and gentlemen carried their hats under their arms."

One relic of the past survives intact in the park—that is, the cow-stalls, which formerly helped to constitute "Milk Fair." Mr. Hare tells us "the vendors are proud of the number of generations through which the stalls have been held in their families."

From Buckingham Palace the Queen went in State on the 17th of July to close Parliament. The carriage, with the eight cream-coloured horses, was used. As far as we can judge, this was the first appearance in her Majesty's reign of "the creams," so dear to the London populace. The carriage was preceded by the Marshalmen, a party of the Yeomen of the Guard in State costumes, and runners. The fourth carriage, drawn by six black horses, contained the Marchioness of Lansdowne, the Duchess of Sutherland, the Duke of Argyle, Lord Steward and Gold Stick in Waiting. The Queen was accompanied by the Earl of Albemarle, Master of the Horse, and the Countess of Mulgrave, the Lady-in-Waiting. The procession, escorted by a squadron of the Horse Guards, moved into Whitehall, and was cheered in Parliament Street by deafening shouts from a mass of spectators lining the streets and covering the house-tops. On arriving opposite the entrance of the House of Lords her Majesty was received by a battalion of the Grenadier Guards, whose splendid band, when she alighted, played the National Anthem. Thus heralded, the young Queen entered the old Houses of Parliament, seated herself on the throne of her ancestors, and accorded her maiden reception to her loyal Lords and faithful Commons. This was the first occasion in a great assembly that people remarked the natural gift which has proved a valuable possession to her Majesty, and has never failed to awaken the admiration of the hearers. We allude to the peculiar silvery clearness, as well as sweetness, of a voice which can be heard in its most delicate modulations through the whole House. In reply to the Speaker of the House of Commons' assurance of the Commons' cordial participation in that strong and universal feeling of dutiful and affectionate attachment which prevailed among the free and loyal people of which they were the representatives, the Queen read her speech in an unfaltering voice, thanking the Parliament for its condolence upon the death of his late Majesty, and for its expressions of attachment and affection to herself, announcing her determination to preserve all the rights, spiritual and civil, of her subjects, touching on the usual topics in a royal speech in its relation to home and foreign affairs, and making the solemn assertion: "I ascend the throne with a deep sense of the responsibility which is imposed upon me, but I am supported by the consciousness of my own right intentions and by my dependence on the protection of Almighty God." Fanny Kemble was present at this memorable scene, and has given her impression of it. Her testimony, as a public speaker, is valuable. "The Queen was not handsome, but very pretty, and the singularity of her great position lent a sentimental and poetical charm to her youthful face and figure. The serene, serious sweetness of her candid brow and clear soft eyes gave dignity to the girlish countenance, while the want of height only added to the effect of extreme youth of the round but slender person, and gracefully moulded hands and arms. The Queen's voice was exquisite, nor have I ever heard any spoken words more musical in their gentle distinctness than "My Lords and Gentlemen," which broke the breathless silence of the illustrious assembly whose gaze was riveted on that fair flower of royalty. The enunciation was as perfect as the intonation was melodious, and I think it is impossible to hear a more excellent utterance than that of the Queen's English by the English Queen."

The accession of Queen Victoria almost coincided with a new era in English history, art and letters, new relations in politics at home and abroad, new social movements undreamt of when she was born. In spite of the strong party spirit, the country was at peace within and without. France, the foreign neighbour of most importance to England, was also at peace under a so-called "citizen-king." The "Tractarian" movement at Oxford was startling the world with a proposed return to the practices of the primitive Church, while it laid the foundation of the High Church and Ritualistic parties in the modern Church of England. The names of Newman and Pusey especially were in many mouths, spoken in various terms of reprobation and alarm, or approval and exultation. Next to Tractarianism, Chartism—the people's demand for a charter which should meet their wants—was a rising force, though it had not reached its full development. Arnold was doing his noble work, accomplishing a moral revolution in the public schools of England. Milman and Grote had arisen as historians. Faraday was one of the chief lights of science. Sir John Herschel occupied his father's post among the stars. Beautiful modest Mary Somerville showed what a woman might do with the Differential Calculus; Brewster had taken the place of Sir Humphry Davy. Murchison was anticipating Robert Dick and Hugh Miller in geology. Alfred Tennyson had already published two volumes of poems; Browning had given to the world his "Paracelsus," and this very year (1837) his Strafford had been performed at Covent Garden, while it was still on the cards that his calling might be that of a great dramatist. Dickens, the Scott of the English lower-middle classes, was bringing out his "Pickwick Papers." Disraeli had got into the House of Commons at last, and his "Vivian Grey" was fully ten years old. So was Bulwer's "Pelbam"—the author of which also aided in forming the literary element of the House of Commons in the Queen's first Parliament. Mrs. Gore, Mrs. Trollope, Miss Mitford, Mrs. S. C. Hail, and Harriet Martinean represented under very different aspects the feminine side of fiction. Macready remained the stage king, but he shared his royalty with the younger Kean. A younger Kemble had also played Juliet well, but the stage queen was Helen Faucit. In painting, Turner was working in his last style; Stanfield's sea-pieces were famous. Mulready and Leslie were in the front as genre painters. Maclise was making his reputation; Etty had struggled into renown, while poor Haydon was sinking into despair. Landseer was already the great animal painter. Sir C. Eastlake had court commissions. Wilkie, too, still had royal commissions, but his best work was done, and he was soon to set out on his last travels in a vain search after health and strength.

Withal the world was a light-hearted world enough—not so hurried as it is to-day, though railways were well established, and the electric telegraph had been hit upon in this same 1837. Young blood continued hot, and play was apt to be riotous. Witness the fantastic frolics of the Marquis of Waterford—public property in those years. He had inherited the eccentricities of the whole Delaval race, and not content with tickling his peers in England, carried his whims and pranks into Scotland and Ireland and across the Channel. Various versions of his grotesque feats circulated and scintillated through all classes, provoking laughter, and tempting to clumsy imitation, till the gentleman may be said to have had a species of world-wide reputation in a madly merry way.

The Queen held a review at Windsor on the 28th of September, 1837. She had dwelt at Windsor before as a cherished guest; but what must it not have been to her to enter these gates as the Queen? The rough hunting-seat of William Rufus had long been the proudest and fairest palace in England. St. George's Tower and battlements are the most royal in these realms. St. George's Hall and St. George's Chapel are the best examples of ancient and modern chivalry. The stately terrace commanding the red turrets of Eton and the silvery reaches of the Thames, where George III. and Queen Charlotte, with their large family and household, were wont to promenade on Sunday afternoons for the benefit of their Majesties' loyal subjects, where the blind old King used to totter along supported by two of his faithful Princesses; the green alleys and glades of the ancient forest, with the great boles of the venerable oaks—Queen Elizabeth's among them; Virginia Water sparkling in the sunshine or glimmering in the moonlight, all make up such a kingly residence, as in many respects cannot be surpassed. What must it not have been to enter the little Court town, another Versailles or Fontainebleau, as its liege Lady, to be hailed and welcomed by the goodly throng of Eton lads—those gay and gallant attendants on royal Windsor pageants—to pass through these halls as their mistress, and fairly recognise that all the noble surroundings were hers, with all England, all Britain and many a great dependency and colony on which the sun never sets—hers to rule over, hers to bless if she would?

At the review, in compliment to her soldiers whom she saw marshalled in their disciplined masses, and saluting her as the Captain of their Captains—even of Wellington himself—the Queen wore a half-military dress—a tight jacket with deep lappels, the blue riband of the Garter across one shoulder, and its jewelled star upon her breast, a stocklike black neckerchief in stiff folds holding up the round throat, and on the head—hiding nearly all the fair hair—a round, high, flatcap with a broad black "snout"; beneath it the soft, open, girlish face, with its single-hearted dignity.

In this month of September the Queen heard that her sister-queen and girl friend, Donna Maria da Gloria, had received consolation for the troubles of her kingdom in becoming the youthful mother of a son and heir, Prince Ferdinand of Portugal.

By November the Court was back at Buckingham Palace, and on the 9th the Queen paid her first visit to the City of London, which received her with magnificent hospitality.

Long before the hour appointed for her Majesty's departure for Guildhall, all the approaches to the palace and the park itself presented dense crowds of holiday folks. At two o'clock the first carriage of the procession emerged from the triumphal arch, and in due time came the royal State carriage, in which sat the Queen, attended by the Mistress of the Robes and the Master of the Horse. Her Majesty's full-dress was a "splendid pink satin shot with silver." She wore a queenly diamond tiara, and, as we are told, looked remarkably well. Her approach was the signal for enthusiastic cheering, which increased as she advanced, while the bells of the city churches rang out merry peals. The fronts of the houses were decorated with bright-coloured cloth, green boughs, and such flowers as November had spared. Devices in coloured lamps waited for the evening illumination to bring them out in perfection. Venetian masts had not been hoisted then in England, but "rows of national flags and heraldic banners were stretched across the Strand at several points, and busts and portraits of her Majesty were placed in conspicuous positions." The only person in the Queen's train who excited much interest was the Duke of Wellington, and he heard himself loudly cheered. The mob was rapidly condoning what they had considered his errors as a statesman, and restoring him to his old eminence, in their estimation, as the hero of the long wars, the conqueror of Bonaparte. Applause or reprobation the veteran met with almost equal coolness. When he had been besieged by raging, threatening crowds, calling upon him to do justice to Queen Caroline, as he rode to Westminster during the wild days of her trial, he had answered "Yes, yes," without a muscle of his face moving, and pushed on straight to his destination. For many a year he was to receive every contrite huzza, as he had received every fierce hiss, with no more than the twinkling of an eyelid or the raising of two fingers.

The gathering at Temple Bar—real, grim old Temple Bar, which had borne traitors' heads in former days—was so great that a detachment of Life Guards, as well as a strong body of police, had work to do in clearing a way for the carriages. The aldermen had to be accommodated with a room in Child's old banking-house, founded by the typical industrious apprentice who married his master's daughter. It sported the quaint old sign of the "Marigold," and was supposed to hold sheaves of papers containing noble, nay, royal secrets, as well as bushels of family jewels, in its strong boxes. It had even a family romance of its own, for did not the great Child of his day pursue his heiress in her flight to Gretna with the heir of the Villiers, who, leaning, pistol in hand, from his postchaise in front, sent a bullet into the near horse of the chaise behind, and escaped with his prize?

Undisturbed by these exciting stories, the aldermen waited in the dim interior—charged with other than money-lending mysteries, till the worthy gentlemen were joined by the Lord Mayor and sheriffs, when they proceeded to mount their chargers in Temple Yard—perhaps the most

1

disturbing proceeding of any, with the riders' minds a little soothed by the circumstance that the horses had been brought from the Artillery barracks at Woolwich, and each was led by the soldier to which it belonged, in the capacity of groom.

"A few minutes before three the approach of the Queen was announced. The Lord Mayor dismounted, and, taking the City sword in his hand, stood on the south side of Temple Bar. As soon as the Queen's carriage arrived within the gateway it stopped, and then, unfortunately, it began to rain." The Queen's weather, which has become proverbial, of which we are given to boast, did not attend her on this occasion. Perhaps it would have been too much to expect of the clouds when the date was the 9th of November. Regardless of the weather, "the Lord Mayor delivered the keys of the City to the Queen, which her Majesty restored in the most gracious manner." At this time the multitude above, around, and below, from windows, scaffolding, roofs, and parapets, cheered long and loud. The Lord Mayor remounted, and, holding the City sword aloft, took his place immediately before the royal carriage, after which the aldermen, members of the Common Council, and civic authorities formed in procession.

Rather a curious ceremony was celebrated in front of St. Paul's. Booths and hustings had been erected in the enclosure for the accommodation of members of the different City companies and the boys of Christ's Hospital. "The royal carriage having stopped in the middle of the road, opposite the cathedral gate, a platform was wheeled out, on which were Mr. Frederick Gifford Nash, senior scholar of Christ's Hospital, and the head master and treasurer. The scholar, in conformity with an old usage, delivered an address of congratulation to her Majesty, concluding with an earnest prayer for her welfare. 'God Save the Queen' was then sung by the scholars and a great part of the multitude."

But already the dreariness and discomfort of a dark and wet November afternoon had been too much even for the staunchest loyalty, and had dispersed the feebler spirits among the onlookers. The Lord Mayor assisted her Majesty to alight at the door of the Guildhall, where the Lady Mayoress was waiting to be presented by her husband. We have a full description of the Council-room and retiring-room, with their draperies of crimson and gold, including the toilet-table, covered with white satin, and embroidered with the initials V. R., a crown and wreath in gold, at which the maiden Queen was understood to receive the last touches to her toilet, while she was attended by such distinguished matrons as the Duchess of Kent, the Duchess of Gloucester, and the Duchess of Cambridge. In the drawing-room the address of the City of London was read by the Recorder, and replied to by the Queen. At twenty minutes past five dinner was announced, and the Queen, preceded by the Lord Mayor and the Lady Mayoress, and conducted by the Lord Chamberlain, in "respectful silence," descended into the hall where the banquet was prepared. The great old hall, with its "glorious timber roof," could hardly have known itself. Gog and Magog—compared by Nathaniel Hawthorne to "playthings for the children of giants"—must have looked down with goggle eyes at the transformation. These were different days from the time when Anne Ascue, of Kelsey, was tried there for heresy, and the brave, keen-witted lady told her judges, when examined on the doctrine of transubstantiation, she had heard that God made man, but that man made God she had never heard; or when gallant Surrey encountered his enemies; or melodious Waller was called to account. It was on the raised platform at the east end of the hall that the Common Council had expended its strength of ornament and lavished its wealth. Here London outdid itself. The throne was placed there. "It was surmounted by an entablature, with the letters V. R. supporting the royal crown and cushion. In the front was an external valance of crimson velvet, richly laced and trimmed with tassels. The back-fluting was composed of white satin, relieved with the royal arms in gold. The curtains were of crimson velvet, trimmed with lace and lined with crimson silk. The canopy was composed of crimson velvet, with radiated centre of white satin enamelled with gold, forming a gold ray from which the centre of velvet diverged; a valance of crimson velvet, laced with gold, depended from the canopy, which was intersected with cornucopia, introducing the rose, thistle, and shamrock, in white velvet. Beneath this splendid canopy was placed the State-chair, which was richly carved and gilt, and ornamented with the royal arms and crown, including the rose, thistle, and shamrock, in crimson velvet. Its proportions were tastefully and judiciously diminished to a size that should in some sort correspond with the slight and elegant figure of the young Sovereign for whom it was provided. The platform on which the throne stood was covered with ermine and gold carpeting of the richest description." ... In front of the throne was placed the royal table, extending the whole width of the platform. It was thirty-four feet long and eight wide, and was covered with a cloth of the most exquisite damask, trimmed with gold lace and fringe. The sides and front of the platform were decked with a profusion of the rarest plants and shrubs. The royal table was on a dais above the level of the hall. A large mirror at each side of the throne reflected the gorgeous scene. From the impromptu dais four long tables extended nearly half-way down the hall, where the Lord and Lady Mayoress presided over the company of foreign ambassadors, Cabinet Ministers, nobility, aldermen, and members of the Common Council. The "royal avenue" led up the middle of the hall to the throne, with the tables on each side. The Queen took her seat on the throne; the Lord and Lady Mayoress stood on either side of her Majesty, but were almost immediately bidden be seated at their table.

The company had now time to study the central figure, the cause and culmination of the assembly. Over her pink and silver she wore the riband and order of the Garter, with the George appended. Besides her diamond tiara she had a stomacher of brilliants, and diamond ear-rings. She sat in the middle of a regal company, only two of the others young like herself. To the rest she must have been the child of yesterday; while to each and all she preserved in full the natural relations, and was as much the daughter, niece, and cousin as of old; yet, at the same time, she was every inch the Queen. What a marvel it must have seemed—still more to those who sat near than to those who stood afar. The Queen was supported by the Dukes of Sussex and Cambridge, the Duchesses of Kent, Gloucester, Cambridge, and Sutherland; and there were present her two cousins, Prince George and Princess Augusta Of Cambridge.

After dinner, Non Bobus Domine was sung; and then, preceded by a flourish of trumpets, the common crier advanced to the middle of the hall and said, "The Right Honourable the Lord Mayor gives the health of our most gracious Sovereign, Queen Victoria."

The company simultaneously rose and drank the toast with enthusiasm. "God Save the Queen" was sung, after which her Majesty rose and bowed repeatedly with marked goodwill.... The common crier then shouted, "Her Majesty gives the Lord Mayor and Prosperity to the City of London." Bishop's "When the Wind Blows" was sung. The only other toast was, "The Royal Family," given by the Lord Mayor.

At half-past eight her Majesty's carriage was announced. The weather was unpleasant, the streets were unusually dirty, but a vast crowd once more greeted her. On arriving at the end of Cheapside, she was hailed out of the glimmering illumination and foggy lamplight by "God Save the Queen," again sung by many hundred voices, accompanied by a band of wind instruments, the performance of the Harmonic Society, and the music was followed all the way by enthusiastic cheering. The Baroness Bunsen remarked of such a scene long afterwards, "I was at a loss to conceive how any woman's sides can 'bear the beating of so strong a throb' as must attend the consciousness of being the object of all that excitement, and the centre of attraction for all those eyes. But the Queen has royal strength of nerve." Not so much strength of nerve, we should say, as strength of single-heartedness and simple sense of duty which are their own reward, together with the comparative immunity produced by long habit.

Still it is a little relief to turn from so much State and strain to a brief glimpse of the girl-Queen in something like the privacy of domestic life. In the month of November, 1837, the Attorney-General, Lord Campbell, with his wife, Lady Stratheden, received an invitation to Buckingham Palace, to dine with her Majesty at seven, and one of the guests wrote thus of the entertainment: "I went, and found it exceedingly agreeable, although by no means so grand as dining at Tarvit with Mrs. Rigg. The little Queen was exceedingly kind to me, and said she had heard from the Duchess of Gloucester that I had the most beautiful children in the world. She asked me how many we had, and when she heard seven, seemed rather appalled, considering this a number which she would never be able to reach. She seems in perfect health, and is as merry and playful as a kitten."

Amongst the other innumerable engagements which engrossed every moment of the Queen from the time of her accession, she had been called on to sit for her portrait to many eager artists— among them Hayter and Sir David Wilkie. The last has recorded his impression of her in his manly, unaffected, half-homely words. "Having been accustomed to see the Queen from a child, my reception had a little the air of that of an early acquaintance. She is eminently beautiful, her features nicely formed, her skin smooth, her hair worn close to her face in a most simple way, glossy and clean-looking. Her manner, though trained to act the Sovereign, is yet simple and natural. She has all the decision, thought, and self-possession of a queen of older years, has all the buoyancy of youth, and from the smile to the unrestrained laugh, is a perfect child. While I was there she was sitting to Pistrucci for her coin, and to Hayter for a picture for King Leopold."

The mention of the coin recalls the "image and superscription" on the gold, silver, and copper that passes through our hands daily, which we almost forget to identify with the likeness of the young Queen. About this time also commenced the royal patronage of Landseer, which resulted later in many a family group, in which numerous four-footed favourites had their place. At the exhibition of Landseer's works after his death, the sight of these groups recalled to elderly men and women who had been his early neighbours, the days when a goodly cavalcade of ladies and gentlemen, with their grooms, on horseback, used to sweep past the windows, and the word went that the young Queen was honouring the painter by a visit to his studio.

On the 20th of November the Queen went in State to the House of Lords to open Parliament for the first time, with as great a crowd of members and strangers present as had flocked to witness the prorogation in July. In the course of the month of December the bills were passed which fixed the Queen's income at three hundred and eighty-five thousand pounds a year, and further raised the Duchess of Kent's annuity from twenty-two thousand, which it had been latterly, to thirty thousand a year. On the 23rd of December the Queen went to give her assent to the bills, and thank her Parliament personally, according to old custom on such an occasion. On presenting the bill the Speaker observed that it had been framed in "a liberal and confiding spirit." The Queen simply bowed her acknowledgement.

Lord Melbourne, "with the tears in his eyes," told Lord Campbell that in one of his first interviews with the Queen she had said to him, "My father's debts must be paid." Accordingly the late Duke of Kent's debts were paid by his daughter, in the name of herself and her mother, in the first year of Queen Victoria's reign. In the second year she discharged the debts which the Duchess of Kent had incurred in meeting the innumerable heavy calls made upon her, not only as the widow of one of the Royal Dukes, but as the mother of the future Sovereign.

The summer of 1838 was gay with the preparations for the Queen's coronation. All classes took the greatest interest in it, so that splenetic people pronounced the nation "coronation mad." Long before the event coronation medals were being struck, coronation songs and hymns written, coronation ribands woven. Every ingenious method by which the world could commemorate the joyful season was put in practice. The sentiment was not confined to the inhabitants of the United Kingdom. "Foreigners of various conditions, and from all quarters of Europe, flocked in to behold the inauguration of the maiden monarch of the British Empire. In the Metropolis for some weeks anterior to the event the excitement was extreme. The thousand equipages which thronged the streets, the plumed retainers of the ambassadors, the streams of swarthy strangers, and the incessant din of preparation, which resounded by night as well as by day, along the intended line of the procession, constituted by themselves a scene of no ordinary animation and interest, and sustained the public mind in an unceasing stretch of expectation."

Some disappointment was experienced on the knowledge that the ancient custom of a royal banquet in Westminster Hall on the coronation day was to be dispensed with. But the loss was compensated by a procession—a modification of the old street pageant—on the occasion.

On the morning of the 28th of June the weather was not promising. It was cold for the season, and some rain fell; but the shower ceased, and the day proved fresh and bright, with sunshine gilding the darkest cloud. The Tower artillery awoke the heaviest City sleepers. It is needless to say a great concourse, in every variety of vehicle and on foot, streamed from east to west through the "gravelled" streets, lined with soldiers and policemen, before the barriers were put up. "The earth was alive with men," wrote an enthusiastic spectator; "the habitations in the line of march cast forth their occupants to the balconies or the house-tops; the windows were lifted out of their frames, and the asylum of private life, that sanctuary which our countrymen guard with such traditional jealousy, was on this occasion made accessible to the gaze of the entire world."

At ten o'clock the Queen left Buckingham Palace in the State coach, to the music of the National Anthem and a salute of guns, and passed beneath the Royal Standard hoisted on the marble arch. A marked feature of the procession was the magnificent carriages and escorts of the foreign ambassadors: the splendid uniform of the German Jagers delighted the populace. A deeper and subtler feeling was produced by the sight of one of Napoleon's marshals, Soult, Wellington's great adversary, rearing his white head in a coach the framework of which had belonged to the State carriage of the Prince de Conde, and figured in the beaux jours of Louis XVI. The consciousness that this worthy foe had come to do honour to the young Queen awoke a generous response from the crowd. Soult was cheered lustily along the whole route, and in the Abbey itself, so that he returned to France not only full of personal gratification at the welcome he had received, but strongly convinced of the goodwill of John Bull to Frenchmen in general. How the balls of destiny roll! Soult feted in London, Ney dead by a traitor's death, filling his nameless grave in Pere la Chaise. The procession, beginning with trumpeters and Life Guards, wound its way in relays of foreign ambassadors, members of the royal family and their suites—the Duchess of Kent first—the band of the Household Brigade, the Queen's bargemaster and her forty-eight watermen—honorary servants for many a day—twelve carriages with her Majesty's suite, a squadron of Life Guards, equerries, gentlemen riders and military officials, the royal huntsmen, yeomen-prickers, and foresters, six of her Majesty's horses, with rich trappings, each horse led by two grooms; the Knight-Marshal, marshalmen, Yeomen of the Guard, the State coach— drawn by eight cream-coloured horses, attended by a Yeoman of the Guard at each wheel, and two footmen at each door—the Gold Stick, Viscount Combermere, and the Captain of the Yeomen of the Guard, the Earl of Ilchester, riding on either side. In the coach sat the Queen, the

Mistress of the Robes (the Duchess of Sutherland), the Master of the Horse (the Earl of Albemarle), and the Captain-General of the Royal Archers (the Duke of Buccleugh). The whole was wound up by a squadron of Life Guards. In this order of stately march, under the June sky, emerging from the green avenues of the park, the procession turned up Constitution Hill, traversed Piccadilly, St. James's Street, Pall Mall, Cockspur Street, and by Charing Cross, Whitehall, and Parliament Street, reached the west door of Westminster Abbey—
Where royal heads receive the sacred gold.

At the Abbey door, at half-past eleven, the Queen was received by the great officers of State, the noblemen bearing the regalia, the bishops carrying the patina, the chalice, and the Bible. Her Majesty proceeded to the robing-room, and there was a hush of expectation in the thronged interior, where the great persons who were to play a part in the ceremony and the privileged ticket-holders had been waiting patiently for long hours.

Underneath the galleries and below the platform were ranged lines of Foot Guards. The platform (under the central tower) was the most conspicuous object. It was covered with cloth of gold, and bore the chair of homage, or throne, facing the altar. Farther on, within the altar-rails, was "St. Edward's Chair," or the chair decorated by "William the Painter" for Edward. Enclosed within it is the "Stone of Destiny," or Fatal Stone of Scone—a sandy stone, supposed to have formed the pillow on which Jacob slept at Bethel, and long used in the coronation of the Scotch kings. In this chair all the kings of England, since the time of Edward I., have been crowned. The altar was covered with massive gold plate.

The galleries of the Abbey were arranged for the members of the House of Commons, the foreign ambassadors, the judges, Knights of the Bath, members of the Corporation, &c. &c. The floor of the transepts was occupied by benches for the peers and peeresses, who may be said to be in their glory at a coronation; the space behind them was for the ticket-holders.

Harriet Martineau has preserved some of the splendours and "humours" of the coronation with her usual clever power of observation and occasional caustic commentary. "The maids called me at half-past two that June morning, mistaking the clock. I slept no more, and rose at half-past three. As I began to dress the twenty-one guns were fired, which must have awakened all the sleepers in London. When the maid came to dress me she said numbers of ladies were already hurrying to the Abbey. I saw the grey old Abbey from the window as I dressed, and thought what would have gone forward within it before the sun set upon it. My mother had laid out her pearl ornaments for me. The feeling was very strange of dressing in crape, blonde, and pearls at five in the morning…. The sight of the rapidly filling Abbey was enough to go for. The stone architecture contrasted finely with the gay colours of the multitude. From my high seat I commanded the whole north transept, the area with the throne, and many portions of galleries, and the balconies which were called the vaultings. Except a mere sprinkling of oddities, everybody was in full dress. In the whole assemblage I counted six bonnets. The scarlet of the military officers mixed in well, and the groups of the clergy were dignified; but to an unaccustomed eye the prevalence of Court dresses had a curious effect. I was perpetually taking whole groups of gentlemen for Quakers till I recollected myself. The Earl-Marshal's assistants, called Gold Sticks, looked well from above, lightly fluttering about in white breeches, silk stockings, blue laced frocks, and white sashes. The throne—an arm-chair with a round back, covered, as was its footstool, with cloth of gold—stood on an elevation of four steps in the centre of the area. The first peeress took her seat in the north transept opposite, at a quarter before seven, and three of the bishops came next. From that time the peers and their ladies arrived faster and faster. Each peeress was conducted by two Gold Sticks, one of whom handed her to her seat, and the other bore and arranged her train on her lap, and saw that her coronet, footstool, and book were comfortably placed. I never saw anywhere so remarkable a contrast between youth and age as in these noble ladies." Miss Martineau proceeds to remark in the strongest and plainest terms on the unbecoming effect of full dress, with "hair drawn to the top of the head, to allow the putting on of the coronet" on these venerable matrons. She goes on to express her admiration of a later generation of peeresses. "The younger were as lovely as the aged were haggard.... About nine the first gleams of the sun slanted into the Abbey and presently travelled down to the peeresses. I had never before seen the full effect of diamonds. As the light travelled each peeress shone like a rainbow. The brightness, vastness, and dreamy magnificence of the scene produced a strange effect of exhaustion and sleepiness.... The great guns told when the Queen had set forth, and there was renewed animation. The Gold Sticks flitted about, there was tuning in the orchestra, and the foreign ambassadors and their suites arrived in quick succession. Prince Esterhazy crossing a bar of sunshine was the most prodigious rainbow of all. He was covered with diamonds and pearls, and as he dangled his hat it cast a dancing radiance all round. "At half-past eleven the guns told that the Queen had arrived, but as there was much to be done in the robing-room, there was a long pause before she appeared."

A little after twelve the grand procession of the day entered the choir. The Prebendaries and Dean of Westminster and Officers-at-Arms, the Comptroller, Treasurer, Vice-Chamberlain, and Lord Steward of her Majesty's Household, the Lord Privy Seal, the Lord President, the Lord Chancellor of Ireland, came first. When these gentlemen were peers their coronets were carried by pages. The Treasurer bore the crimson bag with the medals; the Vice-Chancellor was attended by an officer from the Jewel Office, conveying, on a cushion, the ruby ring and the sword for the offering. Then followed the Archbishops of Canterbury, York, and Armagh, with the Lord Chancellor, each archbishop in his rochet, with his cap in his hand; the princesses of the blood royal, all in "robes of estate" of purple velvet and wearing circlets of gold; the Duchess of Cambridge, her train borne by Lady Caroline Campbell and a gentleman of her household, her coronet by Viscount Villiers; the Duchess of Kent, her train borne by Lady Flora Hastings, and her coronet by Viscount Morpeth; the Duchess of Gloucester, her train borne by Lady Caroline Legge, and her coronet by Viscount Evelyn. (The royal generation next that of George III. was fast dwindling away when these three ladies represented the six daughters and the wives of six of the sons of the old King and Queen. But there were other survivors, though they were not present to-day. The Queen-dowager; Princess Augusta, an aged woman of seventy; Princess Elizabeth, Landgravine of Hesse-Homburg, nearly as old, and absent in Germany; the Queen as well as the King of Hanover, who had figured formerly as Duke and Duchess of Cumberland; and Princess Sophia, who was ten years younger than Princess Augusta, and resident in England, but who was an invalid.) The regalia came next, St. Edward's staff, borne by the Duke of Roxburgh, the golden spurs borne by Lord Byron, the sceptre with the cross borne by the Duke of Cleveland, the third sword borne by the Marquis of Westminster, Curtana borne by the Duke of Devonshire, the second sword borne by the Duke of Sutherland, each nobleman's coronet carried by a page, Black Rod and Deputy-Garter walking before Lord Willoughby d'Eresby, Lord Great Chamberlain of England, with page and coronet.

The princes of the blood royal were reduced to two. The Duke of Cambridge, in his robe of estate, carrying his baton as Field-Marshal, his coronet borne by the Marquis of Granby, his train by Sir William Gomm; the Duke of Sussex, his coronet carried by Viscount Anson, his train by the Honourable Edward Gore.

The High Constable of Ireland, the Duke of Leinster; the High Constable of Scotland, the Earl of

Errol, with their pages and coronets. The Earl-Marshal of England, the Duke of Norfolk, with his staff, attended by two pages; the sword of State, borne by Viscount Melbourne, with his page and coronet; the Lord High Constable of England, the Duke of Wellington, with his staff and baton as Field-Marshal, attended by two pages. The sceptre with the dove, borne by the Duke of Richmond, page and coronet; St. Edward's crown, borne by the Lord High Steward, the Duke of Hamilton, attended by two pages; the orb, borne by the Duke of Somerset, page and coronet. The patina, borne by the Bishop of Bangor; the Bible, borne by the Bishop of Winchester; the chalice, borne by the Bishop of London.

At last the Queen entered, walking between the Bishops of Bath and Wells and Durham, with Gentlemen-at-Arms on each side. She was now a royal maiden of nineteen, with a fair, pleasant face, a slight figure, rather small in stature, but showing a queenly carriage, especially in the pose of the throat and head. She wore a royal robe of crimson velvet furred with ermine and bordered with gold lace. She had on the collars of her orders. Like the other princesses, she wore a gold circlet on her head. Her train was borne by eight "beautiful young ladies," as Sir David Wilkie called them, all dressed alike, some of them destined to officiate again as the Queen's bridesmaids, when the loveliness of the group attracted general attention and admiration. These noble damsels were Lady Adelaide Paget, Lady Fanny Cowper, Lady Anne Wentworth Fitzwilliam, Lady Mary Grimston, Lady Caroline Gordon Lennox, Lady Mary Talbot, Lady Catherine Stanhope, Lady Louisa Jenkinson. The Ladies of her Majesty's Household came next in order, the Duchess of Sutherland, the Mistress of the Robes, walking first, followed by Lady Lansdowne as first Lady of the Bed-chamber. Other ladies of the Bed-chamber, whose names were long familiar in association with that of the Queen, included Ladies Charlemont, Lyttelton, Portman, Tavistock, Mulgrave, and Barham. The Maids of Honour bore names once equally well known in the Court Circular, while the office brought with it visions of old historic Maids prominent in Court gossip, and revealed to this day possibilities of sprightliness reined in by Court etiquette, and innocent little scrapes condoned by royal graciousness and kindness. The Maids of Honour at the Queen's coronation were the Honourable Misses Margaret Dillon, Cavendish, Lister, Spring Rice, Harriet Pitt, Caroline Cocks, Matilda Paget, and Murray. One has heard and read less of the Women of the Bed-chamber, noble ladies also, no doubt, but by the time the superb procession reached them, with the gathering up of the whole in Goldsticks, Captains of the Royal Archers, of the Yeomen of the Guard, of the Gentlemen-at-Arms, though pages and coronets still abounded, the strained attention could take in no more accessories, but was fain to return to the principal figure in the pageant, and dwell with all eyes on her.

"The Queen looked extremely well, and had an animated countenance." The scene within the choir on her entrance was so gorgeous, that, it is said, even the Turkish Ambassador, accustomed we should say to gorgeousness, stopped short in astonishment. As the Queen advanced slowly toward the centre of the choir, she was received with hearty plaudits, everybody rising, the anthem, "I was glad," sung by the musicians, ringing through the Abbey. "At the close of the anthem, the Westminster boys (who occupied seats at the extremity of the lower galleries on the northern and southern sides of the choir) chanted Vivat Victoria Regina. The Queen moved towards a chair placed midway between the chair of homage and the altar, on the carpeted space before described, which is called the theatre." Here she knelt down on a faldstool set for her before her chair, and used some private prayers. She then took her seat in the chair and the ceremonial proceeded.

First came "the Recognition" by the Archbishop of Canterbury, who advanced to the Queen, accompanied by the Lord Chancellor, the Lord Chamberlain, the Lord High Constable, and the

Earl-Marshal, preceded by the Deputy-Garter, and repeated these words: "Sirs, I here present unto you Queen Victoria, the undoubted Queen of this realm, wherefore all you who are come this day to do your homage, are you willing to do the same?" Then burst forth the universal cry from the portion of her Majesty's subjects present, "God save Queen Victoria." The Archbishop, turning to the north, south, and west sides of the Abbey, repeated, "God save Queen Victoria," the Queen turning at the same time in the same direction.

"The Bishops who bore the patina, Bible, and chalice in the procession, placed the same on the altar. The Archbishop of Canterbury and the Bishops who were to read the Litany put on their copes. The Queen, attended by the Bishops of Durham and Bath and Wells, and the Dean of Westminster, with the great officers of State and noblemen bearing the regalia, advanced to the altar, and, kneeling upon the crimson velvet cushion, made her first offering, being a pall or altar-cloth of gold, which was delivered by an officer of the Wardrobe to the Lord Chamberlain, by his lordship to the Lord Great Chamberlain, and by him to the Queen, who delivered it to the Archbishop of Canterbury, by whom it was placed on the altar. The Treasurer of the Household then delivered an ingot of gold, of one pound weight, to the Lord Great Chamberlain, who having presented the same to the Queen, her Majesty delivered it to the Archbishop, by whom it was put into the oblation basin.

"The Archbishop delivered a prayer in the prescribed form. The regalia were laid on the altar by the Archbishop. The great officers of State, except the Lord Chamberlain, retired to their respective places, and the Bishops of Worcester and St. David's read the Litany. Then followed the Communion service, read by the Archbishop of Canterbury and the Bishops of Rochester and Carlisle. The Bishop of London preached the sermon from the following text, in the Second Book of Chronicles, chapter xxxiv. verse 31: 'And the king stood in his place, and made a covenant before the Lord, to walk after the Lord, and to keep his commandments, and his testimonies, and his statutes, with all his heart, and with all his soul, to perform the words of the covenant which are written in this book.'

"In the course of his sermon from this text, the Bishop praised the late king for his unfeigned religion, and exhorted his youthful successor to follow in his footsteps. At the conclusion of the sermon 'the oath' was administered to the Queen by the Archbishop of Canterbury. The form of swearing was as follows: The Archbishop put certain questions, which the Queen answered in the affirmative, relative to the maintenance of the law and the established religion; and then her Majesty, with the Lord Chamberlain and other officers, the sword of State being carried before her, went to the altar, and laying her right hand upon the Gospels in the Bible carried in the procession, and now brought to her by the Archbishop of Canterbury, said, kneeling:

"'The things which I have here before promised I will perform and keep. So help me God.'

"The Queen kissed the book and signed a transcript of the oath presented to her by the Archbishop. She then kneeled upon her faldstool, and the choir sang 'Veni, Creator, Spiritus.'

"'The Anointing' was the next part of the ceremony. The Queen sat in King Edward's chair; four Knights of the Garter—the Dukes of Buccleugh and Rutland, and the Marquesses of Anglesea and Exeter—held a rich cloth of gold over her head; the Dean of Westminster took the ampulla from the altar, and poured some of the oil it contained into the anointing spoon, then the Archbishop anointed the head and hands of the Queen, marking them in the form of a cross, and pronouncing the words, 'Be thou anointed with holy oil, as kings, priests, and prophets were anointed; and as Solomon was anointed king by Zadok the priest, and Nathan the prophet, so be you anointed, blessed, and consecrated Queen over this people, whom the Lord your God hath given you to rule and govern, in the name of the Father, and of the Son and of the Holy Ghost,

Amen.'

"The Archbishop then said the blessing over her.

"The spurs were presented by the Lord Chamberlain, and the sword of State by Viscount Melbourne, who, however, according to custom, redeemed it with a hundred shillings, and carried it during the rest of the ceremony. Then followed the investing with the 'royal robes and the delivery of the orb,' and the 'investiture per annulum et baculum,' by the ring and sceptre.

"The Coronation followed. The Archbishop of Canterbury offered a prayer to God to bless her Majesty and crown her with all princely virtues. The Dean of Westminster took the crown from the altar, and the Archbishop of Canterbury, with the Archbishops of York and Armagh, the Bishops of London, Durham, and other Prelates, advanced towards the Queen, and the Archbishop taking the crown from the Dean reverently placed it on the Queen's head. This was no sooner done than from every part of the crowded edifice arose a loud and enthusiastic cry of 'God save the Queen,' mingled with lusty cheers, and accompanied by the waving of hats and handkerchiefs. At this moment, too, the Peers and Peeresses present put on their coronets, the Bishops their caps, and the Kings-of-Arms their crowns; the trumpets sounding, the drums beating, and the Tower and park guns firing by signal."

Harriet Martineau, who, like most of the mere spectators, failed to see and hear a good deal of the ceremony, was decidedly impressed at this point. "The acclamation when the crown was put on her head was very animating; and in the midst of it, in an instant of time, the Peeresses were all coroneted—all but the fair creature already described." The writer refers to an earlier paragraph in which she had detailed a small catastrophe that broke in upon the harmonious perfection of the scene. "One beautiful creature, with transcendent complexion and form, and coils upon coils of light hair, was terribly embarrassed about her coronet; she had apparently forgotten that her hair must be disposed with a view to it, and the large braids at the back would in no way permit the coronet to keep on. She and her neighbours tugged vehemently at her braids, and at last the thing was done after a manner, but so as to spoil the wonderful effect of the self-coroneting of the Peeresses."

To see "the Enthronement," the energetic Norwich woman stood on the rail behind her seat, holding on by another rail. But first "the Bible was presented by the Archbishop of Canterbury to the Queen, who delivered it again to the Archbishop, and it was replaced on the altar by the Dean of Westminster.

"The Benediction was delivered by the Archbishop, and the Te Deum sung by the choir. At the commencement of the Te Deum the Queen went to the chair which she first occupied, supported by two Bishops; she was then 'enthroned,' or 'lifted,' as the formulary states, into the chair of homage by the Archbishops, Bishops, and Peers surrounding her Majesty. The Queen delivered the sceptre with the cross to the Lord of the Manor of Worksop (the Duke of Norfolk), and the sceptre with the stone to the Duke of Richmond, to hold during the performance of the ceremony of homage. The Archbishop of Canterbury knelt and did homage for himself and other Lords Spiritual, who all kissed the Queen's hand. The Dukes of Sussex and Cambridge, removing their coronets, did homage in these words:—

"'I do become your liege man of life and limb, and of earthly worship; and faith and truth I will bear unto you, to live and die, against all manner of folks, so help me God.'

"They touched the crown on the Queen's head, kissed her left cheek, and then retired. It was observed that her Majesty's bearing towards her uncles was very kind and affectionate. The Dukes and other Peers then performed their homage, the senior of each rank pronouncing the words; as they retired each Peer kissed her Majesty's hand. The Duke of Wellington, Earl Grey, and Lord Melbourne were loudly cheered as they ascended the steps to the throne. Lord Rolle, "who was upwards of eighty, stumbled and fell on going up the steps. The Queen immediately stepped forward and held out her hand to assist him, amidst the loudly expressed admiration of the entire assembly."

"While the Lords were doing homage, the Earl of Surrey, Treasurer of the Household, threw coronation medals, in silver, about the choir and lower galleries, which were scrambled for with great eagerness.

"At the conclusion of the homage the choir sang the anthem, 'This is the day which the Lord hath made.' The Queen received the two sceptres from the Dukes of Norfolk and Richmond; the drums beat, the trumpets sounded, and the assembly cried out—'God save Queen Victoria!'"
[Footnote: Annual Register.]

Harriet Martineau, from her elevated perch, says, "Her small dark crown looked pretty, and her mantle of cloth of gold very regal; she, herself, looked so small as to appear puny." (At a later stage of the proceedings the same keen critic notes that the enormous train borne by her ladies made the figure of the Queen look still less than it really was.) "The homage was as pretty a sight as any: trains of Peers touching her crown, and then kissing her hand. It was in the midst of that process that poor Lord Rolle's disaster sent a shock through the whole assemblage. It turned me very sick. The large infirm old man was held up by two Peers, and had nearly reached the royal footstool when he slipped through the hands of his supporters, and rolled over and over down the steps, lying at the bottom coiled up in his robes. He was instantly lifted up, and he tried again and again, amidst shouts of admiration of his valour. The Queen at length spoke to Lord Melbourne, who stood at her shoulder, and he bowed approval; on which she rose, leaned forward, and held out her hand to the old man, dispensing with his touching the crown. He was not hurt, and his self-quizzing on his misadventure was as brave as his behaviour at the time. A foreigner in London gravely reported to his own countrymen, what he entirely believed on the word of a wag, that the Lords Rolle held their title on the condition of performing the feat at every coronation."

Sir David Wilkie, who was present at the coronation, wrote simply, "The Queen looked most interesting, calm, and unexcited; and as she sat upon the chair with the crown on, the sun shone from one of the windows bright upon her."

Leslie, another painter who witnessed the scene, remarked, "I was very near the altar, and the chair on which the Queen was crowned, when she signed the coronation oath. I could see that she wrote a large, bold hand…. I don't know why, but the first sight of her in her robes brought tears into my eyes, and it had this effect on many people; she looked almost like a child."

"The Archbishop of Canterbury then went to the altar. The Queen followed him, and giving the Lord Chamberlain her crown to hold, knelt down at the altar. The Gospel and Epistle of the Communion service having been read by the Bishops, the Queen made her offering of the chalice and patina, and a purse of gold, which were laid on the altar. Her Majesty received the sacrament kneeling on her faldstool by the chair."

Leslie afterwards painted this part of the ceremony for her Majesty. In his picture are several details which are not given elsewhere. The Peers and Peeresses who had crowned themselves simultaneously with the coronation of the Queen, removed their crowns when she laid aside hers. Among the gentlemen of the royal family was the Duc de Nemours.

After receiving the communion, the Queen put on her crown, "and with her sceptres in her hands, took her seat again upon the throne. The Archbishop of Canterbury proceeded with the Communion service and pronounced the final blessing. The choir sang the anthem, 'Hallelujah! for the Lord God omnipotent reigneth.' The Queen then left the throne, and attended by two

Bishops and noblemen bearing the regalia and swords of State, passed into King Edward's chapel, the organ playing. The Queen delivered the sceptre with the dove to the Archbishop of Canterbury, who laid it on the altar. She was then disrobed of her imperial robe of State and arrayed in her royal robe of purple velvet by the Lord Chamberlain. The Archbishop placed the orb in her left hand. The gold spurs and St. Edward's staff were delivered by the noblemen who bore them to the Dean of Westminster, who placed them on the altar. The Queen then went to the west door of the Abbey wearing her crown, the sceptre with the cross being in the right and the orb in the left hand.... It was about a quarter to four o'clock when the royal procession passed through the nave, in the same order as before, at the conclusion of the ceremony in the Abbey." The coronation lasted three hours, and must have been attended with great fatigue of mind and body to the young girl who bore the burden of the honours. Even the mere spectators, who, to be sure, had been in their places from dawn of day, the moment the stimulus of excitement was removed, awoke to their desperate weariness. "I watched her (the Queen) out at the doors," said Harriet Martineau, "and then became aware how fearfully fatigued I was. I never remember anything like it. While waiting in the passages and between the barriers, several ladies sat or lay down on the ground. I did not like to sink down in dust half a foot deep, to the spoiling of my dress and the loss of my self-respect, but it was really a terrible waiting till my brothers appeared at the end of the barrier."

But the day's business was not ended for the great world, high and low. The return of the procession, though the line was broken, had the special attraction that the Queen wore her crown, and the Peers and Peeresses their coronets. The Queen's crown was a mass of brilliants, relieved here and there by a large ruby or emerald, encircling a purple velvet cap. Among the stories told of the coronation, foremost and favourite of which was the misadventure of poor Lord Rolle, and the pretty gentle way in which the young Queen did her best to help the sufferer; an incident was reported which might have had its foundation in the difficulties described by Miss Martineau as besetting the fair Peeress in the Abbey. It was said that the Queen's crown was too cumbrous, and disturbed the arrangement of those soft braids of hair, the simple, modest fashion of which called forth Sir David Wilkie's praise, and that as her Majesty drove along in her State carriage, she was seen laughingly submitting to the good offices of her beautiful companion seeking with soft hands to loop up afresh the rebellious locks which had broken loose. Leslie, from whom we have already quoted, gives an anecdote of the Queen on her coronation-day, which serves at least to show how deeply the youthfulness of their sovereign was impressed on the public mind. He had been informed that she was very fond of dogs, and that she possessed a favourite little spaniel which was always on the look-out for her. She had been away from him longer than usual on this particular day. When the State coach drove up to the palace on her return, she heard his bark of joy in the hall. She cried, "There's Dash!" and seemed to forget crown and sceptre in her girlish eagerness to greet her small friend. [Footnote: In the list of Sir Edwin Landseer's pictures there is one, the property of the Queen, which was painted in 1838. It includes "Hector," "Nero," "Dash," and "Lorey" (dogs and parrot).]

In spite of the ordeal her Majesty had undergone, she entertained a party of a hundred to dinner, and witnessed from the roof of Buckingham Palace the grand display of fireworks in the Green Park and the general illumination of London. The Duke of Wellington gave a ball at Apsley House, followed next day by official dinners on the part of the Cabinet ministers. The festivities lasted for more than a week in the metropolis. Prominent among them was a fancy fair held for the space of four days in Hyde Park, and visited by the Queen in person. On the 9th of July, a fine, hot day there was a review in Hyde Park. The Queen appeared soon after eleven in an open barouche, with her aides-de-camp in full uniform. The Dukes of Cambridge and Wellington, the Duc de Nemours, Marshal Soult, Prince Esterhazy, Prince Schwartzenburg, Count Stragonoff, were present amidst a great crowd. The Queen was much cheered. The country's old gallant foe, Soult, was again hailed with enthusiasm, though there was just a shade of being exultingly equal to the situation, in the readiness with which, on his having the misfortune to break a stirrup, a worthy firm of saddlers came forward with a supply of the stirrups which Napoleon had used in one of his campaigns. And there might have been something significant to the visitor, in the rapturous greeting which was bestowed on the Iron Duke, round whose erect, impassive figure the multitude pressed, the nearest men and women defying his horse's hoofs and stretching up to shake hands with "the Conquering Hero" amidst a thunder of applause.

The rejoicings pervaded every part of the country from John o' Groat's to Land's End, from the Scilly Isles to Sark. There was merry-making among the English residents in every foreign place, as far as the great colonies in the still remote continents.

To many simple people the Queen did not seem to reign, hardly to exist, till she had put on her crown and taken up her sceptre. It was to do the first honour to their youthful liege lady that June garlands were swung over every village street, bonfires gleamed like carbuncles on mountain cairns, frightening the hill foxes, or lit up the coast-line and were flung back in broken reflections from the tossing waves, scaring the very fish in the depths of the sea, where hardy islanders had kindled the token on some rock of the ocean.

Pen and pencil were soon busy with the great event of the season. Elizabeth Barrett Browning wrote later:—

The Minster was alight that day, but not with fire, I ween,
And long-drawn glitterings swept adown that mighty aisled scene;
The priests stood stoled in their pomp, the sworded chiefs in theirs,
And so the collared knights—and so the civil ministers;
And so the waiting lords and dames—and little pages best
At holding trains—and legates so, from countries east and west;
So alien princes, native peers, and high-born ladies bright
Along whose brows the Queen's new crown'd, flashed coronets to light.
And so, the people at the gates, with priestly hands on high,
Which bring the first anointing to all legal majesty;
And so, the Dead—who lay in rows beneath the Minster floor,
There verily an awful state maintaining evermore—
The statesman, with no Burleigh nod, whate'er court tricks may be;
The courtier, who, for no fair Queen, will rise up to his knee;
The court-dame, who for no court tire will leave her shroud behind;
The laureate, who no courtlier rhymes than "dust to dust" can find;
The kings and queens who having ta'en that vow and worn that crown,
Descended unto lower thrones and darker, deeper adown;
"Dieu et mon Droit," what is't to them? what meaning can it have?
The king of kings, the dust of dust—God's judgment and the grave.
And when betwixt the quick and dead the young fair Queen had vowed,
The living shouted, "May she live! Victoria, live!" aloud,
And as these loyal shouts went up, true spirits prayed between,
The blessings happy monarchs have, be thine, O Crowned Queen!

In the autumn and winter of 1838 Leslie went down to Windsor to get sittings for his picture of the coronation. He had been presented to the Queen on her first visit to the Academy after her accession, as he mentions in one of his pleasant letters to his kindred in America. He was now to come into nearer contact with royalty. He slept at the Castle Inn, Windsor, and went up daily to the Castle. If he found her Majesty and any other sitter engaged, he improved the occasion by copying two of the Queen's fine Dutch pictures, a De Hooghe and a Nicholas Maas. He wrote his experience to his wife in London, and his sister in America. To the latter he said, "I came here on the 29th of last month by appointment to have a sitting of the Queen, and with little expectation of having more than one…. I have been here ever since, with the exception of a day or two in town (I perform the journey in an hour by the railroad), and the Queen has sat five times. She is now so far satisfied with the likeness, that she does not wish me to touch it again. She sat not only for the face, but for as much as is seen of the figure, and for the hands with the coronation-ring on her finger. Her hands, by-the-bye, are very pretty, the backs dimpled, and the fingers delicately shaped. She was particular also in having her hair dressed exactly as she wore it at the ceremony, every time she sat. She has suggested an alteration in the composition of the picture, and I suppose she thinks it like the scene, for she asked me where I sat, and said, 'I suppose you made a sketch on the spot.'

"The Duchess of Kent and Lord Melbourne are now sitting to me, and last week I had sittings of Lord Conyngham and Lady Fanny Cowper [Footnote: Daughter of a beautiful and popular mother, Lady Palmerston, by her first husband, Earl Cowper.] (a very beautiful girl, and one of the Queen's train-bearers), who was here for a few days on a visit to her Majesty. Every day lunch is sent to me, which, as it is always very plentiful and good, I generally make my dinner. The best of wine is sent in a beautiful little decanter, with a V.R. and the crown engraved on it, and the table-cloth and napkins have the royal arms and other insignia on them as a pattern.

"I have two very good friends at the Castle—one of the pages, and a little man who lights the fires. The Queen's pages are not little boys in green, but tall and stout gentlemen from forty to fifty years of age. My friend (Mr. Batchelor) was a page in the time of George III, and was then twenty years old; George IV died in his arms, he says, in a room adjoining the one I am painting in. Mr. Batchelor comes into the room whenever there is nobody there, and admires the picture to my heart's content. My other friend, the fire-lighter, is extremely like Peter Powell, only a size larger. He also greatly admires the picture; he confesses he knows nothing about the robes, and can't say whether they are like or not, but he pronounces the Queen's likeness excellent." [Footnote: Leslie's Autobiography.]

CHAPTER VI. THE MAIDEN QUEEN.

When the great event of the coronation was over the Queen was left to fulfil the heavy demands of business and the concluding gaieties of the season. It comes upon us with a little pathetic shock, to think of one whom we have long known chiefly in the chastened light of the devoted unflagging worker at her high calling, of our lady of sorrows, as a merry girl—girl-like in her fondness, in spite of her noble nature and the serious claims she did not neglect, of a racket of perpetual excitement. We read of her as going everywhere, as the blithest and most indefatigable dancer in her ball-room, dancing out a pair of slippers before the night was over; we hear how reluctant she was to leave town, how eager to return to it.

Inevitably the old and dear friends most interested in her welfare were now regarding this critical period in the Queen's career with anxious eyes. In looking back upon it in after life, she has frankly and gravely acknowledged its pitfalls; "a worse school for a young girl, or one more detrimental to all natural feeling and affection, cannot well be imagined, than the position of a queen at eighteen, without experience, and without a husband to guide and support her. This the Queen can state from painful experience, and she thanks God that none of her dear daughters are exposed to such danger."

The King of the Belgians sought to abridge the period of probation by renewing the project of the worthy marriage to which his niece had been well inclined two years before. But either from the natural coyness and the strain of perversity which are the privilege and the danger of girlhood, or simply because, as she has, stated, "the sudden change from the secluded life at Kensington to the independence of her position as Queen Regnant, at the age of eighteen, put all ideas of marriage out of her head," the bride in prospect demurred. She declared, with the unhesitating decision of her age, that she had no thought of marriage for years to come. She objected, with some show of reason, that both she and Prince Albert were too young, and that it would be better for him to have a little more time to perfect his English education.

The princely cousin who had won her first girlish affections, and the tender sweetness of love in the bud, were by no means forgotten. The idea of marriage never crossed the Queen's mind without his image presenting itself, she has said, and she never thought of herself as wedded to any other man. But every woman, be she Queen or beggar-maid, craves to exercise one species of power at one era of her life. It is her prerogative, and though the ruth of love may live to regret it, and to grudge every passing pang inflicted, half wilfully half unwittingly, on the true heart, it may be questioned whether love would flourish better, whether it would attain its perfect stature, without the test of the brief check and combat for mastery.

But if a woman desires to prove her power, a man cannot be expected to welcome the soft tyranny; the more manly, the more sensitive he is, the more it vexes and wounds him. Here the circumstances were specially trying, and while we have ample sympathy with the young Queen—standing out as much in archness as in imperiousness for a prolonged wooing—we have also sympathy to spare for the young Prince, with manly dignity and a little indignant pain, resisting alike girlish volatility and womanly despotism, asserting what was only right and reasonable, that he could not wait much longer for her to make up her mind—great queen and dear cousin though she might be. It was neither just nor generous that he should be kept hanging on in a condition of mortifying uncertainty, with the risk of his whole life being spoilt, after it was too late to guard against it, by a final refusal on her part. That the Queen had in substance made up her mind is proved by the circumstance that it was by her wish, and in accordance with her written instructions—of which, however, Prince Albert seems to have been ignorant—that Baron Stockmar, on quitting England in 1838, joined the Prince, who had just endured the trial of being separated from his elder brother, with whom he had been brought up in the closest and most brotherly relations, so that the two had never been a day apart during the whole of their previous lives. Prince Albert was to travel in Italy, and Baron Stockmar and Sir Francis (then Lieutenant) Seymour were appointed his travelling companions, visiting with him, during what proved a happy tour, Rome and Naples.

At home, where Baroness Lehzen retained the care of purely personal matters and played her part in non-political affairs and non-political correspondence, Lord Melbourne, with his tact and kindness, discharged the remaining offices of a private secretary. But things did not go altogether well. Party feeling was stronger than ever. The Queen's household was mainly of Whig materials, but there were exceptions, and the lady who had borne the train of the Duchess of Kent at the coronation belonged to a family which had become Tory in politics.

Lady Flora Hastings was a daughter of the Marquis of Hastings and of Flora, Countess of

Loudoun, in her own right. The Countess of Loudoun in her youth chose for her husband Earl Moira, one of the plainest-looking and most gallant officers in the British army. The parting shortly after their marriage, in order that he might rejoin his regiment on active service, was the occasion of the popular Scotch song, by Tannahill, "Bonnie Loudoun's woods and braes." Earl Moira, created Marquis of Hastings, had a distinguished career as a soldier and statesman, especially as Governor-General of India. When he was Governor-General of Malta he died far from Loudoun's woods and braes, and was buried in the little island; but in compliance with an old promise to his wife, who long survived him, that their dust should rest together, he directed that after death his right hand should be cut off, enclosed in a casket, and conveyed to the family vault beneath the church of Loudoun, where the mortal remains of his widow would lie.

Lady Flora Hastings was good, clever and accomplished, dearly loved by her family and friends. But whether she, nevertheless, possessed capabilities of offending her companions in office at Court; whether her conduct in any respect rebuked theirs, and provoked dislike, suspicion, and a desire to find her in the wrong; whether the calamity was sheerly due to that mortal meanness in human nature, which tempts people not otherwise unworthy to receive the most unlikely and injurious evil report of their neighbour, on the merest presumptive evidence, the unhappy sequel remains the same. Lady Flora had been attacked by an illness which caused so great a change in her personal appearance, as to lend colour to a whispered charge that she had been secretly guilty of worse than levity of conduct. The cruel whisper once breathed, it certainly became the duty of every person in authority round a young and maiden Queen to guard her Court jealously from the faintest suspicion of such a reproach. The fault lay with those who uttered the shameful charge on slight and, as it proved, totally mistaken inferences.

When the accusation reached the ears of Lady Flora—last of all, no doubt—the brave daughter of a brave man welcomed such a medical examination as must prove her innocence beyond dispute. Her name and fame were triumphantly cleared, but the distress and humiliation she had suffered accelerated the progress of her malady, and she died shortly afterwards, passionately lamented by her friends. They sought fruitlessly to bring punishment on the accusers, which could not be done since there was no evidence of deliberate insincerity and malice on the part of the circulators of the scandal. The blame of the disastrous gossip fell on two of the Whig Ladies of the Bed-chamber; and just before the sad climax, the other event, which angry Tory eyes magnified to the dignity of a conspiracy, drew double attention to both catastrophes.

In May, 1839, the Whig Government had been defeated in a crucial measure, and the ministry under the leadership of Lord Melbourne resigned office. The Queen sent for the Duke of Wellington, and he recommended that Sir Robert Peel should be called upon to form a new Cabinet. It was the first time that the Queen had experienced a change of Ministers, and she was naturally dismayed at the necessity, and reluctant to part with the friend who had lent her such aid on her accession, whom she trusted implicitly, who in the requirements of his office had been in daily communication with her for the last two years. In her interview with Sir Robert Peel, who in his shyness and constraint appeared to have far fewer personal recommendations for a young Queen's counsellor, she told him with a simple and girlish frankness that she was sorry to have to part with her late Minister, of whose conduct she entirely approved, but that she bowed to constitutional usage. [Footnote: Justin Macarthy.] Sir Robert took the impulsive speech in the straightforward spirit in which it was spoken, while time was to show such a good understanding and cordial regard established between the Queen and her future servant, as has rarely been surpassed in the relations of sovereigns and their advisers. But in the meanwhile a contretemps, which was more than half a blunder, occurred. "The negotiations went on very smoothly as to the colleagues Peel meant to recommend to her Majesty, until he happened to notice the composition of the royal household, as regarded the ladies most closely in attendance on the Queen. For example, he found that the wife of Lord Normanby and the sister of Lord Morpeth were the two ladies in closest attendance on her Majesty. Now it has to be borne in mind—it was proclaimed again and again during the negotiations—that the chief difficulty of the Conservatives would necessarily be in Ireland, where their policy would be altogether opposed to that of the Whigs. Lord Normanby had been Lord Lieutenant of Ireland under the Whigs, and Lord Morpeth, whom we can all remember as the amiable and accomplished Lord Carlisle of later time, Irish Secretary. It certainly would not be satisfactory for Peel to try to work a new Irish policy, whilst the closest household companions of the Queen were the wife and sister of the displaced statesmen, who directly represented the policy he had to supersede. Had this point of view been made clear to the sovereign at first, it is hardly possible that any serious difficulty could have arisen. The Queen must have seen the obvious reasonableness of Peel's request, nor is it to be supposed that the two ladies in question could have desired to hold their places under such circumstances. But unluckily some misunderstanding took place at the very beginning of the conversations on this point. Peel only desired to press for the retirement of the ladies holding the higher offices, [Footnote: This has been the rule in subsequent changes of Ministry.] he did not intend to ask for any change affecting a place lower in official rank than that of Lady of the Bed-chamber. But somehow or other he conveyed to the mind of the Queen a different idea. She thought he meant to insist as a matter of principle upon the removal of all her familiar attendants and household associates. Under this impression she consulted Lord John Russell, who advised her on what he understood to be the facts. On his advice the Queen stated in reply, that she could not "consent to a course which she conceives to be contrary to usage, and is repugnant to her feelings." Sir Robert Peel held firm to his stipulation, and the chance of his then forming a Ministry was at an end. Lord Melbourne and his colleagues had to be recalled, and at a Cabinet meeting they adopted a minute declaring it "reasonable, that the great offices of the Court, and situations in the household held by members of Parliament, should be included in the political arrangements made on a change in the Administration; but they are not of opinion that a similar principle should be applied or extended to the offices held by ladies in her Majesty's household." As an instance of the garbled impression received, and the unhesitating exultation manifested by some of the Whig leaders, we quote from Lord Campbell: "House of Commons, Friday, May 10, 1839. What do you think? Peel has quarrelled with the Queen, and for the present we are all in again. He insisted on her removing all her ladies, which she peremptorily refused. Peel sent his final answer yesterday evening, which she received at dinner, saying that on consulting his colleagues they could not yield, and that his commission was at an end. She then sent for Melbourne, who had not seen her since his resignation. At eleven a meeting of the old Cabinet was called. To-day Melbourne has been with her, and, Bear Ellis says, agreed to go on with the government. Reports differ as to the exact conditions. Our people say that she was willing to give up the wives of Peers; Sir George Clerk asserts she insisted on keeping all, inter alias the Marchioness of Normanby. There never was such excitement in London. I came with hundreds of others to the House of Lords, which met to-day, in the expectation that something would be said, but all passing off in silence." [Footnote: The explanation was made later.]

"Brooks's, Saturday, May 11, 1839. The Cabinet is still sitting, and we know nothing more to-day…. I was several hours at the Queen's ball last night, a scene never to be forgotten. The Queen was in great spirits, and danced with more than usual gaiety. She received Peel with great civility; but after dancing with the Russian Bear, took for her partner Lady Normanby's son. The

Tories looked inconceivably foolish—such whimsical groups."

Calm onlookers, including Stockmar, condemned Lord Melbourne for the position, in which he had allowed the young Queen to be placed, and considered that he had brought discredit on his Government by the circumstances in which he and his colleagues had resumed office. The melancholy death of Lady Flora Hastings following on this overthrow of the ordinary arrangements, intensified the wrath of the Tories, and helped to arouse a sense of general dissatisfaction and doubt.

In the month of July, 1839, an Act of Parliament was passed which was of great consequence to the mass of the people. In 1837 Sir Rowland Hill published his post-office reform pamphlet, and in 1839 the penny-post scheme was embodied in an Act of Parliament.

What stories clustered round the early miniature "heads" of her Majesty in the little dull red stamp! These myths ranged from the panic that the adhesive gum caused cancer in the tongue, to the romance that a desperate young lady was collecting a huge supply of used stamps for the purpose of papering a room of untold dimensions. This feat was the single stipulation on the part of a tyrannical parent, on compliance with which the hapless maiden would be allowed to marry her faithful lover.

CHAPTER VII. THE BETROTHAL.

The Queen's remaining unmarried was becoming the source of innumerable disturbing rumours and private intrigues for the bestowal of her hand. To show the extent to which the public discussed the question in every light, a serious publication like the Annual Register found space in its pages for a ponderous joke on the subject which was employing all tongues. Its chronicle professes to report an interview between her Majesty the Queen and Lord Melbourne, in which the Premier gravely represents to his sovereign the advisability of her marriage, and ventures to press her to say whether there is any man for whom she might entertain a preference. Her Majesty condescends to acknowledge there is one man for whom she could conceive a regard. His name is "Arthur, Duke of Wellington."

Altogether, King Leopold was warranted in renewing his efforts to accomplish the union which would best secure the happiness of his niece and the welfare of a kingdom. He adopted a simple, and at the same time, a masterly line of policy. He sent the Prince, whose majority had been celebrated along with his brother's a few months before, over again to England in the autumn of 1839; Prince Ernest of Saxe-Coburg went once more with Prince Albert, in order to show that this was not a bridegroom come to plead his suit in person; this was a mere cousinly visit of which nothing need come. Indeed, the good king rather overdid his caution, for it seems he led the Prince to believe that the earlier tacit understanding between him and his cousin had come to an end, so that Prince Albert arrived more resolved to relinquish his claims than to urge his rights. In his honest pride there was hardly room for the thought of binding more closely and indissolubly the silken cord of love, which had got loosened and warped in the course of the three years since the pair had parted—a long interval at the age of twenty. All the same, one of the most notably and deservedly attractive young men of his generation was to be brought for the second time, without the compulsory strain of an ulterior motive—declared or unjustifiably implied—into new contact with a royal maiden, whom a qualified judge described as possessing "a keen and quick apprehension, being straightforward, singularly pure-hearted, and free from all vanity and pretension." In the estimation of this sagacious well-wisher, she was fitted beforehand "to do ample justice both to the head and heart of the Prince."

It was at half-past seven on the evening of Thursday, the 10th of October, that the princely brothers entered again on the scene, no longer young lads under the guidance of their father, come to make the acquaintance of a girl-princess, their cousin, who though she might be the heir to a mighty kingdom, was still entirely under the wing of the Duchess, their aunt and her mother, in the homely old Palace of Kensington. These were two young men in the flower of their early manhood, who alighted in due form under the gateway of one of the stateliest of castles that could ever have visited their dreams, and found a young Queen as well as a kinswoman standing first among her ladies, awaiting them at the top of the grand staircase. However cordial and affectionate, and like herself, she might be, it had become her part, and she played it well, to take the initiative, to give directions instead of receiving them, to command where she had obeyed. It was she, and not the mother she loved and honoured, who was the mistress of this castle; and it was for her to come forward, welcome her guests, and graciously conduct them to the Duchess. King Leopold had furnished the brothers with credentials in the shape of a letter, recommending them, in studiously moderate terms, as "good, honest creatures," deserving her kindness, "not pedantic, but really sensible and trustworthy," whom he had told that her great wish was they should be at ease with her.

Both of these simply summed-up guests were fine young men, tall, manly, intelligent, and accomplished. Prince Albert was very handsome and winning, as all his contemporaries must remember him, with a mixture of thought and gentleness in his broad forehead, deep-blue eyes, and sweet smile.

The first incident of the visit was a trifle disconcerting, but not more so than happy, privileged people may be permitted to surmount with a laughing apology; even to draw additional light-hearted jests from the misadventure. The baggage of the Princes by some chance was not forthcoming; they could not appear at a Court dinner in their morning dress, but etiquette was relaxed for the strangers to the extent that later in the evening they joined the circle, which included Lord Melbourne, Lord Clanricarde, Lord and Lady Granville, Baron Brunnow and Lord Normanby, as visitors at Windsor at the time. The pleasant old courtier, Lord Melbourne, immediately told the Queen that he was struck with the resemblance between Prince Albert and herself.

"The way of life at Windsor during the stay of the Princes was much as follows:—the Queen breakfasting at this time in her own room, they afterwards paid her a visit there; and at two o'clock had luncheon with her and the Duchess of Kent. In the afternoon they all rode—the Queen and Duchess and the two Princes, with Lord Melbourne and most of the ladies and gentlemen in attendance, forming a large cavalcade. There was a great dinner every evening, with a dance after it, three times a week." [Footnote: "Early Years of the Prince Consort."] Surely an ideal palace life for the young—born to the Stately conditions, bright with all the freshness of body and sparkle of spirit, unexhausted, undimmed by years and care. Surely a fair field for true love to cast off its wilful shackles, and be rid of its half-cherished misunderstandings, to assert itself master of the situation. And so in five days, while King Leopold was still writing wary recommendations and temperate praise, the prize which had been deemed lost was won, and the Queen who had foredoomed herself to years of maidenly toying with happiness and fruitless waiting, was ready to announce her speedy marriage, with loyal satisfaction and innocent fearlessness, to her servants in council.

At the time, and for long afterwards, there were many wonderful little stories, doubtless fanciful enough, but all taking colour from the one charming fact of the royal lovers. How the Queen, whose place it was to choose, had with maidenly grace made known her worthy choice at one of these palace "dances," in which she had waltzed with her Prince, and subsided from the liege lady into the loving woman. She had presented him with her bouquet in a most marked and significant manner. He had accepted it with the fullest and most becoming sense of the distinction conferred upon him, and had sought to bestow her token in a manner which should prove his devotion and gratitude. But his tight-fitting foreign uniform had threatened to baffle his desire, till, in the exigency of the moment, he took out a pocket-knife (or was it his sword from its sheath?) and cut a slit in the breast of his coat on the left side, over the heart, where he put the flowers. Was this at the end of that second day after the brothers' arrival, on which, as the Prince mentions, in detailing to a friend the turn of the tide, "the most friendly demonstrations were directed towards me?"

On the 14th of October, the Queen told her fatherly adviser, Lord Melbourne, that she had made her choice; at which he expressed great satisfaction, and said to her (as her Majesty has stated in one of the published portions of her Journal), "I think it will be very well received, for I hear that there is an anxiety now that it should be, and I am very glad of it;" adding, in quite a paternal tone, "you will be much more comfortable, for a woman cannot stand alone for any time in whatever position she may be."

In the circumstances, the ordinary role was of necessity strangely reversed, and the ordeal of the declaration fell to the maiden and not to the young man. But the trial could not have come to a better pair. Innate good sense and dignity, and single-hearted affection on the one hand, and manly, delicate-minded tenderness on the other, made all things possible, nay, easy. An intimation was conveyed to the Prince through an old friend, who was in the suite of the brothers on this visit to England, Baron Alvensleben, Master of the Horse to the Duke of Coburg, that the Queen wished to speak to Prince Albert next day. Doubtless, the formality and comparative length of the invitation had its significant importance to the receiver of the message, and brought with it a tumult and thrill of anticipation. But he was called on to show that he had outgrown youthful impetuosity and impatience, and to prove himself worthy of trust and honour by perfect self-restraint and composure. So far as the world knows, he awaited his lady's will without a sign of restlessness or disturbance. If blissful dreams drove away sleep from the pillows on which two young heads rested in Royal Windsor that night, none save the couple needed to know of it. It was not by any means the first time that queenly and princely heads had courted oblivion in vain beneath the tower of St. George, and under the banner of England, but never in more natural, lawful, happy wakefulness.

On the morning of the 15th, behaving himself as if nothing had happened, or was going to happen, according to the code of Saxon Englishmen, Prince Albert went out early, hunting with his brother, but came back by noon, and "half an hour afterwards obeyed the Queen's summons to her room, where he found her alone. After a few minutes' conversation on other subjects, the Queen told him why she had sent for him."

The Prince wrote afterwards to the oldest of his relations: "The Queen sent for me alone to her room a few days ago, and declared to me, in a genuine outburst of love and affection, that I had gained her whole heart, and would make her intensely happy if I would make her the sacrifice of sharing her life with her, for she said she looked on it as a sacrifice; the only thing that troubled her was, that she did not think she was worthy of me. The joyous openness of manner with which she told me this quite enchanted me, and I was quite carried away by it."

"The Prince answered by the warmest demonstration of kindness and affection."

The affair had been settled by love itself in less time than it has taken to tell it.

There is an entry in her Majesty's Journal of this date, which she has, with noble and tender confidence, in the best feelings of humanity, permitted her people to read.

"How I will strive to make him feel, as little as possible, the great sacrifices he has made! I told him it was a great sacrifice on his part, but he would not allow it."

This record has been enthusiastically dwelt upon for its thorough womanliness; and so it is truly womanly, royally womanly. But it seems to us that less weight has been put on the fine sympathetic intuition of the Queen which enabled her to look beyond herself, beyond mere outward appearance and worldly advantages, and see the fact of the sacrifice on the part of such a man as Prince Albert, which he made with all his heart, cheerfully, refusing so much as to acknowledge it, for her dear sake. For the Queen was wisely right, and the Prince lovingly wrong. He not only gave back in full measure what he got, but, looking at the contract in the light of the knowledge which the Queen has granted to us of a rare nature, we recognise that for such a man—so simple, noble, purely scholarly and artistic; so capable of undying attachment; so fond of peaceful household charities and the quiet of domestic life; so indifferent to pomp and show; so wearied and worried in his patience by formality, parade, and the vulgar strife and noise, glare and blare of the lower, commoner ambitions—it was a sacrifice to forsake his fatherland, his father's house, the brother whom he loved as his own soul, the plain living and high thinking, healthful early hours and refined leisure—busy enough in good thoughts and deeds—of Germany, for the great shackled responsibility which should rest on the Queen's husband, for the artificial, crowded, high-pressure life of an England which did not know him, did not understand him, for many a day. If Baron Stockmar was right, that the physical constitution of the Prince in his youth rendered strain and effort unwelcome, and that he was rather deficient in interest in the ordinary work of the world, and in the broad questions which concern the welfare of men and nations, than overendowed with a passion for mastering and controlling them, then the sacrifice was all the greater.

But he made it, led by what was, in him, an overruling sense of right, and by the sweetest compelling motive, for highest duty and for her his Queen. Having put his hand to the plough he never looked back. What his hand found to do, that he did with all his might, and he became one of the hardest workers of his age. In seeing what he resigned, we also see that the fullness of his life was rendered complete by the resignation. He was called to do a grand, costly service, and he did well, at whatever price, to obey the call. Without the sacrifice his life would have been less honourable as an example, less full, less perfect, and so, in the end, less satisfying.

When the troth was plighted, the Queen adds, "I then told him to fetch Ernest, who congratulated us both and seemed very happy. He told me how perfect his brother was."

There were other kind friends to rejoice in the best solution of the problem and settlement of the vexed question. The good mother and aunt, the Duchess of Kent, rendered as secure as mortal mother could be of the future contentment and prosperity of her child; the attached kinsman beyond the Channel; the father of the bridegroom; his female relations; trusty Baron Stockmar; an early comrade, were all to be told and made happy, and in some cases sorry also, for the promotion of Prince Albert to be the Queen's husband meant exile from Germany.

The passages given from the Queen's and Prince's letters to King Leopold and Baron Stockmar are not only very characteristic, the words express what those who loved the writers best would have most wished them to say. The respective utterances are radiant with delight softened by the modest, firm resolves, the humble hearty conscientiousness which made the proposed marriage so auspicious of all it was destined to prove.

The King of the Belgians was still in a state of doubt, writing his earnest but studiously measured praise of his nephews to the Queen. "I am sure you will like them the more, the longer you see them. They are young men of merit, and without that puppy-like affection which is so often found with young gentlemen of rank; and though remarkably well informed, they are very free from pedantry.

"Albert is a very agreeable companion. His manners are so quiet and harmonious that one likes to have him near one's self. I always found him so when I had him with me, and I think his travels have still improved him. He is full of talent and fun, and draws cleverly."

At last there is a plainer insinuation. "I trust they will enliven your sejour in the old castle, and may Albert be able to strew roses without thorns on the pathway of life of our good Victoria. He is well qualified to do so...."

On the very day this letter was written, the Queen was addressing her uncle. "My dearest uncle, this letter will I am sure give you pleasure, for you have always shown and taken so warm an interest in all that concerns me. My mind is quite made up, and I told Albert this morning of it. The warm affection he showed me on learning this, gave me great pleasure. He seems perfection, and I think I have the prospect of very great happiness before me. I love him more than I can say, and shall do everything in my power to render this sacrifice (for such is my opinion it is) as small as I can.... It is absolutely necessary that this determination of mine should be known to no one but yourself and to Uncle Ernest, until after the meeting of Parliament, as it would be considered, otherwise, neglectful on my part not to have assembled Parliament at once to inform them of it.... Lord Melbourne has acted in this business as he has always done towards me, with the greatest kindness and affection. We also think it better, and Albert quite approves of it, that we should be married very soon after Parliament meets, about the beginning of February."

The King's reply from Wiesbaden is like the man, and is pathetic in the depth of its gratification. "My dearest Victoria, nothing could have given me greater pleasure than your dear letter. I had, when I learnt your decision, almost the feeling of Old Simeon: 'Now lettest thou thy servant depart in peace.' Your choice has been for these last years my conviction of what might and would be best for your happiness; and just because I was convinced of it, and knew how strangely fate often changes what one tries to bring about as being the best plan one could fix upon—the maximum of a good arrangement—I feared that it would not happen."

In Prince Albert's letter to Baron Stockmar, written without delay, as he says, "on one of the happiest days of my life to give you the most welcome news possible," he goes on to declare that he is often at a loss to believe that such affection should be shown to him. He quotes as applicable to himself from Schiller's "Song of the Bell," of which the Prince was very fond—

Das Auge sieht den Himmel offen,
Es schwimmt das Herz in seligkeit.

The passage from which these lines are taken is the very beautiful one thus rendered in English by the late Lord Lytton:—

And, lo! as some sweet vision breaks
Out from its native morning skies,
With rosy shame on downcast cheeks,
The virgin stands before his eyes:
A nameless longing seizes him!
From all his wild companions flown;
Tears, strange till then, his eyes bedim,
He wanders all alone.
Blushing he glides where'er she moves,
Her greeting can transport him;
To every mead to deck his love,

The happy wild-flowers court him.
Sweet hope—and tender longing—ye
The growth of life's first age of gold,
When the heart, swelling, seems to see
The gates of heaven unfold.
Oh, were it ever green! oh, stay!
Linger, young Love, Life's blooming may.

In a later letter to Stockmar the Prince writes: "An individuality, a character which shall win the respect, the love, and the confidence of the Queen and of the nation, must be the groundwork of my position.... If therefore I prove a 'noble' Prince in the true sense of the word, as you call upon me to be, wise and prudent conduct will become easier to me, and its results more rich in blessings;" and to his stepmother he makes the thoughtful comment, "With the exception of my relation to her (the Queen), my future position will have its dark sides, and the sky will not always be blue and unclouded. But life has its thorns in every position, and the consciousness of having used one's powers and endeavours for an object so great as that of promoting the good of so many will surely be sufficient to support me."

The brothers remained at Windsor for a happy month, [Footnote: Lady Bloomfield describes a beautiful emerald serpent ring which the Prince gave the Queen when they were engaged.] when the royal lovers saw much of each other, and as a matter of course often discussed the future, particularly with reference to the Prince's position in his new country, and what his title was to be. One can easily fancy how interesting and engrossing such talks would become, especially when they were enlivened by the bright humour, and controlled by the singular unselfishness, of the object of so many hopes and plans. It was already blustering wintry weather, but there was little room to feel the depressing influence of the grey cloudy sky or the chill of the shrilly whistling wind and driving rain. Prince Ernest had the misfortune to suffer from an attack of jaundice, but it was a passing evil, sure to be lightened by ample sympathy, and it did not prevent the friend of the bridegroom from rejoicing greatly at the sound of the bridegroom's voice. Perhaps the fact that a form of secrecy had to be kept up till her Majesty should announce her marriage to the Council only added an additional piquant flavour to the general satisfaction. But this did not cause the Queen to fail in confidence towards the members of her family, for she wrote herself to the Queen-dowager and to the rest of her kindred announcing her intended marriage, and receiving their congratulations.

On the 2nd of November there was a review of the battalion of the Rifle Brigade quartered at Windsor under Colonel, afterwards Sir George Brown, of Crimean fame, in the Home Park. The Queen was present, accompanied by Prince Albert, in the green uniform of the Coburg troops. What a picture, full of joyful content, independent of all accidents of weather, survives of the scene! "At ten minutes to twelve I set off in my Windsor uniform and cap (already described) on my old charger 'Leopold,' with my beloved Albert looking so handsome in his uniform on my right, and Sir John Macdonald, the Adjutant-General, on my left, Colonel Grey and Colonel Wemyss preceding me, a guard of honour, my other gentlemen, my cousin's gentlemen, Lady Caroline Barrington, &c., for the ground.

"A horrid day. Cold, dreadfully blowing, and, in addition, raining hard when we had been out a few minutes. It, however, ceased when we came to the ground. I rode alone down the ranks, and then took my place as usual, with dearest Albert on my right and Sir John Macdonald on my left, and saw the troops march past. They afterwards manoeuvred. The Rifles looked beautiful. It was piercingly cold, and I had my cape on, which dearest Albert settled comfortably for me. He was so cold, being 'EN GRANDE TENUE,' with high boots. We cantered home again, and went in to show ourselves to. poor Ernest, who had seen all from a window."

The Princes left Windsor on the 14th of November, visiting the King of the Belgians on their way home, so that King Leopold could write to his niece, "I find them looking well, particularly Albert. It proves that happiness is an excellent remedy to keep people in better health than any other. He is much attached to you, and modest when speaking of you. He is besides in great spirits, full of gaiety and fun."

The bridegroom also sent kind words to his aunt and future mother-in-law, as well as tender words to his cousin and bride. "Dearest aunt, a thousand thanks for your two kind letters just received. I see from them that you are in close sympathy with your nephew—your son-in-law soon to be—which gratifies me very, very much…. What you say about my poor little bride sitting all alone in her room, silent and sad, has touched me to the heart. Oh, that I might fly to her side to cheer her!"

"For 'the poor little bride' there was no lack of those sweet words, touched with the grateful humility of a manly love, to receive which was a precious foretaste to her of the happiness of the years to come." "That I am the object of so much love and devotion often comes over me as something I can hardly realise," wrote the Prince. "My prevailing feeling is, What am I that such happiness should be mine? For excess of happiness it is to me to know that I am so dear to you." Again, in referring to his grandmother's regret at his departure he added, "Still she hopes, what I am convinced will be the case, that I may find in you, my dear Victoria, all the happiness I could possibly desire. And so I SHALL, I can truly tell her for her comfort." And once more he wrote from "dear old Coburg," brimming over with loyal joy, "How often are my thoughts with you! The hours I was privileged to pass with you in your dear little room are the radiant points of my life, and I cannot even yet clearly picture to myself that I am to be indeed so happy as to be always near you, always your protector." Last and most touching assurance of all, touching as it was solemn, when he mentioned to the Queen that in an hour he was to take the sacrament in church at Coburg, and went on, "God will not take it amiss, if in that serious act, even at the altar, I think of you, for I will pray to Him for you and for your soul's health, and He will not refuse us His blessing."

In the meantime there was much to do in England. On the 20th of November the Queen, with the Duchess of Kent, left Windsor for Buckingham Palace. On the 23rd, the Council assembled there in the Bow-room on the ground floor. The ceremony of declaring her proposed marriage was a mere form, but a very trying form to a young and modest woman called to face alone a gathering of eighty-three elderly gentlemen, and to make to them the announcement which concerned herself so nearly. Of the Privy Councillors some, like the Duke of Wellington, had known the Queen all her life, some had only served her since she came to the throne, but all were accustomed to discuss very different matters with her. How difficult the task was to the Queen we may judge from the significant note. The Queen always wore a bracelet with the Prince's picture, "and it seemed," she wrote in her Journal, "to give me courage at the Council." Her own further account of the scene is as follows: "Precisely at two I went in. The room was full, but I hardly knew who was there. Lord Melbourne I saw looking kindly at me with tears in his eyes, but he was not near me. I then read my short declaration. I felt my hands shook, but I did not make one mistake. I felt most happy and thankful when it was over. Lord Lansdowne then rose, and in the name of the Privy Council asked that this most gracious and most welcome communication might be printed. I then left the room, the whole thing not lasting above two or three minutes. The Duke of Cambridge came into the small library where I was standing and wished me joy."

The Queen's declaration was to this effect: "I have caused you to be summoned at the present time in order that I may acquaint you with my resolution in a matter which deeply concerns the welfare of my people and the happiness of my future life.

"It is my intention to ally myself in marriage with the Prince Albert of Saxe-Coburg and Gotha. Deeply impressed with the solemnity of the engagement which I am about to contract, I have not come to this decision without mature consideration, nor without feeling a strong assurance that, with the blessing of Almighty God, it will at once secure my domestic felicity and serve the interests of my country.

"I have thought fit to make this resolution known to you at the earliest period, in order that you may be apprised of a matter so highly important to me and to my kingdom, and which, I persuade myself, will be most acceptable to all my loving subjects."

The Queen returned to Windsor with the Duchess of Kent the same evening.

On the 16th of January, 1840, the Queen opened Parliament in person, and made a similar statement. "Since you were last assembled I have declared my intention of allying myself in marriage with the Prince Albert of Saxe-Coburg and Gotha. I humbly implore that the Divine blessing may prosper this union, and render it conducive to the interests of my people as well as to my own domestic happiness, and it will be to me a source of the most lively satisfaction to find the resolution I have taken approved by my Parliament. The constant proofs which I have received of your attachment to my person and family persuade me that you will enable me to provide for such an establishment as may appear suitable to the rank of the Prince and the dignity of the Crown."

To see and hear the young Queen, still only in her twenty-first year, when she went to tell her people of her purpose, multitudes lined the streets and cheered her on her way that wintry day, and every seat in the House "was filled with the noblest and fairest of the land" ready to give her quieter but not less heartfelt support. It is no mere courtly compliment to say that Queen Victoria's marriage afforded the greatest satisfaction to the nation at large. Not only was it a very desirable measure on political grounds, but it appealed to the far deeper and wider feelings of humanity. It had that touch of nature which makes the whole world kin. Sir Robert Peel's words, when he claimed the right of the Opposition to join with the Government in its felicitations to both sovereign and country, were not required to convince the people that their Queen was not only making a suitable alliance, but was marrying "for love," according to the oldest, wisest, best plan. They knew the glad truth as if by instinct, and how heartily high and low entered into her happiness and wished her joy! It is said there is one spectacle which, whether the spectators own it or not, hardly ever palls entirely even on the most hardened and worldly, the most weary and wayworn, the poorest and most wretched—perhaps, least of all on the last. It is a bridegroom rejoicing to leave his chamber, and a bride blushing in her sweet bliss. There are after all only three great events in human history which, projected forward or reflected backward, colour all the rest—birth, marriage, and death. The most sordid or sullen population will collect in knots, brighten a little, forget hard fate or mortal wrongs for a moment, in the interest of seeing a wedding company go by. The surliest, the most whining of the onlookers will spare a little relenting, a happier thought, for "two lunatics," "a couple of young fools whose eyes will soon be opened," "a pore delooded lad," "a soft silly of a gal;" who are still so enviable in their brief bright day.

What was it then to know of a pair of royal lovers—a great Queen and her chosen Prince—well mated! It softened all hearts, it made the old young again, with a renewing breath of late romance and tenderness. And, oh! how the young, who are old now, gloried in that ideal marriage! What tales they told of it, what wonderful fancies they had about it! How it knit the hearts of the Queen and her subjects together more strongly than anything else save common sorrow could do! for when it comes to that, sorrow is more universal than joy, sinks deeper, and in this world lasts longer.

Indeed, at this stage, as at every other, it was soon necessary to descend from heaven to earth; and for the royal couple, as for the meanest of the people, there were difficulties in connection with the arrangements, troubles that proved both perplexing and vexatious. It may be said here that the times were not very propitious for asking even the most just and reasonable Parliamentary grants. The usual recurring sufferings from insufficient harvests and from stagnation of trade were depressing the mind of the country. Parliament was called on to act on the occasion of the Queen's marriage, and the House was not only divided into two hostile parties, the hostility had been envenomed by recent contretemps, notably that which prevented Sir Robert Peel and the Tories from taking office and kept in the Whig Government. The unpalatable fruits of the embroilment had to be eaten and digested at the present crisis. Accordingly there were carping faultfinding, and resistance—even defeat—on every measure concerning the Prince brought before the Lords and Commons.

The accusation of disloyal retaliation was made against the Tories. On the other hand the Whigs in power showed such a defiant attitude, in the absence of any attempt to conciliate their antagonists, even when the welfare of the Government's motions, and the interests and feelings of the Queen and the Prince demanded the first consideration, that Lord Melbourne's party were suspected of a crafty determination to let matters take their course for the express purpose of prejudicing Prince Albert against the Tories, and alienating him from them in the very beginning. Lord Melbourne at least did not deserve this accusation. Whatever share he had in the injudicious attitude of the Government, or in the blunders it committed, must be attributed to the sort of high-handed carelessness which distinguished the man. His singular fairness in the business is thus recorded by Baron Stockmar. "As I was leaving the Palace, I met Melbourne on the staircase. He took me aside and used the following remarkable and true words, strongly characteristic of his great impartiality: 'The Prince will doubtless be very much irritated against the Tories. But it is not the Tories alone whom the Prince has to thank for the curtailment of his appanage. It is the Tories, the Radicals, and a good many of our own people.' I pressed his hand in approbation of his remarkable frankness. I said, 'There's an honest man! I hope you will yourself say that to the Prince.'" [Footnote: Lord Melbourne and Baron Stockmar were always on excellent terms. At the same time the English Prime Minister was not without a little jealousy of any suspicion of his Government being dictated to by King Leopold.]

Umbrage was taken by the Duke of Wellington at no mention being made of Prince Albert's Protestantism on the notification of the marriage. With regard to the income and position to be secured to the Prince, the nearest precedent which could be found to guide the discussion was that of Prince George of Denmark, husband to Queen Anne. It was halting in many respects, such as the fact that he had married the Princess long before she was Queen, nay, while her succession to the throne was problematical. Besides, his character and position in the country were only respectable for their harmlessness, and did not recommend him by way of example of any kind, either to Queen or people. Statesmen turned rather to the settlement and dignity accorded to Prince Leopold, when he married Princess Charlotte; but neither was that quite a case in point. The fittest reference, so far as income was concerned, seemed to be to the private purses allowed to the Queen Consorts of the reigning sovereigns of England. To the three last

Queens—Caroline, Charlotte, and Adelaide, the sum of fifty thousand pounds a year had been granted. This also was the annuity settled on Prince Leopold. Therefore fifty thousand was the amount confidently asked by the Government.

After a good deal of wrangling and angry debate, in which, however, the Queen's name was studiously respected, she and the Prince had the mortification to learn that the country, by its representatives, had refused the usual allowance, and voted only thirty thousand a year to the Queen's husband.

The same ill-fortune attended an attempt to introduce into the bill for the naturalisation of the Prince, before the House of Lords, a clause which should secure his taking precedence of all save the Queen. The Duke of Sussex opposed the clause, in the interest of the King of Hanover, and so many jealous objections were urged that it was judged better to let the provision drop than risk a defeat in the House of Lords similar to that in the House of Commons. The awkward alternative remained that Prince Albert's position, so far as it had to do with the Lord Chamberlain and the Heralds' Office, was left undecided and ambiguous. It was only by the issue of letters patent on the Queen's part, at a later date, that any certainty on this point could be attained even in England.

The formation of the Prince's household, which one would think might have been left to his own good feeling and discretion, or at least to the Queen's judgment in acting for him, proved another bone of contention calling forth many applications and implied claims.

Baron Stockmar came to England in January, to see to this important element in the Prince's independence and comfort, as well as to the signing of the marriage contract. But in spite of the able representative, the Prince's written wishes, judicious and liberal-minded as might have been expected, and the Queen's desire to carry them out, at least one of the offices was filled up in a manner which caused Prince Albert anxiety and pain. The gentleman who had been private secretary to Lord Melbourne was appointed private secretary to the Prince, without regard to the circumstance that the step would appear compromising in Tory eyes—the very result which Prince Albert had striven to avoid, and that the official would be forced, as it were, on the Prince's intimacy without such previous acquaintance as might have justified confidence. It was only the sterling qualities of both Prince and secretary which obviated the natural consequences of such an ill-judged proceeding, and ended by producing the genuine liking and honest friendship which ought to have preceded the connection. The grudging, suspicions, selfish spirit thus manifested on all hands, was liable to wound the Queen in the tenderest point, and the disappointment came upon her with a shock, since she had been rashly assured by Lord Melbourne that there would be no difficulty either as regarded income or precedence. The indications were not encouraging to the stranger thus met on the threshold. But his mission was to disarm adverse criticism, to shame want of confidence and pettiness of jealousy, to confer benefits totally irrespective of the spirit in which they might be taken. And even by the irritated party-men as well as by the body of the people, the Prince was to be well received for the Queen's sake, with his merits taken for granted, so far as that went, since the heart of the country was all right, though its Whig and Tory temper might be at fault.

On the 10th of January, 1840, a death instead of a marriage took place in the royal family, but it was that of an aged member long expatriated. Princess Elizabeth, Landgravine of Hesse Homburg, died at Frankfort. It was twenty-two years since she had married and quitted England, shortly before the old Queen's death, a year before the birth of Queen Victoria. The Landgravine had returned once, a widow of sixty-four, and then had gone back to her adopted country. She had survived her husband eleven years, and her sister, resident like herself in Germany, the

Princess Royal, Queen of Wurtemberg, twelve years. The Landgravine as Princess Elizabeth showed artistic talent. She was famous in her middle age for her great embonpoint; as she was also tall she waxed enormous. Baroness Bunsen, when Miss Waddington, saw Princess Elizabeth, while she was still unmarried, dressed for a Drawing-room, with five or six yellow feathers towering above her head, and refers to her huge dimensions then. It was alleged afterwards that it required a chain of her husband's faithful subjects in Homburg to encompass his consort. She accommodated herself wonderfully, though she was an elderly woman before she had ever been out of England, to the curious quaint mixture of State and homeliness in the little German town in which she was held in much respect and regard. The Landgravine was seventy years of age at the time of her death. After her widowhood she resided in Hanover, where her brother, King William, gave her a palace, and then at Frankfort, where she died. Out of her English income of ten thousand a year, it was said she spared six thousand for the needs of Hesse Homburg. Its castle and English garden still retain memories of the English princess who made her quiet home there and loved the place.

The marriage of the Queen was fixed for the 10th of February, and many eager, aspiring young couples throughout the country elected that it should be their wedding-day, also. They wished that the gala of their lives should fit in with hers, and that all future "happy returns of the day" might have a well-known date to go by, and a State celebration to do them honour.

Lord Torrington and Colonel—afterwards General—Grey set out for Gotha to escort the bridegroom to England. They carried with them the Order of the Garter, with which Prince Albert was invested by his father, himself a Knight of the Order, amidst much ceremony.

All the world knows that the Order of the Garter is the highest knightly order of England, dating back to the time of Edward III., and associated by a gay and gallant tradition with the beautiful Countess of Salisbury. The first Chapter of the Order was held in 1340, when twenty-five knights, headed by the King, walked in solemn procession to St. George's Chapel, founded for their use, and for the maintenance of poor knightly brethren to pray for the souls of the Knights-Companions—hence "the Poor Knights of Windsor." The first Knights-Companions dedicated their arms to God and St. George, and held a high festival and tournament in commemoration of the act in presence of Queen Philippa and her ladies. The habit of the knights was always distinguished by its colour, blue. Various details were added at different times by different kings. Henry VIII. gave the collar and the greater and lesser medallions of St. George slaying the dragon. Charles II. introduced the blue riband. It is scarcely necessary to say that the full dress of the knights is very magnificent. "There are the blue velvet mantle, with its dignified sweep, the hood of crimson velvet, the heron and ostrich-plumed cap, the gold medallion, the blazing star, the gold-lettered garter, to all which may be added the accessories that rank and wealth have it in their power to display; as, for example, the diamonds worn by the Marquis of Westminster, at a recent installation, on his sword and badge alone were Worth the price of a small kingdom; or richer still her present Majesty's jewels, that seem to have been showered by some Eastern fairy over her habit of the Order, among, which the most beautiful and striking feature is, perhaps, the ruby cross in the centre of the dazzling star of St. George." [Footnote: Knight's "Old England."] The whole court of Gotha was assembled to see Prince Albert get the Garter; a hundred and one guns were fired to commemorate the auspicious occasion. The younger Perthes, under whom the Prince had studied at Bonn, wrote of the event, "The Grand-ducal papa bound the Garter round his boy's knee amidst the roar of a hundred and one cannon" (the attaching of the Garter, however, was done, not by Prince Albert's father, but by the Queen's brother, the Prince of

Leiningen, another Knight of the Order). "The earnestness and gravity with which the Prince has obeyed this early call to take a European position, give him dignity and standing in spite of his youth, and increase the charm of his whole aspect."

The investiture was followed by a grand dinner, when the Duke proposed the Queen's health, which was drunk by all the company standing, accompanied by several distinct flourishes of trumpets, the band playing "God save the Queen," and the artillery outside firing a royal salute. Already the Prince had written to the Queen, when the marriage was officially declared at Coburg, that the day had affected him very much, so many emotions had filled his heart. Her health had been drunk at dinner "with a tempest of huzzas." The joy of the people had been so great that they had gone on firing in the streets, with guns and pistols, during the whole night, so that one might have imagined a battle was going on. This was a repetition of that earlier festival, only rendered more emphatic and with a touch of pathos added to it by the impending departure of Prince Albert, to lay hold of his high destiny. The leave-takings were earnest and prolonged, with many pretty slightly fantastic German ceremonies, and must have been hard upon a man whose affections were so tender and tenacious. Especially painful was the farewell to his mother's mother, the Dowager Duchess of Gotha, who had partly reared the princely lad. She was much attached to him, and naturally saw him go with little hope of their meeting again in this world.

The Prince was accompanied by his father and brother, with various friends in their train, who, after the celebration of the marriage, were to return to Germany. But Prince Albert carried with him—to remain in his near neighbourhood—two old allies, whose familiar faces would be doubly welcome in a foreign country. The one was his Swiss valet, Cart, a faithful, devoted servant, "the best of nurses," who, had waited on his master since the latter was a boy of seven years of age. The other was the beautiful greyhound, Eos, jet black with the exception of a narrow white streak on the nose and a white foot. Her master had got her as a puppy of six weeks old, when he was a boy in his fourteenth year, and had trained the loving, graceful creature in all imaginable canine, sagacity and cleverness. She had been the constant companion of his youth. She had already come to England with him, on the decisive visit of the previous autumn, and was known and dear to his royal mistress.

It was severe wintry weather when the great cavalcade, in eight travelling carriages, set out for England, and took its way across Germany, Belgium, and the north of France, to the coast The whole journey assumed much of the character of a festive procession. At each halting-place crowds turned out to do the princes honour. Every court and governing body welcomed them with demonstrations of respect and rejoicing. But at Aix-la-Chapelle, in a newspaper which he came across, Prince Albert read the debates and votes in the Houses of Parliament that cut down the ordinary annuity of the English sovereign's consort, and left unsettled the question of his position in the country. The first disappointment told in two ways. Young and sensitive—though he was also resolute and cheerful-minded—he had been a little nervous beforehand about the reception which might be accorded to him in England; he now received a painful impression that the marriage was not popular with the people. He had indulged in generous dreams of the assistance and encouragement which he would be able to bestow on men of letters and artists, when he suddenly found his resources curtailed to nearly half the amount he had been warranted in counting upon. However, at Brussels, the next halting-place, in writing to the Queen, and frankly admitting his mortification at the words and acts of the majority of the members of both English Houses of Parliament, he could add with perfect sincerity, "All I have time to say is, that while I possess your love they cannot make me unhappy."

And King Leopold was there with his sensible, calming counsel, while Baron Stockmar had been careful to have a letter awaiting the Prince, which explained the undercurrent of political, not personal, motives that had influenced the debates.

In fact, so far from being unpopular, the Prince, who was the Queen's choice, was really the most acceptable of all her suitors in the eyes of her people. The sole serious objection urged against him in those days was that of his youth, a fault which was not only daily lessening, but was speedily forgotten in the conviction of the manly and serious attention to duty on his part which he quickly inspired.

On the 5th of February the party arrived at Calais. Lord Clarence Paget had been sent over with the Firebrand to await their arrival, but the usual difficulties of an adverse tide and an insufficient French harbour presented themselves, and the company had to sail on the morning of the 6th in one of the ordinary Dover packet-boats, under a strong gale from the south-east, with a heavy sea, which rendered the horrors of the Channel crossing, at the worst, what only those who have experienced them can realise.

The Prince, like most natives of inland Germany, had been little inured to sailing, and his constitution rendered him specially liable to sea-sickness. As a lad of seventeen, facing the insidious and repulsive foe for the first time, he had expressed his own and his brother's dread of the unequal encounter. Now he was doomed to feel its ignoble clutch to the last moment. "The Duke had gone below, and on either side of the cabin staircase lay the two princes in an almost helpless state."

It was in such unpropitious circumstances that Prince Albert had to rise, pull himself together, and bow his acknowledgements to the crowds on the pier ready to greet him. Who that has rebelled against the calm superiority of the comfortable; amused onlookers at the haggard, giddy sufferers reeling on shore from the disastrous crossing of a stormy ferry, cannot comprehend the ordeal!

The Prince surmounted it gallantly, anticipating the time when, at the call of work or duty, he was known to rise to any effort, to shake off fatigue and indisposition as if he had been the most muscular of giants, and to make a brave fight to the last against deadly illness. He had his reward. The raw inclement day, the disabling, discomfiting malady—which had appeared in themselves a bad beginning, an inhospitable introduction to his future life—the recent misgivings he had entertained, were all forgotten in the enthusiastic reception he received before he put foot on land. A kind heart responds readily to kindness, and the Prince felt, in spite of parliamentary votes, the people were glad to see him, with an overflowing gladness.

It had been fixed that the Prince should not arrive at Buckingham Palace till the 8th. Accordingly there was time for the much-needed rest and refreshment, and for a leisurely conclusion of the long journey. The travellers stayed that night at Dover, the next at Canterbury, the Prince beginning the long list of fatiguing ceremonials which he was to undergo in the days to come, by receiving addresses, holding a reception, and showing himself on the balcony, as well as by the quieter, more congenial interlude of attending afternoon service in Canterbury Cathedral with his brother. The weather was still bad; pouring rain had set in, but it could not damp the spirit of the holiday-makers. As for the hero of the holiday, he was chafing, lover-like, at the formal delay which was all that interposed between him and a blissful reunion. He wrote to the Queen before starting for Canterbury, "Now I am once more in the same country with you. What a delightful thought for me. It will be hard for me to have to wait till to-morrow evening. Still, our long parting has flown by so quickly, and to-morrow's dawn will soon be here…. Our reception has been most satisfactory. There were thousands of people on the quays, and they saluted pus with loud and uninterrupted cheers.".

From Canterbury Prince Albert sent on his valet, Cart, with the greyhound Eos. "Little Dash," if Dash still lived, was to have a formidable rival, and the Queen speaks in her Journal of the pleasure which the sight of "dear Eos," the evening before the arrival of the Prince, gave her." [Footnote: Early Years of the Prince Consort.] Words are not wanted to picture the bright little scene, the light interruption to "affairs of the State," always weighty, often harassing, the gay reaction, the hearty unceremonious recognition on both sides, the warm welcome to the gentle avant courier. This was not a great queen, but a gleeful girl at the height of her happiness, who stroked with white taper hand the sleek black head, looked eagerly into the fond eyes, perhaps went so far as to hug the humble friend, stretching up fleet shapely paws, wildly wagging a slender tail, uttering sharp little yelps of delight to greet her. What wealth of cherished associations, of thrice happy realisation, the mere presence there, once more of "only a dog," brought to the mistress of the palace, the lady of the land!

On Saturday, the 8th of the month, Prince Albert proceeded to London, being cordially greeted along the whole road by multitudes flocking from every town and village to see him and shout their approval. At half-past four, in the pale light of a February afternoon, the travellers arrived at Buckingham Palace, "and were received at the hall door by the Queen and the Duchess of Kent, attended by the whole household," to whom a worthy master had come. The fullness of satisfaction and perfect joy of the meeting to two in the company are sacred.

An hour after his arrival the oath of naturalisation was administered to the Prince, "and the day ended with a great State dinner. Sunday was a rest day. Divine service was performed by the Bishop of London in the Bow-room on the ground floor—the same room in which the Queen had met her assembled Council in the course of the previous November, and announced to them her intended marriage. Afterwards the Prince drove out and paid the visits required of him to the different members of the royal family. In spite of the season and weather, throngs of Londoners surrounded the Palace, and watched and cheered him as he went and came. That day the Queen and Prince exchanged their wedding gifts. She gave him the star and badge of the Garter and the Garter set in diamonds, and he gave her a sapphire and diamond brooch.

CHAPTER VIII. THE MARRIAGE.

The 10th of February rose dark and foggy, with a lowering sky discharging at frequent intervals heavy showers. But to many a loyal heart far beyond the sound of Bow bells the date brought a thrill of glad consciousness which was quite independent of the weather. What mattered dreary skies or stinging sleet! This was the day on which the young Queen was to wed the lover of her youth, the man of her choice.

The marriage was to take place at noon, not in the evening, like former royal weddings, and the change was a great boon to the London public. During the busy morning, Prince Albert found time for a small act, which was nevertheless full of manly reverence for age and weakness, of mindful, affectionate gratitude for old and tender cares which had often made his childhood and youth happy. He wrote a few lines to the loving, venerable kinswoman who had performed the part of second mother to him, who had grieved so sorely over their parting.

"In less than three hours I shall stand before the altar with my dear bride. In these solemn moments I must once more ask your blessing, which I am well assured I shall receive, and which will be my safeguard and my future joy. I must end. God help me (or, rather, God be my stay!), your faithful Grandson." The Prince wrote a similar letter, showing how faithfully he recollected her on the crowning day of his life, to his good stepmother, the Duchess of Coburg.

Among the innumerable discussions on the merits or demerits of the Prince when he was first proposed as the husband for the Queen of England, there had not been wanting in a country where religion is generally granted to be a vital question, and where religious feuds, like other feuds, rage high, sundry probings as to the Prince's Christianity—what form he held, whether he might not be a Roman Catholic, whether he were a Christian at all, and might not rather be an infidel? Seeing that the Prince belonged to a Christian and to one of the most Protestant royal families in Europe, that he had been regularly trained in Christian and Lutheran doctrines, and had made a public profession of his belief in the same—a profession which his practice had in no way contradicted—these suppositions were, to say the least, uncalled for, and not remarkable for liberality or charity. It is easy to answer them substantially. The Prince, reserving his Protestant right of private judgment on all points of his belief, was a deeply religious man, as indicated throughout his career, at every stage, in every event of his life. It is hardly possible even for an irreligious man to conceive that Prince Albert could have been what he was without faith and discipline. His biographer has with reason quoted the "God be my stay!" in the light of the sincerity of the man, in a letter written in the flush of his joy and the very fruition of his desires, as one of the innumerable proofs that the Prince lived consciously and constantly under the all-seeing eye of an Almighty Father.

There were two main points from which out-of-door London could gaze its fill on the gala. The one was St. James's Park, from which the people could see the bride and bridegroom drive from Buckingham Palace to St. James's, where the marriage was to take place, according to old usage, and back again to Buckingham Palace for the wedding breakfast; the other was the Green Park, Constitution Hill, Hyde Park, and Piccadilly, by which most of the guests were to arrive to the wedding. The last point also commanded the route which the young couple would take to Windsor.

It was said that, never since the allied sovereigns visited London in 1814 had such a concourse of human beings made the parks alive, as on this wet February morning, when a dismal solitude was changed to an animated scene, full of life and motion. The Times described the mass of spectators wedged in at the back of Carlton Terrace and the foot of Constitution Hill, and the multitude of chairs, tables, benches, even casks, pressed info. The service, and affording vantage-ground to those who could pay for the accommodation. The dripping trees were also rendered available, and had their branches so laden with human fruit, that brittle boughs gave way, while single specimens and small clusters of men and boys came rattling down on the heads and shoulders of confiding fellow-creatures; but such misadventures were without serious accident, and simply afforded additional entertainment to the self-invited, light-hearted wedding guests.

Parties of cavalry and infantry taking their places, with "orderlies dashing to and fro," lent colour and livelier action to the panorama. At the same time the military were not a very prominent feature in the picture, and the State element was also to some extent wanting. Some state was inevitable, but after all the marriage of the sovereign was not so much a public ceremonial as a private event in her life. As early as eight o'clock in the morning the comparatively limited number of invited guests began to contribute to the satisfaction of the great uninvited by driving up beneath the triumphal arch, and presenting their pink or white cards for inspection. A body of Foot Guards marched forwards, followed by a detachment of the Horse Guards Blue, with their band discoursing wedding music appropriate to the occasion, cheering the hearts of the cold, soaked crowd, and awaking an enthusiastic response from it. Then appeared various members of the nobility, including the Duke of Norfolk, coming always to the front as Grand Marshal, wearing his robe and carrying his staff of office, when the rest of the world were in comparative undress, as more or less private individuals. But this gentleman summed up in his own person "all the blood of all the Howards," and recalled his ancestors great and small—the poet Earl of Surrey, those Norfolks to whom Mary Tudor and Mary Stuart were alike fatal, and that Dicky or Dickon of Norfolk who lent a humorous strain to the tragic tendency of the race.

The Ministers and Foreign Ambassadors came singly or in groups. The Ministers, with one or two exceptions, wore the Windsor uniform, blue turned up with an oak-leaf edging in gold. Viscount Morpeth, Lord John Russell, the Marquis of Normanby, Lord Palmerston, Lord Holland, Lord Melbourne, were well-known figures. The good-natured Duke of Cambridge arrived with his family and suite in three royal carriages. He wore the Orders of the Garter, and the Bath, and carried his baton as Field-Marshal. The Duke of Sussex was in the uniform of Captain-General of the Artillery Company, and wore the Orders of the Garter, the Bath, and St. Andrew. He had on his black skull-cap as usual, and drove up in a single carriage. He had opposed the clause relating to Prince Albert's taking precedence of all, save the Queen, in the Naturalisation Bill. He was to make further objection to the husband's occupying his natural place by the side of his wife when the Queen opened and prorogued Parliament, and to the Prince's rights in the Regency Bill. All the same, by right of birth and years, the Duke of Sussex was to give away his royal niece.

Before eleven o'clock, the Gentlemen and Ladies of the Household were in readiness at Buckingham Palace. The Ladies started first for St. James's. The Gentlemen of the foreign suites—Prince Albert's, and his father's, and brother's—in their dark-blue and dark-green uniforms, mustered in the hall, and dispatched a detachment to receive the Prince on his arrival at the other palace. At a quarter to twelve notice was sent to Prince Albert in his private apartments, and he came forth "like a bridegroom," between his royal supporters, traversed the State-rooms, and descended the grand staircase, preceded by the Chamberlain and Vice-Chamberlain, Comptroller of the Household, equerries and ushers. He was received with eager clappings of hands and wavings of handkerchiefs. The Prince was dressed in the uniform of a British Field-Marshal, and wore only one decoration, that of the Garter, with the collar surmounted by two white rosettes, and his bride's gifts of the previous day, the George and Star set in diamonds, on his breast, and the diamond-embroidered Garter round his knee. His pale, handsome face, with its slight brown moustache, his slender yet manly figure would have become any dress. Indeed, his general appearance, full of "thoughtful grace and quiet dignity," impressed every honest observer most favourably. We can imagine Baron Stockmar watching keenly in the background to catch every furtive glance and remark, permitting himself to rub his hands and exclaim, with sober exultation, "He is liked!"

Prince Albert's father and brother, his dearest friends hitherto, walked beside him. The Duke of Saxe-Coburg and Gotha, with his fatherly heart swelling high, must have looked like one of the quaint stately figures out of old German prints in his long, military boots, the same as those of the Life Guards, and his dark-green uniform turned up with red. He, too, wore the collar and star of the Garter, and the star of his own Order of Coburg Gotha. On the other side of the bridegroom walked Prince Ernest. The wedding was next in importance to him to what it was to his brother, while to the elder playing the secondary part of the couple so long united in every act of their young lives, the marriage ceremony of his other self, which was to deal the decisive blow in the cleaving asunder of the old double existence, must have been full of very mingled feelings of joy and sorrow, pleasure and pain. Prince Ernest was a fine young man, in whose face, possibly a little stern in its repressed emotion, The Times reporter imagined he saw more determination than could be found in the milder aspect of Prince Albert, not guessing how much strength of will and patient steadfastness might be bound up with gentle courtesy. Prince Ernest was in a gay light-blue and silver uniform, and carried his helmet in his hand.

When the group came down the stairs, some privileged company, including a few ladies, stationed behind the Yeoman Guard and about the entrance, clapped their hands and waved their congratulations, and as Prince Albert entered the carriage which was to take him and his father and brother to St. James's, he received for the first time all the honours paid to the Queen. Trumpets sounded, colours were lowered, and arms presented. A squadron of Life Guards attended the party, but as the carriage was closed its occupants were not generally recognised. As soon as the Lord Chamberlain had returned from escorting the Prince, six royal carriages, each with two horses, were drawn up before the entrance to Buckingham Palace, and his Lordship informed the Queen that all was ready for her. Accordingly, her Majesty left her room leaning on the arm of Lord Uxbridge, the Lord Chamberlain. She was supported by her mother, the Duchess of Kent, and followed by a page of honour. The various officers of the Household— the Earl of Belfast, Vice-Chamberlain; the Earl of Albemarle, Master of the Horse; Lord Torrington, Comptroller and Treasurer, &c., walked in advance.

The Queen wore a bride's white satin and orange blossoms, a simple wreath of orange blossoms on her fair hair. Her magnificent veil of Honiton lace did not cover the pale face, but fell on each side of the bent head. Her ornaments were the diamond brooch which had been the gift of the bridegroom, diamond earrings and necklace, and the collar and insignia of the Garter. She looked well in her natural agitation, for, indeed, she was a true woman at such a moment. She was shy and a little shrinking as became a bride, and her eyes were swollen with recent tears—an illustration of the wise old Scotch proverb, "A greetin' (weeping) bride's a happy bride." Here were no haughty indifference, no bold assurance, no thoughtless, heartless gaiety,

A creature breathing thoughtful breath,
A traveller 'twixt life and death.

A maiden leaving one stage of her life, with all its past treasures of affection and happiness, for ever behind her, and going forward, in loving hope and trust, no doubt, yet still in uncertainty of what the hidden future held in store for her of weal and woe, to meet her wifely destiny. As she came down into her great hall she was welcomed with fervent acclamations, but for once she was absorbed in herself, and the usual frank, gracious response was not accorded to the tribute. Her eyes were fixed on the ground; "a hurried glance round, and a slight inclination of the head," were all the signs she gave.

The Duchess of Kent, the good mother who had opened her heart to her nephew as to a son, from the May-day when he came to Kensington, who had every reason to rejoice in the marriage, still shared faithfully in her daughter's perturbation. However glad the Duchess might be, it was still a troubled gladness, for she had long experience. She knew that this day closed the morning glory of a life, brought change, a greater fullness of being, but with the fullness increased duties and obligations, more to dread, as well as more to hope, a heavier burden, though there was a true friend to share it. Illusions would vanish, and though reality is better than illusion to all honest hearts, who would not spare a sigh to the bright dreams of youth—too bright with a rainbow-hued radiance and a golden mist of grand expectations, dim in their grandeur, ever to be fulfilled in this work-a-day world? And the Duchess was conscious that the mother who gives a daughter away, even to the best of sons, resigns the first place in that daughter's heart, the first right to her time, thoughts, and confidence. Queen Victoria belonged to her people, but after that great solemn claim she had till now belonged chiefly to her mother. Little wonder that the kind

Duchess looked "disconsolate" in the middle of her content!

The Duchess of Kent and the Duchess of Sutherland drove in the carriage with her Majesty "at a slow pace," for the royal bride, even on her bridal-day, owed herself to her subjects, while a strong escort of Household cavalry prevented the pressure of the shouting throng from becoming overpowering.

On the arrival of the Queen at St. James's Palace she proceeded to her closet behind the Throne-room, where she remained, attended by her maids of honour and train-bearers, until the Lord Chamberlain announced that all was ready for the procession to the chapel.

Old St. James's had been the scene of many a royal wedding. Besides that of Queen Mary, daughter of James II. and Anne Hyde, who was married to William of Orange at eleven o'clock at night in her bedchamber, Anne and George of Denmark were married, in more ordinary fashion, in the chapel. Following their example, the daughters of George II. and Queen Caroline—another Anne, the third English princess who was given to a Prince of Orange, and who was so ready to consent to the contract that she declared she would have him though he were a baboon, and her sister Mary, who was united to the Landgrave of Hesse-Cassel, were both married here; so was their brother, Frederick, Prince of Wales, to Princess Augusta of Saxe-Coburg. Prince Albert was the third of the Coburg line who wedded with the royal house of England. Already there were two strains of Saxe-Coburg blood in the veins of the sovereign of these realms. The last, and probably the most disastrous, marriage which had been celebrated in St. James's was that of George Frederick, Prince of Wales, and Caroline of Brunswick.

The portions of the palace in use for the marriage included the Presence Chamber, Queen Anne's Drawing-room, the Guard-room, the Grand Staircase, with the Colonnade, the Chapel Royal, and the Throne-room. On the Queen's marriage-day, rooms, staircase, and colonnade were lined with larger and smaller galleries for the accommodation of privileged spectators. The seats had crimson cushions with gold-coloured fringe, warming up the cold light and shade of a February day, while the white and gay-coloured dresses of the ladies and the number of wedding favours contributed to the gaiety of the scene. A Queen's wedding favours were not greatly different from those of humbler persons, and consisted of the stereotyped white riband, silver lace, and orange blossoms, except where loyalty indulged in immense bouquets of riband, and "massive silver bullion, having in the centre what might almost be termed branches of orange blossoms." The most eccentrically disposed favours seem to have been those of the mace-bearers, whose white "knots" were employed to tie up on the wearers' shoulders the large gold chains worn with the black dress of the officials. The uniformity of the gathering was broken by "burly Yeomen of the Guard, with their massive halberts, slim Gentlemen-at-Arms with their lighter 'partisans,'…. elderly pages of State, almost infantile pages of honour, officers of the Lord Chamberlain's Office, officers of the Woods and Forests, embroidered heralds and shielded cuirassiers, robed prelates, stoled priests, and surpliced singing-boys."

Among the guests, though not in the procession, loudly cheered as on other occasions, was the Duke of Wellington, who had seen the bride christened. People thought they noticed him bending under his load of years, tottering to the last step of all, but the old soldier was still to grace many a peaceful ceremony. In his company, far removed this day from the smoke of cannon and the din of battle, walked more than one gallant brother-in-arms, the Marquis of Anglesey, Lord Hill, &c.

The chapel was also made sumptuous for the occasion. Its carved and painted roof was picked out anew. The space within the chancel was lined and hung with crimson velvet, the communion-table covered with magnificent gold plate.

The Queen's procession began with drums and trumpets, and continued with pursuivants, heralds, pages, equeries, and the different officers of the Household till it reached the members of the Royal Family. These ranged from the farthest removed in relationship, Princess Sophia of Gloucester, through the Queen's young cousins in the Cambridge family, with much admiration bestowed on the beautiful child, Princess Mary, and the exceedingly attractive young girl, Princess Augusta, to another and a venerable Princess Augusta—one of the elder daughters of George III., an aged lady upwards of seventy, who then made her final appearance in public. Doubtless she had been among the company who were present at the last royal marriage in St. James's, on the night of the 8th of April, 1795, forty-five years before, a marriage so widely removed in every particular from this happy wedding. The two royal Dukes of Cambridge and Sussex walked next, the Lord Chamberlain and Vice-Chamberlain, with Lord Melbourne between, bearing the Sword of State before the Queen.

Her Majesty's train was carried by twelve unmarried ladies, her bridesmaids. Five of these, Lady Fanny Cowper, Lady Mary Grimston, Lady Adelaide Paget, Lady Caroline Gordon Lennox, and Lady Catherine Stanhope, had been among her Majesty's train-bearers at the coronation. Of the three other fair train-bearers on that occasion, one at least, Lady Anne Wentworth Fitzwilliam, was already a wedded wife. The remaining seven bridesmaids were Lady Elizabeth West, Lady Eleanor Paget, Lady Elizabeth Howard, Lady Ida Hay, Lady Jane Bouverie, Lady Mary Howard, and Lady Sarah Villiers. These noble maidens were in white satin like their royal mistress, but for her orange blossoms they wore white roses. Still more than on their former appearance together, the high-bred English loveliness of the party attracted universal admiration.

The Master of the Horse and the Mistress of the Robes, the Ladies of the Bedchamber, Maids of Honour, and Women of the Bedchamber followed, closed in by Yeomen of the Guard and Gentlemen-at-Arms.

In the chapel there had been a crowd of English nobility and foreign ambassadors awaiting the arrival of Prince Albert, when at twenty minutes past twelve he walked up the aisle, carrying a prayer-book covered with green velvet. He advanced, bowing to each side, followed by his supporters to the altar-rail, before which stood four chairs of State, provided for the Queen, the Prince, and, to right and left of them, Queen Adelaide and the Duchess of Kent. The Queen-dowager was in her place, wearing a dress of purple velvet and ermine; the bridegroom kissed her hand and entered into conversation with her, while his father and brother took their seats near him.

The Queen entered the chapel at twenty-five minutes to one, and immediately proceeded to her chair in front of the altar-rails. She knelt down and prayed, and then seated herself. Her mother was on her left side. Behind her stood her bridesmaids and train-bearers. On stools to right and left sat the members of the Royal Family. The Archbishop of Canterbury and the Bishop of London were already at the altar. In a few minutes the Queen and the Prince advanced to the communion-table. The service was the beautiful, simple service of the Church of England, unchanged in any respect. In reply to the question, "Who giveth this woman to be married to this man?" the Duke of Sussex presented himself. The Christian-names "Albert" and "Victoria" were all the names used. Both Queen and Prince answered distinctly and audibly. The Prince undertook to love, comfort, and honour his wife, to have and to hold her for better, for worse, for richer, for poorer; the Queen promised to obey as well as to love and cherish her husband till death them did part, like any other pair plighting their troth. When the ring was put on the finger, at a concerted signal the Park and Tower guns fired a royal salute and all London knew that her Majesty was a married woman.

The usual congratulations were exchanged amongst the family party before they re-formed themselves into the order of procession. The Duke of Sussex in his character of father kissed his niece heartily on the cheek besides shaking her by the hand. The Queen stepped quickly across and kissed her aunt, Queen Adelaide, whose hand Prince Albert saluted again. The procession returned in the same order, except that the bride and bridegroom walked side by side and hand in hand, the wedding-ring being seen on the ungloved hand. Her Majesty spoke once or twice to Lord Uxbridge, the Lord Chamberlain, as if expressing her wishes with regard to the procession. Her paleness had been succeeded by a little flush, and she was smiling brightly. On the appearance of the couple they were received with clapping of hands and waving of handkerchiefs. In the Throne-room the marriage was attested and the register signed "on a splendid table prepared for the purpose."

The whole company then repaired to Buckingham Palace, Prince Albert driving in the carriage with the Queen. The sight of the pair was hailed everywhere along the short route with loud cheering, to the joyous sound of which "the Queen walked up the grand staircase, in the presence of her court, leaning on her husband's arm."

An eye-witness—the Dowager Lady Lyttelton, who, both as a Lady of the Bedchamber and Governess to the royal children, knew the Queen and Prince well—has recorded her impression of the chief actor in the scene. "The Queen's look and manner were very pleasing, her eyes much swollen with tears, but great happiness in her countenance, and her look of confidence and comfort at the Prince when they walked away as man and wife was very pleasing to see. I understand she is in extremely high spirits since; such a new thing to her to dare to be unguarded in conversation with anybody, and, with her frank and fearless nature, the restraints she has hitherto been under from one reason or another with everybody must have been most painful."

The wedding-breakfast with the toast of the day followed, then the departure for Windsor, on which the skies smiled, for the clouds suddenly cleared away and the sun shone out on the journey and the many thousand spectators on the way.

The Queen and Prince drove in one of the five carriages—four of which contained the suite inseparable from a couple of such rank. The first carriage conveyed the Ladies in Waiting, succeeded by a party of cavalry. The travelling chariot came next in order, and was enthusiastically hailed, bride and bridegroom responding graciously to the acclamations. Her Majesty's travelling dress was bridal-like: a pelisse of white satin trimmed with swans' down, a white satin bonnet and feather. The Prince was in dark clothes. The party left before four, but did not arrive at Windsor till nearly seven—long after darkness had descended on the landscape. Eton and Windsor were in the height of excitement, in a very frenzy of rejoicing. The travellers wended their way through a living mass in brilliantly illuminated streets, amidst the sending up of showers of rockets, the ringing of bells, the huzzaing of the people, the glad shouting of the Eton boys. Her Majesty was handed from the carriage by the Prince, she took his arm and the two entered the castle after a right royal welcome home.

Elizabeth Barrett Browning celebrated this event also in her eloquent fashion.

"She vows to love who vowed to rule, the chosen at her side,
Let none say 'God preserve the Queen,' but rather 'Bless the Bride.'
None blow the trump, none bend the knee, none violate the dream
Wherein no monarch but a wife, she to herself may seem;
Or if you say, 'Preserve the Queen,' oh, breathe it inward, low—
She is a woman and beloved, and 'tis enough but so.
Count it enough, thou noble Prince, who tak'st her by the hand,

And claimest for thy lady-love our Lady of the land.
And since, Prince Albert, men have called thy spirit high and rare,
And true to truth and brave for truth as some at Augsburg were,
We charge thee by thy lofty thoughts and by thy poet-mind,
Which not by glory and degree takes measure of mankind,
Esteem that wedded hand less dear for sceptre than for ring,
And hold her uncrowned womanhood to be the royal thing."

Up in London and all over the country there were feasts and galas for rich and poor. There was a State banquet, attended by very high and mighty company, in the Banqueting-room at St. James's. Grand dinners were given by the members of the Cabinet; the theatres were free for the night to great and small; at each the National Anthem was sung amidst deafening applause; at Drury Lane there was a curious emblematical ballet—like a revival of the old masques, ending with a representation of the Queen and Prince surrounded by fireworks, which no doubt afforded immense satisfaction to the audience.

The Queen's wedding-cake was three hundred pounds in weight, three yards in circumference, and fourteen inches in depth. In recognition of the national interest of the wedding, the figure of Hymen, on the top, was replaced by Britannia in the act of blessing the royal pair, who, as a critic observed, were represented somewhat incongruously in the costume of ancient Rome. At the feet of the image of Prince Albert, several inches high, lay a dog, the emblem of fidelity. At the feet of the image of her Majesty nestled a pair of turtle-doves, the token of love and felicity. A Cupid wrote in a volume, spread open on his knees, for the edification of the capering Cupids around, the auspicious "10th of February, 1840," the date of the marriage; and there were the usual bouquets of white flowers, tied with true lovers' knots of white riband, to be distributed to the guests at the wedding breakfast and kept as mementos of the event.

There were other trophies certain to be cherished and preserved among family treasures, and perhaps shown to future generations, as we sometimes see, turning up in museums and art collections, relics of the marriages of Mary Tudor and Catharine of Aragon. These were the bridesmaids' brooches. They were the royal gift to the noble maidens, several of whom had, two years before, received rings from the same source to commemorate the services of the train-bearers at the Coronation. These brooches were in the shape of a bird, the body being formed entirely of turquoises, the eyes were rubies, and the beak a diamond, the claws were of pure gold, and rested on pearls of great size and value. The design and workmanship were according to the Queen's directions.

The twelve beautiful girls who received the gifts have since fulfilled their various destinies—each has "dreed her weird," according to the solemn, sad old Scotch phrase. Some, perhaps the happiest, have passed betimes into the silent land; the survivors are elderly women, with granddaughters as lovely as they themselves were in their opening day. One became a princess—Lady Sarah Villiers married Prince Nicholas Esterhazy. Two are duchesses—Lady Elizabeth Sackville-West, Duchess of Bedford; and Lady Catherine Stanhope, married first to Lord Dalmeny, eldest son of the Earl of Rosebery, and secondly to the Duke of Cleveland. Three are countesses—Lady Caroline Gordon Lennox, Countess of Bessborough; Lady Mary Grimston, Countess of Radnor; and Lady Ida Hay, Countess of Gainsborough. Lady Fanny Cowper, whose beauty was much admired by Leslie, the painter, married Lord Jocelyn, eldest son of the Earl of Roden. Lord Jocelyn was one of the victims to cholera in 1854. He was seized while on duty at Buckingham Palace, and died after two hours' illness in Lady Palmerston's drawing-room. Lady Mary Howard became the wife of Baron Foley. One bridesmaid, Lady Jane Bouverie, married a simple country gentleman, Mr. Ellis, of Glenaquoich.

CHAPTER IX. A ROYAL PAIR.

The Queen and the Prince were only one whole day holding state by themselves at Windsor. It is not given to a royal couple to flee away into the wilds or to shut themselves up from their friends and the world like meaner people; whether a prolonged interval of retirement be spent in smiling or in sulking, according to cynical bachelors and spinsters, it is not granted to kings and queens. On the single day of grace which her Majesty claimed she wrote to Baron Stockmar the emphatic estimate of the man of her choice. "There cannot exist a dearer, purer, nobler being in the world than the Prince." A young bride's fond judgment; but to her was given the deep joy of finding that time only confirmed the proud and glad conviction of that first day of wedlock.

On Wednesday, the 12th, the royal couple at Windsor were rejoined by the Duchess of Kent, the Duke of Coburg, the hereditary Prince, and the whole Court. Then two more days of holiday were spent with something of the heartiness of old times, when brides and bridegrooms did not seem either as if they were ashamed of their happiness or too selfish to share it with their friends. No doubt there were feasting and toasting, and there was merry dancing each night.

On Friday, the 14th, the Court returned to London, that the principal person might gratify the people by appearing in public and that she might take up once more the burden of a sovereign's duties. Addresses were received from the Houses of Parliament. The theatres were visited in state. On the 19th of the month the Queen held her first levee after her marriage, when the Prince took his place at her left hand. On Sunday, the 20th, the newly-married couple attended divine service together in the Chapel Royal, St. James's, and were loudly cheered on their way through the Park.

Buckingham Palace was to continue the Queen's town residence, but St. James's, by virtue of its seniority in age and priority in historical associations, remained for a considerable time the theatre of all the State ceremonials which were celebrated in town until gradually modifications of the rule were established. A chapel was fitted up in Buckingham Palace, which accommodated the household in comparative privacy, and prevented the inconvenience of driving in all states of the health and the weather for public worship at the neighbouring palace chapel. It was found that there was better accommodation for holding Drawing-rooms, and less crowding and inconvenience to the ladies attending them, when the Drawing-rooms were held at Buckingham Palace instead of St. James's. The levees are nearly all that is left to St. James's, in addition to the fact that it contains the offices of the Lord Chamberlain, &c. But the place where her Majesty was proclaimed Queen and wedded deserves a parting word.

The visitor to St. James's passes up the great staircase, which has been trodden by the feet of so many generations, bound on such different errands. Here and there, from a picture-frame high up on the wall, a painted face looks down immovably on the comings and goings below. The Guard-room has a few stands of glittering arms and one or two women's portraits; altogether a different Guard-room from what it must have been when it received its name. Beyond is the Armoury, where arms bristle in sheaves and piles, surmounted by hauberks and casques, smooth and polished as if they had never been dinted in battle or rusted with blood. Queen Anne's Drawing-room, spacious and stately, is resplendent in yellow satin. Old St. James's has sustained a recent renovation, its faded gorgeousness has been renewed, not without a difficult compromise between the unhesitating magnificence of the past and the subdued taste of the present day. The compromise is honourable to the taste of the decorator, for there is no stinting of rich effect, stinting which would have been out of place, in the great doors, picked out and embossed, the elaborately devised and wrought walls and ceilings, the huge chandeliers, &c. But warm, deep crimson is relieved by cool pale green, and sage wainscot meets the dull red of feathery leaves on other walls. The Queen's Closet, which misses its meaning when it is called a boudoir, with the steel-like embroidery on its walls, matching the grey blue of its cut velvet hangings, recalls the natural pauses in a busy life, when the Queen awaits the call of public duty, or withdraws for a breathing space from the pressure of fatiguing obligations.

In more than one of the principal rooms there are low brass screens or railings drawn across the room, to be used as barricades; and the uninitiated hears with due respect that behind those the ambassadors are supposed to congregate, while these fence the approach to the throne.

In spite of such precautions, large Drawing-rooms became latterly hard-pressed crowds struggling to make their way, and the State-rooms of Buckingham Palace were put in request as affording better facilities for these ceremonies.

There is a picture gallery where a long row of Kings and Queens, in their full-length portraits, stand like Banquo's descendants. The portraits begin with that of bluff King Hal, very bluff and strident. According to Mr. Hare's account, which he has taken from Holinshed, Henry VIII. got St. James's when it was an hospital for "fourteen maidens that were leprous," and having pensioned off the sisters, "reared a fine mansion and park" in the room of the hospital. The picture of his young son is a quaint, slim edition of his father. There is a sad and stiff Mary Tudor, who laid down her embittered and brokenhearted life in this palace, and by her side, as she seldom was in the flesh, a high-ruffed, yellow-haired, peaked-chinned Elizabeth—a noble shrew. The British Solomon has the sword-proof padding of his doublet and trunk hose very conspicuous. A wide contrast is a romantic, tragic King Charles, with a melancholy remembrance in his long face and drooping eyes of the day when he bade farewell to the world at St. James's and left it for the scaffold at Whitehall. His swarthy periwigged sons balance the sister queens, Mary and Anne. St. James's, like Kensington and Hampton Court, seems somehow peculiarly associated with them. Though other and more striking royal figures dwelt there both before and after the two last of the reigning Stuarts, they have left a distinct impression of themselves, together with a Sir Peter Lely and a Sir Godfrey Kneller flavour about all the more prominent quarters of the palace. The likenesses of Mary and Anne occur as they must have appeared before they lost the comeliness of youth, when St. James's was their home, the house of their father, the Duke of York and Anne his Duchess, where the two sisters wedded in turn a princely hero and a princely nobody.

In the Throne-room, amidst the portraits of later sovereigns to which royal robes and the painter's art have supplied an adventitious dignity, there are fine likenesses of the Queen and Prince Albert, which must have been taken soon after their marriage, when they were in the first bloom of their youth and happiness. Her Majesty wears a royal mantle and the riband of the Garter, like her compeers; behind her rise the towers of Windsor.

In the double corridor, along which two streams of company flow different ways to and from the Presence-chamber, as the blood flows in the veins and arteries, are more pictures—those of some charming children. A stout little Prince Rupert before he ever smelt the smoke of battle or put pencil to paper. Representations of almost equally old-world-looking children of the Georgian era by their royal mother's knee, one child bearing such a bow as figures often in the hands of children in the portraits of the period; a princely boy in miniature robes of State, with a queen's hand on his shoulder; a little solitary flaxen-haired child with a tambourine. The bow has long been unbent, the royal mother and child are together again, the music of the tambourine is mute.

In the Banqueting-room there are great battle-pieces by land and sea from

Tournay to Trafalgar, like a memory of the Hall of Battles at Versailles.

The Chapel Royal, where the Queen was made a wife, has ceased in a measure to be a royal place of worship. Still within its narrow bounds and plain walls a highly aristocratic congregation have, if they choose, a right to the services of the dean and sub-dean and the five-and-thirty chaplains—not to say of the bishops duly appointed to officiate on special occasions. Not only is the royal closet still in readiness furnished with its chairs of State, there are other closets or small galleries for the Household, peeresses and their daughters, &c. The simplest pew below belongs to the Lord Chamberlain, the Lord Steward, peers and their sons, or members of Parliament, &c. The Chapel Royal, like the State-rooms, is fresh and spruce from renewal. It has, however, wisely avoided all departure from the original character of the building, which has nothing but the carved roof and the great square window to distinguish it from any other chapel of the same size and style. It is difficult to realise that it was here Queen Mary listened attentively to Bishop Burnet, and Queen Caroline was guilty of talking, while Princess Emily brought her little dog under her arm. Nor is it easy to fancy the brilliance of the scene in the quiet place when it was lined from floor to ceiling with tier upon tier of seats for the noblest in the land, when every inch of standing-room had its fit occupant, and a princely gathering was grouped before the glittering altar to hear a Queen plight her troth.

St. James's has still a royal resident in the sole surviving member of the great family of George III., the venerable Duchess of Cambridge, who lives in the north wing of the palace.

Marlborough House and Clarence House are in the immediate vicinity, indeed the last is so near that it is reached by a covered way. And as if to make the sense of the neighbourhood of a cluster of royal establishments more vivid, and the thought of the younger generation of the Royal Family more present in the old place, as the visitor passes through its corridors the cannon in the park peals forth the announcement of the birth of the last of her Majesty's grandchildren.

On the 28th of February, a little more than a fortnight after the marriage, came the Prince's first practical experience of its cost to him. His father left on his return to Coburg. "He said to me," the Queen wrote in her Journal, "that I had never known a father, and could not therefore feel what he did. His childhood had been very happy. Ernest, he said, was now the only one remaining here of all his earliest ties and recollections; but if I continued to love him as I did now, I could make up for all…. Oh! how I did feel for my dearest, precious husband at this moment! Father, brother, friends, country, all has he left, and all for me. God grant that I may be the happy person, the most happy person to make this dearest, blessed being happy and contented. What is in my power to make him happy I will do."

Prince Ernest remained in England nearly three months after his father had left.

Early in March a step was taken to render the Prince's position clearer and more secure. Letters patent were issued conferring on him precedence next to the Queen. How necessary the step was, even in this country, towards a conclusion which appears to us to-day so natural as to be beyond dispute, may be gathered from the circumstance that, even after the marriage, objections were made to the Prince's sitting by the Queen's side in the State carriage on State occasions, and to his occupying a chair of State next the throne when she opened and prorogued Parliament.

Prince Albert proposed for himself a wise and generous course, which he afterwards embodied in fitting words—"to sink his own individual existence in that of his wife, to aim at no power by himself or for himself, to shun all ostentation, to assume no separate responsibility before the public; continually and anxiously to watch every part of the public business in order to be able to advise and assist her at any moment, in any of the multifarious and difficult questions brought before her—sometimes political, or social, or personal—as the natural head of the family, superintendent of her household, manager of her private affairs, her sole confidential adviser in politics and only assistant in her communications with the affairs of the Government." In fact, the Prince was the Queen's private secretary in all save the name, uniting the two departments, political and social, of such an office which had hitherto been held separately by Lord Melbourne and Baroness Lehzen.

Prince Albert discharged the double duty with the authority of his rank and character, and especially of his relations to the Queen. He expressed his object very modestly in writing to his father: "I endeavour quietly to be of as much use to Victoria in her position as I can." The post was a most delicate and difficult one, and would have been absolutely untenable, had it not been for the perfect confidence and good understanding always existing between the Queen and the Prince, and for his remarkable command of temper, and manly forbearance and courtesy, under every provocation, to all who approached him. Perhaps a still more potent agent was a quality which was dimly felt from the beginning, and is fully recognised to-day—his sincerity of nature and honesty of purpose. In the painful revelations which, alas! time is apt to bring of double-dealing and self-seeking on the part of men in power, no public character of his day stands out more honourably in the strong light which posterity is already concentrating on the words and actions of the past, than does Prince Albert for undeniable truthfulness and disinterestedness. Men may still cavil at his conclusions, and maintain that he theorised and systematised and was tempted to interfere too much, but they have long ceased to question his perfect integrity and single-heartedness, his rooted aversion to all trickery and to deceit in every form. "He was an honest man and a noble prince who did good work," is now said universally of the Queen's husband; and honesty is not only the highest praise, it is a great power in dealing with one's fellows.

But it was not in a day or without many struggles that anything approaching to his aim was achieved. The inevitable irritation caused by the transfer of power and the disturbance of existing arrangements on the part of a new comer, the sensitive jealousy which even the Prince's foreign birth occasioned, had to be overcome before the first approach to success could be attained. We can remember that some of the old Scotch Jacobite songs—very sarcastic where German royal houses were concerned—experienced a temporary revival, certainly more in jest than in earnest, and with a far higher appreciation of the fun than of the malice of the sentiment. The favourite was "The wee, wee German Lairdie," and began in this fashion:—

Wha the Diel hae we gotten for a King,
But a wee, wee German Lairdie?
And when they gaed to bring him hame
He was delvin' in his little kail-yardie.

The last verse declared:—

He'a pu'ed the rose o'English blooms,
He's broken the harp o'Irish, clowns,
But Scotia's thistle will jag his thoomba,
The wee, wee German Lairdie.

A prophecy honoured in its entire breach.

Even tried and trusty friends grown old in Court service could not make up their minds at once to the changed order of affairs, or resign, without an effort to retain it, their rule when it came into collision with the wishes of the new head of the household; Prince Albert, in writing frankly to his old comrade Prince Lowenstein, said he was very happy and contented, but the difficulty in filling his place with proper dignity was that he was only the husband and not the master of the house. The Queen had to assert, like a true woman, when appealed to on the subject, that she had solemnly engaged at the altar to obey as well as to love and honour her husband, and "this sacred obligation she could consent neither to limit nor define."

It may be stated that, in spite of the fidelity and devotion of those who surrounded the Queen, the old system under which the arrangements of the palaces were conducted stood in great need of reform. Anything more cumbrous, complicated, and inconvenient than the plan adopted cannot easily be conceived. The great establishments were not subject to one independent, responsible rule, they were divided into various departments under as many different controlling bodies. Rights and privileges, sinecures and perquisites, bristled on all sides, and he who would reform them must face the unpopularity which is almost always the first experience of every reformer. There is a graphic account of the situation in the "Life of the Prince Consort," and "Baron Stockmar's Memoirs." "The three great Officers of State, the Lord Steward, the Lord Chamberlain, and the Master of the Horse, all of them officials who varied with each change of the Ministry, and were appointed without regard to any special qualifications for their office, had each a governing voice in the regulation of the household.... Thus one section of the palace was supposed to be under the Lord Chamberlain's charge, another under that of the Lord Steward, while as to a third it was uncertain whose business it was to look after it. These officials were responsible for all that concerned the interior of the building, but the outside had to be taken care of by the office of Woods and Forests. The consequence was, that as the inside cleaning of the windows belonged to the Lord Chamberlain's department, the degree of light to be admitted into the palace depended proportionably on the well-timed and good understanding between the Lord Chamberlain's Office and that of Woods and Forests. One portion of the personnel of the establishment again was under the authority of the Lord Chamberlain, another under that of the Master of the Horse, and a third under the jurisdiction of the Lord Steward." "The Lord Steward," writes Baron Stockmar, "finds the fuel and lays the fire, and the Lord Chamberlain lights it.... In the same manner the Lord Chamberlain provides all the lamps, and the Lord Steward must clean, trim, and light them. Before a pane of glass or a cupboard door could be mended, the sanction of so many officials had to be obtained, that often months elapsed before the repairs were made."

One is irresistibly reminded of the dilemma of the unfortunate King of Spain, who died from a feverish attack brought on by a prolonged exposure to a great fire, because it was not etiquette for the monarch to rise, and the grandee whose prerogative it was to move the royal chair happened to be out of the way.

"As neither the Lord Chamberlain nor the Master of the Horse has a regular deputy residing in the palace, more than two-thirds of all the male and female servants are left without a master in the house. They can come on and go off duty as they choose, they can remain absent hours and hours on their days of waiting, or they may commit any excess or irregularity; there is nobody to observe, to correct, or to reprimand them. The various details of internal arrangement whereon depend the well-being and comfort of the whole establishment, no one is cognisant of, or responsible for. There is no officer responsible for the cleanliness, order, and security of the rooms and offices throughout the palace."

Doubtless, it was under this remarkable condition of the royal household that a considerable robbery of silver plate from an attic in which it was stored took place at Windsor Castle in 1841. Massive silver encasings of tables, borders of mirrors, fire-dogs and candelabra, together with the silver ornaments of Tippoo Saib's tent, disappeared in this way.

It took years to remedy such a state of matters, and it was only by the exercise of the greatest tact, which, to be sure, was comparatively easy to the Prince, that the improvement was effected. The necessary reforms were made to proceed from the officers of State themselves, and the enforcement of the new regulations was carried out by a Master of the Household, who resided permanently in the palace which the Queen occupied. Eventually each royal establishment was brought to a high average of order and efficiency. If possible, still greater caution had to be practised in the Prince's dealing with political affairs, for here the jealousy of foreign influence was national, and among the most deeply rooted of insular prejudices. In the beginning of their married life the Prince was rarely with the Queen at her Cabinet Councils, though no objection had been made to his presence, and he did not take much share in business, though Lord Melbourne, especially, urged his being made acquainted with it in all its details. Both in its public and private relations, the path at starting was not an easy one, while the Prince and the Queen shared its anxieties and worries. Happily for all, the two, who were alike in sense, good feeling, and trusting affection, stood firm, and gradually surmounted the contradictions in their brilliant lot. But it was probably under these influences that Baron Stockmar, always exacting in the best interests of those he loved, fancied—even while he had no hesitation in recording the Prince behaved in his difficult position very well—that a friend had reason to dread in the young man not yet twenty-one, the old defects of dislike to intellectual exertion and indifference to politics. No efforts were wanting on the part of the good old mentor, who in his absence kept up a constant correspondence with the Prince, to preserve the latter's "ideal aspirations." Sometimes, the keen observer feared that the object of his dreams and cares was losing courage for his self-imposed Herculean labours, but the brave will and loyal heart proved triumphant.

That spring and the next two springs and summers were gay seasons in London—and London life meant then to the Queen and the Prince an overwhelming amount of engagements, besides the actual part in the government of the country. "Levees, Drawing-rooms, presentations of addresses, great dinners, State visits to the theatre" swelled the long list. The Prince, like most Germans, was fond of the play, and had a great admiration of Shakespeare, whose plays were revived at Covent Garden in 1840, Charles Kemble giving a last glimpse of the glory of the early Kemble performances. The couple presided over many little balls and dances which became a Court where the sovereigns were in the heyday of their youth and happiness. Lady Bloomfield, who as the Hon. Miss Liddell was one of the Queen's Maids of Honour a little later, gives a pleasant account of an episode at one of these dances. "One lovely summer's morning we had danced till dawn, and the quadrangle being then open to the east, her Majesty went out on the roof of the portico to see the sun rise, which was one of the most beautiful sights I ever remember. It rose behind St. Paul's, which we saw quite distinctly; Westminster Abbey and the trees in the Green Park stood out against a golden sky."

All this innocent gaiety was consecrated by the faithful discharge of duty and the reverent observance of sacred obligations. At Easter, which was spent at Windsor, the Queen and the Prince took the Sacrament together for the first time. "The Prince," the Queen has said, "had a very strong feeling about the solemnity of the act, and did not like to appear in company either the evening before or on the day on which, he took it, and he and the Queen almost always dined alone on these occasions." Her Majesty has supplied a brief record, in the "Early Years of the Prince Consort," of one such peaceful evening. "We two dined together. Albert likes being quite alone before he takes the Sacrament; we played part of Mozart's Requiem, and then he read to me out of Stunden den Andacht (Hours of Devotion) the article on Selbster Kentniss (Self-knowledge.)" The whole sounds like a sweet, solemn, blessed pause in the crowded busy life. A sudden shock, which was only that of a great danger happily averted, broke in on the flush of all that was best worth having and doing in existence, and seemed to utter a warning against the instability of life at its brightest and fairest. There was stag-hunting on Ascot Heath, at which the Queen and the Prince were to be present. He was to join in the hunt and she was to follow with Prince Ernest in a pony phaeton. As she stood by a window in Windsor Castle, she saw Prince Albert canter past on a restless and excited horse. In vain the rider turned the animal round several times, he got the bit between his teeth and started at the top of his speed among the trees of the Park; very soon he brushed against a branch and unseated the Prince, who fell, without, however, sustaining any serious injury. The Queen saw the beginning but not the end of the misadventure, and her alarm was only relieved by the return of one of the grooms in waiting, who told the extent of the accident. Noblesse oblige. The Prince mounted a fresh horse and proceeded to the hunt, and the Queen joined him. "Albert received me on the terrace of the large stand and led me up," the Queen wrote in her Journal. "He looked very pale, and said he had been much alarmed lest I should have been frightened by his accident…. He told me he had scraped the skin off his poor arm, had bruised his hip and knee, and his coat was torn and dirty. It was a frightful fall."

On the 20th of April, an event took place in France which at this time naturally was particularly interesting both to the Queen and the Prince. The Duc de Nemours, second son of Louis Philippe and brother to the Queen of the Belgians, married Princess Victoire of Saxe-Coburg, only daughter of the head of the Catholic branch of the family, sister of the King Consort of Portugal, and first cousin both to the Queen and Prince Albert. This marriage drew many intertwined family ties still more closely together. Princess Victoire was a pretty golden-haired girl, and is described afterwards as a singularly sweet, affectionate, reasonable woman. She had spent much of her youth at Coburg, and been a favourite playmate of Prince Albert, whose junior she was by three years. She was the friend of the Queen from girlhood. "We were like sisters," wrote her Majesty, "bore the same name, married the same year…. There was in short a similarity between us, which, since 1839, united us closely and tenderly." The Duc de Nemours, without the intellectual gifts of some of his brothers, resembled his good mother, Queen Amelie, in many respects. He had quiet, domestic tastes, and was affectionately attached to his wife.

CHAPTER X. ROYAL OCCUPATIONS.—AN ATTEMPT ON THE QUEEN'S LIFE.

The family arrangements in the marriage of the Queen and Prince Albert appear to have been made with the kindest, most judicious consideration for what was due to former ties, that all the relations of life might be settled gradually and naturally, on the footing which it was desirable they should assume. The connection between the Queen and the Duchess of Kent was very close. It was that of a mother and child who had been nearly all in all to each other, who, till Queen Victoria's marriage, had not been separated for a day. Since the Duchess of Kent's arrival in England, she had never dwelt alone. It was now deemed advisable that she should have a separate house, which was, however, to be in constant communication with the Queen's, the intercourse between the two continuing to be of the most intimate character, mother and daughter meeting daily and sharing the most of their pleasures. In April, two months after the marriage, the Duchess removed to Ingestrie House, Belgrave Square.

In another month, on the 7th of May, Prince Ernest left England. The parting between the brothers was a severe trial to both. They bade farewell, German student fashion, singing together beforehand the parting song Abschied.

The young couple were now left in a greater measure to themselves to form their life, and lead it to noble conclusions. They spent the Queen's birthday in private at Claremont—a place endeared to her by the happiest associations of her childhood, and very pleasant to him because of its country attractions. There the pair could wander about the beautiful grounds and neighbourhood, as another royal pair had wandered before them, and do much as they pleased, like simple citizens or great folks living in villeggiatura. The custom was then established of thus keeping the real birthday together in retirement, while another day was set apart for public rejoicing. There is a story told of the Queen and Prince Albert's early visits to Claremont—a story certainly not without its parallel in the lives of other popular young sovereigns in their honeymoons, but probable enough in this case. The couple were caught in a shower, during one of their longer rambles, and took refuge in a cottage—the old mistress of which was totally unacquainted with the high rank of her guests. She entertained them with many extraordinary anecdotes of Princess Charlotte and Prince Leopold, the original heroine and hero of Claremont. At last the dame volunteered to give her visitors the loan of her umbrella, with many charges to Prince Albert that it should be taken care of and returned to its owner. The Queen and the Prince started on their homeward way under the borrowed shelter, and it was not for some time that the donor knew with whom she had gossiped, and to whom she had dealt her favours.

The Prince's first appearance as an art patron took place in connection with the Ancient Music Concerts. He had already been named one of the directors who arrange in turn each concert. He made the selections for his concert on the 29th of April, and both he and the Queen appeared at the rehearsal on the 27th. Perhaps the gentle science was what he loved above every other, being a true German in that as in all else. At this time he played and sang much with the Queen; the two played together often on the organ in one of his rooms. Lady Lyttelton has described the effect of his music. "Yesterday evening, as I was sitting here comfortably after the drive by candlelight, reading M. Guizot, suddenly there arose from the room beneath, oh, such sounds! It was Prince Albert, dear Prince Albert, playing on the organ; and with such master skill, as it appeared to me, modulating so learnedly, winding through every kind of bass and chord, till he wound up with the most perfect cadence, and then off again, louder and then softer. No tune, as I was too distant to perceive the execution or small touches so I only heard the harmony, but I never listened with much more pleasure to any music. I ventured at dinner to ask him what I had heard. 'Oh! my organ, a new possession of mine. I am so fond of the organ! It is the first of instruments; the only instrument for expressing one's feelings' (I thought, are they not good feelings that the organ expresses?), 'and it teaches to play; for on the organ a mistake, oh! such misery;' and he quite shuddered at the thought of the sostenuto discord."

But while the Prince was an enthusiastic musician, he was likewise fond of painting; his taste and talent in this respect also having been carefully cultivated. In these sunshiny early days, sunshiny in spite of their occasional clouds, he still possessed a moderate amount of leisure, notwithstanding the late hours night and morning, of which the Queen took the blame, declaring it was her fault that they breakfasted at ten, getting out very little—a practice quite different from their later habits. He seized the opportunity of starting various pursuits which formed afterwards the chief recreation of his and the Queen's laborious days. He tried etching, which afforded the two much entertainment, and he began his essays in landscape gardening, developing a delightful faculty with which she had the utmost sympathy.

On the 1st of June the Prince took the initiatory step in identifying himself with moral and social progress, and in placing himself, as the Queen's representative, at the head of those humane and civilising movements which recommended themselves to his good judgment and philanthropic spirit. He complied with the request that he should be chairman at a meeting to promote the abolition of the slave trade, and made his first public speech in advocacy of justice between man and man. This speech was no small effort to a young foreigner, who, however accomplished, was certainly not accustomed to public speaking in a foreign tongue. It was like delivering a maiden speech under great difficulties, and as it was of importance that he should produce a good impression, he spared no preparation for the task. He composed the speech himself, learnt it by heart, and repeated it to the Queen in the first instance.

Among the crowd present was the young Quaker lady, Caroline Fox, whose "Memories" have been given to the world. She wrote at the time: "The acclamations attending his (the Prince's) entrance were perfectly deafening, and he bore them all with calm, modest dignity, repeatedly bowing with considerable grace. He certainly is a very beautiful young man, a thorough German, and a fine poetic specimen of the race. He uttered his speech in a rather low tone and with the prettiest foreign accent."

On the 18th of the same month great horror and indignation were excited by the report of an attempt to assassinate the Queen. About six o'clock on the June evening, her Majesty was driving, according to her usual custom, with Prince Albert. The low open phaeton, attended by two equeries, was proceeding up Constitution Hill, on its way first to the house of the Duchess of Kent in Belgrave Square and afterwards to Hyde Park. Suddenly a little man leaning against the park railing drew a pistol from under his coat and fired at her Majesty, who was sitting at the farther side from him. He was within six yards of the phaeton—so near, in fact, that the Queen, who was looking another way, neither saw him nor comprehended for a moment the cause of the loud noise ringing in her ears. But Prince Albert had seen the man hold something towards them, and was aware of what had occurred. The horses started and the carriage stopped. The Prince called to the postillions to drive on, while he caught the Queen's hands and asked if the fright had not shaken her, but the brave royal heart only made light of his alarm. He looked again, and saw the same man still standing in a theatrical attitude, a pistol in each hand. The next instant the fellow pointed the second pistol and fired once more. Both the Queen and the Prince saw the aim, as well as heard the shot, on this occasion, and she stooped, he pulling her down that the ball might pass over her head. In another moment the man, who still leant against the railing, pistols in hand, with much bravado and without any attempt to escape, was seized by a bystander. In the middle of the consternation and wrath of the gathering crowd, the Queen and the Prince went on to the Duchess of Kent that they might be the first to tell her what had happened and assure her of the safety of her daughter. A little later, in order to show the people that the Queen had not lost her confidence in them, the couple carried out their original intention of taking a drive in Hyde Park. There they were received with a perfect ovation, a crowd of nobility and gentry in carriages and on horseback forming a volunteer escort on the way back to Buckingham Palace, where another multitude awaited them, vehemently cheering, as the Queen, pale but smiling and bowing, re-entered her palace. The wretched lad who was the author of the attack did not deny it, but seemed rather sorry that it had failed to inflict any injury, though he had no motive to allege for such a crime. In spite of the strictest search no ball could be found, which left the question doubtful whether or not the pistols had been loaded. On further examination it proved that the lad, Edward Oxford—not above eighteen years of age, was a discharged barman from a public-house in Oxford Street. His father, who was dead, had been a working jeweller in Birmingham.

"It would be difficult to describe the state of loyal excitement into which the Metropolis has been thrown by this event," says the Annual Register. "It seems as if only the dastardly deed had been wanted to bring out the full love and devotion of the people to their young Queen," the happy wife and expectant mother, whose precious life might have been cut short by the unlooked-for shot of an assassin. At the different theatres and concerts that evening "God save the Queen" was sung with passionate fervour. When the Queen and Prince Albert drove out the next afternoon in the same phaeton, at the same hour, in Hyde Park, the demonstration of the previous day was repeated with effusion. The crowd was immense, the cheering was again vociferous. An improvised body-guard of hundreds of gentlemen on horseback surrounded the couple. "The line of carriages (calling at Buckingham Palace to make inquiries) extended a considerable way down the Mall." The calls were incessant till the procession from the Houses of Parliament arrived. Thousands of people assembled to witness it. The Sheriffs of London came first in four carriages. Then the Grenadier Guards with their band marched through the gateway, on which the royal standard was hoisted, and took up their position in the entrance court. The Cabinet Ministers and chief Officers of the Household followed. The State carriage of the Speaker led the hundred and nine carriages filled with Members of the House of Commons. The Peers' carriages were upwards of eighty in number. The occupants, beginning with the Barons, rose in rank till they reached the Royal Dukes, and wound up with the Lord Chancellor. "Many of the Lords wore splendid uniforms and decorations and various orders; the Duke of Wellington especially was attired with much magnificence…. The terrace in front of the house was crowded with distinguished persons in grand costume," as on a gala-day. The Queen received the address of congratulation on her escape seated on the throne. What a strange contrast between the scene and its origin—the emphatically stately and dignified display, and the miserable act which gave rise to it! What blended feelings cause and effect must have produced in the principal performers— the inevitable pain and shame for the base reason, the well-warranted pride and pleasure in the honourable result!

The first time the Queen went to the opera afterwards she wrote in her Journal that the moment she and the Prince entered the box "the whole house rose and cheered and waved hats and handkerchiefs, and went on so for some time. 'God save the Queen' was sung…. Albert was called for separately and much cheered."

The trial of Oxford came on during the following month. The question of bullets or no bullets in the pistols was transferred to the jury. Evidence of symptoms of insanity and of confirmed insanity in the prisoner, his father, and grandfather, was shown, and after some difficulty in dealing with the first question the jury found the prisoner guilty, while he was at the same time declared insane. Therefore Oxford, like every other prisoner shielded by the irresponsibility of madness, was delivered up to be dealt with according to her Majesty's pleasure, which signified his imprisonment so long as the Crown should see fit.

The sole reason for the outrage on the Queen proved to be the morbid egotism of an ill-conditioned, ignorant, half-crazy lad; showing that one more danger exists for sovereigns—a peril born entirely of their high and solitary rank with its fascination for envious, irritable, distempered minds.

The following routine of the Queen's life at this time is given in the "Early Years of the Prince Consort": "They breakfasted at nine, and took a walk every morning soon afterwards."

In London, their walks were in Buckingham Palace gardens, fifty acres in extent, part of which was once the pleasant "Mulberry Gardens" of James I. The lake, not far from the palace, covers five acres. Looking across the velvet sward away to the masses of shady trees, it is hard to realise that one is still in London. The Prince had already enlivened these gardens with different kinds of animals and aquatic birds, a modified version of the Thier-Garten so often found in connection with royal residences in Germany.

The Queen mentions that, "in their morning walks in the gardens, it was a great amusement to the Prince to watch and feed these birds. He taught them to come when he whistled to them from a bridge connecting a small island with the rest of the gardens.

"Then came the usual amount of business (far less heavy, however, then than now), besides which they drew and etched a great deal together, which was a source of great amusement, having the plates bit in the house. Luncheon followed at the usual hour of two o'clock. Lord Melbourne, who was generally staying in the house, came to the Queen in the afternoon, and between five and six the Prince usually drove her out in a pony phaeton. If the Prince did not drive the Queen he rode, in which case she drove with the Duchess of Kent or the ladies. The Prince also read aloud most days to the Queen. The dinner was at eight o'clock, and always with the company. In the evening the Prince frequently played at double chess, a game of which he was very fond, and which he played extremely well."

The Prince would return "at a great pace" from his morning rides, which took him into all the districts of London where improvements were going on, and "would always come through the Queen's dressing-room, where she generally was at that time, with that bright loving smile with which he ever greeted her, telling her where he had been, what new buildings he had seen, what studios he had visited."

Her Majesty objected to the English custom of gentlemen remaining in the dining-room after the ladies had left the table. But, by the advice of Lord Melbourne, in which the Prince concurred, no direct change was made in what was almost a national institution. The hour when the whole party broke up, however, was seldom later than eleven.

The story got into circulation that the Queen's habit was to stand conversing with the ladies till the gentlemen joined them, and that knowing her practice, the dining-room was soon left empty. Lord Campbell gives his experience of this portion of a royal dinner some years after the Queen's marriage. "The Queen and the ladies withdrawing, Prince Albert came over to her side of the table, and we remained behind about a quarter of an hour, but we rose within the hour from the time of our sitting down. A snuff-box was twice carried round and offered to all the gentlemen. Prince Albert, to my surprise, took a pinch."

The Prince, who was an exceedingly temperate man at table, rather grudged the time spent in eating and drinking, just as he disliked riding for mere exercise, without any other object. Yet he was a bold and skilled rider, and could, without any privilege of rank, come in first in the hunting-field. It amused the Queen and her husband to find that this accomplishment, more than any other, was likely to make him popular among English gentlemen. But though he liked hunting as a recreation, he did not understand how it or any other sport could be made the business of a man's life.

By the month of July, the prospect of an heir to the throne rendered it advisable that provision should be made for the Queen's possible death, or lengthened disqualification for reigning. The Regency Bill was brought forward with more caution and better success than had attended on the Prince's Annuity Bill. In accordance with the prudent counsels of Baron Stockmar, the Opposition as well as the Ministry were taken into account and consulted. The consequence was that the Duke of Wellington, the mouthpiece of the Tories on the former occasion, was altogether propitious in the name of himself and his party, and it was agreed that the Prince was the proper person to appoint as Regent in case of any unhappy contingency. The Bill was passed unanimously and without objection in both Houses, except for a speech made by the Duke of Sussex in the House of Lords.

This conclusion was gratifying in all respects, not the least so in its testimony to the respect which the Prince's conduct had already called forth. "Three months ago they would not have done it for him," Lord Melbourne told the Queen. "It is entirely his own character." It was also a pleasant proof of the goodwill of the Tories, whom the Prince had done everything in his power to conciliate, employing his influence to impress upon the young Queen the constitutional attitude of impartiality and neutrality towards all political parties.

There was a corresponding withdrawal of the absurd opposition to Prince Albert's taking his place by the Queen's side on all State occasions. "Let the Queen put the Prince where she likes and settle it herself, that is the best way," said the Duke of Wellington cordially. A lively example of the great Duke's want of toleration for the traditions of Court etiquette is given in a note to the "Life of the Prince Consort." The late Lord Albemarle, when Master of the Horse, was very sensitive about his right in that capacity to sit in the sovereign's coach on State occasions. "The Queen," said the Duke, when appealed to for his opinion, "can make Lord Albemarle sit at the top of the coach, under the coach, behind the coach, or wherever else her Majesty pleases."

On the 11th of August the Queen prorogued Parliament, accompanied by her husband for the first time. The following day the Court left for Windsor. The Prince was very fond of the country, and gladly went to it. The Queen, in her early womanhood, had been, as she said, "too happy to go to London, and wretched to leave it." But from the time of her marriage she shared her husband's tastes, and could have been "content and happy never to go to town." How her Majesty has retained the love of nature, which is a refuge of sorrow as well as a crown of happiness, we all know.

In the mornings at Windsor there were shooting in the season, and a wider field for landscape gardening for the Prince before he took to farming. In the evening there were occasional great dinners and little dances as in London. The young couple dispensed royal hospitality to a succession of friendly visitors, who came to see with their own eyes the bright palace home. The King and the Queen of the Belgians rejoiced in the fruits of his work. The Princess of Hohenlohe, herself a happy wife and mother, arrived with her children to witness her sister's felicity. Queen Adelaide did not shrink from revisiting Windsor, and seeing a beloved niece fill well King William and his consort's place.

Prince Albert's birthday was celebrated in England for the first time; there were illuminations in London; down at Windsor the day was kept, for the most part, in the simple family fashion, which is the best. The Prince was awakened by a musical reveille; a German chorale, chosen with loving, ungrudging care, as the first thing which was to greet him, was most certain, on that day of all others, to carry him back in spirit to his native country.

The family circle breakfasted by themselves in a favourite cottage in the park. Princess Feodora's children were in masquerade as Coburg peasants, doubtless hailing the Coburg Prince with an appropriate greeting. In the afternoon, in the fine weather, the Prince drove out the Queen; in the evening, "there was rather a larger dinner than usual."

On the 11th of September the Prince was formally sworn a member of her Majesty's Privy Council. And so conscientiously anxious was he to discharge worthily every duty which could be required of him, that, in the greater leisure of Windsor, he not only read "Hallam's Constitutional History" with the Queen, he began to read English law with a barrister.

In the meantime, an old historical figure, Princess Augusta of England, who had appeared at the Queen's marriage, lay terribly ill at Clarence House. She died on the 22nd of September, having survived her sister, Princess Elizabeth, the Landgravine of Hesse Homburg, only eight months.

Princess Augusta carried away with her many memories of the Court of George III. By a coincidence, the lady who may almost be called the Princess's biographer, at least whose animated sketches and affectionate praises of her "dear Princess Augusta" were destined to give the world of England its principal knowledge of an amiable princess, died at a great age the same year. Madame D'Arblay, as Miss Burney, the distinguished novelist, had been appointed in 1786, in a somewhat whimsical acknowledgement of her talents and services to the reading world, one of the keepers of Queen Charlotte's wardrobe. In this office she resided at Court for five years, and she has left in her diary the most graphic account which we have of the English royal life of the day. "Evelina" and "Cecilia" were old stories even in 1840; it was more than fifty years since Madame D'Arblay had taken royal service, and now her best-beloved young patroness had passed away an aged woman, only a few months later than the gifted and vivacious little keeper of the robes, whose duties, to be sure, had included reading habitually to the Queen when she was dressing, and sometimes to the Court circle. Princess Augusta's funeral went from her house of Frogmore at seven o'clock in the evening of the 2nd of October, one of the last of the night funerals of a past generation, and she was buried with the customary honours in St. George's Chapel, Windsor. Frogmore became from that time the country residence of the Duchess of Kent.

In November the Court returned to Buckingham Palace for the Queen's accouchement. Baron Stockmar, at the Prince's earnest entreaty, came to England for the event, though he remained then as always in the background. On the 21st of November the Princess Royal was born, the good news being announced to London by the firing of the Tower guns. The Cabinet Ministers and Officers of State were in attendance in an adjoining room, and the new-born child, wrapped in flannel, was carried by the nurse, escorted by Sir James Clark, into the presence of those who were to attest her birth, and laid for a moment on a table before them. Both mother and child were well, and although a momentary disappointment was felt at the sex of the infant, it did not detract from the general rejoicing at the Queen's safety with a living successor to the throne. It was said at the time, kindly gossips dwelling on the utterance with the utmost pleasure, that on the Prince expressing a fear that the people might be disappointed, the Queen reassured him in the most cheerful spirit, "Never mind, the next shall be a boy," and that she hoped she might have as many children as her grandmother, Queen Charlotte.

A fresh instance of a diseased appetite for notoriety, grafted on vagrant youthful curiosity and restless love of mischief, astonished and scandalised the English world. On the day after the birth of the Princess Royal a rascally boy named Jones was discovered concealed under a sofa in a room next to the Queen's. The offender was leniently dealt with in consideration of his immature years, but again and again, at intervals of a few months, the flibbertigibbet turned up in the most unlooked-for quarters, impudently asserting, on being questioned, that he had entered "the same way as before," and that he could, any time he pleased, find his way into the palace. It was supposed that he climbed over the wall on Constitution Hill and crept through one of the windows. But he could hardly have done so if it had not been for the confused palace management, for which nobody was responsible, with its inevitable disorder, that had not yet been overcome. The boy had to be committed to the House of Correction as a rogue and vagabond for three months. Afterwards he served on board one of her Majesty's ships, where his taste for creating a sensation seems to have died a natural death.

In the Queen's weakness the young husband and father was continually developing new traits of manly tenderness. "His care and devotion were quite beyond expression." He declined to go anywhere, that he might be always at hand to do anything in his power for her comfort "He was content to sit by her in a darkened room, to read to her and write for her." "No one but himself ever lifted her from her bed to her sofa, and he always helped to wheel her on her bed or sofa into the next room. For this purpose he would come instantly when sent for from any part of the house." "His care for her was like that of a mother, nor could there be a kinder, wiser, more judicious nurse." Happy Queen!

The Queen made an excellent recovery, and the Court was back at Windsor holding Christmas and New Year relieved from all care and full of thankfulness. The peace and goodwill of the season, with the interchange of kindly gifts, were celebrated with pleasant picturesque German, in addition to old English customs. We have all heard wonderful tales of the baron of beef, the boar's head, the peacock with spread tail, the plum soup for which there is only one recipe, and that a royal one. There were fir-trees in the Queen's and the Prince's rooms and in humbler chambers. There was a great gathering of the household in a special corridor, where the Queen's presents were bestowed.

A new year dawned with bright promise on an expectant world. This last year had been so good in one sense that it could hardly be surpassed. What had it not done for the family life! It had given a good and loving wife to a good and loving husband, and a little child, with undreamt-of possibilities in its slumbering eyes and helpless hands. The public horizon was tolerably clear. The Welsh riots had been quelled and other acts of insubordination in the manufacturing districts put down—not without the use of force—but there was room for trust that such mad tumults would not be repeated. Father Matthews was reforming Ireland. There were far-away wars both with China and Afghanistan, certainly, but the wars were far away in more respects than one, distant enough to have their origin in the English protection of the opium trade, and interference—now with a peaceful, timidly conservative race—and again with fiercely jealous and warlike tribes, slurred over and forgotten, and only the successes of the national arms dwelt upon with pride and exultation.

Across "the silver streak" of the Channel there were more remarkable events, marked by a curious inconsistency, than the suitable marriage of the Duc de Nemours. Prince Louis Napoleon Buonaparte landed on the French coast with a handful of men prepared to invade the country, and was immediately overpowered and arrested. He was tried and condemned to imprisonment in the fortress of Ham, from which he escaped in due time, having earned for himself during long years the sobriquet of "the madman of Boulogne." The very same year Prince de Joinville, Louis Philippe's sailor son, was commissioned to bring the ashes of Napoleon from St. Helena to France. The coffin was conveyed in the Prince's frigate, La Belle Poule, to Cherbourg, whence a steamboat sailed with the solemn freight up the Seine to Paris. The funeral formed a splendid pageant, attended by the royal family, the ministers, and a great concourse of spectators. The dust of le petit caporal was deposited in a magnificent tomb in the Hotel des Invalides, before the eyes of a few survivors of his Old Guard.

Spain and Portugal were still the theatres of civil wars—now smouldering, now leaping up with brief fury. In Spain the Queen Regent, Christina, was driven from the kingdom, and had to take refuge in France for a time. In Portugal, in the middle of a political crisis, Maria da Gloria gave birth to a daughter, which died soon after its birth, while for days her own life was despaired of.

CHAPTER XI THE FIRST CHRISTENING.—THE SEASON OF 1841.

The Queen was able to open Parliament in person at the end of January.

The first christening in the royal household had been fixed to take place on the 10th of February, the first anniversary of the Queen's wedding-day, which was thus a double gala in 1841. The day before the Prince again had a dangerous accident. He was skating in the presence of the Queen and one of her ladies on the lake in the gardens of Buckingham Palace when the ice gave way a few yards from the bank, where the water was so deep that the skater had to swim for two or three minutes before he could extricate himself. The Queen had the presence of mind to lend him instant assistance, while her lady was "more occupied in screaming for help," so that the worst consequences of the plunge were a bad cold.

The christening took place at six in the evening in Buckingham Palace. The ceremony was performed by the Archbishop of Canterbury, assisted by the Archbishop of York, the Bishop of London, the Bishop of Norwich, and the Dean of Carlisle. The sponsors were the Duke of Saxe-Coburg Gotha, represented by the Duke of Wellington, King Leopold, the Queen-dowager, the Duchess of Gloucester, the Duchess of Kent, and the Duke of Sussex, the most of whom had been present at the baptism of her Majesty, and were able to compare royal child and royal mother in similar circumstances. The Duke of Cambridge and his son, Prince George, with Prince Edward of Saxe-Weimar, were among the company. The infant was named "Victoria Adelaide Mary Louisa."

The Annual Register for the year has an elaborate description of the new silver-gilt font used on the occasion. It was in the shape of a water-lily supporting a shell, the rim of which was decorated with smaller water-lilies. The base bore, between the arms of the Queen and Prince Albert, the arms of the Princess Royal, surmounted by her Royal Highness's coronet. The water had been brought from the river Jordan.

A simple description of the event was given by Prince Albert in a letter to his grandmother, the Dowager-Duchess of Gotha. "The christening went off very well; your little great-granddaughter behaved with great propriety and like a Christian. She was awake, but did not cry at all, and seemed to crow with immense satisfaction at the lights and brilliant uniforms, for she is very intelligent and observing. The ceremony took place at half-past six P.M. After it there was a dinner, and then we had some instrumental music. The health of the little one was drunk with great enthusiasm."

The lively noticing powers of the Princess Royal when she was between two and three months of age is in amusing contradiction to a report which we remember as current at the time. It was mentioned in order to be denied by Leslie, who was commissioned to paint the royal christening, and worked at the picture so diligently in the long days of the following summer that he was often occupied with the work from nine in the morning till seven or eight in the evening. He wrote in his "Recollections": "In 1841 I painted a second picture for the Queen, the christening of the Princess Royal. I was admitted to see the ceremony, and made a slight sketch of the royal personages as they stood round the font in the room. I made a study from the little Princess a few days afterwards. She was then three months old, and a finer child of that age I never saw. It is a curious proof of the readiness with which people believe whatever they hear to the disadvantage of those placed high in rank above them, that at the time at which I made the sketch it was said everywhere but in the palace and by those who belonged to the royal household, that the Princess was born blind, and by many it was even believed that she was born without feet. The sketch was shown at a party at Mr. Moon's, the evening after I made it, and the ladies all said, 'What a pity so fine a child should be entirely blind!' It was in vain I told them that her eyes were beautifully clear and bright, and that she took notice of everything about her. I was told that, though her eyes looked bright, and though she might appear to turn them to every object, it was certain she was blind."

What Leslie attributes to a species of envy, we think may be more justly regarded as having its foundation in the love of sensationalism to which human nature is prone—sensationalism which appears to become all the racier when it finds its food in high quarters. The particular direction the tendency took was influenced by the blindness of George III. and of his grandson, the Crown Prince of Hanover, which seemed to lend a plausibility to the absurd rumour.

Baron Stockmar states that the Princess Royal was a delicate child, causing considerable apprehension for her successful rearing during the first year of her life. It was only by judicious care that she developed a splendid constitution. Charles Leslie goes on to say: "The most agreeable part of my task in painting the christening of the Princess Royal was in studying the fine head of the wisest and best of living Kings, Leopold, a man whom the people he reigns over scarcely seem to deserve. Nothing could be more agreeable than his manner, and that of his amiable Queen, who was in the room all the time he sat. He speaks English very well, and she also spoke it. After I had painted for some time, she said, "May I look?" and suggesting some alterations, she said, "You must excuse me, I speak honest; but if I am wrong, don't mind me."

In those years the King and Queen of the Belgians were such frequent visitors of her Majesty, who may be said to have been his adopted child, that a whole floor of Buckingham Palace which was set apart for their use is still known as "the Belgian Floor." The portraits of both are in the Palace, and so is his likeness when he was many years younger, and one of the handsomest men in Europe. The last is hanging beside a full-length portrait of his first wife, Princess Charlotte, with her fair face and striking figure. In the summer of 1841 the Queen was farther and longer separated from her mother than she had ever been previously. The Duchess of Kent, secure in her daughter's prosperity and happiness, went to her native Germany, for the first time since she had come to England twenty-two years before. She was warmly received wherever she went. She visited, among other places, Amorbach, the seat of her son, the Prince of Leiningen, in Bavaria, where the Duchess had resided with the Duke of Kent in the first years of their married life. "It is like a dream that I am writing to you from this place," she addressed her daughter. "He (the Prince of Leiningen) has made many alterations in the house. Your father began them just before we left in March, 1819."

A threatened change of Ministry and a general election were pending; but amidst the political anxieties which already occupied much of the Queen and Prince Albert's thoughts, it was a bright summer, full of many interests and special sources of pleasure.

Mademoiselle Rachel, the great French actress, arrived in England. She had already established her empire in Paris by her marvellous revival of Racine's and Corneille's masterpieces. She was now to exercise the same fascination over an alien people, to whom her speech was a foreign tongue. She made her first appearance in the part of Hermione in Racine's Andromaque at the Italian Opera-house. Few who witnessed the spectacle ever forgot the slight figure, the pale, dark, Jewish face, the deep melody of the voice, the restrained passion, the concentrated rage, especially the pitiless irony, with which she gave the poet's meaning.

The Queen and the Prince shared the general enthusiasm. For that matter there was a little jealousy awakened lest there might be too much generous abandon in the royal approval of the great player. Perhaps this feeling arose in the minds of those who, dating from Puritan days, had a conscientious objection to all plays and players, and waxed hotter as time, alas! proved how, in contrast to the honourable reputation of the English Queen of Tragedy, Sarah Siddons, the character and life of the gifted French actress were miserably beneath her genius. There was a little vexed talk, which probably had small enough foundation, of the admission of Rachel into the highest society; of the Duchess of Kent's condescending to give her shawl to the shivering foreigner; of a bracelet with the simple inscription, "From Victoria to Rachel," as if there could be a common meeting-ground between the two, though the one was a queen in art and the other a queen in history. But if there was any imprudence, it might well have been excused as a fault of noble sympathy with art and cordial acknowledgement of it, which leant to virtue's side, a fault which had hitherto been not too common in England. The same year a Kemble, the last of the family who redeemed for a time the fallen fortunes of Covent Garden Theatre, Adelaide, the beautiful and accomplished younger daughter of Charles Kemble, brother to John Kemble and Sarah Siddons, came out as an operatic-singer in the part of "Norma." She was welcomed as her sweet voice, fine acting, and the traditions of her family deserved. She was invited to sing at the palace. From girlhood the Queen had been familiar with the Kembles in their connection with the English stage. The last time she visited the Academy as Princess Victoria, just before the death of King William, Leslie mentions, she asked that Charles Kemble might be presented to her, when the gentleman had the opportunity of making his "best genteel-comedy bow." Now it was on the younger generation of the Kembles that the Queen bestowed her gracious countenance. These were halcyon days for society as well as for the stage, when, in Mrs. Oliphant's words, "the Queen was in the foreground of the national life, affecting it always for good, and setting an example of purity and virtue. The theatres to which she went, and which both she and her husband enjoyed, were purified by her presence, evils which had been the growth of years disappearing before the face of the young Queen...."

On the 13th of June the Queen revisited Oxford in company with her husband, in time for Commemoration. Her Majesty and the Prince stayed at Nuneham, the seat of the Archbishop of York, and drove in to the University city. The Prince was present at a banquet in St. John's and attended divine service at New Inn Hall.

On the 21st of June the Queen and Prince Albert were at Woolwich, for the launch of the good ship Trafalgar. Nothing so gay had been seen at the mouth of the river since King William and Queen Adelaide came down to Greenwich to keep the anniversary of the battle of Trafalgar. The water was covered with vessels, including every sort of craft that had been seen "since the building of Noah's Ark." The shore was equally crowded with an immense multitude of human beings finding standing-ground in the most unlikely places. The Queen drove down to the Dockyard in a travelling-carriage and four. She was received with a royal salute and glad bursts of cheering.

It is hardly necessary to say that the young Queen was exceedingly popular with the blue-jackets. In the course of a visit to Portsmouth she had gone over one of her ships. She was shown through the men's quarters, the sailors being under orders to remain perfectly quiet and abstain from cheering. Her Majesty tasted the men's coffee and pronounced it good. She asked if they got nothing stronger. A glass of grog was brought to her. She put it to her lips, and Jack could contain himself no longer; a burst of enthusiastic huzzas made the ribs of the ship ring.

At Woolwich a discharge of artillery announced the moment when the great vessel slipped from her stays, and "floated gallantly down the river" till she was brought up and swung round with her stern to London.

The King and Queen of the Belgians paid their second visit this year, the Queen remaining six weeks, detained latterly by the illness of her son in England. The long visit confirmed the tender friendship between the two queens. "During this stay, which had been such a happiness for me, we became most intimate," Queen Victoria wrote in her Journal, and she grudged the necessity of having to set out with Prince Albert on a royal progress before the departure of her cherished guest. "To lose four days of her stay, of which, I repeat, every hour is precious, is dreadful," her Majesty told King Leopold.

The short summer progress was otherwise very enjoyable. The Queen and Prince Albert visited the Duke of Bedford at the Russells' stately seat of Woburn Abbey, with its park twelve miles in extent. From Woburn the royal couple went to Panshanger, Earl Cowper's, and Brocket Hall, Lord Melbourne's, returning by Hatfield, the Marquis of Salisbury's. At Brocket the Queen was entertained by her Prime Minister. At Hatfield there were many memories of another Queen and her minister, since the ancient country-house had been a palace of Queen Elizabeth's, passing, in her successor's reign, by an exchange of mansions, from the hands of James I into those of the son and representative of Lord Burleigh, little crooked, long-headed Robert Cecil, first Earl of Salisbury. In Hatfield Park there is an oak still standing which bears the name of "Queen Elizabeth's Oak." It is said Princess Elizabeth was sitting in its shade when the news was brought to her of the death of her sister, Queen Mary, and her own accession to the throne of England. The only difficulty—a pleasant one after all—which was experienced in these progresses, proceeded from the exuberant loyalty of the people. At straw-plaiting Dunstable a volunteer company of farmers joined the regular escort and nearly choked the travellers with the dust the worthy yeomen raised. On leaving Woburn Abbey the same dubious compliment was paid. In the Queen's merry words, "a crowd of good, loyal people rode with us part of the way. They so pressed and pushed that it was as if we were hunting."

The recent election had returned a majority of Conservative members, and soon after the reassembling of Parliament in August a vote of non-confidence in Lord Melbourne's Ministry was carried. The same evening the Prime Minister went to Windsor to announce his resignation. He acted with his natural fairness and generosity, giving due honour to his adversaries, and congratulating the Queen on the great advantage she possessed in the presence and counsel of the Prince, thus softening to her the trial of the first change of Ministers in her reign. He only regretted the pain to himself of leaving her. "For four years I have seen you every day; but it is so different from what it would have been in 1839. The Prince understands everything so well, and has a clever, able head." The Queen was much affected in taking leave of a "faithful and attached friend," as well as Minister, while her words were, that his praise of the Prince gave her "great pleasure" and made her "very proud."

In anticipation of the change of Ministry it had been arranged, with Sir Robert Peel's concurrence, that the principal Whig ladies in the Queen's household—the Duchess of Sutherland, the Duchess of Bedford, and Lady Normanby—should voluntarily retire from office, and that this should be the practice in any future change of Ministry, so that the question of Ministerial interference in the withdrawal or the appointment of the ladies of the Queen's household might be set at rest. [Footnote: The retirement from office is now limited to the Mistress of the Robes.]

On the 3rd of September the new Ministers kissed hands on their appointment at a Cabinet Council held at Claremont. Lord Campbell gives some particulars. "I have just seen here several of our friends returned from Claremont. Both parties met there at once. They were shown into separate rooms. The Queen sat in her closet, no one being present but Prince Albert. The exaunters were called in one by one and gave up the seals or wands of their offices and retired. The new men by mistake went to Claremont all in their Court costume, whereas the Queen at Windsor and Claremont receives her Ministers in their usual morning dress. Nonnanby says taking leave of the Queen was very affecting."

Whatever momentary awkwardness may have attended the substitution of Sir Robert Peel as Prime Minister, it did not at all interfere—thanks to the candid, liberal nature of all concerned—

with the friendly goodwill which it is so desirable should exist between sovereign and minister. We read in the "Life of the Prince Consort," "Lord Melbourne told Baron Stockmar, who had just returned from Coburg, that Sir Robert Peel had behaved most handsomely, and that the conduct of the Prince had throughout been most moderate and judicious."

Sir Robert had experienced considerable embarrassment at the recollection of his share in the debates on the Royal Annuity Bill, but the Prince did not show an equally retentive memory. His seeming forgetfulness of the past and cordiality in the present did more than reassure, it deeply touched and completely won a man who was himself capable of magnanimous self-renunciation. Sir Robert Peel had the pleasure, in his early days in office, of suggesting to the Prince the Royal Commission to promote and encourage the fine arts in the United Kingdom, with reference to the rebuilding of the two Houses of Parliament. Sir Robert proposed that Prince Albert should be placed at the head of the Commission. This was not only a movement after the Prince's own heart, on which he spared no thought and labour for years to come, it was an act in which Prince and Minister—both of them lovers of art—could co-operate with the greatest satisfaction.

CHAPTER XII. BIRTH OF THE PRINCE OF WALES.—THE AFGHAN DISASTERS.—VISIT OF THE KING OF PRUSSIA.—"THE QUEEN'S PLANTAGENET BALL."

On the 9th of November, 1841, the happiness of the Queen and Prince was increased by the birth of the Prince of Wales. The event took place on the morning of the Lord Mayor's Day, as the citizens of London rejoiced to learn by the booming of the Tower guns. In addition to the usual calls of the nobility and gentry, the Lord Mayor and his train went in great state to offer their congratulations and make their inquiries for the Queen-mother and child.

The sole shadow on the rejoicing was the dangerous illness of the Queen-dowager. She had an affection of the chest which rendered her a confirmed invalid for years. At this time the complaint took an aggravated form, and her weakness became so great that it was feared death was approaching. But she rallied—a recovery due in a great measure, it was believed, to her serene nature and patient resignation. She regained her strength in a degree and survived for years.

The public took a keen interest in all that concerned the heir to the crown, though times were less free and easy than they had been—all the world no longer trooped to the Queen's House as they had done to taste the caudle compounded when royal Charlotte's babies were born. There was at least the cradle with the nodding Prince of Wales feathers to gossip about. The patent creating the Duke of Cornwall Prince of Wales and Earl of Chester was issued on the 8th of December, when the child was a month old. It was a quaint enough document, inasmuch as the Queen declared in it that she ennobled and invested her son with the Principality and earldom by girting him with a sword, by putting a coronet on his head and a gold ring on his finger, and also by delivering a gold rod into his hand, that he might preside there, and direct and defend these parts.

The Royal Nursery had now two small occupants, and their wise management, still more than that of the household, engaged the serious consideration of the Queen and the Prince's old friend, Baron Stockmar, and engrossed much of the attention of the youthful parents. They took great delight in the bright little girl, whom her mother named "Pussy," and the charming baby who was so near her in age.

"To think," wrote the Queen in her Journal this Christmas, "that we have two children now, and one who enjoys the sight already" (referring to the Christmas-tree); "it is like a dream."

"This is the dear Christmas Eve on which I have so often listened with impatience to your step which was to usher us into the gift-room," the Prince reminded his father. "To-day I have two children of my own to make gifts to, who, they know not why, are full of happy wonder at the German Christmas-tree and its radiant candles."

On this occasion the New Year was danced into "in good old English fashion. In the middle of the dance, as the clock finished striking twelve, a flourish of trumpets was blown, in accordance with a German custom." The past year had been good also, and fertile in blessings on that roof-tree, though in the world without there were the chafings and mutterings of more than one impending crisis. The corn-laws, with the embargo they laid on free trade, weighed heavily on the minds both of statesmen and people. In Scotland Church and State were struggling keenly once more, though, bloodlessly this time, as they had struggled to the death in past centuries, for mastery where what each considered its rights were in question.

Among the blows dealt by death in 1841, there had been heavy losses to art in the passing away of Chantrey and Wilkie.

In January, 1842, events happened in Afghanistan which brought bitter grief to many an English home, and threw their shadow over the palace itself in the next few months. The fatal policy of English interference with the fiery tribes of Northern India in support of an unpopular ruler had ended in the murder of Sir Alexander Burns and Sir William Macnaghten, and the evacuation of Cabul by the English. This was not all. The march through the terrible mountain defiles in the depth of winter, under the continual assaults of an unscrupulous and cruel enemy, meant simply destruction. The ladies of the party, with Lady Sale, a heroic woman, at their head, the husbands of the ladies who were with the camp, and finally General Elphinstone, who had been the first in command at Cabul, but who was an old and infirm man, had to be surrendered as hostages. They were committed to the tender mercies of Akbar Khan, the son of the exiled Dost Mahomed, the moving spirit of the insurrection against the native puppet maintained by English authority, and the murderer, with his own hand, of Sir William Macnaghten, whose widow was among the prisoners. The surrender of hostages was partly a matter of necessity, in order to secure for the most helpless of the party the dubious protection of Akbar Khan, partly a desperate measure to prevent what would otherwise have been inevitable—the perishing of the women and children in the dreadful hardships of the retreat. The captives were carried first to Peshawur and afterwards to a succession of hill-forts in the direction of the Caucasus, while their countrymen at home, long before they had become familiar with the tragedy of the Indian Rebellion, burned with indignation and thrilled with horror at the possible fate of those victims of a treacherous, vindictive Afghan chief. In the meantime the awful march went on, amidst the rigours of winter, in wild snowy passes, by savage precipices, while the most unsparing guerilla warfare was kept up by the furious natives at every point of vantage. Alas! for the miserable end which we all know, some of us recalling it, through the mists of years, still fresh with the wonder, wrath, and sorrow which the news aroused here. Out of a company of sixteen thousand that left Cabul, hundreds were slain or died of exhaustion every day, three thousand fell in an ambush, and after a night's exposure to such frost as was never experienced in England. At last, on the 13th of January, 1842, one haggard man, Dr. Brydon, rode up, reeling in his saddle, to the gates of Jellalabad. The fortress was still in the keeping of Sir Robert Sale, who had steadfastly refused to retire. It is said his wife wrote to him from her prison, urging him to hold out, because she preferred her own and her daughter's death to his dishonour.

But the Afghan disasters were not fully known in England for months to come. In the interval, the christening of the Prince of Wales was celebrated with much splendour in St. George's

Chapel, Windsor, on the 25th of January. The King of Prussia came over to England to officiate in person as one of the Prince's godfathers. The others were the child's two grand-uncles, the Duke of Cambridge and Prince Ferdinand of Saxe-Coburg, uncle of the Queen and of Prince Albert, and father of the King Consort of Portugal and the Duchesse de Nemours. The godmothers were the Duchess of Kent, proxy for the Duchess of Saxe-Coburg, Prince Albert's stepmother; the Duchess of Cambridge, proxy for the child's great-grandmother, the Duchess of Saxe-Gotha; and the Princess Augusta of Cambridge, proxy for the Princess Sophia of England. The ambassadors and foreign ministers, the Cabinet ministers with their wives in full dress, the Knights of the Garter in their mantles and collars, the Archbishops of Canterbury and York, the Bishops of London, Winchester, Oxford, and Norwich assembled in the Waterloo Gallery; the officers and the ladies of the Household awaited the Queen in the corridor. At noon, certain officers of the Household attended the King of Prussia, who was joined by the other sponsors at the head of the grand staircase, to the chapel.

The Queen's procession included the Duke of Wellington, bearing the Sword of State between the Lord Chamberlain, the Earl De la Warr, and the Lord Steward, the Earl of Liverpool, the three walking before her Majesty and Prince Albert, who were supported by their lords-in-waiting, and followed by the Duke of Sussex, Prince George of Cambridge, Prince Edward of Saxe-Weimar, Prince Augustus and Prince Leopold of Saxe-Coburg, sons of Prince Ferdinand and cousins of the Queen and Prince Albert.

When the sponsors had taken their places, and the other company were seated near the altar, the Lord Chamberlain, accompanied by the Groom of the Stall to Prince Albert, proceeded to the Chapter-house, and conducted in the infant Prince of Wales, attended by the lord and groom in waiting. The Duchess of Buccleuch, the Mistress of the Robes, took the infant from the nurse, and put him in the Archbishop's arms. The child was named "Albert" for his father, and "Edward" for his maternal grandfather, the Duke of Kent. The baby, on the authority of The Times, "behaved with princely decorum." After the ceremony, he was reconducted to the Chapter-house by the Lord Chamberlain. By Prince Albert's desire "The Hallelujah Chorus," which has never been given in England without the audience rising simultaneously, was played at the close of the service.

The Queen afterwards held a Chapter of the Order of the Garter, at which the King of Prussia, "as a lineal descendant of George I.," was elected a Knight Companion, the Queen buckling the garter round his knee. There was luncheon in the White Breakfast-room, and in the evening there was a banquet in St. George's Hall. The table reached from one end of the hall to the other, and was covered with gold plate. Lady Bloomfield, who was present, describes an immense gold vessel—more like a bath than anything else, capable of containing thirty dozens of wine. It was filled with mulled claret, to the amazement of the Prussians. Four toasts were drunk—that to his Royal Highness the Prince of Wales taking precedence; toasts to his Majesty the King of Prussia, the Queen and Prince Albert followed. A grand musical performance in the Waterloo Gallery wound up the festivities of the day.

The presence of the King of Prussia added additional dignity to the proceedings. He was a great ally whose visit on the occasion was a becoming compliment. Besides, his personal character was then regarded as full of promise, and excited much interest. His attainments and accomplishments, which were really remarkable, won lively admiration. His warm regard for a man like Baron Bunsen seemed to afford the best augury for the liberality of his sentiments. As yet the danger of impracticability, discouragement, confusion, and paralysis of all that had been hoped for, was but faintly indicated in the dreaminess and fancifulness of his nature.

Lady Bloomfield describes the King as of middle size, rather fat, with an excellent countenance and little hair. The Queen met him on the grand staircase, kissed him twice, and made him two low curtseys. Her Majesty says in her Journal: "He was in common morning costume, and complained much of appearing so before me…. He is entertaining, agreeable, and witty, tells a thing so pleasantly, and is full of amusing anecdotes."

Madame Bunsen, who was privileged to see a good deal of the gay doings during the King of Prussia's visit, has handed down her experience. "28th January, 1842, came by railway to Windsor, and found that in the York Tower a comfortable set of rooms were awaiting us. The upper housemaid gave us tea, and bread and butter—very refreshing; when dressed we went together to the corridor, soon met Lord De la Warr, the Duchess of Buccleugh, and Lord and Lady Westmoreland—the former showed us where to go—that is, to walk through the corridor (a fairy scene—lights, pictures, moving figures of courtiers unknown), the apartments which we passed through one after another till we reached the magnificent ball-room where the guests were assembled to await the Queen's appearance. Among these guests stood our King himself, punctual to quarter-past seven o'clock; soon came Prince Albert, to whom Lord De la Warr named me, when he spoke to me of Rome. We had not been there long before two gentlemen walking in by the same door by which we had entered, and then turning and making profound bows towards the open door, showed that the Queen was coming. She approached me directly and said, with a gracious smile, 'I am very much pleased to see you,' then passed on, and after speaking a few moments to the King took his arm and moved on, 'God save the Queen' having begun to sound from the Waterloo Gallery, where the Queen has always dined since the King has been with her. Lord Haddington led me to dinner, and one of the King's suite sat on the other side. The scene was one of fairy tales, of undescribed magnificence, the proportions of the hall, the mass of light in suspension, the gold plate, and the table glittering with a thousand lights in branches of a proper height not to meet the eye. The King's health was drunk, then the Queen's, and then the Queen went out, followed by all her ladies. During the half-hour or less that elapsed before Prince Albert and the King followed the Queen, she did not sit, but went round to speak to the different ladies. She asked after my children, and gave me an opportunity of thanking her for the gracious permission to behold her Majesty so soon after my arrival. The Duchess of Kent also spoke to me, and I was very glad of the notice of Lady Lyttelton, who is very charming. As soon as the King came the Queen went into the ball-room and made the King dance a quadrille with her, which he did with all suitable grace and dignity, though he has long ceased to dance. At half-past eleven, after the Queen had retired, I set out on my travels to my bed-chamber. I might have looked and wandered about some miles before I had found my door of exit, but was helped by an old gentleman, I believe Lord Albemarle."

The same thoughtful observer was present when the King of Prussia saw the Queen open Parliament. "February, 1842, Thursday. The opening of the Parliament was the thing from which I expected most, and I was not disappointed; the throngs in the streets, in the windows, in every place people could stand upon, all looking so pleased; the splendid Horse Guards, the Grenadiers of the Guard—of whom might be said as the King said on another occasion—'An appearance so fine, you know not how to believe it true;' the Yeomen of the Body Guard; then in the House of Lords, the Peers in their robes, the beautifully-dressed ladies with very many beautiful faces; lastly, the procession of the Queen's entry and herself, looking worthy and fit to be the converging-point of so many rays of grandeur. It is self-evident that she is not tall, but were she ever so tall, she could not have more grace and dignity, a head better set, a throat better arching; and one advantage there is in her looks when she casts a glance, being of necessity cast up and not down, that the effect of the eyes is not lost, and they have an effect both bright and pleasing. The composure with which she filled the throne while awaiting the Commons, I much admired— it was a test, no fidget, no apathy. Then her voice and enunciation cannot be more perfect. In short it could not be said that she did well, but that she was the Queen—she was, and felt herself to be, the descendant of her ancestors. Stuffed in by her Majesty's mace-bearers, and peeping over their shoulders, I was enabled to struggle down the emotions I felt, at thinking what mighty pages in the world's history were condensed in the words so impressively uttered by that soft and feminine voice. Peace and war—the fate of millions—relations and exertions of power felt to the extremities of the globe! Alterations of corn-laws, birth of a future sovereign, with what should it close, but the heartfelt aspiration, God bless her and guide her for her sake, and the sake of all." Lady Bloomfield, who was also present, mentions that when the Queen had finished speaking and descended from the throne, she turned to the King of Prussia and made him a low curtsey. The same eye-witness refers to one of the "beautiful faces" which Madame Bunsen remarked; it was that of one of the loveliest and most accomplished women of her time: "Miss Stewart (afterwards Marchioness of Waterford) was there, looking strikingly handsome. She wore a turquoise, blue velvet which was very becoming, and she was like one of the Madonnas she is so fond of painting."

The Queen and the Prince's hearts were gladdened this spring by the news of the approaching marriage of his brother, Prince Ernest, to Princess Alexandrine of Baden. In a family so united such intelligence awoke the liveliest sympathy. The Queen wrote eagerly on the subject to her uncle, and the uncle of the bridegroom, King Leopold. "My heart is full, very full of this marriage; it brings back so many recollections of our dear betrothal—as Ernest was with us all the time and longed for similar happiness… I have entreated Ernest to pass his honeymoon with us, and I beg you to urge him to do it, for he witnessed our happiness and we must therefore witness his."

There were warm wishes for Prince Albert's presence at the ceremony at Carlsruhe on the 3rd of May; but though his inclination coincided with these wishes, he believed there were grave reasons for his remaining in England, and, as was usual with him, inclination yielded to duty. The times were full of change and excitement. The people were suffering. Rioting had occurred in the mining districts, both in England and Scotland. Lord Shaftesbury, then Lord Ashley, a champion of hard-pressed humanity, was able to obtain an Act of Parliament which redeemed women from the degradation and slavery of their work as beasts of burden in the mines, and he was pushing forward his "Factories Bill," to release little children from the unchildlike length of small labour, which was required from them in mills. The Anti-corn Law League was stirring up the country through its length and breadth. The twin names of Cobden and Bright, men of the people, were becoming associated everywhere with eloquent persistent appeals for "Free Trade"—cheap bread to starving multitudes. Fears were entertained of the attitude of the Chartists. The true state of matters in Afghanistan began to break on the public. America was sore on what she considered the tampering with her flag in the interests of the abolition of the slave trade. Sir Robert Peel's income-tax, in order to replenish an ill-filled exchequer, was pending. Notwithstanding, the season was a gay one, though the gaiety might be a little forced in some quarters. Certainly an underlying motive was an anxious effort to promote trade by a succession of "dinners, concerts, and balls."

One famous ball is almost historical. It is still remembered as "the Queen's Plantagenet Ball." It was a very artistic and wonderfully perfect revival, for one night at Buckingham Palace, of the age of Chaucer and the

Court of Edward III. and Queen Philippa.

Nothing could exceed the enthusiasm with which the idea was taken up in the great world. All aristocratic London set themselves to study the pages of Chaucer and Froissart. At the same time, though the Court was to be that of Edward III and his Queen, no limit was put to the periods and nationalities to be selected by the guests. The ball was to be a masque, and perhaps it would have lost a little of its motley charm had it been confined entirely to one age in history, and to one country of the world. A comical petition had to be presented, that the masquers might remain covered before the Queen, lest the doffing of hats should cause the displacement of wigs.

The great attraction lay in the fact that not only did her Majesty represent one of her predecessors, an ancestress however remote, but that many of the guests were enabled to follow her example. They appeared—some in the very armour of their forefathers, others in costumes copied from family pictures, or in the dress of hereditary offices still held by the representatives of the ancient houses. For it was the sons and daughters of the great nobles of England that held high revelry in Buckingham Palace that night. There was an additional picturesqueness, as well as a curious vividness, lent to the pageant by the circumstance that in many cases the blood of the men and the women represented ran in the veins of the ball circulated beforehand. It was said that eighteen thousand persons were engaged in it. The Earl of Pembroke was to wear thirty-thousand pounds' worth of diamonds—the few diamonds in his hat alone would be of the value of eighteen thousand pounds. He was to borrow ten thousand pounds' worth of diamonds from Storr and Mortimer at one per cent, for the night. These great jewellers' stores were reported to be exhausted. Every other jeweller and diamond merchant was in the same condition. It almost seemed as if the Prince of Esterhazy must be outdone, even though the report of his losses from falling stones on the Coronation-day had risen to two thousand pounds. One lady boasted that she would not give less than a thousand pounds for her dress alone. Lord Chesterfield's costume was to cost eight hundred pounds. Plain dresses could not be got under two hundred; the very commonest could not be bought under fifty pounds. A new material had been invented for the occasion—gold and silver blonde to replace the heavy stuffs of gold and silver, since the nineteenth century did not always furnish strength or endurance to bear such a burden in a crowded ball-room on a May night. Truly one description of trade must have received a lively impetus.

Both The Times and the Morning Post give full accounts of the ball. "The leading feature…. was the assemblage and meeting of the Courts of Anne of Brittany (the Duchess of Cambridge) and Edward III. and Philippa (her Majesty and Prince Albert). A separate entrance to the Palace was set apart for the Court of Brittany, the Duchess of Cambridge assembling her Court in one of the lower rooms of the Palace, while the Queen and Prince Albert, surrounded by a numerous and brilliant circle, prepared to receive her Royal Highness in the Throne-room, which was altered so as to be made as much as possible to harmonize with the period. The throne was removed and another erected, copied from an authentic source of the time of Edward III. It was lined (as well as the whole alcove on which the throne was placed) with purple velvet, having worked upon it in gold the crown of England, the cross of St. George, and emblazoned shields with the arms of England and France. The State chairs were what might be called of Gothic design, and the throne was surmounted with Gothic tracery. At the back of the throne were emblazoned the royal arms of England in silver. Seated on this throne, her Majesty and Prince Albert awaited the arrival of the Court of Anne of Brittany."

Her Majesty's dress was entirely composed of the manufactures of Spitalfields. Over a skirt with a demi-train of ponceau velvet edged with fur there was a surcoat of brocade in blue and gold lined with miniver (only her Majesty wore this royal fur). From the stomacher a band of jewels on gold tissue descended. A mantle of gold and silver brocade lined with miniver was so fastened that the jewelled fastening traversed the jewelled band of the stomacher, and looked like a great jewelled cross on the breast. Her Majesty's hair, folded a la Clovis, was surmounted by a light crown of gold; she had but one diamond in her crown, so large that it shone like a star. It was valued at ten thousand pounds.

Prince Albert, as Edward III., wore a cloak of scarlet velvet, lined with ermine and trimmed with gold lace—showing oak-leaves and acorns, edged with two rows of large pearls. The band connecting the cloak was studded with jewels; so was the collar of the full robe, or under-cloak, of blue and gold brocade slashed with blue velvet. The hose were of scarlet silk, and the shoes were richly jewelled. The Prince had on a gold coronet set with precious stones.

The suite were in the costume of the time. The Hon. Mrs. Anson and Mrs. Brand, Women of the Bedchamber, had dresses bearing the quarterings of the old arms of England, with lions and fleurs-de-lys. The Maids of Honour had dresses and surcoats trimmed with gold and silver. The Duke of Buccleugh figured as one of the original Knights of the Garter. The Countess of Rosslyn appeared as the beautiful Countess of Salisbury.

About half-past ten, the heralds marshalled the procession from the lower suite of rooms up the grand white marble staircase, and by the Green Drawing-room to the Throne-room, all the State-rooms having been thrown open and brilliantly illuminated. The Duchess of Cambridge entered magnificently dressed as Anne of Brittany, led by the Duke of Beaufort, richly clad as Louis XII., and followed by her court. It included the Earl of Pembroke as the Comte d'Angouleme, with Princess Augusta of Cambridge as Princess Claude; Prince George of Cambridge as Gaston de Foix, with the Marchioness of Ailesbury as the Duchesse de Ferrare; Lord Cardigan as Bayard, with Lady Exeter as Jeanne de Conflans; Lord Claud Hamilton as the Comte de Chateaubriand, with Lady Lincoln as Ann de Villeroi…. The Duchess of Gloucester and the Duchess of Saxe-Weimar represented two French Chatelaines of the period. Each gentleman, leading a lady, passed before the Queen and Prince Albert, and did obeisance.

Among the most famous quadrilles which followed that of France were the German quadrille, led by the Duchess of Sutherland, and the Spanish quadrille, led by the Duchess of Buccleugh. There were also Italian, Scotch, Greek and Russian quadrilles, a Crusaders' quadrille led by the Marchioness of Londonderry, and a Waverley quadrille led by the Countess De la Warr.

One of the two finest effects of the evening was the passing of the quadrilles before the Queen, a ceremony which lasted for an hour. On leaving the Throne-room, the quadrille company went by the Picture Gallery to join the general company in the ballroom. The Queen and the Prince then headed their procession, and walked to the ballroom, taking their places on the haut pas under a canopy of amber satin, when each quadrille set was called in order, and danced in turn before the Queen, the Scotch set dancing reels. The court returned to the Throne-room for the Russian mazurkas. The Russian or Cossack Masquers were led by Baroness Brunnow in a dress of the time of Catherine II., a scarlet velvet tunic, full white silk drawers, and white satin boots embroidered with gold, a Cossack cap of scarlet velvet with heron's feathers. The appearance of the Throne-room with its royal company and brilliant picturesque groups, when the mazurkas were danced, is said to have been striking and beautiful.

The diamonds of the Queen, the Duchess of Cambridge, and the Marchioness of Londonderry outshone all others. Lady Londonderry's very gloves and shoes were resplendent with brilliants. The Duke and Duchess of Beaufort—the one as Louis XII. of France, the other as Isabelle of Valois, Queen of Spain, in the French and Spanish quadrilles, were magnificent figures. Among the beauties of the evening, and of Queen Victoria's earlier reign, were Lady Clementina Villiers as Vittoria Colonna; Lady Wilhelmina Stanhope as her ancestress, Anne Stanhope, Duchess of Somerset; Lady Frances and Lady Alexandrina Vane as Rowena and Queen Berengaria; and the Ladies Paget in the Greek quadrille led by the Duchess of Leinster. Another group of lovely sisters who took part in three different quadrilles, were the Countess of Chesterfield, Donna Florinda in the Spanish quadrille; the Honourable Mrs. Anson, Duchess of Lauenburg in the German quadrille; and Miss Forrester, Blanche de St. Pol in the French quadrille.

Of the ladies and gentlemen who came in the guise of ancient members of their families, or in the costumes of old hereditary offices, Lady De la Warr appeared as Isabella Lady De la Warr, daughter of the Lord High Treasurer of Charles I.; Lady Colville as the wife of Sir Robert Colville, Master of the Horse to James IV. of Scotland; Viscountess Pollington, daughter of the Earl of Orford, as Margaret Rolle, Baroness Clinton, in her own right, and Countess of Orford; and the Countess of Westmorland as Joan Beaufort, daughter of John of Gaunt and wife of Ralph Neville, first Earl of Westmoreland. Earl De la Warr wore the armour used by his ancestor in the battle of Cressy, and the Marquis of Exeter the armour of Sir John Cecil at the siege of Calais.

The Earl of Warwick went as Thomas Beauchamp, Earl of Warwick, Marshal-General of the army at the battle of Poietiers; the Duke of Norfolk as Thomas Howard, Earl-Marshal in the reign of Elizabeth; the Earl of Rosslyn as the Master of the Buckhounds; the Duke of St. Albans as Grand Falconer-hereditary offices.

Mr. Monckton Milnes, the poet, presented himself as Chaucer. The historical novelist of the day, Sir Edward Lytton Bulwer, contented himself with a comparatively humble anonymous dress, a doublet of dark velvet slashed with white satin. The Duke of Roxburgh as David Bruce, the captive King of Scotland, encountered no rival royal prisoner, though a ridiculous report had sprung up that a gentleman representing John of France was to form a prominent feature of the pageant, to walk in chains past the Queen. This stupid story not only wounded the sensitive vanity of the French, to whom the news travelled, it gave rise to a witty canard in the Morning Chronicle professing to give a debate on the affront, in the Chamber of Deputies.

The tent of Tippoo Saib was erected in the upper or Corinthian portico communicating with the Green Drawing-room, and used as a refreshment-room. At one o'clock, the Earl of Liverpool, the Lord High Steward, as an ancient seneschal, conducted the Queen to supper, which was served in the dining-room. The long double table was covered with shields, vases, and tankards of massive gold plate. Opposite the Queen, where she sat at the centre of the horseshoe or cross table, a superb buffet reached almost to the roof, covered with plate, interspersed with blossoming flowers. After supper her Majesty danced in a quadrille with Prince George of Cambridge, opposite the Duke of Beaufort and the Duchess of Buccleugh. The Queen left the ball-room at about a quarter to three o'clock, and dancing was continued for an hour afterwards. Thus ended the most unique and splendid fete of the reign. About a fortnight afterwards, the Queen and the Prince went in state to a ball given at Covent Garden Theatre, for the relief of the Spitalfields weavers. Society followed the Queen's example. There was another fancy ball at Stafford House, and a magnificent rout at Apsley House. Fanny Kemble was present at both, and retained a vivid remembrance of "the memorable appearance" of two of the belles of the evening at the last fete,

"Lady Douro and Mdlle. D'Este, [Footnote: Daughter of the Duke of Sussex, by his morganatic marriage with Lady Augusta Murray. Mdlle. D'Este became the wife of Lord Chancellor Truro.] who, coming into the room together, produced a most striking effect by their great beauty and their exquisite dress. They both wore magnificent dresses of white lace over white satin, ornamented with large cactus flowers, those of the blonde Marchioness being of the sea-shell rose colour, and the dark Mademoiselle D'Este's of deep scarlet, and in the bottom of each of those large veined blossoms lay, like a great drop of dew, a single splendid diamond. The women were noble samples of fair and dark beauty, and their whole appearance, coming in together attired with such elegance and becoming magnificent simplicity, produced an effect of surprise and admiration on the whole brilliant assembly." Of this year's Drawing-rooms we happen to have two characteristic reports. Baroness Bunsen attended one on April 8th, and wrote: "I was extremely struck with the splendour of the scene at the Drawing-room, and had an excellent place near enough to see everybody come up to the Queen [Footnote: "At a Levee or Drawing-room it is his (the Lord Chamberlain's) duty to stand next to the Queen and read out the names of each one approaching the royal presence…. Any peeress on presentation, as also daughters of dukes, marquises, and earls, have the privilege of being kissed by her Majesty; all other ladies make the lowest Court curtsey they can, and lifting the Queen's hand, which she offers, on the palm of their hand, it is gently kissed…. It seems unnecessary to say that of course the right-hand glove is removed before reaching the Presence Chamber."—"Old Court Customs and Modern Court Rule," by the Hon. Mrs. Armytage.] and pass off again. I was very much entertained, and admired a number of beautiful persons. But nobody did I admire more than Mrs. Norton, whom I had never seen before, and Lady Canning's face always grows upon me." Fanny Kemble also attended a Drawing-room and described it after her fashion. "You ask about my going to the Drawing-room, which happened thus. The Duke of Rutland dined some little time ago at the Palace, and speaking of the late party at Belvoir, mentioned me, when the Queen asked why I didn't have myself presented? The Duke called next day, at my house, but we did not see him, and he being obliged to go out of town, left a message for me with Lady Londonderry to the effect that her Majesty's interest about me (curiosity would have been the more exact word I suspect) rendered it imperative that I should go to the Drawing-room; and indeed Lady Londonderry's authoritative 'Of course you'll go,' given in her most gracious manner, left me no doubt whatever as to my duty in that respect…."

"You ask me how I managed about diamonds to go to Court in?" she wrote afterwards in reply to a friend's question. "I used a set of the value of seven hundred pounds, which I also wore at the fete at Apsley House; they were only a necklace and earrings, which I wore … stitched on scarlet velvet and as drops in the middle of scarlet velvet bows in my hair, and my dress being white satin and point lace, trimmed with white Roman pearls, it all looked nice enough.

"I suffered agonies of nervousness, and I rather think did all sorts of awkward things; but so I dare say do other people in the same predicament, and I did not trouble my head much about my various mis-performances. One thing, however, I can tell you, if her Majesty has seen me, I have not seen her, and should be quite excusable in cutting her wherever I met her. 'A cat may look at a king,' it is said; but how about looking at the Queen? In great uncertainty of mind on this point I did not look at my sovereign lady. I kissed a soft white hand which I believe was hers; I saw a pair of very handsome legs in very fine silk stockings, which I am convinced were not hers, but am inclined to attribute to Prince Albert; and this is all I perceived of the whole Royal family of England, for I made a sweeping curtsey to the 'good remainders of the Court' and came away, with no impression but that of a crowded mass of full-dressed confusion, and neither know how I got in or out of it."

We might furnish a third sketch of a Drawing-room from one of the letters of Bishop, then Archdeacon, Wilberforce, who was often at Court about this time. In the early part of 1842 he paid a visit to Windsor, of which he has left a graphic account. "All went on most pleasantly at the Castle. My reception and treatment throughout was exceedingly kind. The Queen and the Prince were both at church, as was also Lord Melbourne, who paid his first visit at the same time. The Queen's meeting with him was very interesting. The exceeding pleasure which lighted up her countenance was quite touching. His behaviour to her was perfect—the fullest attentive deference of the subject with a subdued air of 'your father's friend' that was quite fascinating. It was curious to see (for I contemplated myself at the moment objectively—and free from the consciousness of subjectivity), sitting round the Queen's table, (1) the Queen, (2) the Prince, (3) Lord Melbourne, (4) Archdeacon, (5) Lady F. Howard, (6) Baron Stockmar, (7) Duchess of Kent, (8) Lady Sandwich, in the evening, discussing Coleridge, German literature, &c., with 2 and 3, and a little with 4 and 6, who is a very superior man evidently. The remarks of 3 were highly characteristic, his complaints of 'hard words,' &c., and 2 showed a great deal of interest and taste in German and English literature, and a good deal of acquaintance with both. I had orders to sit by the Duchess of Kent at dinner, just opposite to 1 and 2, 3 sitting at I's right, and the conversation, especially after dinner, was much more general across the table on etymology," &c. &c.

CHAPTER XIII. FRESH ATTEMPTS AGAINST THE QUEEN'S LIFE.—MENDELSSOHN.—DEATH OF THE DUC D'ORLEANS.

On the 30th of May a renewed attempt to assassinate the Queen, almost identical in the circumstances and the motive—or no motive, save morbid vanity—with the affair of Oxford, awoke the same disgust and condemnation. This was a double attack, for on the previous day, Sunday, at two o'clock, as the Queen and the Prince were driving home from the Chapel Royal, St. James's, in passing along the Mall, near Stafford House, amidst a crowd of bowing, cheering spectators, the Prince saw a man step out and present a pistol at him. He heard the trigger snap, but the pistol missed fire. The Queen, who had been bowing to the people on the opposite side, neither saw nor heard anything. On reaching the Palace the Prince questioned the footmen in attendance, but neither had they noticed anything, and he could judge for himself that no commotion, such as would have followed an arrest, had taken place. He was tempted to doubt the evidence of his senses, though he thought it necessary to make a private statement before the Inspector of Police. Confirmation came in the story of a stuttering boy named Pearse. He had witnessed the scene, and after a little delay arrived of his own accord at the Palace, to report what had happened. Everybody concerned was now convinced of the threatened danger, but it was judged best to keep it secret. The Prince, writing afterwards to his father, mentions in his simple straightforward fashion that they were both naturally much agitated, and that the Queen was very nervous and unwell; as who would not be with the sword of Damocles quivering ready to fall on the doomed head? Her Majesty's doctor wished that she should go out, and the wish coincided with the quiet courage and good sense of the Royal couple. To have kept within doors might have been to shut themselves up for months, and the Queen said later, "she never could have existed under the uncertainty of a concealed attack. She would much rather run the immediate risk at any time than have the presentiment of danger constantly hovering over her." But the brave, generous woman, a true queen in facing the dastardly foe, was careful to save others from unnecessary exposure. The Annual Register of the year mentions that she did not permit her female attendants to accompany her according to her usual practice, on that dangerous drive. Lady Bloomfield, who as Miss Liddell was one of the Maids of Honour in waiting, amply confirms the statement. No whisper of what was expected to occur had reached the ladies of the Household. They waited at home all the afternoon counting on being summoned to drive with the Queen. Contrary to her ordinary habit and to her wonted consideration for them, they were neither sent for to accompany her, nor apprised in time that they were not wanted, so that they might have disposed of their leisure elsewhere. The Queen went out alone with Prince Albert. When she returned and everybody knew what she had encountered, she said to Miss Liddell: "I dare say, Georgy, you were surprised at not driving with me this afternoon, but the fact was that as we returned from church yesterday, a man presented a pistol at the carriage window, which flashed in the pan; we were so taken by surprise that we had not time to escape, so I knew what was hanging over me, and was determined to expose no life but my own." The young Maid of Honour, in speaking warmly of the Queen's courage and unselfishness, shrewdly reminds her readers that had three ladies driven rapidly by instead of one, the would-be assassin might have been bewildered and uncertain in his aim. The Queen and the Prince had driven in the direction of Hampstead in "superb weather," with "hosts of people on foot" around them—a strange contrast in their ease and tranquillity to the beating hearts and watchful eyes in the Royal carriage. There had been no misadventure and nothing suspicious observed, though every turn, almost every face was scanned, till on the way home, between the Green Park and the garden wall, at the same spot, though on the opposite side from where Oxford had stood two years before, a shot was fired about five paces off. The Prince immediately recognised the man who had aimed at him the day before, "a little swarthy ill-looking rascal," who had been already seized, though too late to stop the shot, by a policeman close at hand.

When the worst was over without harm done, "We felt as if a load had been taken off our hearts," wrote the Prince, "and we thanked the Almighty for having preserved us a second time from so great a danger." The Prince added, "Uncle Mensdorff [Footnote: The Duchess of Kent's eldest sister married a private gentleman, originally a French emigre, afterwards a distinguished officer in the Austrian service. His sons were Prince Albert's early companions and intimate friends.] and mamma were driving close behind us. The Duchess Bernhard of Weimar was on horseback—not sixty paces from us."

It was said that when the Queen arrived at the Palace and met the Duchess of Kent, whom Count Mensdorff had conducted thither, the poor mother was deeply affected and fell upon her daughter's neck with a flood of tears, "while the Queen endeavoured to reassure her with cheerful words and affectionate caresses." Indeed the Queen was greatly relieved, and in the reaction she recovered her spirits. She wrote to the King of the Belgians the day afterwards, "I was really not at all frightened, and feel very proud at dear Uncle Mensdorff calling me 'very courageous,' which I shall ever remember with peculiar pride, coming from so distinguished an officer as he is." We may mention that the general impression made on the public by the Queen's bearing under these treacherous attacks was that of her utter fearlessness and strength of nerve; a corresponding idea, which we think quite mistaken, was that the Prince showed himself the more nervous of the two.

A great crowd assembled to cheer the Queen when she drove out on the following day. "One long shout of hurrahs," with waving of hats and handkerchiefs, greeted her. She bowed and smiled and appeared calm and collected, though somewhat flushed; but when she came back from what is described as like a triumphal progress, it was observed that, in spite of her gratification, she looked pale and not so well as she had done on the day preceding the attack.

The bravest heart in a woman's breast could not surmount unmoved such an ordeal; she was at the Italian Opera the same evening, however, and heard the national anthem interrupted at every line by bursts of cheering.

In this case, as in the other, the offender was a mere lad, little over twenty, named John Francis. He was the son of a stage-carpenter, and had himself been a young carpenter who had led an irregular life, and been guilty of dishonesty. He behaved at first with much coolness and indifference, jeering at the magistrates. Francis was tried in the month of June for high treason, and sentenced to death, when his bluster ceased, and he fell back in a fainting fit in the arms of the turnkey.

The Queen was exceedingly anxious that the sentence should not be executed, though "fully conscious of the encouragement to similar attempts—which might follow from such leniency," and the sentence of death was commuted to banishment for life.

On the very day after the commutation of the sentence had been announced, Sunday, the 3rd of July, the Queen was again fired at as she sat by the side of her uncle, King Leopold, on her way to the Chapel Royal, St. James's. The pistol missed fire, and the man who presented it, a hunchback, was seized by a boy of sixteen called Dasset. So ridiculous did the group seem, that the very policemen pushed away both captor and captive as actors in a bad practical joke. Then the boy Dasset, who retained the pistol, was in danger of being taken up as the real culprit, trying to throw the blame upon another. At last several witnesses proved the true state of the case. The pistol was discovered to contain only powder, paper, and some bits of a tobacco-pipe rammed together. On examination it was found that the hunchback, another miserable lad named Bean, was a chemist's assistant, who had written a letter to his father declaring that he "would never see him again, as he intended doing something which was not dishonest, but desperate."

The Queen was not aware of Bean's attempt till she came back from St. James's, "when she betrayed no alarm, but said she had expected a repetition of the attempts on her life, so long as the law remained unaltered by which they could be dealt with only as acts of high treason."

"Sir Robert Peel hurried up from Cambridge on hearing what had occurred, to consult with the Prince as to the steps to be taken. During this interview her Majesty entered the room, when the Minister, in public so cold and self-controlled, in reality so full of genuine feeling, out of his very manliness, was unable to control his emotion, and burst into tears;" [Footnote: "Life of the Prince Consort"] an honourable sequel to the difficulties and misunderstanding which had heralded the Premier's entrance on office.

It was, indeed, high time that a suitable provision should be made to meet what seemed likely to be a new and base abuse of Royal clemency.

In the meantime, Prince Albert's fair and fearless treatment of the whole matter was very remarkable. He wrote that he could imagine the circumstance of Bean's attempt being made the day after Francis received his pardon would excite much surprise in Germany. But the Prince was satisfied that Bean's letter making known his intention had been written days before. Prince Albert was convinced that, as the law then stood, Francis's execution, notwithstanding the verdict of the jury, would have been nothing less than a judicial murder, as it was essential that the act should be committed with intent to kill or wound, and in Francis's case this, to all appearance, was not the fact; at least it was open to grave doubt. There was no proof that Francis's pistol was loaded. "In this calm and wise way," observes Mr. Justin M'Carthy, "did the husband of the Queen, who had always shared with her whatever of danger there might be in the attempts, argue as to the manner in which they ought to be dealt with." The historian adds, "The ambition which moved most or all the miscreants who thus disturbed the Queen and the country, was that of the mountebank rather than the assassin." It merited contempt no less than severity. A bill was brought forward on the 12th of July, and passed on the 16th, making such attacks punishable, as high misdemeanours, by transportation for seven years, or imprisonment with or without hard labour for a term not exceeding three years; the culprit to be publicly or privately whipped as often and in such manner and form as the court shall direct, not exceeding thrice. Bean was tried by this law on the 25th of August, and sentenced to eighteen months' imprisonment.

One of the attractions of the season was the reappearance of Rachel, ravishing all hearts by her acting of Camille in Les Horaces, and winning ovations of every kind up to roses dropped from the Queen's bouquet.

Mendelssohn was also in London, and went to Buckingham Palace. He has left a charming account of one of his visits in a letter to his mother. "I must tell you," he writes, "all the details of my last visit to Buckingham Palace…. It is, as G. says, the one really pleasant and thoroughly comfortable English house where one feels a son aise. Of course I do know a few others, but yet on the whole I agree with him. Joking apart, Prince Albert had asked me to go to him on Saturday at two o'clock, so that I might try his organ before I left England; I found him alone, and as we were talking away, the Queen came in, also alone, in a simple morning-dress. She said she was obliged to leave for Claremont in an hour, and then, suddenly interrupting herself, exclaimed, 'But, goodness, what a confusion!' for the wind had littered the whole room, and even the pedals of the organ (which, by the way, made a very pretty picture in the room), with leaves of music from a large portfolio that lay open. As she spoke she knelt down, and began picking up the music; Prince Albert helped, and I too was not idle. Then Prince Albert proceeded to explain the stops to me, and she said that she would meanwhile put things straight.

"I begged that the Prince would first play me something, so that, as I said, I might boast about it in Germany. He played a chorale by heart, with the pedals, so charmingly, and clearly, and correctly, that it would have done credit to any professional; and the Queen, having finished her work, came and sat by him and listened, and looked pleased. Then it was my turn, and I began my chorus from St. Paul, "How lovely are the messengers." Before I got to the end of the first verse they both joined in the chorus, and all the time Prince Albert managed the stops for me so cleverly—first a flute, at the forte the great organ, at the D major part the whole register, then he made a lovely diminuendo with the stops, and so on to the end of the piece, and all by heart—that I was really quite enchanted. Then the young Prince of Gotha came in, and there was more chatting; and the Queen asked if I had written any new songs, and said she was very fond of singing my published ones. 'You should sing one to him,' said Prince Albert, and after a little begging she said she would try the 'Fruhlingslied' in B flat. 'If it is still here,' she added, 'for all my music is packed up for Claremont.' Prince Albert went to look for it, but came back saying it was already packed. 'But one might, perhaps, unpack it,' said I. 'We must send for Lady ——,' she said (I did not catch the name). So the bell was rung, and the servants were sent after it, but without success; and at last the Queen went herself, and while she was gone, Prince Albert said to me, 'She begs you will accept this present as a remembrance,' and gave me a little case with a beautiful ring, on which is engraved 'V. R., 1842.'

"Then the Queen came back and said, ' Lady —— is gone, and has taken all my things with her. It really is most annoying.' You can't think how that amused me. I then begged that I might not be made to suffer for the accident, and hoped she would sing another song. After some consultation with her husband, he said, 'She will sing you something of Gluck's.' Meantime, the Princess of Gotha had come in, and we five proceeded through various corridors and rooms to the Queen's sitting-room. The Duchess of Kent came in too, and while they were all talking, I rummaged about amongst the music, and soon discovered my first set of songs; so, of course, I begged her rather to sing one of those than the Gluck, to which she very kindly consented; and which did she choose? 'Schoner und schoner schmuck sich,' sang it quite charmingly, in strict time and tune, and with very good execution. Only in the line 'Der Prosa Lasten und muh,' where it goes down to D, and then comes up again by semi-tones, she sang D sharp each time, and as I gave her the note the two first times, the last time she sang D, where it ought to have been D sharp. But with the exception of this little mistake it was really charming, and the last long G I have never heard better, or purer, or more natural, from any amateur. Then I was obliged to confess that Fanny had written the song (which I found very hard; but pride must have a fall), and to beg her to sing one of my own also. 'If I would give her plenty of help she would gladly try,' she said, and then she sang 'Pilgerspruch,' 'Lass dich nur,' really quite faultlessly, and with charming feeling and expression. I thought to myself, one must not pay too many compliments on such an occasion, so I merely thanked her a great many times, upon which she said. 'Oh, if only I had not been so frightened! generally I have such long breath.' Then I praised her heartily, and with the best conscience in the world; for just that part with the long C at the close, she had done so well, taking it and the three notes next to it all in the same breath, as one seldom hears it done, and therefore it amused me doubly that she herself should have begun about it.'

"After this Prince Albert sang the 'Arndle-lied,' 'Es ist ein schnitter,' and then he said I must play him something before I went, and gave me as themes the chorale which he had played on the organ, and the song he had just sung. If everything had gone as usual I ought to have improvised dreadfully badly, for it is almost always so with me when I want it to go well, and then I should have gone away vexed with the whole morning. But just as if I were to keep nothing but the pleasantest, most charming recollection of it, I never improvised better; I was in the best mood for it, and played a long time, and enjoyed it myself so much that, besides the two themes, I brought in the songs that the Queen had sung quite naturally; and it all went off so easily, that I would gladly not have stopped; and they followed me with so much intelligence and attention, that I felt more at my ease than I ever did in improvising to an audience. The Queen said several times she hoped I would soon come to England again, and pay them a visit, and then I took leave; and down below I saw the beautiful carriages waiting, with their scarlet outriders, and in a quarter of an hour the flag was lowered, and the Court Circular announced, 'Her Majesty left the palace at twenty minutes past three.'"

The Queen and the Prince were enjoying the company of Prince Albert's brother, Prince Ernest, the hereditary Prince of Saxe-Coburg Gotha, and his newly-wedded wife, who were both with the Court during its short stay at Claremont. There the news reached her Majesty of the sad and sudden death of the Duc d'Orleans, the eldest son of Louis Philippe, and the favourite brother of the Queen of the Belgians. The Duc d'Orleans had been with the King and Queen of France at Neuilly, from which he was returning in order to join the Duchesse d'Orleans at Plombieres, when the horses in his carriage started off near the Porte Maillot. Fearing that he should be overturned the Prince rashly leaped out, when his spurs and his sword caught in his cloak and helped to throw him to the ground with great violence. The result was concussion of the brain, from which he died within three hours, never recovering consciousness. The Duc d'Orleans was a young man of great promise, and his death was not only a source of deep distress to all connected with him, it was in the end, so far as men can judge, fatal to the political interests of his family. Many of us can recollect still something of the agonised prayer of the poor mother by the dying Prince, "My God, take me, but save my child!" and the cry of the bereaved father, the first time he addressed the Chamber afterwards, when he broke down and could utter nothing save the passionate lamentation of David of old, "My son, my son!" The Queen and Prince Albert were doubly and trebly allied to the Orleans family by the marriages of the Queen of the Belgians, the Duc de Nemours, and later of Princess Clementine, to three members of the Coburg family—the uncle and two of the cousins of Queen Victoria and Prince Albert. They felt much for the unhappy family in their terrible bereavement. The Queen grieved especially for her particular friend, Queen Louise, and for the young widow, a cultured, intellectual German Princess, with her health already broken. "My poor dearest Louise, how my heart bleeds for her. I know how she loved poor Chartres, [Footnote: The Duc de Chartres was the earlier title of the Duc d'Orleans, which he bore when his father was still Duc d'Orleans, before he became King of France as "Louis Philippe." Apparently the son continued "Chartres" to his intimate friends.] and deservedly, for he was so noble and good. All our anxiety now is to hear how poor dear frail Helene (the Duchesse d'Orleans) has borne this too dreadful loss. She loved him so, and he was so devoted to her."

During the night of the 27th of July this year, London was visited by the most violent thunderstorm which had been experienced for many summers. It lasted for several hours. The fine spire of the church of St. Martin-in-the-Fields was struck by the lightning and practically destroyed.

On the 9th of August the Queen prorogued Parliament, when the Prince and Princess of Saxe-Coburg Gotha witnessed the interesting ceremony, occupying chairs near the chair of State, kept vacant for the Prince of Wales to the right of the Queen, while Prince Albert sat in the chair to her left.

The Prince of Wales was still at a considerable distance from the occupancy of that chair. Even as we see him here, in a copy of Mrs. Thornycroft's graceful statue, he is in the character of a shepherd lad, like David of old, and not in that of the heir-apparent to the throne.

At the close of this season, the Queen's old friend and servant Baroness Lehzen withdrew from Court service and retired to Germany to end her days in her native country, in the company of a sister. Lady Bloomfield saw the Baroness Lehzen in her home at Buckeburg, within a day's journey of Hanover, a few years subsequently. "She resided with her sister in a comfortable small house, where she seemed perfectly contented and happy. She was as much devoted to the Queen as ever, and her rooms were filled with pictures and prints of her Majesty." The Prince and Princess of Buckeburg were very kind to her, and she had as much society as she liked or desired. What a change from the great monarchy of England to the tiny princedom of Buckeburg! But the Baroness was a German, and could reconcile the two ideas in her mind. She was also an ageing woman, to whom the rest and freedom of domestic life were sweet and the return to the customs of her youth not unacceptable..

CHAPTER XIV. THE QUEEN'S FIRST VISIT TO SCOTLAND.

The Queen had never been abroad. It was still well-nigh an unconstitutional step for a sovereign of England to claim the privilege, enjoyed by so many English subjects, of a foreign tour, let it be ever so short. However, this year the proposal of a visit to her uncle King Leopold at Brussels, where several members of Louis Philippe's family were to have met her, was made. But the lamentable death of the Duc d'Orleans put an end for the present to the project. Neither were affairs at home in so flourishing a condition as to encourage any great departure from ordinary rule and precedent. The manufacturing districts were in a most unsettled state. The perpetually recurring riots—so long as the corn laws stood in the way of a sure and abundant supply of grain, which meant cheap bread, and as the people believed prosperous trade—had broken out afresh in

Lancashire, Yorkshire, and the Midland counties. The aspect of Manchester alone became so threatening, that all the soldiers who could be spared from London, including a regiment of the Guards, were dispatched to the North of England. Happily, the disturbances were quelled, though not without bloodshed; and it was resolved, notwithstanding the fact that similar rioting had taken place in Lanarkshire, the Queen and the Prince should pay their first visit to Scotland, a country within her dominions, but different in physical features and history from the land in which she had been born and bred. How much the royal visitors were gratified, has been amply shown; but to realise what the Queen's visit was to the Scotch people, it is necessary to go back to the nation's loyalty and to the circumstance that since the exile of the Stewarts, nay, since the days when James VI. left his ancient capital to assume the crown of England, the monarchs had shown their faces rarely in the north; while in the cases of Charles I. and Charles II. there had been so much of self-interest and compulsion in their presence as to rob it of its grace. George IV. had come and gone certainly, but though he was duly welcomed, it was difficult even for his most zealous supporters to be enthusiastic about him. At the proposed arrival of the young Queen, who was well worthy of the most ardent devotion, the "leal" heart of Scotland swelled with glad anticipation. The country had its troubles like the rest of the world. In addition to vexed questions between perplexed mill-masters, shipbuilders, and mine-owners on the one side, and on the other, penniless mechanics and pitmen, the crisis which more than all others rent the Covenanting church, so dear to the descendants of the old Whigs, was close at hand. All was forgotten for the hour in the strange resemblance which exists between one strain of the character of the staid Scotch, and a vein in the nature of the impulsive French, two nations that used to be trusty allies. There is, indeed, a bond to unite "Caledonia stern and wild" and "the sunny land of France;" a weft of passionate poetry crosses alike the woof of the simple cunning of the Highlander and the slow canniness of the Lowlander. Scotland as well as France has been The chosen home of chivalry, the garden of romance.

The news that the Queen and the Prince were coming, travelled with the rapidity of the ancient clansmen's fiery cross from the wan waters of the south to the stormy friths of the north, and kindled into a blaze the latent fire in every soul. The fields, the pastures, the quarries, the shootings, were all very well, and the Kirk was still better; but the Queen was at the door—the Queen who represented alike Queen Mary, King Jamie—all the King Jamies,—King William, the good friend of religious liberty, and of "Cardinal Carstairs," "Bonnie Prince Charlie," at once pitied and condemned, and King George, "honest man!" not unfair or unmerciful, whatever his minister Walpole might advise. The Queen was, above all, herself the flower of her race. Who would not hurry to meet and greet her, to give her the warmest reception?

All the traditions, all the instincts of the people thrilled and impelled them. Multitudes formed of broadly and picturesquely contrasting elements flocked to Edinburgh to hail her Majesty's landing. Manifold preparations were made for her entrance into the capital, the one regret being that she was not to dwell in her own beautiful palace of Holyrood—unoccupied by royal tenants since the last French exiles, Charles X., the Dauphin and the Dauphiness (the Daughter of the Temple), and the Duchesse de Berri, with her two children, the young Duc de Bourdeaux and his sister, found a brief refuge within its walls. The Queen, like her uncle George IV., was to be in the first place the guest of the Duke of Buccleugh at Dalkeith Palace.

Her Majesty and the Prince left Windsor at five o'clock on the morning of the 29th August, 1842, and after journeying to London and Woolwich, embarked on board the Royal George yacht under a heavy shower of rain. The yacht was attended by a squadron of nine vessels, the Trinity House steamer, and a packet, besides being followed for some distance, in spite of the unpropitious weather, by innumerable little pleasure-boats. The squadron was both for safety and convenience; certain vessels conveyed the ladies and gentlemen of the suite, and one took the two dogs, the chosen companions of their master and mistress, "Eos," and another four-footed favourite, "Cairnach." [Footnote: Sir Edwin Landseer painted these two dogs for the Queen, "Eos" with the Princess Royal in 1841, "Eos" alone, a sketch for a large picture in 1842, "Cairnach" in 1841. In 1838, the great animal painter had painted for her Majesty "little Dash" along with two other dogs, and "Lorey," a pet parrot belonging to the Duchess of Kent.]

The voyage was both tedious and trying, the sea was rough, and the royal voyagers were ill. On the morning of the 31st they were only coasting Northumberland, when the Queen saw the Fern Islands, where Grace Darling's lighthouse and her heroic story were still things of yesterday. Before her Majesty's return to England, she heard what she had not known at the time, that the brave girl had died within twenty-four hours of the royal yacht's passing the lighthouse station. The Queens first remark on the Scotch coast, though it happened to be the comparatively tame east coast, was "very beautiful—so dark, rocky, bold, and wild—totally unlike our coast." All her observations had the naive freshness and sympathetic willingness to be pleased, of an unexhausted, unvitiated mind. She noticed everything, and was gratified by details which would have signified nothing to a sated, jaded nature, or, if they had made an impression, would only have called forth more weariness, varied by contemptuous criticism. The longer light in the north, that dear summer gloaming which is neither night nor day, but borrows something from both—from the silence and solemn mystery of the latter, and from the clear serenity of the former—a leisure time which is associated from youth to age with a host of happy, tender associations; the pipes playing in one of the fishing-boats; the reel danced on board an attendant steamer; the bonfires on the coast—nothing was too trivial to escape the interested watcher, or was lost upon her, Queen though she was.

The anchor of the royal yacht was let down in Leith Roads at midnight. At seven o'clock on the morning of the 1st of September the Queen saw before her the good town of Leith, where Queen Mary had landed from France; and in the background, Edinburgh half veiled in an autumn fog, lying at the foot of its semicircle of hills—the grim couchant lion of Arthur's seat; Salisbury Crags, grey and beetling; the heatherly slopes of the Pentlands in the distance. A little after eight her Majesty landed at Granton Pier, amidst the cheers of her Scotch subjects. The Duke of Buccleugh, whose public-spirited work the pier was, stood there to receive his sovereign, when she put her foot on shore, as he had already been on board the yacht to greet her arrival in what was once called Scotland Water.

When Queen Mary landed at Leith, it took her more than one day, if we remember rightly, to make a slow progress to her capital. Things are done faster in the nineteenth century; a few minutes by railway now separate Granton from Edinburgh. But the Edinburgh and Granton railway did not exist in 1842. Her Majesty and the Prince drove in a barouche, followed by the ladies and gentlemen of her suite in other carriages, and escorted by the Duke of Buccleugh and several gentlemen on horseback, to the ancient city of her Stewart ancestry. An unfortunate misconception robbed the occasion of the dignified ceremony and the exhibition of fervent personal attachment which had awaited it. All the previous day the authorities and the crowd had been on the look-out for the great event, and in the delay had passed the time quite happily in watching the preparations, and the decorations and devices for the coming illumination. The Lord Provost, Sir James Forrest, had taken the precaution to send a carriageful of bailies over night, or by dawn of day, to catch the first sign of the Queen's landing, and drive with it, post-haste, to the chief magistrate, who with his fellows was to be stationed at the barrier erected in the High Street, to present the keys of the city to the sovereign claiming admittance. But whether the bailies blundered over their instructions or slept at their post, or lost their way, no warning of the Queen's approach reached the Provost and his satellites in time. They were calm in the confident persuasion that the Queen would not arrive till noon—at the soonest—a persuasion which was based on the conviction that the event was too great to be hurried over, and which left out of sight the consideration of the disagreeable sea-voyage, and the natural desire to be on solid ground, and at rest, on the part of the travel-tossed voyagers. "We both felt dreadfully tired and giddy," her Majesty wrote of herself and the Prince when they reached Dalkeith.

The result was that these gentlemen in office were seated at breakfast as usual, or were engaged in getting rid betimes of some of the numerous engagements which beset busy men on a busy day, when the cry arose that the Queen was there, in the midst of them, with nobody to meet her, no silver keys on a velvet cushion to be respectfully offered and graciously returned. The ancient institution of the Royal Archer Guard, one of the chief glories of the situation, was only straggling by twos and threes to its muster-ground. The Celtic Society was in a similar plight, headed in default of the Duke of Argyle by the Marquis of Lorn, a golden-haired stripling in a satin kilt of the Campbell set, who looked all the slighter and more youthful, with more dainty calves in his silken hose, because of the big burly chieftains—Islay conspicuous among them—whom he led. The stands, the windows, the very grand old streets were half empty as yet, in the raw September morning. No King or Queen had visited Edinburgh for a score of years, and when at last the Queen of Hearts did come, the citizens were found napping—a sore mortification with which her Majesty deals very gently in her Journal, scarcely alluding to the inopportune accident. In truth only a moiety of early risers—those mostly country folks who had trooped into the town—restless youthful spirits, ardent holiday-makers, who could not find any holiday too long—or gallant devoted innocent Queen-worshippers, sleepless with the thought that the Queen was so near and might already be stirring—were abroad and intent on what was passing, looking at the vacant places, speculating on how they would be choke full in a couple of hours, amusing themselves easily with the idlest trifles, by way of whetting the appetite for the great sight, which they were to remember all their lives. These spectators were startled by seeing a gentleman, said afterwards to have been Lord John Scott, the popular but somewhat madcap brother of the Duke of. Buccleugh, gallop up the street bareheaded, waving his hat above his head and shouting "The Queen, the Queen!" The listeners looked at each other and laughed. How well the hoax was gone about; but who would presume to play such a trick, it was too much even from Lord John—did not somebody say it was Lord John? On the line of route too! What were the police thinking of? Then swift corroboration followed, in the train of carriages rolling up, the first attended by a few of the Royal Archers, in their picturesque costumes of green and gold, each with his bow in one hand and his arrows in his belt. But the calmest had his equanimity disturbed by the consciousness that the main body of his comrades, all noblemen and gentlemen of Scotland, were running pell-mell behind, in a desperate effort to form into rank and march in due order. One eager confused glance, one long-drawn breath, one vehement heart-throb for her who was the centre of all, and the disordered pageant had swept past.

The Queen wrote in her Journal that the Duke of Roxburgh and Lord Elcho were the members of the Body Guard on her side of the carriage, and that Lord Elcho, whom she did not know at the time, pointed out the various monuments and places of interest.

Both the Queen and Prince Albert were much struck by the beautiful town, the massive stone houses, the steep High Street, the tall buildings, "and the Castle on the grand rock in the middle of the town, and Arthur's Seat in the background, a splendid spectacle."

On the country road to Dalkeith, the cottages built of stone, the walls ("dry stane dykes") instead of fences, the old women in their close caps ("sou-backed mutches"), the girls and children of the working classes, with flowing hair, often red, and bare feet, all the little individual traits, which impress us on our first visit to a foreign country, were carefully noted down. The Duke and Duchess of Buccleugh proved a noble host and hostess, but they could provide no such cicerone for the Queen as was furnished for George IV., when Sir Walter Scott showed him Edinburgh, and for the Governor of the Netherlands, when Rubens introduced him to Antwerp. Neither did any peer or chief appear on the occasion of the Queen's visit, with such a telling accompaniment as that ruinous "tail" of wild Highlanders, attached to Glengarry, when he waited on the King. On the "rest day," which succeeded that of her Majesty's arrival at Dalkeith, she had three fresh experiences, chronicled in her Journal. She tasted oatmeal porridge, which she thought "very good," and "Finnan haddies," of which she gave no opinion, and she was stopped and turned back in her drive by "a Scotch mist." Indeed, not all the Queen's proverbial good luck in the matter could now or at any future time greatly modify the bane of open-air enjoyment amidst the beautiful scenery of Scotland—the exceedingly variable, even inclement, weather which may be met with at all seasons.

Saturday, the 3rd of September, afforded abundant compensation for all that had been missed on the Queen's entrance into Edinburgh. She paid an announced and formal visit from Dalkeith Palace to the town, in order to accomplish the balked ceremony of the presentation of the keys and to see the Castle on its historic rock. By Holyrood Chapel and Holyrood Palace, which the Queen called "a royal-looking old place," but where she did not tarry now, because there was fever in the neighbourhood; up the old world Cannon-gate, and the High Street, where the Setouns and the Leslies had their brawl, and the Jacobites went with white cockades in their cocked hats and white roses at their breasts, braving the fire of the Castle, to pay homage to Prince Charlie; on to the barrier. Edinburgh was wide awake this time. The streets were densely crowded, every window, high and low, in the tall grey houses framed a galaxy of faces, stands had been erected, and platforms thrown out wherever stand and platform could find space. The very "leads" of the public buildings bore their burden of sightseers. The Lord Provost and his bailies stood ready, and the Queen came wearing the royal Stewart tartan, "A' fine colours but nane o' them blue," to show that she was akin to the surroundings. She heard and replied to the speech made to her by the representative of the old burghers, and gave him back the token of his rule. She reached the Castle, after having passed the houses of Knox and the Earl of Moray. She saw the Scotch regalia, and heard anew how it had once been saved by a minister's brave wife, who carried it hidden in a bundle of yarn in her lap, out of the northern castle, which was in the hands of the enemy; and how it had been concealed again—only too well, forgotten in the course of a generation or two, and actually lost sight of for a hundred years. She entered the room, "such a very, very small room," she wrote, in her wonder at the rude and scanty accommodation of those days, in which James VI. was born. No doubt "Mons Meg," the old Flemish cannon and grim darling of the fortress, was presented to her. But what seems to have moved her most was the magnificent view, which included the rich Lothians and the silver shield of the Frith, and stretched, but only, when the weather was fine enough, in the direction of Stirlingshire, to the round-backed Ochils and the blue giants, the Grampians, while at her feet lay the green gardens of Princes Street and the handsome street itself—once the Nor' Loch and the Burgh Muir—Allan Ramsay's house and Heriot's Hospital, or "Wark," the princely gift of the worthy jeweller to his native town.

A little incident, the motive of which was unknown to her Majesty, occurred on her drive back to

Dalkeith. An enthusiastic active young fellow, who had seen the presentation of the keys, hurried out the length of a mile on the country road to Dalkeith, and choosing a solitary point, stationed himself on the summit of a wall, where he was the only watcher, and awaited the return of the carriages. The special phaeton drove up with the young couple, talking and laughing together in the freedom of their privacy. The single spectator took off his hat at the risk of losing his precarious footing, and in respectful silence, bowed, or "louted low"—another difficult proceeding under the circumstances. Prince Albert, who was sitting with his arms crossed on his breast, treated the demonstration as not meant for him. The smiling Queen inclined her head, and the eager lad had what he sought, a mark of her recognition given to him alone. To the day of his death no more loyal heart beat for his Queen throughout her wide dominions.

The Queen drove to Leith on another day, and she and the Prince were still more charmed with the view, which he called "fairylike." After the fashion of most strangers, the travellers had their attention attracted by the Newhaven fish-wives, who offered a curious contrast to the rest of the population. Their Flemish origin announced itself, for her Majesty pronounced them "very clean and very Dutch-looking with their white caps and bright-coloured petticoats." It was about this time that a great author made them all his own, by "choosing a fit representative for his heroine, and describing a fisherman's marriage on the island of Inchcolm.

On Sunday, Dean Kamsay, whose memory is so linked with Scotch stories, read prayers. On Monday, the Queen held a Drawing-room at Dalkeith Palace. It was an antiquarian question whether there had been another Drawing-room since the Union. Well might the stay-at-home ladies of Scotland plume themselves.

Afterwards, her Majesty received addresses from the Magistrates of Edinburgh, the Scotch Church, and Universities.

The Queen's stay at Dalkeith was varied by drives about the beautiful grounds on the two Esks, and short visits to neighbouring country seats, characteristic and interesting, Dalmeny, Dalhousie, &c. &c. In the evening, it is said, Scotch music was frequently given for her Majesty's delectation, and that among the songs were some of the satires and parodies poured forth on the unfortunate Lord Provost and bailies, who had robbed the town of the full glory of the Queen's arrival. The cleverest of these was an adaptation of an old Jacobite ditty, itself a cutting satire which a hundred years before had taunted the Georgian general, Sir John Cope, with the excess of caution that led him to shun an engagement, withdraw his forces over night, and leave the country open to the Pretender to march southward. The mocking verses thus challenged the defaulter—

Hey! Johnnie Cope, are ye waukin' yet?
Or are your drums a-beatin' yet?

Now, with a slight variation on the words the measure ran—

Hey! Jamie Forrest, are ye waukin' yet?
Or are your bailies snorin' yet?

Then, after proceeding to run over the temptations which might he supposed to have overmastered the party, the writer dwelt with emphasis on a favourite breakfast dish in Scotland—

For kipper it is savoury food,
Sae early in the mornin'.

Common rumour would have it that Lord John Scott, whose good qualities included a fine voice and a love for Scotch songs, to which his wife contributed at least one exquisite ballad, sang this squib to her Majesty. An improvement on the story, which is at least strictly in keeping with the

Prince's character, added, that when another song was suggested, and the "Flowers of the Forest" mentioned, Prince Albert, unacquainted with the song in question, and misled by a word in the title, exclaimed kindly, "No, no; let the poor man alone, he has had enough of this sort of thing." From Dalkeith the Queen and the Prince started for the Highlands, on a bright, clear, cold, frosty morning. They crossed the Forth and landed at Queen's Ferry, which bore its name from another queen when she was going on a very different errand; for there it is said the fugitive Margaret, the sister of the Atheling, after she had been wrecked in Scotland Water, landed and took her way on foot to Dunfermline to ask grace of Malcolm Cean Mohr, who made her his wife. Queen Victoria only saw Dunfermline and the abbey which holds the dust of King Robert the Bruce from a distance, as she journeyed by Kinross and Loch Leven, getting a nearer glimpse of Queen Mary's island prison, to Perthshire.

At Dupplin the 42nd Highlanders, in their kilts, were stationed appropriately. Perth, with its fair "Inches" lying on the brimming Tay, in the shadow of the wooded hills of Kinnoul and Moncrieff, delighted the royal strangers, and reminded Prince Albert of Basle.

The old Palace of Scone, under the guardianship of Lord Mansfield, was the restingplace for the night. Next day the Queen saw the mound where the early kings of Scotland were crowned. A sort of ancient royal visitors' book was brought out from Perth to her Majesty, and the Queen and the Prince were requested to write their names in it. The last names written were those of James VI. and Charles I. Her Majesty and Prince Albert gave their mottoes as well as their names. Beneath her signature she wrote, "Dieu et mon Droit;" beneath his he wrote, "Treu und Fest."

From Scone the party proceeded to Dunkeld, passing through Birnam Pass, the first of the three "Gates," into the Highlands, where the prophecy against Macbeth was fulfilled, and entered what is emphatically "the Country" by the lowest spur of the mighty Grampians.

The romantic, richly-wooded beauty of Dunkeld was increased by a picturesque camp of Athole Highlanders, to the number of a thousand men, with their piper in attendance. They had been called out for her Majesty's benefit by the late Duke of Athole, then Lord Glenlyon, who was suffering from temporary blindness, so that he had to be led about by Lady Glenlyon, his wife. At Dunkeld the Queen lunched, and walked down the ranks of Highland soldiers. The piper played, and a reel and the ancient sword-dance, over crossed swords—the nimble dancer avoiding all contact with the naked blades—were danced. The whole scene—royal guests, noble men and women, stalwart clansmen in their waving dusky tartans—must have been very animated and striking in the lovely autumn setting of the mountains when the ling was red, the rowan berries hung like clusters of coral over the brown burns, and a field of oats here and there came out like a patch of gold among the heather. To put the finishing-touch to the picture, the grey tower of Gawin Douglas's Cathedral, still and solemn, kept watch over the tomb of the Wolf of Badenoch.

But Dunkeld was not the Queen's destination. She was going still farther into the Highlands. She left the mountains of Craig-y-barns and Craig-vinean behind her, and travelled on by Aberfeldy to Taymouth, the noble seat of the Marquis of Breadalbane. Lord Glenlyon's Highlanders gave place to Lord Breadalbane's, the Murrays, in their particular set of tartan with their juniper badge, to the Campbells and the Menzies, in their dark green and red and white kilts, with the tufts of bog myrtle and ash in their bonnets. The pipers were multiplied, and a company of the 92nd Highlanders replaced the 42nd, in kilts like their neighbours. "The firing of the guns," wrote the Queen, "the cheering of the great crowd, the picturesqueness of the dresses, the beauty of the surrounding country with its rich background of wooded hills, altogether formed one of the finest scenes imaginable. It seemed as if a great chieftain in olden feudal times was receiving his sovereign. It was princely and romantic."

Such a "sovereign" of such a "chief" is the crowned lady, every inch a queen, represented in Durham's bust reproduced in the illustration.

Lord Breadalbane was giving his Queen a royal welcome. Lady Breadalbane, a childless wife, had been one of the beautiful Haddington Baillies, descendants of Grizel Baillie; she was suffering from wasting sickness, and her beauty, still remarkable, was "as that of the dead."

Some of the flower of the Scotch nobility were assembled in the house to meet the Queen and the Prince—members of the families of Buccleugh, Sutherland, Abercorn, Roxburgh, Kinnoul, Lauderdale &c. &c. The Gothic dining-room was dined in for the first time; the Queen was the earliest occupant of her suite of rooms. After dinner, the gardens were illuminated, the hills were crowned with bonfires, and Highlanders danced reels to the sound of the pipes by torchlight in front of the house. "It had a wild and very gay effect."

The whole life, with its environment, was like a revelation of new possibilities to the young English Queen who had never been out of England before. It was at the most propitious moment that she made her first acquaintance with the Scotch Highlands which she has learned to love so well; she enjoyed everything with the keen sense of novelty and the buoyance of unquenched spirits. Looking back upon it all, long afterwards, she wrote with simple pathos, "Albert and I were then only twenty-three, young and happy."

At Taymouth there was shooting for the Prince; and there was much pleasant driving, walking, and sketching for the Queen—with the drives walks, and sketches unlike anything that she had been accustomed to previously. The weather was not always favourable; the sport was not always so fortunate as on the first day, when the Prince shot nineteen roe-deer, several hares and pheasants, three brace of grouse, and wounded a capereailzie, which was afterwards brought in; but the travellers made the best of everything and became "quite fond of the bagpipes," which were played in perfection at breakfast, at luncheon, whenever the royal pair went out and in, and before and during dinner. One evening there was a ball for the benefit of the county people, at which the Queen danced a quadrille with Lord Breadalbane; Prince Albert and the Duchess of Buccleugh being the vis-a-vis.

On September 10th, a fine morning, the Queen left Taymouth. She was rowed up Loch Tay, past Ben Lawers with Benmore in the distance. The pipers played at intervals, the boatmen sang Gaelic songs, and the representative of Macdougal of Lorn steered. At Auchmore, where the party lunched, they were rejoined by the Highland Guard. As her Majesty drove round by Glen Dochart and Glen Ogle, the latter reminded her of the fatal Kyber Pass with which her thoughts had been busy in the beginning of the year. By the time Loch Earn was reached, the fine weather had changed to rain. By Glenartney and Duneira, earthquake-haunted Comrie, Ochtertyre, where grows "the aik," and Crieff with the "Knock," on which the last Scotch witch was burnt, the travellers journeyed to Drummond Castle, belonging to Lady Willoughby d'Eresby, where her Majesty was to make her next stay. Lady Willoughby was a chieftainess in her own right, the heiress of the old Drummonds, Earls of Perth. Lord Willoughby was the representative of the lucky English Burrells and the Welsh Gwydyrs, one of whom had married a Maid of Honour to Catharine of Aragon, and come to grief, because, unlike her royal mistress, she and her husband adopted the Protestant religion, and fell into dire disgrace in the reign of Bloody Mary. The Drummonds. like the Murrays and unlike the Campbells, had been staunch Jacobites. The mother of the first and last Duke of Perth caused the old castle to be blown up after her two sons had joined the rebellion in the '45, lest the keep should fall into the hands of King George's soldiers. [Footnote: She is said to have been the heroine of the popular Jacobite song, "When the King comes over the water."] The Queen alludes in her Journal to the steep ascent to the castle. The long narrow avenue leads up by the side of the fine castle rock, tufted with wild strawberries, ferns, and heather, to the courtyard. Her Majesty also mentions the old terraced garden; "like an old French garden," or like such an Italian garden as was a favourite model for the gardens of its day.

The Willoughby Highlanders, wearing the Drummond tartan and the holly badge, were now the Queen's guard. The lady of the castle and her daughters wore the Drummond tartan and the holly when they met the Queen.

It was at Drummond Castle that Prince Albert made his first attempt at deer-stalking, under the able guidance of Campbell of Moonzie. The Prince's description of the sport was that it was "one of the most interesting of pursuits," in which the sportsman, clad in grey, in order to remain unseen, had to keep under the hill, beyond the possibility of scent, and crawl on hands and knees to approach his prey.

There was a story told at the time of the Prince and Campbell of Moonzie. Prince Albert had arranged to return at a particular hour to drive with the Queen. Moonzie, who was the most ardent and agile deer-stalker in the neighbourhood, had got into the swing of the sport, till then unsuccessful, when, as the men lay crouching among the heather, waiting intently for the herd expected to come that way, the Prince said it was, time to return.

"But the deer, your Royal Highness," faltered the Highlander, looking aghast, and speaking in the whisper which the exigencies of the case required.

The Prince explained that the Queen expected him.

It is to be feared the Highlander, in the excitement of the moment, and the marvel that any man—not to say any prince—could give up the sport at such a crisis, suggested that the Queen might wait, while the deer certainly would not.

"The Queen commands," said her true knight, with a quiet smile and a gentle rebuke.

In the evening there was company, as at Taymouth, some in kilts. Campbell of Moonzie showed himself as great in reels as in deer-stalking. (Ah! the wild glee and nimble grace of a Highland reel well danced.) The Queen danced one country dance with Lord Willoughby, while Prince Albert had the eldest daughter of the house, Lady Carington, for his partner.

The next day the royal party, starting as early as nine on a hazy morning, reached Stirling and visited the castle, which figures so largely in the lives of the old Stewart kings. The Queen saw the room in which James II. slew Douglas, John Knox's pulpit, the field of Bannockburn, which saved Scotland from a conquest, and the Knoll or "Knowe" where the Scotch Queens and the Court ladies sat to look down on their knights "Riding the Ring" or playing at the boisterously boyish game of "Hurleyhacket." But the autumn mists shut out the "Highland hills," already receding in the background, and the Links of Forth, where the river winds like the meshes of a chain through the fertile lowlands to the sea. Soon Drummond Castle and Taymouth, with their lochs and mountains and "plaided array," would be like a wonderful dream, to be often recalled and recounted at Windsor and Buckingham Palace.

From Stirling the Queen travelled back to Dalkeith, where she arrived the same night. During her Majesty's last day in Scotland, which she expressed herself as "very sorry to leave," she drove to Roslin Chapel, where twenty "barons bold" of the house of St. Clair wear shirts of mail for shrouds, then went on to storied Hawthornden—a wooded nest hung high over the water, where the poet Drummond entertained his English brother-of-the-pen, Ben Jonson.

On Thursday, the 15th of September, the Queen embarked in the Trident, a large steamboat, likely to be swifter than the Royal George, and surrounded by the flotilla, which, with the exception of one, fell behind, and out of sight in the course of the voyage, sailed for England, past Berwick Law, Tantallon, the ruined keep of the Douglases, and the Bass, where a gloomy state prison once frowned on a rock, now given up to seagulls and Solan geese. The weather was favourable and the moonlight fine. The voyage became enjoyable as the young couple ate a "pleasant little dinner on deck in a tent, made of flags," or paced the deck in the moonlight, or read the "Lay of the Last Minstrel," and played on the piano in the cabin. Notwithstanding the good time, winds and waves are not to be trusted, and the roar of the guns which announced that the vessel was at the Nore was a welcome awakening at three o'clock on the morning of Saturday, the 17th. The sun smiled through a slight haze on the sail up the river, among the familiar English sights and sounds. The tour, which had delighted the pair, was over; but home, where a loving mother and little children awaited them, was sweet.

CHAPTER XV. A MARRIAGE, A DEATH, AND A BIRTH IN THE ROYAL FAMILY.—A PALACE HOME.

The rest of the autumn and early winter passed in busy quiet and domestic happiness. In November, the Queen honoured the Duke of Wellington by a second visit to Walmer. She was no longer the girl-princess—a solitary figure, but for her devoted mother, she was the Queen-wife, taking with her not only her good and noble husband, but her two fine children, to show her old servant, the great soldier of a former generation, who had known her from her childhood, how rich she had become in all womanly blessings. During her stay her Majesty went to Dover, and included the guardian castle of England, on the chalk cliffs which overlook the coast of France, among the venerable fortresses she had inspected this year.

In the meantime, the agitation for Free Trade was exciting the country in one direction, and O'Connell was thundering for a repeal of the union between England and Ireland in another. On the 20th of January, 1843, a public crime was committed which shocked the whole nation and aroused the utmost sympathy of the Queen and Prince Albert. A half-crazy man named Macnaughten, who conceived he had received a political injury from Sir Robert Peel, planned to waylay and shoot the Premier in Downing Street. The man mistook his victim, and fatally wounded Sir Robert's private secretary, Mr. Drummond, who perished in the room of his chief. The plea of insanity accepted by the jury on the trial was so far set aside by the judges.

The descendants of the numerous family of George III. and Queen Charlotte, in the third generation, only numbered five princes and princesses. Apart from her German kindred, the Queen had only four cousins—her nearest English relations after her uncles and aunts. Of these the Crown Prince of Hanover, German born but English bred as Prince George of Cumberland, and long regarded as, in default of Princess Victoria, the heir to the crown, married at Hanover, on the 18th of February, Princess Mary of Saxe-Altenburg. The Crown Prince was then twenty-four years of age. Though he had no longer any prospect of succeeding to the throne of England, he was the heir to a considerable German kingdom. But the terrible misfortune which had cost him his eyesight did not terminate his hard struggle with fate. His father, whose ambition had been built upon his son from his birth, appeared to have more difficulty in submitting to the sore conditions of the Prince's loss than the Prince himself showed. By a curious self-deception, the King of Hanover never acknowledged his son's blindness, but persisted in treating him, and causing others to treat him, as if he saw. The Queen of Hanover, once a bone of contention at the English Court, and Queen Charlotte's bete noire, as the divorced wife of one of her two husbands prior to her third marriage with the Duke of Cumberland, had died two years before. It was desirable in every light that she should find a successor—a princess—to preside over the widowed Court, and be the mother to the future kings of Hanover, supposing Hanover had remained on the roll of the nations. A fitting choice was made, and the old King took care that the marriage should be celebrated with a splendour worthy of the grandson of a King of England. Twenty-four sovereigns and princes, among them the King of Prussia, graced the ceremony. The bride wore cloth of silver and a profusion of jewels, and whatever further troubles were in store for the blind bridegroom, whose manly fortitude and uprightness of character—albeit these qualities were not without their alloy of pride and obstinacy—won him the respect of his contemporaries, Providence blessed him on that February day with a good, bright, devoted wife. On the 25th of March, the Thames Tunnel, which at the time was fondly regarded as the very triumph of modern engineering, and a source of the greatest convenience to London, was opened for foot-passengers by a procession of dignitaries and eminent men, including in their ranks the Lord Mayor, Sir Robert Inglis, Lord Lincoln, Joseph Hume, Messrs. Babbage and Faraday, &c. &c. The party descended by one staircase, shaft, and archway which carried them to Wapping, and, ascending again, returned by the other archway to Rotherhithe. Some of the Thames watermen hoisted black flags as a sign that they considered their craft doomed.

For the first time since her accession, the Queen had been unable, from the state of her health, to open Parliament or to hold the usual spring levees. Prince Albert relieved her of this, as of so many of her burdens, and Baron Stockmar paid a visit to England, at the Prince's urgent request, that the Baron's sagacity and experience might be brought to bear on what remained of the arduous task of getting a Queen's household into order and directing a royal nursery. The care of the Queen's Privy Purse had been transferred to the Prince on the departure of Baroness Lehzen. These various obligations, together with his rapidly increasing interest in public affairs, and the number of persons who claimed his attention, especially when he was in London, become a serious tax on his strength, a tax which the Queen even at this early date feared and sought to guard against. Baron Stockmar was greatly pleased with the aspect of the family. He proudly proclaimed that the Prince was quickly showing what was in him, among other things that he was rich in that very practical talent in which the Baron had feared the young man might be deficient; at the same time the old family friend remarked that the Prince, in the midst of his industry and happiness, frequently looked "pale, worried, and weary."

An instance of Prince Albert's cordial interest in the welfare of the humbler ranks is to be found in one of Bishop Wilberforce's letters, dated March, 1843: "After breakfast with the Prince, for three-quarters of an hour talked about Sunday. Told him that I thought 'Book of Sports' did more than anything to shock the English mind. He urged want of amusements for common people of an innocent class—no gardens. In Coburg, with ten thousand inhabitants, thirty-two gardens, frequented by different sorts of people, who meet and associate in them. 'I never heard a real shout in England. All my servants marry because they say it is so dull here, nothing to interest-good living, good wine, but there is nothing to do but turn rogue or marry.'"

On the 20th of April, Prince Augustus of Saxe-Coburg was married to Princess Clementine of France, the youngest daughter of Louis Philippe. On the following day, the 21st, the Queen's uncle, the Duke of Sussex, who had long been infirm, and for a little time seriously ailing, died at Kensington Palace, at the age of seventy years. The body lay in state there on the 3rd of May, all persons in decent mourning being admitted to witness the sight. Twenty-five thousand persons availed themselves of the permission. On the following morning, the funeral of the first of the Royal Dukes, who was buried by daylight and not in the royal vault at Windsor, took place. There was a great procession, a mile in length, beginning and ending with detachments of Horse and Foot Guards, their bands playing at intervals the "Dead March in Saul," in acknowledgement of the military rank of the deceased. The hearse, drawn by eight black horses, was preceded and followed by twenty-two mourning-coaches and carriages, each with six horses, and upwards of fifty private carriages, one of these containing Sir Augustus d'Este, the son of the dead Duke and of Lady d'Ameland (Lady Augusta Murray). [Footnote: The Duke of Sussex made a second morganatic marriage, after Lady d'Ameland's death, with Lady Cecilia Buggin, daughter of the second Earl of Arran, and widow of Sir George Buggin. She was created Duchess of Inverness. She survived the Duke of Sussex thirty years.] The Duke of Cambridge acted as chief mourner. The cortege passed along the High Street to Kensal Green Cemetery, where Prince Albert, Prince George of Cambridge, and the Grand Duke of Mecklenburg-Strelitz, whose son was about to become the husband of Princess Augusta of Cambridge, awaited its arrival. The service was read by the Bishop of Norwich in the cemetery chapel, and the coffin was deposited in the vault prepared for it. It was observed of Prince Albert that "he seemed to be more affected than any person at the funeral."

An old face, once very familiar, had passed away: a young life had dawned. In the interval between the Duke of Sussex's death and funeral, five days after the death, on the 24th of April, 1843, a second princess was born. The Queen was soon able to write to King Leopold that the baby was to be called "Alice," an old English name, "Maud," another old English name, and "Mary," because she had been born on the birthday of the Duchess of Gloucester. The godfathers were the Queen's uncle, the King of Hanover, and Prince Albert's brother, by their father's retirement, already Duke of Coburg. The King of Hanover came to England, though, unfortunately, too late to be present at the christening, so that one likes to think of the Princess, whose name is associated with all that is good and kind, as having served from the first in the light of a messenger of peace to heal old feuds. The godmothers were the Princess of Hohenlohe and Princess Sophia Matilda of Gloucester.

In the illustration Princess Alice is given as she represented "Spring" in the family mask in 1854. On the 18th of May, 1843, the prolonged contest between the civil and ecclesiastical courts in Scotland reached its climax—in many respects striking and noble, though it may be also one-sided, high-handed, and erring. The chief civil law-court in Scotland—the Court of Session—had overruled the decisions of the chief spiritual court—the General Assembly of the Church of Scotland—and installed, by the help of soldiers, in the parishes, which patronage had presented to them, two ministers, disliked by their respective congregations, and resolutely rejected by them, though neither for moral delinquencies nor heretical opinions. The Government, after a vain attempt to heal the breach and reconcile the contending parties, not only declined to interfere, but asserted the authority of the law of the land over a State church.

Once more the representatives of the Scotch clergy and laity, of all shades of opinion, met, as their forefathers had done for centuries, in the Assembly Hall, in Edinburgh, in the month of May. Then, after the usual introductory ceremonies, the moderator, or chairman, delivered a solemn protest against the State's interference with the spiritual rights of the Church, declared that the sovereignty of its Divine Head was invaded, and, in the name of himself and his brethren, rejected, a union which compelled submission to the civil law on what a considerable proportion of the population persisted in regarding as purely spiritual questions. Four hundred and seventy ministers of one of the poorest churches in Christendom had appended their names to the protest. Churches, manses, livings were laid down, the mass following their leaders. Among them, though many a good and gifted man remained with equal conscientiousness behind, there were men of remarkable ability as well as Christian worth; and there was one, Dr. Chalmers, with a world-wide reputation for genius, eloquence, and splendid benevolence. The band formed themselves into a procession of black-coated soldiers of a King—not of this world—marched along the crowded streets of Edinburgh, hailed and cheered by an enthusiastic multitude, and entering a building temporarily engaged for the purpose, constituted themselves a separate church, and flung themselves on the liberality of their portion of the people, on whom they were thenceforth entirely dependent for maintenance. And their people, who, with their compatriots, are regarded among the nations as notably close-fisted and hard-headed, responded generously, lavishly, to the impassioned appeal. All Scotland was rent and convulsed then, and for years before and after, by the great split in what lay very near its heart—its church principles and government. These things were not done in a corner, and could not fail to arouse the interest of the Queen and Prince, whatever verdict their judgment might pronounce on the dispute, or however they might range themselves on the constitutional side of the question, as it was interpreted by their political advisers—indeed, by the first statesmen, Whig or Tory, of the day. Six years later, Sir Edwin Landseer painted the picture called "The Free Kirk," which became the property of her Majesty.

The Royal Commission on the Fine Arts, at the head of which was Prince Albert, in view of the decoration of the new Houses of Parliament, had an exhibition of prize cartoons in Westminster Hall during the summer of 1843. Great expectations were entertained of the effect of such patronage on painting in its higher branches. Many careful investigations were made into the best processes of fresco painting, of which the Prince had a high opinion, and this mode of decoration was ultimately adopted, unfortunately, as it proved, for in spite of every precaution, and the greatest care on the part of the painters—some of whom, like Dyce, were learned in this direction, while others went to Italy to acquire the necessary knowledge—the result has been to show the perishable nature of the means used, in this climate at least, since the pictures on the walls of the Houses of Parliament have become but dim, fast-fading shadows of the original representations. In the early days of the movement the Prince, in order the better to test and encourage a new development of art in this country, gave orders for a series of fresco paintings from Milton's "Comus," in eight lunettes, to decorate a pavilion in the grounds of Buckingham Palace. Among the painters employed were Landseer, Maclise, Leslie, Uwins, Dyce, Stanfield, &c. &c. Two of them—Leslie and Uwins—record the lively interest which the Queen and the Prince took in the painting of the pavilion, how they would come unannounced and without attendants twice a day, when the Court was at Buckingham Palace, and watch the painters at work. Uwins wrote, that in many things the Queen and her husband were an example to the age. "They have breakfasted, heard morning prayers with the household in the private chapel, and are out some distance from the Palace, talking to us in the summer-house, before half-past nine o'clock—sometimes earlier. After the public duties of the day, and before the dinner, they come out again, evidently delighted to get away from the bustle of the world to enjoy each other's society in the solitude of the garden…. Here, too, the royal children are brought out by the nurses, and the whole arrangement seems like real domestic pleasure."

The square of the Palace, with a park on either hand, and its main entrance fronting the Mall, has green gardens of its own, velvet turf, shady trees, shining water—now expanding into a great round pond, like that in Kensington Gardens, only larger—now narrowing till it is crossed by a rustic bridge. These cheat the eye and the fancy into the belief that the dwellers in the Palace have got rid of the town, and furnish pleasant paths and pretty effects of landscape gardening within a limited space.

But the Palace has a public as well as a private side. The former looks out on the parks and drives, which belong to all the world, and in the season are crowded with company.

The great white marble staircase leads to many a stately corridor, with kings and queens looking down from the walls, to many a magnificent room with domed and richly fretted roofs, ball-room with a raised dais for court company, and a spot where royal quadrilles are danced, banqueting-room, music-room, white, crimson, blue, and green drawing-rooms, crimson and gold throne-room. There are finely-wrought white marble chimney-pieces with boldly-carved heads, angelic figures, and dragons in full relief. There are polished pillars of purple-blue, and red scagliola, hugs china vases—oriental, Dresden, unpolished Sevres—and glittering timepieces of every shape and device.

King George and Queen Charlotte in shadowy form preside once and again, as well they may, seeing this was her house when it was named the Queen's House. Their family, too, still linger in their portraits. George IV. in very full-blown kingly state, the Duke of York and his Duchess, the Duke of Kent and his Duchess, the King of Hanover, King William and Queen Adelaide, the Duke of Sussex. But not one of their lives is so linked with the place as the life of Queen Victoria has been, especially the double life of the Queen and the Prince Consort in their "blooming time." Buckingham Palace was their London home, to which they came every season as regularly as Park Lane and Piccadilly, with the squares and streets of Belgravia, find their fitting occupants. From this Palace the girl-Queen drove to Westminster, to be crowned, and returned to watch in the soft dusk of the summer evening all London illuminated in her honour. Here she announced her intended marriage to her Lords in Council; here she met her princely bridegroom come across the seas to wed her. From that gateway she drove in her bridal white and orange blossoms, and it was up these steps she walked an hour-old wife, leaning on the arm of her husband. Most of their children were born here. The Princess Royal was baptized here, and she went from Buckingham Palace to St. James's, like her mother before her, to be married. In the immediate neighbourhood occurred some of the miserable attempts on the Queen's life, and it was round Buckingham Palace that nobility and people thronged to convince themselves of her Majesty's safety, and assure her of their hot indignation and deep sympathy. On that balcony she has shown herself, to the thousands craving for the sight, on the opening-day of the first Exhibition and on the morning when the Guards left for the Crimea. Through these corridors and drawing-rooms streamed the princely pageant of the Queen's Plantagenet Ball. Kingly and courtly company, the renowned men and the fair women of her reign, have often held festival here. Along these quiet garden walks the Queen was wont to stroll with her husband-lover; from that rustic bridge he would summon his feathered favourites around him; in yon sheet of water he swam for his life among the broken ice, the day before the christening of the Princess Royal. In the little chalet close to the house the Queen loved to carry on her correspondence on summer-days, rather than to write within palace walls, because she, whose life has been pure and candid as the day, has always loved dearly the open air of heaven. In the pavilion where the first English artists of the time strove to do their Prince's behest, working sometimes from eight in the morning to six or seven in the evening, her Majesty and the Prince delighted to watch Maclise put in Sabrina releasing the Lady from the enchanted chair, and Leslie make Comus offering the cup of witchery.

As in the case of King George and Queen Charlotte, it is well that portraits and marble statues of the Queen and the Prince, in the flower of their age, should remain here as unfailing links with the past which was spent within these walls.

In later years the widowed Queen has dwelt little at Buckingham Palace, coming rarely except for the Drawing-rooms, which inaugurate the season and lend the proper stamp to the gilded youth of the kingdom. What tales that Throne-room could tell of the beating hearts of debutantes and the ambitious dreams of care-laden chaperons! The last tale is of the kind consideration of the liege lady. From the room where the members of the royal family assemble apart, she walks, not to take her seat on the throne, but to stand in front of the steps which lead to it, that the ladies who advance towards her in single file may not have to climb the steps with stumbling feet, often caught in their trailing skirts, till the wearers were in danger of being precipitated against the royal knees as the ladies bent to kiss the Queen's hand. In the same manner, the slow and painful process of walking backwards with long trains, of which such stories were told in Queen Charlotte's day, is graciously dispensed with. A step or two, and the trains are thrown over their owners' arms by the pages in waiting, while the ladies are permitted to retire, like ordinary mortals, in a natural, easy, and what is really a more seemly fashion. A royal chapel has for a considerable time taken the place of a great conservatory, so that the Queen and the Prince could worship with their household, without the necessity of repairing to the neighbouring Chapel Royal of St. James's.

There are other suites of rooms besides the private apartments, notably the Belgian floor, full of memories of King Leopold and Queen Louise.

Among the portraits of foreign sovereigns, the correctly beautiful face of the Emperor Alexander of Russia, and the likeness of his successor, Nicholas, occur repeatedly. The portraits of the Emperor and Empress of Germany, when as Prince and Princess of Prussia they won the cordial friendship of the Queen, are here. There is a pleasant picture of Queen Victoria's girl friend, Maria da Gloria, and a companion picture of her husband, the Queen and the Prince's cousin. The burly figure of Louis Philippe appears in the company of two of his sons. Another ruler of France, the Emperor Napoleon III., looks sallow and solemn beside his Empress at the height of her loveliness. Other royal portraits are those of the King of Saxony, the present King and Queen of the Belgians, as Duke and Duchess of Brabant; the late blind King of Hanover and his devoted Queen; the Duke of Mecklenburg-Strelitz, now blind also, and his Duchess, who was the handsome and winning Princess Augusta of Cambridge; her not less charming sister, Princess Mary, Duchess of Teck; the familiar face of their soldierlike brother, the Duke of Cambridge; the Maharajah Dhuleep Singh, in his slender youth and eastern dress, &c. &c.

In the sister country of France, one has a feeling that there are blood stains on all the palaces. Let us be thankful that, as a rule, it is not so in England. But there are tragic faces and histories here too, mocking the glories of rank and State. There is a fine picture of Matilda of Denmark, to whom—but for the victim's fairer hair—her collateral descendant, Queen Victoria, is said to bear a great resemblance. The Queen's ancestress was herself a princess and a queen, yet she was fated to fall under an infamous, unproven charge, and to pine to an early death in a prison fortress.

Here, with a pathos all her own, in her pale dark girlish face and slight figure, is the Queen's Indian god-daughter, Princess Gouromma, the child of the Rajah of Coorg. She was educated in England, and married a Scotch gentleman named Campbell. But the grey northern skies and the bleak easterly winds were cruel to her, as they would have been to one of her native palm-trees, and she found an early grave.

A graceful remembrance of a peculiarly graceful tribute to the faithful service and devotion of a lifetime appears in a picture of the old Duke of Wellington—after whom the Queen named her third son—presenting his godfather's token of a costly casket to the infant Prince Arthur, seated on the royal mother's knee. Another laughing child, in the arms of another happy mother, is the Queen herself, held by the Duchess of Kent.

The long picture gallery contains valuable specimens of Dutch and Flemish art, a remnant of

George IV.'s collection, and a portion, of the Queen's many fine examples of these schools. Here are Tenierses, full of riotous life; exquisite Metzus, Terburgs, and Gerard Dows; cattle by Paul Potter; ships by Van de Velde; skies by Cuyp; landscapes, with white horses, by Wouvermanns; driving clouds and shadow-darkened plains by Ruysdael, who, though he died in a workhouse, yet lives in his pictures in kings' palaces.

Lady Bloomfield has given the world a delightful glimpse of what the life at Windsor and Buckingham Palace was from 1842 to 1845; how much real friendliness existed in it; what simplicity and naturalness lay behind its pomp and magnificence. Dissipation and extravagance found no place there. That palace home—whether in town or country, where all sacred obligations and sweet domestic affections reigned supreme, where noble work had due prominence and high-minded study paved the way for innocent pleasure—was, indeed, a pattern to every home in the kingdom. The great household was like a large family, with a queenly elder sister and a royal brother at its head; for the Queen and the Prince were still in their first prime, and very kindly, as well as very wise, were their relations with old and young. It is good to read of the tenderly-united pair; of their well-regulated engagements—punctually performed as clockwork, and rarely jostling each other; of their generous consideration for others, their faithful regard for old friends, so that to this day the ranks of the Queen's household are replenished from the households of her youth. It has been pointed out how rarely the Duchess of Kent allowed any change in the little Princess's guardians and teachers. In like manner, as whoever will examine Court calendars may learn for themselves, this middle-aged Mistress of the Robes, or that elderly Lady in Waiting, was in former times a young Maid of Honour, and the youngest page of to-day is very likely the grandson of a veteran courtier, and has a hereditary interest in his surroundings. When her Majesty was still young, there was the frankest sympathy with the young girls who were so proud to be in their Queen's service—a sympathy showing itself in a thousand unmistakable ways; in concern for each noble maiden's comfort and happiness; in interest in her friends pursuits, and prospects; by the kindly informal manner in which each member of the girlish suite was addressed by her familiar christian-name, sometimes with its home abbreviation; by the kiss with which she was greeted on her return from her six months' absence. We do not always connect such lovable attributes with kings' and queens' courts, and it is an excellent thing for us to know that the greatest, towards whom none may presume, can also he the most ready to oblige, the least apt to exact, the most cordial and trustful.

We hear from Lady Bloomfield that the sum total of a Maid of Honour's obligations, when she is in residence, like a canon, is to give the Queen her bouquet before dinner every other day. In reality, the young lady and her companions, as well as the older and more experienced Ladies and Women of the Bedchamber, are in waiting to drive, ride, or walk with the Queen when she desires their society, to sit near her at dinner, to share her occupations—such as reading, music, drawing, needlework—when she wishes it, to help to make up any games, dances, &c. &c. These favoured damsels enjoy a modest income of three hundred a year, and wear a badge—the Queen's picture, surrounded with brilliants on a red bow—such as the public may have seen in the portraits of several of the Maids of Honour belonging to the Queen which were exhibited on the walls of the Academy within recent years. The hours of "the Maids" never were so early as those of their royal mistress, while their labours, like their responsibilities, have been light as thistledown in comparison with hers.

The greatest restriction imposed on these youthful members of the Household, when Lady Bloomfield as Miss Liddell figured among them, seems to have been that they were expected to be at their posts, and they were not at liberty to entertain all visitors in their private sitting-rooms, but had to receive some of their friends in a drawing-room which belonged to the ladies in common.

The routine of the Palace passes before us, unpretentious in its dignity as the actual life was led: the waiting of the ladies in the corridor to meet the Queen when she left her apartments and accompany her to dinner; the talk at the dinner-table; the round game of cards—vingt-et-un, or some other in the evening, for which the stakes were so low, that the players were accustomed to provide themselves with a stock of new shillings, sixpences, and fourpenny pieces, and the winnings were now threepence, now eightpence; the workers and talkers in the background. In spite of different times and different manners, there is a slight flavour of Queen Charlotte's drawing-room, in Miss Burney's day, about the whole scene.

The ordinary current was broken by varying eddies of royal visits and visitors, with their accompanying whirl and bubble of excitement, and by ceremonies, like the opening and proroguing of Parliament, State visits to the City, royal baptisms. In addition there were the more tranquil and homely diversions of the festivals of the seasons and family festivals. There was Christmas, when everybody gave and received Christmas-boxes; and this happy individual had a brooch, "of dark and light blue enamel, with two rubies and a diamond in the shape of a bow;" and another had a bracelet, with the Queen's portrait; while to all there were pins, rings, studs, shawls, &c. &c. Or it was the Duchess of Kent's birthday, when the Court went to dine and dance, and wish the kind Duchess many happy returns of the day, at Frogmore. On one occasion the little ball ended in a curious dance, called "Grand-pere," a sort of "Follow my Leader." "The Prince and the Duchess of Kent led the way, and it was great fun, but rather a romp." Solemn statesmen, hoary soldiers, reverent churchmen, foreign diplomatists, were frequently consigned for companionship and entertainment to the "ladies of the Household," and relaxed and grew jocular in such company, under the spring sunshine of girlish smiles and laughter.

More mature and distinguished figures stood out among the women, to match the men—whose names will be household words so long as England keeps her place among the nations. Sagacious Baroness Lehzen, the incomparable early instructress and guide of the Queen, so good to all the young people who came under her influence, before she retired to her quiet home at Buckeburg; Lady Lyttelton, who had been with the Queen as one of the ladies-in-waiting ever since her Majesty came to the throne, who, after the most careful selection, was appointed governess to the Royal children, and was well qualified to discharge an office of such consequence to the Queen and the nation. It is impossible to read such portions of her letters as have been published without being struck by their wise womanliness and gentle motherliness. Beautiful Lady Canning, with her artist soul, was another star in an exalted firmament.

Little feet pattered amongst the brilliant groups. The Princess Royal was a remarkably bright, lively child; the Prince of Wales a beautiful good-tempered baby, in such a nautilus-shell cradle as Mrs. Thorneycroft copied in modelling the likeness of Princess Beatrice. We have the pretty fancy before us: the exquisite curves of the shell, its fair round-limbed occupant, one foot and one arm thrown out with the careless grace of childhood, as if to balance and steer the fairy bark, the other soft hand lightly resting on the breast, over which the head and face, full of infant innocence and peace, are inclined.

Both children were fond of music, as the daughter and son of parents so musical might well be. When the youthful pair were a little older they would stand still and quiet in the music-room to hear the Prince-father discourse sweet sounds on his organ, and the Queen-mother sing with one of her ladies, "in perfect time and tune," with a fine feeling for her songs, as Mendelssohn has described her. The small people furnished a never-ending series of merry anecdotes and witticisms all their own, and would have gone far to break down the highest dead wall of stiffness and reserve, had such a barrier ever existed. Now it was the little Princess, a quaint tiny figure "in dark-blue velvet and white shoes, and, yellow kid gloves," keeping the nurseries alive with her sports, showing off the new frocks she had got as a Christmas-box from her grandmamma, the Duchess of Kent, and bidding Miss Liddell put on one. Now it was the Queen offending the dignity of her little daughter by calling her "Missy," and being told in indignant remonstrance, "I'm not Missy—I'm the Princess Royal." Or it was Lady Lyttelton who was warned off with the dismissal in French, from the morsel of royalty, not quite three, "N'approchez pas moi, moi ne veut pas vous;" or it was the Duke of Wellington, with a dash of old chivalry, kissing the baby-hand and bidding its owner remember, him. Or the child was driving in Windsor Park with the Queen and three of her ladies, when first the Princess imagined she saw a cat beneath the trees, and announced, "Cat come to look at the Queen, I suppose." Then she longed for the heather on the bank, and asked Lady Dunmore to get her some; when Lady Dunmore said she could not do that, as they were driving so fast, the little lady observed composedly, "No, you can't, but those girls," meaning the two Maids of Honour, in the full dignity of their nineteen or twenty summers and their office, "might get me some."

Windsor Castle in the height of summer, Windsor in the park among the old oaks and ferns, Windsor on the grand terrace with its glorious English view, might well leave bright lingering memories in a susceptible young mind. So we hear of a delightful ride, when the kind Queen mounted her Maid of Honour on a horse which had once belonged to Miss Liddell's sister, and in default of Miss Liddell's habit, which was not forthcoming, lent her one of the Queen's, with hat, cellar and cuffs to suit, and the two cantered and walked over the greensward and down many a leafy glade for two hours and a half. Once, we are told, the Queen, the Prince, and the whole company went out after dinner in the warm summer weather, and promenaded in the brilliant moonlight, a sight to see, with the lit-up castle in the background, the men in the Windsor uniform, the women in full dress, like poor Marie Antoinette's night promenades at Versailles, or a page from Boccaccio.

Running through all the young Maid of Honour's diary is the love which makes all service light; the loyal innocent sense of hardship at being in waiting and not seeing the Queen "at least once a day;" the affectionate regret to lose any of her Majesty's company; the pride and pleasure at being selected by the Queen for special duties.

CHAPTER XVI. THE CONDEMNATION OF THE ENGLISH DUEL.— ANOTHER MARRIAGE.—THE QUEEN'S VISIT TO CHATEAU D'EU.

On the 1st of July, 1843, duelling received its death-blow in England by a fatal duel—so unnatural and so painful in its consequences that it served the purpose of calling public attention to the offence—long tolerated, even advocated in some quarters, and to the theory of military honour on which this particular duel took place. Two officers, Colonel Fawcett and Lieutenant Munro, who were also brothers-in-law, had a quarrel. Colonel Fawcett was elderly, had been in India, was out of health and exceedingly irritable in temper. It came out afterwards that he had given his relation the greatest provocation. Still Lieutenant Munro hung back from what up to that time had been regarded as the sole resource of a gentleman, especially a military man, in the circumstances. He showed great reluctance to challenge Colonel Fawcett, and it was only after the impression—mistaken or otherwise—was given to the insulted man that his regiment expected him to take the old course, and if he did not do so he must be disgraced throughout the service, that he called out his brother-in-law.

The challenge was accepted, the meeting took place, Colonel Fawcett was shot dead, and the horrible anomaly presented itself of two sisters—the one rendered a widow by the hand of her brother-in-law, and a family of children clad in mourning for their uncle, whom their father had slain. Apart from the bloodshed, Lieutenant Munro was ruined by the miserable step on which he had been thrust. Public feeling was roused to protest against the barbarous practice by which a bully had it in his power to risk the life of a man immeasurably his superior, against whom he happened to have conceived a dislike. Prince Albert interested himself deeply in the question, especially as it concerned the army. Various expedients were suggested; eventually an amendment was inserted into the Articles of War which was founded on the more reasonable, humane, and Christian conclusion, that to offer an apology, or even to make reparation where wrong had been committed, was more becoming the character of an officer and a gentleman, than to furnish the alternative of standing up to kill or to be killed for a hasty word or a rash act.

On the 28th of July, Princess Augusta of Cambridge was married in the chapel at Buckingham Palace to the hereditary Grand Duke of Mecklenburg-Strelitz. Princess Augusta was the elder of the two daughters of the Duke of Cambridge, was three years younger than the Queen, and at the time of her marriage was twenty-one years of age. In the cousins' childhood and early youth, during the reign of King William, the Duke of Cambridge had acted as the King's representative in Hanover, so that his family were much in Germany. At the date of the Queen's accession, Princess Augusta, a girl of fifteen, was considered old enough to appear with the rest of the royal family at the banquet at Guildhall, and in the other festivities which commemorated the beginning of the new reign. She figures in the various pictures of the Coronation, the Queen's marriage, &c. &c., and won the enthusiastic admiration of Leslie when he went to Cambridge House to take the portraits of the different members of the family for one of his pictures. Only a year before she had, in the character of Princess Claude of France, been one of the most graceful masquers at the Queen's Plantagenet Ball, and among the bridesmaids on the present occasion were two of the beauties at the ball, Lady Alexandrina Vane and Lady Clementina Villiers. Princess Augusta was marrying a young German prince, three years her senior, a kinsman of her father's through his mother, Queen Charlotte. She was going to the small northern duchy which had sent so brave a little queen to England.

Queen Victoria, Prince Albert, and all the royal family in the country, including the King of Hanover, who had remained to grace the ceremony, were present at the wedding, which, in old fashion, took place in the evening. Among the foreign guests were the King and Queen of the Belgians, the Prince and Princess of Oldenburg, the Crown Prince of Wurtemburg, &c. &c. The ambassadors, Cabinet Ministers, and officers of State were in attendance. The Archbishops of Canterbury and York, and the Bishops of London and Norwich, officiated. The marriage was registered and attested in the great dining room at Buckingham Palace. Then there passed away from the scene the Princess who had been for some years the solitary representative of the royal young ladyhood of England, as her sister, Princess Mary, was eleven years Princess Augusta's junior, and still only a little girl of ten. Princess Augusta had an annuity of three thousand a year voted to her by Parliament on her marriage.

A month later, on the 28th of August, the Queen went by railway to Southampton, in order to go on board the royal yacht for a trip to the Isle of Wight and the Devonshire coast. At Southampton Pier, the rain was falling heavily. Her Majesty had been received by the Mayor and Corporation, the Duke of Wellington, and other official personages, when it was discovered that there was not sufficient covering for the stage or gangway, which was to be run out between the pier and the yacht. Then the members of the Southampton Corporation were moved to follow the example of

Sir Walter Raleigh in the service which introduced him to the notice of Queen Elizabeth. They pulled off their red gowns, spread them on the gangway, and so procured a dry footing for her Majesty.

Lady Bloomfield, as Miss Liddell, in the capacity of Maid of Honour in waiting, was with the Queen, and has furnished a few particulars of the pleasant voyage. The Queen landed frequently, returning to the yacht at night and sleeping on board. At the Isle of Wight she visited Norris Castle, where she had stayed in her youth, asking to see some of the rooms, and walking on the terrace. She told her companions that she would willingly have bought the place but could not afford it. At one point all the party except Lady Canning were overcome by sea sickness, which is no respecter of persons. At Dartmouth the Queen entered her barge and was rowed round the harbour, for the better inspection of the place, and the gratification of the multitude on the quays and in every description of sailing craft. At Plymouth the visitors landed and proceeded to Mount Edgcumbe, the beautiful seat of the Edgcumbe family. Wherever her Majesty went she made collections of flowers, which she had dried and kept as mementoes of the scenes in which they had been gathered. In driving through Plymouth, the crowd was so great, and pressed so much on the escort, that the infantry bayonets crossed in the carriages.

At Falmouth, the Queen was again rowed in her barge round the harbour, but the concourse of small boats became dangerous, as their occupants deserted the helms and rushed to one side to see the Queen, and the royal barge could only be extricated by the rowers exerting their utmost strength and skill, and forcing a passage through the swarming flotilla. The Mayor of Falmouth was a Quaker, and asked permission to keep on his hat while reading his address to the Queen. The Mayor of Truro, who with the Mayor of Penryn had accompanied their official brother when he put off in a small boat to intercept her Majesty in her circuit round the harbour, was doomed to play a more undignified part. He unluckily overleaped himself and fell into the water, so that he and his address, being too wet for presentation, were obliged to be put on shore again.

On board the Queen used to amuse herself with a favourite occupation of the ladies of the day, plaiting paper so as to resemble straw plait for bonnets. She was sufficiently skilled in the art to instruct her Maid of Honour in it.

On one occasion the Queen chanced to have her camp-stool set where it shut up the door of the place that held the sailors' grog-tubs. After much hanging about and consulting with the authorities, she was made acquainted with the fact, when she rose on condition that a glass of grog should be brought to her. She tasted it and said, "I am afraid I can only make the same remark I did once before, that I think it would be very good if it were stronger," an observation that called forth the unqualified delight of the men. Sometimes in the evening the sailors, at her Majesty's request, danced hornpipes on deck.

But the Queen's cruises this year were not to end on English or even Scotch ground. She was to make the first visit to France which had been paid by an English sovereign since Henry VIII. met Francis I. on the field of the Cloth of Gold. Earlier in the year two of Louis Philippe's sons, the sailor Prince Joinville, "tall, dark, and good looking, with a large beard, but, unfortunately for him, terribly deaf," and his brother, the man of intellect and culture if not of genius, the Duc d'Aumale, "much shorter and very fair," had been together at Windsor; and had doubtless arranged the preliminaries of the informal visit which the Queen was to pay to Louis Philippe. The King of France and his large family were in the habit of spending some time in summer or autumn at Chateau d'Eu, near the seaport of Treport, in Normandy; and to this point the Queen could easily run across in her yacht and exchange friendly greetings, without the elaborate preparations and manifold trouble which must be the accompaniment of a State visit to the

Tuileries.

Accordingly the Queen and Prince Albert, on the 1st of September, sailed past the Eddystone Lighthouse, where they were joined by a little fleet of war-ships, and struck off for the coast of France. Besides her suite, the Queen was accompanied by two of her ministers, Lords Aberdeen and Liverpool. With the first, a shrewd worthy Scot, distinguished as a statesman by his experience, calm sagacity, and unblemished integrity, her Majesty and Prince Albert were destined to have cordial relations in the years to come.

In the meantime, French country people were pouring into Treport, where the King's barge lay ready. It was provided with a crimson silk awning, having white muslin curtains over a horseshoe-shaped seat covered with crimson velvet, capable of containing eleven or twelve persons. The rowers were clad in white, with red sashes and, red ribands round their hats.

The Queen was to land by crossing the deck of a vessel moored along the quay and mounting a ladder, the steps of which were covered with crimson velvet. At five o'clock in the afternoon the King and his whole family, a great cortege, arrived on horseback and in open chars-a-bancs. Prince Joinville had met the yacht at Cherbourg and gone on board. As soon as it lay-to the King came alongside in his barge. The citizen King was stout, florid, and bluff-looking, with thick grizzled hair brushed up into a point. As the exiled Duke of Orleans, in the days of the great Revolution, he had been a friend of the Queen's father, the Duke of Kent. The King did not fail to remind his guest of this, after he had kissed her on each check, kissed her hand, and told her again and again how delighted he was to see her. When the two sovereigns entered the barge the standards of England and France were hoisted together, and amidst royal salutes from the vessels in the roads and from the batteries on shore, to the music of regimental bands, in the sunset of a fine autumn evening the party landed.

At the end of the jetty the ladies of the royal family of France with their suites stood in a curved line. Queen Amelie, with her snowy curls and benevolent face, was two paces in advance of the others. Behind her were her daughter and daughter-in-law, the Queen of the Belgians and the widowed Duchesse d'Orleans, who appeared in public for the first time since her husband's death a year before. A little farther back stood Madame Adelaide, the King's sister, and the other princesses, the younger daughter and the daughters-in-law of the house. Louis Philippe presented Queen Victoria to his Queen, who "took her by both hands and saluted her several times on both cheeks with evident warmth of manner." Queen Louise, and at least one of the other ladies, were well known to the visitor, whom they greeted gladly, while the air was filled with shouts of "Vive la Reine Victoria!" "Vive la Reine d'Angleterre!"

The Queen, who was dressed simply, as usual, in a purple satin gown, a black mantilla trimmed with lace, and a straw bonnet with straw-coloured ribands and one ostrich feather, immediately entered the King's char-a-bancs, which had a canopy and curtains that were left open. Lady Bloomfield describes it as drawn by twelve large clumsy horses. There was a coachman on the box, with three footmen behind, and there was "a motley crowd of outriders on wretched horses and dressed in different liveries." The other chars-a-bancs with six horses followed, and the whole took their, way to the Chateau, a quaint and pleasant dwelling, some of it as old as the time of the Great Mademoiselle.

A stately banquet was held in the evening in the banqueting-room, hung round with royal portraits and historical pictures, the table heavy with gold and silver plate, including the gold plateau and the great gold vases filled with flowers. The King, in uniform, sat at the centre of the table. He had on his right hand Queen Victoria, wearing a gown of crimson velvet, the order of the garter and a parure of diamonds and emeralds, but having her hair simply braided. On her other side sat Prince Joinville. On the King's left hand was Queen Louise. The Duchesse d'Orleans, in accordance with French etiquette for widows in their weeds, did not come to the dinner-table. Opposite the King sat his Queen, with Prince Albert on her right hand and the Duc d'Aumale on her left. The royal host and hostess carved like any other old-fashioned couple. The Queen received the same lively impressions from her first visit to France that she had experienced on her first visit to Scotland. Apart from the scenery there was yet more to strike her. The decidedly foreign dresses of the people, the strange tongue, the mill going on Sunday, the different sound of the church bells—nothing escaped her. There was also, in the large family of her brother king and ally—connected with her by so many ties, every member familiar to her by hearsay, if not known to her personally—much to interest her. The Queen had been, to all intents and purposes, brought up like an only child, and her genial disposition had craved for entire sympathy and equal companionship. She seems to have regarded wistfully, as an only child often regards, what she had never known, the full, varied, yet united life of a large, happy, warmly attached family circle. When she saw her children possessed of the blessing which had been denied to her in her early days, she was tempted to look back on the widowed restricted household in Kensington Palace as on a somewhat chill and grey environment. She has more than once referred to her childhood as dull and sad by comparison with what she lived to know of the young life of other children.

But the great royal household of France at this date, in addition to its wealth of interests and occupations, and its kindness to the stranger who was so quick to respond to kindness, was singularly endowed with elements of attractiveness for Queen Victoria. It appeared, indeed, as if all life at its different stages, in its different aspects, even in its different nationalities, met and mingled with a wonderful charm under the one roof-tree. Besides the old parent couple and the maiden aunt, who had seen such changes of fortune, there were three young couples, each with their several careers before them. There was the bride of yesterday, the youngest daughter of the house, Princess Clementine, with her young German husband, the Queen and Prince Albert's kinsman; there was Nemours, wedded to another German cousin, the sweet-tempered golden-haired Princess Victoire; there was Joinville, with his dark-haired Brazilian Princess. [Footnote: A kinswoman of Maria da Gloria's] It had been said that he had gone farther, as became a sailor, in search of a wife than any other prince in Europe. She was very pretty in a tropical fashion, very piquante, and, perhaps, just a little sauvage. She had never seen snow, and the rules and ceremonies of a great European court were almost as strange to her. Lady Bloomfield mentions her as if she were something of a spoilt child who could hardly keep from showing that the rigid laws of her new position fretted and bored her. She wore glowing pomegranate blossoms in her hair, and looked pensive, as if she were pining for the gorgeous little hummingbirds and great white magnolias—the mixture of natural splendour and ease, passion and languor, of a typical South American home.

D'Aumale and Montpensier were still gay young bachelors, and well would it have been for the welfare of the Orleans family and the credit of Louis Philippe if one of them had remained so. There was a widow as well as a bride in the house. There were the cherished memories of a dearly-prized lost son and daughter to touch with tender sorrow its blithest moments and lightest words. The Queen had to make the acquaintance of Helene, Duchesse d'Orleans; [Footnote: Princess Helena of Mecklenburg-Schwerin.] tall, thin and pale, not handsome, but better than handsome, full of character and feeling, shrinking from observation in her black dress, with the shadow of a life-long grief over her heart and life. And the visitor had to hear again of the gifted Princess Marie, the friend of Ary Scheffer, whose statue of Jeanne d'Arc is the best monument of a life cut down in its brilliant promise. Princess Marie's devoted sister Louise, Queen of the Belgians, in her place as the eldest surviving daughter of France, had long been Queen Victoria's great friend. Finally, there was the third generation, headed by the fatherless boy, "little Paris," with regard to whom few then doubted that he would one day sit on the throne of France.

It was not principally because the Chateau d'Eu was in France that the Queen wrote, the first morning she awoke there, the fulfilment of her favourite air-castle of so many years was like a dream, or that she grieved when her visit was over. She sought to find, and believed she had found, a whole host of new friends and kindred—another father and mother, more brothers and sisters, nephews and nieces, to make her life still richer and more full of kindly ties.

The speciality in the form of entertainment at Chateau d'Eu was drives in the sociable chars-a-bancs in the neighbouring forest, ending in dejeuners and fetes-champetres, which the Queen enjoyed heartily, both because they were novel to her and because they were spontaneous and untrammelled. "So pretty, so merry, so rural," she declared. "Like the fetes in Germany," Prince Albert said. The long, frequently rough drives under the yellowing trees in the golden September light, the camp-chairs, the wine in plain bottles, the improvised kitchen hidden among the bushes, the many young people of high rank all so gay, the king full of liveliness and brusqueness, his queen full of motherliness and consideration for all—everything was delightful. One pathetic little incident occurred when the guests were being shown over the parish church of Notre Dame. As they came to the crypt, with its ancient monuments of the Comtes d'Eu, the Duchesse d'Orleans was overcome with emotion, and the Queen of the Belgians drew her aside. When the rest of the party passed again through the church, on their way back, they came upon the two mourning women prostrate before one of the altars, the Duchesse weeping bitterly.

The King presented Queen Victoria with fine specimens of Gobelin tapestry and of Sevres china. He went farther in professions and compliments. He was not content to leave the discussion of politics to M. Guizot and Lord Aberdeen. Louis Philippe volunteered to the Queen's minister the statement that he would not give his son to Spain (referring to a proposed marriage between the Duc de Montpensier and the Infanta Luisa, the sister of the young Queen Isabella, who had been lately declared of age), even if he were asked. To which the stout Scot replied, without beating about the bush, "that except one of the sons of France, any aspirant whom Spain might choose would be acceptable to England."

Louis Philippe, Queen Amelie, and the whole family escorted the Queen and the Prince on board the yacht, parting with them affectionately. Prince Joinville accompanied the couple to the Pavilion, Brighton. In the course of the sail there was a race between his ship and the Black Eagle, in which the English vessel won, to the French sailors' disgust.

Louis Philippe felt great satisfaction at a visit which proved his cordial relations with England, and served to remove the reproach which he seemed to think clung to him and prevented the other European royal families from fraternising with him and his children as they would otherwise have done—namely, that he was not the representative of the elder, and what many were pleased to consider the legitimate, branch of the Bourbons. He was but a king set up by the people, whom the people might pull down again. There was not much apparent prospect of this overthrow then, though the forces were at work which brought it about. In token of his gratification, and as a memorial of what had given him so much pleasure, the King caused a series of pictures to be taken of Queen Victoria's landing, and of the various events of her stay. These pictures remain, among several series, transferred to the upper rooms of one of the French palaces, and furnish glimpses of other things that have vanished besides the fashion of the day. There the various groups reappear. Queen Amelie with her piled-up curls, the citizen King and their numerous young people doing honour to the young Queen of England and her husband, both looking juvenile in their turn—all the more so for a certain antiquated cut in their garments at this date, a formality in his hat and neckerchief, a demureness in her close bonnet, and a pretty show of youthful matronliness in the little lace cap which, if we mistake not, she wears on one occasion.

CHAPTER XVII. THE QUEEN'S TRIP TO OSTEND:—VISITS TO DRAYTON, CHATSWORTH, AND BELVOIR.

"Ce n'est que le premier pas qui coute." In the course of another week the Queen took a second trip to the Continent, sailing to Ostend to pay the most natural visit in the world—the only thing singular about it was that it had been so long delayed—to her uncle, King Leopold. The yacht, which had been lying off Brighton, was accompanied by eight other steamers, and joined at Walmer by two ships of the line. At Dover a salute was fired from the castle. At Deal the Duke of Wellington came on board and dined with the royal party, the Queen watching with some anxiety the return of the old man in his boat, through a considerable surf which wetted him thoroughly, before he mounted his horse and rode off to Walmer, to superintend the illumination of the Castle in lines of light. In like manner every ship lying in the Downs glittered through the darkness.

At two o'clock on the following afternoon the Queen and the Prince reached Ostend, where they were received by King Leopold and Queen Louise. There had been some uncertainty whether the travellers, after not too smooth a passage, would be equal to the fatigue of a banquet at the Hotel de Ville that evening. But repose is the good thing to which royalty can rarely attain, so it was settled that the banquet should go on. The display was less, and there was more of undress among the chief personages than there had been at the opening banquet at Chateau d'Eu. The Queen must have looked to her host not far removed from the docile young niece he had so carefully trained and tutored, as she sat by him in white lace and muslin, with flowers in her hair—only bound by a ferroniere of diamonds. The King and Prince Albert were in plain clothes, save that they showed the ribands and insignia of the orders of the Garter and the Bath; the Queen of the Belgians wore a white lace bonnet. It was in the main a simple family party made for the travellers.

The next day the Prince and Princess of Hohenlohe arrived, when the elder sister would have knelt and paid her homage to the younger, had not her Majesty prevented her with a sisterly embrace. Ostend was the head-quarters of the royal party, from which in the mellow autumn time they visited Bruges and Ghent. "The old cities of Flanders had put on their fairest array and were very tastefully decorated with tapestries, flowers, trees, pictures, &c. &c." The crowds of staid Flemings were stirred up to joyous enthusiasm.

The Queen's artistic tastes, in addition to her fresh sympathies and her affection for her uncle and his wife, rendered the whole scene delightful to her. She was fitted to relish each detail, from the carillons to the carvings. She inspected all that was to be seen at Bruges, from the Palace of Justice to the Chapel of the Holy Blood. At Ghent, she went to the church of St. Bavon, where the Van Eycks have left the best part of their wonderful picture before the altar while the dust of Hubert and Margaret, rests in the crypt below. She saw the fragment of the palace in which John of Gaunt was born, when an English queen-consort, Philippa, resided there five hundred years before. She visited the old Beguinage, with the shadowlike figures of the nuns in black and white flitting to and fro.

From Ostend the Queen and Prince Albert proceeded to the cheerful, prosperous, and, by comparison, modern town of Brussels, King Leopold's capital, and stayed a night at his palace of Lacken, which had been built by Prince Albert's ancestor and namesake, Duke Albert of Sechsen, when he governed the Netherlands along with his wife the Archduchess Christina, the favourite daughter of Maria Theresa and the sister of Marie Antoinette. From Brussels the travellers journeyed to Antwerp, where they saw another grand cathedral and witnessed the antique spectacle of "the Giant" before the palace in the Place de Mer.

On leaving Antwerp, the Queen and the Prince sailed for England, escorted so far on their way by King Leopold and Queen Louise. "It was such a joy to me," her Majesty wrote to her uncle, soon after their parting, "to be once again under the roof of one who has ever been a father to me." The vessel lay all night in Margate Roads, and the next morning arrived at Woolwich.

In the month of October her Majesty and the Prince visited Cambridge, where he received his degree of LL.D. A witty letter, written by Professor Sedgwick, describing the royal visit to the Woodwardian Museum, is quoted by Sir Theodore Martin

"….I received a formidable note from our master telling me of an intended royal visit to the Woodwardian den of wild beasts, immediately after Prince Albert's degree; and enjoining me to clear a passage by the side entrance through the old divinity schools. This threw me off my balance, for since the building of the new library this place of ancient theological disputation has been converted into a kind of lumber-room, and has filled from end to end with every kind of unclean things—mops, slop-pails, chimney-pots, ladders, broken benches, rejected broken cabinets, two long ladders, and an old rusty scythe were the things that met the eye, and all covered with half an inch of venerable dust. There is at the end of the room a kind of gallery or gangway, by which the undergraduates used to find their way to my lecture-room, but this was also full of every kind of rubbish and abomination. We did our best; soon tumbled all impediments into the area below, spread huge mats over the slop-pails, and, in a time incredibly short, a goodly red carpet was spread along the gangway, and thence down my lecture-room to the door of the Museum. But still there was a dreadful evil to encounter. What we had done brought out such a rank compound of villanous smells that even my plebeian nose was sorely put to it; so I went to a chemist's, procured certain bottles of sweet odours, and sprinkled them cunningly where most wanted.

"Inside the Museum all was previously in order, and inside the entrance door from the gangway was a huge picture of the Megatherium, under which the Queen must pass to the Museum, and at that place I was to receive her Majesty. So I dusted my outer garments and ran to the Senate House, and I was just in time to see the Prince take his degree and join in the acclamations. This ended, I ran back to the feet of the Megatherium, and in a few minutes the royal party entered the mysterious gangway above described. They halted, I half thought in a spirit of mischief, to contemplate the furniture of the schools, and the Vice-chancellor (Whewell) pointed out the beauties of the dirty spot where Queen Bess had sat two hundred and fifty years before, when she presided at the Divinity Act. A few steps more brought them under the feet of the, Megatherium. I bowed as low as my anatomy would let me, and the Queen and Prince bowed again most graciously, and so began act first. The Queen seemed happy and well pleased, and was mightily taken with one or two of my monsters, especially with the 'Plesiosaurus,' and a gigantic stag. The subject was new to her; but the Prince evidently had a good general knowledge of the old world, and not only asked good questions and listened with great courtesy to all I had to say, but in one or two instances helped me on by pointing to the rare things in my collection, especially in that part of it which contains the German fossils. I thought myself very fortunate in being able to exhibit the finest collection of German fossils to be seen in England. They fairly went the round of the Museum, neither of them seemed in a hurry, and the Queen was quite happy to hear her husband talk about a novel subject with so much knowledge and spirit. He called her back once or twice to look at a fine impression of a dragon-fly which I have in the Solenhope slate. Having glanced at the long succession of our fossils, from the youngest to the oldest, the party again moved into the lecture-room. The Queen was again mightily taken with the long neck of the Plesiosaurus; under it was a fine head of an Ichthyosaurus which I had just been unpacking. I did not know anything about it, as I had myself never seen its face before, for it arrived in my absence. The Queen asked what it was. I told her as plainly as I could. She then asked whence it came; and what do you think I said? That I did not know the exact place, but I believed it came as a delegate from the monsters of the lower world to greet her Majesty on her arrival at the University. I did not repeat this till I found that I had been overheard, and that my impertinence had been talked of among my Cambridge friends. All was, however, taken in good part, and soon afterwards the royal party again approached the mysterious gangway. The Queen and Prince bowed, the Megatherium packed up his legs close under the abdominal region of his august body, the royal pageant passed under, and was soon out of my sight and welcomed by the cheers of the multitude before the library.

"I will only add that I went through every kind of backward movement to admiration of all beholders, only having once trodden on the hinder part of my cassock, and never once having fallen during my retrogradations before the face of the Queen. In short, had I been a king crab, I could not have walked backwards better."

When in Cambridgeshire the Queen and the Prince visited Lord Hardwicke at Wimpole, where the whole county was assembled at a ball, and Earl De la Warr at Bourne.

In this month of October the great agitator for the repeal of the Irish Union, Daniel O'Connell, was arrested, in company with other Irish agitators, on a charge of sedition and conspiracy. After a prolonged trial, which lasted to the early summer of the following year, he was sentenced to a year's imprisonment and the payment of a fine of two thousand pounds, with recognisances to keep the peace for seven years. The sentence lapsed on technical grounds, but its moral effect was considerable.

In the month of September the Queen and Prince Albert visited Sir Robert Peel at Drayton, travelling by railroad, with every station they passed thronged by spectators. At Rugby the pupils of the great school, headed by Dr. Tait, were drawn up on the platform. Sir Robert Peel received his guests in a pavilion erected for the occasion, and conducted her Majesty to her carriage, round which was an escort of Staffordshire yeomanry. At the entrance to the town of Tamworth, the mayor, kneeling, presented his mace, with the words, "I deliver to your Majesty the mace;" to which the Queen replied, "Take it, it cannot be in better hands."

At eight o'clock in the evening Sir Robert Peel conducted the Queen, who wore pink silk and a profusion of emeralds and diamonds, to the dining-room, Prince Albert giving his arm to Lady Peel. Among the guests were the Duke of Wellington and the Duke and Duchess of Buccleugh. The Duchess on one occasion during the visit wore an old brocade which had belonged to a great grand-aunt of the Duke's, and was pronounced very beautiful. After dinner the party withdrew to the library. Either on this evening or the next the Queen played at the quaint old game of "Patience," with some of her ladies, while the gentlemen "stood about."

On the following day her Majesty walked in the grounds, while Prince Albert gratified an earnest wish by visiting Birmingham and inspecting its manufactures, undeterred, perhaps rather allured, by the fact that the great town of steel and iron was regarded as one of the centres of Chartism.

This did not prevent its mighty population from displaying the most exultant loyalty as they pressed round the carriage in which the Prince and the Mayor, reported to be a rank Chartist, drove to glass and silver-plate manufactories and papier-mache works, the town hall, and the schools.

At the railway station the Prince was joined by the Queen-dowager and Prince Edward of Saxe-Weimar, who came from Whitley Court to accompany him back to Drayton. The next morning was devoted to shooting, when Prince Albert confirmed his good character as a sportsman by bringing down sixty pheasants, twenty-five hares, eight rabbits, one woodcock, and two wild ducks. In the afternoon the Queen visited Lichfield, to which she had gone as "the young Princess." Indeed, the next part of the tour was over old ground in Derbyshire, for from Drayton the royal couple proceeded to Chatsworth, and spent several days amidst the beauties of the Peak. Twenty thousand persons were assembled in the magnificent grounds at Chatsworth, and artillery had been brought from Woolwich to fire a salute. Many old friends, notably members of the great Whig houses—Lord Melbourne, Lord and Lady Palmerston, the Marquis and Marchioness of Normanby—met to grace the occasion. There was a grand ball, at which the aristocracy of invention and industry, trade and wealth, represented by the Arkwrights and the Strutts, mingled with the autocracy of ancient birth and landed property. Mrs. Arkwright was presented to the Queen. Her Majesty opened the ball with the Duke of Devonshire, dancing afterwards with Lord Morpeth and Lord Leveson—in the last instance, "a country dance, with much vigour"—and waltzing with Prince Albert. On the 2nd of December the party visited Haddon Hall, the ancient seat of the Vernons, where Dorothy Vernon lived and loved. On their return in the evening, the great conservatory was brilliantly illuminated, and there was a display of fireworks.

On the 3rd, Sunday, the Queen walked through the kitchen gardens and botanical gardens, and drove to Edensor. On the return of the party by the Home Farm, they went to see a prize-pig, weighing seventy pounds. The day ended with a concert of sacred music.

On Monday, the 4th, the Queen and the Prince parted from the Duke of Devonshire at Derby, and proceeded to Nottingham—not to visit what remained of the Castle so long associated with John and Lucy Hutchinson, or to penetrate to the cradle of hosiery, daring an encounter with the "Nottingham Lambs," the roughest of roughs, who at election times were wont to add to their natural beauties by painting their faces red, white, and blue, as savages tattoo themselves—but as a step on the way to Belvoir, the seat of the Duke of Rutland. There her Majesty entered that most aristocratic portion of England known as "The Dukeries." The Duke of Rutland, attended by two hundred of his tenantry on horseback, awaited his guests at Red Mile, and rode with them the three miles to Belvoir. Soon after the Queen's arrival, Dr. Stanton presented her Majesty with the key of Stanton Town, according to the tenure on which that estate is held.

Belvoir was a sight in itself, even after the stately lawns of Chatsworth. "I do not know whether you ever saw Belvoir," writes Fanny Kemble; "it is a beautiful place; the situation is noble, and the views, from the windows of the castle, and the terraces and gardens hanging over the steep hill crowned by it, is charming. The whole vale of Belvoir, and miles of meadow and woodland, lie stretched below it, like a map unrolled to the distant horizon, presenting extensive and varied prospects in every direction; while from the glen which surrounds the castle-hill, like a deep moat filled with a forest, the spring winds swell up as from a sea of woodland, and the snatches of birds' carolling, and cawing rooks' discourse, float up to one from the topmost branches of tall trees, far below one's feet, as one stands on the battlemented terraces."

December was not the best time for seeing some of the attractions of Belvoir; but Lady Bloomfield has written of her Majesty's proverbial good fortune in these excursions: "The Queen yachts during the equinox, and has the sea a dead calm; visits about in the dead of winter, and has summer weather." There were other respects in which Belvoir was in its glory in midwinter—it belonged to a hunting neighbourhood and a hunting society. Whereas at Drayton and Chatsworth the royal pair had been principally surrounded by Tory and Whig statesmen, at Belvoir, while the Queen-dowager and some of the most distinguished members of the company at Chatsworth were again of the party, the Queen and the Prince found themselves in the centre of the fox-hunters of Melton Mowbray.

Happily, the Prince could hunt with the best, and the Queen liked to look on at her husband's sport, so that the order of the day was the throwing off of the hounds at Croxton. In the evening the Queen played whist. The next day there was a second splendid meet royally attended, with cards again at night. The Prince wrote of one of these "runs," to Baron Stockmar, that he had distinguished himself by keeping up with the hounds all through. "Anson" and "Bouverie" had both fallen on his left and right, but he had come off "with a whole skin." We are also told that the Prince's horsemanship excited the amazed admiration of the spectators, to the Queen's half-impatient amusement. "One can scarcely credit the absurdity of the people," she wrote to her uncle, King Leopold; "but Albert's riding so boldly has made such a sensation that it has been written all over the country, and they make much more of it than if he had done some great act." Apparently the Melton Mowbray fox-hunters had, till now, hardly appreciated that fine combination of physical and mental qualities, which is best expressed in two lines of an old song:—

　His step is foremost in the ha',
　His sword in battle keen.

On the 7th of December the visitors left for Windsor, passing through endless triumphal arches on the road, greeted at Leicester by seven thousand school children.

Shortly after the Queen's return home, she and the Prince heard, with regret, of the death of Thomas Graham, Lord Lynedoch. The veteran fell, indeed, like a shock of corn ripe for the garner, until it had been difficult to recognise in the feeble, nearly blind old man, upwards of ninety, the stout soldier of Barossa and Vittoria. But he carried with him many a memory which could never be recalled. Gallant captain though he was, his whole life was touched with tender romance. Born only four years after the Jacobite rebellion of '45, married in 1774, when he was twenty-five years of age, to his beautiful wife, the Hon. Mary Cathcart—whose sister Jane was married on the same day to John, Duke of Athole—for eighteen years Mr. Graham lived the quiet life of a country gentleman in Lynedoch Cottage, the most charming of cottages ornes, thatch-roofed, with a conservatory as big as itself, set down in a fine park. The river Almond flowed by, serving as a kind of boundary, and marking the curious limit which the plague kept in its last visit to Scotland. On a green "haugh" beneath what is known as the Burnbraes, within a short distance of Lynedoch Cottage, may be seen the carefully-kept double grave of two girls heroines of Scotch song, who died there of the "pest," from which they were fleeing.

Mr. Graham was happy in his marriage, though it is said Mrs. Graham did not relish that element in her lot which had made her the wife of a simple commoner, while her sister, not more fair, was a duchess. Death entered on the scene, and caused the distinctions of rank to be forgotten. The cherished wife was laid in a quiet grave in Methven kirk-yard, and the childless widower mourned for the desire of his heart with a grief that refused to be comforted. By the advice of his friends, who feared for his reason or his life, he went abroad, where he joined Lord Hood as a volunteer. It is said he fought his first battle in a black coat, with the hope that, being thus rendered conspicuous in any act of daring which he might perform, he would be stricken down before the day was done. Honours, not death, were to be his portion in his new career. A commission, rapid promotion, the praise of his countrymen followed. He received the thanks of both Houses of Parliament. It was on this occasion that Sheridan said eloquently, in allusion to the soldier's services in the retreat to Corunna, "In the hour of peril Graham was their best adviser, in the hour of disaster Graham was their surest consolation." A peerage, which there was none to share or inherit, a pension, the Orders of the Bath, of St. Michael and St. George, &c. &c., were conferred upon him. It seemed only the other day since Lord Lynedoch, hearing of her Majesty's first visit to Scotland, hurried home from Switzerland to receive his queen. A place in Westminster Abbey was ready for all that was mortal of him, but he had left express injunctions that he was to be buried in Methven kirk-yard, beside the wife of his youth, dead more than half a century before.

Most people know the history of Gainsborough's lovely picture of Mrs. Graham, the glory of the Scotch National Gallery—that it was not brought home till after the death of the lady, whose husband could not bear to look on her painted likeness, and sent it, in its case, to the care of a London merchant, in whose keeping it remained unopened, and well-nigh forgotten, for upwards of fifty years. On Lord Lynedoch's death, the picture came into the possession of his heir, Mr. Graham, of Redgorton, who presented it—a noble gift—to the Scotch National Academy.

CHAPTER XVIII. ALLIES FROM AFAR.—DEATH AND ABSENCE.— BIRTHDAY GREETINGS.

Lady Bloomfield describes a set of visitors at Windsor this year such as have not infrequently come a long way to pay their homage to the Queen, and to see for themselves the wonders of civilisation. The party consisted of five Indian chiefs, two squaws, a little girl, and a half-breed, accompanied by Mr. Catlin as interpreter. The Queen received the strangers in the Waterloo Gallery. The elder chief made a speech with all the dignity and self-confidence of his race. It was to the effect that he was much pleased the Great Spirit had permitted him to cross the large lake (the Atlantic) in safety. They had wished to see their great mother, the Queen. England was the light of the world; its rays illuminated all nations, and reached even to their country. They found it much larger than they expected, and the buildings were finer than theirs, and the wigwam (Windsor Castle) was very grand, and they were pleased to see it. Nevertheless, they should return to their own country and be quite happy and contented. They thanked the Great Spirit they had enough to eat and drink. They thought the people in England must be very rich, and they looked pleased and happy. They (the Chippewas) had served under the English sovereigns and had fought their battles. He—the chief—had served under ——, the greatest chief that had ever existed or had ever been known. He had been on the field of battle when his general was killed and had helped to bury him. He had received kindness from the English nation, for which he thanked them; their wigwams at home had been made comfortable with English goods. He had nothing more to say. He had finished.

These Indians had their faces tattooed and were clad in skins, with large bunches of feathers on their heads. The men were armed with tomahawks, clubs, wooden swords, bows, and spears. The women were in the height of squaw-fashion, with long black hair, dresses reaching to their feet, and quantities of coloured beads. Two war-dances were danced before the Queen, one of the chiefs playing a sort of drum, the music being assisted by shrieks and cries and the shaking of a rattle. The dance began by the dancers quivering in every joint, then passed into a slow movement, which ended in violent action.

Such an interlude was welcome in the necessary monotony of Court life to those who do not penetrate into its inmost circle. Lady Bloomfield writes, "Everything else changes; the life at Court never does; it is exactly the same from day to day and year to year." And she records, as an agreeable diversion from the set routine, the mistake of one of the pages, by which an equerry-in-waiting, in the absence of another official, received a wrong order about dinner. When the Queen dines in private there is a purely Household dinner in the room appointed for the purpose. In those days the Queen rarely dined two days consecutively in private, so that her suite were surprised by the announcement that there were to be two Household dinners—the one after the other. The ladies and gentlemen sat down together in the Oak Room at eight o'clock, and had finished their soup and fish, when a message came from the Queen to know who had given the order that they were to dine without her. The company stared blankly at each other, finished their dinner with what appetite they might, and adjourned to the drawing-room, when they were told that her Majesty was coming. One can fancy the consternation of the courtiers, who were "only in plain evening coats," instead of Windsor uniform. Happily it occurred to the defaulters that it would be but right to anticipate her Majesty, so that all rushed off to the corridor to meet the Queen and the Prince, who were much amused by the blunder.

There is a pleasant little picture of the young family at Windsor in one of the Prince's letters this winter: "The children, in whose welfare you take so kindly an interest, are making most favourable progress. The eldest, "Pussy" (the Princess Royal at three years of age), is now quite a little personage. She speaks English and French with great fluency and choice of phrase…. The little gentleman (the Prince of Wales) is grown much stronger than he was…. The youngest (Princess Alice) is the beauty of the family, and is an extraordinarily good and merry child."

January, 1844, brought a severe trial to Prince Albert, and through him to the Queen, in the sudden though not quite unexpected death of his father at Gotha, at the comparatively early age of sixty years. Father and son were much attached to each other, they had been parted for nearly four years since the Prince's marriage, and the early meeting to which they had been looking forward was denied to them.

The Queen wrote to Baron Stockmar, in the beginning of February, "Oh, if you could be here now with us: My darling stands so alone, and his grief is so great and touching…. He says (forgive my bad writing, but my tears blind me) I am now all to him. Oh, if I can be, I shall be only too happy; but I am so disturbed and affected myself, I fear I can be but of little use."

"I have been with the Queen a good deal, altogether,"—Lady Lyttelton refers to this time; "she is very affecting in her grief, which is in truth all on the Prince's account; and every time she looks at him her eyes fill afresh. He has suffered dreadfully, being very fond of his father, and his separation from him and the suddenness of the event, and his having expected to see him soon, all contribute to make him worse."

The Prince himself wrote to his trusty friend, "God will give us all strength to bear the blow becomingly. That we were separated gives it a peculiar poignancy; not to see him, not to be present to close his eyes, not to help to comfort those he leaves behind, and to be comforted by them is very hard. Here we sit together, poor Mama (the Duchess of Kent, the late Duke of Coburg's sister), Victoria and myself, and weep, with a great cold public around us, insensible as stone."

The Prince had one source of consolation, that of a good son who had never caused his father pain. He had another strong solace in the reality and worth of the new ties which were replacing the old, both in his own case and in that of his brother. "The good Alexandrine," Prince Albert remarked, referring to his sister-in-law, "seems to me in the whole picture like the consoling angel." Then he goes on, "Just so is Victoria to me, who feels and shares my grief and is the treasure on which my whole existence rests. The relation in which we stand to each other leaves nothing to desire. It is a union of heart and soul, and is therefore noble; and in it the poor children shall find their cradle, so as to be able one day to ensure a like happiness for themselves."

Lady Lyttelton describes a sermon which Archdeacon Wilberforce preached at Windsor at this season, February, 1844. "Just before church time the Queen told me that Archdeacon Wilberforce was going to preach, so I had my treat most unexpectedly, mercifully I could call it, for the sermon, expressed in his usual golden sweetness of language, was peculiarly practical and useful to myself—I mean, ought to be. 'Hold thee still in the Lord and abide patiently upon him,' was the text, and the peace, trust and rest which breathed in every sentence, ought to do something to assuage any and every worret, temporal and spiritual. There were some beautiful passages on looking forward into 'the misty future,' and its misery to a worldly view, and the contrary. The whole was rather the more striking from its seeming to come down so gently upon the emblems of earthly sorrow (referring to the mourning for Prince Albert's father), we are in such 'a boundless contiguity of shade.' There was a beautiful passage—I wish you could have heard it, because you could write it out—about growth in grace being greatest when mind and heart are at rest, and in stillness like the first shoot of spring which is not forwarded by the storm or hurricane, but by the silent dews of early dawn; another upon the melancholy of human life, 'most beautiful because most true.'"

It was judged desirable that the Prince should go to Germany for a fortnight at Easter. It was his first separation from the Queen since their marriage, and both felt it keenly. Lady Lyttelton wrote of her Majesty on the occasion: "The Queen has been behaving like a pattern wife as she is, about the Prince's tour; so feeling and so wretched and yet so unselfish; encouraging him to go, and putting the best face on it to the last moment…. We all feel sadly wicked and unnatural in his absence, and I am actually counting the days on my part as her Majesty is on hers," adds the kindly, sympathetic woman. The Queen of the Belgians,—and later, King Leopold, came over to console their niece by their company during part of her solitude. But her best refreshment must have been the letters with which couriers were constantly riding to and fro, full of a lover's tenderness and a brother's care, from the first to the last; these dispatches came unfailingly. They breathed "the tender green of hope," like the spring which was on the land at the time.

From Dover the husband wrote: "My own darling…. I have been here about an hour and regret the lost time which I might have spent with you. Poor child, you will, while I write, be getting ready for luncheon, and you will find a place vacant where I sat yesterday; in your heart, however, I hope my place will not be vacant. I, at least, have you on board with me in spirit. I reiterate my entreaty, 'Bear up,' and do not give way to low spirits, but try to occupy yourself as much as possible; you are even now half a day nearer to seeing me again; by the time you get this letter you will be a whole one—thirteen more and I am again within your arms."

From Ostend he wrote, "I occupy your old room." From Cologne, "Your picture has been hung up everywhere, and been very prettily wreathed with laurel, so that you will look down from the walls on my tete-a-tete with Bouverie" (the Prince's equerry)…. "Every step takes me farther from you—not a cheerful thought." From Gotha, in the centre of his kinsfolk, he told her what delight her gifts had given, and added, "Could you have witnessed the happiness my return gave my family, you would have been amply repaid for the sacrifice of our separation. We spoke much of you." From Reinhardtsbrunn and Rosenau he sent the flowers he had gathered for her. He wrote of the toys he had got for the children, the presents he was bringing for her. At

Kalenberg—one of his late father's country seats—he broke out warmly, "Oh, how lovely and friendly is this dear old country; how glad I should be to have my little wife beside me, that I might share my pleasure with her."

Coburg had grown marvellously in beauty. In company with his stepmother, brother, and sister-in-law, he went to the town church and was deeply moved by the devotional singing, and "an admirable sermon" from the pastor, who had confirmed the two brothers. Afterwards they rode together to their father's last resting-place. The Prince's biographer closes the account of this tour with a few significant words from Prince Albert's diary, in which he noted down in the briefest form the events of each day: "Crossed on the 11th. I arrived at six o'clock in the evening at Windsor. Great joy."

As a surprise for the Queen's birthday this year, the Prince had privately ordered a little picture of angels from Sir C. Eastlake, who had received a similar commission from the Queen for a picture with which she intended to greet the Prince.

A still more welcome surprise to Her Majesty was a miniature of Prince Albert in armour, according to a fancy of the Queen's, by Thorburn, a likeness which proved the best of all the portraits taken of the Prince, the most successful in catching the outward look when it expressed most characteristically the man within. This picture, together with that of the angels holding a medallion bearing the inscription "Heil und segen" (Health and Blessing), and all the other presents were placed in a room "turned into a bower by dint of enormous garlands."

The Queen and the Prince's relations with artists were naturally, from the royal couple's artistic tastes, intimate and happy. Accordingly, many pictures not only of great personages in State ceremonies, but of family groups in the simplicity of domestic life, survive as a proof of the connection. Vandyck did not paint Charles I. and Henrietta Maria more frequently than Landseer and some of his contemporaries painted her Majesty, with her husband and children, in the bright and unclouded summer of her life; and Vandyck, never painted his royal patrons in such easy unaffected guise and everyday circumstances. There is such a picture of Landseer's, well known from engravings, in which the Prince is represented in a Highland dress returned late from shooting, seated, surrounded by the trophies of his sport in deer, blackcock, &c. &c., and by a whole colony of delighted dogs,—beautiful Eos conspicuous by her sobriety and reserve, while an enraptured terrier presses forward to lick his master's hand. The Queen, dressed for dinner and still girlish-looking in her white satin, stands talking to the Prince. The Princess Royal, a chubby child of two or three, is prowling childlike among the dead game, curiously making her investigations.

Of many stories told of royal visits to studios, there are two which refer to an enfant terrible, the baby son of one of the painters. This small man having undertaken to be cicerone to his father's work, sought specially to point out to her Majesty that two elves were likenesses of himself and a little brother, "only, you know, we don't go about without clothes at home," he volunteered the confidential explanation.

The same child horrified an attentive audience by declining to receive a gracious advance made to him by the Queen, asserting with the utmost candour, "I don't like you."

"But why don't you like me, my boy?" inquired the loving mother of other little children, in some bewilderment.

"Because you are the Queen of England and you killed Queen Mary," the ardent champion of the slain Queen answered boldly.

The story goes on, that after a little laughter at the anachronism, Her Majesty took some trouble to explain to the malcontent that he was wrong, she did not kill Queen Mary, she had been very sorry for her fate. So far from killing her, she, Queen Victoria, was one of Queen Mary's descendants, and it was because she came of the old Stewart line that she reigned over both England and Scotland.

CHAPTER XIX. ROYAL VISITORS.—THE BIRTH OP PRINCE ALFRED.—A NORTHERN RETREAT.

The year 1844 may be instanced as rich in royal visitors to England. On the 1st of June the King of Saxony arrived and shortly after him a greater lion, the Emperor of Russia. The King of Saxony came as an honest friend and sightseer, entering heartily into the obligations of the latter. There was more doubt as to the motives of the Czar of all the Russias, and considerable wariness was needed in dealing with the northern eagle, whose real object might be, if not to use his beak and claws on the English nation, to employ them on some other nation after he had got an assurance that England would not interfere with his game. Indeed, jealousy of the French, and of the friendship between the Queen and Louis Philippe, was at the bottom of the Emperor's sudden appearance on the scene.

The Emperor had paid England a previous visit so far back as 1816, in the days of George, Prince Regent, when Prince Leopold and Princess Charlotte were the young couple at Claremont. He had then won much admiration and popularity by his strikingly handsome person, stately politeness, and gallant devotion to the English ladies who caught his fancy. He was still a handsome man—over six feet, with regular features, remarkable eyes, and bushy moustaches. He wore on his arrival a cloth cloak lined with costly fur, and a kind of cap which looked like a turban—rather a telling costume.

But time and the man's life and character had stamped themselves on what had once been a goodly mould. There was something oppressive in his elaborate politeness. There was a glare, not far removed from ferocity, in the great grey eyes, so little shaded by their lids and light eyelashes that occasionally a portion of the white eyeball above the iris was revealed, and there was an intangible brooding melancholy about the autocrat whose will was still law to millions of his fellow-creatures.

The Queen received her distinguished guest in the great hall at Buckingham Palace Shortly afterwards there was a dejeuner, at which some of the Emperor's old acquaintances in the royal family and out of it, met him—the Duchess of Gloucester, the Princess Sophia, the Duke of Cambridge, the Duke of Wellington, &c. &c. In the evening there was a banquet.

The Emperor followed the Queen to Windsor, where, amidst the gaieties of the Ascot week, he was royally entertained. Two visits were paid to the racecourse, with which the new-comer associated his name by founding the five hundred pounds prize. There was a grand review in Windsor Park, at which both the Emperor of Russia and the King of Saxony were present, as well as Her Majesty and Prince Albert and the royal children. The Emperor in a uniform of green and red, the King of Saxony in a uniform of blue and gold, and Prince Albert in a field-marshal's uniform—all the three wearing the insignia of the Garter—were the observed of all observers in the martial crowd. The only incidents of the day which struck Lady Lyttelton were "the very fine cheer on the old Duke of Wellington passing the Queen's carriage, and the really beautiful salute of Prince Albert, who rode by at the head of his regiment, and of course lowered his sword in full military form to the Queen, with such a look and smile as he did it! I never saw so many pretty feelings expressed in a minute."

On the return of the Court with its guests to Buckingham Palace, the Emperor went with Prince Albert to a fete at Chiswick, given by the Duke of Devonshire, and attended by seven or eight hundred noble guests. The Czar returned from it loud in the praise of the beauty of English women, while staunchly faithful to the belles he had admired twenty-eight years before. The same evening he accompanied the Queen to the opera, when she took his hand and made him stand with her in the front of the box, that the brilliant assemblage might see and welcome him. The Emperor was an adept at saying courteous things. He remarked to the Queen, of Windsor, which he greatly admired, "It is worthy of you, Madame." He wished Prince Albert were his son. When the hour of leave-taking came he found the Queen in the small drawing-room with her children. He declared with emotion that he might at all times be relied upon as her most devoted servant, and prayed God to bless her. He kissed her hand and she kissed him; he embraced and blessed the children. He besought her to go no farther with him. "I will throw myself at your knees; pray let me lead you to your room." "But," wrote the Queen, "of course I would not consent, and took his arm to go to the hall…. At the top of the few steps leading to the lower hall he again took most kindly leave, and his voice betrayed his emotion. He kissed my hand and we embraced. When I saw him at the door I went down the steps, and from the carriage he begged I would not stand there; but I did, and saw him drive off with Albert to Woolwich."

The Emperor was rather suspiciously fond of declaring, "I mean what I say, and what I promise I will perform." Some of his speeches were emphatic enough. "I esteem England highly, but as for what the French say of me I care not; I spit upon it." He felt awkward in evening dress; he was so accustomed to wear military uniform that without it he said he felt as if they had taken off his skin. To humour him, uniform was worn every evening at Windsor during his stay. Among his camp habits was one which he had formed in his youth and kept up to the last: it was that of sleeping every night on clean straw stuffed into a leathern case. The first thing his valets did on being shown their master's bedroom in Windsor Castle was to send out for a truss of straw for the Emperor's bed. The last thing got for him at Woolwich was the same simple stuffing for his rude mattress.

On the 15th of June, 1844, Thomas Campbell, author of the "Pleasures of Hope," "Ye Mariners of England," &c., died at Boulogne at the age of sixty-seven. Although he had not quite reached the threescore and ten, the span of man's life on earth, he had long survived the authors, Scott, Byron, &c., with whom his name is linked. He was one of many well-known men in very different spheres who passed away in 1844. Sir Augustus Callcott, the painter; Crockford with his house of Turf celebrity; Beckford, the eccentric author of "Vathek," and the owner of the art-treasures of Fonthill; Lord Sidmouth, the well-known statesman of the "Addington Administration;" Sir Francis Burdett, who in recent times was lodged in the Tower under a charge of high treason.

In the same year an attempt was made to honour the memory of a greater poet than Thomas Campbell, one whose worldly reward had not been great, whose history ended in a grievous tragedy. The Scotchmen of the day seized the opportunity of the return of two of Robert Burns's sons from military service in India to give them a welcome home which should do something to atone for any neglect and injustice that had befallen their father. The festival was not altogether successful, as such festivals rarely are, but it excited considerable enthusiasm in the poet's native country, especially in his county of Ayrshire. And when the lord of the Castle of Montgomery presided over the tribute to the sons of the ploughman who had "shorn the harvest" with his Highland Mary on the Eglinton "lea-riggs," and Christopher North made the speech of the day, the demonstration could not be considered an entire failure.

Scotch hearts warmed to the belief that the Queen understood and admired Burns's poetry, and proud reference was made to the circumstance that during one of her Highland excursions she applied the famous descriptive passage in the "Birks of Aberfeldy" to the scene before her:

> The braes ascend like lofty wa'e,
> The foamy stream deep roaring fa's,
> O'erhung with fragrant spreading shaws,
> The birks of Aberfeldy.
> The hoary cliffs are crown'd wi' flowers,
> White o'er the linn the burnie pours,
> And rising, weets wi' misty showers
> The birks of Aberfeldy.

This summer, brown Queen Pomare, and the affairs of far-off Tahiti, had a strange, inordinate amount of attention from the English public. French interference in the island, the imprisonment of an English consul and Protestant missionary, roused the British lion. The dusky island-queen claimed the help of her English allies, and till Louis Philippe and M. Guizot disowned the policy which had been practised by their representatives in the South Seas, there was actually fear of war between England and France, in spite of the friendly visit to Chateau d'Eu. Happily the King and his minister made, or appeared to make, reparation as well as explanation, and the danger blew over.

On the 31st of July, down at Windsor a humble but affectionately loved friend died. Prince Albert's greyhound Eos—his companion from his fourteenth to his twenty-fifth year, his avant courier when he came as a bridegroom to claim his bride—was found dead, without previous symptom of illness. She lies buried on the top of the bank above the Slopes, and a bronze model of her marks the spot.

On the 6th of August the Queen's second son was born at Windsor Castle. The Prince of Prussia (the present Emperor of Germany), the third royal visitor this year, came over in time for the christening, when the little prince received the name of the great Saxon King of England, Alfred, together with the names of his uncle, Ernest, and his father, Albert. The godfathers were Prince George of Cambridge, the Queen's cousin, represented by his father; and the Prince of Leiningen, the Queen's brother, represented by the Duke of Wellington; while the godmother was the Queen and Prince Albert's sister-in-law, the Duchess of Coburg-Gotha, represented by the Duchess of Kent. "To see these two children there too," the Queen wrote of the Princess Royal and the Prince of Wales, "seems such a dream to me … May God bless them all, poor little things." The engraving represents the sailor-Prince in his childhood.

A tour in Ireland had been projected for the Queen's holiday, but the excitement in the country consequent on the liberation of O'Connell and his companions rendered the time and place unpropitious for a royal visit, so it was decided that Her Majesty should go again to Scotland. On this occasion the Queen and the Prince took their little four-year-old daughter with them. The route was not quite the same as formerly. The party went by a shorter way to the Highlands, the yacht sailing to Dundee, the great manufacturing city so fortunate in its situation, where the rushing Tay calms and broadens into a wide Frith, with a background of green hills and a foreground of the pleasantly broken shores of Forfar and Fife. The trades held high holiday, and gave the Queen a jubilant welcome, the air ringing with shouts of gladness as she landed from the yacht, leaning on Prince Albert's arm, while he led by the hand the small daughter who reminded the Queen so vividly of herself—as the little Princess of past years.

The Queen, escorted by the Scots Greys, proceeded by Cupar Angus to Dunkeld, stopping at one of the hotels to get "some broth for the child," who proved an excellent traveller, sleeping in her carriage at her usual hours, not put out or frightened at noise or crowds—an excellent thing in a future empress—standing bowing to the people from the windows like a great lady.

At Moulinearn her Majesty tasted that luscious compound of whisky, honey, and milk known as "Athol brose."

The Queen's destination was Blair Castle, the seat of Lord Glenlyon—a white, barrack-like building in the centre of some of the grandest scenery of the Perthshire Highlands. There a strong body of Murrays met her Majesty at the gate and ran by the side of the carriages to the portico of the Castle, where the clansmen, pipers and all, were drawn up in four companies of forty each, to receive the guests. The Queen occupied the Castle during her stay, Lord and Lady Glenlyon, with their son and the other members of their family, being quartered in the lodge for the time.

The Queen and the Prince led the perfectly retired and simple life which was so agreeable to them. Spent among romantic and interesting scenery, it was doubly delightful to the young couple. They dispensed as much as possible with state and ceremony. The Highland Guard were ordered not to present arms more than twice a day to the Queen, and once a day to the Prince and the Princess Royal; but in other respects the Guard were so much impressed by their responsibility that not only would they permit no stranger to pass their cordon without giving the password, which was changed every day, they stopped Lord Glenlyon's brother for want of the necessary "open sesame," telling him that, lord's brother or not, he could not pass without the word.

Her Majesty's piper, Mackay, had orders to play a pibroch under her windows every morning at seven o'clock. At the same early hour a bunch of fresh heather, with a draught of icy-cold water from Glen Tilt, was brought to the Queen. The Princess Royal, on her Shetland pony, accompanied the Queen and the Prince in their morning rambles. Sometimes the little one was carried in her father's arms, while he pointed out to her any object that would amuse her and call forth her prattle. "Pussy's cheeks are on the point of bursting, they have grown so red and plump," wrote the Prince to his stepmother. "She is learning Gaelic, but makes wild work with the names of the mountains."

So free was the life that one morning when a lady, plainly dressed and unaccompanied, left the Castle about seven o'clock no notice was taken of her, and it was only after she had gone some distance that the rank of the pedestrian was discovered. With a little hesitation, a body-guard was told off and followed her Majesty, but she intimated that she would dispense with their attendance, and went on alone as far as the lodge, where she inquired for Lord Glenlyon. It was understood afterwards that she had chosen to be her own messenger with regard to some arrangements to be made respecting a visit to the Falls of the Bruar.

Lord Glenlyon was not out of bed, and the deputy-porter was electrified by being told that the Queen had called on his master. On her Majesty's return to the house she took a different road and lost her way, so that she had to apply to some Highland reapers whom she met, trudging to one of the isolated oatfields, to direct her to the Castle. They told her civilly, but without ceremony, to cross one of the "parks" (fields or meadows) and climb over a paling—instructions which she obeyed literally, and found herself at home again.

On a fine September morning the two who were so happy in each other's company rode on a dun and a grey pony, attended only by Sandy McAra, who led the Queen's pony through the ford, up the grassy hill of Tulloch, "to the very top." There they saw a whole circle of stupendous Bens— Ben Vrackie, Ben-y-Ghlo, Ben-y-Chat, as well as the Falls of the Bruar and the Pass of Killiecrankie, which the Hanoverian troopers likened to "the mouth of hell" on the day that Dundee fell on the field at Urrard.

"It was quite romantic," declared the Queen joyfully. "Here we were with only this Highlander behind us holding the ponies—for we got off twice and walked about; not a house, not a creature near us, but the pretty Highland sheep, with their horns and black faces, up at the top of Tulloch, surrounded by beautiful mountains … the most delightful, the most romantic ride I ever had." There was much more riding and driving in Glen Tilt, with its disputed "right of way" ease, but there was none to bar the Queen's progress. Her Majesty showed herself a fearless rider, abandoning the cart-roads and following the foot-tracks among the mountains. She grew as fond of her homely Highland pony, Arghait Bhean, with which Lord Glenlyon supplied her, as she was of her Windsor stud, with every trace of high breeding in their small heads, arching necks, slender legs, and dainty hoofs.

One day the foresters succeeded in driving a great herd of red-deer, with their magnificent antlers, across the heights, so that the Queen had a passing view of them. On another day she was able to join in the deer-stalking, scrambling for hours in the wake of the hunters, among the rocks and heather, when she was not "allowed," as she described it, to speak above a whisper, in case she should spoil the sport. It was a brief taste of an ideal, open-air, unsophisticated life, upon which there was no intrusion, except when stolid sightseers flocked to the little parish church of Blair Athol for the chance of "seeing royalty at its prayers, and hardly a regret beyond the lack of time to sketch the groups of keepers and dogs, the deer, the mountains.

The Queen, as usual, enjoyed and admired everything there was to admire—the pretty jackets or "short gowns" of the rustic maidens; the "burns," clear as glass; the mossy stones; the peeps between the trees; the depth of the shadows; the corn-cutting or "shearing," when a patch of yellow oats broke the purple shadow of the moor; Ben-y-Ghlo standing like a mighty sentinel commanding the course of the Garry, as when many a lad "with his bonnet and white cockade," sped with fleet foot by the flashing waters, "leaving his mountains to follow Prince Charlie;" Chrianean, where the eagles sometimes sat; the sunsets when the sky was "crimson, golden red, and blue," and the hills "looked purple and lilac," till the hues grew softer and the outlines dimmer. Prince Albert, an ardent admirer of natural scenery, was in ecstasy with the mountain landscape. But her Majesty has already permitted her people to share in the halcyon days of those Highland tours.

On the homeward journey to Dundee, Lord Glenlyon and his brother, Captain Murray, performed the loyal feat of riding fifty miles, the whole distance from Blair, by the Queen's carriage.

CHAPTER XX. LOUIS PHILIPPE'S VISIT.—THE OPENING OF THE ROYAL EXCHANGE.

The Queen and the Prince returned to Windsor to receive a visit from Louis Philippe. The King, who had spent part of his exiled youth in England, had not been back since 1815, when he took refuge there again during "the Hundred Days," after Napoleon's return from Elba and Louis XVIII.'s withdrawal to Ghent, till the battle of Waterloo restored the heads of the Bourbon and Orleans families to the Tuileries and the Palais Royal.

The King arrived on the 6th of October, accompanied by his son, the Duc de Montpensier, M. Guizot, and a numerous suite. They had sailed from Treport in the steamer Gomer, attended by three other, steamers, and arrived at Portsmouth, where the Corporation came on board to present an address.

The King answered in English, with much effusion and affability, shaking hands with the whole batch of magistrates, telling those who were too slow in removing their white gloves, "Oh! never mind your gloves, gentlemen," and recalling a former visit to Portsmouth when he was an exile.

Prince Albert and the Duke of Wellington went on board the steamer, when the enthusiastic elderly gentleman saluted the Prince on both cheeks, to which he submitted, though he did not reply in kind, contenting himself with shaking his guest by the hand. It would seem as if the Prince had some perception of the wiliness which was one quality of the big, bluff citizen king, and of the discretion which must be practised in dealing with him, no less than with the Russian bear. For in writing from Blair to a kinswoman, in anticipation of the visit, the writer states, with a dash of humour, that after a preliminary training on the sea, the bold deerstalker and mountaineer would have to transform himself into a courtier to receive and entertain a King of the French, and play the part of a staid and astute diplomatist.

The king wore the French uniform of a Lieutenant-General—blue with red facings. The moment he ascended the stairs of the jetty, he turned with his hand on his heart and bowed to the multitude of spectators.

The Queen met her visitor in the grand vestibule fronting George the Fourth's Gate at Windsor Castle; the Duchess of Kent and the ladies of the Household, Sir Robert Peel and Lord Liverpool, and the officers of the Household, were with her Majesty. The moment the carriage drew up, the Queen advanced and extended her arms to her father's old friend. The two sovereigns embraced, and she led the way to the suite of rooms which had been previously occupied by the Emperor of Russia.

Lady Lyttelton has supplied her version of the arrival. "At two o'clock he arrived, this curious king, worth seeing if ever a body was. The Queen having graciously permitted me to be present, I joined the Court in the corridor, and we waited an hour, and then the Queen of England came out of her room to go and receive the King of France—the first time in history! Her Majesty had not long to wait (in the armoury, as she received him in the State apartments, his own private rooms; very civil); and from the armoury, amidst all the old trophies and knights' armour, and Nelson's bust, and Marlborough's flag, and Wellington's, we saw the first of the escort enter, the Quadrangle, and down flew the Queen, and we after her, to the outside of the door on the pavement of the Quadrangle, just in time to see the escort clattering up and the carriage close behind. The old man was much moved, I think, and his hand rather shook as he alighted, his hat quite off, and grey hair seen. His countenance is striking—much better than the portraits—and his embrace of the Queen was very parental, and nice. Montpensier is a handsome youth, and the courtiers and ministers very well-looking, grave, gentlemenlike people. It was a striking piece of real history—made one feel and think much."

"He is the first king of France who comes on a visit to the sovereign of this country," wrote the Queen in her Journal.... "The King said, as he went up the grand staircase to his apartments, 'Heavens! how beautiful!'.... I never saw anybody more pleased or more amused in looking at every picture, every bust. He knew every bust, and knew everything about everybody here in a most wonderful way. Such a memory! such activity! It is a pleasure to show him anything, as he is so pleased and interested. He is enchanted with the Castle, and repeated to me again and again (as did also his people) how delighted he was to be here; how he had feared that what he had so earnestly wished since I came to the throne would not take place, and 'Heavens! what a pleasure it is to me to give you my arm!'" The dinner was comparatively private, in the Queen's dining-room.

On the 8th of the month the whole royal party went on a little pilgrimage to Claremont and Twickenham, to the house in which Louis Philippe, as Duc d'Orleans, had resided, and wound up the day by a great banquet in St. George's Hall. The Queen records of this excursion, "We proceeded by Staines, where the King recognised the inn and everything, to Twickenham, where we drove up to the house where he used to live, and where Lord and Lady Mornington, who received us, are now living. It is a very pretty house, much embellished since the King lived there, but otherwise much the same, and he seemed greatly pleased to see it again. He walked round the garden, in spite of the heavy shower which had just fallen.... The King himself directed the postillion which way to go to pass by the house where he lived for five years with his poor brothers, before his marriage. From here we drove to Hampton Court, where we walked over Wolsey's Hall and all the rooms. The King remained a long time in them, looking at the pictures, and marking on the catalogue numbers of those which he intended to have copied for Versailles. We then drove to Claremont. Here we got out and lunched, and after luncheon took a hurried walk in the grounds.... We left Claremont after four, and reached Windsor at a little before six."

Of the conversation during the banquet her Majesty wrote, "He talked to me of the time when he was 'in a school in the Grisons, a teacher merely,' receiving twenty pence a day, having to brush his own boots, and under the name of Chabot. What an eventful life his has been!" On the 9th there was an installation of a Knight of the Garter. Sir Theodore Martin reminds his readers, 'with regard to the ceremony, that it "must have been pregnant with suggestions to all present who remembered that the Order had been instituted by Edward III. after the battle of Cressy, and that its earliest knights were the Black Prince and his companions, whose prowess had been so fatal to France. "In the Throne-room, in a State chair, sat Queen Victoria, in the (blue velvet) mantle of the Order, its motto inscribed on a bracelet that encircled her arm; a diamond tiara on her head. The chair of State by her side was vacant. Round the table before her sat the knights-companions of the highest rank; on the steps of the throne behind the Queen's chair were seated the high civil ministers of the two sovereigns, and some officers of the French suite. At the opposite end of the room were the royal ladies (members of the royal family) and the two young Princes (the Duc de Montpensier and Prince Edward of Saxe-Weimar) visiting at the Castle.... The King, dressed in a uniform of dark blue and gold, was introduced by Prince Albert and the Duke of Cambridge, preceded by Garter King-at-Arms, the Queen and the knights all standing. The sovereign (Queen Victoria) in French announced the election. The declaration having been pronounced by the Chancellor of the Order, the new knight was invested by the Queen and Prince Albert with the Garter and the George, and received the accolade."

"Albert then placed the Garter round the King's leg," wrote the Queen. "I pulled it through while the admonition was being read, and the King said to me, 'I wish to kiss this hand,' which he did afterwards, and I embraced him."

"Taking the King's arm, her Majesty conducted him in state to his own apartments," the Annual Register ends its account of an interesting episode.

"At four o'clock we again went over to the King's room," wrote the Queen, "and I placed at his feet a large cup representing St. George and the dragon, with which he was very much pleased." That night there was a splendid banquet in St. George's Hall to commemorate the installment. On the 12th the King was to have left, but first the Corporation of London went down to Windsor in civic state to present Louis Philippe with an address. This unusual compliment from the City was due partly to the general satisfaction which the visit, with, its promise of continued friendly relations between England and France, gave to the whole country, partly to the circumstance that it was judged inadmissible, in view of the susceptibility of the French nation, for the King of France to pay a formal visit to London, since the Queen of England, in her recent trip to Treport, had not gone to Paris. A somewhat comical contretemps occurred in the preparation of the reply to this address. It was written by the person who usually acted for the

King in such matters, and brought to him shortly before the arrival of the Corporation, when Louis Philippe found to his disgust that the speech was so French in spirit, and expressed in such bad English, he could not hope to make it understood. "It is deplorable.... It is cruel," cried the mortified King. "And to send it to me at one o'clock! They will be here immediately!" No time was to be lost; the King had to sit down and, with the help of his host and hostess, who had come to his rooms opportunely, to write out a more suitable answer.

In M. Guizot's "Memoirs" he tells a curious incident of this visit. On retiring to his room at night he lost his way, and appeared to wander, as Baroness Bunsen feared she might do on a similar occasion, along miles of corridors and stairs. At last, believing he recognised his room-door, he turned the handle, but immediately withdrew, on getting a glimpse of a lady seated at a toilet-table, with a maid busy about her mistress's hair. It was not till next day that from some smiling words addressed to him by the Queen the horrified statesman discovered he had been guilty of an invasion of the royal apartments.

Louis Philippe started on his homeward journey accompanied by her Majesty and Prince Albert, who were to go on board the Gomer and there take leave of their guest. Afterwards they were to embark in the royal yacht and cross to the Isle of Wight. But the stormy weather overturned all these plans. The swell in the sea was so great that it was feared the King could not land at Treport. Eventually he parted from the Queen and the Prince on shore, returned in the evening to London, went to New Cross—where he found the station on fire—proceeded by train to Dover, and sailed next day, amidst wind and rain, in French steamer to Calais. In order to soften the disappointment to the officers and crew of the Gomer, the Queen and Prince Albert breakfasted on board that vessel before they proceeded to the Isle of Wight.

The cause of the cruise of the Queen and the Prince at this season was the wish to see for themselves the house and grounds of Osborne, belonging to Lady Isabella Blatchford. They were to be sold, and had been, suggested by Sir Robert Peel to her Majesty and the Prince as exactly constituted to form the retired yet not too remote country and seaside home—not palace, for which the royal couple were looking out. It is unnecessary to say that the personal visit was quite satisfactory, though the purchase was not made till some months later. The engraving gives a pleasant idea of the Osborne of to-day, with its double towers—seen out at sea—its terraces, and its fountains.

On the 21st of October the Queen and the Prince happened to be yachting off Portsmouth. It was the anniversary of the battle of Trafalgar, and the Victory lay in the roads, adorned with wreaths and garlands from stem to stern. The Queen expressed her desire to visit the ship. She went at once to the quarter-deck to see the spot where Nelson fell. It is marked by a brass plate with an inscription, on this day surrounded by a wreath of laurel. The Queen gazed in silence, the tears rising to her eyes. Then she plucked a couple of leaves from the laurel wreath, and asked to be shown the cabin in which Nelson died. The cockpit was lit up while the party were inspecting the poop of the Victory, which bears the words of the great Admiral's last signal, "England expects every man to do his duty." In the cockpit, long associated with merry, mischievous sprites of "middies," there had been for many a year the representation of a funeral urn, with the sentence, "Here Nelson died." The visitors looked at the spot without speaking. There, on this very day in the fast-receding past, amidst the hardly subdued din of a great naval battle, the dying hero with his failing breath made the brief, tender appeal to his faithful captain, "Kiss me, Hardy." The Queen requested that there might be no firing when she left the ship, and was sped on her way only by "the three tremendous British cheers of the sailors manning the yards."

On the 28th of October the great civic ceremonies of the opening of the new Royal Exchange by the Queen took place. The morning had been foggy, but cleared up into brilliant autumn sunshine, a happy instance of the Queen's weather, when a considerable part of the programme, as a matter of necessity, was enacted under the open sky.

Crowds almost as great as on the day of the Coronation six years before occupied the line of route, swarming in St. James's Park and St. Paul's Churchyard and at Charing Cross, while the Poultry—deriving its name from the circumstance that it was once filled with poulterers' shops—was reserved for the Livery of the City Companies. Every window which could command the passing of the pageant was filled with spectators. The Queen, in her State coach, drawn by her cream-coloured horses, drove through the marble arch at Buckingham Palace about eleven o'clock. She was accompanied by Prince Albert, and attended by Lady Canning in the absence of the Duchess of Buccleugh, Mistress of the Robes, and by the Earl of Jersey, Master of the Horse. The great officers of her Household in long procession preceded her, and she was followed by an escort of Life Guards. At this time the Queen's popularity was a very active principle, though not more heartfelt and abiding than it is to-day. As she appeared, it is said the words "God bless you," uttered by some loyal subject, were caught up and passed from lip to lip, running through the vast concourse. The simply-clad lady of the Highlands was magnificently dressed to-day, to do honour to her City of London, in white satin and silver tissue, sparkling with jewels. On her left side she wore the star of the Order of the Garter, and round her left arm the Garter itself, with the motto set in diamonds. She had at the back of her head a miniature crown entirely composed of brilliants, while above her forehead she wore a diamond tiara. Prince Albert was in the uniform of a colonel of artillery.

The City magnates as usual had gathered at Child's Bank, from which they went to Temple Bar. The common councilmen were in their mazarine-blue cloaks and cocked hats, the aldermen in their scarlet robes, the Lord Mayor in a robe of crimson velvet, with a collar of SS, and, strange to say, a Spanish hat and feather. In truth a goodly show. The gates of Temple Bar, which had been previously closed, were thrown open to admit the royal procession. The Queen's carriage drew up. The Lord Mayor advanced on foot before the spikes on which many a traitor's head had been stuck, and with a profound reverence offered to her Majesty the City sword, which, the Queen touched as a sign of acceptance, and then waved it back to the Lord Mayor. Nothing can read better, but accidents will happen.

From Lady Bloomfield, on the authority of the late Sir Robert Peel, who told the story in the maid-of-honour's hearing, we have additional particulars. The Lord Mayor, in his Spanish hat and feather, was at this very moment in as awkward a predicament as ever befell an unlucky chief magistrate. He had drawn on a pair of jack-boots over his shoes and stockings, to keep the mud off till the moment of action. Unfortunately the boots proved too tight, and could not be got off when the sign was given that the Queen was coming. One of the victim's spurs caught in the fur trimming of an alderman's robe, and rendered the confusion worse. The Lord Mayor stood with a leg out, and several men tugging at his boot. In the meantime the Queen was coming nearer and nearer; she was only a few paces off, while the representative of her good City of London struggled in an agony with one boot on and one off. At last he became beside himself, and cried wildly, "For God's sake put that boot on again." He only got it on in time to make his obeisance to her Majesty. He had to wear the detestable boots till the banquet; just before it, he was successfully stripped of his encumbrances.

As the procession went on, the civic body fell into its place, the Lord Mayor on horseback, where his jack-boots would not look amiss, with three footmen in livery on each side of him, carrying the City sword before the

Queen's coach.

The Royal Exchange, at the end of the Poultry, with the Mansion House on the right and the Bank of England on the left, has been twice burnt. Sir Thomas Gresham's Exchange, which was built after an Antwerp model, while it bore the Greshams' grasshopper crest conspicuous on the front, was opened by good Queen Bess, and perished in the Great Fire of London. This building's successor was burnt down in 1838, one of the bells which rang tunes pealing forth, in the middle of the fire, the only too appropriate melody, "There's nae luck about the house." In the large cloistered court of the present Royal Exchange, the stage of this day's festivities, stands a statue of Queen Victoria. There is an allegorical figure of Commerce on the front of the building. The inscription on the pedestal, selected by Dean Milman, is due to a suggestion of Prince Albert's to the sculptor, Westmacott, that there should be the recognition of a superior Power. The well-chosen words declare "The earth is the Lord's and the fullness thereof."

At the Royal Exchange the body of the procession went in by the northern entrance, only to hurry to the western door to receive the Queen. She entered the building leaning on the arm of Prince Albert, and the royal standard was immediately hoisted. The procession was again formed. She set forth "in slow State" to make her circuit of the roofless quadrangle, round the corridor and through the inner court, all in the open air. At the foot of the campanile the bells chimed for the first time "God save the Queen." Her Majesty went upstairs and passed through the second banqueting-room to show herself, then walked on to the throne-room, hung with crimson velvet and cloth, and furnished with a throne of crimson velvet. The Queen took her seat, Prince Albert standing on her right and the Duchess of Kent and the Duke of Cambridge on her left, Sir Robert Peel and Sir James Graham being near. The Lord Mayor and the rest of the Corporation formed a semicircle facing the Queen. The Recorder read the loyal and congratulatory address welcoming his sovereign, and recalling Queen Elizabeth's visit to open the first Exchange. Did anybody remember the picture of the Virgin Queen with the outshone goddesses fleeing abashed before her virtues, with which the child-princess reared at Kensington must have been familiar?

The speaker concluded by asking her Majesty's "favourable regard and sanction for the work which her loyal citizens of London had now completed." The Queen returned a gracious reply, gave the Lord Mayor her hand to kiss, and doubtless consoled him for any misadventure by announcing her intention to create him a baronet in remembrance of the day.

In the great room of the underwriters, ninety-eight feet long by forty wide, a dejeuner was served, at which the Queen, the Prince, the Duchess of Kent, and the Duke and Duchess of Cambridge, with other persons of rank, including the foreign ambassadors and their wives, sat on the dais at the cross-table. At the long table beneath the dais, among the Cabinet ministers and their wives, members of Parliament, judges, the Court of Aldermen, and many other distinguished and privileged persons, sat Sir Robert and Lady Sale, in another scene than any they had known among the defiles and forts of Afghanistan. The Bishop of London said grace. The usual toasts, "Her gracious Majesty, Queen Victoria"—no longer the young girl who bore her part so well at the Guildhall dinner, but the woman in her flower, endowed with all which makes life precious—"Prince Albert, the Prince of Wales, and the rest of the royal family," were drunk, and replied to by the comprehensive wish, "Prosperity to the City of London."

At twenty minutes after two the Queen and the Prince went downstairs again to the quadrangle, in the centre of which her Majesty stopped, while the Ministers and the Corporation formed a circle round her. The heralds made proclamation and commanded silence; the Queen, after receiving a slip of paper from Sir James Graham, announced in clear, distinct tones, "It is my royal will and pleasure that this building be hereafter called "The Royal Exchange." This ceremony concluded the day's programme, and her Majesty left shortly afterwards. Great festivities in the City wound up the gala. The Lord Mayor entertained at the Mansion House, the Lady Mayoress gave a ball, the Livery Companies dined in their respective halls.

A little adventure occurred at the Opera in November, 1844. The Queen went, not in State, or even semi-state, but privately, to hear Auber's opera of "The Siren," when Mr. Bunn, the lessee, was found to have made known without authority her Majesty's intention. The result was a great house, but some inconvenience to the first lady in the land. The Queen was called for, but declined to come forward, and for ten minutes there was a commotion, the audience refusing to let the opera go on. At last the National Anthem was played, the Queen showed herself, and this section of her subjects was appeased and passed from clamorous discontent to equally clamorous satisfaction.

During the winter Sir Robert and Lady Sale paid the Queen a visit at Windsor, while Miss Liddell was maid-of-honour in waiting. The lively narrator of the events of these days describes Lady Sale, as tall, thin, and rather plain, but with a good countenance, while Sir Robert was stout. Lady Sale told these wondering listeners, in a palace that she started from Cabul in a cloth habit, which got wet the first day, and became like a sheet of ice, while it was nine days before she could take it off. She was wounded in the arm on the second day's march, the ball passing first below the elbow and coming out at the wrist, while there were other balls which passed through her habit; Mrs. Sturt's fatherless child, Lady Sales's grand-daughter, was born in a small room without light and almost without air. The captive ladies often slept in the open air on the snow, with the help of sheepskins, half of which were under and half over the sleepers. They washed their clothes by dipping them in the rivers and patting the garments till they became dry. Sometimes the prisoners were twenty-four hours without food, and when served it consisted of dishes of rice with sheeps' tails in the middle, and melted fat like tallow poured over them. The captivity lasted ten weary months, while the captives were dragged from place to place, over fearful roads, amidst the snows of the Caucasus. Lady Sale was told she was kept by Akbar Khan as a hold on her "devil of a husband."

END OF VOL. I.

Volume II.

CHAPTER I. ROYAL PROGRESSES TO BURGHLEY, STOWE, AND STRATHFIELDSAYE.

On the 29th of November the Queen went on one of her visits to her nobility. We are told, and we can easily believe, these visits were very popular and eagerly contested for. In her Majesty's choice of localities it would seem as if she loved sometimes to retrace her early footsteps by going again with her husband to the places where she had been, as the young Princess, with the Duchess of Kent. The Queen went at this time to Burghley, the seat of the Marquis of Exeter. The tenantry of the different noblemen whose lands she passed through lined the roads, the mayors of the various towns presented addresses, the school children sang the National Anthem. At Burghley, too, Queen Elizabeth had been before Queen Victoria. She also had visited a Cecil. The Maiden Queen had travelled under difficulties. The country roads of her day had been so nearly impassable that her only means of transit had been to use a pillion behind her Lord Steward. Her seat in the chapel was pointed out to the Queen and Prince Albert when they went there for morning prayers. Whether or not both queens whiled away a rainy day by going over the whole manor-house, down to the kitchen, we cannot say; but it is not likely that her Majesty's predecessor underwent the ordeal to her gravity of passing through a gentleman's bedroom and finding his best wig and whiskers displayed upon a block on a chest of drawers. And we are not aware that Queen Elizabeth witnessed such an interesting family rite as that which her Majesty graced by her presence. The youngest daughter of the Marquis and Marchioness of Exeter was christened in the chapel, at six o'clock in the evening, before the Queen, and was named for her "Lady Victoria Cecil," while Prince Albert stood as godfather to the child. After the baptism the Queen kissed her little namesake, and Prince Albert presented her with a gold cup bearing the inscription, "To Lady Victoria Cecil, from her godfather Albert." At dinner the newly-named child was duly toasted by the Queen's command.

The next day the royal party visited "Stamford town," from which the Mayor afterwards sent Prince Albert the gift of a pair of Wellington boots, as a sample of the trade of the place. The drive extended to the ruins of another manor-house which, Lady Bloomfield heard, was built by the Cecils for a temporary resort when their house of Burghley was swept. The Queen and the Prince planted an oak and a lime, not far from Queen Elizabeth's lime. The festivities ended with a great dinner and ball, at which the Queen did not dance. Most of the company passed before her chair of State on the dais, as they do at a drawing-room.

On the 29th of December an aged English kinswoman of the Queen's died at the Ranger's House, Blackheath, where she held the somewhat anomalous office of Ranger of Greenwich Park. This was Princess Sophia Matilda, daughter of the Duke of Gloucester, George III.'s brother, and sister of the late Duke of Gloucester, the husband of his cousin, Princess Mary.

Her mother's history was a romance. She was the beautiful niece of Horace Walpole, the illegitimate daughter of his brother, the Earl of Oxford. She married first the Earl of Waldegrave, and became the mother of the three lovely sisters whom Sir Joshua Reynolds's brush immortalised. The widowed countess caught the fancy of the royal Duke, just as it was said, in contemporary letters, that another fair young widow turned the head of another brother of the King's. George III. refused at first to acknowledge the Duke of Gloucester's marriage, but finally withdrew his opposition. If, as was reported, the Duke of York married Lady Mary Coke, the marriage was never ratified. The risk of such marriages caused the passing of the Royal Marriage Act, which rendered the marriage of any member of the royal family without the consent of the reigning sovereign illegal. The children of the Duke of Gloucester and his Duchess were two— Prince William and Princess Sophia Matilda. They held the somewhat doubtful position, perhaps more marked in those days, of a family royal on one side of the house only. The brother, if not a very brilliant, an inoffensive and not an illiberal prince, though wicked wags called him "Silly Billy," improved the situation by his marriage with the amiable and popular Princess Mary, to whom a private gentleman, enamoured by hearsay with her virtues, left a considerable fortune. We get a passing glimpse of the sister, Princess Sophia Matilda, in Fanny Burney's diary. She was then a pretty, sprightly girl, having apparently inherited some of her beautiful mother's and half-sisters' attractions. She was admitted to terms of considerable familiarity and intimacy with her royal cousins; and yet she was not of the circle of Queen Charlotte, neither could she descend gracefully to a lower rank. No husband, royal or noble, was found for her. One cannot think of her without attaching a sense of loneliness to her princely estate. She survived her brother, the Duke of Gloucester, ten years, and died at the age of seventy-two at the Ranger's House, Blackheath, from which she had dispensed many kindly charities. At her funeral the royal standard was hoisted half- mast high on Greenwich Hospital, the Observatory, the churches of St. Mary and St. Alphege, and on Blackheath. She was laid, with nearly all her royal race for the last two generations, in the burial-place of kings, St. George's Chapel, Windsor. Prince Albert occupied his stall as a Knight of the Garter, with a mourning scarf across his field- marshal's uniform.

In the middle of January, 1845, the Queen and Prince Albert went on a visit to the Duke of Buckingham at Stowe, which was still unstripped of its splendid possessions and interesting antiquarian relics. The huge gathering of neighbours and tenants included waggons full of labourers, admitted into the park to see the Queen's arrival and the illumination of the great house at night.

The amusements of the next two days, the ordinary length of a royal visit, began with battues for the Prince, when the accumulation of game was so enormous that, in place of the fact being remarkable that "he hit almost everything he fired at," it would have been singular if a good shot could have avoided doing so. Fifty beaters, so near each other that their sticks almost touched, entered a thick cover and drove the game past the place where the sportsmen were stationed, into the open space of the park. Out the hares rushed from every quarter, "so many of them, that it was often impossible to stop more than one out of half-a-dozen. The ground immediately in front of the shooters became strewn with dead and dying…. It was curious to behold the evident reluctance with which the hares left their retreat, and then their perplexity at finding themselves so beset without. Many actually made for the canal, and swam like dogs across a piece of water nearly a hundred yards wide, shaking themselves upon landing, and making off without any apparent distress. The pheasants were still more averse 'to come and be killed.' For some time not one appeared above the trees. The cocks were heard crowing like domestic fowls, as the numerous tribe retreated before the sticks of the advancing army of beaters. Upon arriving, however, at the edge of the wood, quite a cloud ascended, and the slaughter was proportionately great."

"Slaughter," not sport, is the appropriate word. One cannot help thinking that so it must have struck the Prince; nor are we surprised that, on the next opportunity he had of exercising a sportsman's legitimate vocation, with the good qualities of patience, endurance, and skill, which it is calculated to call forth, emphatic mention is made of his keen enjoyment.

Besides shooting there was walking for both ladies and gentlemen, to the number of twenty guests, "in the mild, clear weather," in the beautiful park. There was the usual county gathering, in order to confer on the upper ten thousand, within a radius of many miles, the much-prized honour of "meeting" the Queen at a dinner or a ball. Lastly, her Majesty and the Prince planted the oak and the cedar which were to rank like heirlooms, and be handed down as trophies of a royal visit and princely favour, to future generations.

The Queen and Prince Albert returned to Windsor on the evening of Saturday, the 18th of January, and on the afternoon of Monday, the 20th, they started again to pay a long-projected visit to her old friend the Duke of Wellington at Strathfieldsaye. It was known that the Duke had set his heart on entertaining his sovereign in his own house, and she not only granted him the boon, but in consideration of his age, his laurels, and the long and intimate connection between them, she let the visit have more of a private and friendly character than the visits of sovereigns to subjects were wont to have. However, the country did not lose its gala. Arches of winter evergreens instead of summer flowers, festive banners, loyal inscriptions, yeoman corps, holiday faces, met her on all sides. At Swallowfield—a name which Mary Russell Mitford has made pleasant to English ears—"no less a person than the Speaker of the House of Commons," the representative of an old Huguenot refugee, the Right Honourable John Shaw Lefevre, commanded the troop of yeomanry.

The Iron Duke met his honoured guests in the hall and conducted them to the library. Every day the same formula was gone through. "The Duke takes the Queen in to dinner, sits by her Majesty, and after dinner gets up and says, 'With your Majesty's permission I give the health of her Majesty,' and then the same to the Prince. They then adjourn to the library, and the Duke sits on the sofa by the Queen (almost as a father would sit by a daughter) for the rest of the evening until eleven o'clock, the Prince and the gentlemen being scattered about in the library or the billiard-room, which opens into it. In a large conservatory beyond, the band of the Duke's grenadier regiment plays through the evening."

There was much that was unique and kindly in the relations between the Queen and the greatest soldier of his day. He had stood by her baptismal font; she had been his guest, when she was the girl- Princess, at Walmer. He had sat in her first Council; he had witnessed her marriage; she was to give his name to one of her sons; in fact, he had taken part in every event of her life. The present arrangements were a graceful, well-nigh filial, tribute of affectionate regard for the old man who had served his country both on the battle-field and in the senate, who had watched his Queen's career with the keenest interest, and rejoiced in her success as something with which he had to do.

The old soldier also gave the Prince shooting, but it was the "fine wild sport" which might have been expected from the host, and which seemed more to the taste of the guest. And in the party of gentlemen who walked for miles over the ploughed land and through the brushwood, none kept up the pace better than the veteran.

The weather was broken and partly wet during the Queen's stay at Strathfieldsaye, and in lieu of out-of-door exercise, the tennis-court came into request. Lord Charles Wellesley, the Duke's younger son, played against professional players, and Prince Albert engaged Lord Charles and one of the professional players, the Queen looking on.

When the visit was over, the Duke punctiliously performed his part of riding on horseback by her Majesty's carriage for the first stage of her journey.

Comical illustrations are given of the old nobleman and soldier's dry rebuffs, administered to the members of the press and the public generally, who haunted Strathfieldsaye on this occasion. The first was in reply to a request for admission to the house on the plea that the writer was one of the staff of a popular journal commissioned to give the details of the visit. "Field-Marshal the Duke of Wellington presents his compliments to Mr. —-, and begs to say he does not see what his house at Strathfieldsaye has to do with the public press." The other was in the form of a still more ironical notice put up in the grounds, "desiring that people who wish to see the house may drive up to the hall-door and ring the bell, but that they are to abstain from walking on the flagstones and looking in at the windows."

In February the Queen opened Parliament in person for what was destined to be a stormy session, particularly in relation to Sir Robert Peel's measure proposing an increased annual grant of money to the Irish Roman Catholic priests' college of Maynooth. In the Premier's speech, in introducing the Budget, he was able to pay a well-merited compliment on the wise and judicious economy shown in the management of her Majesty's income, so that it was equal to meet the heavy calls made upon it by the visits of foreign sovereigns, who were entertained in a manner becoming the dignity of the sovereign, "without adding one tittle to the burdens of the country. And I am not required, on the part of her Majesty," went on Sir Robert Peel, "to press for the extra expenditure of one single shilling on account of these unforeseen causes of increased expenditure. I think, to state this is only due to the personal credit of her Majesty, who insists upon it that there shall be every magnificence required by her station, but without incurring a single debt." In order to show how the additional cost of such royal hospitality taxed the resources even of the Queen of England, it may be well to give an idea of the ordinary scale of housekeeping at Windsor Castle. Lady Bloomfield likens the kitchen-fire to Nebuchadnezzar's burning fiery furnace. Even when there was no company, from fifteen to twenty joints hung roasting there. In one year the number of people fed at dinner in the Castle amounted to a hundred and thirteen thousand!

Shall we be accused of small moralities and petty lessons in thrift if we say that this passage in Sir Robert Peel's speech recalls the stories of the child-Princess's training, in a wholesome horror of debt, and the exercise of such little acts of self-denial as can alone come in a child's way; that it brings to mind the Tunbridge anecdote of the tiny purchaser on her donkey, bidden to look at her empty purse when a little box in the bazaar caught her eye, and prohibited from going further in obtaining the treasure, till the next quarter's allowance was due? Well might the nation that had read the report of Sir Robert Peel's speech listen complacently when it heard in the following month, of the Queen's acquisition of a private property which should be all her own and her husband's, to do with, as they chose. Another country bestowed, upon quite different grounds, on one of its sovereigns the honourable title of King Honest Man. Here was Queen Honest Woman, who would not buy what she could not afford, or ask her people to pay for fancies in which she indulged, regardless of her means. A different example had been presented by poor Louis XVI. and Marie Antoinette, who, after a course of what their most faithful servants admitted to be grievous misrule and misappropriation of public dignities and funds—to satisfy the ambition and greed of favourites or their friends—in the face of national bankruptcy, private ruin, and widespread disaffection, in the very death-throes of the Revolution, chose that time of all others to buy—under whatever specious pretext of exchange and indemnification—for him who had already so many hunting-seats, the fresh one of Rambouillet; for her, who had Little Trianon in its perfection, the new suburban country house of St. Cloud.

Osborne abounded in the advantages which the royal couple sought. It was in the Isle of Wight, which her Majesty had loved in her girlhood, with the girdle of sea that gave such assurance of the much-courted, much-needed seclusion, as could hardly be procured elsewhere— certainly not within a reasonable distance of London. It was a lovely place by nature, with no end of capabilities for the practice of the Prince's pleasant faculty of landscape-gardening, with which he had already done wonders in the circumscribed grounds of Buckingham Palace and the larger field of Windsor. There were not only woods and valleys and charming points of view—among them a fine look at Spithead; the woods went down to the sea, and the beach belonged to the estate. Such a quiet country home for a country and home-loving Queen and Prince, and for the little children, to whom tranquillity, freedom, the woods, the fields, and the sea-sands were of such vital and lasting consequence, was inestimable.

In addition to other outlets for an active, beneficent nature, Osborne, with its works of building, planting, and improving going on for years to come, had also its farms, like the Home Farm at Windsor. And the Prince was fond of farming no less than of landscape-gardening —proud of his practical success in making it pay, deeply interested in all questions of agriculture and their treatment, so as to secure permanent employment and ample provision for the labourers. Prince Albert's love of animals, too, found scope in these farming operations. When the Queen and the Prince visited the Home Farm the tame pigeons would settle on his hat and her shoulders. The accompanying engraving represents the pasture and part of the Home Farm at Osborne. "The cow in the group was presented to her Majesty by the Corporation of Guernsey, when the Queen visited the Channel Islands; the animal is a beautiful specimen of the Alderney breed, and is a great favourite ... on the forehead of the cow is a V distinctly marked; a peculiarity, it may be presumed, which led to the presentation; the other animals are her calves."

In the course of this session of Parliament, the Queen sought more than once to mark her acknowledgment of the services of Sir Robert Peel, round whose political career troubles were gathering. She acted as sponsor to his grandchild—the heir of the Jersey family—and she offered Sir Robert, through Lord Aberdeen, the Order of the Garter, an offer which the Prime Minister respectfully declined in words that deserve to be remembered. He sprang from the people, he said, and was essentially of the people, and such an honour, in his case, would be misapplied. His heart was not set upon titles of honour or social distinction. His reward lay in her Majesty's confidence, of which, by many indications, she had given him the fullest assurance; and when he left her service the only distinction he courted was that she should say to him, "You have been a faithful servant, and have done your duty to your country and to myself."

CHAPTER II.THE QUEEN'S POWDER BALL.

On the evening of the 6th of June, 1845, her Majesty, who was at Buckingham Palace for the season, gave another great costume ball, still remembered as her Powder Ball—a name bestowed on it because of the universally-worn powder on hair and periwigs. It was not such a novelty as the Plantagenet Ball had been, neither was it so splendidly fantastic nor apparently so costly a performance; not that the materials used in the dresses were less valuable, but several of them — notably the old lace which was so marked a feature in the spectacle that it might as well have been called "The Lace Ball"—existed in many of the great houses in store, like the family diamonds, and had only to be brought out with the other heirlooms, and properly disposed of, to constitute the wearer en grande tenue. No doubt trade was still to be encouraged, and Spitalfields, in its chronic adversity, to be brought a little nearer to prosperity by the manufacture of sumptuous stuffs, in imitation of gorgeous old brocades, for a portion of the twelve hundred guests. But these motives were neither so urgent nor so ostensible, and perhaps the ball originated as much in a wish to keep up a good custom once begun, and to show some cherished guests a choice example of princely hospitality, as in an elaborate calculation of forced gain to an exotic trade.

The period chosen for the representation was much nearer the present. It was only a hundred years back, from 1740 to 1750. It may be that this comparative nearness fettered rather than emancipated the players in the game, and that, though civil wars and clan feuds had long died out, and the memory of the Scotch rebellion was no more than a picturesque tragic romance, a trifle of awkwardness survived in the encounter, face to face once more, in the very guise of the past, of the descendants of the men and women who had won at Prestonpans and lost at Culloden. It was said that a grave and stately formality distinguished this ball—a tone attributed to dignified, troublesome fashions—stranger then, but which since these days have become more familiar to us.

No two more attractive figures presented themselves that night than the sisters-in-law, the Duchess of Kent and the Duchess of Gloucester, the one in her sixtieth the other in her seventieth year. The third royal duchess in the worthy trio, who represented long and well the royal matronhood of England, the Duchess of Cambridge, was, along with her Duke, prevented from being present at the Queen's ball in consequence of a recent death in her family. The Duchess of Kent wore a striped and "flowered" brocade, with quantities of black lace relieving the white satin of her train. The Duchess of Gloucester, sweet pretty Princess Mary of more than fifty years before, came in the character of a much less happy woman, Marie Leczinska, the queen of Louis XV. She must have looked charming in her rich black brocade, and some of the hoards of superb lace—which she is said to have inherited from her mother, Queen Charlotte—edged with strings of diamonds and agraffes of diamonds, while over her powdered hair was tied a fichu capuchin of Chantilly.

Among the multitude of guests assembled at Buckingham Palace, the privileged few who danced in the Queen's minuets, as well as the members of the royal family, arrived by the Garden Gate and were received in the Yellow Drawing-room. Included in this select company was a German princess who had lately married an English subject— Princess Marie of Baden, wife of the Marquis of Douglas, not the first princess who had wedded into the noble Scotch house of Hamilton, though it was many a long century since Earl Walter received—

all Arran's isle To dower his royal bride

The Queen had special guests with her on this occasion—her brother the Prince of Leiningen, the much-loved uncle of the royal children; and the favourite cousin of the circle, the young Duchesse de Nemours, with her husband. The Queen and Prince Albert, accompanied by their visitors, the various members of the English royal family present at the ball, and the different suites, passed into the ball-room at half- past ten. The first dance, the graceful march of the German polonaise, was danced by all, young and old, the bands striking up simultaneously, and the dance extending through the whole of the State apartments, the Queen leading the way, preceded by the Vice- Chamberlain, the Comptroller and Treasurer of the Household, and two gentlemen ushers to clear a space for her. After the polonaise the company passed slowly before the Queen. A comical incident occurred in this part of the programme through the innocent mistake of an old infantry officer, who in his progress lifted his peaked hat and gave the Queen a military salute, as he walked by.

Then her Majesty left the ball-room and repaired to the throne-room, where the first minuet was formed. It is only necessary to recall that most courtly of slow and graceful dances to judge how well suited it was for this ball. The Queen danced with her cousin, Prince George of Cambridge. Her Majesty wore a wonderful dress of cloth of gold and cloth of silver, with daisies and poppies worked in silks, and shaded the natural colours; trimmings and ruffles of exquisite old lace, stomacher covered with old lace and jewels, the sacque set off with scarlet ribands, the fair hair powdered under a tiara and crown of diamonds, dainty white satin shoes with scarlet rosettes—a diamond in each rosette, the Order of the Garter on the arm, the Star and Riband of the Order. Prince George was less fortunate in the regimentals of a cavalry officer a century back; for, as it happened, while the costume of 1740-50 was favourable to women and to civilians, it was trying to military men.

Prince Albert danced with the Duchesse de Nemours. These two had been early playmates who never, even in later and sadder days, got together without growing merry over the stories and jokes of their childhood in Coburg. The Prince must have been one of the most graceful figures there, in a crimson velvet coat edged with gold and lined with white satin, on the left breast the splendid Star of the Order of the Garter, shoulder-strap and sword inlaid with diamonds, white satin waistcoat brocaded with gold, breeches of crimson velvet with gold buttons, shoes of black kid with red heels and diamond buckles, three- cornered hat trimmed with gold lace, edged with white ostrich feathers, a magnificent loop of diamonds, and the black cockade of the Georges, not the white cockade of the Jameses.

His golden-haired partner was in a tastefully gay and fantastic as well as splendid costume of rose-coloured Chinese damask, with gold blonde and pearls, over a petticoat of point d'Alençon, with a deep border of silver and silver rosettes. The stomacher of brilliants and pearls, on the left shoulder a nosegay with diamond wheat-ears interspersed, shoes of purple satin with fleurs-de-lys embroidered in gold and diamonds, as became a daughter of France, and gloves embroidered with similar fleurs-de-lys.

There were many gay and gallant figures and fair faces in that minuet of minuets. Prince Edward of Saxe-Weimar was meant to dance with the young Marchioness of Douro, but she by some strange chance came too late for the honour, and her place was supplied by another young matron and beauty, Lady Jocelyn, formerly Lady Fanny Cowper. Prince Leiningen, who wore a white suit faced with blue and a buff waistcoat edged with silver lace, danced with Lady Mount-Edgcumbe. The Duke of Beaufort once more disputed with the Earl of Wilton the distinction of being the finest gentleman present.

The Queen danced in four minuets, standing up in the second with Prince Albert. This minuet also included several of the most beautiful women of the time and of the Court; notably Lady Seymour, one of the Sheridan sisters, the Queen of Beauty at the Eglinton tournament; and Lady Canning.

After the second minuet the Queen and all the company returned to the ball-room, where two other minuets, those of Lady Jersey and Lady Chesterfield, were danced, and between them was given Lady Breadalbane's strathspey. There was such crowding to see these dances that the Lord Chamberlain had difficulty in making room for them. While Musard furnished special music for the minuets and quadrilles, adapting it in one case from airs of the '45, the Queen's piper, Mackay, gave forth, for the benefit of the strathspey and reel- dancers, the stirring strains of "Miss Drummond of Perth," "Tullochgorum," and "The Marquis of Huntly's Highland Fling," which must have rung with wild glee through the halls of kings.

Lady Chesterfield's minuet was the last dance before supper, served with royal splendour in the dining-room, to which the Queen passed at twelve o'clock. After supper the Queen danced in a quadrille and in the two next minuets. Her first partner was the Duc de Nemours, who wore an old French infantry general's uniform—a coat of white cloth, the front covered with gold embroidery, sleeves turned up with crimson velvet, waistcoat and breeches of crimson velvet, stockings of crimson silk, and red-heeled shoes with diamond buckles. In the second minuet her Majesty had her brother, the Prince of Leiningen, for her partner. The ball was ended, according to a good old English fashion, by the quaint changing measure of "Sir Roger de Coverley," known in Scotland as "The Haymakers," in which the Queen had her husband for her partner. This country-dance was danced in the picture gallery.

Let who would be the beauty at the Queen's ball, there was at least one poetess there in piquant black and cerise, with cerise roses and priceless point à l'aiguille, Lady John Scott, who had been the witty heiress, Miss Spottiswoode of Spottiswoode. She wrote to an old refrain one of the most pathetic of modern Scotch ballads—

Douglas, Douglas, tender and true

The beauty of the ball was the Marchioness of Douro, who not so long ago had been the beauty of the season as Lady Elizabeth Hay, daughter of the Marquis of Tweeddale, when she caught the fancy of the elder, son and heir of the Duke of Wellington. In this case beauty was not unadorned, for the lovely Marchioness, [Footnote: Her likeness is familiar to many people in an engraving from a well-known picture of the Duke of Wellington showing his daughter-in-law the field of Waterloo] the Greek mould of whose head attracted the admiration of all judges, was said to wear jewels to the value of sixty thousand pounds, while the superb point-lace flounce to her white brocade must have been a source of pious horror to good Roman Catholics, since it was believed to have belonged to the sacred vestments of a pope.

We have said that lace and jewels gave the distinguishing stamp to the ball—such lace!—point d'Alençon, point de Bayeux, point de Venise, point a l'aiguille, Mechlin, Guipure, Valenciennes, Chantilly, enough to have turned green with envy the soul of a cultured petit- maître, an aesthetic fop of the present day.

Some of the jewels, no less than the lace, were historical. The
Marchioness of Westminster, besides displaying sabots of point-
lace, which had belonged to Caroline, queen of George II., wore the
Nassuk and Arcot diamonds.

Miss Burdett-Coutts wore a lustrous diadem and necklace that had once graced the brow and throat of poor Marie Antoinette, and had found their way at last into jewel-cases no longer royal, owing their glittering contents to the wealth of a great city banker.

A word about the antiquated finery of the Iron Duke, with which the old soldier sought to please his young mistress. It provoked a smile or two from the more frivolous as the grey, gaunt, spindle-shanked old man stalked by, yet it was not without its pathetic side. The Duke wore a scarlet coat, a tight fit, laced with gold, with splendid gold buttons and frogs, the brilliant star of the Order of the Garter, and the Order of the Golden Fleece, a waistcoat of scarlet cashmere covered with gold lace, breeches of scarlet kerseymere trimmed with gold lace; gold buckles, white silk stockings, cocked hat laced with gold, sword studded with rose diamonds and emeralds.

It is nearly forty years since these resplendent masquers trod the floors of Buckingham Palace, and if the changes which time has brought about had been foreseen, if the veil which shrouds the future had been lifted, what emotions would have been called forth!

Who could have borne to hear that the bright Queen and giver of the fete would pass the years of her prime in the mournful shade of disconsolate widowhood? That the pale crown of a premature death was hovering over the head of him who was the life of her life, the active promoter and sustainer of all that was good and joyous in that great household, all that was great and happy in the kingdom over which she ruled?

Who would have ventured to prophesy that of the royal kindred and cherished guests, the Prince of Leiningen was to die a landless man, the Duc de Nemours to spend long years in exile, the Duchesse to be cut down in the flower of her womanhood? Who would have guessed that this great nobleman, the head of an ancient house, was to perish by a miserable accident in a foreign hotel; that his sister, the wife of an unfortunate statesman, was to be dragged through the mire of a divorce court; that the treasures of a princely home were to pass away from the race that had accumulated them, under the strokes of an auctioneer's hammer? Who could have dreamt that this fine intellect and loving heart would follow the lord of their destiny to Hades, and wander there for evermore distracted, in the land of shadows, where there is no light of the sun to show the way, no firm ground to stay the tottering feet and groping hands? As for these two fair sisters in Watteau style of blue and pink, and green and pink taffetas, lace, and pearls, and roses—surely the daintiest, most aristocratic shepherdesses ever beheld—one of them would have lost her graceful equanimity, reddened with affront, and tingled to the finger-tips with angry unbelief if she had been warned beforehand that she would be amongst the last of the high-born, high-bred brides who would forfeit her birthright and her presence at a Queen's Court by agreeing to be married at the hands of a blacksmith instead of a bishop, before the rude hymeneal altar at Gretna.

But to-night there was no alarming interlude, like a herald of evil, to shake the nerves of the company—nothing more unpropitious than the contretemps to an unlucky lady of being overcome by the heat and seized with a fainting-fit, which caused her over-zealous supporters to remove her luxuriant powdered wig in order to give her greater air and coolness, so that she was fain, the moment she recovered, to hide her diminished head by a rapid discomfited retreat from what remained of the revelry.

On the 21st of June the Queen and the Prince, with the Lords of the Admiralty, inspected the fleet off Spithead. The royal yacht was attended by a crowd of yachts belonging to the various squadrons, a throng of steamboats and countless small boats. The Queen visited and went over the flagship—which was the St. Vincent—the Trafalgar, and the Albion. On her return to the yacht she held a levee of all the captains of the fleet. A few days afterwards she reviewed her fleet in brilliant, breezy weather. The royal yacht took up its position at Spithead, and successive signals were given to the squadron to "Lower sail," "Make sail," "Shorten sail and reef," and "Furl topgallant sails," all the manoeuvres—including the getting under way and sailing in line to St. Helen's—being performed with the very perfection of nautical accuracy. The review ended with the order, "Furl sails, put the life-lines on, and man yards," which was done as only English sailors can accomplish the feat, while the royal yacht on its return passed through the squadron amidst ringing cheers.

During the earlier part of the summer Sir John Franklin sailed with his ships, the Erebus and Terror, in search of that North Pole which, since the days of Sir Hugh Montgomery, "a captain tall," has been at once the goal and snare of many a gallant English sailor. The good ships disappeared under the horizon, never to reach their haven. By slow degrees oblivion, more or less profound, closed over the fate of officers and men, while, for lack of knowledge of their life or death, the light of many a hearth was darkened, and faithful hearts sickened with hope deferred and broke under the strain. As one instance, out of many, of the desolation which the silent loss of the gallant expedition occasioned, sorrow descended heavily on one of the happy Highland homes among which the Queen had dwelt the previous summer. Captain, afterwards Lord James, Murray, brother of Lord Glenlyon, was married to Miss Fairholme, sister of one of the picked men of whom the explorers were composed. When no tidings of him came, year after year, from the land of mist and darkness, pining melancholy seized upon her and made her its prey.

In the month of July the King of the Netherlands, who, as Prince of Orange, had served on the Duke of Wellington's staff at the close of the Peninsular War, came to England and took up his quarters at Mivart's Hotel, the Queen being in the Isle of Wight, where he joined her. Prince Albert met the King at Gosport and escorted him to Osborne. On his return to London the King, who was already a general in the English army, received his appointment as field-marshal, and reviewed the Household troops in Hyde Park. He paid a second visit to the Queen at Osborne before he left Woolwich for Holland.

A curious accident happened when the Queen prorogued Parliament on the 9th of August. The Duke of Argyle, an elderly man, was carrying the crown on a velvet cushion, when, in walking backwards before the Queen, he appeared to forget the two steps, leading from the platform on which the throne stands to the floor, and stumbled, the crown slipping from the cushion and falling to the ground, with the loss of some diamonds. The Queen expressed her concern for the Duke instead of for the crown; but on her departure the keeper of the House of Lords appeared in front of the throne, and prevented too near an approach to it, with the chance of further damage to the dropped jewels. The misadventure was naturally the subject of a good deal of private conversation in the House.

CHAPTER III. THE QUEEN'S FIRST VISIT TO GERMANY.

On the evening of the day that she prorogued Parliament, the Queen and the Prince with the Earl of Aberdeen as the minister in attendance, started from Buckingham Palace that she might pay her first visit to Germany. Surely none of all the new places she had visited within the last few years could have been of such surpassing interest to the traveller. It was her mother's country as well as her husband's, the home of her brother and sister, the place of which she must have heard, with which she must have had the kindliest associations from her earliest years.

The first stage of the journey—in stormy weather, unfortunately—was to Antwerp, where the party did not land till the following day, when they proceeded to Malines, where they were met by King Leopold and Queen Louise, who parted from their royal niece at Verviers. On the Prussian frontier Lord Westmoreland, the English ambassador, and Baron Bunsen met her Majesty. "To hear the people speak German," she wrote in her Journal, "to see the German soldiers, seemed to me so singular. I overheard people saying that I looked very English."

At Aix-la-Chapelle the King and Prince of Prussia received the visitors and accompanied them to Cologne. The ancient dirty town of the Three Kings gave the strangers an enthusiastic reception. The burghers even did their best to get rid of the unsavoury odours which distinguish the town of sweet essences, by pouring eau-de-Cologne on the roadways.

At Bruhl the Queen and the Prince were taken to the palace, where they found the Queen of Prussia, whose hostility to English and devotion to Russian interests when Lord Bloomfield represented the English Government at Berlin, are recorded by Lady Bloomfield. With the Queen was her sister-in-law, the Princess of Prussia, and the Court. The party went into one of the salons to hear the famous tatoo played by four hundred musicians, in the middle of an illumination by means of torches and coloured lamps. The Queen was reminded that she was in a land of music by hearing at a concert, in which sixty regimental bands assisted, "God save the Queen" better played than she had ever heard it before. "We felt so strange to be in Germany at last," repeats her Majesty, dwelling on the pleasant sensation, "at Bruhl, which Albert said he used to go and visit from Bonn."

The next day the visitors went to Bonn, accompanied by the King and Queen of Prussia. At the house of Prince Furstenberg many professors who had known Prince Albert were presented to the Queen, "which interested me very much," the happy wife says simply. "They were greatly delighted to see Albert and pleased to see me.... I felt as if I knew them all from Albert having told me so much about them." The experience is known to many a bride whose husband takes her proudly to his old alma mater.

The day was made yet more memorable by the unveiling of a statue to Beethoven. But, by an unlucky contretemps, the royal party on the balcony found the back of the statue presented to their gaze. The Freischutzen fired a feu-de-joie. A chorale was sung. The people cheered and the band played a Dusch—such a flourish of trumpets as is given in Germany when a health is drunk.

The travellers then went to the Prince's "former little house." The Queen writes, "It was such a pleasure for me to be able to see this house. We went all over it, and it is just as it was, in no way altered.... We went into the little bower in the garden, from which you have a beautiful view of the Kreuzberg—a convent situated on the top of a hill. The Siebengebirge (seven mountains) you also see, but the view of them is a good deal built up."

This visiting together the ground once so familiar to the Prince formed an era in two lives. It was the fulfilment of a beautiful, brilliant expectation which had been half dim and vague when the ardent lad was a quiet, diligent student, living simply, almost frugally, like the other students at the university on the Rhine, and his little cousin across the German Ocean, from whom he had parted in the homely red-brick palace of Kensington, had been proclaimed Queen of a great country. The prospect of their union was still very uncertain in those days, and yet it must sometimes have crossed his mind as he built air-castles in the middle of his reading; or strolled with a comrade along those old-fashioned streets, among their population of "wild-looking students," with long fair hair, pipes between their lips, and the scars of many a sword-duel on forehead and cheek; or penetrated into the country, where the brown peasant women, "with curious caps and handkerchiefs," came bearing their burden of sticks from the forest, like figures in old fairy tales. He must have told himself that the time might come when something like the transformation of a fairy-tale would be effected on his account; the plain living and high-thinking and college discipline of Bonn be exchanged for the dignity and influence of an English sovereign's consort. Then, perhaps, he would bring his bride to the dear old "fatherland," and show her where he had dreamt about her among his books.

At the banquet in the afternoon the accomplished King gave the Queen's health in a speech fit for a poet. He referred to a word sweet alike to British and German hearts. Thirty years before it had echoed on the heights of Waterloo from British and German tongues, after days of hot and desperate fighting, to mark the glorious triumph of their brotherhood in arms. "Now it resounds on the banks of our fair Rhine, amidst the blessings of that peace which was the hallowed fruit of the great conflict. That word is 'Victoria.' Gentlemen, drink to the health of her Majesty the Queen of the United Kingdom of Great Britain and Ireland, and to that of her august consort."

"The Queen," remarked Bunsen, "bowed at the first word, but much lower at the second. Her eyes brightened through tears, and as the King was taking his seat again, she rose and bent towards him and kissed his cheek, then took her seat again with a beaming countenance."

After the four-o'clock dinner, the royal party returned to Cologne, and from a steamer on the Rhine saw, through a drizzle of rain which did not greatly mar the spectacle, a splendid display of fireworks and illumination of the town, in which the great cathedral "seemed to glow with fire."

We quote a picturesque description of the striking scene. "The Rhine was made one vast feu-de-joie. As darkness closed in, the dim city began to put forth buds of light. Lines of twinkling brightness darted like liquid gold or silver from pile to pile, then by the bridge of boats across the river, up the masts of the shipping, and along the road on the opposite bank. Rockets now shot from all parts of the horizon. The royal party embarked in a steamer at St. Tremond and glided down by the river. As they passed the banks blazed with fireworks and musketry. At their approach the bridge glowed with redoubled light, and, opening, let the vessel pass to Cologne, whose cathedral burst forth a building of light, every detail of the architecture being made out in delicately-coloured lamps—pinkish, with an underglow of orange. Traversing in carriages the illuminated and vociferous city, the King and his companions returned by the railroad to Bruhl."

Next morning there was a great concert at Bonn—part of the Beethoven festival, in which much fine music was given, but, oddly enough, not much of Beethoven's, to her Majesty's regret. The Queen drove to the University—in the classrooms of which the Prince had sat as a student—and saw more of the professors who had taught him, and of students similar to those who had been his class-fellows. Then she went once more to Cologne, and visited its glory, the cathedral, at that time unfinished, returning to Bruhl to hail with delight the arrival of the King and Queen of the Belgians. "It seems like a dream to them and to me to see each other in Germany," the Queen wrote once more. The passages from her Majesty's Journal read as if she were pleased to congratulate herself on being at last with Prince Albert in his native country.

The last day at Cologne ended in another great concert, conducted by Meyerbeer, for which he had composed a cantata in honour of the Queen. Jenny Lind sang in the concert. It was her Majesty's first opportunity of hearing the great singer, who, of all her sister singers, has most identified herself with England, and from her noble, womanly character and domestic virtues, endeared herself to English hearts.

The tutelary genius of the river which is the Germans' watchword was not able to procure the Queen her weather for her sail on its green waters. Rain fell or threatened for both of the days. Not even the presence of three queens—of England, Prussia, and Belgium—two kings, a prince consort, an archduke, and a future emperor and empress, could propitiate the adverse barometer, or change the sulky face of the sky. Between showers the Queen had a glimpse of the romantic scenery, and perhaps Ehrenbreitstein was most in character when the smoke from the firing of twenty thousand troops "brought home to the imagination the din and lurid splendours of a battle."

The halt was made at Schlossenfels, which included among its distinguished guests Humboldt and Prince Metternich. Next day the King and Queen of Prussia took leave of their visitors, still under heavy rain. The weather cleared afterwards for a time, however, and beautiful Bingen, with the rest of the Rhenish country, was seen in sunshine. The only inconvenience remaining was the thunder of cannons and rattle of muskets which every loyal village kept up.

At Mayence the Queen was received by the Governor, Prince William of Prussia, and the Austrian commander, while the Prussian and Austrian troops, with their bands, gave a torchlight serenade before the hotel windows. On the rest-day which Sunday secured, the Queen saw the good nurse who had brought the royal pair into the world. Her Majesty had also her first introduction to one of her future sons-in-law—an unforeseen kinsman then—Prince Louis of Hesse, whom she noticed as "a very fine boy of eight, nice, and full of intelligence."

There were still long leagues to drive, posting, before Coburg could be reached, and the party started from Mayence in two travelling carriages as early as seven o'clock next morning. They went by Frankfort to Aschaffenburg, where they were met by Bavarian troops and a representative of the King on their entrance into Bavaria. Through woodland scenery, and fields full of the stir of harvest, where a queenly woman did not relish the spectacle of her sister-women treated as beasts of burden, the travellers journeyed to Wurzburg. There Prince Luitpold of Bavaria met and welcomed them to a magnificent palace, where the luggage, which ought to have preceded the wearied travellers, was not forthcoming. Another long day's driving, beginning at a little after six in the morning, would bring the party to Coburg. By one o'clock they were at the old prince-bishop's stately town of Bamberg. In the course of the afternoon the Queen had changed horses for the last time in Franconia. "I began," she wrote, "to feel greatly moved, agitated indeed, in coming near the Coburg frontier. At length we saw flags and people drawn up in lines, and in a few minutes more were welcomed by Ernest (the Duke of Coburg) in full uniform.... We got into an open carriage of Ernest's with six horses, Ernest sitting opposite to us."

The rest of the scene was very German, quaintly picturesque and warm-hearted. "The good people were all dressed in their best, the women in pointed caps, with many petticoats, and the men in leather breeches. Many girls were there with wreaths of flowers." A triumphal arch, a Vice-Land-Director, to whose words of greeting the Queen replied, his fellow-officials on either side, the people welcoming their prince and his queen in "a really hearty and friendly way."

The couple drove to what had been the pretty little country house of their common grandmother, the late Dowager-Duchess of Coburg, and found King Leopold and Queen Louise awaiting them there. He also was an honoured son of Coburg, pleased to be present on such a proud day for the little State. He and his queen took their places beside Queen Victoria and Prince Albert—Ernest Duke of Coburg mounting on horseback and riding beside the carriage as its chief escort. In this order the procession, "which looked extremely pretty," was formed. At the entrance to the town there was another triumphal arch, beneath which the Burgomaster addressed the royal couple. "On the other side stood a number of young girls dressed in white, with green wreaths and scarfs, who presented us with bouquets and verses."

Oh! what anxious, exciting, girlish rehearsals must have been gone through beforehand.

"I cannot say how much I felt moved on entering this dear old place, and with difficulty I restrained my emotion. The beautifully-ornamented town, all bright with wreaths and flowers, the numbers of good affectionate people, the many recollections connected with the place—all was so affecting. In the Platz, where the Rathhaus and Rigierungshaus are, which are fine and curious old houses, the clergy were assembled, and Ober-Superintendent Genzler addressed us very kindly—a very young-looking man for his age, for he married mamma to my father, and christened and confirmed Albert and Ernest." Neither was the motherly presence of her whose marriage vow the Ober-Superintendent had blessed, who had done so much to contribute to the triumph of this day, wanting to its complete realization of all that such a day should have been. The Duchess of Kent was already on a visit to her nephew, standing on the old threshold—once so well known to her—ready to help to welcome her daughter, prepared to show her the home and cherished haunts of her mother's youth. As the carriage drew up, young girls threw wreaths into it. Beside the Duchess of Kent were the Duchess and Dowager-Duchess of Coburg, Prince Albert's sister-in-law and stepmother. The staircase was full of cousins. "It was an affecting but exquisite moment, which I shall never forget," declared the Queen.

But in the middle of the gratification of the son of the house who thus brought his true wife under its roof-tree, and of his satisfaction of being with her there, the faithful hearts did not forget the late sovereign and house-father who had hoped so eagerly to welcome them to the ancestral home. They were there, but his place was filled by another. At Coburg and at Rosenau, which had been one of the old Duke's favourite resorts, his memory haunted his children. "Every sound, every view, every step we take makes us think of him and feel an indescribable hopeless longing for him."

By an affectionate, thoughtful provision for their perfect freedom and enjoyment, Rosenau, Prince Albert's birthplace, was set apart for the Queen and the Prince's occupation on this very happy occasion when they visited Coburg, and still it is the widowed Queen's residence when she is dwelling in the neighbourhood. Beautiful in itself among its woods and hills, it was doubly beautiful to both from its associations. The room in which the Queen slept was that in which the Prince had been born. "How happy, how joyful we were," the Queen wrote, "on awaking to find ourselves here, at the dear Rosenau, my Albert's birthplace, the place he most loves.... He was so happy to be here with me. It is like a beautiful dream."

Fine chorales were sung below the window by some of the singers in the Coburg theatre. Before breakfast the Prince carried off the Queen to see the upper part of the house, which he and his brother had occupied when children. "It is quite in the roof, with a tiny little bedroom on each side, in one of which they both used to sleep with Florschutz, their tutor. [Footnote: The Prince was then such a mere child that the tutor used to carry him in his arms up and down stairs. One is reminded of the old custom of appointing noble governors for royal children of the tenderest years, and of the gracious pathetic relations which sometimes existed between bearded knights and infant kings. Such was the case where Sir David Lindsay of the Mount and little King James V. were concerned, when the pupil would entreat the master for a song on the lute with childish peremptoriness, "P'ay, Davie Lindsay, p'ay!"] The view is beautiful, and the paper is still full of holes from their fencing; and the very same table is there on which they were dressed when little."

The days were too short for all that was to be seen and done. The first day there was a visit to the fortress overhanging the town, which looks as far away as the sea of trees, the Thuringerwald. It has Luther's room, with his chair and part of his bed.

In the evening the Queen went to the perfect little German theatre, where Meyerbeer's Huguenots was given, and the audience sang "God save the Queen" to German words.

The next day the visitors drove to Kalenberg, another of the Duke's seats. In the evening they held a reception at the palace, when not only those persons who had the magic prefix von to their names were admitted, but deputations of citizens, merchants, and artisans were presented, the Queen praising their good manners afterwards.

The following day was the Feast of St. Gregorius, the children's festival, in which thirteen hundred children walked in procession through Coburg, some in fancy dresses, most of the girls in white and green. Three girls came up to the palace balcony and sang a song in honour of the Queen. Then great and small repaired to the meadow— fortunately the fine weather had set in— where there were tents decorated with flowers, in which the royal party dined, while the band played and the children danced "so nicely and merrily, waltzes, polkas, and it was the prettiest thing I ever saw," declared the Queen. "Her Majesty talked to the children, to their great astonishment, in their own language. Tired of dancing and processions, and freed from all awe by the ease of the illustrious visitors, the children took to romps, 'thread my needle,' and other pastimes, and finally were well pelted by the royal circle with bon-bons, flowers and cakes" is the report of another observer.

The day ended with a great ball at the palace.

The next day was spent more quietly in going over old favourite haunts, among them the cabinet or collection of curiosities, stuffed birds, fossils, autographs, &c., which had been formed partly by the Princes when boys. Prince Albert continued to take the greatest interest in it, and had made the Queen a contributor to its treasures. At dinner the Queen tasted bratürste (roasted sausages), the national dish of Coburg, and pronounced it excellent, with its accompaniment of native beer. A royal neighbour, Queen Adelaide's brother, the Duke of Saxe-Meiningen, joined the party at dinner, and the company witnessed the performance of Schiller's Bride of Messina at the theatre.

On Sunday the August weather was so hot that the Queen and the Prince breakfasted for the second time out of doors. In the course of the morning they drove over with Duke Ernest and the Duchess to St. Moritz Kirche—equivalent to the cathedral of the town. The clergy received the party at the door of the church, and the Ober-Superintendent Genzler made a brief oration "expressive of his joy at receiving the great Christian Queen who was descended from their Saxon dukes, who were the first Reformers, and at the doors of the church where the Reformation was first preached." The Queen describes the service as like the Scotch Presbyterian form, only with more ceremony and more singing. The last impressed her deeply. The pastor preached a fine sermon. The afternoon's drive led through scenery which, especially in its pine woods, resembled the Scotch Highlands, and ended in the Thiergarten, where the Duke reared his wild boars.

"I cannot think," the Queen wrote longingly, "of going away from here. I count the hours, for I have a feeling here which I cannot describe— a feeling as if my childhood also had been spent here." No wonder; Coburg was home to her, like her native air or her mother tongue; she must have learnt to know it at her mother's knee. Her husband's experience was added to the earlier recollection of every salient point, every Haus-Mahrchen; and never were husband and wife more in sympathy than the two who now snatched a short season of delight from a sojourn in the cradle of their race.

Another brilliant sunshiny day—which the brother Princes spent together reviving old associations in the town, while the Queen sketched at Rosenau—closed with the last visit to the theatre, when the people again sang "God save the Queen," adding to it some pretty farewell verses.

The last day which the Queen passed in Coburg was, by a happy circumstance, the Prince's birthday—the first he had spent at Rosenau since he was a lad of fifteen, and, in spite of all changes, the day dawned full of quiet gladness. "To celebrate this dear day in my beloved husband's country and birthplace is more than I ever hoped for," wrote her Majesty, "and I am so thankful for it; I wished him joy so warmly when the singers sang as they did the other morning." The numberless gifts had been arranged by no other hands than those of the Queen and the Prince's brother and sister-in-law on a table "dressed with flowers.'" Peasants came in gala dress, [Footnote: The Queen admired greatly many of the peasant costumes, often as serviceable and durable as they were becoming, which she saw in Germany. She expressed the regret so often uttered by English travellers that English labourers and workers at handicrafts, in place of retaining a dress of their own, have long ago adopted a tawdry version of the fashions of the upper classes. Unfortunately the practice is fast becoming universal.] with flowers, music, and dancing to offer their good wishes. In the afternoon all was quiet again, and the Queen and the Prince took their last walk together, for many a day, at Rosenau, down into the hayfields where the friendly people exchanged greetings with them, drank the crystal clear water from the stream, and looked at the fortifications which two princely boys had dug and built, as partly lessons, partly play.

The next day at half-past eight the travellers left "with heavy hearts," measuring the fateful years which were likely to elapse before Coburg was seen again. The pain of parting was lessened by the presence of the Duke and Duchess of Coburg, who accompanied their guests to the Duke's other domain of Gotha. The way led through Queen Adelaide's country of Meiningen, and at every halting-place clergymen with addresses more or less discursive, and "white and green young ladies," literally bombarded the travellers with speeches, flowers, and poems. At last the Duke of Coburg's territory was again entered after it was dark; and the party reached the lovely castellated country-seat of Reinhardtsbrunn, amidst forest and mountain scenery, with its lake in front of the house, set down in the centre of a mining population that came up in quaint costumes, with flaming torches, to walk in procession past the windows. The Queen was charmed with Reinhardtsbrunn, and would fain have lingered there, but time pressed, and she was expected in the course of the next afternoon at Gotha, on a visit to the Prince's aged grandmother who had helped to bring him up, and was so fondly attached to her former charge. The old lady at seventy-four years of age anticipated the visit. She travelled the distance of eight miles before breakfast, in order to take her grandchildren by surprise. "I hastened to her," is the Queen's account, "and found Albert and Ernest with her. She is a charming old lady, and though very small, remarkably nice-looking, erect and active, but unfortunately very deaf.... She was so happy to see us, and kissed me over and over again. Albert, who is the dearest being to her in the world, she was enraptured to see again, and kissed so kindly. It did one's heart good to see her joy."

In the afternoon the travellers proceeded to Gotha, which was in a state of festival and crowded with people. The Queen and the Prince resided at the old Duchess's house of Friedrichsthal, where the greatest preparations, including the hanging of all her pictures in their rooms, had been made for them. The first visit they paid in Gotha was a solemn one, to the chapel which formed the temporary resting-place of the body of the late Duke, till it could be removed to its vault in Coburg. Then the rooms in which the father had died were visited. These were almost equally melancholy, left as they had been, unchanged, with the wreaths that had decorated the room for his last birthday still there; "and there is that sad clock which stopped just before he died." Who that has seen in Germany these faded wreaths, with their crushed, soiled streamers of white riband, can forget the desolate aspect which they lend to any room in which they are preserved! There was a cabinet or museum here, too, to inspect, and the curious old spectacle of the popinjay to be witnessed, in company with the Grand Duke of Weimar and his son. This kind of shooting was harmless enough, for the object aimed at was a wooden bird on a pole. The riflemen, led by the rifle-king (schutzen-konig), the public officials, and deputations of peasants marched past the platform where the Queen stood, like a pageant of the Middle Ages. All the princes, including King Leopold, fired, but none brought down the bird; that feat was left for some humbler hero.

On the Queen's return from the popinjay she had the happiness to meet Baroness Lehzen, her old governess, who had come from Buckeburg to see her Majesty. During the next few days the old friends were often together, and the Queen speaks with pleasure of the Baroness's "unchanged devotion," only she was quieter than formerly. It must have appeared like another dream to both, that "the little Princess" of Kensington, travelling with her husband, should greet her old governess, and tell her, under the shadow of the great Thuringerwald, of the four children left behind in England.

The next day the forest itself was entered, when "the bright blue sky, the heavenly air, the exquisite tints," gave a crowning charm to its beauties. The road lay through green glades which occasionally commanded views so remote as those of the Hartz Mountains, to Jagersruh, a hunting-lodge on a height "among stately firs that look like cedars." Here the late Duke had excited all his skill and taste to make a hunter's paradise, which awoke again the regretful thought, "How it would have pleased him to have shown all this himself to those he loved so dearly!"

But Jagersruh was not the goal of the excursion; it was a "deer-drive" or battue, which in Germany at least can be classed as "a relic of mediaeval barbarism." A considerable space in the forest was cleared and enclosed with canvas. In the centre of this enclosure was a pavilion open at the sides, made of branches of fir-trees, and decorated with berries, heather, and forest flowers; in short, a sylvan bower provided for the principal company, outside a table furnished with powder and shot supplied a station for less privileged persons, including the chasseurs or huntsmen of the Duke, in green and gold uniforms.

Easy-chairs were placed in the pavilion for the Queen, the Queen of the Belgians, and the Duchess Alexandrina, while Prince Albert, King Leopold, the Prince of Leiningen, and Duke Ferdinand of Saxe-Coburg, the Prince's uncle, stood by the ladies. Stags to the number of upwards of thirty, and other game, were driven into the enclosure, and between the performances of a band which played at intervals, the gentlemen loaded their rifles, and fired at the helpless prey in the presence of the ladies.

Her Majesty records in her Journal, "As for the sport itself, none of the gentlemen like this butchery." She turns quickly from the piteous slaughter to the beautiful, peaceful scenery.

A quiet Sunday was spent at Gotha. Monday was the Lieder fest, or festival of song, to which, on this occasion, not only the townspeople and villagers from all the neighbouring towns and villages came with their banners and bands, but every small royalty from far and near flocked to meet the Queen of England. These innumerable cousins repaired with the Queen to the park opposite the Schloss, and shared in the festival. The orchestra, composed of many hundreds of singers, was opposite the pavilion erected for the distinguished visitors. Among the fine songs, rendered as only Germans could render them, songs composed by Prince Albert and his brother, and songs written for the day, were sung. Afterwards there was a State dinner and a ball.

The last day had come, with its inevitable sadness. "I can't—won't think of it," wrote the Queen, referring to her approaching departure. She drove and walked, and, with her brother-in-law and his Duchess, was ferried over to the "Island of Graves," the burial-place of the old Dukes of Gotha when the duchy was distinct from that of Coburg. An ancient gardener pointed out to the visitors that only one more flower-covered grave was wanted to make the number complete. When the Duchess of Gotha should be laid to rest with her late husband and his fathers, then the House of Gotha, in its separate existence, would have passed away.

One more drive through the hayfields and the noble fir-trees to the vast Thuringerwald, and, "with many a longing, lingering look at the pine-clad mountains," the Queen and the Prince turned back to attend a ball given in their honour by the townspeople in the theatre.

On the following day the homeward journey was begun. After partings, rendered still more sorrowful by the fact that the age of the cherished grandmother of the delightful "dear" family party rendered it not very probable that she, for one, would see all her children round her again, the Duke and Duchess of Coburg went one stage with the travellers, and then there was another reluctant if less painful parting.

The Queen and the Prince stopped at the quaint little town of Eisenach, which Helen of Orleans was yet to make her home. They were received by the Grand Duke and Hereditary Duchess of Saxe-Weimar, with whom the strangers drove through the autumn woods to the famous old fortress of the Wartburg, which, in its time, dealt a deadly blow to Roman Catholicism by sheltering, in the hour of need, the Protestant champion, Luther. Like the good Protestants her Majesty and the Prince were, they went to see the great reformer's room, and looked at the ink-splash on the wall—the mark of his conflict with the devil—the stove at which he warmed himself, the rude table at which he wrote and ate, and above all, the glorious view over the myriads of tree-tops with which he must have refreshed his steadfast soul. But if Luther is the hero of the Wartburg, there is also a heroine—the central figure of that "Saint's Tragedy" which Charles Kingsley was to give to the world in the course of the next two or three years—St. Elizabeth of Thuringia, the tenderest, bravest, most tortured soul that ever received the doubtful gain of canonization. There is the well by which she is said to have ministered to her sick poor, half-way up the ascent to the Wartburg, and down in the little town nestling below, may be seen the remains of an hospital bearing her name.

From Fulda, where the royal party slept, they journeyed to Goethe's town of Frankfort, where Ludwig I., who turned Munich into a great picture and sculpture gallery, and built the costly Valhalla to commemorate the illustrious German dead, dined with her Majesty.

At Biberich the Rhine was again hailed, and a steamer, waiting for the travellers, carried them to Bingen, where their own little vessel, The Fairy, met and brought them on to Deutz, on the farther side from Cologne. The Queen says naively that the Rhine had lost its charm for them all—the excitement of novelty was gone, and the Thuringerwald had spoilt them. Stolzenfels, Ehrenbreitstein, and the Sieben-Gebirge had their words of praise, but sight-seeing had become for the present a weariness, and after Bonn, with its memories, had been left behind, it was a rest to the royal travellers—as to most other travellers at times—to turn away their jaded eyes, relinquish the duty of alert observation, forget what was passing around them, and lose themselves in a book, as if they were in England. Perhaps the home letters had awakened a little home-sickness in the couple who had been absent for a month. At least, we are given to understand that it was of home and children the Queen and the Prince were chiefly thinking when they reached Antwerp, to which the King and Queen of the Belgians had preceded them, and re-embarked in the royal yacht Victoria and Albert, though it was not at once to sail for English waters. In gracious compliance with an urgent entreaty of Louis Philippe's, the yacht was to call, as it were in passing, at Tréport.

On the morning of the 8th of September the Queen's yacht again lay at anchor off the French seaport. The King's barge, with the King, his son, and son-in-law, Prince Joinville, and Prince Augustus of Saxe- Coburg, and M. Guizot, once more came alongside. After the friendliest greetings, the Queen and Prince Albert landed with their host, though not without difficulty. The tide would not admit of the ordinary manner of landing, and Louis Philippe in the dilemma fell back on a bathing-machine, which dragged the party successfully if somewhat unceremoniously over the sands.

The Queen of the French was there as before, accompanied among others by her brother, the Prince of Salerno and his Princess, sister to the Emperor of Austria. The crowd cheered as loudly as ever; there seemed no cloud on the horizon that bright, hot day; even the plague of too much publicity and formality had been got rid of at Château d'Eu. The Queen was delighted to renew her intercourse with the large, bright family circle—two of them her relations and fast friends. "It put me so much in mind of two years ago," she declared, "that it was really as if we had never been away;" and the King had to show her his Galerie Victoria, a room fitted up in her honour, hung with the pictures illustrating her former visit and the King's return visit to Windsor. Although she had impressed on him that she wished as much as possible to dispense with state and show on this occasion, the indefatigable old man had been at the trouble and expense of erecting a theatre, and bringing down from Paris the whole of the Opéra Comique to play before her, and thus increase the gaiety of the single evening of her stay.

Only another day was granted to Château d'Eu. By the next sunset the King was conducting his guests on board the royal yacht and seizing the last opportunity, when Prince Albert was taking Prince Joinville over the Fairy, glibly to assure the Queen and Lord Aberdeen that he, Louis Philippe, would never consent to Montpensier's marriage to the Infanta of Spain till her sister the Queen was married and had children.

At parting the King embraced her Majesty again and again. The yacht lay still, and there was the most beautiful moonlight reflected on the water. The Queen and the Prince walked up and down the deck, while not they alone, but the astute statesman Aberdeen, congratulated themselves on how well this little visit had prospered, in addition to the complete success of the German tour. With the sea like a lake, and sky and sea of the deepest blue, in the early morning the yacht weighed anchor for England. Under the hot haze of an autumn noonday sun the royal travellers disembarked on the familiar beach at Osborne. The dearest of welcomes greeted them as they "drove up straight to the house, for there, looking like roses, so well and so fat, stood the four children."

The Queen referred afterwards to that visit to Germany as to one of the happiest times in her life. She said when she thought of it, it made her inclined to cry, so pure and tender had been the pleasure.

CHAPTER IV.RAILWAY SPECULATION—FAILURE OF THE POTATO CROP—SIR ROBERT PEEL'S RESOLUTIONS—BIRTH OF PRINCESS HELENA—VISIT OF IBRAHIM PASHA.

One thousand eight hundred and forty-five had begun with what appeared a fresh impetus to national prosperity—a new start full of life and vigour, by which the whole resources of the country should be at once stirred up and rendered ten times more available than they had ever been before. This was known afterwards as "the Railway Mania," which, like other manias, if they are not mere fever-fits of speculation, but are founded on real and tangible gains, had its eager hopeful rise, its inflated disproportioned exaggeration, its disastrous collapse, its gradual recovery, and eventually its solid reasonable success. In 1845 the movement was hurrying on to the second stage of its history.

The great man of 1845 was Hudson the railway speculator, "the Railway King." Fabulous wealth was attributed to him; immense power for the hour was his. A seat in Parliament, entrance into aristocratic circles, were trifles in comparison. We can remember hearing of a great London dinner at which the lions were the gifted Prince, the husband of the Queen, and the distorted shadow of George Stephenson, the bourgeois creator of a network of railway lines, a Bourse of railway shares; the winner, as it was then supposed, of a huge fortune. It was said that Prince Albert himself had felt some curiosity to see this man and hear him speak, and that their encounter on this occasion was prearranged and not accidental.

The autumn of 1845 revealed another side to the country's history. The rainy weather in the summer brought to sudden hideous maturity the lurking potato disease. Any one who recalls the time and the aspect of the fields must retain a vivid recollection of the sudden blight that fell upon acres on acres of what had formerly been luxuriant vegetation, under the sunshine which came late only to complete the work of destruction; the withering and blackening of the leaves of the plant, the sickening foetid odour of the decaying bulbs, which tainted the heavy air for miles; the dismay that filled the minds of the people, who, in the days of dear corn, had learnt more and more to depend upon the cultivation of potatoes, to whom their failure meant ruin and starvation. This was especially the case in Ireland and the Highlands of Scotland, where the year closed in gloom and apprehension; famine stalked abroad, and doles of Indian corn administered by Government in addition to the alms of the charitable, alone kept body and soul together in fever-stricken multitudes.

About this time also, like another feature of the spirit of adventure which sent Franklin to the North Pole, and operated to a certain extent in the flush of railway enterprise, England was talking half chivalrously, half commercially, and alas! more than half sceptically, of Brook and Borneo, and the new attempt to establish civilization and herald Christianity under English influence in the far seas. All these conflicting elements of new history were felt in the palace as in other dwellings, and made part of Queen Victoria's life in those days.

A great statesman closed his eyes on this changing world. Earl Grey, who had been in the front in advocating change in his time, died.

A brave soldier fell in the last of his battles. Sir Robert Sale, who had been the guest of his Queen a year before, having returned to India and rejoined the army of the Sutlej on fresh disturbances breaking out in the Punjab, was killed at the battle of Moodkee.

Something of the wit and humour of the country was quenched or undergoing a transformation and passing into other hands. Two famous English humorists, Sydney Smith and Tom Hood the elder, went over to the great majority.

By the close of 1845 it had become clear that a change in the Corn Laws was impending. In the circumstances Sir Robert Peel, who, though he had been for some time approaching the conclusion, was not prepared to take immediate steps—who was, indeed, the representative of the Conservative party—resigned office. Lord John Russell, the great Whig leader, was called upon by the Queen to summon a new Ministry; but in consequence of difficulties with those who were to have been his colleagues, Lord John was compelled to announce himself unable to form a Cabinet, and Sir Robert Peel, at the Queen's request, resumed office, conscious that he had to face one of the hardest tasks ever offered to a statesman. He had to encounter "the coolness of former friends, the grudging support of unwilling adherents, the rancour of disappointed political antagonists."

In February, 1846, the royal family spent a week at Osborne, glad to escape from the strife of tongues and the violent political contention which they could do nothing to quell. The Prince was happy, "out all day," directing the building which was going on, and laying out the grounds of his new house; and the Queen was happy in her husband and Children's happiness. During this short absence Sir Robert Peel's resolutions were carried, and his Corn Bill, which was virtually the repeal of the Corn Laws, passed. He had only to await the consequences.

In the middle of the political excitement a single human tragedy, which Sir Robert Peel did something to prevent, reached its climax. Benjamin Haydon, the painter, the ardent advocate, both by principle and practice, of high art, took his life, driven to despair by his failure in worldly success—especially by the ill-success of his cartoons at the exhibition in Westminster Hall.

On the 25th of May a third princess was born, and on the 20th of June Sir Robert Peel's old allies, the Tories, who had but bided their time for revenge, while his new Whig associates looked coldly on him, conspired to defeat him in a Government measure to check assassination in Ireland, so that he had no choice save to resign. He had sacrificed himself as well as his party for what he conceived to be the good of the nation. His reign of power was at an end; but for the moment, at least, he was thankful.

To Lord John Russell, who was more successful than on an earlier occasion, the task of forming a new Ministry was intrusted. The parting from her late ministers, on the 6th of July, was a trial to the Queen, as the same experience had been previously. "Yesterday," her Majesty wrote to King Leopold, "was a very hard day for me. I had to part from Sir Robert Peel and Lord Aberdeen, who are irreparable losses to us and to the country. They were both so much overcome that it quite upset me. We have in them two devoted friends. We felt so safe with them. Never during the five years that they were with me did they ever recommend a person or a thing that was not for my or the country's best, and never for the party's advantage only.... I cannot tell you how sad I am to lose Aberdeen; you cannot think what a delightful companion he was. The breaking up of all this intercourse during our journeys is deplorable."

In the separation the Queen turned naturally to a nearer and dearer friend, whom only death could remove from her. "Albert's use to me, and I may say to the country, by his firmness and sagacity in these moments of trial, is beyond all belief." And beyond all gainsaying must have been the deep satisfaction with which the uncle, who was like a father, heard the repeated assurance of how successful had been his work—what a blessing had rested upon it.

Here is a note of exultation on the political changes from the opposite side of the House. Lord Campbell wrote: "The transfer of the ministerial offices took place at Buckingham Palace on the 6th of July. I ought to have been satisfied, for I received two seals, one for the Duchy of Lancaster and one for the County Palatine of Lancaster. My ignorance of the double honour which awaited me caused an awkward accident, for, when the Queen put two velvet bags into my hand, I grasped one only, and the other with its heavy weight fell down on the floor, and might have bruised the royal toes, but Prince Albert good-naturedly picked it up and restored it to me."

In July the Court again paid a short visit to Osborne, that the Queen's health might be recruited before the baptism of the little Princess. Her Majesty earnestly desired that the Queen of the Belgians might be present, as the baby was to be the godchild of the young widow of Queen Louise's much-loved brother, the late Duc d'Orleans. Unfortunately the wish could not be fulfilled. The child was christened at Buckingham Palace. She received the names of "Helena Augusta Victoria." Her sponsors were the Duchesse d'Orleans, represented by the Duchess of Kent; the Duchess of Cambridge; and the Hereditary Grand Duke of Mecklenburg-Strelitz. The illustration represents the charming little Princess at rather a more advanced age.

At the end of July Prince Albert was away from home for a few days. He visited Liverpool, which he had greatly wished to see, in order to lay the foundation-stone of a Sailors' Home and open the Albert Dock. In the middle of the bustle and enthusiasm of his reception he wrote to the Queen: "I write hoping these lines, which go by the evening post, may reach you by breakfast time to-morrow. As I write you will be making your evening toilette, and not be ready in time for dinner. [Footnote: The Queen dressed quickly, but sometimes she relied too much on her powers in this respect, and failed in her wonted punctuality.] I must set about the same task and not, let me hope, with the same result. I cannot get it into my head that there are two hundred and fifty miles between us.... I must conclude and enclose, by way of close, two touching objects—a flower and a programme of the procession."

The same day the Queen wrote to Baron Stockmar: "I feel very lonely without my dear master; and though I know other people are often separated for a few days, I feel habit could not make me get accustomed to it. This I am sure you cannot blame. Without him everything loses its interest.... It will always be a terrible pang for me to separate from him even for two days." Then she added with a ring of foreboding, "And I pray God never to let me survive him." She concluded with the true woman's proud assertion, "I glory in his being seen and heard."

CHAPTER V.AUTUMN YACHTING EXCURSIONS—THE SPANISH MARRIAGES—WINTER VISITS.

In the beginning of August the Queen and the Prince, accompanied by the King and Queen of the Belgians, went again to Osborne. This autumn the Queen, the Prince and their two elder children, made pleasant yachting excursions, of about a week's duration each, to old admired scenes and new places. In one of these Baron Stockmar was with them, since he had come to England for a year's visit. He expressed himself as much gratified by the Prince's interest and judgment in politics, and his opinion of the Queen was more favourable than ever. "The Queen improves greatly," he noted down as the fruits of his keen observation, "and she makes daily advances in discernment and experience. The candour, the tone of truth, the fairness, the considerateness with which she judges men and things, are truly delightful; and the ingenuous self-knowledge with which she speaks of herself is simply charming." The yachting excursions included Babbicombe, with the red rocks and wooded hills, which gave the Queen an idea of Italy, where she had never been, "or rather of a ballet or play where nymphs are to appear;" and Torbay, where William of Orange landed. It was perhaps in reference to that event that her Majesty made her little daughter "read in her English history." It seems to have been the Queen's habit, in these yachting excursions, to take upon herself a part, at least, of the Princess Royal's education. "Beautiful Dartmouth" recalled—it might be all the more, because of the rain that fell there—the Rhine with its ruined castles and its Lurlei. Plymouth Harbour and the shore where the pines grew down to the sea, led again to Mount Edgcumbe, always lovely. But first the Queen and the Prince steamed up the St. Germans and the Tamar rivers, passing Trematon Castle, which belonged to the little Duke of Cornwall, and penetrated by many windings of the stream into lake-like regions surrounded by woods and abounding in mines, which made the Prince think of some parts of the Danube. The visitors landed at Cothele, and drove up to a fine old house unchanged since Henry VII.'s time. When they returned in the Fairy to the yacht proper, they found it in the centre of a shoal of boats, as it had been the last time it sailed in these waters.

Prince Albert made an excursion to Dartmoor, and could have believed he was in Scotland, while her Majesty contented herself with another visit to Mount Edgcumbe, the master of which, a great invalid, yet contrived to meet her near the landing-place at which his wife and sons, with other members of the family, had received the royal visitor. The drowsy heat and the golden haze were in keeping with the romantically luxuriant glories of the drive, which the Queen took with her children and her hostess. The little people went in to luncheon while the Queen sketched. After Prince Albert's return in the afternoon, the visit was repeated. "The finest and tallest chestnut-trees in existence," and the particularly tall and straight birch-trees, were inspected, and Sir Joshua Reynolds's portraits examined. Well might they flourish at Mount Edgcumbe, since Plymouth was Sir Joshua's native town, and some of the Edgcumbe family were among his first patrons, when English art stood greatly in need of such patronage.

The next excursion was an impromptu run in lovely weather to Guernsey, which had not been visited by an English sovereign since the days of King John. The rocky bays, the neighbouring islands, the half-foreign town of St. Pierre, with "very high, bright-coloured houses," illuminated at night, pleased her Majesty greatly. On the visitors landing they were met by ladies dressed in white singing "God save the Queen," and strewing the path with flowers. General Napier, a white- haired soldier, received the Queen and presented her with the keys of the fort. The narrow streets through which she drove were "decorated with flowers and flags, and lined with the Guernsey militia." The country beyond, of which she had a glimpse, was crowned with fine vegetation.

Whether or not it was to prevent Jersey, with St. Helier's, from feeling jealous, ten days later the Queen and the Prince, the Prince of Wales, and the Princess Royal, the usual suite, Lord Spencer, and Lord Palmerston, set out on a companion trip to the sister island. The weather was colder and the sea not so calm. Indeed, the rolling of the vessel in Alderney Race was more than the voyagers had bargained for. After it became smoother the little Prince of Wales put on a sailor's dress made by a tailor on board, and great was the jubilation of the Jack Tars of every degree. The whole picturesque coast of Jersey was circumnavigated in order to reach St. Helier's, which was gained when the red rocks were gilded with the setting sun. A little later the yacht was hauled up under the glow of bonfires and an illumination. On a splendid September day, which lent to the very colouring a resemblance to Naples, the Queen passed between the twin towers of Noirmont Point and St. Aubin, and approached Elizabeth Castle, with the town of St. Helier's behind it. The Queen landed amidst the firing of guns, the playing of military bands, and the roar of cheers, the ladies of the place, as before, strewing her path with flowers, and marshalling her to a canopy, under which her Majesty received the address of the States and the militia. The demonstrations were on a larger and more finished scale than in Guernsey, greater time having been given for preparation.

The French tongue around her arrested the Queen's attention. So did a seat in one of the streets filled with French women from Granville, "curiously dressed, with white handkerchiefs on their heads." The Queen drove through the green island, admiring its orchards without end, though the season of russet and rosy apples was past for Jersey. The old tower of La Hogue Bie was seen, and the castle of Mont Orgueil was still more closely inspected, the Queen walking up to it and visiting one of its batteries, with a view across the bay to the neighbouring coast of France. Mont Orgueil is said to have been occupied by Robert of Normandy, the unfortunate son of William the Conqueror. Her Majesty heard that it had not yet been taken, but found this was an error, though it was true the island of Guernsey had never been conquered.

The close of the pleasant day was a little spoilt by the heat and glare, which sent the Queen ill to her cabin. The next day saw the party bound for Falmouth, where they arrived under a beautiful moon, with the sea smooth as glass—not an unacceptable change from the rolling swell of the first part of the little voyage.

Something unexpected and unwelcome had happened before the close of the excursion, while the French coast which the Queen had hailed with so much pleasure was still full in sight. Whether the news which arrived with the other dispatches had anything to do with the fit of indisposition that rendered the heat and glare unbearable, it certainly marred the enjoyment of the last part of her trip. Before quitting Jersey the Queen was made acquainted with the fact that Louis Philippe's voluntary protestations with regard to the marriage of his son, the Duc de Montpensier, had been so many idle words. He had stolen a march both upon England and Europe generally. The marriage of the Due de Montpensier with the Infanta Luisa of Spain was announced simultaneously with the marriage of her sister, the Queen of Spain, to her cousin the Due de Cadiz.

Everybody knows at this date how futile were Louis Philippe's schemes for the aggrandisement of his family, and how he learnt by bitter experience, as Louis XIV. had done before him, that a coveted Spanish alliance, in the very fact of its attainment, meant disaster and humiliation for France.

Louis Philippe had the grace, as we sometimes say, to shrink from writing to announce the double marriage against which he had so often solemnly pledged himself to the Queen. He delegated the difficult task to Queen Amélie, who discharged it with as much tact as might have been expected from so devoted a wife and kind a woman.

The Queen of England's reply to this begging of the question is full of spirit and dignity:—

"OSBORNE, September 10, 1846.

"MADAME,—I have just received your Majesty's letter of the 8th, and I hasten to thank you for it. You will, perhaps remember what passed at Eu between the King and myself. You are aware of the importance which I have always attached to the maintenance of our cordial understanding, and the zeal with which I have laboured towards this end. You have no doubt been informed that we refused to arrange the marriage between the Queen of Spain and our cousin Leopold (which the two Queens [Footnote: The reference is to the young Queen of Spain and her mother the Queen-dowager Christina.] had eagerly desired) solely with the object of not departing from a course which would be more agreeable to the King, although we could not regard the course as the best. [Footnote: The confining of the Queen of Spain's selection of a husband to a Bourbon prince, a descendant of Philip V.] You will therefore easily understand that the sudden announcement of this double marriage could not fail to cause us surprise and very keen regret.

"I crave your pardon, Madame, for speaking to you of politics at a time like this, but I am glad that I can say for myself that I have always been sincere with you. Begging you to present my respectful regards to the King, I am, Madame, your Majesty's most devoted friend,

"VICTORIA."

The last yachting excursion of the season was to Cornwall. The usual party accompanied the Queen and the Prince, the elder children, and the ladies and gentlemen in waiting, her Majesty managing, as before, to hear her little daughter repeat her lessons. Lizard Point and Land's End were reached. At Penzance Prince Albert landed to inspect the copper and serpentine-stone works, while the Queen sketched from the deck of the Fairy. As the Cornish boats clustered round the yacht, and the Prince of Wales looked down with surprise on the half- outlandish boatmen, a loyal shout arose, "Three cheers for the Duke of Cornwall."

The romantic: region of St. Michael's Mount, dear to the lovers of Arthurian legends, was visited, the Queen climbing the circuitous path up the hill to enter the castle, the Prince mounting to the tower where "St Michael's chair," the rocky seat for betrothed couples, still tests their courage and endurance. Each man and woman races up the difficult path, and the winner of the race who first sits down in the chair claims the right to rule the future home.

The illustration from a painting by Stanfield represents the imposing pile of the "old religious house" crowning the noble rock, the royal yacht lying off the shore commanding St. Michael's Mount, the numerous spectators on shore and in boats haunting the royal footsteps—in short, the whole scene in the freshness and stir which broke in upon its sombre romance.

On Sunday service was held under the awning with its curtains of flags, Lord Spencer—a captain in the navy—reading prayers "extremely well." On Monday there was an excursion to the serpentine rocks, where caves and creeks, cormorants and gulls, lent their attractions to the spot. At Penryn the corporation came on board, "very anxious to see the Duke of Cornwall." The Queen makes a picture in writing of the quaint interview. "I stepped out of the pavilion on deck with Bertie. Lord Palmerston told them that that was the Duke of Cornwall, and the old mayor of Penryn said he hoped 'he would grow up a blessing to his parents and his country.'"

The party were rowed up the beautiful rivers Truro and Tregony, between banks covered with stunted oaks or woods of a more varied kind down to the water's edge, past charming pools, creeks, and ferries, with long strings of boats on the water and carts on the shore, and a great gathering of people cheering the visitors, especially when the little Duke of Cornwall was held up for them to see. The Queen took delight in the rustic demonstration, so much in keeping with the place, and the simple loyalty of the people.

Her Majesty went to Fowey, and had the opportunity of driving through some of the narrowest, steepest streets in England, till she reached the hilly ground of Cornwall, "covered with fields, and intersected with hedges," and at last arrived at her little son's possession, the ivy-covered ruin of the old castle of Restormel, an appanage of the Duchy of Cornwall, in which the last Earl of Cornwall had resided five hundred years before.

The Queen also visited the Restormel iron-mines. She was one of the comparatively few ladies who have ventured into the nether darkness of a pit. She saw her underground subjects as well as those above ground, and to the former no less than to the latter she bore the kindly testimony that she found them "intelligent good people." We can vouch for this that these hewers and drawers of ore, in their dark-blue woollen suits, the arms bare, and caps with the candles or lamps stuck in the front, lighting up the pallid grimy faces, would be fully conscious of the honour done them, and would yield to no ruddy, fustian-clad ploughman or picturesque shepherd, with his maud and crook in loyalty to their Queen.

The Queen and the Prince got into a truck and were drawn by the miners, the mineral agent for Cornwall bringing up the rear, into the narrow workings, where none could pass between the truck and the rock, and "there was just room to hold up one's head, and not always that." As it is with other strangers in Pluto's domains, her Majesty felt there was something unearthly about this lit-up cavern-like place, where many a man spent the greater part of his life. But she was not deterred from getting out of the truck with me Prince, and scrambling along to see the veins of ore, from which Prince Albert was able to knock off some specimens. Daylight was dazzling to the couple when they returned to its cheerful presence.

The last visit paid in Cornwall was by very narrow stony lanes to "Place," a curious house restored from old plans and drawings to a fac-simile of a Cornwall house of the past as it had been defended by one of the ancestresses of the present family, the Treffrys, against an attack made upon her, by the French during her husband's absence. The hall was lined with Cornwall marble and porphyry.

On the 15th of September the new part of Osborne House was occupied for the first time by its owners. Lady Lyttelton chronicled the pleasant event and some ceremonies which accompanied it. "After dinner we were to drink the Queen and Prince's health as a 'house-warming.' And after it the Prince said very naturally and simply, but seriously, 'We have a hymn' (he called it a psalm) 'in Germany for such occasions. It begins'—and then he repeated two lines in German, which I could not quote right, meaning a prayer to 'bless our going out and coming in.' It was long and quaint, being Luther's. We all perceived that he was feeling it. And truly entering a new house, a new palace, is a solemn thing to do, to those whose probable span of life in it is long, and spite of rank, and health, and youth, down-hill now."

Sir Theodore Martin, who quotes Lady Lyttelton's letters in the "Life of the Prince Consort," gives such a hymn, which is a paraphrase of the 121st Psalm, as it appears in the Coburg Gesang-Buch, and supplies a translation of the verse in question.

Unsern ausgang segne Gott,
  Unsern erngang gleicher massen,
Segne unser taglich brod,

Segne unser thun und lassen.
Segne uns mit sel'gem sterben,
  Und mach uns zu Himmel's Erben
* * * * *

By Tre, Con and Pen,
  You may know the Cornish men
God bless our going out, nor less
  Our coming in, and make them sure,
God bless our daily bread, and bless
  Whate'er we do, whate'er endure,
In death unto his peace awake us,
  And heirs of his salvation make us

"I forgot," writes Lady Lyttelton again, "much the best part of our breaking in, which was that Lucy Kerr (one of the maids of honour) insisted on throwing an old shoe into the house after the Queen, as she entered for the first night, being a Scotch superstition. It looked too strange and amusing. She wanted some melted lead and sundry other charms, but they were not forthcoming. I told her I would call her Luckie, and not Lucy."

During the autumn the Princess of Prussia, who was on a visit to her aunt, Queen Adelaide, went to Windsor Castle, where Madame Bunsen met her. "I arrived here at six," writes Madame Bunsen "and at eight went to dinner in the great hall, hung round with Waterloo pictures, the band playing exquisitely, so placed as to be invisible, so that what with the large proportions of the hall and the well-subdued lights, and the splendours of plate and decorations, the scene was such as fairy tales present; and Lady Canning, Miss Stanley, and Miss Dawson were beautiful enough to represent an ideal queen's ideal attendants.

"The Queen looked well and rayonnante, with the expression of countenance that she has when pleased with what surrounds her, and which you know I like to see. The old Duke of Cambridge failed not to ask after you.

"This morning at nine we were all assembled at prayers in the private chapel, then went to breakfast, headed by Lady Canning, after which Miss Stanley took the Countess Haach and me to see the collection of gold plate. Three works of Benvenuto Cellini, and a trophy from the Armada, an immense flagon or wine-fountain, like a gigantic old- fashioned smelling-bottle, and a modern Indian work—a box given to the Queen by an Indian potentate—were what interested me the most. Then I looked at many interesting pictures in the long corridor.

"I am lodged in what is called the Devil's Tower, and have a view of the Round Tower, of which I made a sketch as soon as I was out of bed this morning."

In October the Queen and the Prince spent several days on a private visit to the Queen-dowager at her country house of Cashiobury. From Cashiobury the royal couple went on, in bad weather, to Hatfield House, which had once been a palace, but had long been the seat of the Cecils, Marquises of Salisbury. Here more than anywhere else Queen Victoria was on the track of her great predecessor, Queen Elizabeth, while the virgin queen was still the maiden princess, considerably oppressed by her stern sister Queen Mary. Queen Victoria inspected all the relics of the interesting old place, "the vineyard," the banqueting-room fallen down into a stable, and the oak still linked with the name of Queen Bess.

At Hatfield there was a laudable innovation on the usual round of festivities. From four to five hundred labourers were regaled on the lawn with a roasted ox and hogsheads of ale.

On the 1st of December, the Queen and Prince, who had been staying at Osborne, paid the Duke of Norfolk a visit at Arundel. Not only was the Duke the premier duke and Earl-Marshal of England, but he held at this time the high office in the Household of Master of the Horse. The old keep and tower at Arundel were brilliantly illuminated in honour of the Queen's presence, and bonfires lit up the surrounding country. The Duke of Wellington was here also, walking about with the Queen, while the younger men shot with Prince Albert. On the second day of her stay her Majesty received guests in the state drawing-room. The third day included the usual commemorative planting of trees in the Little Park. In the evening there was dancing, in which the Queen joined.

There were great changes, ominous of still further transitions, in the theatrical and literary world. Liston, the famous comedian who had delighted a former generation, was dead, and amateur actors, led by authors in the persons of Charles Dickens, Douglas Jerrold, &c. &c., had come to the front, and were winning much applause, as well as solid benefits for individuals and institutions connected with literature requiring public patronage. A man and a woman unlike in everything save their cordial admiration for each other, bore down all opposition in the reading world: William Makepeace Thackeray, in 1846, in spite of the discouragement of publishers, started his "Vanity Fair," and Charlotte Brontë, from the primitive seclusion of an old- fashioned Yorkshire parsonage, took England by storm with her impassioned, unconventional "Jane Eyre." The fame of these two books, while the authors were still in a great measure unknown, rang through the country.

Art in England was still following the lines laid down for the last twenty or thirty years, unless in the case of Turner, who had entered some time before on the third period of his work, the period marked by defiance and recklessness as well as by noble power.

CHAPTER VI.INSTALLATION OF PRINCE ALBERT AS CHANCELLOR OF CAMBRIDGE.

One thousand eight hundred and forty-seven began with the climax of the terrible famine in Ireland, and the Highlands, produced by the potato disease, which, commencing in 1845, had reappeared even more disastrously in 1846. In the Queen's speech in opening Parliament, she alluded to the famine in the land with a perceptibly sad fall of her voice.

In spite of bad trade and bad times everywhere, two millions were advanced by the Government for the relief of the perishing people, fed on doles of Indian meal; yet the mortality in the suffering districts continued tremendous.

In February, 1847, Lord Campbell describes an amusing scene in the Queen's closet. "I had an audience, that her Majesty might prick a sheriff for the county of Lancaster, which she did in proper style, with the bodkin I put into her hand. I then took her pleasure about some Duchy livings and withdrew, forgetting to make her sign the parchment roll. I obtained a second audience, and explained the mistake. While she was signing, Prince Albert said to me, 'Pray, my lord, when did this ceremony of pricking begin?' CAMPBELL. 'In ancient times, sir, when sovereigns did not know now to write their names.' QUEEN, as she returned me the roll with her signature, 'But we now show we have been to school.'" In the course of the next month his lordship gives a lively account of dining along with his wife and daughter at Buckingham Palace. "On our arrival, a little before eight, we were shown into the picture gallery, where the company assembled. Bowles, who acted as master of the ceremonies, arranged what gentlemen should take what lady. He said, 'Dinner is ordered to be on the table at ten minutes past eight, but I bet you the Queen will not be here till twenty or twenty-five minutes after. She always thinks she can dress in ten minutes, but she takes about double the time.' True enough, it was nearly twenty-five minutes past eight before she appeared; she shook hands with the ladies, bowed to the gentlemen, and proceeded to the salle à manger. I had to take in Lady Emily de Burgh, and was third on her Majesty's right, Prince Edward of Saxe- Weimar and my partner being between us. The greatest delicacy we had was some very nice oat-cake. There was a Highland piper standing behind her Majesty's chair, but he did not play as at State dinners. We had likewise some Edinburgh ale. The Queen and the ladies withdrawing, Prince Albert came over to her side of the table, and we remained behind about a quarter of an hour, but we rose within the hour from the time of our sitting down to dinner.... On returning to the gallery we had tea and coffee. The Queen came up and talked to me. She does the honours of the palace with infinite grace and sweetness, and considering what she is both in public and domestic life, I do not think she is sufficiently loved and respected. Prince Albert took me to task for my impatience to get into the new House of Lords, but I think I pacified him, complimenting his taste. A dance followed. The Queen chiefly delighted in a romping sort of country-dance, called the Tempête. She withdrew a little before twelve."

The beginning of the season in London was marked by two events in the theatrical and operatic world. Fanny Kemble (Mrs. Pierce Butler) reappeared on the stage, and was warmly welcomed back. Jenny Lind sang for the first time in London at the Italian Opera House in the part of "Alice" in Roberto il Diavolo, and enchanted the audience with her unrivalled voice and fine acting.

In the month of May, in the middle of the Irish distress, the great agitator of old, Daniel O'Connell, died in his seventy-second year, on his way to Rome. The news of his death was received in Ireland as only one drop more in the full cup of national misery. In the same month of May another and a very different orator, Dr. Chalmers, the great impassioned Scotch divine, philosopher, and philanthropist, one of the leaders in the disruption from the Church of Scotland, died in Edinburgh, in his sixty-eighth year.

Prince Albert had been elected Chancellor of Cambridge University—a well-deserved compliment, which afforded much gratification both to the Queen and the Prince. They went down to Cambridge in July for the ceremony of the installation, which was celebrated with all scholarly state and splendour.

"The Hall of Trinity was the scene of the ceremony for which the visit was paid. Her Majesty occupied a chair of state on a dais. The Chancellor, the Prince in his official robes, supported by the Duke of Wellington, Chancellor of Oxford, the Bishop of Oxford, the Vice- Chancellor of Cambridge, and the Heads of the Houses entered, and the Chancellor read an address to her Majesty congratulatory on her arrival. Her Majesty made a gracious reply and the Prince retired with the usual profound obeisances, a proceeding which caused her Majesty some amusement," so says the Annual Register. This part of the day's proceedings seems to have made a lively impression on those who witnessed it.

Bishop Wilberforce gives his testimony. "The Cambridge scene was very interesting. There was such a burst of loyalty, and it told so on the Queen and Prince. E—— would not then have thought that he looked cold. It was quite clear that they both felt it as something new that he had earned, and not she given, a true English honour; and so he looked so pleased and she so triumphant. There was also some such pretty interludes when he presented the address, and she beamed upon him and once half smiled, and then covered the smile with a gentle dignity, and then she said in her clear musical voice, 'The choice which the University has made of its Chancellor has my most entire approbation.'" The Queen records in her Diary, "I cannot say how it agitated and embarrassed me to have to receive this address and hear it read by my beloved Albert, who walked in at the head of the University, and who looked dear and beautiful in his robes, which were carried by Colonel Phipps and Colonel Seymour. Albert went through it all admirably, almost absurd, however, as it was for us. He gave me the address and I read the answer, and a few kissed hands, and then Albert retired with the University."

After luncheon a Convocation was held in the Senate House, at which the Queen was present as a visitor. The Prince, as Chancellor, received her at the door, and led her to the seat prepared for her. "He sat covered in his Chancellor's chair. There was a perfect roar of applause," which we are told was only tamed down within the bounds of sanity by the dulness of the Latin oration, delivered by the public orator. Besides the princes already mentioned, and several noblemen and gentlemen, Sir George Grey, Sir Harry Smith (of Indian fame), Sir Roderick Murchison, and Professor Muller, received university honours.

Her Majesty and the new Chancellor dined with the Vice-Chancellor at Catherine Hall— probably selected for the honour because it was a small college, and could only accommodate a select party. After dinner her Majesty attended a concert in the Senate House—an entertainment got up in order to afford the Cambridge public another opportunity of seeing their Queen. Later the Prince went to the Observatory, and her Majesty walked in the cool of the evening in the little garden of Trinity Lodge, with her two ladies.

The following day the royal party again went to the Senate House, the Prince receiving the Queen, and conducting her as before to her seat. With the accompaniment of a tremendous crowd, great heat, and thunders of applause, the prize poems were read, and the medals distributed by the Prince. Then came the time for the "Installation Ode," written at the Prince's request by Wordsworth, the poet laureate, set to music, and sung in Trinity Hall in the presence of the Queen and Prince Albert with great effect. Poetry, of all created things, can least be made to order; yet the ode had many fine passages and telling lines, besides the recommendation claimed for it by Baroness Bunsen: "The Installation Ode I thought quite affecting, because the selection of striking points was founded on fact, and all exaggeration and humbug were avoided."

The poem touched first on what was so prominent a feature in the history of Europe in the poet's youth—the evil of unrighteous and the good of righteous war, identifying the last with the successes of England when Napoleon was overthrown.

  Such is Albion's fame and glory,
  Let rescued Europe tell the story
Then the measure changes to a plaintive strain.
  But lo! what sudden cloud has darkened all
  The land as with a funeral pall?
  The rose of England suffers blight,
  The flower has drooped, the isle's delight
  Flower and bud together fall,
  A nation's hopes he crushed in Claremont's desolate hall
Hope and cheer return to the song.
  Time a chequered mantle wears,
  Earth awakes from wintry sleep,
  Again the tree a blossom bears
  Cease, Britannia, cease to weep,
  Hark to the peals on this bright May morn,
  They tell that your future Queen is born

A little later is the fine passage—

Time in his mantle's sunniest fold
Uplifted on his arms the child,
And while the fearless infant smiled
Her happy destiny foretold
Infancy, by wisdom mild,
Trained to health and artless beauty,
Youth by pleasure unbeguiled
From the lore of lofty duty,
Womanhood, in pure renown
Seated on her lineal throne,
Leaves of myrtle in her crown
Fresh with lustre all their own,
Love, the treasure worth possessing
More than all the world beside,
This shall be her choicest blessing,
Oft to royal hearts denied.

After a brief period of rest, which meant a little quiet "reading, writing, working, and drawing"—a far better sedative for excited nerves than entire idleness—the Queen and the Prince attended a flower-show in the grounds of Downing College, walking round the gardens and entering into all the six tents, "a very formidable undertaking, for the heat was beyond endurance and the crowd fearful." In the evening there was a great dinner in Trinity Hall. "Splendid did that great hall look," is Baroness Bunsen's admiring exclamation; "three hundred and thirty people at various tables … the Queen and her immediate suite at a table at the raised end of the hall, all the rest at tables lengthways. At the Queen's table the names were put on the places, and anxious was the moment before one could find one's place." Then the Queen gave a reception in Henry VIII.'s drawing-room, when the masters, professors and doctors, with their wives, were presented. When the reception was over, at ten o'clock, in the soft dim dusk, a little party again stole out, to see with greater leisure and privacy those noble trees and hoary buildings. Her Majesty tells us the pedestrians were in curious costumes: "Albert in his dress-coat with a mackintosh over it, I in my evening dress and diadem, and with a veil over my head, and the two princes in their uniforms, and the ladies in their dresses and shawls and veils. We walked through the small garden, and could not at first find our way, after which we discovered the right road, and walked along the beautiful avenues of lime-trees in the grounds of St. John's College, along the water and over the bridges. All was so pretty and picturesque, in particular the one covered bridge of St. John's College, which is like the Bridge of Sighs at Venice. We stopped to listen to the distant hum of the town; and nothing seemed wanting but some singing, which everywhere but here in this country we should have heard. A lattice opened, and we could fancy a lady appearing and listening to a serenade."

Shade of quaint old Fuller! thou who hast described with such gusto Queen Elizabeth's five days' stay at Cambridge, what wouldst thou not have given, hadst thou lived in the reign of Victoria, to have been in her train this night? Shades more formidable of good Queen Bess herself, Bluff King Hal, Margaret Countess of Richmond, and that other unhappy Margaret of Anjou, what would you have said of this simple ramble? In truth it was a scene from the world of romance, even without the music and the lady at the lattice. An ideal Queen and an ideal Prince, a thin disguise over the tokens of their magnificence, stealing out with their companions, like so many ghosts, to enjoy common sights and experiences and the little thrill of adventure in the undetected deed.

On the last morning there was a public breakfast in the grounds of Trinity College, attended by thousands of the county gentry of Cambridge and Lincolnshire. "At one the Queen set out through the cloisters and hall and library of Trinity College, to pass through the gardens and avenues, which had been connected for the occasion by a temporary bridge over the river, with those of St. John's." Madame Bunsen and her companions followed her Majesty, and had the best opportunity of seeing everything, and in particular "the joyous crowd that grouped among the noble trees." The Queen ate her déjeuner in one of the tents, and on her return to Trinity Lodge, she and Prince Albert left Cambridge at three o'clock for London. Baroness Bunsen winds up her graphic descriptions with the statement, "I could still tell much of Cambridge— of the charm of its 'trim gardens,' of how the Queen looked and was pleased, and how well she was dressed, and how perfect in grace and movement."

CHAPTER VII.THE QUEEN'S VISIT TO THE WESTERN ISLANDS OP SCOTLAND AND STAY AT ARDVERIKIE.

On the 11th of August her Majesty and Prince Albert, with the Prince of Wales, the Princess Royal, and the Prince of Leiningen, attended by a numerous suite, left Osborne in the royal yacht for Scotland. They followed a new route and succeeded, in spite of the fogs in the Channel, in reaching the Scilly Isles. The voyage, to begin with, was not a pleasant one. There had been a rough swell on the sea as well as fogs off shore. The children, and especially the Queen, on this occasion suffered from sea-sickness. However, her Majesty landed on the tiny island of St. Mary's.

As the royal party approached Wales the sea became calmer and the sailing enjoyable. The yacht and its companions lay in the great harbour of Milford Haven, under the reddish-brown cliffs. Prince Albert and the Prince of Leiningen went to Pembroke, while the Queen sat on the deck and sketched.

On a beautiful Sunday the Queen sailed through the Menai Straits in the Fairy, when the sight of "Snowdon rising splendidly in the middle of the fields and woods was glorious." The "grand old Castle of Caernarvon" attracted attention; so did Plas Newydd, where her Majesty had spent six weeks, when she had visited Wales as Princess Victoria, in one of her girlish excursions with the Duchess of Kent. The Isle of Man, with the town of Douglas, surmounted by bold hills and cliffs, a castle and a lighthouse, looked abundantly picturesque, but the landing there was reserved for the return of the voyagers, though it was on this occasion that a tripping Manxman described Prince Albert, in a local newspaper, as leading the Prince Regent by the hand; a slip which drew from the Prince the gay rejoinder that "usually one has a regent for an infant, but in Man it seems to be precisely the reverse."

The Mull of Galloway was the first Scotch land that was sighted, and just before entering Loch Ryan the huge rock, Ailsa Craig, with its moving clouds of sea-fowl, rose to view.

Arran and Goatfell, Bute and the Bay of Rothesay, were alike hailed with delight. But the islands were left behind for the moment, till more was seen of the Clyde, and Greenock, of sugar-refining and boat-building fame, was reached. It was her Majesty's first visit to the west coast of Scotland, and Glasgow poured "down the water" her magistrates, her rich merchants, her stalwart craftsmen, her swarms from the Gorbels and the Saut Market, the Candle-rigs and the Guse-dibs. Multitudes lined the quays. No less than forty steamers over- filled with passengers struggled zealously in the wake of royalty. "Amidst boats and ships of every description moving in all directions," the little Fairy cut its way through, bound for Dumbarton.

On the Queen's return to Greenock she sailed past Roseneath, and followed the windings of Loch Long, getting a good view of the Cobbler, the rugged mountain which bears a fantastic resemblance to a man mending a shoe. At the top of the loch, Ben Lomond came in sight. "There was no sun, and twice a little mist; but still it was beautiful," wrote the Queen.

On "a bright fresh morning" in August, when the hills were just "slightly tipped with clouds," the Queen sailed through the Kyles of Bute, that loveliest channel between overtopping mountains, and entered Loch Fyne, another fine arm of the sea, of herring celebrity.

A Highland welcome awaited the Queen at the little landing-place of Inverary, made gay and fragrant with heather. Old friends, whom she was honouring by her presence, waited to receive her, the Duke and Duchess of Argyle—the latter the eldest daughter of the Duchess of Sutherland, who was also present with her son, Lord Stafford, her unmarred daughter, Lady Caroline Leveson-Gower, and her son-in-law and second daughter, Lord and Lady Blantyre. An innocent warder stood in front of the old feudal keep. In the course of the Queen's visit to Germany she had made the acquaintance, without dreaming of what lay concealed in the skirts of time, of one of her future sons-in-law in a fine little boy of eight years. Now her Majesty was to be introduced, without a suspicion of what would be the result of the introduction, to the coming husband of another daughter still unborn. Here is the Queen's description of the son and heir of the house of Argyle, who was yet to win a princess for his bride. "Outside, stood the Marquis of Lorne, just two years old—a dear, white, fat, fair little fellow, with reddish hair but very delicate features, like both his mother and father; he is such a merry, independent little child. He had a black velvet dress and jacket, with a 'sporran,' scarf, and Highland bonnet."

Her Majesty lunched at the castle, "the Highland gentlemen standing with halberts in the room," and returned to the Fairy, sailing down Loch Fyne when the afternoon was at its mellowest, and the long shadows were falling across the hillsides. At five Lochgilphead was reached, when Sir John Orde lent his carriage to convey the visitors to the Crinan Canal. The next day's sail, in beautiful weather still, was through the clusters of the nearest of the western islands, up the Sound of Jura, amidst a flotilla of small boats crowned with flags. Here were fresh islands and mountain peaks, until the strangers were within hail of Staffa.

It is not always that an approach to this northern marvel of nature is easy or even practicable; but fortune favours the brave. Her Majesty has described the landing. "At three we anchored close before Staffa, and immediately got into the barge, with Charles, the children, and the rest of our people, and rowed towards the cave. As we rounded the point the wonderful basaltic formation came into sight. The appearance it presents is most extraordinary, and when we turned the corner to go into the renowned Fingal's Cave the effect was splendid, like a great entrance into a vaulted hall; it looked almost awful as we entered, and the barge heaved up and down on the swell of the sea. It is very high, but not longer than two hundred and twenty-seven feet, and narrower than I expected, being only forty feet wide. The sea is immensely deep in the cave. The rocks under water were all colours— pink, blue, and green, which had a most beautiful and varied effect. It was the first time the British standard, with a queen of Great Britain and her husband and children, had ever entered Fingal's Cave, and the men gave three cheers, which sounded very impressive there."

On the following day the Atlantic rains had found the party, though for the present the affliction was temporary. It poured for three hours, during which her Majesty drew and painted in her cabin. The weather cleared in the afternoon; sitting on the deck was again possible, and Loch

Linnhe, Loch Eil, and the entrance to Loch Leven were not lost.

At Fort William the Queen was to quit the yacht and repair to the summer quarters of Ardverikie. Before doing so she recorded her regret that "this delightful voyage and tour among the western lochs and isles is at an end; they are so beautiful and so full of poetry and romance, traditions and historical associations."

Rain again, more formidable than before, on Saturday, the 21st of August. It was amidst a hopeless drenching drizzle, which blots out the chief features of a landscape, that the Queen went ashore, to find "a great gathering of Highlanders in their different tartans" met to do her honour. Frasers, Forbeses, Mackenzies, Grants, replaced Campbells, Macdonalds, Macdougals, and Macleans. By a wild and lonely carriage-road, the latter part resembling Glen Tilt, her Majesty reached her destination.

Ardverikie, which claimed to have been a hunting-seat of Fergus, king of the Scots, was a shooting lodge belonging to Lord George Bentinck, rented from him by the Marquis of Abercorn, and lent by the marquis to the Queen. It has since been burnt down. It was rustic, as a shooting lodge should be, very much of a large cottage in point of architecture, the bare walls of the principal rooms characteristically decorated with rough sketches by Landseer, among them a drawing of "The Stag at Bay," and the whole house bristling with stags' horns of great size and perfection. In front of the house lay Loch Laggan, eight miles in length.

The Queen remained at Ardverikie for four weeks, and doubtless would have enjoyed the wilds thoroughly, had it not been for the lowest deep of persistently bad weather, when "it not only rained and blew, but snowed by way of variety."

Lord Campbell heard and wrote down these particulars of the royal stay at Ardverikie. "The Queen was greatly delighted with the Highlands in spite of the bad weather, and was accustomed to sally for a walk in the midst of a heavy rain, putting a great hood ever her bonnet, and showing nothing of her features but her eyes. The Prince's invariable return to luncheon about two o'clock, in spite of grouse-shooting and deer-stalking, is explained by his voluntary desire to please the Queen, and by the intense hunger which always assails him at this hour, when he likes, in German fashion, to make his dinner."

In a continuance of the most dismally unpropitious weather, the Queen and her children left Ardverikie on the 17th of September, the Prince having preceded her for a night that he might visit Inverness and the Caledonian Canal. The storm continued, almost without intermission, during the whole of the voyage home.

CHAPTER VIII.THE FRENCH FUGITIVES—THE PEOPLE'S CHARTER.

Long before the autumn of 1847, the mischievous consequences of the railway mania, complicated by the failure of the potato crop, showed itself in great bankruptcies in the large towns all over the country.

The new year came with trouble on its wings. The impending storm burst all over Europe, first in France. Louis Philippe's dynasty was overthrown.

In pairs or singly, sometimes wandering aside in a little distraction, so as to be lost sight of for days, the numerous brothers and sisters, with the parent pair, reached Dreux and Eu, and thence, with the exception of the Duchesse d'Orleans and her sons, straggled to England.

One can guess the feelings of the Queen and Prince Albert when they heard that their late hosts, doubly allied to them by kindred ties, were fugitives, seeking refuge from the hospitality of a foreign nation. And the first confused tidings of the French revolution which reached the Queen and Prince Albert were rendered more trying, by the almost simultaneous announcement of the death of the old Dowager- Duchess of Gotha, to whom all her grandchildren were so much attached.

The ex-King and Queen arrived at Newhaven, Louis Philippe bearing the name of Mr. Smith. Queen Victoria had already written to King Leopold on the 1st of March: "About the King and Queen (Louis Philippe and Queen Amélie) we still know nothing…. We do everything we can for the poor family, who are, indeed, sorely to be pitied. But you will naturally understand that we cannot make common cause with them, and cannot take a hostile position to the new state of things in France. We leave them alone; but if a Government which has the approbation of the country be formed, we shall feel it necessary to recognise it in order to pin them down to maintain peace and the existing treaties, which is of the greatest importance. It will not be pleasant to do this, but the public good and the peace of Europe go before one's personal feelings."

As soon as it could be arranged under the circumstances, the Queen had an interview with the exiles. What a meeting after the last parting, and all that had come to pass in the interval! This interview took place on the 6th of March, when Louis Philippe came privately to Windsor.

The same intelligent chronicler, Lady Lyttelton, who gave such a graphic account of the Citizen-King's first visit to Windsor, had also to photograph the second. Once more she uses with reason the word "historical." "To-day is historical, Louis Philippe having come from Claremont to pay a private (very private) visit to the Queen. She is really enviable now, to have in her power and in her path of duty, such a boundless piece of charity and beneficent hospitality. The reception by the people of England of all the fugitives has been beautifully kind."

That day the Queen wrote sadly to Baron Stockmar: "I am quite well; indeed, particularly so, though God knows we have had since the 25th enough for a whole life—anxiety, sorrow, excitement; in short, I feel as if we had jumped over thirty years' experience at once. The whole face of Europe is changed, and I feel as if I lived in a dream." She added, with the tenderness of a generous nature, referring to the very different circumstances in which her regard for the Orleans house had been established, and to the alienation which had arisen between her and some of its members: "You know my love for the family; you know how I longed to get of terms with them again … and you said, 'Time will alone, but will certainly, bring it about.' Little did I dream that this would be the way we should meet again and see each other, all in the most friendly way.

That the Duchesse de Montpensier, about whom we have been quarrelling for the last year, and a half, should be here as a fugitive and dressed in the clothes I sent her, and should come to thank me for my kindness, is a reverse of fortune which no novelist would devise, and upon which one could moralise for ever."

It was a comfort to the Queen and Prince Albert that Belgium, which had at first appeared in the greatest danger, ended by standing almost alone on the side of its King and Government.

The tide of revolution, which swept over the greater states, did not spare the small. The Duke of Coburg-Gotha's subjects, who had seemed so happily situated and so contented at the time of the Queen's visit, were in a ferment like the rest of their countrymen. Bellona's hot breath was in danger of withering the flowers of that Arcadia. The Princes of Leiningen and Hohenlohe, the Queen's brother and brother- in-law, were practically dispossessed of seigneurial rights and lands, and ruined. The Princess of Hohenlohe wrote to her sister: "We are undone, and must begin a new existence of privations, which I don't care for, but for poor Ernest" (her husband) "I feel it more than I can say."

In the meantime, on the 18th of March a fourth English Princess was born. There was more than usual congratulation on the safety and well- being of mother and child, because of the great shocks which had tried the Queen previously, and the anxiety which filled all thoughtful minds for the result of the crisis in England. Her Majesty's courage rose to the occasion. She wrote to King Leopold in little more than a fortnight: "I heard all that passed, and my only thoughts and talk were political. But I never was calmer or quieter, or less nervous. Great events make one calm; it is only trifles that irritate my nerves."

England had its own troubles and was in high excitement about an increased grant of money for the support of the army and navy, and the continuance of the income-tax. The Chartists threatened to make a great demonstration on Kennington Common.

The first threat in London, for the 13th of March, a few days before the birth of the little Princess, ended in utter failure. The happy termination was assisted by the state of the weather, great falls of rain anticipating the work of large bodies of police prepared to scatter the crowd. But as another demonstration, with the avowed intention of walking in procession to present to the House of Commons a monster petition, miles long, for the granting of the People's Charter, was announced to take place on the 10th of April, great uncertainty, and agitation filled the public mind. It was judged advisable that the Queen should go to the Isle of Wight for a short stay at Osborne, though it was still not more than three weeks since her confinement.

The second demonstration collapsed like the first. Only a fraction— not more than twenty-three thousand of the vast multitude expected to appear—assembled at the meeting-place, and the people dispersed quietly. But it is only necessary to mention the precautions employed to show how great had been the alarm. The Duke of Wellington devised and conducted the steps which were taken beforehand. On the bridges were massed bodies of foot and horse police, and special constables, of whom nearly two hundred thousand—one of them Prince Louis Napoleon, the future Emperor of the French—are said to have been sworn in. In the immediate neighbourhood of each bridge strong forces of military, while kept out of sight, were ready "for instant movement." Two regiments of the line were at Millbank Penitentiary, twelve hundred infantry at Deptford Dockyard, and thirty pieces of heavy field ordnance at the Tower prepared for transport by hired steamers to any spot where help might be required. Bodies of troops were posted in unexpected quarters, as in the area of the untenanted Rose Inn yard, but within call. The public offices at Somerset House and in the City were liberally supplied with arms. Places like the Bank of England were "packed" with troops and artillery, and furnished with sand-bag parapets for their walls, and wooden barricades with loopholes for firing through, for their windows.

"Thank God," her Majesty wrote to the King of the Belgians, "the Chartist meeting and procession have turned out a complete failure. The loyalty of the people at large, has been very striking, and their indignation at their peace being interfered with by such wanton and worthless men immense."

Never was cheerfulness more wanted to lighten a burden of work and care. In this year of trouble "no less than twenty-eight thousand dispatches were received or sent out from the Foreign Office." All these dispatches came to the Queen and Prince Albert, as well as to Lord Palmerston, the Minister for Foreign Affairs.

Across the Channel the inflammatory speeches and writings of Messrs. Mitchel, Meagher, and Smith O'Brien became so treasonable in tone that, after the passing of a Bill in Parliament for the better repression of sedition, the three Irish leaders were arrested and brought to trial, the jury refusing to commit in the case of Meagher and Smith O'Brien, but in that of Mitchel, who was tried separately, finding him guilty, and sentencing him to transportation for fourteen years.

On the 2nd of May the Court returned to Buckingham Palace, and the baptism of the infant princess took place on the 13th, in the private chapel of Buckingham Palace, when the Archbishop of Canterbury officiated. The sponsors were Duke Augustus of Mecklenburg-Schwerin, represented by Prince Albert, and the Duchess of Saxe-Meiningen and the Grand-Duchess of Mecklenburg-Strelitz, represented by the Queen- dowager and the Duchess of Cambridge. The names given to the child were, "Louise Caroline Alberta," the first and last for the child's grandmother on the father's side and for the royal father himself. A chorale was performed, which the Prince had adapted from an earlier composition written to the hymn—

In life's gay morn, ere sprightly youth
  By vice and folly is enslaved,
Oh! may thy Maker's glorious name
  Be on thy infant mind engraved;
So shall no shades of sorrow cloud
  The sunshine of thy early days,
But happiness, in endless round,
  Shall still encompass all thy ways.

Bishop Wilberforce describes the scene. "The royal christening was a very beautiful sight, in its highest sense of that word 'beauty.' The Queen, with the five royal children around her, the Prince of Wales and Princess Royal hand-in-hand, all kneeling down quietly and meekly at every prayer, and the little Princess Helena alone, just standing, and looking round with the blue eyes of gazing innocence."

When the statues of the royal children were executed by Mrs. Thornycroft, Princess Helena was modelled as Peace. The engraving is a representation of the graceful piece of sculpture, in which a slender young girl, wearing a long loose robe and having sandalled feet, holds the usual emblematic branch and cluster—one in each hand.

As one Princess was born, another of a former generation, whose birth had been hailed with equal rejoicing, passed away, on the 27th of May, immediately after the Birthday Drawing-room. Princess Sophia, the youngest surviving daughter and twelfth child of George III. and Queen Charlotte, died in her arm-chair in the drawing-room of her house at Kensington, aged seventy-one. At her own request she was buried at Kensal Green, where the Duke of Sussex was interred.

CHAPTER IX. THE QUEEN'S FIRST STAY AT BALMORAL.

From France, in June, came the grievous news of the three days' fighting in the streets of Paris, because no Government provision could secure work and bread for the artisans. The insurrection was only put down by martial law under the Dictator, General Cavaignac.

In Sardinia the King, Charles Albert, fighting gallantly against the Austrian rule, was defeated once and again, and driven back.

In England, though the most swaggering of the Chartists still blustered a little, attention could be given to more peaceful concerns. In July Prince Albert went to York, though he could "ill be spared" from the Queen's side in those days of startling events and foreign turmoil, to be present at a meeting of the Royal Agricultural Society, of which he had been governor for half-a-dozen years. The acclamations with which the Prince was received, were only the echo of the tempest of cheers which greeted and encouraged her Majesty every time she appeared in public this year. In August strong measures had again to be taken in Ireland. These included the gathering together of a great military force in the disturbed districts, and the assemblage of a fleet of war-steamers on the coast. As in the previous instance, little or no resistance was offered. In the course of a few days the former leaders, Meagher, Smith O'Brien, and Mitchel, were arrested.

They were brought to trial in Dublin, convicted of high treason, and sentenced to death—a sentence commuted into transportation for life.

The Queen had the pleasure of finding her brother, the Prince of Leiningen, appointed head of the department of foreign affairs in the short-lived Frankfort assembly of the German states. It showed at least the respect in which he was held by his countrymen.

On the 5th of September the Queen went in person to prorogue Parliament, which had sat for ten months. The ceremony took place in the new House of Lords. There was an unusually large and brilliant company present on this occasion, partly to admire the "lavish paint and gilding," the stained-glass windows, with likenesses of kings and queens, and Dyce's and Maclise's frescoes, partly to enjoy the emphatically-delivered sentence in the royal speech, in which the Queen acknowledged, "with grateful feelings, the many marks of loyalty and attachment which she had received from all classes of her people."

The Queen and the Prince, with three of their children and the suite, sailed from Woolwich for a new destination in Scotland—a country-house or little castle, which they had so far made their own, since the Prince, acting on the advice of Sir James Clark, the Queen's physician, had acquired the lease from the Earl of Aberdeen.

The royal party were in Aberdeen Harbour at eight o'clock in the morning of the 7th September. On the 8th Balmoral was reached. The first impression was altogether agreeable. Her Majesty has described the place, as it appeared to her, in her Journal. "We arrived at Balmoral at a quarter to three. It is a pretty little castle in the old Scottish style. There is a picturesque tower and garden in the front, with a high wooded hill; at the back there is a wood down to the Dee, and the hills rise all around."

During the first stay of the Court at Balmoral, the Queen has chronicled the ascent of a mountain. On Saturday, the 16th of September, as early as half-past nine in the morning, her Majesty and Prince Albert drove in a postchaise four miles to the bridge in the wood of Ballochbuie, where ponies and guides awaited them. Macdonald, a keeper of Farquharson of Invercauld's and afterwards in the service of the Prince, a tall, handsome man, whom the Queen describes as "looking like a picture in his shooting-jacket and kilt," and Grant, the head-keeper at Balmoral, on a pony, with provisions in two baskets, were the chief attendants.

Through the wood and over moss, heather, and stones, sometimes riding, sometimes walking; Prince Albert irresistibly attracted to stalk a deer, in vain; across the stony little burn, where the faithful Highlanders piloted her Majesty, walking and riding again, when Macdonald led the bridle of the beast which bore so precious a burden; the views "very beautiful," but alas! mist on the brow of Loch-na-gar. Prince Albert making a detour after ptarmigan, leaving the Queen in the safe keeping of her devoted guides, to whom she refers so kindly as "taking the greatest care of her." Even "poor Batterbury," the English groom, who seems to have cut rather a ridiculous figure in his thin boots and gaiters and non-enjoyment of the expedition, "was very anxious also" for the well-being of his royal lady, whose tastes must have struck him as eccentric, to say the least.

The mist intensified the cold when the citadel mountain was reached, so that it must have been a relief to try a spell of walking once more, especially as the first part of the way was "soft and easy," while the party looked down on the two lochans, known as Na Nian. Who that has any knowledge of the mountains cannot recall the effect of these solitary tarns, like well-eyes in the wilderness, gleaming in the sunshine, dark in the gloom? The Prince, good mountaineer as he was, grew glad to remount his pony and let the docile, sure-footed creature pick its steps through the gathering fog, which was making the ascent an adventure not free from danger.

Everything not within a hundred yards was hidden. The last and steepest part of the mountain (three thousand seven hundred and seventy-seven feet from the sea-level) was accomplished on foot, and at two o'clock, after four hours' riding and walking, a seat in a little nook where luncheon could be taken was found; for, unfortunately, there was no more to be done save to seek rest and refreshment. There was literally nothing to be seen, in place of the glorious panorama which a mountain-top in favourable circumstances presents.

This was that "dark Loch-na-gar" whose "steep frowning glories" Lord Byron rendered famous, for which he dismissed with scorn, "gay landscapes and gardens of roses."

No doubt the snowflakes, in corries on the mountain-side, do look deliciously cool on a hot summer day. But such a drizzling rain as this was the other side of the picture, which her Majesty, with a shiver, called "cold, wet, and cheerless." In addition to the rain the wind began to blow a hurricane, which, after all, in the case of a fog was about the kindest thing the wind could do, whether or not the spirits of heroes were in the gale.

At twenty minutes after two the party set out on their descent of the mountain. The two keepers, moving on as pioneers in the gloom, "looked like ghosts." When walking became too exhausting, the Queen, "well wrapped in plaids," was again mounted on her pony, which she declared "went delightfully," though the mist caused the rider "to feel cheerless."

In the course of the next couple of hours, after a thousand feet of the descent had been achieved, by one of those abrupt transitions which belong to such a landscape, the mist below vanished as if by magic, and it was again, summer sunshine around.

But the world could not be altogether shut out at Balmoral, and the echoes which came from afar, this year, were of a sufficiently disturbing character. Among the most notable, Sir Theodore Martin mentions the Frankfort riots, in which two members of the German States Union were assassinated, and the startling death of the Conservative leader, Lord George Bentinck, who had suddenly exchanged the rôle of the turf for that of Parliament, and come to the front during the struggle over the abolition of the Corn Laws.

A third strangely significant omen was the election of Prince Louis Napoleon, by five different French Departments, as a deputy to the new French Chamber.

The Court left Balmoral on the 28th of September, stayed one night in London, and then proceeded for ten days to Osborne. On the return of the Queen and the Prince to Windsor, on the 9th of October, a sad accident occurred in their sight. As the yacht was crossing on a misty and stormy day to Portsmouth, she passed near the frigate Grampus, which had just come back from her station in the Pacific. In their eagerness to meet their relations among the crew on board, five unfortunate women had gone out in an open boat rowed by two watermen, though the foul-weather flag was flying. "A sudden squall swamped the boat" without attracting the attention of anyone on board the Grampus or the yacht. But one of the watermen, who was able to cling to the overturned boat, was seen by the men in a Custom-house boat, who immediately aroused the indignation of Lord Adolphus Fitzclarence and his brother-officers by steering, apparently without any reason, right across the bows of the Fairy. Prince Albert, who was on deck, was the first to discover the cause of the inexplicable conduct of the men in the Custom-house boat. "He called out that he saw a man in the water;" the Queen hurried out of her pavilion, and distinguished a man on what turned out to be the keel of a boat. "Oh dear! there are more!" cried Prince Albert in horror, "which quite overcame me," the Queen wrote afterwards. "The royal yacht was stopped and one of its boats lowered, which picked up three of the women—one of them alive and clinging to a plank, the others dead." The storm was violent, and the responsibility of keeping the yacht exposed to its fury lay with Lord Adolphus. Since nothing further could be attempted for the victims of their own rashness, he did not think it right that the yacht should stay for the return of the boat, as he held the delay unsafe, although both the Queen and the Prince, with finer instincts, were anxious this should be done. "We could not stop," wrote her Majesty again, full of pity. "It was a dreadful moment, too horrid to describe. It is a consolation to think we were of some use, and also that, even if the yacht had remained, they could not have done more. Still, we all keep feeling we might, though I think we could not.... It is a terrible thing, and haunts me continually."

The Magyar War under Kossuth was raging in Hungary. In the far-away Punjab the Sikh War, in which Lieutenant Edwardes had borne so gallant a part in the beginning of the year, was still prolonged, with Mooltan always the bone of contention.

In October all aristocratic England was excited by the sale of the Art treasures of Stowe, which lasted for forty days. Mrs. Gaskell made a fine contribution to literature in her novel of "Mary Barton," in which genius threw its strong light on Manchester life.

The Queen had a private theatre fitted up this year in the Rubens Room, Windsor Castle. The first of the dramatis personae in the best London theatres went down and acted before the Court, giving revivals of Shakespeare—which it was hoped would improve the taste for the higher drama—varied by lighter pieces.

On the 24th of November the Queen heard of the death of her former Minister and counsellor William Lamb, Viscount Melbourne. "Truly and sincerely," her Majesty wrote in her Journal, "do I deplore the loss of one who was a most disinterested friend of mine, and most sincerely attached to me. He was, indeed, for the first two years and a half of my reign, almost the only friend I had, except Stockmar and Lehzen, and I used to see him constantly, daily. I thought much and talked much of him all day."

CHAPTER X.PUBLIC AND DOMESTIC INTERESTS—FRESH ATTACK UPON THE QUEEN.

The Queen and the Prince were now pledged—alike by principle and habit—to hard work. They were both early risers, but before her Majesty joined Prince Albert in their sitting-room, where their writing-tables stood side by side, we are told he had already, even in winter, by the light of the green German lamp which he had introduced into England, prepared many papers to be considered by her Majesty, and done everything in his power to lighten her labours as a sovereign.

Lord Campbell describes an audience which he had from the Queen in February. "I was obliged to make an excursion to Windsor on Saturday, and have an audience before Prince Albert's lunch. I was with the Queen in her closet, solus cum solâ. But I should first tell you my difficulty about getting from the station at Slough to the Castle. When we go down for a council we have a special train and carriages provided for us. I consulted Morpeth, who answered, 'I can only tell you how I went last—on the top of an omnibus; but the Queen was a little shocked.' I asked how she found it out. He said he had told her himself to amuse her, but that I should be quite en règle by driving up in a fly or cab. So I drove up in my one horse conveyance, and the lord-in-waiting announced my arrival to her Majesty. I was shown into the royal closet, a very small room with one window, and soon she entered by another door all alone. My business was the appointment of a sheriff for the County Palatine, which was soon despatched. We then talked of the state of the finances of the Duchy, and I ventured to offer her my felicitations on the return of this auspicious day—her wedding-day. I lunched with the maids of honour, and got back in time to take a part in very important deliberations in the Cabinet."

In February, 1849, the Queen opened Parliament in person. Perhaps the greatest source of anxiety was now the Sikh War, in which the warlike tribes were gaining advantages over the English troops, though Mooltan had been reduced the previous month. A drawn battle was fought between Lord Gough's force and that of Chuttar Singh at Chillianwallah. While the English were not defeated, their losses in men, guns and standards were sore and humiliating to the national pride. Sir Charles Napier was ordered out, and, in spite of bad health, obeyed the order. But in the meantime Lord Gough had retrieved his losses by winning at Goojerat a great victory over the Sikhs and Afghans, which in the end compelled the surrender of the enemy, with the restoration of the captured guns and standards. On the 29th of March the kingdom of the Punjaub was proclaimed as existing no longer, and the State was annexed to British India; while the beneficial influence of Edwardes and the Lawrences rendered the wild Sikhs more loyal subjects, in a future time of need, than the trained and petted Sepoy mercenaries proved themselves.

On the afternoon of the 19th of May, after the Queen had held one of her most splendid Drawing-rooms, when she was driving in a carriage with three of her children up Constitution Hill, she was again fired at by a man standing within the railings of the Green Park. Prince Albert was on horseback, so far in advance that he did not know what had occurred, till told of it by the Queen when he assisted her to alight. But her Majesty did not lose her perfect self-possession. She stood up, motioned to the coachman, who had stopped the carriage for an instant, to go on, and then diverted the children's attention by talking to them. The man who had fired was immediately arrested. Indeed, he would have been violently assaulted by the mob, had he not been protected by the police. He proved to be an Irishman, named Hamilton, from Limerick, who had come over from Ireland five years before, and worked as a bricklayer's labourer and a navvy both in England and France. Latterly he had been earning a scanty livelihood by doing chance jobs. There was this to distinguish him from the other dastardly assailants of the Queen: he was not a half-crazed, morbidly conceited boy, though he also had no conceivable motive for what he did. He appears to have taken his measures, in providing himself with pistol and powder, from a mere impulse of stolid brutality. His pistol contained no ball, so that he was tried under the Felon's Act, which had been provided for such offences, and sentenced to seven years' transportation.

The education of their children was a subject of much thought and care to the Queen and Prince Albert. Her Majesty wrote various memoranda on the question which was of such interest to her. Some of these are preserved in the life of the Prince Consort. She started with the wise maxim, "that the children should be brought up as simply and in as domestic a way as possible; that (not interfering with their lessons) they should be as much as possible with their parents, and learn to place their greatest confidence in them in all things." She dwelt upon a religious training, and held strongly the conviction that "it is best given to a child, day by day, at its mother's knee." It was a matter of tender regret to the Queen when "the pressure of public duty" prevented her from holding this part of her children's education entirely in her own keeping. "It is already a hard case for me," was the pathetic reflection of the young mother in reference to the childhood of the Princess Royal, "that my occupations prevent me being with her when she says her prayers." At the same time the Queen and the Prince had strong opinions on the religious training which ought to be given to their children, and strove to have them carried out. The Queen wrote, still of the Princess Royal, "I am quite clear that she should be taught to have great reverence for God and for religion, but that she should have the feelings of devotion and love which our Heavenly

Father encourages His earthly children to have for Him, and not one of fear and trembling; and that the thoughts of death and an after life should not be represented in an alarming and forbidding view, and that she should be made to know as yet no difference of creeds, and not think that she can only pray on her knees, or that those who do not kneel are less fervent and devout in their prayers."

Surely these truly reverent, just, and liberal sentiments on the religion to be imparted to young children must recommend themselves to all earnest, thoughtful parents.

In the accompanying engraving the girl-Princesses, Helena and Louise, who are represented wearing lilies in the breasts of their frocks, look like sister-lilies—as fresh, pure, and sweet.

In 1849 Mr. Birch, who had been head boy at Eton, taken high honours at Cambridge, and acted as one of the under masters at Eton, was appointed tutor to the Prince of Wales when the Prince was eight years of age.

CHAPTER XI. THE QUEEN'S FIRST VISIT TO IRELAND.

Parliament was prorogued by commission, and the Queen and the Prince, with their four children, sailed on the 1st of August for Ireland. Lady Lyttelton watching the departing squadron from the windows of Osborne, wrote with something like dramatic emphasis, "It is done, England's fate is afloat; we are left lamenting. They hope to reach Cork to-morrow evening, the wind having gone down and the sky cleared, the usual weather compliment to the Queen's departure."

The voyage was quick but not very pleasant, from the great swell in the sea. At nine o'clock, on the morning of the 2nd, Land's End was passed, and at eight o'clock in the evening the Cove of Cork was so near that the bonfires on the hill and the showers of rockets from the ships in the harbour to welcome the travellers, were distinctly visible. Unfortunately the next day was gray and "muggy"—a quality which the Queen had been told was characteristic of the Irish climate. The saluting from the various ships sent a roar through the thick air. The large harbour with its different islands—one of them containing a convict prison, another a military depot—looked less cheerful than it might have done. The captains of the war-steamers came on board to pay their respects; so did the Lord-Lieutenant, Lord Bandon, and the commanders of the forces at Cork. Prince Albert landed, but the Queen wrote and sketched till after luncheon. The delay was lucky, for the sun broke out with splendour in the afternoon. The Fairy, with its royal freight, surrounded by rowing and sailing boats, went round the harbour, all the ships saluting, and then entered Cove, and lay alongside the gaily-decorated crowded pier. The members, for Cork, the clergymen of all denominations, and the yacht club presented addresses, "after which," wrote the Queen, "to give the people the satisfaction of calling the place 'Queenstown,' in honour of its being the first spot on which I set foot upon Irish ground, I stepped on shore amid the roar of cannon (for the artillery was placed so close as quite to shake the temporary room which we entered), and the enthusiastic shouts of the people.".

The Fairy lay alongside the pier of Cork proper, and the Queen received more deputations and addresses, and conferred the honour of knighthood on the Lord Mayor. The two judges, who were holding their courts, came on board in their robes.

Then her Majesty landed and entered Lord Bandon's carriage, accompanied by Prince Albert and her ladies, Lord Bandon and General Turner riding one on each side. The Mayor went in front, and many people in carriages and on horseback joined the royal cortege, which took two hours in passing through the densely-crowded streets and under the triumphal arches. Everything went well and the reception was jubilant. To her Majesty Cork looked more like a foreign than an

English town. She was struck by the noisy but good-natured crowd, the men very "poorly, often-raggedly, dressed," many wearing blue coats and knee-breeches with blue stockings. The beauty of the women impressed her, "such beautiful dark eyes and hair, and such fine teeth; almost every third woman was pretty, and some remarkably so. They wear no bonnets, and generally long blue cloaks."

Re-embarking at Cork, the visitors sailed to Waterford, arriving in the course of the afternoon. The travellers sailed again at half-past eight in the morning, having at first a rough passage, with its usual unacceptable accompaniment of sea-sickness, but near Wexford the sea became gradually smooth, and there was a fine evening. At half-past six Dublin Bay came in sight. The war-steamers, four in number, waiting for her Majesty, were at their post. Escorted by this squadron, the yacht "steamed slowly and majestically" into Kingstown Harbour, which was full of ships, while the quays were lined with thousands of spectators cheering lustily. The sun was setting as this stately "procession of boats" entered the harbour, and her Majesty describes in her Journal "the glowing light" which lit up the surrounding country and the fine buildings, increasing the beauty of the scene.

Next morning, while the royal party were at breakfast, the yacht was brought up to the wharf lined with troops. The Lord-Lieutenant, Lord Clarendon, and Lady Clarendon, Prince George of Cambridge, Lords Lansdowne and Clanricarde, the Archbishop of Dublin, &c. &c., came on board, an address was presented from the county by the Earl of Charlemont, to which a written reply was given. At ten Lord Clarendon, bowing low, stepped before the Queen on the gangway, Prince Albert led her Majesty on shore, the youthful princes and princesses and the rest of the company following, the ships saluting so that the very ground shook with the heavy 68-pounders, the bands playing, the guard of honour presenting arms, the multitude huzzaing, the royal standard floating out on the breeze.

Along a covered way, lined with ladies and gentlemen, and strewn with flowers, the Queen proceeded to the railway station, and after a quarter of an hour's journey reached Dublin, where she was met by her own carriages, with the postillions in the Ascot liveries.

The Queen and Prince Albert, the Prince of Wales and the Princess Royal, occupied one carriage, Prince Alfred and Princess Alice, with the ladies-in-waiting, another. The Commander-in-chief of the soldiers in Ireland, Sir Edward Blakeney, rode on one side of the Queen's carriage, Prince George of Cambridge on the other, followed by a brilliant staff and escort of soldiers. "At the entrance of the city a triumphal arch of great size and beauty had been erected, under which the civic authorities—Lord Mayor, town-clerk, swordbearer, &c. &c.— waited on their sovereign." The Lord Mayor presented the keys and her Majesty returned them. "It was a wonderful and stirring scene," she described her progress in her Journal; "such masses of human beings, so enthusiastic, so excited, yet such perfect order maintained. Then the number of troops, the different bands stationed at certain distances, the waving of hats and handkerchiefs, the bursts of welcome that rent the air, all made it a never-to-be-forgotten scene when one reflected how lately the country had been under martial law."

The Queen admired Dublin heartily, and gave to Sackville Street and Merrion Square their due meed of praise. At the last triumphal arch a pretty little allegory, like a bit of an ancient masque, was enacted. Amidst the heat and dust a dove, "alive and very tame, with an olive- branch round its neck," was let down into the Queen's lap.

The viceregal lodge was reached at noon, and the Queen was received by Lord and Lady Clarendon and their household.

On the 7th of August, a showery day, the Queen drove into Dublin with her ladies, followed by the gentlemen, but with no other escort. Her Majesty was loudly cheered as she proceeded to the bank, the old Parliament House before the Union, where Curran and Grattan and many a "Monk of the Screw" had debated, "Bloody Toler" had aroused the rage of the populace, and Castlereagh had looked down icy cold on the burning commotion. The famous Dublin schools were next visited. Their excellent system of education and liberal tolerant code delighted the Prince. At Trinity College, with its memories of Dean Swift and "Charley O'Malley," the Queen and the Prince wrote their names in St. Columba's book, and inspected the harp said to have belonged to "King O'Brian." After their return to the lodge, when luncheon had been taken, and Prince Albert went into Dublin again, the Queen refreshed herself with a bit of home life. She wrote and read, and heard her children say some of their lessons.

At five the Queen drove to Kilmainham Hospital, Lord Clarendon accompanying her and her ladies, while the Prince and the other gentlemen rode. The Irish Commander-in-chief and Prince George received her Majesty, who saw and no doubt cheered the hearts of the old pensioners, going into their chapel, hall, and governor's room. Afterwards she drove again into Dublin, through the older quarters, College Green—where Mrs. Delany lived when she was yet Mrs. Pendarvis and the belle of the town, and where there still stands the well- known, often maltreated statue of William III., Stephen's Green, &c. &c. The crowds were still tremendous.

On the 8th of August, before one o'clock, the Queen and her ladies in evening dress, and Prince Albert and the gentlemen in uniform, drove straight to the castle, where there was to be a levee the same as at St. James's. Her Majesty, seated on the throne, received numerous addresses— those of the Lord Mayor and corporation, the universities, the Archbishop and bishops (Protestant and Catholic), the different Presbyterians, and the Quakers. No fewer than two thousand presentations took place, the levee lasting till six o'clock—some five hours.

On the following day there was a review of upwards of six thousand soldiers and police in the Phoenix Park.

The Queen and the Prince dined alone, but in the course of the evening they drove again into Dublin, to the castle, that she might hold a Drawing-room. Two or three thousand people were there; one thousand six hundred ladies were presented. Then her Majesty walked through St. Patrick's Hall and the other crowded rooms, returning through the densely-filled, illuminated streets, and the Phoenix Park after midnight.

On the 10th of August, the Queen had a little respite from public duties in a private pleasure. She and Prince Albert, in company with Lord and Lady Clarendon and the different members of the suite, went on a short visit to Carton, the seat of "Ireland's only Duke," the Duke of Leinster. The party passed through Woodlands, with its "beautiful lime-trees," and encountered a number of Maynooth students near their preparatory college. At Carton the Queen was received by the Duke and Duchess and their eldest son, the Marquis of Kildare, with his young wife, Lady Caroline Leveson-Gower, one of the daughters of the Duchess of Sutherland. All the company walked, to the music of two bands, in the pretty quaint garden with its rows of Irish yews. Was it the same in 1798, when a son of the Leinster house, after thinking to be a king, was hunted down in a poor Dublin lodging, fought like a lion for his life, was taken a wounded prisoner to the castle, and then to Newgate to die?

The Duke led the Queen round the garden, while Prince Albert conducted the Duchess. Her Majesty wrote warmly of her host that "he was one of the kindest and best of men." After luncheon the country people danced jigs in the park, the men in their thick coats, the women in their shawls; one man, "a regular Irishman, with his hat on, one ear," the music furnished by three old and tattered pipers. Her Majesty pronounced the steps of the dancers "very droll."

The Duke and Duchess took their guests a drive, the people riding, running, and driving with the company, but continuing perfectly well- behaved, and ready to obey any word of the Duke's. It must have been a curious scene, in which all ranks took part. The Queen could not get over the spectacle of the countrymen running the whole way, in their thick woollen coats, in the heat.

On the Queen's departure from Kingstown she was followed by the same enthusiasm that had greeted her on her arrival. "As the yacht approached the extremity of the pier near the lighthouse, where the people were most thickly congregated and were cheering enthusiastically, the Queen suddenly left the two ladies-in-waiting with whom she was conversing, ran with agility along the deck, and climbed the paddle-box to join Prince Albert, who did not notice her till she was nearly at his side. Reaching him and taking his arm, she waved her right hand to the people on the piers." As she stood with the Prince while the yacht steamed out of the harbour, she waved her handkerchief in "a parting acknowledgment" of her Irish subjects' loyalty. As another compliment to the enthusiastic farewells of the people, the Queen gave orders "to slacken speed." The paddlewheels became still, the yacht floated slowly along close to the pier, and three times the royal standard was lowered by way of "a stately obeisance" made in response to the last ringing cheers of the Irish. Lord Clarendon wrote afterwards, that "there was not an individual in Dublin who did not take as a personal compliment to himself the Queen's having gone upon the paddle-box and ordered the royal standard to be lowered three times." It was a happy thought of her own.

The weather was thick and misty, and the storm which was feared came on in a violent gale before the yacht entered Belfast Harbour, early on the morning of the 11th of August. The Mayor and other officials came on board to breakfast, and in the course of the forenoon the Queen and the Prince, with the ladies and gentlemen in attendance, entered the barge to row to the Fairy. Though the row was only of two minutes' duration, the swell on the water was so great that the embarkation in the Fairy was a matter of difficulty; and when the smaller yacht was gained the Queen had to take shelter in the pavilion from the driving spray. In such unpropitious circumstances her Majesty passed Carrickfergus, the landing-place of William III., and arrived at the capital of Ulster just as the sun came out and lent its much-desired presence to the gala. Lord Londonderry and his wife and daughters, Lord Donegal, the proprietor of the greater part of Ulster, &c. &c., came on board with various deputations, especially of Presbyterians and members of the linen trade. The Queen knighted the mayor, as she had knighted his brother-magistrate at Cork.

By an odd blunder the gangway, which had been carefully constructed for the Queen's use, was found too large. Some planks on board the yacht had to form an impromptu landing-stage; but the situation was not so awkward as when Louis Philippe had to press a bathing-machine into the royal service at Tréport. The landing-place was covered in and decorated, the Londonderry carriage in waiting, and her Majesty's only regret was for Lord Londonderry, a big man, crowded on the rumble along with specially tall and large sergeant-footmen.

The Scotch-descended people of Belfast had outdone themselves in floral arches and decorations. The galleries for spectators were thronged. There was no stint in the honest warmth of the reception. But the Irish beauty, and doubtless also something of the Irish spirit and glee, had vanished with the rags and the tumbledown cabins. The douce, comfortable people of Ulster were less picturesque and less demonstrative.

Linen Hall, the Botanic Gardens, and the new college were visited, and different streets driven through in returning to the place of embarkation at half-past six on an evening so stormy that the weather prevented the yacht from setting sail. As it lay at anchor there was an opportunity for seeing the bonfires, streaming in the blast, on the neighbouring heights. Before quitting Ireland the Queen determined to create her eldest son "Earl of Dublin," one of the titles borne by the late Duke of Kent.

CHAPTER XII.SCOTLAND AGAIN—GLASGOW AND DEE-SIDE.

In the course of the afternoon the yacht sailed for Loch Ryan. The object of this second visit to the West of Scotland was not so much for the purpose of seeing again the beautiful scenery which had so delighted the Queen and the Prince, as with the view of making up for the great disappointment experienced by the townspeople of Glasgow on her Majesty's having failed to visit what was, after London, one of the largest cities in her empire.

The weather was persistently bad this time, squally and disagreeable. On August 15th the Fairy, with the Queen and Prince on board, sailed for Glasgow, still in pouring rain and a high wind. The storm did not prevent the people from so lining the banks that the swell from the steamer often broke upon them. Happily the weather cleared at last, and the day was fine when the landing-place was reached. As usual, the Lord Provost came on board and received the honour of knighthood, after he had presented one of the many addresses offered by the town, the county, the clergy of all denominations, and the House of Commerce. The Queen landed, with the Prince and all the children that had accompanied her. Sheriff Alison rode on one side of her carriage, the general commanding the forces in Scotland on the other. The crowd was immense, numbering as many as five hundred thousand men, women, and children. The Queen admired the streets, the fine buildings, the quays, the churches. At the cathedral she was received by a man who seemed as venerable as the building itself, Principal MacFarlane. He called her Majesty's attention to what was then the highest chimney in the world, that of the chemical works of St. Rollax. The inspection of the fine cathedral, which the old Protestants of the west protected instead of pulling down, included the crypt. The travellers proceeded by railway to Stirling and Perth.

Early on the morning of the 15th the party started, the Queen having three of the children in the carriage with herself and the Prince, on the long drive through beautiful Highland scenery to Balmoral.

This year her Majesty made her first stay at Alt-na-guithasach, the hut or bothie of "old John Gordon," the situation of which had taken her fancy and that of the Prince. They had another hut built for themselves in the immediate vicinity, so that they could at any time spend a day or a couple of days in the wilds, with a single lady-in- waiting and the most limited of suites. On the 30th of August the Queen, the Prince, and the Honourable Caroline Dawson, maid of honour, set out on their ponies, attended only by Macdonald, Grant, another Highlander, and an English footman. The rough road had been improved, and riding was so easy that Prince Albert could practise his Gaelic by the way.

The Queen was much pleased with her new possession, which meant "a charming little dining-room, sitting-room, bedroom, and dressing-room all en suite; a little bedroom for Miss Dawson and one for her maid, and a pantry." In the other hut were the kitchen where the Gordon family sat, a room where the servants dined, a storeroom, and a loft where the men slept. All the people in attendance on the small party were the Queen's maid, Miss Dawson's maid, Prince Albert's German valet, a footman, and Macdonald, together with the old couple, John Gordon and his wife. After luncheon the visitors went to Loch Muich—a name which has been interpreted "darkness" or "sorrow"—and got into a large boat with four rowers, while a smaller boat followed, having a net. The excursion was to the head of the loch, which joins the Dhu or Black

Loch. "Real severe Highland scenery," her Majesty calls it, and to those who know the stern sublimity of such places, the words say a great deal. "The boat, the net, and the people in their kilts in the water and on the shore," called for an artist's pencil. Seventy trouts were caught, and several hawks were seen. The sailing was diversified by scrambling on shore. The return in the evening was still more beautiful. At dinner the German valet and Macdonald, the Highland forester, helped the footman to wait on the company. Whist, played with a dummy, and a walk round the little garden, "where the silence and solitude, only interrupted by the waving of the fir-trees, were very striking," ended the day.

The Queen and her family left Balmoral on the 27th. Travelling by Edinburgh and Berwick, they visited Earl Grey at Howick. Derby was the next halting-place. At Reading the travellers turned aside for Gosport, and soon arrived at Osborne.

Already, on the 16th of September, a special prayer had been read in every church in England, petitioning Almighty God to stay the plague of cholera which had sprung up in the East, travelled across the seas, and broken out among the people. But the dreaded epidemic had nothing to do with the sad news which burst upon the Queen and Prince Albert within, a few days of their return to the south. Both were much distressed by receiving the unexpected intelligence of the sudden death of Mr. Anson, who had been the Prince's private secretary, and latterly the keeper of the Queen's privy purse.

The offices which Mr. Anson filled in succession were afterwards worthily held by Colonel Phipps and General Grey.

CHAPTER XIII.OPENING OF THE NEW COAL EXCHANGE—THE DEATH OF QUEEN ADELAIDE.

On the 30th of October the new Coal Exchange, opposite Billingsgate, was to have been opened by the Queen in person. A slight illness—an attack of chicken-pox—compelled her Majesty to give up her intention, and forego the motherly pleasure of seeing her two elder children, the Prince of Wales and the Princess Royal, make their first appearance in public. Prince Albert, with his son and daughter, accompanied by the Duke of Norfolk as Master of the Horse, drove from Buckingham Palace at twelve o'clock, and embarked on the Thames in the royal barge, "a gorgeous structure of antique design, built for Frederic, Prince of Wales, the great-great-grandfather of the Prince and Princess who now trod its deck." It was rowed by twenty-seven of the ancient craft of watermen, restored for a day to the royal service, clad in rich livery for the occasion, and commanded by Lord Adolphus Fitzclarence. Commander Eden, superintendent of Woolwich Dockyard, led the van in his barge. Then came Vice-Admiral Elliot, Commander-in-chief at the Nore; next the Lord Mayor's bailiff in his craft, preceding the Lord Mayor in the City barge, "rearing its quaint gilded poop high in the air, and decked with richly emblazoned devices and floating ensigns…. Two royal gigs and two royal barges escorted the State barge, posted respectively on its port and starboard bow, and its port and starboard quarter. The Queen's shallop followed; the barges of the Admiralty and the Trinity Corporation barge brought up the rear." [Footnote: Annual Register.] According to ancient custom one barge bore a graceful freight of living swans to do honour to the water procession. Such a grand and gay pageant on the river had not been seen for a century back. It only wanted some of the "water music," which Handel composed for George II., to render the gala complete.

It would be difficult to devise a scene more captivating for children of nine and ten, such as the pair who figured in it. Happily the day, though it was nearly the last of October, was beautiful and bright, and from the position which the royal party occupied in their barge when it was in the middle of the river, "not only the other barges and the platformed steamers and lighters with their living loads, but the densely-crowded banks, must have formed a memorable spectacle. The very streets running down from the Strand were so packed with spectators as to present each one a moving mass. Half a million of persons were gathered together to witness the unwonted sight; the bridges were hung over with them like swarms of flies, and from the throng at intervals shouts of welcome sounded long and loud." Between Southwark and London Bridge the rowers lay on their oars for a moment, in compliment to the ardent loyalty of the scholars of Queen Elizabeth's Grammar School. The most picturesque point was "at the moment the vessels emerged from London Bridge and caught sight of the amphitheatre of shipping in the Upper Pool—a literal forest of masts, with a foliage of flags more variously and brilliantly coloured than the American woods after the first autumn frost. Here, too, the ear was first saluted by the boom of guns, the Tower artillery firing as the procession swept by."

The landing-place on the Custom House Quay was so arranged, by means of coloured canvas, as to form a covered corridor the whole length of the quay, to and across Thames Street, to the principal entrance to the Coal Exchange.

Prince Albert and the young Prince and Princess passed down the corridor, "bowing to the citizens on either side," a critical ordeal for the simply reared children. When the Grand Hall of the Exchange was reached, the City procession came up, headed by the Lord Mayor, and the Recorder read aloud an address "with such emphatic solemnity," it was remarked, that the Prince of Wales seemed "struck and almost awed by his manner." Lady Lyttelton takes notice of the same comical effect produced on the little boy. Prince Albert replied.

At two o'clock the déjeuner was served, when the Lord Mayor and the Lady Mayoress, at Prince Albert's request, sat near him. The usual toasts were given; the health of the Queen was drunk with "loudest cheers," that of the Queen-Dowager with "evident feeling," called forth by the fact that King William's good Queen, who had for long years struggled vainly with mortal disease, was, as everybody knew, drawing near her end. The toast of the Prince of Wales and the Princess Royal was received with an enthusiasm that must have tended at once to elate and abash the little hero and heroine of the day.

At three o'clock the royal party re-embarked in the Fairy. As Prince Albert stepped on board, while expressing his gratification with the whole proceedings, he said to his children, with the gracious, kindly tact which was natural to him, "Remember that you are indebted to the Lord Mayor for one of the happiest days of your lives."

Before December wound up the year it was generally known that the Queen-Dowager Adelaide, who had in her day occupied a prominent place in the eyes of the nation, was to be released from the sufferings of many years.

In November Queen Victoria paid her last visit to the Queen-Dowager. "I shall never forget the visit we paid to the Priory last Thursday,", the Queen wrote to King Leopold. "There was death written in that dear face. It was such a picture of misery, of complete prostration, and yet she talked of everything. I could hardly command my feelings when I came in, and when I kissed twice that poor dear thin hand…. I love her so dearly; she has ever been so maternal in her affection to me. She will find peace and a reward for her many sufferings."

Queen Adelaide died quietly on the 2nd of December, at her country seat of Bentley Priory, in the fifty-eighth year of her age. Her will, which reflected her genuine modesty and humility, requested that she should be conveyed to the grave "without any pomp or state;" that she should have as private a funeral as was consistent with her rank; that her coffin should be "carried by sailors to the chapel;" that, finally, she should give as little trouble as possible.

The Queen-Dowager's wishes were strictly adhered to. There was no embalming, lying in State, or torchlight procession. The funeral started from the Priory at eight o'clock on a winter morning, and reached Windsor an hour after noon. There was every token of respect and affection, but an entire absence of show and ostentation. Nobody was admitted to St. George's Chapel except the mourners and those officially connected with the funeral. Few even of the Knights of the Garter were present. Among the few was the old Duke of Wellington, sitting silent and sad; Prince Albert and the Duke of Cambridge also occupied their stalls. The Duchess of Kent and the Duchess of Cambridge, with the Duchess of Saxe-Weimar and two Princesses of Saxe- Weimar, the late Queen's sister and nieces, were in the Queen's closet.

The Archbishop of Canterbury officiated. Ten sailors of the Royal Navy "gently propelled" the platform on which the coffin was placed to the mouth of the vault. Among the supporters of the pall were Lord Adolphus and Lord Frederick Fitzclarence. The chief mourner was the Duchess of Norfolk. Prince George of Cambridge and Prince Edward and Prince Gustaf of Saxe-Weimar, nephews of the late Queen, followed. Then came the gentlemen and ladies of her household. All the gentlemen taking part in the funeral were in plain black with black scarfs; each lady had a large black veil over her head.

After the usual psalms and lessons, Handel's anthem, "Her body is buried in peace," was sung. The black velvet pall was removed and the crown placed on the coffin, which, at the appropriate time in the service, was lowered to the side of King William's coffin. Sir Charles Young, King-at-Arms, proclaimed the rank and titles of the deceased. The late Queen's chamberlain and vice-chamberlain broke their staves of office amidst profound silence, and kneeling, deposited them upon the coffin. The organ played the "Dead March in Saul," and the company retired.

Long years after Queen Adelaide had lain in her grave, the publication of an old diary revived some foul-mouthed slanders, which no one is too pure to escape. But the coarse malice and gross falsehood of the accusations were so evident, that their sole result was to rebound with fatal effect on the memory of the man who retailed them.

CHAPTER XIV.PREPARATION FOR THE EXHIBITION—BIRTH OF THE DUKE OF CONNAUGHT—THE BLOW DEALT BY FATE— FOREIGN TROUBLES—ENGLISH ART.

The first great public meeting in the interest of the Exhibition was held in London in the February of this year, and on the 21st of March a banquet was given at the Mansion House to promote the same cause. Prince Albert was present, with the ministers and foreign ambassadors; and the mayors and provosts of all the principal towns in the United Kingdom were also among the guests. The Prince delivered an admirable speech to explain his view of the Exhibition.

It was at this time that the Duke of Wellington made the gratifying proposal that the Prince should succeed him as Commander-in-chief of the army, urging the suggestion by every argument in his power, and offering to supply the Prince with all the information and guidance which the old soldier's experience could command. After some quiet consideration the Prince declined the proposal, chiefly on the ground that the many claims which the high office would necessarily make on his time and attention, must interfere with his other and still more binding duties to the Queen and the country.

On May-day, 1850, her Majesty's third son and seventh child was born. The Prince, in announcing the event to the Dowager-Duchess of Coburg, says: "The little boy was received by his sisters with jubilates. 'Now we are just as many as the days of the week,' was the cry, and then a bit of a struggle arose as to who was to be Sunday. Out of well-bred courtesy the honour was conceded to the new-comer."

The circumstance that the 1st of May was the birthday of the Duke of Wellington determined the child's name, and perhaps, in a measure, his future profession. The Queen and the Prince were both so pleased to show this crowning mark of friendship from a sovereign to a subject, that they did not allow the day to pass without intimating their intention to the Duke. "It is a singular thing," the Queen wrote to Baron Stockmar, "that this so much wished-for boy should be born on the old Duke's eighty-first birthday. May that, and his beloved father's name, bring the poor little infant happiness and good fortune!"

An amusing episode of the Queen's visit to Ireland had been the passionate appeal of an old Irishwoman, "Och, Queen, dear! make one of them Prince Patrick, and all Ireland will die for you!" Whether or not her Majesty remembered the fervent request, Prince Arthur had Patrick for one of his names, certainly in memory of Ireland, and William for another, partly in honour of one of his godfathers—the present Emperor of Germany—and partly because it would have pleased Queen Adelaide, whose sister, Duchess Ida of Saxe-Weimar, was godmother. Prince Albert's name wound up the others. The child was baptized on the 22nd of June at Buckingham Palace. The two godfathers were present; so were the Duchesses of Kent and Cambridge (the Duke of Cambridge lay ill), Prince George and Princess Mary of Cambridge, the Prince of Leiningen, and Prince Edward of Saxe-Weimar, the ministers and foreign ambassadors. The Archbishop of Canterbury, the Bishops of London and Oxford, &c. &c., officiated. Prince Albert's chorale, "In life's gay morn," was performed again. After the christening there was a State banquet in the picture gallery. Prince Arthur was the finest of all the Queen's babies, and the royal nurseries still retain memories of his childish graces.

Before the ceremony of the christening, and within a month of the birth of her child, her Majesty was subjected to one of the most wanton and cowardly of all the attacks which half-crazed brains prompted their owners to make upon her person. She had driven out about six o'clock in the evening, with her children and Lady Jocelyn, to inquire for her uncle, the Duke of Cambridge, who was suffering from his last illness. While she was within the gates of Cambridge House, a tall, gentlemanlike man loitered at the entrance, as it appeared with the by no means uncommon wish to see the Queen. But when her carriage drove out, while it was leisurely turning the corner into the road, the man started forward, and, with a small stick which he held, struck the Queen a sharp blow on the face, crushing the bonnet she wore, and inflicting a severe bruise and slight wound on the forehead. The fellow was instantly seized and the stick wrested from his grasp, while he was conveyed to the nearest police-station.

The Queen drove home, and was able to show herself the same evening at the Opera, where she was received with the singing of the National Anthem and great cheering.

The offender was neither a boy nor of humble rank. He proved to be a man of thirty—a gentleman by birth and education.

The Prince wrote of the miserable occurrence to Baron Stockmar that its perpetrator was a dandy "whom you must often have seen in the Park, where he has made himself conspicuous. He maintains the closest silence as to his motives, but is manifestly deranged. All this does not help to make one cheerful."

The man was the son of a gentleman named Pate, of wealth and position, who had acted as sheriff of Cambridgeshire. The son had had a commission in the army, from which he had been requested to retire, on account of an amount of eccentricity that had led at least to one serious breach of discipline. He could give no reason for his conduct beyond making the statement that he had acted on a sudden uncontrollable impulse. He was tried in the following July. The jury refused to accept the plea of insanity, and he was sentenced, like his predecessor, to seven years' transportation.

At the date of the attack the minds of the Queen and the Prince, and indeed of a large portion of the civilised world, were much occupied with a serious foreign embroilment into which the Government had been drawn by what many people considered the restless and interfering policy of Lord Palmerston, the Secretary of State for Foreign Affairs. He had gone so far as to send a fleet into Greek waters for the protection of two British subjects claiming assistance, and in the act he had offended France and Russia.

Much political excitement was aroused, and there were keen and protracted debates in both Houses of Parliament. In the House of Lords something like a vote of censure of the foreign policy of the Government was moved and carried. In the House of Commons the debate lasted five nights, and the fine speech in which Lord Palmerston, a man in his sixty-sixth year, defended his policy, was continued "from the dusk of one day to the dawn of the next."

Apart from these troubles abroad, the country, on the whole, was in a prosperous and satisfactory condition. Trade was flourishing. Neither had literature fallen behind. Perhaps it had rarely shown a more brilliant galaxy of contemporary names, including those of John Stuart Mill in logic, Herbert Spencer in philosophy, Charles Darwin in natural science, Ruskin in art criticism, Helps as an essayist. And in this year Tennyson brought out his "In Memoriam," and Kingsley his "Alton Lock". It seemed but natural that the earlier lights should be dying out before the later; that Lord Jeffrey, the old king of critics, should pass beyond the sound of reviews; and Wordsworth, after this spring, be seen no more among the Cumberland hills and dales; and Jane Porter, whose innocent high-flown romances had been the delight of the young reading world more than fifty years before, should end her days, a cheerful old lady, in the prosaic town of Bristol.

In the Academy's annual exhibition the same old names of Landseer (with his popular picture of the Duke of Wellington showing his daughter-in-law, Lady Douro, the field of Waterloo), Maclise, Mulready, Stanfield, &c. &c., came still to the front. But a new movement, having a foreign origin, though in this case an English development, known as the pre-Raphaelite theory, with Millais, Holman Hunt, and Rossetti as its leaders, was already at work. This year there was a picture by Millais—still a lad of twenty-one—in support of the protest against conventionality in the beautiful, which did not fail to attract attention, though it excited as much condemnation as praise. The picture was "Christ in the House of His Parents," better known as "The Carpenter's Shop."

CHAPTER XV. THE DEATHS OF SIR ROBERT PEEL, THE DUKE OF CAMBRIDGE, AND LOUIS PHILIPPE.

The Court had been at Osborne for the Whitsun holidays, and the Prince had written to Germany, "In our island home we are wholly given up to the enjoyment of the warm summer weather. The children catch butterflies, Victoria sits under the trees, and I drink the Kissingen water, Ragotzky. To-day mamma-aunt (the Duchess of Kent) and Charles (Prince of Leiningen) are come to stay a fortnight with us; then we go to town to compress the (so-called) pleasures of the season into four weeks. God be merciful to us miserable sinners."

There was more to be encountered in town this year, than the hackneyed round of gaieties—from which even royalty, with all the will in the world, could not altogether free itself. The first shock was the violent opposition, got up alike by the press and in Parliament, to Hyde Park as the site of the building required for the Exhibition. Following hard upon it came the melancholy news of the accident to Sir Robert Peel, which occurred at the very door, so simply and yet so fatally. Sir Robert, who, was riding out on Saturday, the 29th of June, had just called at Buckingham Palace and written his name in her Majesty's visiting-book. He was going up Constitution Hill, and had reached the wicket-gate leading into the Green Park, when he met Miss Ellis, Lady Dover's daughter, with whom he was acquainted, also riding. Sir Robert exchanged greetings with the young lady, and his horse became restive, "swerved towards the rails of the Green Park," and threw its rider, who had a bad seat in the saddle, sideways on his left shoulder. It was supposed that Sir Robert held by the reins, so as to drag the animal down with its knees on his shoulder. He was taken home in a carriage, and laid on a sofa in his dining- room, from which he was never moved. At his death he was in his sixty- third year.

The vote of the House of Commons settled the question that Hyde Park should be the site of the Exhibition, and Punch's caricature, which the Prince enjoyed, of Prince Albert as "The Industrious Boy," cap in hand, uttering the petition—

"Pity the troubles of a poor young Price,
Whose costly scheme has borne him to your door,"

lost all its sting, when such a fund was guaranteed as warranted the raising of the structure according to Sir Joseph Paxton's beautiful design.

The Queen and the Prince had many calls on their sympathy this summer. On the 8th of July the Duke of Cambridge died, aged seventy-six. He was the youngest of George III and Queen Charlotte's sons who attained manhood. He was one of the most popular of the royal brothers, notwithstanding the disadvantages of having been educated partly abroad, taken foreign service, and held appointments in Hanover which caused him to reside there for the most part till the death of William IV. Neither was he possessed of much ability. He had not even the scientific and literary acquirements of the Duke of Sussex, who had possessed one of the best private libraries in England. But the Duke of Cambridge's good-nature was equal to his love of asking questions— a hereditary trait. He was buried, according to his own wish, at Kew.

The House of Commons voted twelve thousand a year to Prince George, on his becoming Duke of Cambridge, in lieu of the twenty-seven thousand a year enjoyed by the late Duke.

Osborne was a more welcome retreat than ever at the close of the summer, but even Osborne could not shelter the Queen from political worry and personal sorrow. There were indications of renewed trouble from Lord Palmerston's "spirited foreign policy."

The Queen and the Prince believed they had reason to complain of Lord Palmerston's carelessness and negligence, in not forwarding in time copies of the documents passing through his department, which ought to have been brought under the notice both of the sovereign and the Prime Minister, and to have received their opinion, before the over- energetic Secretary for Foreign Affairs acted upon them on his own responsibility.

In these circumstances her Majesty wrote a memorandum of what she regarded as the duty of the Secretary of State for Foreign Affairs towards the Crown. The memorandum was written in a letter to Lord John Russell, which he was requested to show to Lord Palmerston.

Except the misunderstanding with Sir Robert Peel about the dismissal of the ladies of her suite, which occurred early in the reign, this is the only difference on record between the Queen and any of her ministers.

During this July at Osborne, Lady Lyttelton wrote her second vivid description, quoted in the "Life of the Prince Consort," of Prince Albert's organ-playing. "Last evening such a sunset! I was sitting, gazing at it, and thinking of Lady Charlotte Proby's verses, when from an open window below this floor began suddenly to sound the Prince's organ, expressively played by his masterly hand. Such a modulation! Minor and solemn, and ever changing and never ceasing. From a piano like Jenny Lind's holding note up to the fullest swell, and still the same fine vein of melancholy. And it came on so exactly as an accompaniment to the sunset. How strange he is! He must have been playing just while the Queen was finishing her toilette, and then he went to cut jokes and eat dinner, and nobody but the organ knows what is in him, except, indeed, by the look of his eyes sometimes."

Lady Lyttelton refers to the Prince's cutting jokes, and the Queen has written of his abiding cheerfulness. People are apt to forget in their very admiration of his noble thoughtfulness, earnestness, and tenderness of heart that he was also full of fun, keenly relishing a good story, the life of the great royal household.

The Queen had been grieved this summer by hearing of the serious illness of her greatest friend, the Queen of the Belgians, who was suffering from the same dangerous disease of which her sister, Princess Marie, had died. Probably it was with the hope of cheering King Leopold, and of perhaps getting a glimpse of the much-loved invalid, that the Queen, after proroguing Parliament in person, sailed on the 21st of August with the Prince and their four elder children in the royal yacht on a short trip to Ostend, where the party spent a day. King Leopold met the visitors—the younger of whom were much interested by their first experience of a foreign town. The Queen had the satisfaction of finding her uncle well and pleased to see her, so that she could call the meeting afterwards a "delightful, happy dream;" but there was a sorrowful element in the happiness, occasioned by the absence of Queen Louise, whose strength was not sufficient for the journey to Ostend, and of whose case Sir James Clark, sent by the Queen to Laeken, thought badly.

The poor Orleans family had another blow in store for them. On Prince
Albert's thirty-first birthday, the 26th of August, which he passed at
Osborne, news arrived of the death that morning, at Claremont, of
Louis Philippe, late King of the French, in his seventy-seventh year.

The Queen and the Prince had been prepared to start with their elder children for Scotland the day after they heard of the death, and by setting out at six o'clock in the morning they were enabled to pay a passing visit to the house of mourning.

We may be permitted to remark here, by what quiet, unconscious touches in letters and journals we have brought home to us the dual life, full of duty and kindliness, led by the highest couple in the land. Whether it is going with a family of cousins to take the last look at a departed kinsman, or in getting up at daybreak to express personal sympathy with another family in sorrow, we cannot fail to see, while it is all so simply said and done, that no painful ordeal is shirked, no excuse is made of weighty tasks and engrossing occupations, to free either Queen or Prince from the gentle courtesies and tender charities of everyday humanity; we recognise that the noblest and busiest are also the bravest, the most faithful, the most full of pity.

CHAPTER XVI. THE QUEEN'S FIRST STAY AT HOLYROOD—LIFE IN THE HIGHLANDS—THE DEATH OF THE QUEEN OF THE BELGIANS.

This year the Queen went north by Castle Howard, the fine seat of the Earl of Carlisle, the Duchess of Sutherland's brother, where her Majesty made her first halt. After stopping to open the railway bridges, triumphs of engineering, over the Tyne and the Tweed, the travellers reached Edinburgh, where, to the gratification of an immense gathering of her Scotch subjects, her Majesty spent her first night in Holyrood, the palace of her Stewart ancestors. The place was full of interest and charm for her, and though it was late in the afternoon before she arrived, she hardly waited to rest, before setting out incognito, so far as the old housekeeper was concerned, to inspect the historical relics of the building. She wandered out with her "two girls and their governess" to the ruins of the chapel or old abbey, and stood by the altar at which Mary Stewart, the fair young French widow, wedded "the long lad Darnley," and read the inscriptions on the tombs of various members of noble Scotch houses, coming to a familiar name on the slab which marked the grave of the mother of one of her own maids of honour, a daughter of Clanranald's. The Queen then visited Queen Mary's rooms, being shown, like other strangers, the closet where her ancestress had sat at supper on a memorable night, and the stair from the chapel up which Ruthven, risen from a sick-bed, led the conspirators who seized Davie Rizzio, dragged him from his mistress's knees, to which he clung, and slew him pitilessly on the boards which, according to old tradition, still bear the stain of his blood. After that ghastly token, authentic or non-authentic, which would thrill the hearts of the young princesses as it has stirred many a youthful imagination, Darnley's armour and Mary's work-table, with its embroidery worked by her own hand, must have fallen comparatively flat.

The next morning the Queen and the Prince, with their children, took their first drive round the beautiful road, then just completed, which bears her name, and, encircling Arthur's Seat, is the goal of every stranger visiting Edinburgh, affording as it does in miniature an excellent idea of Scotch scenery. On this occasion the party alighted and climbed to the top of the hill, rejoicing in the view. "You see the beautiful town, with the Calton Hill, and the bay with the island of Inchkeith stretching out before you, and the Bass Rock quite in the distance, rising behind the coast.... The view when we gained the carriage hear Dunsappie Loch, quite a small lake, overhung by a crag, with the sea in the distance, is extremely pretty.... The air was delicious." In the course of the forenoon the Prince laid the foundation stone of the Scotch National Gallery, and made his first speech (which was an undoubted success) before one of those Edinburgh audiences, noted for their fastidiousness and critical faculty. The afternoon drive was by the beautiful Scott monument, the finest modern ornament of the city, Donaldson's Hospital, the High Street, and the Canongate, and the lower part of the Queen's Drive, which encloses the Queen's Park. "A beautiful park indeed," she wrote, "with such a view, and such mountain scenery in the midst of it."

In the evening there was assembled such a circle as had not been gathered in royal old Holyrood since poor Prince Charlie kept brief state there. Her Majesty wrote in her journal, "The Buccleuchs, the Roxburghs, the Mortons, Lord Roseberry, Principal Lee, the Belhavens, and the Lord Justice General, dined with us. Everybody so pleased at our living at my old palace." The talk seems to have been, as was fitting, on old times and the unfortunate Queen Mary, the heroine of Holyrood. Sir Theodore Martin thinks it may have been in remembrance of this evening that Lord Belhaven, on his death, left a bequest to the Queen "of a cabinet which had been brought by Queen Mary from France, and given by her to the Regent Mar, from whom it passed into the family of Lord Belhaven." The cabinet contains a lock of Queen Mary's golden hair, and a purse worked by her.

On the following day the royal party left Holyrood and travelled to Balmoral. The Queen, with the Prince and her children, and the Duchess of Kent, with her son and grandson, were at the great gala of the district, the Braemar gathering, where the honour of her Majesty's presence is always eagerly craved.

Another amusement was the leistering, or spearing, of salmon in the Dee. Captain Forbes of Newe, and from forty to fifty of his clan, on their return to Strathdon from the Braemar gathering, were attracted by the fishing to the river's edge, when they were carried over the water on the backs of the Queen's men, who volunteered the service, "Macdonald, at their head, carrying Captain Forbes on his back." The courteous act, which was quite spontaneous, charmed the Queen and the Prince. The latter in writing to Germany gave further details of the incident. "Our people in the Highlands are altogether primitive, true-hearted and without guile....

Yesterday the Forbeses of Strath Don passed through here. When they came to the Dee our people (of Strath Dee) offered to carry them across the river, and did so, whereupon they drank to the health of Victoria and the inmates of Balmoral in whisky (schnapps), but as there was no cup to be had, their chief, Captain Forbes, pulled off his shoe, and he and his fifty men drank out of it."

The Forbeses got permission to march through the grounds of Balmoral, "the pipers going, in front. They stopped and cheered three times three, throwing up their bonnets." The Queen describes the characteristic demonstration, and she then mentions listening with pleasure "to the distant shouts and the sound of the pibroch."

There were two drawbacks to the peace and happiness of Balmoral this year. The one was occasioned by an unforeseen vexatious occurrence, and the complications which arose from it. General Haynau, the Austrian officer whose brutalities to the conquered and to women during the Hungarian war had aroused detestation in England, happened to visit London, and was attacked by the men in Barclay's brewery. Austria remonstrated, and Lord Palmerston made a rash reply, which had to be recalled.

The other care which darkened the Balmoral horizon in 1850 was the growing certainty of a fatal termination to the illness of the Queen of the Belgians. Immediately after the Court returned to Osborne the blow fell. Queen Louise died at Ostend on the 11th of October, 1850. She was only in her thirty-ninth year, not more than eight years older than Queen Victoria. She was the second daughter of Louis Philippe, Princess Marie having been the elder sister.

CHAPTER XVII. THE PAPAL BULL—THE GREAT EXHIBITION.

In the winter of 1850 the whole of England was disturbed by the Papal Bull which professed to divide England afresh into Roman Catholic bishoprics, with a cardinal-archbishop at their head. Protestant England hotly resented the liberty the Pope had taken, the more so that the Tractarian movement in the Church seemed to point to treachery within the camp. Lord John Russell took this view of it, and the announcement of his opinion intensified the excitement which expressed itself, in meetings all over the county and numerous addresses to the Queen, condemning the act of aggression and urging resistance. The protests of the Universities of Oxford and Cambridge, and of the Corporation of London, were presented to her Majesty in St. George's Hall, Windsor Castle, on the 10th of December. The Oxford address was read by the Chancellor of Oxford, the Duke of Wellington, the old soldier speaking "in his peculiar energetic manner with great vigour and animation." The Cambridge address was read by the Chancellor of Cambridge, Prince Albert, "with great clearness and well-marked emphasis." The Queen replied "with great deliberation and with decided accents." Her Majesty, while repelling the invasion of her rights and the offence to the religious principles of the country, held, with the calmer judges of the situation, that no pretence, however loudly asserted, could constitute reality. The Pope might call England what he liked, but he could not make it Catholic.

In January, 1851, the Court had a great loss in the retirement of Lady Lyttelton from her office of governess to the royal children, which she had filled for eight years; while her service at Court, including the time that she had been a lady-in-waiting, had lasted over twelve years. Thenceforth her bright sympathetic accounts of striking events in the life at Windsor and Osborne cease. The daughter of the second Earl of Spenser married, at twenty-six years of age, the third Lord Lyttelton. She was forty-two when she became a lady-in-waiting, and fifty-four when she resigned the office of governess to the Queen's children. She desired to quit the Court because, as she said, she was old enough to be at rest for whatever time might be left her. In the tranquillity and leisure which she sought, she survived for twenty years, dying at the age of seventy-four in 1870. The parting in 1851 was a trial to all. "The Queen has told me I may be free about the middle of January," wrote Lady Lyttelton, "and she said it with all the feeling and kindness of which I have received such incessant proofs through the whole long twelve years during which I have served her. Never by a word or look has it been interrupted." Neither could Lady Lyttelton say enough in praise of the Prince, of "his wisdom, his ready helpfulness, his consideration for others, his constant kindness." "In the evening I was sent for to my last audience in the Queen's own room," Lady Lyttelton wrote again, "and I quite broke down and could hardly speak or hear. I remember the Prince's face, pale as ashes, and a few words of praise and thanks from them both, but it is all misty; and I had to stop on the private staircase and have my cry out before I could go up again."

Lady Lyttelton was succeeded in her office by Lady Caroline Barrington, sister of Earl Grey, who held the post for twenty-four years, till her death in 1875. She too was much and deservedly esteemed by the Queen and the royal family.

The Exhibition was the event in England of 1851. From the end of March till the opening-day, for which May-day was fitly chosen, Prince Albert strove manfully day and night to fulfil his important part in the programme, and it goes without saying that the Queen shared in much of his work, and in all his hopes and fears and ardent desires.

Already the building, with its great transept and naves, lofty dome, transparent walls and roof, enclosing great trees within their ample bounds, the chef-d'-oeuvre of Sir Joseph Paxton—who received knighthood for the feat—the admiration of all beholders, had sprung up in Hyde Park like a fairy palace, the growth of a night. Ships and waggons in hundreds and thousands, laden by commerce, science and art, were trooping from far and near to the common destination. Great and small throughout the country and across the seas were planning to make the Exhibition their school of design and progress, as well as their holiday goal.

It must be said that the dread of what might be the behaviour of the vast crowds of all nations gathered together at one spot, and that spot London, assailed many people both at home and abroad. But as those who are not "evil-doers" are seldom "evil-dreaders," the Queen and the Prince always dismissed the idea of such a danger with something like bright incredulous scorn, which proved in the end wiser than cynical suspicion and gloomy apprehension.

The Exhibition of 1851, with its reverent motto, chosen by Prince Albert, "The earth is the Lord's, and the fullness thereof; the compass of the world, and they that dwell therein," is an old story now, and only elderly people remember some of its marvels—like the creations of the "Arabian Nights'" tales—and its works of art, which, though they may have been excelled before and since, had never yet been so widely seen and widely criticised. The feathery palm-trees and falling fountains, especially the great central cascade, seemed to harmonize with objects of beauty and forms of grace on every side. The East contended with the West in soft and deep colours and sumptuous stuffs. Huge iron machines had their region, and trophies of cobweb lace theirs; while "walking-beams" clanked and shuttles flew, working wonders before amazed and enchanted-eyes.

Especially never had there been seen, such modern triumphs in carved woodwork, in moulded iron, zinc, and bronze, in goldsmiths' work, in stoneware and porcelain, in designs for damasks in silk and linen.

The largest diamond in the world, the Koh-i-Noor or "mountain of light," found in the mines of Golconda, presented to the great Mogul, having passed through the hands of a succession of murderous and plundering Shahs, had been brought to England and laid at the feet of Queen Victoria as one of the fruits of her Afghan conquests, the year before the Exhibition. It was now for the first time publicly displayed. Like many valuable articles, its appearance, marred by bad cutting, did not quite correspond with the large estimate of its worth, about two millions. In order to increase its effect, the precious clumsily-cut "goose's egg," relieved against a background of crimson velvet in its strong cage, was shown by gas-light alone. Since those days, the jewel has been cut, so that its radiance may have full play when it is worn by her Majesty on great occasions. To keep the Koh-i-Noor in company, one of the largest emeralds and one of the largest pearls in the world were in this Exhibition. So were "le saphir merveilleux"—of amethystine colour by candle-light, once the property of Egalité Orleans, and the subject of a tale by Madame Genlis-and a renowned Hungarian opal.

Hiram Powers's "Greek Slave" from America more than rivalled Monti's veiled statue from Italy, while far surpassing both in majesty was Kiss's grand group of the "Mounted Amazon defending herself from, the attack of a Lioness," cast in zinc and bronzed. Statues and statuettes of the Queen abounded, and must have constantly met her eye, from Mrs. Thornycroft's spirited equestrian statue to the great pedestal and statue, in zinc, of her Majesty, crowned, in robes of State, with the sceptre in one hand and the orb in the other, modelled by Danton, which stood in the centre of the foreign nave.

What enhanced the fascination of the scene to untravelled spectators was that without the deliberate contrivance brought to perfection in the great Paris Exhibition, real Chinamen walked among their junks and pagodas, Russians stood by their malachite gates, Turks hovered about their carpets.

Women's quaint or exquisite work, whether professional or amateur, was not absent. It was notable in the magnificent covers for the head and footboard of a bed which had occupied thirty girls for many weeks, and in a carpet worked in squares by a company of ladies, and presented as a tribute of their respect and love for the most unremittingly diligent woman in England, her Majesty the Queen.

CHAPTER XVIII.THE QUEEN'S ACCOUNT OF THE OPENING OF THE EXHIBITION.

Of all the many descriptions of the Exhibition of 1851, which survive after more than thirty years, the best are those written by the Queen, which we gratefully borrow, as we have already borrowed so many of the extracts from her journal in the Prince's "Life."

Sir Theodore Martin has alluded to the special attraction lent to the Exhibition on its opening day by the excitement of the glad ceremonial, the throng of spectators, the Court element with "its splendid toilets" and uniforms, while Thackeray has a verse for the chief figure.

Behold her in her royal place,
A gentle lady, and the hand
That sways the sceptre of this land,

How frail and weak
Soft is the voice and fair the face;
She breathes amen to prayer and hymn
No wonder that her eyes are dim,
And pale her cheek.

But she has deigned to speak for herself, and no other speaks words so noble and tender in their simplicity.

"May 1st. The great event has taken place, a complete and beautiful triumph, a glorious and touching sight, one which I shall ever be proud of for my beloved Albert and my country…. Yes, it is a day which makes my heart swell with pride and glory and thankfulness.

"We began it with tenderest greetings for the birthday of our dear little Arthur. At breakfast there was nothing but congratulations…. Mamma and Victor (the Queen's nephew, son of the Princess of Hohenlohe, now well-known as Count Gleichen) were there, and all the children and our guests. Our humble gifts of toys were added to by a beautiful little bronze replica of the 'Amazon' (Kiss's) from the Prince (of Prussia), a beautiful paper-knife from the Princess (of Prussia), and a nice little clock from mamma.

"The Park presented a wonderful spectacle, crowds streaming through it, carriages and troops passing quite like the Coronation day, and for me the same anxiety; no, much greater anxiety, on account of my beloved Albert. The day was bright, and all bustle and excitement…. At half-past eleven the whole procession, in State carriages, was in motion…. The Green Park and Hyde Park were one densely crowded mass of human beings in the highest good-humour and most enthusiastic. I never saw Hyde Park look as it did, as far as the eye could reach. A little rain fell just as we started, but before we came near the Crystal Palace the sun shone and gleamed upon the gigantic edifice, upon which the flags of all the nations were floating. We drove up Rotten Row and got out at the entrance on that side.

"The glimpse of the transept through the iron gates—the waving palms, flowers, statues, myriads of people filling the galleries and seats around, with the flourish of trumpets as we entered, gave us a sensation which, I can never forget, and I felt much moved. We went for a moment to a little side-room, where we left our shawls, and where we found mamma and Mary (now Duchess of Teck), and outside which were standing the other Princes. In a few seconds we proceeded, Albert leading me, having Vicky at his hand, and Bertie holding mine. The sight as we came to the middle, where the steps and chair (which I did not sit on) were placed, with the beautiful crystal fountain in front of it, was magical—so vast, so glorious, so touching. One felt, as so many did whom I have since spoken to, filled with devotion, more so than by any service I have ever heard. The tremendous cheers, the joy expressed in every face, the immensity of the building, the mixture of palms, flowers, trees, statues, fountains—the organ (with two hundred instruments and six hundred voices, which sounded like nothing), and my beloved husband the author of this peace festival, which united the industry of all nations of the earth—all this was moving indeed, and it was and is a day to live for ever. God bless my dearest Albert, God bless my dearest country, which has shown itself so great to-day! One felt so grateful to the great God who seemed to pervade all and to bless all. The only event it in the slightest degree reminded me of was the Coronation, but this day's festival was a thousand times superior. In fact it is unique and can bear no comparison, from its peculiarity, beauty, and combination of such different and striking objects. I mean the slight resemblance only as to its solemnity; the enthusiasm and cheering, too, were much more touching, for in a church naturally all is silent.

"Albert left my side after "God save the Queen" had been sung, and at the head of the commissioners, a curious assemblage of political and distinguished men, read me the report, which is a long one, and to which I read a short answer; after which the Archbishop of Canterbury offered up a short and appropriate prayer, followed by the "Hallelujah Chorus," during which the Chinese mandarin came forward and made his obeisance. This concluded, the procession began. It was beautifully arranged and of great length, the prescribed order being exactly adhered to. The nave was full, which had not been intended; but still there was no difficulty, and the whole long walk, from one end to the other, was made in the midst of continued and deafening cheers and waving of handkerchiefs. Everyone's face was bright and smiling, many with tears in their eyes. Many Frenchmen called out "Vive la Reine!" One could, of course, see nothing but what was near in the nave, and nothing in the courts. The organs were but little heard, but the military band at one end had a very fine effect as we passed along. They played the march from Athalie.... The old Duke and Lord Anglesey walked arm in arm, which was a touching sight. I saw many acquaintants among those present. We returned to our own place, and Albert told Lord Breadalbane to declare that the Exhibition was opened, which he did in a loud voice: 'Her Majesty commands me to declare this Exhibition open,' which was followed by a flourish of trumpets and immense cheering. All the commissioners, the executive committee, who worked so hard, and to whom such immense praise is due, seemed truly happy, and no one more so than Paxton, who may be justly proud; he rose from being a common gardener's boy. Everybody was astonished and delighted, Sir George Grey (Home Secretary) in tears.

"The return was equally satisfactory, the crowd most enthusiastic, the order perfect. We reached the palace at twenty minutes past one, and went out on the balcony and were loudly cheered, the Prince and Princess (of Prussia) quite delighted and impressed. That we felt happy, thankful, I need not say; proud of all that had passed, of my darling husband's success, and of the behaviour of my good people. I was more impressed than I can say by the scene. It was one that can never be effaced from my memory, and never will be from that of any one who witnessed it. Albert's name is immortalised, and the wicked reports of dangers of every kind, which a set of people, viz. the soi disant fashionables, the most violent Protectionists, spread, are silenced. It is therefore doubly satisfactory, and that all should have gone off so well, and without the slightest accident or mishap.... Albert's emphatic words last year, when he said that the feeling would be that of deep thankfulness to the Almighty for the blessings which He has bestowed on us here below this day realised....

"I must not omit to mention an interesting episode of this day, viz:— the visit of the good old Duke on this his eighty-second birthday to his little godson, our dear little boy. He came to us both at five, and gave him a golden cup and some toys, which he had himself chosen, and Arthur gave him a nosegay.

"We dined en famille, and then went to the Covent Garden Opera, where we saw the two finest acts of the Huguenots given as beautifully as last year. I was rather tired, but we were both so happy, so full of thankfulness! God is indeed our kind and merciful Father."

In answer to Lord John Russell's statement, on the close of the Exhibition, that the great enterprise and the spirit in which it had been conducted would contribute "to give imperishable fame to Prince Albert," the Queen asserted that year would ever remain the happiest and proudest of her life.

CHAPTER XIX. THE QUEEN'S "RESTORATION BALL" AND THE "GUILDHALL BALL."

The season of the first Exhibition was full of movement and gaiety, in which the Queen and Prince Albert joined. They had also the pleasure of welcoming their brother and sister, the Duke and Duchess of Saxe Coburg, who arrived to witness the Prince's triumph. As usual he came forward on every occasion when his services, to which his position and personal gifts lent double value, were needed—whether he presided at an Academy dinner, or at a meeting of the Society for the Propagation of the Gospel, or laid the foundation of the Hospital for Consumption, or attended the meeting of the British Association, and the Queen delighted in his popularity and usefulness.

On the 4th of May Baroness Bunsen was at Stafford House "when her there," and thus describes the Queen. "The Queen looked charming, and I could not help the same reflection that I have often made before, that she is the only piece of female royalty I ever saw who was also a creature such as almighty God has created. Her smile is a real smile, her grace is natural; although it has received a high polish from cultivation, there is nothing artificial about it. Princes I have seen several whose first characteristic is that of being men rather than princes, though not many. The Duchess of Sutherland is the only person I have seen, when receiving the Queen, not giving herself the appearance of a visitor in her own house by wearing a bonnet."

On the 16th of May the Queen and the Prince were at Devonshire House, when Lord Lytton's comedy of "Not so Bad as we Seem" was played by Dickens, Foster, Douglas Jerrold, on behalf of the new "Guild of Literature and Art," in which hopes for poor authors were cheerfully entertained.

On the 23rd of May Lord Campbell was anticipating the Queen's third costume ball with as much complacency as if the eminent lawyer had been a young girl. "We are invited to the Queen's fancy ball on the 13th of June," he wrote "where we are all to appear in the characters and costume of the reign of Charles II. I am to go as Sir Matthew Hale, Chief Justice, and I am now much occupied in considering my dress, that is to say, which robe I am to wear—scarlet, purple, or black. The only new articles I shall have to order are my black velvet coif, a beard with moustaches, and a pair of shoes with red heels, and red rosettes."

The period chosen for the Restoration Ball was the time midway between the dates of the Plantagenet and the Powder Ball.

As on former occasions, the Court walked in procession to the throne- room, where each quadrille passed in turn before the Queen and Prince Albert.

Her Majesty's dress was of grey watered silk, trimmed with gold and silver lace, and ornamented with bows of rose-coloured riband fastened by bouquets of diamonds. The front of the dress was open, and the under-skirt was made of cloth of gold embroidered in a shawl pattern in silver. The gloves and shoes were embroidered alternately with roses and fleurs-de-lys in gold. On the front of the body of the dress were four large pear-shaped emeralds of great value. The Queen wore a small diamond crown on the top of her head, and a large emerald set in diamonds, with pearl loops, on one side of the head; the hair behind plaited with pearls.

Prince Albert wore a coat of rich orange satin, brocaded with gold, the sleeves turned up with crimson velvet, a pink silk epaulette on one shoulder; a baldrick of gold lace embroidered with silver for the sword; the breeches of crimson velvet with pink satin bows and gold lace, the stockings of lavender silk, the sash of white silk, gold fringed.

There were four national quadrilles. The English Quadrille was led by the Marchioness of Ailesbury; the Scotch Quadrille was under the guidance of the young Marchioness of Stafford, daughter-in-law of the Duke of Sutherland; the French Quadrille was led by Countess Flahault, the representative of the old barons Keith, and the wife of a brilliant Frenchman; the Spanish

Quadrille was marshalled by Countess Granville. There were two more Quadrilles, the one under the control of the Countess of Wilton, the other, called the "Rose Quadrille," led by Countess Grey.

With all due deference to the opinion of the late Mr. Henry Greville, the accounts of these quadrilles leave the impression not only that they were arranged with finer taste, but that a considerable advance had been made in artistic perception and sense of harmony. The ladies in each quadrille were dressed alike, so were the gentlemen; thus there were no harsh contrasts. In the English set the ladies wore blue and white silk gowns with trimmings of rose-colour and gold. The gentlemen were in scarlet and gold, and blue velvet. Lady Waterford was in this set, and Lady Churchill, daughter of the Marquis of Conyngham, long connected with the Court. The Duke of Cambridge and Prince Edward of Saxe Weimar were among the gentlemen in the set. Certainly it is a little hard to decide on what principle the exceedingly piquant costume of the ladies in the Scotch Quadrille was classed as Scotch. The ladies wore riding-habits of pale green taffeta ornamented with bows of pink ribbon, and had on grey hats with pink and white feathers. Lady Stafford carried a jewelled riding-whip. The gentlemen were in Highland costume.

In the French Quadrille the ladies wore white satin with bows of light blue ribbon opening over cloth of gold. The gentlemen were in the uniform of Mousquetaires. In this quadrille danced Lady Clementina Villiers, with her "marble-like beauty." She had ceased to be a Watteau shepherdess, and she had lost her companion shepherdess of old, but her intellectual gifts and fine qualities were developing themselves more and more. In the same dance was Lady Rose Lovell, the young daughter of the Duke of Beaufort, whose elopement at the age of seventeen with a gallant one-armed soldier had been condoned, so that she still played her part in the Court gala.

In the Spanish Quadrille the ladies wore black silk over grey damask, trimmed with gold lace and pink rosettes, and Spanish mantillas. The gentlemen were in black velvet, with a Spanish order embroidered in red silk on coat and cloak, grey silk stockings, and black velvet hats with red and yellow feathers. In this quadrille were the matronly beauties Lady Canning, Lady Jocelyn, and Lady Waldegrave.

After the quadrilles had been danced, the ladies falling into lines, advanced to the throne and did reverence, the gentlemen forming in like manner and performing the same ceremony. Her Majesty, and Prince Albert then proceeded to the ballroom, where Lady Wilton's and Lady Grey's quadrilles were danced. In the Rose Quadrille the ladies wore rose-coloured skirts over white moire, with rose-coloured bows and pearls, rose colour and pearls in the hair. Each lady wore a single red rose on her breast.

After the quadrilles, the Queen opened the general ball by dancing the Polonnaise with Prince Albert, the Duke of Cambridge, and Prince Edward of Saxe Weimar; Prince Albert dancing next with the Duchess of Norfolk, the premier peeress present. The Queen danced after supper with the Prince of Leiningen. He was at the Restoration as he had been at the Powder Ball, and wore black velvet and gold lace with orange ribbons.

The characters seem to have been chosen with more point than before.

The Countess of Tankerville personated a Duchesse de Grammont, in right of her mother-in-law, Corisande de Grammont, grand-daughter of Marie Antoinette's friend Gabrielle de Polignac.

Lady Ashburton was Madame de Sevigné, whose fashion of curls beginning in rings on the forehead and getting longer and longer towards the neck, was as much in demand for the ladies, as Philip Leigh's lovelocks were for the gentlemen.

Lady Hume Campbell was "La Belle Duchesse de Bourgogne;" Lady Middleton, Lucy Percy, Countess of Carlisle. Mrs. Abbot Lawrence vindicated her American nationality by representing Anna Dudley, the wife of an early governor of Massachusetts; Mr. Bancroft Davies, secretary of the United States legation, figured as William Penn.

Lady Londonderry and Miss Burdett Coutts were still remarkable for the splendour of their jewels. Lady Londonderry wore a girdle of diamonds, a diamond berthe, and a head-dress a blaze of precious stones, the whole valued roughly at a hundred and fifty thousand pounds. Miss Burdett Coutts displayed a band of jewels, after the fashion of the gentlemen's baldricks, passing over one shoulder and terminating in a diamond clasp fastening back the upper skirt. After diamonds, which, like the blossom of the gorse, may be considered as always à la mode, the specialities of the Restoration Ball were Honiton lace, which was reckoned in better keeping with falling collars than old point, and an enormous expenditure of ribbons. Some of the magnificent collars, such as that of Lord Overton, were manufactured for the occasion. As for ribbons, not only did ladies' dresses abound in bows and rosettes, the gentlemen's doublets, "trunks," and sleeves, were profusely beribboned. The very shirt-sleeves, exposed by the coat-sleeves terminating at the elbow, were bound and festooned with ribbons; while from the ends of the waistcoat hung a waterfall of ribbons, like a Highlander's philabeg. Verily, the heart of Coventry must have rejoiced; the Restoration Ball might have been got up for its special benefit. The Duke of Wellington was in the scarlet and gold uniform of the period, but he alone of all the gentlemen was privileged to wear his own scanty grey hair, which rendered him conspicuous. The old man walked between his two daughters-in-law, Lady Douro and Lady Charles Wellesley.

Lord Galway wore a plain cuirass and gorget so severely simple that it might have been mistaken for the guise of one of Cromwell's officers, who were otherwise unrepresented.

Mr. Gladstone was there as Sir Leoline Jenkins, judge of the High Court of Admiralty in Charles's reign. His dress was copied from an engraving in the British Museum. It was quiet enough, but it is difficult to realise "the grand old man" of to-day in a velvet coat turned up with blue satin, ruffles and collar of old point, black breeches and stockings, and shoes with spreading bows.

Sir Edwin Landseer, whom Miss Thackeray has described as helping to dress some of the ladies for this very ball, was so studiously plain that it must have looked like a protest against the use of "properties" in his apparel. He wore a dress of black silk, with no cloak, no mantle, no skirts to his coat. Round his neck was a light blue scarf, hanging low behind. He had on a grey wig, imitating partial baldness. There could have been no doubt of the historical correctness of the dress, though there might have been some question of its becomingness.

There were changes of some importance in the royal household at this time, caused by the retirement of General, afterwards Sir George Bowles, the Master of the Household, and of Mr. Birch, tutor to the Prince of Vales. With the assistance of Baron Stockmar, fitting successors for those gentlemen were found in Sir Thomas Biddulph and Mr. Frederick Gibbes.

The ball at Guildhall had been fixed for the 2nd of July, but the day was changed when it was remembered that the 2nd was the anniversary of the death of Sir Robert Peel. The entertainment was a very splendid affair. The city was continually progressing in taste and skill in these matters, and the times were so prosperous as to admit of large expenditure without incurring the charge of reckless extravagance. The Queen, Prince Albert, and their suite left Buckingham Palace, in State carriages, at nine o'clock on the summer evening, and drove through brilliantly illuminated streets, densely crowded with large numbers of foreigners as well as natives.

The great hall where the ball took place was magnificently fitted up, many ideas for the decoration being borrowed from the Exhibition. Thus there was a striking array of banners emblazoned with the arms of the nations and cities which had contributed to the Exhibition. "Above the centre shaft of each cluster of columns, shot up towards the roof a silver palm-tree, glittering and sparkling in the brilliant light so profusely shed around. On touching the roof these spread forth and ended in long branches of bright clustering broad leaves of green and gold, from which hung pendant rich bunches of crimson and ruby sparkling fruit." The compartments beneath the balconies were filled with pictures of the best known and most admired foreign contributions to the Exhibition—such as the Amazon group, the Malachite gates, the Greek Slave; &c., &c. Huge griffins had their places at the corners of the dais supporting the throne, while above it a gigantic plume of Prince of Wales's feathers reared itself in spun glass. The chambers and corridors of the Mansion House were fitted up with "acres of looking-glass, statuary, flowers, &c., &c.," provided for the crowd of guests that could not obtain admittance to the hall, where little room was left for dancing. The supper, to which the Queen was conducted, was in the crypt. It was made to resemble a baronial hall, "figures in mediaeval armour being scattered about as the bearers of the lights which illuminated the chamber." Before leaving, in thanking the Lord Mayor (Musgrove) for his hospitality, the Queen announced her intention of creating him a baronet. Her Majesty and the Prince took their departure at one o'clock, returning to Buckingham Palace through the lit streets and huzzaing multitude.

CHAPTER XX.ROYAL VISITS TO LIVERPOOL AND MANCHESTER—CLOSE OF THE EXHIBITION.

On the 27th of August the Court left for Balmoral, travelling for the most part by the Great Northern Railway, but not, as now, making a rapid night and day journey. On the contrary, the journey lasted three days, with pauses for each night's rest between. Starting from Osborne at nine, the Royal party reached Buckingham Palace at half-past twelve. Halting for an hour and a half, they set off again at two. They stopped at Peterborough, where old Dr. Fisher, the Bishop, was able to greet in his Queen the little Princess who had repeated her lessons to him in Kensington Palace. No longer a solitary figure but for the good mother, she was herself a wife and mother, the happiest of the happy in both relations. The train stopped again at Boston and Lincoln for the less interesting purpose of the presentation and reception of congratulatory addresses on the Exhibition. The same ceremony was gone through at Doncaster where the party stayed for the night at the Angel Inn.

Leaving before nine on the following morning, after changing the line of railway at York, and stopping at Darlington and Newcastle, Edinburgh was reached in the course of the afternoon. Her Majesty and the Prince, with their children, proceeded to Holyrood, and before the evening was ended drove for an hour through the beautiful town. Here, too, the Exhibition bore its fruit in the honour of knighthood conferred on the Lord Provost.

On the third morning the travellers left again at eight o'clock, and journeyed as far as Stonehaven, where the royal carriages met them, and conveyed them to Balmoral, which was reached by half-past six. The Prince had now bought the castle and estate, seven miles in length, and four in breadth, and plans were formed for a new house more suitable for the accommodation of so large a household.

On the day after the Queen and Prince Albert's arrival in the
Highlands, he received the news of the death of his uncle, brother to
the late Duke of Coburg and to the Duchess of Kent, Duke Ferdinand of

Saxe-Coburg.

There is little to record of the happy sojourn in the North this year, with its deer-stalking, riding and driving, except that Hallam, the historian, and Baron Liebig, the famous chemist, visited Sir James Clark, the Queen's physician, at Birkhall, which he occupied, and were among the guests at Balmoral.

It had been arranged that the Queen and the Prince should visit Liverpool and Manchester on their way south, in order to give the great cities of Lancashire the opportunity of greeting and welcoming their Sovereign. It was the 8th of October before the royal party set out on their homeward journey, ending the first of the shortening days at Holyrood.

On the following day the strangers went on to the ancient dull little town of Lancaster, and drove to the castle, where the keys were presented, and an address read under John O'Gaunt's gateway. The tower stairs were mounted for the view over Morcambe Bay and the English lake country on the one hand, and away across level lands to the sea on the other. Every native of the town "wore a red rose or a red rosette, as emblems of the House of Lancaster."

The Queen and the Prince then proceeded to Prescot, where they left the railway, driving through Lord Derby's fine park at Knowsley, to be the guests of the Earl of Sefton at Croxteth. Next morning, when Liverpool was to be visited, a contretemps occurred. The weather was hopelessly wet; the whole party had to go as far as possible in closed carriages; afterwards the downpour was so irresistible that the Prince's large cloak had to be spread over the Queen and her children to keep them dry. But her Majesty's commiseration is almost entirely for the crowd on foot, "the poor people so wet and dirty." They spoil her pleasure in her enthusiastic reception and the fine buildings she passes.

The royal party drove along the docks, and in spite of the rain got out at the appointed place of embarkation, went on board the Fairy, accompanied by the Mayor and other officials, and sailed along the quays round the mouth of the Mersey, surveying the grand mass of shipping from the pavilion on deck as well as the dank mist would permit. On landing, the Town Hall and St. George's Hall were visited in succession. In the first the Queen received an address and knighted the Mayor. She admired both buildings—particularly St. George's, which she called "worthy of ancient Athens," and said it delighted Prince Albert. At both halls she presented herself on balconies in order to gratify the multitudes below.

The Queen left Liverpool by railway, going as far as Patricroft, where she was received by Lady Ellesmere and a party from Worsley, including the Duke of Wellington, Lord and Lady Westminster, and Lord and Lady Wilton. Her Majesty was to try a mode of travelling new to her. She had arrived at the Bridgewater Canal, one of the greatest feats of engineering in the last century, constructed by the public-spirited, eccentric Duke of Bridgewater, and Brindley the engineer. The Queen went on board a covered barge drawn by four horses. She describes the motion as gliding along "in a most noiseless and dream-like manner, amidst the cheers of the people who lined the sides of the canal." Thus she passed under the "beautifully decorated bridges" belonging to Lord Ellesmere's colliery villages.

Only at the hall-door of Worsley were Lord Ellesmere, lame with gout, and Lord Brackley, his son, "terribly delicate" from an accident in the hunting-field, the husband of one of the beautiful Cawdor Campbells, able to meet their illustrious guests. Henry Greville says her Majesty brought with her four children, two ladies-in-waiting, two equerries, a physician, a tutor, and a governess. Men of mechanical science seem to belong to Worsley, so that it sounds natural for the Queen and the Prince to have met there, during the evening, Nasmyth, the inventor of the steam-hammer, and to have examined his maps of his investigations in the moon, and his landscape-drawings, worthy of his father's son. The Queen and Prince Albert derived great pleasure from their passing intercourse with a man of varied gifts, whose sterling qualities they could well appreciate.

The next morning, the 10th of October, the weather was all that could be wished, but another and even more unfortunate complication threatened the success of the arrangements, on which the comfort of a few and the gratification of many thousands of persons depended. Prince Albert, never strong, was always liable to trying attacks of sleeplessness and sickness. In the course of the night he had been "very unwell, very sick and wretched for several hours." "I was terrified for our Manchester visit" wrote the Queen in her journal. "Thank God! by eight o'clock he felt much better, and was able to get up" indefatigable as ever.

At ten the party started to drive the seven miles to Manchester, escorted by Yeomanry and a regiment of Lancers, Lord Cathcart and his staff riding near the Queen's carriage through an ever-increasing crowd. The Queen was greatly interested in the rows of mill-workers between whom she passed, "dressed in their best, ranged along the streets, with white rosettes in their button-holes"—that patient, easily pleased crowd, which has an aspect half comical, half pathetic. Her Majesty admired the intelligent expression of both men and women, but was painfully struck with their puniness and paleness. In the Peel Park the visitors were greeted by a great demonstration, which her Majesty calls "extraordinary and unprecedented," of no less than eighty-two thousand school children, of every denomination, Jews as well as Christians. The Queen received and replied to an address, from her carriage, and the immense body of children sang "God save the Queen."

The party then drove through the principal streets of Salford and Manchester—the junction of the two being marked by a splendid triumphal arch, under which the Mayor and Corporation (dressed for the first time in robes of office—so democratic was Manchester), again met the Queen and presented her with a bouquet. At the Exchange she alighted to receive another address, to which she read an answer, and knighted the Mayor. Her Majesty missed "fine buildings," of which, with the exception of huge warehouses and factories, Manchester had then none to boast; but she was particularly struck by the demeanour of the inhabitants, in addition to what she was pleased to call their "most gratifying cheering and enthusiasm." "The order and good behaviour of the people, who were not placed behind any barriers, were the most complete we have seen in our many progresses through capitals and cities—London, Glasgow, Dublin, Edinburgh—for there never was a running crowd, nobody moved and therefore everybody saw well, and there was no squeezing...." The Queen heard afterwards that she had seen a million of human beings that day. In the afternoon her Majesty and the Prince, returned to Worsley.

Henry Greville tells an almost piteous incident of this visit, in relation to the Duke of Wellington and his advanced age, with the infirmities that could no longer be repelled. After saying that in order to prevent the procession's becoming too large, no other guest at Worsley was admitted into it, except the privileged old Duke, whom the teller of the story describes as driving in the carriage with Henry Greville's sister, Lady Enfield, one of the ladies in attendance on the Queen, he goes on to mention "he (the Duke) was received with extraordinary enthusiasm; notwithstanding Lady Enfield had to nudge him constantly, to keep him awake, both going and coming, with very little success." Lady Enfield adds a note to her brother's narrative. "The whole scene was one of the most exciting I ever saw in my life. Being carried away by the general enthusiasm, and feeling that the people would be disappointed if no notice was taken of their cheering, I at last exclaimed 'Duke, Duke, that's for you.' Thereupon he opened his eyes, and obediently made his well-known salutation, two fingers to the brim of his hat."

The next morning when the Prince had started by seven o'clock to inspect a model factory near Bolton, while there was a long and busy day before them, the Queen made a little entry in her journal which will find a sorrowful echo in many a faithful heart, "This day is full of sad recollections, being the anniversary of the loss of my beloved Louise (Queen of the Belgians), that kind, precious friend, that angelic being whose loss I shall ever feel."

The same pleasant passage was made by the canal back to Patricroft, where the railway carriages were entered and the train steamed to Stockport. Crewe, Stafford—there another old soldier, Lord Anglesey, was waiting—Rugby, Weedon, Wolverton, and Watford, then at five o'clock the railway journey ended. The royal carriages were in attendance, and rest and home were near at hand. The day had been hot and fatiguing, but the evening was soft and beautiful with moonlight; a final change of horses at Uxbridge, the carriage shut when the growing darkness prevented any farther necessity for seeing and being seen; at half-past seven, Windsor, and the three little children still up and at the door "well and pleased."

From Windsor the Court went for some days to London for the closing of the Exhibition. The number of visitors had been six millions two hundred thousand, and the total receipts five hundred thousand pounds. There had not been a single accident, "We ought, indeed, to be thankful to God for such a success," the Prince wrote reverently. On the 14th of October the Queen paid a farewell visit to the place in which she had been so much interested, with the regret natural on such an occasion. "It looked so beautiful," she wrote in her journal, "that I could not believe it was the last time I was to see it." But already the dismantling had begun.

The Queen refers in the next breath to a heroine of the Exhibition, an old Cornish woman named Mary Kerlynack, who had found the spirit to walk several hundreds of miles to behold the wonder of her generation. This day she was at one of the doors to see another sight, the Queen. "A most hale old woman" her Majesty thought Mary, "who was near crying at my looking at her."

On the 15th, a cheerlessly wet day, in keeping with a somewhat melancholy scene, Prince Albert and his fellow commissioners closed the Exhibition—a ceremony at which it was not judged desirable the Queen should be present, though she grieved not to witness the end as well as the beginning. "How sad and strange to think this great and bright time has passed away like a dream," her Majesty wrote once more in her diary. The day of the closing of the Exhibition happened to be the twelfth anniversary of the Queen's betrothal to the Prince.

The tidings arrived in the course of November of the death, in his eighty-first year, in the old palace of Herrenhausen, on the 18th of the month, of the King of Hanover, the fifth, and last surviving son of George III and Queen Charlotte. He had been more popular as a king than as a prince.

The arrival of Kossuth in England in the autumn of 1851 had brought a disturbing element into international politics. But it was left for Louis Napoleon's coup d'état in Paris on the 2nd of December, when the blood shed so mercilessly on the Boulevards was still fresh in men's minds, to get Lord Palmerston into a dilemma, from which there was no disentanglement but the loss of office on his part.

An impetus, great though less lasting than it seemed, was given this year to emigration to Australia, by the discovery in the colony of gold in quartz beds, under much the same conditions that the precious metal had been found in California. The diggings, with the chance of a large nugget, became for a time the favourite dream of adventurers. Nay, the dream grew to such an absorbing desire, that men heard of it as a disease known as "the gold fever." And quiet people at home were told that it was hardly safe for a ship to enter some of the Australian harbours, on account of the certainty of the desertion of the crew, under whatever penalties, that they might repair to the last El Dorado.

The successful ambition of Louis Napoleon and his power over the French army, began to excite the fears of Europe with regard to French aggression, and a renewal of the desolating wars of the beginning of the century; before the talk about the Exhibition and the triumphs of peace had well died on men's lips. The Government was anxious to fall back on the old resource of calling out the militia, with certain modifications and changes—brought before Parliament in the form of a Militia Bill. It did not meet with the approval of the members any more than of the Duke of Wellington, whose experience gave his opinion much weight. Lord Palmerston spoke with great ability against the measure. The end was that the Government suffered a defeat, and the Ministry resigned office in February, 1852. This time Lord Derby was successful in forming a new Cabinet, in which Mr. Disraeli was Chancellor of the Exchequer. A fresh Militia Bill was brought forward and carried by the new Government, after it had received the warm advocacy of the Duke of Wellington. The old man spoke in its favour with an amount of vigour and clear-headedness which showed that however his bodily strength might be failing, his mental power remained untouched.

CHAPTER XXI. DISASTERS—YACHTING TRIPS—THE DEATH OF THE DUKE OF WELLINGTON.

The month of February, 1852, was unhappily distinguished by three great English calamities, accompanied by extensive loss of life. The first was the destruction of the West India mail steamer Amazon by fire, as she was entering the Bay of Biscay, in which a hundred and forty persons perished, among them Eliot Warburton, the accomplished traveller and author.

The second was the wreck of her Majesty's troop-ship Birkenhead near the Cape of Good Hope, with the loss of upwards of four hundred lives, in circumstances when the discipline and devotion of the men were of the noblest description. The third was the bursting of the Bilberry Reservoir in midland England, with the sacrifice of nearly a hundred lives and a large amount of property.

When the season commenced, and it was this year, as last, particularly gay, a reflection of the general prosperity of the country, with the high hopes inspired by the Australian gold-fields, the Queen wrote to the King of the Belgians in order to re-assure him with regard to a fear which seems to have arisen in the elderly man's mind, that she whom he remembered at the beginning of her reign as fond of pleasure and untiring in her amusements, might be swept away in the tide. "Allow me just to say one word about the London season. The London season for us consists of two State balls and two concerts. (The State balls and concerts are given to this day, though her Majesty, since her widowhood, has ceased to attend them. The Queen's place and that of Prince Albert in these social gaieties, have been naturally taken by the Prince and Princess of Wales.) We are hardly ever later than twelve o'clock at night, and our only dissipation is going three or four times a week to the play or opera, which is a great amusement and relaxation to us both. As for going out as people do here every night, to balls and parties, and to breakfasts and teas all day long besides, I am sure no one would stand it worse than I should; so you see, dearest uncle, that in fact the London season is nothing to us."

So much higher, and more solid and lasting, as they should have been, were the pursuits and gratifications of the woman, the wife and mother, than of the young girl.

The Queen added that the only one who was fagged was the Prince, and that from business and not pleasure, a result which made her often anxious and unhappy. Indeed, this suspicion of precarious health on Prince Albert's part was the cloud the size of a man's hand that kept hovering on the horizon in the summer sky.

Parliament was prorogued and dissolved at the same time at an unusually early date, the first of July, so that the season itself came to a speedy end.

Before the Queen left London, she was present at the baptism and stood sponsor for the young Hindoo Princess Gouromma, the pale, dark, slender girl whose picture looks down on the visitor at Buckingham Palace. She had been brought to England by her father, the Rajah of Coorg, a high caste Hindoo, who desired that she should be brought up a Christian. He was one of the princes of Northern India, whose inheritance had become a British possession. He lived at Benares under the control of the East India Company, and had an allowance from Government as well as a large private fortune. The little princess was the same age as the Princess Royal, eleven years. She was the daughter of the Rajah's favourite wife, who had died immediately after the infant's birth. The ceremony took place in the private chapel of Buckingham Palace. The Archbishop of Canterbury officiated. Besides the Queen, the sponsors were Lady Hardinge, Mr. Drummond, and Sir James Weir Hogg, the chairman of the East India Company. The little girl received the name "Victoria." The Rajah returned soon afterwards to India.

The Court had longer time to enjoy the sea air and quiet of Osborne, where, however, sorrow intruded in the shape of the news of the death of Count Mensdorff, the uncle by marriage both of the Queen and Prince Albert, to whom they were warmly attached. Though he had been no prince, only a French emigrant officer in the Austrian service, when he married the sister of the Duchess of Kent, he was held in high esteem by his wife's family for the distinction with which he had served as a soldier, and for his many good qualities.

Princess Hohenlohe, with a son and daughter, came to Osborne as a stage to Scotland and Abergeldie, where she was to visit her mother, the Duchess of Kent, and where she could also best enjoy the Queen's society. The poor Princess, who made a stay of several months in this country, had need of a mother's and a sister's sympathy. A heavy sorrow had lately befallen her. The eldest daughter of the Hohenlohe family, Princess Elise, a girl of great promise, had died at Venice of consumption in her twenty-first year.

Yachting excursions were again made to Devonshire and Cornwall, to Torquay and the often-visited beauties of Mount Edgcumbe and the banks of the Tamar. There was a proposal of a visit to the King of the Belgians, with the Channel Islands to be touched at on the way. One part of the programme had to be given up, on account of the tempestuous weather. The yacht, after waiting to allow Prince Albert to pay a flying visit—the last—to the Duke of Wellington at Walmer, ran up the Scheldt in one of the pauses in the storm, and the travellers reached Antwerp at seven o'clock on the morning of the 11th of August, "in a hurricane of wind and rain."

But the weather is of little consequence when friends meet. King Leopold was waiting for his welcome guests, and immediately carried them off to his country palace, for their visit this time was to him and not to any of the old Flemish towns.

The Queen and Prince Albert, with their children, stayed at Laeken for three days, returning to Antwerp in time for a visit to the cathedral and the museum, before sailing in the same unpropitious weather for Flushing. The intention was still to cross on the following morning to the Channel Islands, but the wet, wild weather did not change, and the yacht remained where it was, the Queen indemnifying herself for the disappointment by landing and going over an old Dutch town and a farmhouse, with which she was much pleased.

On the 30th of August the Court went to Balmoral by Edinburgh. Soon after her arrival the Queen had the gratifying intelligence that a large legacy, about two hundred and fifty thousand pounds, had been left to her and her heirs by one of her subjects—Mr. Campden Nield— a gentleman without near relatives, who had lived in the most penurious way, denying himself the very necessaries of life.

The Queen's comment on the bequest to King Leopold was like her. "It is astonishing, but it is satisfactory to see that people have so much confidence that it will not be thrown away, and so it certainly will not be." Baron Stockmar held with some justice that it was "a monument reared to the Queen during her life, in recognition of her simple, honourable, and constitutional career."

Her Majesty and Prince Albert went on the 16th of September for their customary two days' stay by Loch Muich, though they had been startled in the morning by a newspaper report of the death of the Duke of Wellington at Walmer. But the rumour had arisen so often during these many years that nobody believed it, now that it was true.

The little party started in the course of the forenoon on a showery day. Arrived at the Loch, the Queen walked up the side to Alt-na- Dearg, a "burn" and fall, then rode up the ravine hung with birch and mountain-ash, and walked again along the top of the steep hills to points which command a view of Lord Panmure's country, "Mount Keen and the Ogilvie Hills."

A little farther on, while resting and looking down on the Glassalt Shiel and the head of the loch, the Queen, by a curious coincidence, missed the watch which the Duke of Wellington had given her. Her Majesty sent back a keeper to inquire about her loss; in the meanwhile she walked on and descended by the beautiful falls of the Glassalt, one hundred and fifty feet in height, which she compares to those of the Bruar. The cottage or shiel of the Glassalt had just been built for the Queen, and offered accommodation in its dainty little dining- room and drawing-room for her to rest and refresh herself. After she had eaten luncheon, she set out again on a pony, passed another waterfall, called the Burn of the Spullan, and reached the wild solitary Dhu Loch.

The Queen had sat down to sketch when the keeper returned to tell her that the watch was safe at home; but that was not all. He brought a letter from Lord Derby with a melancholy confirmation of the report of the morning. The Duke of Wellington was dead. The Queen calls the news "fatal," and with something of the fond exaggeration of a daughter, writes of the dead man as "England's—rather Britannia's—pride, her glory, her hero, the greatest man she ever had produced."

We can understand it, when we remember how closely connected he was with all her previous career, from her cradle till now. He had taken pride in her, advised her, obeyed her, with half a father's, half a servant's devotion. The King of the Belgians was hardly more her second father than the Duke of Wellington had been.

Besides, the Duke was not only a soldier; he had been a statesman, tried and true as far as his vision extended; brave here no less than in the stricken field, honest with an upright man's straightforwardness, wise with a practical man's sense of what could and could not be done, what must be yielded when the time came.

The Queen might well mourn for her grey-bearded captain, her faithful old councillor. There was one comfort, that the Duke had reached a good old age, and died after a few hours illness, without suffering. He simply fell asleep, and awoke no more in this world. His old antagonist, Marshal Soult, had pre-deceased him only by a few months.

The Queen sums up the position: "One cannot think of this country without 'the Duke,' our immortal hero."

Her Majesty hastened down on foot to the head of Loch Muich, and rode back in the rain to Alt-na-Giuthasach to write to Lord Derby and Lord Charles Wellesley, who had been with his father in his last hours. She wrote mournfully in her journal: "We shall soon stand sadly alone.

Aberdeen is almost the only personal friend of that kind left to us. Melbourne, Peel, Liverpool, now the Duke, all gone!...."

Invitations were countermanded, and the Court went into mourning. The Queen was right that the sorrow was universal. The ships in the Thames and in all the English ports had their flags half-mast high, the church bells were tolled, business was done "with the great exchanges half-shuttered," garrison music was forbidden.

The Duke had left no directions with regard to his funeral, and it was fitting that it should receive the highest honour Sovereign and people could pay. But the Queen refrained from issuing an order, preferring that the country should take the initiative. It was necessary to wait till the 11th of November, when Parliament must meet. In the meantime the body of the Duke was placed under a Guard of Honour at Walmer. Viscount Hardinge was appointed Commander-in-Chief. The Court left Balmoral on the 12th of October, about a month after the Duke of Wellington's death, and on the 11th—a day which the Queen calls in her journal "a very happy, lucky, and memorable one"—her Majesty and Prince Albert, with their family, household, tenants, servants, and poorer neighbours, ascended Craig Gowan, a hill near Balmoral, for the purpose of building a cairn, which was to commemorate the Queen and the Prince's having taken possession of their home in the north. At the "Moss House," half-way up, the Queen's piper met her, and preceded her, playing as he went. Not the least welcome among the company already collected were the children of the keepers and other retainers, with whom her Majesty was familiar in their own homes. She calls them her "little friends," and enumerates them in a motherly way, "Mary Symons, and Lizzie Stewart, the four Grants, and several others."

The Queen laid the first stone of the cairn, Prince Albert the next. Their example was followed by the Princes and Princesses, according to their ages, and by the members of the household. Finally every one present "came forward at once, each person carrying a stone and placing it on the cairn." The piper played, whiskey was handed round. The work of building went on for an hour, during which "some merry reels were danced on a flat stone opposite." All the old people danced, apparently to her Majesty's mingled gratification and diversion. Again the happy mother of seven fine children notices particularly the children and their performance. "Many of the children—Mary Symons and Lizzie Stewart especially—danced so nicely, the latter with her hair all hanging down."

There is another little paragraph which is very characteristic of the love of animals, and the faithful remembrance of old landmarks, well- known features in the Queen's character. "Poor dear old Monk, Sir Robert Gordon's (the former owner of Balmoral) faithful old dog, was sitting there among us all."

When the cairn ("seven or eight feet high") was all but finished, Prince Albert climbed to the top and deposited the last stone, when three cheers were given. The Queen calls it "a gay, pretty, and touching sight," that almost made her cry. "The view was so beautiful over the dear hills; the day so fine, the whole so gemüthlich." She ends reverently, "May God bless this place, and allow us to see it and enjoy it many a long year."

CHAPTER XXII. THE IRON DUKE'S FUNERAL.

On the 11th of November the Parliament met and voted the Duke a public funeral in the City cathedral of St. Paul's, by the side of Nelson, the great soldier and the great sailor bearing each other company in their resting-place, in the middle of the people whom they had saved from foreign dominion.

The hearse with the body had left Walmer at seven o'clock on the morning of the 10th, minute guns being fired in succession from the castles of Walmer, Deal, and Sandown, startling the sea-mews hovering over the Goodwin Sands, causing the sailors in the foreign vessels in the Downs to ask if England had gone to war. From the railway station in London, the coffin was escorted by Life Guards to Chelsea, where it was received by the Lord Chamberlain and conducted to the great hall for the lying-in-state, which occupied four days.

The fine old hospital, where so many of the Duke's soldiers had found refuge, which Wilkie had painted for him at the moment when the pensioners were listening to the reading of the Gazette that announced the victory of Waterloo, was carefully prepared for the last scene but one of a hero's life. Corridors, vestibule, and hall were hung with black cloth and velvet, and lit with tall candles in silver candelabra. Trophies of tattered banners, the spoils of the many victories of him who had just yielded to the last conqueror, were surmounted by the royal standard; Grenadiers lined hall and vestibule, their heads bent over their reversed arms. A plumed canopy of black velvet and silver was raised over a dais, with a carpet of cloth of gold, on which rested the gilt and crimson coffin. At the foot of the bier hung the mace and insignia of the late Duke's numerous orders of knighthood; and on ten pedestals, with golden lions in front, were the eight field-marshals' batons of eight different kingdoms, which had been bestowed on him. On the ninth and tenth pedestals were placed the Great Banner and the banner of Wellesley.

The Queen and Prince Albert came privately with their children, early on the first day, a windy, rainy Saturday in November, to view the lying-in-state.

On the night before the funeral the coffin was removed to the Horse Guards, over which Wellington had so long presided, where it is said that in the early days of his career he met Nelson. Early next morning the coffin was conveyed to a pavilion on the parade, whence it was lifted to the car which was to convey it to St. Paul's.

Not later than six o'clock on the morning of the 18th, the troops in large numbers began to muster in Hyde Park, under the direction of the Duke of Cambridge. The streets and windows were lined with seats covered with black cloth. Barriers were raised at the mouths of the side streets in the line of route, to prevent the danger of any side rush. In the dread of missing the sight, hundreds of people took up their position the night before, and kept it during the dark hours, in spite of wind and rain. All the richer classes were in mourning; indeed, whoever could bring out a scrap of black did so. There was a peculiar hush and touch of solemnity, which had its effect on the roughest in the million and a half of spectators.

At a quarter before eight, nineteen minute guns were fired in the park, the walls of the pavilion were suddenly drawn up, revealing the funeral car and its sacred burden. Instantly the troops presented arms for the last time to their late commander, and the drums beat "a long and heavy roll, increasing like the roll of thunder." The words "to reverse arms" were then given, and the funeral procession began to move. First came battalion after battalion of infantry, commencing with the rifles, the bands playing "The Dead March in Saul," the trumpets of the cavalry taking up "the wailing notes." "As the dark mass of the rifles appeared, and the solemn dead march was heard, the people were deeply affected, very many of both sexes to tears…. Great interest was felt as the Duke's regiment, the 33rd, passed." Squadrons of cavalry were succeeded by seventeen guns; the Chelsea Pensioners, old men, like him whose remains they followed, to the number of eighty three—his years on earth; one soldier from every regiment in her Majesty's service, to say that none had been left out, when their leader was borne to his grave; standards and pennons; deputations from public bodies—Merchant Taylors' Company, East India Company, and the deputation from the Common Council of London, joining the procession at Temple Bar; more standards, high officials, Sheriffs, and Knights of the Bath; the Judges, members of the Ministry, and Houses of Parliament; the Archbishop of Canterbury; the Lord Mayor of London carrying the City Sword; His Royal Highness Prince Albert, attended by the Marquesses of Exeter and Abercorn— Lord Chamberlain and Groom of the Stole; the Great Banner, borne by an officer, and supported by two officers on horseback; the Field- marshals' batons—each carried by a foreign officer of high rank— which every country in Europe, except France and Austria, had entrusted to the care of the Great Duke. To the imposing scene to-day France, like an honorable enemy, sent a representative; but Austria, still smarting under the affront to Haynau, was conspicuous by absence. The English Field-marshal's baton was borne on its cushion by the Duke's old comrade in arms, the Marquis of Anglesey. The Duke's coronet followed. Then the pall-bearers—eight generals in mourning coaches. At length the huge funeral car, heavily wrought and emblazoned and inscribed with the names of the Duke's battles, drawn by twelve horses, with five officers on horseback, bearing the banneroles of the lineage of the deceased, riding on either side. On the car was placed the coffin, and on the coffin rested the hat and sword of the dead commander.... Every emotion, save that of solemn awe, was hushed. The massive structure moved on its course with a steady pressure, and produced a heavy dull sound, as it ground its path over the road.... But the car, apart from its vast size, passed unnoticed, for on its highest stage rested a red velvet coffin, which contained all that was mortal of England's greatest son. It seemed that a thousand memories of his great and long career were awakened at the sight of that narrow tenement of so great a man.... The voice which had cried "Up, Guards, and at them!" at the critical moment on the afternoon of that rainy Sunday at Waterloo, thirty-seven years before, was silent for ever. The sagacious and skilled brain which had planned so well the defence of London from the threatened outbreak of the Chartists, would plan no more for Queen and country. No longer would the shouting crowd press round him on every gala, and strangers watch patiently near the Horse Guards for one of the sights of London— the eagle face of the conqueror of him who conquered Europe.

"No more in soldier fashion would he greet,
  With lifted hand, the gazer in the street."

Wellington was making his way from the Horse Guards for the last time, attended by such a mighty multitude as seldom waits on the steps of Kings, hardly ever with such mute reverence as they gave him that day. The "good grey head" of "the last Great Englishman" was about to be laid in the dust, and his best epitaph was Tennyson's line—

"One that sought but duty's iron crown."

Behind the car came the chief mourner, accompanied by his younger brother, with cousins and relatives to the last degree of kindred, and friends filling a long train of mourning coaches. Then followed what moved the people more than all the splendour, because it came like a touch of homely nature appealing to all, in a familiar part of the life that was gone, the late Duke's horse, led by John Mears, his aged groom. The horse might have been "Copenhagen," which had borne the Duke in the thick of his greatest battle, and died long since at Strathfieldsaye, so eagerly did the crowds gaze on it. More carriages and troops closed the march.

And she was not absent who had held the dead man in such high esteem, whom he had so loved and honoured. From two different points—as if she were reluctant to see the last of her old friend—from the balcony of Buckingham Palace, where the Royal Standard floated half-mast high, as the funeral passed up Constitution Hill, and again from the windows of St. James's Palace, as the melancholy train went down St. James's Street, the Queen, surrounded by her children and her young cousins from Belgium, looked down on the solemn pageant.

Nearly twenty thousand privileged persons—many of them of high rank, filled St. Paul's, black-draped and gas-lit on the dark November day. After the funeral company were seated, the body, which had been received at the west entrance by the Bishop of London and the other clergy of the Cathedral, was carried up the nave to the chanting of "I am the Resurrection and the Life." The spurs were borne by one herald, the helmet and crest by another, the sword and target by a third, the surcoat by a fourth, the foreign batons by their foreign bearers, the English baton by Lord Anglesey.

Among the psalms and anthems, a dirge accompanied by trumpets was sung, "And the King said to all the people that were with him, rend your clothes and gird you with sackcloth and mourn. And the King himself followed the bier. And they buried him; and the King lifted up his voice and wept at the grave, and all the people wept. And the King said unto his servants, Know ye not that there is a prince and a great man fallen this day in Israel."

An affecting incident occurred, when, at the conclusion of this dirge, the body was lowered into the crypt to the "intensely mournful" sound of "The Dead March in Saul." As the coffin with the coronet and baton slowly descended, and thus the great warrior departed from the sight of men, a sense of heavy depression came on the whole assembly. Prince Albert was deeply moved, and the aged Marquess of Anglesey, the octogenarian companion in arms of the deceased, by an irresistible impulse stepped forward, placed his hand on the sinking coffin that contained the remains of his chief in many battles, and burst into tears.

"In the vast Cathedral leave him;
God accept him, Christ receive him."

CHAPTER XXIII. THE EMPEROR NAPOLEON III. AND THE EMPRESS EUGÉNIE—FIRE AT WINDSOR— THE BIRTH OF PRINCE LEOPOLD.

At the close of 1852 Mr. Disraeli announced his Budget in one famous speech, to which Mr. Gladstone replied in another, the first of those memorable speeches—at once a fine oration and a convincing argument— so often heard since then. The Derby Ministry, already tottering to its fall on the ground of its opposition to Free-trade principles, was defeated, and the same night Lord Derby resigned office, and Lord Aberdeen, who was able to unite the Whigs and the followers of the late Sir Robert Peel, took his place.

On the 2nd of December, the anniversary of the coup d'état, the
Empire was declared in France, and Louis Napoleon entered Paris as
Emperor on the following day.

On the 22nd of January, 1853, the Emperor of the French made public his approaching marriage to the beautiful Eugénie de Montigo, Comtesse de Théba.

A serious fire broke out at Windsor Castle on the night of the 19th of March, the very day that the Court had come down for Easter. It was the result of an accident from the over-heating of a flue, which might have been doubly disastrous.

The scene of the fire was the upper stories of the Prince of Wales's Tower, above the Gothic dining-room, which is in the same suite with the Crimson, Green, and White drawing-rooms, in the last of which the Queen and Prince Albert were sitting, at ten o'clock in the evening, when the smell of smoke and burning aroused an alarm.

Besides the suite of drawing-rooms, with their costly furniture, the plate-rooms were beneath the Gothic dining-room; and on the other side—beyond a room known as the Octagon-room—was the Jewelled Armoury. The fire had taken such hold that the utmost exertions were needed to keep it under, and prevent it from spreading, and it remained for hours doubtful whether the rest of the Castle would escape. Prince Albert, the gentlemen of the household, and the servants, with seven hundred Guards brought from the barracks and stationed in the avenues to prevent further disorder, strove to supplement the work of the fire-engines. The Gothic dining-room was stripped of its furniture, including the gold vase or bath for wine, valued at ten thousand pounds. The Crimson drawing-room and the Octagon-room were dismantled. The plate-rooms were considered fireproof, but the Jewelled Armoury was emptied of its treasures, among them the famous peacock of Tippoo Sahib.

More than five hours passed before the danger was over. The Queen, in writing to reassure the King of the Belgians, said, "Though I was not alarmed, it was a serious affair, and an acquaintance with what a fire is, and with its necessary accompaniments, does not pass from one's mind without leaving a deep impression. For some time it was very obstinate, and no one could tell whether it would spread or not. Thank God, no lives were lost."

Less than three weeks after the fire, the Queen's fourth son, and eighth child, was born at Buckingham Palace on the 7th of April. Within a fortnight her Majesty was sufficiently recovered to write to the King of the Belgians, and here the wound which had been felt so keenly bled afresh. "My first letter is this time, as last time, addressed to you. Last time it was because dearest Louise—to whom the first announcement had heretofore always been addressed, was with me, alas! Now," she goes on to remind him affectionately, "Stockmar will have told you that Leopold is to be the name of our fourth young gentleman. It is a mark of love and affection which I hope you will not disapprove. It is a name which is the dearest to me after Albert, one which recalls the almost only happy days of my sad childhood. To hear "Prince Leopold" [Footnote: When Prince Leopold's title was merged into that of Duke of Albany, our readers may remember that some reluctance was expressed at the change, and that there was an attempt to preserve the earlier name, by arranging that his Royal Highness should be styled "Prince Leopold, Duke of Albany."] again will make me think of all those days. His other names will be George, Duncan, Albert, and the sponsors will be the King of Hanover, Ernest Hohenlohe (the Queen's brother-in-law), the Princess of Prussia, and Mary of Cambridge. George is after the King of Hanover, and Duncan is a compliment to dear Scotland."

In the Royal Academy this year one of the pre-Raphaelites, who had been at first treated with vehement opposition and ridicule, came so unmistakably to the front as to stagger his former critics, and render his future success certain. Even the previous year Millais's "Huguenot" had made a deep impression, and his "Order of Release" this year carried everything before it. In the same Academy exhibition were Sir Edwin Landseer's highly poetic "Night" and "Morning."

On the Court's return from Osborne to London, the Queen and Prince Albert were present with their guests, the King and Queen of Hanover, and the Duke and Duchess of Coburg, on the 21st of June, in the camp at Chobham, when a sham-fight and a series of military manoeuvres over broken ground were carried out with great spirit and exactness, to the admiration of a hundred thousand spectators. Her Majesty, as in the early years of her reign, wore a half-military riding-habit, and was mounted on a splendid black horse, on which she rode down the lines before witnessing the mock battle from an adjoining height.

Four days afterwards Prince Albert returned to the camp to serve for a couple of days with his brigade, the Guards. The Prince experienced something of the hardships of bivouacing in stormy weather, and suffered in consequence. He came back labouring under a bad cold, to be present at the baptism of his infant son on the 28th. All the sponsors were there in person. The Lord Chamberlain conducted the baby-prince to the font; the Archbishop of Canterbury performed the sacred rite. The usual State banquet and evening party followed. But illness, not very deadly, yet sufficiently prostrating, was hovering over the royal pair and their guests. The Prince of Wales was already sick of measles. Prince Albert, pre-disposed by the cold he had caught, got the infection from his son, had a sharp attack of the same disease, and we are told "at the climax of the illness showed great nervous excitement," symptomatic of a susceptible, highly-strung, rather fragile temperament.

Though the country was unaware of the extent of the Prince's illness, we can remember the public speculation it excited, and the contradictory assertions that the Queen would claim her wife's prerogative of watching by her husband's sick-bed, and that she would be forbidden to do so, for State reasons, her health or sickness, not to say the danger to her life, being of the utmost importance to the body politic. It is easy to see that if such a question had arisen, it would have been peculiarly trying to one who had been brought up to regard her duty to the country as a primary obligation, while at the same time every act of her life showed how precious and binding were her conjugal relations. But the matter settled itself. After the Princess Royal and Princess Alice had also been attacked by the epidemic, the Queen was seized with it, happily in the mildest form, which was of short duration. But the mischief did not confine itself to the English royal family. The juvenile malady of measles became for a time the scourge of princes, a little to the diversion of the world, since no great harm was anticipated, or came to pass, while the ailment invaded a succession of Courts. The guests at Prince Leopold's baptism carried the seeds of the disease to Hanover, in the person of the little Hanoverian cousin, King George's son, who had been a visitor in the English royal nurseries; to Brussels, in the case of the Duke and Duchess of Coburg, who unconsciously handed on the unwelcome gift to King Leopold's sons, the Due de Brabant and the Comte de Flandres, the former on the eve of his marriage, before the illness was taken across Germany to Coburg.

By the 6th of August, the birthday of Prince Alfred, the Queen and the Prince were sufficiently recovered to pay a second visit with their children to Chobham, when a fresh series of manoeuvres were performed prior to the breaking up of the camp.

A great cluster of royal visitors had arrived in England, making the season brilliant. It was, perhaps, significant that these visitors included three Russian archduchesses, in spite of the fact that a war with Russia was in the air, being only held back by the strenuous efforts of statesmen, against the wishes of the people. Other visitors were the Crown Prince and Princess of Wurtemberg, near akin to Russia, and the Prince of Prussia—the later came from Ostend, on an invitation to witness a sight well calculated to recommend itself to his martial proclivities—a review, on the grandest scale, of the fleet at Spithead, on the 11th of August. The weather was fine, and the spectacle, perfect of its kind, was seen by all the royal company, by what was in effect "the House of Commons with the Speaker at its head," and by multitudes in more than a hundred steamers, besides, the crowds viewing the scene from the shores of the Isle of Wight and Hampshire. On the 21st of August, a French sailor whose name has become a household word in England, died far away amidst the horrors of the north seas, in a gallant effort to rescue Sir John Franklin and his crew. Among the brave men who sailed on this perilous quest, none earned greater honour and love than young Bellot.

On the 22nd of August, a marriage of some interest to the Queen was celebrated at Brussels. King Leopold's eldest son, the Due de Brabant, was married in St. Gudule's to the Archduchess Marie Henriette of Austria. The bridegroom was only eighteen years of age, the bride as young; but it was considered desirable that the heir-apparent should marry, and Queen Louise's place had remained vacant while her daughter, Princess Charlotte, was still unfit to preside over the

Court in her mother's room.

On the 29th of August, Sir Charles Napier, the dauntless, eccentric conqueror of Scinde, follows his old commander to the grave. Though more than ten year's younger, Sir Charles's last public appearance was at the Duke's funeral. He was the grandson of Lord Napier, and the son of the beautiful Lady Sarah Lennox.

A great art and industrial exhibition at Dublin—the first of the numerous progeny of the Great Exhibition of two years before—was held this year. Naturally, the Queen and the Prince were much interested in its fortunes, and had promised to be present at the opening, but were prevented by the outbreak of measles in June. It was possible, however, to visit the Irish Exhibition before its close, and this her Majesty and Prince Albert did on their way to Balmoral. Proceeding by train to Holyhead, where they were detained a day and a night by a violent storm, the travellers sailed on the 29th of August for Kingstown, which was reached next morning. On landing they were received by the Lord-Lieutenant, Lord St. Germains and Lady St. Germains, the Archbishop of Dublin, the Duke of Leinster, &c., &c., together with an immense number of people, lining the dock walls and hailing her Majesty's arrival with vociferous cheers, as on her last visit to Ireland. Enthusiasm, equal to what had been shown before, was displayed on the railway route and the drive through the thronged streets to the Viceregal Lodge. Not long after her arrival, the Queen, as energetic as ever, was seen walking in the Phoenix Park, and in the evening she took a drive in the outskirts of the city. At night Dublin was illuminated. The next day the Queen and the Prince, with their two elder sons, paid a State visit to the exhibition, full to overflowing with eager gazers. The royal party were conducted to a dais, where the Queen, seated on the throne prepared for her, received the address of the commissioners thanking her for the support she had lent to the undertaking by her presence, and by her contributions to the articles exhibited.

The Queen replied, expressing her satisfaction that the worthy enterprise had been carried out in a spirit of energy and self- reliance, "with no pecuniary aid but that derived from the patriotic munificence of one of her subjects." That subject, Mr. Dargan, who had erected the exhibition building at his own expense, was present, and kissed hands amidst the cheers of the assembly. The Queen and the Prince afterwards made the circuit of the whole place, specially commending the Irish manufactures of lace, poplin, and pottery.

In, the afternoon her Majesty and Prince Albert, to the high gratification of the citizens of Dublin, drove out through pouring rain to Mount Annville, the house of Mr. Dargan, saw its beautiful grounds, and conversed with the host and hostess. His manner struck the Queen as "touchingly modest and simple," and she wrote in her journal, "I would have made him a baronet, but he was anxious it should not be done."

Every morning during their week's stay the royal pair returned unweariedly to the exhibition, and by their interest in its productions, stimulated the interest of others. The old engagements—a review, visits to the castle, and the national schools—occupied what time was left.

On Saturday, the 3rd of September, a beautiful day succeeding miserable weather, the Queen drove slowly through the Dublin streets, "unlined with soldiers," feeling quite sorry that it was the last day after what she called "such a pleasant, gay, and interesting tune in Ireland." Loyal multitudes waited at the station and at Kingstown, cheering the travellers. Lord and. Lady St. Germains went on board the yacht, and dined with hen Majesty and Prince Albert.

On the following morning, the Victoria and Albert crossed to Holyhead.

A glad event at Balmoral that year was the laying of the foundation- stone of the new house. The rite was done with all the usual ceremonies, Mr. Anderson, then the minister of Crathie, praying for a blessing on the work.

CHAPTER XXIV.THE EASTERN QUESTION—APPROACHING WAR—GROSS INJUSTICE TO PRINCE ALBERT—DEATH OF MARIA DA GLORIA.

The return of the Court to England was hastened by what had disturbed the peace of the stay in the North. The beginning of a great war was imminent. The Eastern Question, long a source of trouble, was becoming utterly unmanageable. Russia and Turkey were about to take up arms. Indeed, Russia had already crossed the Danube and occupied the Principalities.

Turkey, in a fever-heat, declared war against Russia, crossed the Danube, and fought with desperate valour and some success at Oltenitza and Kalafat; but matters were brought to a crisis by the nearly utter destruction of the Turkish fleet at Sinope, one of the Turkish ports on the shores of the Black Sea. The French and English Governments uttered a practical protest by informing the Czar, that if his fleet in the south made any further movement against the Turks, the English and French fleets already in the Dardanelles would immediately enter the Black Sea and take active steps in defence of their ally.

In the meantime there had been some commotion in the English Cabinet. Lord Palmerston suddenly resigned, and as quickly resumed office. The ostensible cause of difference between him and his colleagues was the new Reform Bill; but the real motive is believed to have been the Government's tactics with regard to the threatened war. These changed all at once, the change coinciding with the return of Lord Palmerston to office, and suiting the fighting mood of the people. He was once more the favourite of the hour, and in the popular pride and confidence in him, a great injustice was done to another. Startled and angered by Lord Palmerston's withdrawal from the Government, the old clamour about Court prejudice and intrigue, and German objections to Liberal statesmen, broke out afresh, and raged more hotly than ever. Prince Albert was openly mentioned as the hostile influence "behind the throne," and in the Cabinet of which he was a member, against the man who was prepared to assert the dignity of England in spite of all opposition; the man who had uniformly sided with the weak, and spoken the truth of tyrants, let them be in ever so high places; the man at the same time who had approved of the coup d'état. The most unfounded charges of unfaithfulness to English interests, and personal interference for the purpose of gaining his own ends, and working into the hands of foreign Governments, were brought against the Queen's husband. His birth as a German, and his connection with the King of the Belgians and the Orleans family, were loudly dwelt upon. It was treated as an offence on his part that he should attend the Cabinet counsels of which he was a member, and be in the confidence of the Queen, who was his loving wife. He was attacked alike by Liberals and Protectionists; assailed, with hardly an assumption of disguise, both in public and private, and in many of the principal newspapers. The man who little more than two years before, at the time of the Great Exhibition, had been hailed as a general benefactor, and praised as the worthiest of patriots, was now almost the best-abused man in England, pursued with false accusations and reproaches equally false.

"One word more about the credulity of the public," wrote Prince Albert to Baron Stockmar; "you will scarcely credit that my being committed to the Tower was believed all over the country; nay, even 'that the Queen had been arrested!' People surrounded the Tower in thousands to see us brought to it."

All this ingratitude and stupidity must have been galling to its object, in spite of his forbearance, and, if possible, still more exquisitely painful to the Queen, who had felt a natural and just pride, not merely in her husband's fine qualities, but in her people's appreciation of them. The Prince wrote in the same letter, "Victoria has taken the whole affair greatly to heart, and was exceedingly indignant at the attacks." And the Queen wrote with proud tender pain to Lord Aberdeen, "In attacking the Prince, who is one and the same with the Queen herself, the throne is assailed; and she must say she little expected that any portion of her subjects would thus requite the unceasing labours of the Prince."

This unscrupulous accusation was grave enough to demand a refutation in Parliament, which Lord Aberdeen and Lord John Russell were ready to give as soon as the House should meet. During this trying winter, the Queen heard of the melancholy death of her sister queen and girlish acquaintance, who had become a kinswoman by marriage—Maria da Gloria. The two queens were the same in age— thirty-four—and each had become the mother of eight children, but there the similarity ceased. At the birth of her last child—dead born—the Queen of Portugal ended a life neither long nor happy, though she had been fortunate in her second husband. Queen Maria da Gloria lacked Queen Victoria's reasonableness and fairness. The Queen of Portugal started on a wrong course, and continued with it, notwithstanding the better judgment of her husband. She supported the Cabrals—the members of a noble Portuguese family, who held high offices under her government—in ruling unconstitutionally and corruptly. She consented to her people's being deprived of the liberty of the press, and burdened with taxes, till, though her private life was irreproachable, she forfeited their regard. In 1846 civil war broke out, and the Cabrals were compelled to resign; the Count of Soldanha and his party took the place of the former ministers. But the insurrection spread until it was feared the Queen and her husband would be driven out of the country. Suddenly the tide turned; the better portion of the army declared for the Queen, her cause was upheld by the English Government, and peace and the royal authority were restored. But in spite of a pledge that the Cabrals should be excluded from the Government, the elder brother again became Premier, with the old abuse of power. A second revolution was accomplished by Soldanha, to whose control Maria da Gloria had to yield, much against the grain. She was succeeded by her eldest son, Don Pedro, still a minor, with the King-Consort his father for regent, an arrangement which proved satisfactory to the distracted kingdom.

A different event was the premature death of perhaps the most beautiful, and the most fortunate, in the eyes of the world, of the Queen's fair bridesmaids. Lady Sarah Villiers, who had become a princess by her marriage with the son of one of the richest, most aristocratic subjects in Europe, Prince Nicholas Esterhazy—of diamond notoriety, died at Torquay in her thirty-second year.

When Parliament met in January, 1854, the Prince was triumphantly vindicated by the leaders on both sides, but it was not till his death that his character was done full justice to. In the meantime the cloud had broken, and the royal couple rejoiced unaffectedly. The Queen wrote to Baron Stockmar that there was "an immense concourse" of people assembled, and they were very friendly when she went to the House of Lords. The anniversary of the marriage was hailed with fresh gratitude and gladness, and with words written to Germany that fall pathetically on our ears to-day. "This blessed day is full of joyful, tender emotions," are her Majesty's words. "Fourteen happy and blessed years have passed, and I confidently trust many more will, and find us in old age as we are now, happy and devotedly united. Trials we must have; but what are they if we are together?"

It was on this occasion that there was a family masque, of which Baroness Bunsen, who was present, has given a full description. She tells how, between five and six o'clock in the evening, the company followed the Queen and the Prince to a room where a red curtain was let down. They all sat in darkness till the curtain was drawn aside, "and the Princess Alice, who had been dressed to represent 'spring,' recited some verses taken from Thomson's "Seasons," enumerating the flowers which the spring scatters around, and she did it very well, spoke in a distinct and pleasing manner, with excellent modulation, and a tone of voice like that of the Queen. Then the curtain was drawn up, and the whole scene changed, and the Princess Royal represented 'summer,' with Prince Arthur lying upon some sheaves, as if tired with the heat of the harvest work; the Princess Royal also recited verses. Then again there was a change, and Prince Alfred, with a crown of vine-leaves and a panther's skin, represented 'autumn,' and recited also verses and looked very well. Then there was a change to a winter landscape, and the Prince of Wales represented 'winter,' with a white beard and a cloak with icicles or snow-flakes (or what looked like such), and the Princess Louise, warmly clothed, who seemed watching the fire; and the Prince also recited well a passage altered from Thomson.... Then another change was made, and all the seasons were grouped together, and far behind, on high, appeared the Princess Helena, with a long veil hanging on each side down to her feet, and a long cross in her hand, pronouncing a blessing on the Queen and Prince in the name of all the seasons. These verses were composed for the occasion. I understood them to say that St. Helena, remembering her own British extraction, came to utter a blessing on the rulers of her country; and I think it must have been so intended, because Helena the mother of Constantine, the first Christian emperor, was said to have discovered the remains of the cross on which our Saviour was crucified, and so when she is painted she always has a cross in her hand. But grandpapa understood that it was meant for Britannia blessing the royal pair. At any rate, the Princess Helena looked very charming. This was the close; but when the Queen ordered the curtain to be drawn back, we saw the whole royal family, and they were helped to jump down from their raised platforms; and then all came into the light and we saw them well; and the baby, Prince Leopold, was brought in by his nurse, and looked at us all with big eyes, and wanted to go to his papa, Prince Albert. At the dinner-table the Princesses Helena and Louise and Prince Arthur were allowed to come in and stand by their mamma, the Queen, as it a was festival day.... In the evening there was very fine music in St. George's Hall, and the Princess Royal and Princess Alice, and the Prince of Wales and Prince Alfred, were allowed to stop up and hear it, sitting to the right and left of the chairs where sat the Queen and Prince Albert and the Duchess of Kent." Some of the graceful figures in the pretty masque were given, with modifications, by the sculptor's art. Four are reproduced in the engravings in this book, that of the Princess Royal at page 146, that of Princess Alice at page 190, that of the Prince of Wales at page 153, and that of Prince Alfred at page 224, Volume First. On the 7th of February Baron Brunnow, who had been Russian ambassador in England for fifteen years, quitted London. Notes were dispatched on the 27th from London and Paris to St. Petersburg, calling on Russia to evacuate the Principalities, a summons to which the Czar declined to reply. War was declared in a supplemental gazette, and on the 31st of March the declaration was read, according to ancient usage, from the steps of the Royal Exchange by the Sergeant-at-Arms of the City of London, to a great crowd that wound up the ceremony by giving three cheers for the Queen. Part of the troops had already embarked, their marching and embarkation being witnessed by multitudes with the utmost interest and enthusiasm. The chief sight was the departure of the Guards, the Grenadiers leaving by gaslight on the winter morning, the Fusiliers marching to Buckingham Palace, where at seven o'clock the Queen and the Prince, with their children, were ready to say good-bye. "They formed line, presented arms, and then cheered us very heartily, and went off cheering," the Queen wrote to the King of the Belgians.... "Many sorrowing friends were there, and one saw the shake of many a hand. My best wishes and prayers went with them all." It was a famous scene, which is remembered to this day. Another episode was that of the Duchess of Cambridge and her daughter, the Princess Mary, taking leave of the brigade with which the Duke of Cambridge, the only son and brother, left.

Her Majesty and the Prince started for Osborne in the course of the next fortnight, to visit the superb fleet which was to sail from Spithead under Sir Charles Napier. "It will be a solemn moment," the Queen wrote again to Lord Aberdeen; "many a heart will be very heavy, and many a prayer, including our own, will be offered up for its safety and glory." In spite of the bad weather, which marred the arrangements, the Queen sailed from Portsmouth in the Fairy, and passing the Victory, with its heroic associations, went through the squadron of twenty great vessels, amidst the booming of the guns, the manning of the yards, and the cheers of the sailors. The following day the little Fairy, with its royal occupants, played a yet more striking part. At the head of the outward-bound squadron, it sailed with the ships for several miles, then stopped for the fleet to pass by, the Queen standing waving her handkerchief to the flag-ship. Her Majesty was, as she said, "very enthusiastic" about her army and navy, and wished she had sons in both of them, though she foresaw how she would suffer when she heard of the losses of her brave men. If she had not sons in either service, her cousin, the Duke of Cambridge, was with the Guards for a time, and her young nephews, Prince Victor of Hohenlohe and Prince Ernest Leiningen, were with their ships. The Queen paid the same compliment of giving a farewell greeting to the second division of the fleet.

When the address to the Throne in reply to the Queen's message announcing the declaration of war was presented, her Majesty and the Prince were accompanied to the House for the first time by the Prince of Wales, a boy of thirteen.

In the middle of the worry, the season was gay as if no life-blood was drained in strong currents from the country; and Varna, with its cholera swamps, where the troops had encamped on Turkish soil, was not present to all men's minds. The Queen set an example in keeping up the social circulation without which there would be a disastrous collapse of more than one department of trade. On May-day, Prince Arthur's birthday, there was a children's ball, attended by two hundred small guests, at Buckingham Palace. Sir Theodore Martin quotes her Majesty's merry note, inviting the Premier to come and see "a number of happy little people, including some of his grandchildren, enjoying themselves." Among the grandchildren of Lord Aberdeen were the young sons of Lord Haddo—sinking under a long wasting illness—George, sixth Earl of Aberdeen, who, when he came to man's estate, served as an ordinary seaman in a merchant ship, where his rank was unsuspected, and who perished by being washed overboard on a stormy night; and the Honourable James Gordon, who died from the bursting of his gun when he was keeping his terms at Cambridge.

The Queen honoured Count Walewski, the French ambassador, by her presence at one of the most brilliant of costume balls. A great Court ball was followed by a great Court concert, at which Lablache sang again in England after an interval of many years. Among the visitors to London in June were poor Maria da Gloria's sons, Coburgs on the father's side, young King Pedro of Portugal, and his brother, the Duke of Oporto, fine lads who were much liked wherever they went.

The Queen and the Prince spent her Majesty's birthday at Osborne, and commemorated it to their children by putting them in possession of the greatest treasure of their happy childhood—the Swiss cottage in the grounds, about a mile from the Castle, in which youthful princes and princesses played at being men and women, practised the humbler duties of life, and kept natural history collections and geological specimens, as their father and uncle had kept theirs in the museum at Coburg. Another great resource consisted of the plots of ground—among which the Princess Royal's was a fair-sized garden, ultimately nine in number, where the amateur gardeners studied gardening in the most practical manner, and had their tiny tool-house, with the small spades and rakes properly grouped and duly lettered, "Prince Alfred" or "Princess Louise," as the case might be. A third idea, borrowed like the first from Coburg, was the miniature fort, with its mimic defences, every brick of which was made and built, and the very cannon-balls founded, by the two sons destined to be soldiers—the Prince of Wales and Prince Arthur.

Before the end of the season cholera broke out in London. Among its victims was Lord Jocelyn, eldest son of Lord Roden, and husband of Lady Fanny Cowper. He had been on guard at the palace, and died after an illness of not more than two hours' duration in the drawing-room of his mother-in-law, Lady Palmerston.

The Queen came up to town to prorogue Parliament in person. Afterwards her Majesty and the Prince spent his birthday at Osborne, when one of the amusements, no doubt with a view to the entertainment of the children as well as of the grown-up people, was Albert Smith's "Ascent of Mont Blanc," which was then one of the comic sights of London.

Early in September Prince Albert, in compliment to the alliance between England and France, went, by the Emperor's invitation, to visit the French camp at St. Omer, and was absent four or five days. The Prince's letters were as constant and lover-like as ever.

On the 15th of September the Court arrived at Balmoral, and the same day the Queen received the news of the sailing of the English and French soldiers for the Crimea. An anxious but brief period of suspense followed. Six days later came the tidings of the successful landing, without opposition, in the neighbourhood of Eupatoria.

Lord Aberdeen came on a visit to Balmoral, and had just left when the glad tidings arrived of the victory of the Alma, followed immediately by a false report of the fall of Sebastopol.

During this year's stay in the north, her Majesty met for the first time a remarkable Scotchman whom she afterwards honoured with her friendship. Both the Queen and Dr. Macleod describe the first sermon he preached before her, on Christian life. He adds, "In the evening, after daundering in a green field with a path through it which led to the high-road, and while sitting on a block of granite, full of quiet thoughts, mentally reposing in the midst of the beautiful scenery, I was roused from my reverie by some one asking me if I was the clergyman who had preached that day. I was soon in the presence of the Queen and Prince, when her Majesty came forward and said with a sweet, kind, and smiling face, 'We wish to thank you for your sermon.' She then asked me how my father was, what was the name of my parish, &c.; and so, after bowing and smiling, they both continued their quiet evening walk alone." [Footnote: Life of Dr. Norman Macleod.]

The Court returned from Balmoral by Edinburgh. At Hull, and again at Grimsby, the Queen and the Prince inspected the docks, of which he had laid the foundation stones.

CHAPTER XXV. THE BATTLE OF INKERMANN—FLORENCE NIGHTINGALE—THE DEATH OF THE EMPEROR NICHOLAS.

In the beginning of November England heard with mingled triumph and pain of the repulsed attack on the English at Balaclava on the 25th of October, and of the charge of the Light Brigade. The number of the English soldiers in the field fell lower and lower. The Queen wrote to King Leopold, "We have but one thought, and so has the nation, and that is—Sebastopol. Such a time of suspense, anxiety, and excitement, I never expected to see, much less to feel."

On the 13th of November telegrams arrived with the news of the battle of Inkermann, fought against terrible odds on the 5th.

The Queen wrote herself to Lord Raglan to tell of her "pride and joy" at receiving the intelligence of "the glorious, but alas! bloody victory of the 5th." She conferred upon him the baton of a Field-Marshal. Her Majesty also addressed a kind and sympathising letter to the widow of Sir George Cathcart.

The Queen wrote with high indignation to the King of the Belgians after the battle of Inkermann: "They (the enemy) behaved with the greatest barbarity; many of our poor officers who were only slightly wounded were brutally butchered on the ground. Several lived long enough to say this. When poor Sir G. Cathcart fell mortally wounded, his faithful and devoted military secretary (Colonel Charles Seymour) ... sprang from his horse, and with one arm—he was wounded in the other—supported his dying chief, when three wretches came and bayoneted him. This is monstrous, and requisitions have been sent by the two commanders-in-chief to Menschikoff to remonstrate...."

The winter of 1854-55 was a sorrowful and care-laden time. Little or no progress was made in the war, while in the meanwhile the sufferings of the soldiers from a defective commissariat, a rigorous climate, and the recurring ravages of cholera, were frightful. The very winds and waves seemed to fight against the allies and to side with "Holy Russia." Never had the Black Sea been visited by such storms and wrecks.

From the palace to the cottage, women's fingers worked eagerly and unweariedly knitting comforters and muffatees to protect the throats and wrists of the shivering men. We have heard that the greatest lady in the land deigned thus to serve her soldiers. We have been told of a cravat worked in crochet by a queen's fingers which fell to the share of a gallant young officer in the trenches—the same brave lad who had carried, unscathed, the colours of his regiment to the heights of the Alma.

The hospitals were in as disorganised a state as the commissariat, and Mr. Sydney Herbert, well-nigh in despair, had the bright inspiration of sending to the seat of war Florence Nightingale, the daughter and co-heiress of a Derbyshire squire, with a staff of nurses.

Such reformation of abuses was wrought by a capable devoted woman, such order brought out of disorder, such comfort and consolation carried to wounded and dying men, that the experiment became a triumphant success. Many were the stories told of the soldiers' boundless reverence for the woman who had left country and friends and all the good things that wealth and rank can command to relieve her fellow-creatures; how one of them was seen to kiss her shadow on the wall of his ward as she passed; how the convalescents engaged in strange and wonderful manufactures of gifts to offer to her.

A second large instalment of nurses was sent out after the first, the latter led by Mary Stanley, daughter of the Bishop of Norwich, and sister of the Dean of Westminster, who had already been a sister to the poor in her father's diocese.

The Queen wrote again to Lord Raglan, "The sad privations of the army, the bad weather, and the constant sickness, are causes of the deepest concern and anxiety to the Queen and the Prince. The braver her noble troops are, the more patiently and heroically they bear all their trials and sufferings, the more miserable we feel at their long continuance. The Queen trusts that Lord Raglan will be very strict in seeing that no unnecessary privations are incurred by any negligence of those whose duty it is to watch over their wants.

"The Queen heard that their coffee was given them green instead of roasted, and some other things of this kind, which have distressed her, as she feels so anxious that they should be as comfortable as circumstances can admit of. The Queen earnestly trusts that the large amount of warm clothing sent out has not only reached Balaclava, but has been distributed, and that Lord Raglan has been successful in procuring the means of hutting for the men. Lord Raglan cannot think how much we suffer for the army, and how painfully anxious we are to know that their privations are decreasing…. The Queen cannot conclude without wishing Lord Raglan and the whole of the army, in the Prince's name and her own, a happy and glorious new year."

No sooner had Parliament reassembled than Mr. Roebuck brought forward his famous motion for the appointment of a committee to inquire into the state of the army and the management of the War Department of the Government.

Lord John Russell resigned office, and there was a threatened resignation of the whole Ministry, an ill-timed step, which was only delayed till Mr. Roebuck's motion was carried, by a large majority, not amidst the cheers, but to the odd accompaniment of the derisive laughter of the Liberal members who had voted for the motion. Lord Aberdeen's Ministry immediately resigned office; and after an abortive attempt on the part of Lord Derby, at the request of the Queen, to form a new Ministry, Lord Lansdowne and Lord John Russell were in succession asked to take the leadership, but each in his turn had to own his inability to get the requisite men to act under him. In summoning Lord John Russell to become Premier, the Queen had expressed a wish that Lord Palmerston—the man to whom the country looked as the only proper war minister—should take office. The wish, especially flattering and acceptable to Lord Palmerston, because it indicated that old differences were forgotten, was in marked keeping with a certain magnanimity and candour—excellent qualities in a sovereign— which have been prominent features in her Majesty's character.

Lord John Russell having been as unsuccessful as his predecessors in forming a Ministry, Lord Palmerston was sent for by the Queen and offered the premiership, and the most popular minister of the day was soon able, to the jubilation of the country, to construct a Cabinet.

On the 10th of February, the anniversary of the Queen's marriage-day, there was this year, as usual, a home festival, with the nursery drama of "Little Red Riding Hood" performed by the younger members of the family, and appropriate verses spoken by Princess Alice, who seems to have been the chosen declaimer among the princes and princesses. But beneath the rejoicing there were in the elders anxiety, sympathetic suffering, and the endurance of undeserved suspicion. The committee carrying out the inquiry proposed by Mr. Roebuck's motion, conceived most unjustly that the Prince's hostile influence prevented them from obtaining the information they desired. The Queen's health was suffering from her distress on account of the hardships experienced by her soldiers, so that when Lord Cardigan returned to England, repaired to Windsor, and had the royal children upon his knee, they said, "You must hurry back to Sebastopol and take it, else it will kill mamma!"

On the 2nd of March the strange news burst upon Europe, exciting rather a sense of solemnity than any less seemly feeling, of the sudden death of the Emperor Nicholas, former guest and fervent friend of the Queen—for whom she seems to have retained a lingering, rueful regard— grasper at an increase of territory, disturber of the peace of Europe, dogged refuser of all mediation. He had an attack of influenza, but the real cause of his death is said to have been bitter disappointment and mortification at his failure to drive the allies out of the Crimea. The "Generals, January and February," on whom he had counted to work his will, laid him low.

CHAPTER XXVI.INSPECTION OF THE HOSPITAL AT CHATHAM—

VISIT OF THE EMPEROR AND EMPRESS OF THE FRENCH— DISTRIBUTION OF WAR MEDALS.

On the 3rd of March, the Queen and the Prince, with the Prince of Wales, Prince Alfred and the Duke of Cambridge, visited the hospital at Chatham, to which many of the wounded and sick soldiers had been brought home. The whole of the invalids who were in a condition to leave their beds "were drawn up on the lawn," each having a card containing his name and services, his wounds, and where received. Her Majesty passed along the line, saying a few kind words to those sufferers who particularly attracted her notice, or to those whose services were specially commended. It is easy to imagine how the haggard faces would brighten and the drooping figures straighten themselves in that royal and gentle presence.

In the course of the month, at an exhibition and sale of water-colour drawings and pictures by amateurs, in aid of a fund for the widows and orphans of officers in the Crimea, the artistic talent of which there have been many proofs in the Queen's and the Prince's children, was first publicly shown. A water-colour drawing by the Princess Royal, already a fine girl of fifteen—whose marriage was soon to be mooted, in which she had represented a woman weeping over a dead grenadier, displayed remarkable merit and was bought for a large price.

On the 16th of April the Emperor and Empress of the French arrived in England on a visit to the Queen. The splendid suite of rooms in Windsor Castle which includes the Rubens, Zuccarelli, and Vandyck rooms, were destined for the imperial guests. And we are told that, by the irony of fate, the Emperor's bedroom was the same that had been occupied on previous occasions by the late Emperor Nicholas and King Louis Philippe. Sir Theodore Martin refers to a still more pathetic contrast which struck the Queen. He quotes from her Majesty's journal a passage relating to a visit paid by the old Queen Amélie to Windsor two or three days before. "It made us both so sad to see her drive away in a plain coach with miserable post-horses, and to think that this was the Queen of the French, and that six years ago her husband was surrounded by the same pomp and grandeur which three days hence would surround his successor."

Prince Albert received the travellers at Dover in the middle of a thick mist which had delayed the corvette, hidden the English fleet, and somewhat marred what was intended to have been the splendour of the reception. After the train had reached London, the drive was through densely crowded streets, in which there was no lack of enthusiasm for the visitors.

The strangers did not reach Windsor till past seven. The Queen had been waiting for them some time in one of the tapestry rooms near the guard-room. "The expectation and agitation grew more intense," her Majesty wrote in her diary. "The evening was fine and bright. At length the crowd of anxious spectators lining the road seemed to move; then came a groom; then we heard a gun, and we moved towards the staircase. Another groom came. Then we saw the advanced guard of the escort; then the cheers of the crowd burst forth. The outriders appeared, the doors opened, I stepped out, the children and Princes close behind me; the band struck up "Partant pour la Syrie," the trumpets sounded, and the open carriage, with the Emperor and Empress, Albert sitting opposite to them, drove up, and they got out.

"I cannot say what indescribable emotions filled me, how much all seemed like a wonderful dream. These great meetings of sovereigns, surrounded by very exciting accompaniments, are always very agitating. I advanced and embraced the Emperor, who received two salutes on either cheek from me, having first kissed my hand. I next embraced the very gentle, graceful, and evidently very nervous Empress. We presented the Princes (the Duke of Cambridge and the Prince of Leiningen, the Queen's brother) and our children (Vicky, with very alarmed eyes, making very low curtsies); the Emperor embraced Bertie; and then we went upstairs, Albert leading the Empress, who in the most engaging manner refused to go first, but at length with graceful reluctance did so, the Emperor leading me, expressing his great gratification at being here and seeing me, and admiring Windsor." [Footnote: Life of the Prince Consort.]

Her Majesty was pleased with the Emperor; his low soft voice and quiet manner were very attractive. She was delighted with the Empress, of whom she repeatedly wrote with admiration and liking. "She is full courage and spirit," the Queen described her visitor, "yet so gentle, with such innocence and enjouement, that the ensemble is most charming. With all her great liveliness, she has the prettiest and most modest manner." There were morning walks during the visitors' stay, and long conversations about the war. A deputation from the Corporation of London came down to Windsor, and presented the Emperor with an address. There was a review of the Household troops in the Great Park, to which the Queen drove with the Empress. The Emperor, the Prince, and the Duke of Cambridge rode. There was a tremendous enthusiastic crowd in the Long Walk, and considerable pushing at the gates. The Queen was alarmed because of the spirited horse the Emperor rode.

The day ended with a ball in the Waterloo Room, when the Queen danced a quadrille with the Emperor, who, she wrote, "danced with great dignity and spirit. How strange" she added "to think that I, the grand-daughter of George III., should dance with the Emperor Napoleon, nephew of England's great enemy, now my nearest and most intimate ally, in the Waterloo Room, and this ally only sixteen years ago living in this country in exile, poor and unthought of."

A Council of War was held the day after the Emperor's arrival, at which the Queen was not present. It was attended by the Emperor, the Prince, Lords Palmerston, Panmure, Hardinge, Cowley (English ambassador in Paris), Count Walewski (French ambassador in London), Marshal Vaillant, &c., &c. It met at eleven, and had not separated at two, the hour of luncheon, after which a chapter of the Order of the Garter—for which special toilettes were indispensable, was to be held. The Empress went and told Lord Cowley how late it was, in vain. She advised the Queen to go to them. "I dare not go in, but your Majesty may; it is your affair." The Queen passed through the Emperor's bedroom, which was next to the council-room, knocked, and entered to ask what was to be done, perhaps a solitary instance of a queen having to go in search of her guests. Both the Emperor and the Prince rose and said they would come, but business was so enchaining that still they delayed, and the ladies had to take luncheon alone.

The Emperor was invested with the Order of the Garter in the Throne-room. The forms were the same as those followed in the investiture of Louis Philippe, and no doubt the one scene recalled the other vividly enough. Bishop Wilberforce was present and gives some particulars: "A very full chapter. The Duke of Buckingham (whose conduct had not been very knightly) came unsummoned, and was not asked to remain to dinner. The Emperor looked exulting and exceedingly pleased." After the chapter, the Emperor sent for the Bishop, that he might be presented. His lordship's opinion was that Louis Napoleon was "rather mean-looking, small, and a tendency to embonpoint; a remarkable way, as it were, of swimming up a room, with an uncertain gait; a small grey eye, looking cunning, but with an aspect of softness about it too. The Empress, a peculiar face from the arched eye-brows, blonde complexion; an air of sadness about her, but a person whose countenance at once interests you. The banquet was magnificent. At night," ends Bishop Wilberforce, "the Queen spoke to me. 'All went off very well, I think; I was afraid of making some mistake; you would not let me have in writing what I was to say to him. Then we put the riband on wrong, but I think it all went off well on the whole.'"

The Emperor and Empress were invited to a banquet at Guildhall. They went from Buckingham Palace, to which the Queen and Prince Albert had accompanied them. The Queen wrote in her journal that their departure from Windsor made her sad. The passing through the familiar rooms and descending the staircase to the mournful strains of "Partant pour la Syrie" (composed by the Emperor's mother, Queen Hortense, and heard by her Majesty fourteen different times that April day), the sense that the visit about which there had been so much excitement was nearly over, the natural doubt how and when the group would meet again, touched her as with a sense of foreboding.

The Emperor and Empress drove from Buckingham Palace to Guildhall in six of the Queen's State carriages, the first drawn by the famous cream-coloured horses. The whole route was packed with people, who gave the visitors a thorough ovation. The City hall was decorated with the flags of England, France, and Turkey; and the lion and the eagle conjointly supported devices which bore the names "Alma, Balaclava, and Inkermann." At the déjeuner sherry was served which had reached the venerable age of one hundred and nine years, was valued at £600 the butt, and had belonged to the great Napoleon. The same evening, the Queen and the Prince, with their guests, went in State to the Italian Opera, where Fidelio was performed. "We literally drove through a sea of human beings, cheering and pressing near the carriage." The illuminated streets bore many devices—of N.E. and V.A., which the Emperor remarked made the word "Neva"—a coincidence on which he appears to have dwelt with his share of the superstition of the Buonapartes. The Opera-house and the royal box were richly decorated for the occasion. On entering, her Majesty led the Emperor, and Prince Albert the Empress, to the front of the box, amidst great applause. The audience was immense, a dense mass of ladies and gentlemen in full dress being allowed to occupy a place behind the singers on the stage.

The next day, a beautiful April day, the Queen discovered was the forty-seventh birthday of the Emperor; and when she went to meet him in the corridor, she wished him joy and gave him a pencil-case. He smiled and kissed her hand, and accepted with empressment two violets— the Buonapartes' flower—brought to him by Prince Arthur. All along the thronged road to Sydenham, cries of "Vive l'Empereur!" and "Vive l'Impératrice!" alternated with cheers for the Queen. The public were not admitted while the royal party were in the palace, but they gathered twenty thousand strong on the terrace; and when her Majesty, with her guests, came out on the balcony to enjoy the beautiful view, such shouts of loyalty and welcome filled the spring air as struck even ears well accustomed to public greetings. After luncheon the Queen and her visitors returned to the Palace, having to pass through an avenue of people lining the nave, to reach the balcony from which the strangers were to see the fine spectacle of the fountains playing. The Queen owned afterwards she was anxious; yet, she added, "I felt as I leant on the emperor's arm, that I was possibly a protection for him. All thoughts of nervousness for myself were lost. I thought only of him; and so it is, Albert says, when one forgets oneself, one loses this great and foolish nervousness." A sentence worthy of him and of her.

Alas for fickle fortune and the changes which time brings! The present writer was accidentally present on the occasion of the Emperor and Empress's last visit to the Crystal Palace. They came from Chislehurst without any announcement, when they were not expected, on an ordinary shilling day in autumn, the company happening to be few. A slight stir and one or two policemen coming to the front, suggested that some theft had been committed, and that the offender was about to be taken into custody and removed from the building. Then an official walked bareheaded down the cleared nave, and behind him came a little yellow-skinned shrunken man in plain clothes, on whose arm a lady in a simple black silk walking-dress and country hat leant lightly, as if she were giving instead of receiving support. He made a slight attempt to acknowledge the faint greetings of the spectators, some of them ignorant of the identity of the visitors, all of them taken by surprise. She smiled and bowed from side to side, a little mechanically, as if anxious to overlook no courtesy and to act for both. It was not long after the battle of Sedan and the imprisonment at Wilhelmshöhe, and the hand of death was already upon him. The couple hurried on, as if desirous of not being detained, and could not have tarried many minutes in the building when a few straggling cheers announced their departure.

In the afternoon of the 20th of April a second council relating to the war in the Crimea was held, at which the Queen was present. With her large interest in public affairs, her growing experience, and her healthy appetite for the work of her life, she enjoyed it exceedingly. "It was one of the most interesting scenes I was ever present at," she wrote in her journal. "I would not have missed it for the world."

On Saturday, the 21st of April, the visitors left, after the Emperor had written a graceful French sentence in the Queen's album, and an admonitory verse in German, which had originally been written for himself, in the Prince of Wales's autograph book. The Queen accompanied her visitors to the door, and parted from them with kindly regret. As they drove off she "ran up" to see the last of the travellers from the saloon they had just quitted. "The Emperor and Empress saw us at the window," she wrote, "turned round, got up, and bowed…. We watched them, with the glittering escort, till they could be seen no more…." The Prince escorted the Emperor and Empress to Dover. The Queen wrote in a short memorandum her view of the Emperor's character, and what she expected from the visit in a political light. Through the good sense of the paper one can see how the confiding friendly nature had survived the rough check given to it by Louis Philippe's manoeuvres and dissimulation.

On the 1st of May the Academy opened with Millais's "Rescue of children from a burning house," and with a remarkable picture by a young painter who has long since vindicated the reception it met with. It was Mr. F. Leighton's "Procession conveying Cimabue's Madonna through the streets of Florence."

On the 18th of May her Majesty distributed medals to some of the heroes of the war still raging. The scene was both picturesque and pathetic, since many of the recipients of the honour were barely recovered from their wounds. The presentation took place in the centre of the parade of the Horse Guards, where a dais was erected for the ceremony, while galleries had been fitted up in the neighbouring public offices for the accommodation of members of the royal family and nobility. Barriers shut off the actors in the scene, and a great gathering of officers, from the crowd which filled every inch of open space and flowed over into St. James's Park.

The Queen, the Prince, with many of the royal family, the Court, the Commander-in-Chief, the Secretary for War, and "a host of generals and admirals," arrived about eleven o'clock. The soldiers who kept the ground formed four deep, making three sides of a square, and the men to be decorated passed up the open space, until "the Queen stood face to face with a mass of men who had suffered and bled in her cause."

The Deputy-Adjutant-General read over the list of names, and each person, answering to the call, presented to an officer a card on which was inscribed his name, rank, wounds, and battles. As the soldiers passed in single file before the Queen, Lord Panmure handed to her Majesty the medal, which she gave in turn to the medal-holder. He saluted and passed to the rear, where friends and strangers gathered round him to inspect his trophy.

The first to receive the medal were the Queen's cousin and contemporary, the Duke of Cambridge, Lords Lucan, Cardigan, Major- General Scarlett, Sir John Burgoyne, Sir De Lacy Evans, and Major- General Torrens. It is needless to say how keenly the public were moved by the sight of their brave defenders, several of them scarred and mutilated, many tottering from weakness, some wearing on their sleeves bands of crape, tokens of mourning for kinsmen lying in Russian earth.

To every wounded man, officer or private, her Majesty spoke, some of those addressed blushing like girls under their bronze, and the tears coming into their eyes. The idea of personally presenting the medals to the soldiers was the Queen's own, and she must have been amply rewarded by the gratification she bestowed.

Three officers unable to walk were wheeled past her Majesty in bath- chairs. Among them was young Sir Thomas Troubridge, both of whose feet had been carried off by a round shot, while he had continued commanding his battery till the battle was over, refusing to be taken away, only desiring his shattered limbs to be raised in order to check the loss of blood. The Queen leant over Sir Thomas's chair and handed him his medal, while she announced to him his appointment as one of her aides-de-camp. He replied, "I am amply repaid for everything."

CHAPTER XXVII.DEATH OP LORD RAGLAN—VISIT OF THE QUEEN AND PRINCE ALBERT TO THE EMPEROR AND EMPRESS OF THE FRENCH—FALL OF SEBASTOPOL.

A Sardinian contingent had now, by a stroke of policy on the part of Count Cavour, the Sardinian Minister, joined the English and French in arms in the Crimea; but an unsuccessful attack, made with heavy loss by the combined forces of the English and French on Sebastopol, filled the country with disappointment and sorrow. The attack was made on the 18th of June, a day which, as the anniversary of Waterloo, had been hitherto associated with victory and triumph.

Lord Raglan had never approved of the assault, but he yielded to the urgent representations of General Pelissier. The defeat was the last blow to the old English soldier, worn by fatigue and chagrin. He was seized with illness ending in cholera, and died in his quarters on the 29th of June, eleven days after the repulse. He was in his sixty- seventh year. The Queen wrote to Lady Raglan the day after the tidings of the death reached England.

During the summer the Queen received visits from King Leopold and his younger children, and from her Portuguese cousins. During the stay of the former in England scarlet fever broke out in the royal nurseries. Princess Louise, Prince Arthur, Prince Leopold, and finally Princess Alice, were attacked; but the disease was not virulent, and the remaining members of the family escaped the infection.

In the early morning of the 16th of August, the Russians marched upon the French lines, and were completely routed in the battle of the Tchernaya, which revived the allies' hopes of a speedy termination of the war.

In the meantime, the Queen and Prince Albert, accompanied by the Prince of Wales and the Princess Royal, paid a visit to the Emperor and Empress of the French, near Paris. The palace of St. Cloud was set apart for the use of the Queen and the Prince.

Her Majesty landed at Boulogne during the forenoon of the 18th of August. She was received by the Emperor, who met her on the gangway, first kissed her hand, and then kissed her on both cheeks. He led her on shore, and rode by the side of her carriage to the railway station.

Paris, where no English sovereign had been since the baby Henry VI. was crowned King of France, was not reached till evening. The city had been en fête all day with banners, floral arches, and at last an illumination. Amidst the clatter of soldiers, the music of brass bands playing "God save the Queen," and endless cheering, her Majesty drove through the gathering darkness by the Bois de Boulogne to St. Cloud. To the roar of cannon, the beating of drums, and the echoing of vivats, she was greeted and ushered up the grand staircase by the Empress and the Princess Mathilde. Everybody was "most civil and kind," and in the middle of the magnificence all was "very quiet and royal."

The next day was Sunday, and after breakfast there was a drive with the Emperor through the beautiful park, where host and guests were very cheerful over good news from Sebastopol. The English Church service was read by a chaplain from the Embassy in one of the palace rooms. In the afternoon the Emperor and the Empress drove with their guests to the Bois de Boulogne, and to Neuilly—so closely associated with the Orleans family—lying in ruins. General Canrobert, just returned from the Crimea, was an addition to the dinner party.

On Monday the weather continued lovely. The Emperor fetched his guests to breakfast, which, like luncheon, was eaten at small round tables, as in her Majesty's residences in England. She remarked on the cookery that it was "very plain and very good." After breakfast the party started in barouches for Paris, visiting the Exposition des Beaux Arts and the Palais d'Industrie, passing through densely crowded streets, amidst enthusiastic shouts of "Vive l'Empereur!" "Vive la Reine d'Angleterre!" At the Elysée the corps diplomatique were presented to the Queen. In the meantime, the Emperor himself drove the boy Prince of Wales in a curricle through Paris. Afterwards the Queen and Prince Albert, in the company of the Emperor, visited the beautiful Sainte Chapelle and the Palais de Justice. On the way the Emperor pointed out the conciergerie as the place where he had been imprisoned.

Nôtre Dame, where the Archbishop of Paris and his clergy met the visitors, and the Hôtel de Ville, followed in the regular order of sightseeing.

The Queen dwells not only on the kindness but on the quietness of the Emperor as a particular "comfort" on such an occasion.

Les Demoiselles de St. Cyr was acted in the evening. In the Salle de Mars all the company passed before the Queen, the Empress presenting each in turn. The Emperor and Empress, preceded by their gentlemen, always took the Queen and the Prince to their rooms.

On, Tuesday Versailles was the visitors' destination. They went in many carriages. Troops and national guards, and especially gendarmes, were to be seen everywhere. The gardens and the fountains, with throngs of company, were much admired.

The Queen visited the two Trianons. At the larger the Emperor showed her the room and bed provided for her, in the expectation of her visiting Paris, by "poor Louis Philippe;" Madame Maintenon's sedan- chair, by which Louis XIV. was wont to walk; and the little chapel in which "poor Marie (Louis Philippe's daughter) was married to Alexander of Wurtemberg in 1838," two years before the Queen's marriage.

At Little Trianon the Empress (who had a passion for every relic of Marie Antoinette) joined the party, and luncheon was eaten in one of the cottages where princes and nobles were wont to play at being peasants.

In the evening the Emperor, with his guests, paid a State visit to the opera-house in the Rue Lepelletier. Part of the performance was a representation of Windsor Castle, with the Emperor's reception there, when "God save the Queen" was splendidly sung, and received with acclamation. The Emperor's happy animation, in contrast to his usual impassiveness, was remarked by the audience.

Wednesday's visit, in the continuously fine August weather, was to the French Exhibition, which the Queen and the Prince were so well calculated to appreciate. They rejoiced in the excellent manner in which England was represented, particularly in pottery. The specially French productions of Sèvres, Goblins, and Beauvais were carefully studied. The Queen also examined the French Crown jewels, the crown bearing the renowned Regent diamond, which, though less large than the Koh-i-noor, is more brilliant. The Emperor presented the Prince with a magnificent Sèvres vase, a souvenir of the Exhibition of 1851. The Tuileries was visited, and luncheon taken there in rooms containing pictures and busts or Napoleon I., Josephine, &c., &c. The Queen received the Prefect and consented to attend the ball to be given in her honour.

After a visit to the British Embassy, the Queen and the Prince, with the Princess Royal and one of the ladies of the suite, took a drive incognito through Paris, which they enjoyed exceedingly. They went in an ordinary remise, the three ladies wearing common bonnets and mantillas, and her Majesty having a black veil over her face.

On Thursday morning the Queen rested, walking about the gardens with her young daughter, and sketching the Zouaves at the gate. The afternoon was spent at the Louvre, where the Queen mentions the heat as "tropical."

After dinner at the Tuileries, the party stood laughing together at an old-fashioned imperial cafetière which would not let down the coffee, listening to the music, the carriages, and the people in the distance, and talking of past times; as how could people fail to talk at the Tuileries! The Emperor spoke of having known Madame Campan (to whose school his mother was sent for a time), and repeated some of the old court dresser's anecdotes of Marie Antoinette and the Great Revolution.

In her Majesty's full dress for the ball given to her by the City of
Paris, she wore a diadem in which the Koh-i-noor was set. Through the
illuminated, crammed streets, the Queen proceeded to the Hotel de
Ville, and entered among flags, flowers, and statues, "like the
Arabian Nights," the Emperor said.

The royal visitors occupied chairs on a dais. One quadrille and one valse were danced, the Emperor being the Queen's partner, while Prince Albert danced with Princess Mathilde (the Empress was in delicate health); Prince Napoleon and Madame Haussman (the wife of the Prefect of the Seine), and Prince Adalbert of Bavaria and Lady Cowley (wife of the English ambassador) completing the set.

Several Arabs in long white burnouses were among the guests, and kissed the hands of the Queen and the Emperor. Her Majesty made the tour of the stately suite of rooms, lingering in the one in which "Robespierre was wounded, Louis Philippe proclaimed, and from the windows of which Lamartine spoke for so many hours in 1848."

On Friday there was a second visit to the Exhibition, and in the afternoon a grand review of troops in the Champ de Mars, which the Queen admired much, regretting that she had not been on horseback, though the day was not fine. From the Champ de Mars the visitors drove to the Hôtel des Invalides, and there occurred the most striking scene in the memorable visit, of which the passages from the Queen's journal in the "Life of the Prince Consort," give so many graphic, interesting details. Passing between rows of French veterans, the Queen and the Prince went to look by torchlight at the great tomb, in which, however, all that was mortal of Napoleon I. had not yet been laid. The coffin still rested in a side chapel, to which her Majesty was taken by the Emperor. The coffin was covered with black velvet and gold, and the orders, hat, and sword of "le Petit Caporal" were placed at the foot. The Queen descended for a few minutes into the vault, the air of which struck cold on the living within its walls.

The Emperor took his guests in the evening to the Opéra Comique. It was not a State visit, but "God save the Queen" was sung, and her Majesty had to show herself in front of the Emperor's private box. On Saturday the royal party went to the forest of St. Germain's, and a halt was made at the hunting-lodge of La Muette. The Grand Veneur and his officials in their hunting-dress of dark-green velvet, red waistcoats, high boots, and cocked hats, received the company. The dogs were exhibited, and a fanfare sounded on the huntsmen's horns.

The strangers repaired to the old palace of St. Germain's, where her Majesty saw the suite of rooms which had served as a home for her unhappy kinsman, James II. It is said she went also to his tomb, and stood by it in thoughtful silence for a few minutes. On the return drive to St. Cloud detours were made to Malmaison, where the Emperor remembered to have seen his grandmother, the Empress Josephine, and to the fortress of St. Valérien.

The same night there was a State ball at Versailles. At the top of the grand staircase stood the Empress—"like a fairy queen or nymph," her Majesty writes, "in a white dress trimmed with bunches of grass and diamonds, ..." wearing her Spanish and Portuguese orders. The enamoured Emperor exclaimed in the hearing of his guests, "Comme tu es belle!" (how beautiful you are!) The long Galerie de Glaces, full of people, was blazing with light, and had wreaths of flowers hanging from the ceiling. From the windows the illuminated trellis was seen reflected in the splashing water of the fountains. The balconies commanded a view of the magnificent fireworks, among which Windsor Castle was represented in lines of light.

The Queen danced two quadrilles, with the Emperor and Prince Napoleon,
Prince Albert dancing with Princess Mathilde and the Princess of
Augustenburg. Among the guests presented to her Majesty was Count
Bismarck, Prussian Minister at Frankfort.

The Queen waltzed with the Emperor, and then repaired to the famous Oeil-de-Boeuf, hung with Beauvais tapestry. After the company had gone to supper, the Queen and the Emperor's procession was formed, and headed by guards, officers, &c. &c, they passed to the theatre, where supper was served. The whole stage was covered in, and four hundred people sat in groups of ten, each presided over by a lady, at forty small tables. Innumerable chandeliers and garlands of flowers made the scene still gayer. The boxes were full of spectators, and an invisible band was playing. The Queen and Prince Albert, with their son and daughter, the Emperor and the Empress, Prince Napoleon, Princess Mathilde, and Prince Adalbert of Bavaria, sat at a small table in the central box. Her Majesty seems to have been much struck with this Versailles ball, which was designed and arranged by the Empress from a plate of the time of Louis XV. It was said there had been no ball at Versailles since the time of Louis XVI. The last must have been the ball in the Orangery, on the night that the Bastille fell.

Sunday was Prince Albert's birthday, which was not forgotten among these brilliant doings. Loving hands laid out the flower-decorated table with its gifts. At luncheon the Emperor presented the Prince with a picture by Meissonier. The Empress gave a pokal, or mounted cup, carved in ivory. During a quiet drive with the Emperor through the park in the morning, the Queen, with her characteristic sincerity, courageously approached a topic which was a burden on her mind, on which Baron Stockmar had long advised her to act as she was prepared to do. She spoke of her intercourse with the Orleans family, on which the French ambassador in London had laid stress as likely to displease the Emperor. She said they were her friends and relations, and that she could not drop them in their adversity, but that politics were never touched upon between her and them. He professed himself perfectly satisfied, and sought in his turn to explain his conduct in the confiscation and forced sale of the Orleans property.

The English Church service was read in a room at St. Cloud as before. In the afternoon the Emperor took his guests to the memorial Chapelle de St. Ferdinand, erected on the spot where the late Duc d'Orleans was killed.

On Monday, the 27th of August, the Queen wrote in her diary her deep gratitude for "these eight happy days, for the delight of seeing such beautiful and interesting places and objects," and for the reception she had met with in Paris and France. The Emperor arrived to say the Empress was ready, but could not bring herself to face the parting, and that if the Queen would go to her room it would make her come. "When we went in," writes her Majesty, "the Emperor called her: 'Eugénie, here is the Queen,' and she came," adds her Majesty, "and gave me a beautiful fan, and a rose and heliotrope from the garden, and Vicky a beautiful bracelet, set with rubies and diamonds, containing her hair...."

The morning was beautiful as the travellers, accompanied by the Emperor and Empress, drove for the last time through the town of St. Cloud, with its Zouaves and wounded soldiers from the Crimea, under the Arc de Triomphe, where the ashes of the great Napoleon had passed, to Paris and the Tuileries. There was talk of future meetings at Windsor and Fontainbleau. (And now of the places which the Queen admired so much, St. Cloud and the Tuileries are in ruins like Neuilly, while the Hôtel de Ville has perished by the hands of its own children.) Leave was taken of the Empress not without emotion;

At the Strasbourg railway station the Ministers and municipal authorities were in attendance, and the cordiality was equal to the respect shown by all.

Boulogne, to which the Emperor accompanied his guests, was reached between five and six in the afternoon. There was a review of thirty- six thousand infantry, besides cavalry, on the sands. The Queen describes the beautiful effect of the background of calm, blue sea, while "the glorious crimson light" of the setting sun was gilding the thousands of bayonets, lances, &c. It was the spot where Napoleon I. inspected the army with which he was prepared to invade England; while Nelson's fleet, which held him in check, occupied the anchorage where the Queen's squadron lay. Before embarking, her Majesty and Prince Albert drove to the French camps in the neighbourhood.

At last, when it was only an hour from midnight, in splendid moonlight, through a town blazing with fireworks and illuminations, with bands playing, soldiers saluting, and a great crowd cheering as if it was noonday, the Queen and the Prince returned to their yacht, accompanied by the Emperor. As if loth to leave them, he proposed to go with them a little way. The parting moment came, the Queen and the Emperor embraced, and he shook hands warmly with the Prince, the Prince of Wales, and the Princess Royal. Again at the side of the vessel, her Majesty pressed her late host's hand, and embraced him with an, "Adieu, sire." As he saw her looking over the side of the ship and watching his barge, he called out, "Adieu, Madame, au revoir," to which the Queen answered, "Je l'espère bien."

On the 6th of September the Court went to Scotland, staying a night at Holyrood, as usual in those years. On the Queen's arrival she drove through the old castle of Balmoral, the new house being habitable, though much of the building was still unfinished. An old shoe was thrown after her Majesty, Scotch fashion, for luck, as she entered the northern home, where everything charmed her.

On the 10th of September the Duchess of Kent, who was staying at Abergeldie, dined with the Queen. At half-past ten despatches arrived for her Majesty and Lord Granville, the Cabinet Minister in attendance. The Queen began reading hers, which was from Lord Clarendon, with news of the destruction of Russian ships. Lord Granville said, "I have still better news," on which he read, "'From General Simpson. Sebastopol is in the hands of the allies.'" "God be praised for it," adds the Queen.

Great was the rejoicing. Prince Albert determined to go up Craig Gowan and light the bonfire which had been ready the year before, had been blown down on the day of the battle of Inkermann, and was at last only waiting to be lit. All the gentlemen, in every species of attire, all the servants, and gradually the whole population of the little village, keepers and gillies, were aroused and started, in the autumn night, for the summit of the hill. The happy Queen watched from below the blazing light above. Numerous figures surrounded it, "some dancing, all shouting; Ross (the Queen's piper) playing his pipes (surely the most exultant of pibrochs), and Grant and Macdonald firing off guns continually," the late Sir E. Gordon's old Alsatian servant striving to add his French contribution to the festivities by lighting squibs, half of which would not go off. When Prince Albert returned he described the health-drinking in whiskey as wild and exciting.

CHAPTER XXVIII.BETROTHAL OF THE PRINCESS ROYAL— QUEEN'S SPEECH TO THE SOLDIERS RETURNED FROM THE CRIMEA—BALMORAL.

An event of great importance to the Queen and her family was now impending. A proposal of marriage for the Princess Royal—still only fifteen years of age—had been made by the Prince of Prussia, the heir of the childless king, in the name of the Prince's only son, Prince Frederick William, a young man of four-and-twenty, nearly ten years the Princess's senior. From the friendship which had long existed between the Queen and the Prince and the Princess of Prussia, their son was well-known and much liked in the English royal family, and the youthful Princess Royal was favourably inclined to him. The proposal was graciously received, on certain conditions. Of course the marriage of the young Princess could not take place for some time. She had not even been confirmed. She ought to be allowed to know her mind fully. The couple must become better acquainted. It was agreed at first that nothing should be said to the Princess Royal on the subject till after her confirmation. But when the wooer arrived to pay a delightfully private visit to the family in their Highland retreat, the last interdict was judged too hard, and he was permitted to plead his cause under the happiest auspices.

We have pleasant little glimpses in her Majesty's journal, and Prince Albert's letters, of what was necessarily of the utmost moment to all concerned; nay, as the contracting parties were of such high estate, excited the lively sympathies of two great nations. The Prince writes in a half tender, half humorous fashion, of the young couple to Baron Stockmar, "The young man, 'really in love,' 'the little lady' doing her best to please him." The critical moment came during a riding party up the heathery hill of Craig-na-Ban and down Glen Girnock, when, with a sprig of white heather for "luck" in his hand, like any other trembling suitor, the lover ventured to say the decisive words, which were not repulsed. Will the couple ever forget that spot on the Scotch hillside, when they fill the imperial throne of Charlemagne? They have celebrated their silver wedding-day with loud jubilees, may their golden wedding still bring welcome memories of Craig-na-Ban and its white heather.

The Court had travelled south to Windsor, and in the following month, in melancholy contrast to the family circumstances in which all had been rejoicing, her Majesty and the Prince had the sorrowful intelligence that her brother, the Prince of Leiningen, while still only in middle age, just over fifty, had suffered from a severe apoplectic attack.

In November the King of Sardinia visited England. His warm welcome was due not only to his patriotic character, which made Victor Emmanuel's name a household word in this country, but to the fact that the Sardinians were acting along with the French as our allies in the Crimea. He was royally entertained at Windsor, saw Woolwich and Portsmouth, received an address at Guildhall, and was invested with the Order of the Garter. He left before five the next morning, when, in spite of the early hour, the intense cold, and a snowstorm, the Queen took a personal farewell of her guest.

In the beginning of 1896 the Queen and the Prince were again wounded by newspaper attacks on him, in consequence of his having signed his name, as Colonel of the Grenadier Guards, among the other officers of the Guards, to a memorial to the Queen relating to the promotion and retirement of the officers.

On the 31st of January her Majesty opened Parliament amidst much enthusiasm, in a session which was to decide the grave question of peace or war. In March the welcome news arrived that the Empress of the French had given birth to a son.

On the 20th of March the ceremony of the confirmation of the Princess Royal took place in the private chapel, Windsor. The Archbishop of Canterbury and the Bishop of Oxford, Lord High Almoner, officiated, in the presence of the Queen and the royal family, the Ministers, Officers of State, &c. Prince Albert led in the Princess; her Godfather, King Leopold, followed with the Queen. Bishop Wilberforce made a note of the scene in a few words. "To Windsor Castle. The confirmation of Princess Royal. Interesting. She devout, composed, earnest. Younger sister much affected. The Queen and Prince also."

On the 30th of March peace was signed. London became aware of it by the firing of the Park and the Tower guns at ten o'clock at night. The next morning the Lord Mayor, on the balcony of the Mansion House, read a despatch from the Secretary of State, to a large crowd assembled in the street, who received the tidings with loud cheers. At noon his Lordship, preceded by the civic functionaries, went on foot to the Exchange and read the despatch there.

The Tower guns were again fired, the church-bells rang merry peals, flags were hung out from all the public buildings. A few days afterwards the Queen conferred on Lord Palmerston the Order of the Garter—a frank and cordial acknowledgment of his services, which the high-spirited statesman received with peculiar pleasure.

On the 18th of April her Majesty and Prince Albert went to Aldershot to commemorate the completion of the camp and review the troops, when the Queen spent her first night in camp, in the pavilion prepared for her use. On one of the two days she wore a Field-Marshal's uniform, with the Star and Order of the Garter, and a dark blue riding habit. Within a week, in magnificent weather, Her Majesty and Prince Albert inspected a great fleet at Spithead.

After Easter Lord Ellesmere, in his last appearance in the House of Lords, moved the address to the Queen on the peace, and spoke the feelings of the nation when he expressed in the words of a poet the country's deep debt of gratitude to Florence Nightingale. On the 8th of May the Lords and Commons went in procession to Buckingham Palace to present their addresses to the Queen. The same evening she gave a State ball—the first in the new ball-room—to celebrate the peace. Lord Dalhousie returned in this month of May from India, where he had been Governor-General. He was a hopeless invalid, while still only in his forty-fifth year. The moment the Queen heard of his arrival, she wrote to him a letter of welcome, for which her faithful servant thanked her in simple and touching words, as for "the crowning honour of his life." He could not tell what the end of his illness might be, but he ventured to say that her Majesty's most gracious words would be a balm for it all.

On the 19th of May the Queen laid the foundation of the military hospital at Netley, which she had greatly at heart.

In June a serious accident, which might have been fatal, occurred to the Princess Royal while her promised bridegroom was on a visit to this country. Indeed he was much in England in those days, appearing frequently in public along with the royal family, to the gratification of romantic hearts that delighted to watch young royal lovers. She was sealing a letter at a table when the sleeve of her light muslin dress caught fire and blazed up in a moment. Happily she was not alone. The Princess's governess, Miss Hildyard, was at the same table, and Princess Alice was receiving a lesson from her music-mistress in the room. By their presence of mind in wrapping the hearthrug round the Princess Royal, who herself showed great self possession under the shock and pain of the accident, her life was probably saved. The arm was burnt from below the elbow to the shoulder, though not so as to be permanently disfigured. Lady Bloomfield has a pretty story about this accident. She has been describing the Princess as "quite charming. Her manners were so perfectly unaffected and unconstrained, and she was full of fun." The writer goes on to say, "When she, the Princess, burnt her arm, she never uttered a cry; she said 'Don't frighten mamma—send for papa first.'" She wrote afterwards to her music- mistress, dictating the letter and signing it with her left hand, to tell how she was, because she knew the lady, who had been present when the accident happened, would be anxious.

King Leopold, his younger son, and his lovely young daughter, Princess Charlotte, were among the Queen's visitors this summer, and a little later came the Prince and Princess of Prussia to improve their acquaintance with their future daughter-in-law.

In July the Queen and the Prince were again at Aldershott to review the troops returned from the Crimea. But the weather, persistently wet, spoilt what would otherwise have been a joyous as well as a glorious scene. During a short break in the rain, the Crimean regiments formed three sides of a square round the carriage in which the Queen sat. The officers and four men of each of the troops that had been under fire "stepped out," and the Queen, standing up in the carriage, addressed them. "Officers, non-commissioned officers, and soldiers, I wish personally to convey through you to the regiments assembled here this day my hearty welcome on their return to England in health and full efficiency. Say to them that I have watched anxiously over the difficulties and hardships which they have so nobly borne, that I have mourned with deep sorrow for the brave men who have fallen in their country's cause, and that I have felt proud of that valour which, with their gallant allies, they have displayed on every field. I thank God that your dangers are over, while the glory of your deeds remains; but I know that should your services be again required, you will be animated with the same devotion which in the Crimea has rendered you invincible."

When the clear, sweet voice was silent, a cry of "God save the Queen!" sprang to every lip. Helmets, bearskins, and shakos were thrown into the air; the dragoons waved their sabres, and a shout of loyal acclamation, caught up from line to line, rang through the ranks.

The next day, in summer sunshine, the Queen and her City of London welcomed home the Guards. In anticipation of a brilliant review in the park, she saw them march past from the central balcony of Buckingham Palace, as she had seen them depart on the chill February morning more than two years before: another season and another scene—not unchastened in its triumph, for many a once-familiar face was absent, and many a yearning thought wandered to Russian hill and plain and Turkish graveyard, where English sleepers rested till the great awakening.

An old soldier figured before the Queen and the Prince in circumstances which filled them with sorrow and pity. Lord Hardinge, the Commander-in-Chief, was having an audience with the Queen, when he was suddenly struck by paralysis. He resigned his post, to which the Duke of Cambridge was appointed. Lord Hardinge died a few months afterwards.

After several yachting excursions, marred by stormy weather, the Court went north, and reached Balmoral on the 30th of August. The tower and the offices, with the terraces and pleasure-grounds, were finished, and every trace of the old house had disappeared. The Balmoral of to-day, though it still lacked what has become some of its essential features, stood before the Queen. We are fain to make it stand before our readers as it is now.

The road to Balmoral may be said to begin with the Strath at Aberdeen. The farther west the railway runs, the higher grow the mountains and the narrower waxes the valley. Yet the Highlands proper are held to commence only at Ballater, the little northern town with its gray square, and its pleasant inn by the bridge over the rushing Dee. The whole is set between the wooded hills of Pannanich and Craigendarroch, the last-named from the oak wood which crowns its summit. The Prince of Wales's house, Birkhall, stands back from the road on a green eminence with the mountain rising behind, and in front the river Muich running down to join the Dee.

At Ballater the railway ends, and two picturesque roads follow the course of the river, one on each side, the first passing Crathie, the other going through the fir and birch woods of Abergeldie on the same side as Balmoral. Both command grand glimpses of the mountains, which belong to the three great ranges of the district—Cairngorm, Glengairn, and Loch-na-Gar.

Approaching on the Crathie side, the stranger is struck with the frequent tokens of a life that was once the presiding genius of this place, which passing away in its prime, has left the shadow of a great grief, softened by the merciful touch of time. The haunting presence, mild in its manliness and gentle in its strength, of a princely benefactor common to all, has displaced the grim phantoms of old chieftains and reigns in their stead. It hovers over the dearly loved Highland home with its fitting touch of stateliness in the middle of its simplicity, over the forest where a true sportsman stalked the deer, over the streams and lochs in which he fished, and the paths he trod by hill and glen. We are made to remember that Balmoral was the Prince Consort's property, that he bought it for his possession, as Osborne was the Queen's, and that it was by a bequest in his will that it came, with all its memories, to his widow. Three different monuments to the Prince, on as many elevations above the castle, at once attract the eye. The highest and most enduring, seen from many quarters and at considerable distances, is a gable-like cairn on the summit of a hill. It is here that such of the Prince's sons as are in the neighbourhood, and all the tenantry and dependents who can comply with the invitation, assemble on the Prince Consort's birthday and drink to his memory.

Lower down stands a representation of the noble figure of the Prince, attended by his greyhound, Eos. On another spur of the same hill is an obelisk, erected by the tenantry and servants to the master who had their interests so deeply at heart.

The castle, like its smaller predecessor of which this pile of building has taken the place, stands in a haugh or meadow at the foot of a hill, within a circle of mountain-tops. The porter's ledge and gate might belong to the hunting-seat of any gentleman of taste and means; only the fact that, even when her Majesty is not in residence, a constable of police is in attendance, marks the difference between sovereign and subject.

Within the gate the surroundings are still wild and rural, in keeping with nature free and unshackled, and have a faint flavour of German parks where the mowing-machine is not always at work, but a sweet math of wild flowers three or four feet high is supposed to cheat the dweller in courtly palaces into a belief that he too is at liberty to breathe the fresh air without thought or care, and roam where he will, free from the fetters of form and etiquette.

Great innocent moon-daises, sprightly harebells, sturdy heather, bloom profusely and seem much at home within these royal precincts, under the brow of the hills and within sight and sound of the flashing Dee. Gradually the natural birch wood shows more traces of cultivation, and is interspersed with such trees and shrubs as suit the climate, and the rough pasture gives place to the smooth lawn, with a knot of bright flower-beds on one side.

The house is built of reddish granite in what is called the baronial style, with a sprinkling of peaked gables and pepper-box turrets, and a square tower with a clock which is said to keep the time all over the parish. Above the principal entrance are the coats of arms, carved, coloured, and picked out with gold. There are two bas-reliefs serving to indicate the character of the building— a hunting-lodge under the patronage of St. Hubert, supported by St. Andrew of Scotland and St. George of England, the stag between whose antlers the sacred cross sprang, forming part of the representation. The other bas-relief shows groups of men engaged in Highland games.

Within doors many a relic of the chase appears in antlered heads surmounting inscriptions in brass of the date of the slaying of the stag and the name of the slayer. The engravings on the walls are mostly of mountain landscapes and sporting scenes, in which Landseer's hand is prominent, and of family adventures in making this ascent or crossing that ford.

The furniture is as Scotch as may be—chairs and tables, with few exceptions, of polished birch hangings and carpets with the tartan check on the velvet pile, the royal "sets" in all their bewildering variety: "royal Stewart," strong in scarlet; "Victoria," with the check relieved on a white ground; "Albert," on a deep blue, and "hunting Stewart," which suddenly passes into a soft vivid green, crossed by lines of red and yellow.

Drawing-room, dining-room, billiard-room, and library are spacious enough for royalty, while small enough for comfort when royalty is in happy retreat in little more than a large family circle rusticating from choice. The corridors look brown and simple, like the rest of the house, and lack the white statuary of Osborne, and the superb vases, cabinets, and pictures of Buckingham Palace and Windsor. By the chimney-piece in the entrance hall rest the tattered colours once borne through flood and field by two famous regiments, one of them "the Cameronians."

In the drawing-room is a set of chairs with covers in needlework sewed by a cluster of industrious ladies-in-waiting. In the library hangs a richly wrought wreath of flowers in porcelain, an offering from Messrs. Minton to the Queen. On the second story are the private rooms of her Majesty and the different members of the royal family. Perhaps the ballroom, a long hall, one story in height, running out from the building like an afterthought, is one of the most picturesque features of the place. The decorations consist of devices placed at intervals on the walls. These devices are made up of Highland weapons, Highland plaids, Highland bonnets bearing the chief's feather or the badge of the clan. Doubtless tufts of purple heather and russet bracken, with bunches of the coral berries of the rowan, will supplement other adornments as the occasion calls for them; and when the lights gleam, the pipers strike up, and the nimble dancers foot it with grace and glee through reel [Footnote: "Yesterday we had the Gillies' Ball, at which Arthur distinguished himself and was greatly applauded in the Highland reels. Next to Jamie Gow, he was the 'favourite in the room.'"—Extract from one of the Prince Consort's letters.] and sword- dance, the effect must be excellent of its kind. For long years the balls at Balmoral have been mostly kindly festivals to the humble friends who look forward to the royal visits as to the galas of the year, the greater part of which is spent in a remote solitude not without the privations which accompany a northern winter.

The parish church of Crathie, a little, plain, white building, well situated on a green, wooded knoll, looks across the Dee to Balmoral. The church is notable for its wide, red-covered gallery seats, to which the few plain pews in the area below bear a small proportion. The Queen's arms are in front of the gallery, which contains her seat and that of the Prince of Wales. Opposite are two stained-glass windows, representing King David with his harp, and St. Paul with the sword of the Spirit and the word of God, gifts of the Queen in memory of her sister, the Princess of Hohenlohe, and of Dr. Norman Macleod. Famous speakers and still more famous hearers have worshipped together in this simple little country church. Macleod, Tulloch, Caird, Macgregor—the foremost orators in the Church of Scotland—have taken their turn with the scholarly parish minister, while in the pews, bearing royalty company, have sat statesmen and men of letters of whom the world has heard: Lord Derby, Mr. Gladstone, Dean Stanley, Sir Arthur Helps, &c., &c.

The old churchyard in which John Brown, the Queen's trusty Scotch servant, faithful as a squire of old, sleeps, lies down in the low land near the Dee. John Brown's house, solid and unpretending like the man himself, which he only occupied once, when his coffin lay for a night in the dining-room, is in the neighbourhood.

The Queen has white cottages not far from the castle gate, built on the model of the Osborne cottages, pretty and convenient homes of keepers, keepers' widows, &c., &c., with the few artisans whose services are necessary for the small population. There are other cottages of the old, homely sort, containing no more than "the butt and the benn" of stereotyped Scotch architecture, with the fire made of "peats" or of sticks on the hearth-floor. In some of these, the walls of the better rooms are covered with good plates and photographs of every member of the royal family, with whose lineaments we are familiar, from the widowed Queen to the last royal couple among her grandchildren. These likenesses are much-valued gifts from the originals.

As a nucleus to the cottages, there is the shop or Highland store with a wide door and a couple of counters representing two branches of trade in the ordinarily distinct departments of groceries and haberdashery. Probably this is the one shop in her Majesty's domains in which, as we have evidence in her journal, [Footnote: "Life in the Highlands"—Queen's journal. "Albert went out with Alfred for the day, and I walked out with the two girls and Lady Churchill, stopped at the shop and made some purchases for poor people and others. Drove a little way, got out and walked up the hill to Balnacroft, Mrs. P. Farquharson's, and she walked round with us to some of the cottages to show me where the poor people lived, and to tell them who I was…. I went into a small cabin of old Kitty Kear's, who is eighty-six years old, quite erect, and who welcomed us with a great air of dignity. She sat down and spun. I gave her, also, a warm petticoat; she said, 'May the Lord ever attend ye and yours, here and hereafter, and may the Lord be a guide to ye and keep ye from all harm.' … We went into three other cottages—to Mrs. Symons's (daughter-in-law to the old widow living next door) who had an 'unwell boy,' then across a little burn to another old woman's, and afterwards peeped into Blair's, the fiddler. We drove back and got out again to visit old Mrs. Grant (Grant's mother), who is so tidy and clean, and to whom I gave a dress and a handkerchief; and she said, 'You're too kind to me, you're over kind to me, ye give me more every year, and I get older every year.' After talking some time to her, she said, 'I am happy to see ye looking so nice.' She had tears in her eyes, and speaking of Vicky's going said, 'I'm very sorry, and I think she is sorry hersel'.'…"] she avails herself of the feminine privilege of shopping. For the Queen can live the life of a private lady—can show herself the most considerate and sympathetic of noble gentlewomen in this primitive locality. She can walk or drive her ponies, or visit on foot her commissioner or her minister, or look in at her school, or call on her sick, aged, and poor, and take to them the comforts she has provided for them, the tokens of her remembrance they prize so much. She can enjoy their simple friendliness and native shrewdness. She can read to them words of lofty promise and tender consolation. She can do all as if she were not crowned Queen and ruler of a great kingdom. In hardly any other part of her empire would such pleasant familiar intercourse and gentle personal charities be possible for her. The association has been deepened and strengthened by a duration of more than thirty years. The Queen came while still a young wife to Balmoral, and she has learnt to love and be loved by her neighbours in the long interval which leaves her a royal widow of threescore. Her children were fair-haired little boys and girls, making holiday here, playing at riding and shooting, getting into scrapes like other children, [Footnote: There is a story told of one of the little princes having chased an old woman's hen and been soundly scolded by her for the offence. Her neighbours remonstrated with her, and her heart failed her when, a few days afterwards, she saw the Prince Consort coming up the path to her house leading the small offender. But the visit was one of courteous deprecation, in order that the little hunter of forbidden game might personally apologise for his delinquency.] prattling to the old women in "mutches" and "short gowns," whose houses were so charmingly queer and convenient, with the fires on the hearths to warm cold little toes, and the shadowy nooks ready for hide-and-seek. These children are now older than their mother was when she first came up Dee-side, heads of houses in their turn, but they have not forgotten the friends of their youth.

The rustic community is pervaded in an odd and fascinating manner with the fine flavour of a Court. It has, as it were, a touch of Arcady. Among tales of the great storms and fragments of old legends, curious reflections of high life and gossip of lords and ladies crop up. Not only are noble names and distinguished personages, everyday sounds and friendly acquaintances in this privileged region, but when the great world follows its liege lady here, it is to live in villiagiatura, to copy her example in adapting itself to the ways of the place and in cultivating the natives. Courtiers are only courtly in being frankly at ease with the whole human race. Ladies-in-waiting and maids of honour lose their pride of rank and worldly ambition—if they ever had any, stroll about, drop into this or that cottage at will, and have their cronies there as in loftier localities. We hear of this or that marriage, which has yet to be announced in the Morning Post; how a noble duke, who was conveniently in attendance on the Prince, once walked with a fair and gentle lady, whose father was in waiting on the Queen, through the birch woods and by the brawling Dee, and a marriage, only too shortlived, came of it. And we end by listening to the piteous details of the swift fading away of the much-loved young duchess. Other names, with which the Court Calendar has made us familiar, are constantly coming to the surface in the conversation, generally in association with some act of cheery good fellowship. The son of an earl found a dog for his mother at one of these cottage hearths, and never returned to the neighbourhood without punctually reporting himself to tell its old mistress how well her former pet was thriving—that it had its dinner with the family in the dining-room, and drove every day with the countess in her carriage.

The fine old white house of Abergeldie, with its single-turreted tower, has become the Scotch home of a genial prince and a beautiful princess, who, we may remember, remained steadfastly settled there during the darkening, shortening days of a gloomy autumn, in devoted watch over her lady-in-waiting lying sick, nigh unto death with fever. Abergeldie has another cherished memory, that of the good old Duchess of Kent, for whom Prince Albert first rented the castle, who often stayed in it, accompanied by her son, the Prince of Leiningen, her daughter, the Princess of Hohenlohe, or some member of their families. The peculiar cradle which used to be swung across the Dee here, conveying passengers as well as parcels, has been removed in consequence of the last disaster which befell its progress. An earlier tragedy of a hapless bride and bridegroom who perished in making the passage is still remembered. Remoter traditions, like that of the burning of a witch on Craig-na-Ban, linger in the neighbourhood.

Beyond Balmoral, in the Braemar direction, stretches the fine deer- forest—a great fir-wood on broken ground—of Ballochbuie, a remnant of the old forest of Mar, where a pretended hunting expedition meant a projected rebellion. It is said an earl of that name bestowed it on a Farquaharson in exchange for so small a matter as a plaid. It is now part of the estate of Balmoral. The hills of Craig Nortie and Meal Alvie lie not far off, while on the opposite side rise Craig-na-Ban and Craig Owsel.

Of all the Queen's haunts, that which she has made most her own, where she has stayed for a day or two at a time, seeming to prefer to do so when the hills have received their first powdering of snow, [Footnote: "A little shower of snow had fallen, but was succeeded by brilliant sunshine. The hills covered with snow, the golden birch-trees on the lower brown hills, and the bright afternoon sky, were indescribably beautiful"—Extract from the Queen's journal.] almost every year during her residence in Aberdeenshire, is that which includes Alt-na- Giuthasach and the Glassalt Shiel. This retreat is now reached by a good carriage-road over a long tract of moorland among brown hills, opening now and then in different directions to show vistas closed in by the giant heads and shoulders—here of dark Loch-na-Gar, there of Ben Macdhui, both of them presenting great white splashes on their seamed and scarred sides—wide patches of winter snow on this July day, far more than usual at the season, which will not melt now while the year lasts. "Burns," the Girnoch and the Muich, trot by turns along with us, singing their stories, half blythe, half plaintive. Once or twice a lowly farmhouse has a few grass or oat-fields spread out round it, with the solitude of the hills beyond. A cross-road to such a house was so bad that a dog-cart brought up to it, had been unyoked and left by the side of the main road, while its occupants trudged to their destination on foot, leading with them the horse, which needed rest and refreshment still more than its masters. The blue waters of Loch Muich come in sight with bare precipitous hills round; a little wood clothes the mouth of the pass and the loch, and helps to shelter Alt-na-Ginthasach. The hut is now the Prince of Wales's small shooting-lodge. The modest blue stone building, with its brown wooden porch and its offices behind, is built on a knoll, and commands a beautiful view of the loch and the steep rocky crags to those who care for nature at the wildest. The only vestige of soft green is the knoll on which the hut stands. All the rest is bleak and brown, or purple when the heather is in bloom. The hills, torn by the winter torrents, are glistening after a summer shower with a hundred silver threads in the furrows of the watercourses.

There are fences and gates to the royal domicile, but there is hardly an attempt to alter its character within, unless by a round plot of rhododendrons offering a few late blossoms. But all nature, however stern and savage, smiles on a July day. The purple heather-bell is in bloom, the tiny blue milkwort and the yellow rock-rose help to make a summer carpet which is rendered still gayer by many a pale peach- coloured orchis and by an occasional spray of wild roses, deeper in the rose than the same flower is in the low countries, or by a tall white foxglove. Loch Muich may be desolation itself when the heather and bracken are sere, when the lowering sky breathes nothing save gloom, and chill mist-wreaths creep round its precipices; but when the air is buoyant in its tingling sharpness, when the dappled white clouds are reflected in water—blue, not leaden, and there is enough sunshine to cast intermittent shadows on the hillsides and the loch, though a transient darkness and a patter of raindrops vary the scene, it has its day and way of blossoming.

The Queen's house or shiel of the Glassalt stands near the head of the two miles long loch, just beyond the point where the Glassalt burn comes leaping and dashing down the hillside. Here, too, is a small sheltering fir and birch plantation, though not large enough to hide the full view of the sentinel hills. A "roundel" of Alpenrosen, or dwarf rhododendrons, is the only break in the growth of moss and heather. The loch is so near the house that a stone thrown by a child's hand from the windows of the principal rooms would fall into the watery depths.

The interior is almost as simple and limited in accommodation as Alt- na-Giuthasach was when the Queen described it in her journal. The dining-room and drawing-room might, in old fashioned language, be called "royal closets"—cosy and sweet with chintz hangings and covers to chairs and couches, a small cottage piano, a book-tray in which Hill Burton's "History of Scotland" and Sir Walter Scott's "Tales of a Grandfather," find their place among Scotch poetry old and new. The engravings on the walls tell of that fidelity to the dead which implies truth to the living. There are likenesses of the Prince—who died before this house was built, as in the great palaces; the Duchess of Hesse—best known in the north as Princess Alice; the Princess of Hohenlohe, with her handsome matronly face, full of sense and kindness, and her young daughter, Princess Elise, who passed away in the springtime of her life. In these rustic sitting-rooms and the adjacent bedrooms and dressing-rooms we come again on many a portrait of the humble friends of the family—the dogs which we seem to know so well; the early group of little Dash and big Nero, and Hector with the parrot Lorey; Cairnach, Islay, Deckel, &c. [Footnote: An anecdote of the royal kennels states that when no notice has been given, the servants shall know of her Majesty's presence in the vicinity, and will say among themselves, "The Queen is at Frogmore" by the actions of the dogs, the stir and excitement, the eager listening, sniffing of the air, wagging of tails, and common desire to break bounds and scamper away to greet their royal mistress.]

Behind the house a winding footpath leads up the hill to the rocky cleft from which issues in a succession of white and foamy twists and downward springs, the Falls of the Glassalt. Turning round from the spectacle, the stranger looks down on the loch in its semicircle of mountains. Gaining the crest of the hill and descending the edge on the opposite side, the foot of the grim giant Loch-na-Gar is reached.

Among the visitors at Balmoral in 1858 was Florence Nightingale. The Queen had before this presented her with a jewel in remembrance of her services in the Crimea. The design was as follows: a field of white enamel was charged with a St. George's cross in ruby red enamel, from which shot rays of gold. This field was encircled by a black band bearing the scroll "Blessed are the merciful." The shield was set in a framework of palm-branches in green enamel tipped with gold, and united at the bottom by a riband of blue enamel inscribed "Crimea" in gold letters. The cypher V.R. surmounted by a crown in diamonds, was charged upon the centre of the cross. On the back was a gold tablet which bore an inscription from the hand of her Majesty.

While the Queen was in Scotland the marriage in Germany of one of the daughters of the Princess of Hohenlohe took place. Princess Adelaide, like her sister Princess Elise, possessed of many attractions, became the wife of Prince Frederick of Schleswig Holstein Sonderberg-Augustenberg, the brother of Prince Christian, destined to become the husband of Princess Helena.

CHAPTER XXIX.DEATH OF THE PRINCE Of LEININGEN—BIRTH OF PRINCESS BEATRICE—BESTOWAL

OF THE VICTORIA CROSS—INDIAN MUTINY.

The court returned to Windsor in October, and in November a severe blow struck the Queen in the death of her brother, the Prince of Leiningen. A second fit of apoplexy ended his life while his sister, the Princess of Hohenlohe, watched by his death-bed. Prince Leiningen was fifty-two years of age. He had served in the Bavarian army, and was a man of recognised influence among his countrymen in the German troubles of 1848, which cost him his principality. He had married in 1829, when he was twenty-seven years of age and when the Queen was only a little girl of ten, Marie (née) Countess of Kletelsberg. He left two sons, the eldest of whom, Prince Ernest, entered the English navy.

Her Majesty's references to the death in her letters to King Leopold are very pathetic. "Oh! dearest uncle, this blow is a heavy one, my grief very bitter. I loved my dearest, only brother, most tenderly." And again, "We three were particularly fond of each other, and never felt or fancied that we were not real geschwister (children of the same parents). We knew but one parent, our mother, so became very closely united, and so I grew up; the distance which difference of age placed between us entirely vanished...." The aged Duchess of Kent was "terribly distressed, but calm and resigned."

Baron Stockmar was with the royal family at this time. It was his last visit to England. His company, always earnestly coveted, especially by the Prince, was apt to be bestowed in an erratic fashion characteristic of the man. Some one of the royal children would unexpectedly announce, "Papa, do you know the Baron is in his room," which was the first news of his arrival.

During the stay of the Court at Osborne in December, the graceful gift of the Resolute was made by the Americans to the Queen, and accepted by her Majesty in person, with marked gratification. The Resolute was one of the English ships which had gone to the north seas in search of Sir John Franklin. It had been abandoned in the ice, found by an American vessel, taken across the Atlantic, refitted, and by a happy thought offered as a suitable token to the Queen.

On the 14th of April, 1857, the Queen's fifth daughter and ninth and last child was born at Buckingham Palace. A fortnight afterwards the Duchess of Gloucester, the last of George the III. and Queen Charlotte's children, died in her eighty-third year. The Queen wrote of her to King Leopold, who must have been well acquainted with her in his youth, "Her age, and her being a link with bygone times and generations, as well as her great kindness, amiability, and unselfishness, rendered her more and more dear and precious to us all, and we all looked upon her as a sort of grandmother." Sixty-two years before, when the venerable Princess was a charming maiden of eighteen, she had gloried in the tidings of her princely cousin's laurels, won on the battlefields of Flanders. More than twenty years afterwards, when Princess Charlotte descended the staircase of Carlton House after her marriage with Prince Leopold, "she was met at the foot with open arms by the Princess Mary, whose face was bathed in tears." The first wedding had removed the obstacle to the second, which was celebrated a few weeks later. The Duchess lived for eighteen years happily with her husband, then spent more than twenty years in widowhood. She ended her long life at Gloucester House, Park Lane. At her earnest request, she was buried without pomp or show with her people in the family vault at Windsor.

Before the late Duchess of Gloucester's funeral, Prince Albert, according to a previous pledge, opened, on the 5th of May, the great Art Exhibition at Manchester, to which the Queen contributed largely.

On the announcement to Parliament of the Princess Royal's approaching marriage, the House of Commons voted in a manner gratifying to the Queen and the Prince a dowry of forty thousand, with an annuity of eight thousand a year to the Princess.

At Osborne the Queen had a flying visit from one of her recent enemies, the Archduke Constantine, the Admiral-in-Chief of the Russian navy.

On the 14th of June, the young Archduke Maximilian of Austria arrived. He was an object of peculiar interest to the Queen and the Prince, as the future husband of their young cousin, Princess Charlotte of Belgium. He seemed in every way worthy of the old king's careful choice for his only daughter. Except in the matter of looks, he was all that could have been wished—good, clever, kind. But man proposes and God disposes; so it happened that the marriage attended by such bright and apparently well-founded hopes resulted in one of the most piteous tragedies that ever befell a noble and innocent royal pair. Another bridegroom, Prince Frederick William, was in England to meet the Archduke, and a third was hovering in the background in the person of Don Pedro of Portugal, whose marriage with Princess Stephanie of Hohenzollern Prince Albert had been requested to negotiate. Marriage-bells were in the air, and that must indeed have been a joyous christening at which two of the bridegrooms were present. Prince Frederick William of Prussia acted as godfather to his future little sister-in-law, while his betrothed bride was one of the godmothers. The infant was named as her Majesty explained to King Leopold: "She is to be called Beatrice, a fine old name, borne by three of the Plantaganet princesses, and her other names will be Mary (after poor Aunt Mary), Victoria (after mamma and Vicky, who with Fritz Wilhelm are to be the sponsors), and Feodore (the Queen's sister)." Her Majesty's last baby was a beautiful infant, soon to exhibit bright and winning ways, the pet plaything of her brothers and sisters, and especially of her father.

On the 25th of June the Queen conferred on Prince Albert, by letters patent, the title of "Prince Consort." The change was desirable, to insure the proper recognition of his rank, as her Majesty's husband, at foreign courts.

On the following day, the 26th, the interesting ceremony of the first bestowal of the Victoria Cross took place in Hyde Park before many thousands of spectators. The idea was to provide a decoration which might be earned by officers and soldiers alike, as it should be conferred for a single merit—the highest a soldier could possess, yet in its performance open to all—devoted, unselfish courage. Thus arose the most coveted and honourable of English orders, which confers more glory on its wearer than the jewelled star of the Order of the Garter gives distinction. In excellent keeping with the motive of the creation, the Maltese cross is of the plainest material, iron from the cannon taken at Sebastopol; in the centre is the crown, surmounted by the lion; below it the scroll "For Valour." On the clasp are branches of laurel; the cross hangs suspended from it by the letter V—a red riband being for the army, a blue for the navy. The decoration includes a pension of ten pounds a year. The arrangements for the ceremony were similar to those at the distribution of the medals, except that her Majesty was on horseback. She rode a grey roan, and wore a scarlet jacket with a black skirt. Stooping from her seat on horseback, she pinned the cross on each brave man's breast, while the Prince saluted him with "a gesture of marked respect." [Footnote: "Life of the Prince Consort."] Prince Frederick William was with the royal party.

A few days afterwards, the Queen, the Prince, their two elder daughters and two elder sons and Prince Frederick William of Prussia, a large party, paid a visit to Manchester, staying two nights at Worsley Hall. They inspected the great picture exhibition, received addresses, and traversed the streets to Peel Park, where a statue to her Majesty had been recently erected, the whole amidst much rejoicing.

In the end of June, King Leopold arrived with his daughter on a farewell visit before her marriage, so that there were two young brides comparing experiences and anticipating what the coming years would bring, under her Majesty's wing. The princesses were nearly of an age, neither quite seventeen. They had been playmates and friends since childhood, but the fates in store for them were very different.

In the second week of July the freedom of the City of London was presented to Prince Frederick William of Prussia; the Prince Consort was sworn in master of the Trinity House, and the Queen and the Prince visited the camp at Aldershott. On the 27th the marriage of the Princess Charlotte of Belgium and the Archduke Maximilian was celebrated at Brussels. The Prince went abroad for a few days, to make one in the group of friends and relations, among whom was the old French Queen Amélie, the grandmother of the bride. Queen Victoria wrote to King Leopold, that she was present with them in spirit, and that she could not have given a greater proof of her love than she had shown in urging her husband to go. "You cannot think how much this costs me," she added, "or how completely forlorn I am and feel when he is away, or how I count the hours till he returns. All the numerous children are as nothing to me when he is away. It seems as if the whole life of the house and the home were gone."

On the 6th of August, the Emperor of the French's yacht, with the Emperor and Empress on board, arrived on the English coast, and a private visit of a few days' length was paid to the Queen and the Prince at Osborne. On the 19th of August Her Majesty and the Prince, with six of their children, in the royal yacht, paid an equally private visit to Cherbourg, in the absence of the Emperor and Empress. During the short stay there was a long country drive to an old chateau, when darkness overtook the adventurous party, and all was agreeably fresh and foreign.

By the beginning of September terrible tidings arrived from India. The massacre of the English women and children at Cawnpore, after the surrender of the fort, and the perilous position of the garrison at Lucknow, darkened the usually joyous stay at Balmoral, to which the Princess Royal was paying her last visit. Another source of distress to the Queen and the Prince, when the mutiny began to be put down, was the indiscriminate vengeance which a section of the rulers in India seemed inclined to take on the natives for the brutalities of the rebels. At length Lucknow was relieved, and England breathed freely again, though the country had to mourn the death of Havelock. Sir Colin Campbell completed the defeat of the enemy, and the first steps were taken to put an end to the complications of government in India, by bringing the great colony directly under the rule of the Queen, and causing the intermediate authority of the East India Company to cease.

CHAPTER XXX. THE MARRIAGE OF THE PRINCESS ROYAL.

In the end of 1857 there were many preparations for the marriage of the Princess Royal in the month of January in the coming year. In the interval a calamity occurred at Claremont which revived the recollection of the great disaster in the early years of the century, and was deeply felt by the Queen and the Prince Consort. The pretty and gentle Victoire, Duchesse de Nemours, the Queen and the Prince Consort's cousin, and his early playfellow, had given birth to a princess, and appeared to be recovering, in spite of her presentiment to the contrary. The Queen had gone to see and congratulate her. The old Queen Amélie and the Duc de Nemours had been at Windsor full of thankfulness for the happy event. The Duchess was sitting up in bed, looking cheerfully at the new dress in which she was to rejoin the family circle next day, when in a second she fell back dead.

Another shock was the news of the Orsini bomb, which exploded close to the Emperor and Empress of the French as they were about to enter the opera-house.

The marriage of the Princess Royal was fixed for the 25th of January, 1858. On the 15th the Court left Windsor for Buckingham Palace, when the Queen's diary records the sorrow with which the young bride relinquished many of the scenes and habits of her youth. One sentence recalls vividly the kindly family ties which united the royal children. Her Majesty writes, "She slept for the last time in the same room with Alice." In the course of the next few days all the guests had assembled, including, King Leopold and his sons, the Prince and Princess of Prussia, the Duke of Saxe Coburg, with minor princes and princesses, to the number of nearly thirty, so that even Buckingham Palace was hardly large enough to hold the guests and their suites. At the nightly dinner party from eighty to ninety covers were laid. But one old friend was absent, to the regret of all, and not least so of the bride. Baron Stockmar was too ill to accept the invitation to be present at the ceremony. One of his sons was to accompany the Princess to Berlin as her treasurer.

"Such bustle and excitement," wrote the Queen, and then she describes an evening party with a "very gay and pretty dance" on the 18th, when Ernest, Duke of Coburg, said, "It seemed like a dream to him to see Vicky dance as a bride, just as I did eighteen years ago, and I am still (so he said) looking very young. In 1840 poor dear papa (late Duke of Coburg) danced with me, as Ernest danced with Vicky." In truth, neither the father nor the mother of the bride of seventeen had reached the age of forty.

The first of the public festivities were three of the four State visits to Her Majesty's Theatre, "when the whole of the boxes on one side of the grand tier had been thrown into one" for the royal company gracing the brilliant audience—which, as on a former occasion, filled the back of the stage as well as the rest of the house. The plays and operas were, Macbeth, in which Helen Faucit acted, [Footnote: Another great actress had just passed away in her prime. Mademoiselle Rachel had died in the beginning of this month, near Cannes.] Twice Killed, The Rose of Castille, Somnambula. At the first performance, the Queen sat between the King of the Belgians and the Prince of Prussia. After the play, "God save the Queen" was sung with much enthusiasm. As when her own marriage had occurred, all the nation sympathised with Her Majesty. It was as if from every house a cherished young daughter was being sent with honour and blessing. The Princess Royal, always much liked, appealed especially to the popular imagination at this time because of her extreme youth, her position as a bride, and the circumstance that she was the first of the Queen's children thus to quit the home-roof. But, indeed, we cannot read the published passages in the Queen's journal that refer to the marriage without a lively realisation of the touch of nature which makes the whole world kin, without a sense that good true hearts beat alike everywhere, and that strong family affection—an elixir of life—is the same in the palace as in the cottage.

In fine frosty weather, on Saturday, the 23rd, the Prince Consort, after a walk in Buckingham Palace Gardens with the Queen and the child so soon to be parted from them, started to bring the bridegroom, who had landed in England that morning. He arrived in the middle of the day, and was received in the presence of the Court. The Queen found him looking pale and nervous, but no doubt alive to her warm greeting, at the bottom of the grand staircase. At the top a still sweeter reward awaited him, for the Princess Royal, with her fifteen years' old sister, Princess Alice, to keep her company, stood there.

On the 24th, all the gifts to the young couple, which the Queen calls "splendid," were shown in the large drawing-room—the Queen's, the Prince Consort's, the Duchess of Kent's, &c., on one table; the Prussian and other foreign gifts on another. Of the bride-groom's gift—a single string of large pearls, said to have been worth five thousand pounds, her Majesty remarks that they were the largest she ever saw. The Queen gave a necklace of diamonds, the Prince Consort a set of diamonds and emeralds, the Prince of Wales a set of diamonds and opals, the King and Queen of Prussia a diamond tiara, the Prince of Prussia a diamond and turquoise necklace, King

Leopold a Brussels lace dress, valued at a thousand pounds. On a third table were the candelabra which the Queen and the Prince gave to their son-in-law. The near relations of the bride and bridegroom brought the young couple into the room, and witnessed their pleasure at the magnificent sight. Before the Sunday service the Princess Royal gave the Queen a brooch with the Princess's hair, clasping her mother in her arms as she did so, and telling her—precious words for such a mother to hear, nobly fulfilled in the days to come—that she hoped to be worthy to be her child.

Wilberforce, Bishop of Oxford, preached an eloquent sermon.

"Very busy, interrupted and disturbed every instant," the record runs on. Many can enter into the feelings which prompted the Queen and the Prince, after the duties of hospitality were discharged, to accompany their child to her room for the last time, and to kiss and bless her while she clung to them. It is necessary to remember that every rank has its privations. Not the least penalty of such a station as that which the Princess Royal was to occupy arose from the fact that its many and weighty obligations precluded the hope of her returning frequently or for any length of time to the home where she had been so happy, which she was so grieved to quit, though social customs have improved in this respect, and royal marriages no longer mean, as a matter of course, banishment for life from the bride's native country.

On the wedding morning, the Queen declared very naturally that she felt as if she were being married over again herself, "only much more nervous," since now it was for another, and a dearer than herself, that her heart was throbbing. Besides, she said, she had not "that blessed feeling, elevating and supporting, of giving herself up for life to him whom she loved and worshipped—then and ever." She was comforted by her daughter's coming to her while the Queen was dressing, showing herself quiet and composed. The day was fine, with a winter sun shining brightly, as all England, especially all London knew, for many a pleasure-seeker was abroad betimes to enjoy the holiday. The marriage was to take place, like the Queen's marriage, in the little Chapel Royal of St. James's. Before setting out, a final daguerreotype was taken of the family group, father, mother, and daughter, "but I trembled so," the Queen writes, "my likeness has come out indistinct."

In the drive from Buckingham Palace to St James's, the Princess Royal in her wedding dress was in the carriage with her Majesty, sitting opposite to her, when "the flourish of trumpets and the cheering of thousands" made the Queen's motherly heart sink. In the bride's dressing-room, fitted up for the day, to which the Queen took the Princess, were the Prince Consort and King Leopold, both in field- marshals' uniform, and carrying batons, and the eight bridesmaids, "looking charming in white tulle, with wreaths and bouquets of pink roses and white heather."

Her Majesty left the bride and repaired to the royal closet, where she found the Duchess of Kent and the Duchess of Cambridge with her son and daughter. Old and new relations were claiming the Queen at the same time. Her thoughts were perpetually straying back to that former wedding-day. She spared attention from her daughter to bestow it on her mother, "looking so handsome in violet velvet, trimmed with ermine and white silk and violets." And as the processions were formed, her Majesty exclaimed, perhaps with a vague pang, referring to the good old Duchess still with her, and still able to play her part in the joyful ceremony, "How small the old royal family has become!" Indeed, there were but two representatives—the Duchesses of Kent and Cambridge. The Princess Mary of Cambridge, the farthest removed from the throne, walked first of the English royal family, her train borne by Lady Arabella Sackville West; then the Duke of Cambridge; the Duchess of Cambridge followed, her train borne by Lady Geraldine Somerset. The Duchess of Kent, with her train borne the Lady Anna Maria Dawson, walked next to the present royal family. They were preceded by Lord Palmerston, bearing the sword of state. The Prince of Wales, and Prince Alfred, fresh from his naval studies, lads of sixteen and fourteen, in Highland costumes, were immediately before the Queen, who walked between Prince Arthur and Prince Leopold, children of eight and five years of age. Her Majesty's train was of lilac velvet, petticoat of lilac and silver moiré—antique, with a flounce of Honiton lace; corsage ornamented with diamonds, the Koh-i- noor as a brooch; head-dress, a magnificent diadem of diamonds and pearls. The three younger princesses—Alice, Helena, and Louise, girls of fifteen, twelve, and ten—went hand-in-hand behind their mother. They wore white lace over pink satin, with daisies and blue cornflowers in their hair.

Most of the foreign princes were already in the chapel, which was full of noble company, about three hundred peers and peeresses being accommodated there. White and blue prevailed in the colours of the ladies dresses, blue in compliment to Prussia. At the altar, set out with gold plate of Queen Anne's reign, were the Archbishop of Canterbury, the Bishops of London, Oxford, and Chester, and the Dean of Windsor. As the Queen entered, she and the Princess of Prussia exchanged profound obeisances. Near her Majesty were her young princes and princesses; behind her the Duchess of Kent; opposite her the Princess of Prussia, with the foreign princes behind her.

The drums and trumpets and the organ played as the bridegroom's and the bride's processions approached, and the Queen describes the thrilling effect of the music drawing nearer and nearer. The bridegroom entered between his supporters, his father and brother-in- law, the Prince of Prussia and Prince William of Baden. Prince Frederick William, soldierly and stately, wore the blue uniform of a Prussian general, with the insignia of the Black Eagle, and carried in his hand his polished silver helmet. He looked pale and agitated, but was quite master of himself. He bowed low to the Queen and to his mother, then knelt with a devotion which attracted attention. The bride walked as at her confirmation, between her father and godfather— her grand-uncle King Leopold. Her blooming colour was gone, and she was pale almost as her white dress of moiré and Honiton lace, with wreaths of orange and myrtle blossoms. Her train was borne by eight bridesmaids—daughters of dukes, marquises, and earls—Lady Susan Clinton, Lady Emma Stanley, Lady Susan Murray, Lady Victoria Noel, Lady Cecilia Gordon Lennox, Lady Katherine Hamilton, Lady Constance Villiers, and Lady Cecilia Molyneux.

One can well conceive that the young princess looked "very touching and lovely, with such an innocent, confiding, and serious expression, her veil hanging back over her shoulders."

As the Princess advanced to the altar, she paused and made a deep obeisance to her mother, colouring high as she did so, and the same to the Princess of Prussia. The bridegroom when he took the bride's hand bent one knee.

Once more as the Prince Consort gave her daughter away, her Majesty had a bright vision of her own happy marriage on that very spot; again she was comforted by her daughter's self-control, and she could realise that it was beautiful to see the couple kneeling there with hands joined, the bridesmaids "like a cloud of maidens hovering near her (the bride) as they knelt."

When the ring was placed on the Princess's finger cannon were fired, and a telegram was sent off to Berlin that the same compliment might be paid to the pair there. The close of the "Hallelujah Chorus" was sung at the end of the ceremony.

The usual congratulations followed. The bride flung herself into her mother's arms and was embraced by her again and again, then by her bridegroom and her father. Prince Frederick William kissed first the hand and then the cheek of his father and mother, saluted the Prince Consort and King Leopold foreign fashion, and was embraced by the Queen. Princess Frederick

William would have kissed her father-in- law's hand, but was prevented by his kissing her cheek. The bride and bridegroom left the chapel hand-in-hand to the sound of Mendelssohn's "Wedding March." The register was signed in the Throne-room first by the young couple, then by their parents, and afterwards by all the princes and princesses—including the Maharajah Duleep Singh "resplendent in pearls."

The newly wedded pair drove to Buckingham Palace, to which the Queen and the Prince Consort followed, with the Prince and Princess of Prussia, through an immense multitude, amidst ringing cheers. The whole party showed themselves on the balcony before the window over the grand archway, where the Queen had appeared on so many memorable occasions. First her Majesty with her children came out, then the Queen led forward the bride, who stood hand-in-hand with her bridegroom; afterwards the rest of the circle joined them. It was a matter of lively satisfaction to her Majesty and the Prince Consort to witness the loyal, affectionate interest which the people took in their daughter, and the Queen and the Prince were ready to gratify the multitude by what is dear to every wedding crowd, "a sight of the bride and bridegroom."

The wedding cake was six feet high. The departure of the couple for Windsor, where they were to spend their honeymoon, was no more than a foreshadowing of that worse departure a week later. The Queen and the Princess of Prussia accompanied their children to the grand entrance; the Prince Consort escorted his daughter to her carriage. The bride wore a while épinglé dress and mantle trimmed with grebe, a white bonnet with orange blossoms, and a Brussel's lace veil. At the family dinner after the excitement and fatigue of the day were over, the Queen felt "lost" without her eldest daughter. In the evening a messenger arrived from Windsor, bringing a letter from the bride telling how the Eton boys had dragged the carriage from the station to the castle, though she might not know that they, had flung up their hats in the air, many of them beyond recovery, the wearers returning bareheaded to their college. When the Queen and the Prince read this letter all London was illuminated, and its streets filled with huzzaing spectators. At the palace the evening closed quietly with a State concert of classic music.

The Princess Royal's honeymoon so far as a period of privacy was concerned, did not last longer than the Queen's. Two days after the marriage the Court followed the young couple to Windsor, where a chapter of the Order of the Garter was held, and Prince Frederick William was created a knight, a banquet being held in the Waterloo Gallery. On the 29th of January, the Court- including the newly married pair-returned to Buckingham Palace, and in the evening the fourth state visit was paid to Her Majesty's Theatre, when The Rivals and The Spitalfields Weaver were given. The bride was in blue and white, the Prussian colours, and wore a wreath of sweet peas on her hair.

On the 30th of January, the addresses from the City of London and other cities and towns of the Empire, many of them accompanied by wedding gifts, were received, and there was a great and of course specially brilliant Drawing-room, which lasted for four hours. On Sunday the thought of the coming separation pressed heavily on those loving hearts, "but God will carry us through, as He did on the 25th," wrote the Queen reverently, "and we have the comfort of seeing the dear young people so perfectly happy."

On Monday, the Queen in noting that it was the last day of their dear child's being with them, admitted she was sick at heart, and the poor young bride confided to her mother, "I think it will kill me to take leave of dear papa."

Tuesday, the 2nd of February, was dark and cold, with snow beginning to fall, unpropitious weather for a long journey, unless in the Scotch saying which declares that a bride is happy who goes "a white gate" (road:) All were assembled in the hall, not a dry eye among them, the Queen believed. "I clasped her in my arms, and blessed her, and knew not what to say." The royal mother shared all good mother's burdens. "I kissed good Fritz, and pressed his hand again and again. He was unable to speak, and the tears were in his eyes." One more embrace of her daughter at the door of the open carriage, into which the Prince Consort and the Prince of Wales went along with the Prince and Princess Frederick William, the band struck up, and they were gone.

The embarkation was at Gravesend. The Londoners assembled in crowds to see the last of their Princess on her route to the coast by the Strand, Cheap, and London Bridge. Many persons recall to this day the sorrowful scene in the cheerless snowy weather. This was the reverse side of all the splendid wedding festivities-the bride of seventeen quitting family, home, and native country, sitting grave and sad beside her equally pale, and silent father—the couple so tenderly attached, on the eve of the final parting. At Gravesend, where young girls, in spite of the snow, strewed flowers before the bride's steps, the Prince waited to see the ship sail—not without risk in the snowstorm—for Antwerp. But no daughter appeared for a last look; the passionate sorrow of youth hid itself from view.

Away at Buckingham Palace the Queen could not bear to look at the familiar objects—all linked with one vanished presence. The very baby princess, so great a darling in the household, only brought the thought of how fond her elder sister had been of her; how but yesterday the two had played together.

The Princess wrote home from the steamer, and every telegram and letter, together with the personal testimony of Lady Churchill and Lord Sydney, who had accompanied the travellers to Berlin, conveyed the most gratifying and consoling intelligence of the warm welcome the stranger had met with, and how well she bore herself in difficult circumstances. "Quiet and dignified, but with a kind word to say of everybody; on the night of her public entry into Berlin and reception at Court, when she polonaised with twenty-two princes in succession." [Footnote: Lady Bloomfield.] The Princess Frederick William continued to write "almost daily, sometimes twice a day," to her mother, and regularly once a week to her father. And another fair young daughter was almost ready to take the Princess Royal's place at the Queen's side. From the date of her sister's marriage, the Prince Consort's letters and the Queen's journal tell that the Princess Alice, with her fine good sense and unselfishness, almost precocious at her age, was a great help and comfort in the royal circle.

CHAPTER XXXI.DEATH OF THE DUTCHESS D'ORLEANS—THE PRINCE CONSORT'S VISIT TO GERMANY—THE QUEEN AND PRINCE CONSORT'S VISIT TO PRINCE AND PRINCESS FREDERICK WILLIAM AT BABELSBERG.

In February, Lord Palmerston's ministry resigned after a defeat on the Conspiracy Bill, and Lord Derby, at the Queen's request, formed a short-lived Cabinet. The Prince of Wales was confirmed on Maundy Thursday in the chapel at Windsor.

In April, the young Queen of Portugal, Princess Stéphanie of Hohenzollern, visited England with her father on her way to her husband—to whom she had been married by proxy—and her future home. Her charm and sweetness greatly attracted the Queen and the Prince. In May, only seven months after the death of Victoire, Duchesse de Nemours, the sympathies of her Majesty and the

Prince Consort were awakened afresh for the Orleans family. Helene, Duchesse d'Orleans, died suddenly from the effects of influenza at Cranbourne House, Richmond. How many of the large family party with which the Queen had been so delighted when she visited Chateau d'Eu had already passed away—the old King, Queen Louise, the Duchesse de Nemours, and now the Duchesse d'Orleans! Her two young sons—the elder the Comte de Paris, not yet twenty—were specially adopted by Queen Amélie.

In the end of May the Prince started for a short visit to Germany, with the double intention of getting a glimpse of his daughter, and revisiting his country for the first time after thirteen years absence. He accomplished both purposes, and heard "the watchman's horn" once more before he retired to rest in the old home. He sent many a loving letter, and tender remembrance to England in anticipation of his speedy return. On his arrival in London he was met by the Queen at the Bricklayers' Arms station.

In the course of a very hot June, the Queen and the Prince went to Warwickshire, which she had known as a young girl, in order to pay a special visit to Birmingham. They were the guests for two nights of Lord and Lady Leigh, at Stoneleigh. Her Majesty had the privilege of seeing Birmingham without a particle of smoke, while a mighty multitude of orderly craftsmen, with their wives and children, stood many hours patiently under the blazing sun, admiring their banners and flags, and cheering lustily for their Queen. One of the objects of the visit was that her Majesty might open a people's museum and park at Aston for the dwellers in the Black country. The royal party drove next day to one of the finest old feudal castles in England— Warwick Castle, with its noble screen of woods, mirroring itself in the Avon— and were entertained at luncheon by Lord and Lady Warwick. In the evening, in the middle of a violent thunderstorm, the Queen and the Prince returned to Buckingham Palace.

This season as usual, there was a visit from the King of the Belgians and several of his family. The first Atlantic cable was laid, and lasted just long enough for the exchange of messages of proud congratulation on the wonderful annihilation of distance between Europe and America, so far as the thoughts of men were concerned.

After a month's stay at Osborne, during one of the warmest Julys ever known in this country, when the condition of the river Thames threatened to drive the Parliament from Westminster, the Queen and the Prince Consort, with the Prince of Wales and their suites, paid a state visit to Cherbourg. The great fort was nearly completed, and the harbour was full of French war-vessels as her Majesty steamed in, on the evening of the 4th of August, receiving such a salute from the ships and the fortress itself as seemed to shake earth and sky. The Emperor and Empress, who arrived the same day, came on board at eight o'clock, and were cordially received by the Queen and the Prince, though the relations between France and England were not quite so assured as when their soldiers were brothers-in-arms in the Crimea. After the visitors left, the Queen's journal records that she went below and read, and nearly finished "that most interesting book 'Jane Eyre.'"

When the Queen and the Prince landed next day, which was fine, they were received by the Emperor and Empress, entered with them one of the imperial carriages, and drove through the town to the Prefecture, where the party breakfasted or rather lunched. In the afternoon the fort with its gigantic ramparts and magnificent views was visited. There was a State dinner in the evening, in the French ship Bretagne. The Emperor received the Queen at the foot of the ladder. The dinner was under canvas on deck amidst decorations of flowers and flags. The Queen sat between the Emperor and the Duke of Cambridge; the Empress sat between the Prince Consort and the Prince of Wales. The speechmaking, to which one may say all Europe was listening, was a trying experience. The Emperor, though he changed colour, spoke well "in a powerful voice," proposing the health of the Queen, the Prince, and the royal family, and declaring his adherence to the French alliance with England. The Prince replied. "He did it very well, though he hesitated once," the Queen reported. "I sat shaking, with my eyes riveted to the table." The duty done, a great relief was felt, as the speechmakers, with the Queen and the Empress, retired to the privacy of the cabin, shook hands, and compared notes on their nervousness.

A splendid display of fireworks was witnessed from the deck of the Bretagne. In the middle of it the Queen and the Prince returned to the yacht, escorted by the Emperor and Empress, when they took their departure in turn. They were followed by showers of English rockets and rounds of English cheers.

The next morning the Emperor and Empress paid a farewell visit on board the yacht, which sailed at last under "heavy salutes." At five o'clock in the afternoon the beach at Osborne was reached. The sailor Prince, whose fourteenth birthday it was, stood on the pier. All the children, including the baby, were at the door. The dogs added their welcome. The young Prince's birthday-table was inspected. There was still time to visit the Swiss Cottage, to which Princess Alice and the Queen drove the other members of the family. The children's castle, where they had lunched in honour of the day, was gay with flags. Prince Alfred with Princess Alice was promoted to join the royal dinner party. The little princes, Arthur and Leopold, appeared at dessert. "A band played," writes the Queen, "and after dinner we danced, with the three boys and the three girls and the company, a merry country-dance on the terrace—a delightful finale to the expedition! It seemed a dream that this morning at twelve we should have been still at Cherbourg, with the Emperor and Empress on board our yacht."

On the 11th of August, the Queen and the Prince arrived in the yacht at Antwerp, on their way to Germany, to pay their first eagerly anticipated visit to the Princess Royal—then a wife of six months standing—in her Prussian home.

The travellers proceeded by railway to Malines, where they were met by King Leopold with his second son, and escorted to Verviers in a progress which was to be as far as possible without soldiers, salutes, addresses; and at Aix-la-Chapelle the Prince of Prussia joined the party. The halt for the night was at Dusseldorf, where the Prince and Princess of Hohenzollern were waiting. The Queen and the Prince Consort quitted their hotel to dine with the Hohenzollern family, in whose members they were much interested. The Queen made the acquaintance of a young son who is now Prince of Roumania, and a handsome girl-princess who has become the wife of the Comte de Flanders, King Leopold's younger son.

The next day, long looked forward to as that which was to bring about a reunion with the Princess Royal, was suddenly overclouded by the news of the sad, unexpected death of the Prince's worthy valet, "Cart," who had come with him to England, and been in his service twenty-nine years—since his master was a child of eight The Prince entered the room as the Queen was dressing, carrying a telegram, and saying "My poor Cart is dead." Both felt the loss of the old friend acutely. "All day long," wrote the Queen, "the tears would rush into my eyes." She added, "He was the only link my loved one had about him which connected him with his childhood, the only one with whom he could talk over old times. I cannot think of my dear husband without Cart." It was no day for sorrow, yet the noble, gentle hearts bled through all their joys.

Before seven the royal party, including the Prince of Prussia, were on their way through Rhenish Prussia. As the train rushed by the railway platform at Buckeburg there stood the aged Baroness Lehzen, the Queen's good old governess, waving her handkerchief. In the station at Hanover were the King and Queen of Hanover, Princess Frederick Charles of Prussia, and her Majesty's niece, the Princess Feodore of Hohenlohe, a charming girl of nineteen, with her betrothed husband, the Duke of Saxe-Meiningen, a widower of thirty-two.

The Queen then made the acquaintance of one of the cradles of her race, driving out to the country palace of Herrenhausen, which had been the home of the Electress Sophia, and where George I. was residing when he was summoned to be king of England. At five o'clock, in the heat and the dust, her Majesty resumed her journey, "with a racking headache." At Magdeburg Prince Frederick William appeared, "radiant," with the welcome intelligence that his Princess was at the Wildpark station. "There on the platform stood our darling child, with a nosegay in her hand." The Queen described the scene. "She stepped in, and long and warm was the embrace, as she clasped me in her arms; so much to say, and to tell, and to ask, yet so unaltered; looking well, quite the old Vicky still! It was a happy moment, for which I thank God!" It was eleven o'clock at night before the party reached Babelsberg—a pleasant German country house, with which her Majesty was much pleased. It became her headquarters for the fortnight during which her visit lasted. In addition to enjoying the society of her daughter, the Queen became familiar with the Princess's surroundings. Daily excursions were made to a succession of palaces connected with the past and present Prussian royal family. In this manner her Majesty learnt to know the King's palace in Berlin, while the poor King, a wreck in health, was absent; Frederick the Great's Schloss at Potsdam; his whimsical Sans Souci with its orange-trees, the New Palais, and Charlottenburg with its mausoleum. The Queen also attended two great reviews, gave a day to the Berlin Museum, and met old Humboldt more than once. Among the other guests at Babelsberg were the Duke of Saxe- Coburg and Baron Stockmar. The Prince Consort's thirty-ninth birthday was celebrated in his daughter's house. At last with struggling tears and a bravely said "Auf baldiges wiedersehn" (to a speedy meeting again), the strongly attached family party separated. The peculiar pang of separation to the Queen, she expressed in words which every mother will understand. "All would be comparatively easy were it not for the one thought, that I cannot be with her (the Princess Royal), at that very critical moment when every other mother goes to her child."

The royal travellers stayed over the Sunday at Deutz, and again saw Cologne illuminated, the cathedral like "a mass of glowing red fire." On reaching Osborne on the 31st of August, the Queen and the Prince were met by Prince Alfred—who had just passed his examination and been appointed to a ship—"in his middy's jacket, cap, and dirk."

On their way to Scotland the Queen and the Prince Consort, accompanied by the Princesses Alice and Helena, visited Leeds, for the purpose of opening the Leeds Town Hall. The party stayed at Woodley House, the residence of the mayor, who is described in her Majesty's journal as a "perfect picture of a fine old man." In his crimson velvet robes and chain of office he looked "the personification of a Venetian doge." The Queen as usual made "the tour of the town amidst a great concourse of spectators." She remarked on the occasion, "Nowhere have I seen the children's names so often inscribed. On one large arch were even 'Beatrice and Leopold,' which gave me much pleasure...." a result which, had they known it, would have highly gratified the loyal clothworkers. After receiving the usual addresses, the Queen knighted the mayor, and by her command Lord Derby declared the hall open.

While her Majesty was at Balmoral, the marriages of a niece and nephew of hers took place in Germany—Princess Feodore, the youngest daughter of the Princess of Hehenlohe, married the Duke of Saxe-Meiningen; and Ernest, Prince of Leiningen, the eldest son of the late Prince of Leiningen, who was in the English navy, married Princess Marie Amélie of Baden.

More of the English royal children were taking flight from the parent nest. Mr. Bruce, Lord Elgin's brother, was appointed Governor to the Prince of Wales, and was about to set out with him on a tour in Italy. Prince Alfred was with his ship at Malta.

CHAPTER XXXII.BIRTH OF PRINCE WILLIAM OF PRUSSIA— DEATH OF PRINCE HOHENLOHE— VOLUNTEER REVIEWS— SECOND VISIT TO COBURG—BETROTHAL OF PRINCESS ALICE.

One of the beauties of the Queen's early Court, Lady Clementina Villiers, daughter of the Earl of Jersey, died unmarried at her father's seat of Middleton Park in 1858. She was as good and clever as she was beautiful. Like her lovely sister, Princess Nicholas Esterhazy, Lady Clementina died in the prime of life, being only thirty-four years of age.

On the 27th of January, 1859, the Queen and the Prince received the good news of the birth of their first grandchild, a fine boy, after great suffering on the part of the young mother. He had forty-two godfathers and godmothers.

In April Princess Alice was confirmed. Her Majesty's estimate of her daughter's character was amply borne out in the years to come. "She is very good, gentle, sensible, and amiable, and a real comfort to me." Without her sister, the Princess Royal's, remarkable intellectual power, Princess Alice had fine intelligence. She was also fair to see in her royal maidenhood. The two elder sons were away. The Prince of Wales was in Italy, Prince Alfred with his ship in the Levant. At home the volunteer movement, which has since acquired such large proportions, was being actively inaugurated. The war between Austria and France, and a dissolution of Parliament, made this spring a busy and an anxious time. The first happy visit from the Princess Royal, who came to join in celebrating her Majesty's birthday at Osborne, would have made the season altogether joyous, had it not been for a sudden and dangerous attack of erysipelas from which the Duchess of Kent suffered. The alarm was brief, but it was sharp while it lasted.

In June her Majesty opened the new Parliament, an event which was followed in a fortnight by the resignation of Lord Derby's Ministry, and Lord Palmerston became Prime Minister with a strong Cabinet.

At the close of the season the sad news arrived of the sudden death from diphtheria of the year-old wife, the young Queen of Portugal.

In August the Queen and the Prince made one of their yachting excursions to the Channel Islands. The Duchess of Kent's seventy-third birthday was kept at Osborne. During the autumn stay of the Court at Balmoral, the Prince presided over the British Association for the Promotion of Science, which met that year at Aberdeen. He afterwards entertained two hundred members of the association, filling four omnibuses, in addition to carriages, at a Highland gathering at Balmoral. The day was cold and showery, but with gleams of sunshine. It is unnecessary to say that the attendance was large, and the games and dancing were conducted with much spirit. In honour of the country, the Prince and his sons appeared in kilts, the Queen and the Princesses in royal Stewart tartan skirts and shawls over black velvet bodices.

In 1859 the Queen made no less than three successful ascents of Highland mountains, Morvem, Lochnagar, and at last Ben Macdhui, the highest mountain in Scotland, upwards of four thousand feet. On the return of the royal party they went from Edinburgh to Loch Katrine, in order to open the Glasgow Waterworks, the conclusion of a great undertaking which was marred not inappropriately by a very wet day. The Queen and the Prince made a detour on their homeward route, as they had occasionally done before, visiting Wales and Lord Penryn at Penryn Castle. This year saw the publication of a memorable book, "Adam Bede," for which even its precursor, "Scenes from Clerical Life," had not prepared the world of letters. The novel was much admired in the royal circle. In one of the rooms at Osborne, as a pendant to a picture from the "Faery Queen," there hangs a representation from a very different masterpiece in English literature, of the young Squire watching Hetty in the dairy.

In the beginning of winter the Prince suffered from an unusually severe fit of illness. In November the Princess Royal again visited England, accompanied by her husband.

There were cheery winter doings at Osborne, when the great household, like one large family, rejoiced in the seasonable snow, in a slide "used by young and old," and in a "splendid snow man." The new year was joyously danced in, though the children who were wont to assemble at the Queen's dressing-room door to call in chorus "Prosit Neu Jahr," were beginning to be scattered far and wide.

In January, 1860, the Queen opened Parliament in person, when for the first time the Princesses Alice and Helena were present.

On the twentieth anniversary of the Queen's wedding-day she wrote to Baron Stockmar, "I wish I could think I had made one as happy as he has made me."

In April the Prince of Hohenlohe-Langenberg, the Queen's brother-in-law, who was now an old man, died at Baden, after a long illness. He had been an upright, unlucky German prince, trusted by his contemporaries, a good husband and father—whose loss was severely felt by the widowed Princess. Her sorrow was reflected in the Queen's sympathy for her sister.

This year's Academy Exhibition contained Millais's "Black Brunswicker," Landseer's "Flood in the Highlands," and Phillips's "Marriage of the Princess Royal," now in the great corridor at Windsor Castle. "The Idyls of the King," much admired by the Prince, were the poems of the year.

Among the guests at Windsor Castle for Ascot week, in addition to King Leopold, who came to look once more on the old scene, were Prince Louis of Hesse and his younger brother. In a letter of the Prince Consort's, written soon afterwards, he alludes to an apparent "liking" between Prince Louis and Princess Alice.

Sir Arthur Helps, whose subsequent literary relations with the Queen were so friendly, was sworn in Clerk of the Council on the 23rd of June.

The first great volunteer review took place in Hyde Park this summer. The Queen was present, driving with Princess Alice, Prince Arthur, and King Leopold, while the Prince Consort rode. The display of the twenty thousand citizen soldiers, at that time reckoned a large volunteer force, was in every respect satisfactory. As a sequel her Majesty was also present during fine weather, in an exceptionally wet summer, at the first meeting of the National Rifle Association at Wimbledon, when the first shot was fired by the Queen, the rifle being so arranged that a touch to the trigger caused the bullseye to be hit, when the shooter scored three points.

At the close of the season the Prince of Wales sailed for Canada, after he had accepted the President of the United States' invitation to visit him at Washington. At the same time another distant colony was to be graced by the presence of royalty; it was settled that Prince Alfred was to land at the Cape of Good Hope. The Queen's sons were to serve her by representing her race and rule in her far distant dominions.

In July the Princess Royal became the medium, in a letter home, of the overtures of the Hesse family for a marriage between Prince Louis and Princess Alice—overtures favourably received by the Queen and the Prince, who were much attracted by the young suitor. Immediately afterwards came the intelligence of the birth of the Princess Royal's second child—a daughter. The eyes of all Europe began to be directed to Garibaldi as the champion of freedom in Naples and Sicily.

In August the Court went North, staying longer than usual in Edinburgh for the purpose of holding a volunteer review in the Queen's Park, which was even a greater success than that in Hyde Park. The summer day was cloudless; the broken nature of the ground heightened the picturesqueness of the spectacle. There was much greater variety in the dress and accoutrements of the Highland and Lowland regiments, numbering rather more than their English neighbours. The martial bearing of many of the men was remarkable, and the spectators crowding Arthur's Seat from the base to the summit were enthusiastic in their loyalty. The Queen rejoiced to have the Duchess of Kent by her side in the open carriage. The old Duchess had not appeared at any public sight for years, and her presence on this occasion recalled former days. She was not venturing so far as Abergeldie, but was staying at Cramond House, near Edinburgh. Soon after the Queen and the Prince's arrival at Balmoral the news reached them of the death of their aunt, the Duchess of Kent's only surviving sister, the widow of the Grand- Duke Constantine of Russia.

This year the Queen and the Prince, with the Princesses Alice and
Helena, made, in fine weather, a second ascent of Ben Macdhui.

The success of such an excursion led to a longer expedition, which meant a night spent on the way at what was little better than a village inn. Such a step was only possible when entire secrecy, and even a certain amount of disguise, were maintained. Indeed, the little innocent mystery, with all the amusement it brought, was part of the pleasure. The company consisted of the Queen and the Prince, Lady Churchill and General Grey, with two keepers for attendants. Their destination, reached by driving, riding, and walking through the shiel of the Geldie, Glen Geldie, Glen Fishie, &c, was Grantown, where the party spent the night, and were waited on, in all unconsciousness, by a woman in ringlets in the evening and in curl-papers in the morning. But before Grantown was left, when the truth was known, the same benighted chambermaid was seen waving a flag from the window of the dining and drawing-room in one, which had been lately so honoured, while the landlady on the threshold made a vigorous use of her pocket-handkerchief, to the edification and delight of an excited crowd in the street.

The Court returned to Osborne, and on the 22nd of September the Queen, the Prince, and Princess Alice, with the suite, sailed from Gravesend for Antwerp en route for Coburg, where the Princess Royal was to meet them with her husband and the child-prince, whom his grandparents had not yet seen.

The King of the Belgians, his sons and daughter-in-law met the travellers with the melancholy intelligence that the Prince's stepmother, the Duchess-Dowager of Coburg, who had been ill for some time, but was looking forward to this visit, lay in extremity. At Verviers a telegram announced that she had died at five o'clock that morning—a great shock to those who were hastening to see her and receive her welcome once more. Royal kindred met and greeted the party at each halting-place, as by Aix-la-Chapelle, Frankfort, where they slept, the valley of the Maine and the Thuringen railway, the travellers approached Coburg. Naturally the Queen grew agitated at the thought of the arrival, so different from what she had expected and experienced on her last visit, fifteen years before. At the station were the Duke of Saxe-Coburg and Prince

Frederick William of Prussia, in deep mourning. Everything was quiet and private. At the door of the palace, in painful contrast to the gala faces and dresses of her earlier reception, stood the Grand Duchess and the Princess Royal in the deepest German mourning, with long black veils, the point hanging over the forehead. Around were the ladies and gentlemen of the suites. "A tender embrace, and then we walked up the staircase," wrote the Queen; "I could hardly speak, I felt so moved, and quite trembled." Her room was that which had formerly belonged to the Duchess of Kent when she was a young Coburg princess. One of its windows looked up a picturesque narrow street with red roofs and high gables, leading to the market-place. His English nurse led in the Queen's first grandchild, aged two years, "in a little white dress with black bows." He was charming to his royal grandmother. She particularised his youthful attractions—"A beautiful white soft skin, very fine shoulders and limbs, and a very dear face, ... very fair curly hair." The funeral of the Dowager-Duchess took place at seven o'clock on the morning of the 27th September, at Gotha, and was attended by the gentlemen of the party, while the ladies in deep mourning, wearing the pointed veils, were present at a commemorative service in the Schloss Kirche at Coburg.

Then followed a quiet happy time, among the pleasures of which were the daily visits from the little grandchild, the renewal of intercourse with Baron Stockmar, whom Germans called the familiar spirit of the house of Coburg; the acquaintance of the great novelist, Auerbach; a visit to Florrschutz, the Prince's old tutor, in the pretty house which his two pupils had built for him.

The holiday was alarmingly interrupted by what might have been a grave accident to the Prince Consort. He was driving alone in an open carriage with four horses, which took fright and dashed along at full gallop in the direction of the railway line, where a waggon stood in front of a bar, put up to guard a level crossing. Seeing that a crash was inevitable, the Prince leapt out, escaping with several bruises and cuts, while the driver, who had remained with the carriage, was thrown out when it came in contact with the railway-bar, and seriously hurt. One of the horses was killed, the others rushed along the road to Coburg. They were met by the Prince's equerry, Colonel Ponsonby, who in great anxiety procured a carriage and drove with two doctors to the spot, where he found the Prince lending aid to the injured man. Colonel Ponsonby was sent to intercept the Queen as she was walking and sketching with her daughter and sister-in-law, to tell her of the accident and of the Prince's escape, before she could hear a garbled version of the affair from other quarters.

In deep gratitude for the Prince's preservation, her Majesty afterwards set aside the sum deemed necessary—rather more than a thousand pounds—to found a charity called the "Victoria Stift," which helps a certain number of young men and women of good character in their apprenticeship, in setting them up in trade, and marriage.

The royal party returned at the end of a fortnight by Frankfort and Mayence. At Coblentz, where they spent the night, her Majesty was attacked by cold and sore throat, though she walked and drove out next day, inspecting every object she was asked to see in suffering and discomfort. It was her last day with the Princess Royal and "the darling little boy," whom his grandmother was so pleased to have with her, running about and playing in her room. The following day was cold and wet, and the Queen felt still worse, continuing her journey so worn out and unwell that she could only rouse herself before reaching Brussels, where King Leopold was at the station awaiting her. By the order of her doctor, who found her labouring under a feverish cold with severe sore throat, she was confined to her room, where she had to lie down and keep quiet. Never in the whole course of her Majesty's healthful life, save in one girlish illness at Ramsgate, of which the world knew nothing, had she felt so ailing. Happily a night's rest restored her to a great extent; but while a State dinner which had been invited in her honour was going on, she had still to stay in her room, with Lady Churchill reading to her "The Mill on the Floss," and the door open that the Queen might hear the band of the Guides.

On the 17th of October the travellers left Brussels, and on the 17th arrived at Windsor, where they were met by the younger members of the family.

On the 30th of October the great sea captain, Lord Dundonald, closed his chequered life in his eighty-fifth year.

In December two gallant wooers were at the English Court, as a few years before King Pedro, the Arch-Duke Maximilian, and Prince Frederick William were all young bridegrooms in company. On this occasion Prince Louis of Hesse-Darmstadt came to win Princess Alice, and the hereditary Prince of Hohenzollern Seigmaringen was on his way to ask the hand of Donna Antoine, sister of King Pedro. Lord Campbell paid a visit to Windsor at this time, and made his comment on the royal lovers. "My stay at Windsor was rather dull, but was a little enhanced by the loves of Prince Louis of Hesse and the Princess Alice. He had arrived the night before, almost a stranger to her" (a mistake), "but as her suitor. At first they were very shy, but they soon reminded me of Ferdinand and Miranda in the Tempest, and I looked on like old Prospero."

The betrothal of Princess Alice occurred within the week. Her Majesty has given an account in the pages of her journal, transferred to the "Life of the Prince Consort," how simply and naturally it happened. "After dinner, whilst talking to the gentlemen, I perceived Alice and Louis talking before the fireplace more earnestly than usual, and when I passed to go to the other room both came up to me, and Alice in much agitation said he had proposed to her, and he begged for my blessing. I could only squeeze his hand and say 'Certainly,' and that we would see him in our room, later. Got through the evening work as well as we could. Alice came to our room … agitated but quiet…. Albert sent for Louis to his room, went first to him, and then called Alice and me in…." The bride was only seventeen, the bridegroom twenty-three years of age—but nearly two years were to elapse, with, alas! sad changes in their course, before the marriage thus happily settled was celebrated.

This winter her Majesty's old servant and friend, Lord Aberdeen, died.

In December the Empress of the French, who had recently lost her sister, the Duchess of Alba, in order to recover health and cheerfulness, paid a flying visit in private to England and Scotland. From Claridge's Hotel she went for a day to Windsor to see the Queen and the Prince. Towards the close of the year the Prince had a brief but painful attack of one of the gastric affections becoming so common with him.

In January, 1861, the Queen received the news of the death of the invalid King of Prussia at Sans Souci. His brother, the Crown Prince, who had been regent for years, succeeded to the throne, of which the husband of the Princess Royal was now the next heir.

In the beginning of the year the Prince of Wales matriculated at Cambridge.

In February the Queen opened Parliament. The twenty-first anniversary of the royal wedding-day falling on a Sunday, it was celebrated quietly but with much happiness. The Queen wrote to her uncle, King Leopold, "Very few can say with me that their husband, at the end of twenty-one years, is not only full of the friendship, kindness, and affection which a truly happy marriage brings with it, but of the same tender love as in the very first days of our marriage."

CHAPTER XXXIII.DEATH OF THE DUCHESS OF KENT.

The Duchess of Kent was now seventy-five years of age. For the last few years she had been in failing health, tenderly cared for by her children. When she had been last in town she had not gone to her own house, Clarence House, but had stayed with her daughter in the cheerful family circle at Buckingham Palace.

A loss in her household fell heavily on the aged Duchess. Sir George Cooper, her secretary, to whose services she had been used for many years, a man three years her junior, died in February, 1860.

In March the Duchess underwent a surgical operation for a complaint affecting her right arm and rendering it useless, so that the habits of many years had to be laid aside, and she could no longer without difficulty work, or write, or play on the piano, of which her musical talent and taste had made her particularly fond. The Queen and the Prince visited the Duchess at Frogmore on the 12th of March, and found her in a suffering but apparently not a dangerous condition.

On the 15th good news, including the medical men's report and a letter from Lady Augusta Bruce, the Duchess of Kent's attached lady-in- waiting, came from Frogmore to Buckingham Palace, and the Queen and the Prince went without any apprehension on a visit to the gardens of the Horticultural Society at Kensington. Her Majesty returned alone, leaving the Prince to transact some business. She was "resting quite happily" in her arm-chair, when the Prince arrived with a message from Sir James Clark that the Duchess had been seized with a shivering fit— a bad symptom, from which serious consequences were apprehended.

In two hours the Queen, the Prince, and Princess Alice were at Frogmore. "Just the same," was the sorrowful answer given by the ladies and gentlemen awaiting them.

The Prince Consort went up to the Duchess's room and came back with tears in his eyes; then the Queen knew what to expect. With a trembling heart she followed her husband and entered the bedroom. There "on a sofa, supported by cushions, the room much darkened," sat the Duchess, "leaning back, breathing heavily in her silk dressing- gown, with her cap on, looking quite herself"

For a second the sight of the dear familiar figure, so little changed, must have afforded a brief reprieve, and lent a sense of almost glad incredulity to the distress which had gone before. But the well-meant whisper of one of the attendants of "Ein sanftes ende" destroyed the passing illusion. "Seeing that my presence did not disturb her," the Queen wrote afterwards, "I knelt before her, kissed her dear hand and placed it next my cheek; but though she opened her eyes, she did not, I think, know me. She brushed my hand off, and the dreadful reality was before me that for the first time she did not know the child she had ever received with such tender smiles. I went out to sob.... I asked the doctors if there was no hope; they said they feared none whatever, for consciousness had left her.... It was suffusion of water on the chest which had come on."

The long night passed in sad watching by the unconscious sufferer, and in vain attempts at rest in preparation for the greater sorrow that was in store.

A few months earlier, on the death of the King of Prussia, the Prince Consort had written to his daughter that her experience exceeded his, for he had never seen any person die. The Queen had been equally unacquainted with the mournful knowledge which comes to most even before they have attained mature manhood and womanhood. Now the loving daughter knelt or stood by the mother who was leaving her without a sign, or lay painfully listening to the homely trivial sounds which broke the stillness of the night—the crowing of a cock, the dogs barking in the distance; the striking of the old repeater which had belonged to the Queen's father, that she had heard every night in her childhood, but to which she had not listened for twenty-three years— the whole of her full happy married life. She wondered with the vague piteous wonder—natural in such a case—what her mother, would have thought of her passing a night under her roof again, and she not to know it?

In the March morning the Prince took the Queen from the room in which she could not rest, yet from which she could not remain absent. When she returned windows and doors were thrown open. The Queen sat down on a footstool and held the Duchess's hand, while the paleness of death stole over the face, and the features grew longer and sharper. "I fell on my knees," her Majesty wrote afterwards, "holding the beloved hand which was still warm and soft, though heavier, in both of mine. I felt the end was fast approaching, as Clark went out to call Albert and Alice, I only left gazing on that beloved face, and feeling as if my heart would break.... It was a solemn, sacred, never-to-be-forgotten scene. Fainter and fainter grew the breathing; at last it ceased, but there was no change of countenance, nothing; the eyes closed as they had been for the last half-hour.... The clock struck half-past nine at the very moment. Convulsed with sobs I fell on the hand and covered it with kisses. Albert lifted me up and took me into the next room, himself entirely melted into tears, which is unusual for him, deep as his feelings are, and clasped me in his arms. I asked if all was over; he said, "Yes." I went into the room again after a few minutes and gave one look. My darling mother was sitting as she had done before, but was already white. Oh, God! how awful, how mysterious! But what a blessed end. Her gentle spirit at rest, her sufferings over."

By the Prince's advice the Queen went at once to the late Duchess's sitting-room, where it was hard to bear the unchanged look of everything, "Chairs, cushions ... all on the tables, her very work-basket with her work; the little canary bird which she was so fond of, singing!"

In one of the recently published letters of Princess Alice to the Queen, the former recalled after an interval of eight years the words which her father had spoken to her on the death of her grandmother, when he brought the daughter to the mother and said, "Comfort mamma," a simple injunction which sounded like a solemn charge in the sad months to come.

The melancholy tidings of the loss were conveyed by the Queen's hand to the Duchess's elder daughter, the Princess of Hohenlohe; to the Duchess's brother, the King of the Belgians—the last survivor of his family—and to her eldest grand-daughter, the Crown Princess of Prussia.

The moment the Princess Royal heard of the death she started for England, and arrived there two days afterwards.

The unaffected tribute of respect paid by the whole country, led by the Houses of Parliament, to the virtues of the late Duchess, was very welcome to the mourners. The Duchess of Kent by her will bequeathed her property to the Queen, and appointed the Prince Consort her sole executor. "He was so tender and kind," wrote the Queen, "so pained to have to ask me distressing questions, but spared me so much. Everything done so quickly and feelingly."

The funeral took place on the 25th of March, in the vault beneath St. George's Chapel, Windsor. The Prince Consort acted as chief mourner, and was supported by two of the grandchildren of the late Duchess, the Prince of Wales and the Prince of Leiningen. The pallbearers were six ladies; among whom was Lady Augusta Bruce. Neither the Queen nor her daughters were present. They remained, in the Queen's words, "to pray at home together, and to dwell on the happiness and peace of her who was gone." On the evening of the funeral the Queen and the Prince dined alone; afterwards he read aloud to her letters written by her mother to a German friend, giving an account of the illness and death of the Duke of Kent more than forty years before. The Queen continued the allowances which the Duchess of Kent had made to her elder daughter, the Princess Hohenlohe, and to two of the duchess's grandsons, Prince Victor Hohenlohe and Prince Edward Leiningen. Her Majesty pensioned the Duchess's servants, and appointed Lady Augusta Bruce, who had been like a daughter to the dead Princess, resident bedchamber woman to the

Queen.

Frogmore had been much frequented by Queen Charlotte and her daughters, and was the place where they held many of their family festivals. It had been the country house of Princess Augusta for more than twenty years. On her death it was given to the Duchess of Kent. It is an unpretending white country house, spacious enough, and with all the taste of the day when it was built expended on the grounds, which does not prevent them from lying very low, with the inevitable sheet of water almost beneath the windows. Yet it is a lovely, bowery, dwelling when spring buds are bursting and the birds are filling the air with music; such a sheltered, peaceful, home-like house as an ageing woman well might crave. On it still lingers, in spite of a period when it passed into younger hands, the stamp of the old Duchess, with her simple state, her unaffected dignity, her affectionate interest in her numerous kindred. The place is but a bowshot from the old grey castle of Windsor. It was a chosen resort of the royal children, to whom the noble, kind, grandame was all that gracious age can be. Here the Queen brought the most distinguished of her guests to present them to her mother, who had known so many of the great men of her time. Here the royal daughter herself came often, leaving behind her the toils of government and the ceremonies of rank, where she could always be at ease, was always more than welcome. Here she comes still, after twenty years, to view old scenes—the chair by which she sat when the Duchess of Kent occupied it, the piano she knew so well, the familiar portraits, the old-fashioned furniture, suiting the house admirably, the drooping trees on the lawn, under which the Queen would breakfast in fine weather, according to an old Kensington —an old German—custom.

The long verandah was wont to contain vases of flowers and statues of the Duchess's grandchildren, and formed a pleasant promenade for an old lady. Within the smaller, cosier rooms, with the softly tinted pink walls covered with portraits, was led the daily life which as it advanced in infirmity necessarily narrowed in compass, while the State rooms remained for family and Court gatherings. The last use made of the great drawing-room by its venerable mistress was after her death, when she lay in state there.

Half-length portraits of the Duke and Duchess of Kent are in the place usually occupied by the likenesses of the master and mistress of the house. Among the other pictures are full-length portraits of the Queen and Prince Albert in their youth, taken soon after their marriage— like the natural good end to the various pictures of her Majesty in her fair English childhood and maidenhood, with the blonde hair clustering about the open innocent forehead, the fearless blue eyes, the frank mouth. The child, long a widow in her turn, a mother, grandmother, great-grandmother, must look with strange mingled feelings on these shadows of her early, unconscious self.

There are innumerable likenesses of the Queen's children such as a loving grandmother would delight to accumulate, from the baby Princess Royal with the good dog Eos curled round by her side, the child's tiny foot on the hound's nose, to the same Princess a blooming girl-bride by the side of her bridegroom, Prince Frederick William of Prussia.

The Duchess's other children and grandchildren are here on canvas, with many portraits of her brothers and sisters and their children. A full-length likeness of the former owner of Frogmore, Princess Augusta, Fanny Burney's beloved princess, hangs above a chimneypiece; while on the walls of another room quaintly painted floral festoons, the joint work of the painter, Mary Moser, and the artistic Princess Elizabeth, are still preserved.

Frogmore was for some years the residence of Princess Christian of Schleswig-Holstein. When she removed to Cumberland House, the furniture which had belonged to the Duchess of Kent was brought back, and the place restored as much as possible to the condition in which she had left it, which implies the presence of many cherished relics— such as the timepiece which was the last gift of the Queen and the Prince, and a picture said to have been painted by both representing Italian peasants praying beside a roadside calvary. There are numerous tokens of womanly tastes in the gay, bright fashion of the Duchess's time, among them a gorgeously tinted inlaid table from the first Exhibition, and elaborate specimens of Berlin woolwork, offerings from friends of the mistress of the house and from the ladies of her suite. In one of the simply furnished bedrooms of quiet little Frogmore, as it chanced, the heir of the Prince of Wales first saw the light. For here was born unexpectedly, making a great stir in the little household, Prince Victor Albert of Wales.

CHAPTER XXXIV.LAST VISIT TO IRELAND—HIGHLAND EXCURSIONS—MEETING OF THE PRINCE OF WALES AND THE PRINCESS ALEXANDRA OF DENMARK—DEATH OF THE KINO OF PORTUGAL AND HIS BROTHERS

In the retirement of Osborne the Queen mourned her mother with the tender fidelity which her people have learnt to know and reverence.

In April the Court returned to Buckingham Palace, when the Queen announced the marriage of the Princess Alice to the Privy Council It was communicated to Parliament, and was very favourably received. The Princess had a dowry of thirty thousand, and an annuity of six thousand pounds from the country.

The Queen's birthday was celebrated at Osborne without the usual festivities. During the Whitsun holidays Prince Louis, who was with the family, had the misfortune to be attacked by measles, which he communicated to Prince Leopold. The little boy had the disease severely, and it left bad results.

In June King Leopold and one of his sons paid the Queen a lengthened visit of five weeks. The Princess Royal, with her husband and children, arrived afterwards, and there was a happy family meeting, tinged with sorrow.

In July the most exalted Order of the Star of India was instituted, and conferred first on the Maharajah Dhuleep Singh, Lord Clyde, Sir John Lawrence, &c., &c. That summer saw the death of two statesmen who had been men of mark in the Crimean war—Count Cavour, the Sardinian Prime Minister, and Lord Herbert of Lea. The royal visitors in London and at Osborne included the Archduke Maximilian and his young wife, and the King of Sweden and his son.

Towards the close of August the Queen went to Frogmore with the Prince and Princess Alice, in order to keep the birthday of the late Duchess of Kent, whose remains had been already removed from St. George's chapel to the mausoleum prepared for them in the grounds of her former home. The Queen wrote of the first evening at Frogmore as "terribly trying;" but it comforted her in the beautiful morning to visit the grand simple mausoleum, and to help to place on the granite sarcophagus the wreaths which had been brought for the purpose.

The day after the return of Prince Alfred from the West Indies, the Queen and the Prince, their second son and the Princesses Alice and Helena, sailed from Holyhead in the Victoria and Albert for Kingstown. This visit to Ireland meant also the royal presence on a field-day in the Curragh camp, where the Prince of Wales was serving, and a run down to Killarney in very hot weather. At the lakes the Queen was the guest of Lord Castleross and Mr. Herbert. The wild luxuriant scenery, the size and beauty of the arbutus-trees, and the enthusiastic shriek of the blue-cloaked women, made their due impression. In a row on one of the lakes her Majesty christened a point. The Prince's birthday came round during the stay in Ireland, and was marked by the usual loving tokens, though the Queen noted sadly the difference between this and other anniversaries: the lack of festivities, the absence from home, the separation from the younger children, and the missing the old invariable gift from the Duchess of Kent.

Balmoral was reached in the beginning of September. Prince Louis came speedily, and another welcome guest, Princess Hohenlohe, who travelled north with Lady Augusta Bruce. Dr. Norman Macleod gives a glimpse of the circumstances and the circle. He preached to the Queen, and she thanked him for the comfort he gave her. Lady Augusta Bruce talked to him of "that noble, loving woman, the Duchess of Kent, and of the Queen's grief." He found the Queen's half-sister "an admirable woman" and Prince Alfred "a fine gentlemanly sailor."

The Queen's greatest solace this year was in long days spent on the purple mountains and by the sides of the brown lochs, and in a second private expedition, like that of the previous year to Grantown, when she slept a night at the Ramsay Arms in the village of Fettercairn, and Prince Louis and General Grey were consigned to the Temperance Hotel opposite. The whole party walked out in the moonlight and were startled by a village band. The return was by Blair, where the Queen was welcomed by her former host and hostess, the Duke and Duchess of Athole. Her Majesty had a look at her earlier quarters, at the room in which the little Princess Royal had been put to bed in two chairs, and saw Sandy Macara, grown old and grey.

After an excursion to Cairn Glaishie, her Majesty recorded in her journal, "Alas! I fear our last great one." Six years afterwards the sorrowful confirmation was given to words which had been written with a very different meaning, "It was our last one."

The Prince of Wales was on a visit to Germany, ostensibly to witness the manoeuvres of the Prussian army, but with a more delicate mission behind. He was bound, while not yet twenty, to make the acquaintance of the Princess Alexandra of Denmark, not quite seventeen, with the probability of their future marriage—a prospect which, to the great regret of the Prince Consort, got almost immediately into the newspapers. The first meetings of the young couple took place at Speyer and Heidelberg, and were altogether promising of the mutual attachment which was the desired result.

On the 18th of October the King of Prussia was crowned at Könisburg—a splendid ceremonial, in which the Princess Royal naturally, as the Crown Princess, bore a prominent part.

On the return of the Court to Windsor, Prince Leopold, then between eight and nine years of age, was sent, with a temporary household, to spend the winter in the south of France for the sake of his health.

Suddenly a great and painful shock was given to the Queen and the Prince by the news of the disastrous outbreak of typhoid fever in Portugal among their royal cousins and intimate friends, the sons of Maria de Gloria. When the tidings arrived King Pedro's brother, Prince Ferdinand, was already dead, and the King ill. Two more brothers, the Duke of Oporto and the Duke of Beja, were in England, on their way home from the King of Prussia's coronation. The following day still sadder news arrived—the recovery of the young king, not more than twenty-five, was despaired of. His two brothers started immediately for Lisbon, but were too late to see him in life. The younger, the Duke of Beja, was also seized with the fatal fever and died in the course of the following month. The Queen and the Prince lamented the King deeply, finding the only consolation in the fact that he had rejoined the gentle girl-wife for whose loss he had been inconsolable.

CHAPTER XXXV.THE DEATH OF THE PRINCE CONSORT.

The news of the terrible mortality in the Portuguese royal family, especially the death of the King, to whom the Prince was warmly attached, had seriously affected his health, never strong, and for the last few years gradually declining, with gastric attacks becoming more frequent and fits of sleeplessness more confirmed. At the same time the Prince's spirit was so unbroken, his power of work and even of enjoyment so unshaken, while the patience and unselfishness which treated his own bodily discomfort as a matter of little moment had grown so much the habit of his mind, that naturally those nearest to him failed in their very love to see the extent of the physical mischief which was at work. Nevertheless there is abundant evidence that the Queen was never without anxiety on her husband's account, and Baron Stockmar expressed his apprehensions more than once.

Various causes of care troubled the Prince, among them the indisposition contracted by the Princess Royal at the coronation of her father-in-law, the King of Prussia, and the alarming illness at Cannes of Sir Edward Bowater, who had been sent to the south of France in charge of Prince Leopold. After a fortnight of sleeplessness, rheumatic pains, loss, of appetite, and increasing weakness, the Prince drove in close wet weather to inspect the building of the new Military Academy at Sandhurst, and it is believed that he there contracted the germs of fever. But he shot with the guests at the Castle, walked with the Queen to Frogmore and inspected the mausoleum there, and visited the Prince of Wales at Cambridge afterwards.

Then the affair of the Trent suddenly demanded the Prince's close attention and earnest efforts to prevent a threatened war between England and America. In the course of the civil war raging between the Northern and Southern states the English steamer Trent sailed with the English mails from Savannah to England, having on board among the other passengers several American gentlemen, notably Messrs. Mason and Slidell, who had run the blockade from Charlestown to Cuba, and were proceeding to Europe as envoys sent by the Confederates to the Courts of England and France. A federal vessel fired on the English steamer, compelling her to stop, when the American Captain Wilkes, at the head of a large body of marines, demanded the surrender of Mason and Slidell, with their companions. In the middle of the remonstrances of the English Government agent at the insult to his flag and to the neutral port from which the ship had sailed, the objects of the officer's search came forward and surrendered themselves, thus delivering the English commander from his difficulty.

But the feeling in England was very strong against the outrage which had been committed, and it was only the most moderate of any political party who were willing to believe—either that the American Government might not be cognisant of the act done in its name, or that it might be willing to atone by honourable means for a violation of international law—enough to provoke the withdrawal of the English ambassador from Washington, and a declaration of war between the two countries.

Cabinet councils were summoned and a dispatch prepared. A draft of the dispatch was forwarded to Windsor to be read by the Queen, when it struck both her and, the Prince that it was less temperate and conciliatory than it might have been, while still consistent with perfect dignity. The Prince Consort's last public work for his Queen and country was to amend this draft. He rose as usual at seven o'clock, and faint and ill as he was, scarcely able to hold a pen, drew out an improved version of the dispatch, which was highly approved of by the Ministers and favourably received by the American Government. As the world knows, the President, in the name of his countrymen, declared that Captain Wilkes had acted without official instructions, and ordered the release of the gentlemen who had been taken prisoners.

In the meantime the shadows were darkening round the royal home which had been so supremely blest. The Prince was worse. Still he walked out on one of the terraces, and wrapped in a coat lined with fur he witnessed a review of the Eton College volunteers, from which his absence would have been remarked. The ill-omened chilly feeling continued, but there were guests at the Castle and he appeared at dinner. On Sunday, the 1st of December, the Prince walked out again on the terrace and attended service in the chapel, insisting "on going through all the kneeling," though very unwell.

Next morning something was said by the doctors of low fever. No wonder the Queen was distressed after the recent calamity at Lisbon, but concealing her feelings as such watchers must, she strove to soothe and amuse her sick husband. The members of the household who had been at Lisbon arrived with the particulars of the young King of Portugal's death. After listening to them the Prince said "that it was well his illness was not fever, as that, he felt sure, would be fatal to him."

One of the guests at the Castle was Lord Palmerston. In spite of his natural buoyancy of temperament he became so much alarmed by what he heard that he suggested another physician should be called in. Her Majesty had not been prepared for this step, and when she appealed to the two medical men in attendance, Sir James Clark and Dr. Jenner, they comforted her by their opinion that there was nothing to alarm her, and that the low fever which had been feared might pass off.

The next few days were spent in alternations of hope and fear. Which of us is so happy as not to have known that desperate faith when to doubt would be to despair? The Prince liked to be read to, but "no book suited him." The readers were the Queen and Princess Alice, who sought to cheat themselves by substituting Trollope for George Eliot, and Lever for Trollop, and by speaking confidently of trying Sir Walter Scott "to-morrow." To-morrow brought no improvement. Sir James Clark, though still sanguine, began to drop words which were not without their significance. He hoped there would be no fever, which all dreaded, with too sure a presentiment of what would follow. The Prince must eat, and he was to be told so; his illness was likely to be tedious, and completely starving himself would not do.

As if the whole atmosphere was heavy with sorrow, and all the tidings which came from the world without in these days only reflected the ache of the hearts within, the news came from Calcutta of the death of the wife of the Governor-General, beautiful, gifted Lady Canning, so long the Queen's lady-in-waiting and close companion.

The doctors began to sit up with the patient, another stage of the terrible illness. When her Majesty came to the Prince at eight in the morning she found him sitting up in his dressing-room, and was struck with "a strange wild look" which he had, while he talked in a baffled way, unlike him, of what his illness could be, and how long it might last. But that day there was a rally; he ate and slept a little, rested, and liked to be read to by Princess Alice. He was quite himself again when the Queen came in with his little pet child, Princess Beatrice, in whom he had taken such delight. He kissed her, held her hand, laughed at her new French verses, and "dozed off," as if he only wanted sleep to restore him.

The doctor in attendance was anxious that the Prince should undress and go to bed, but this he would not do. Throughout the attack, with his old habit of not giving way and of mastering his bodily feelings by sheer force of will, he had resisted yielding to his weakness and submitting to the ordinary routine of a sick-room. After it was too late the doctor's compliance with the Prince's wishes in this respect was viewed by the public as rash and unwise. On this particular occasion he walked to his dressing-room and lay down there, saying he would have a good night—an expectation doomed to disappointment. His restlessness not only kept him from sleeping, it caused him to change his room more than once during the night.

The morning found him up and seated in his sitting-room as before. But he was worse, and talked with a certain incoherence when he told the Queen that he had been listening to the little birds, and they had reminded him of those he had heard at the Rosenau in his childhood. She felt a quick recoil, and when the doctors showed that their favourable opinion of the day before had undergone a change, she went to her room and it seemed to her as if her heart would break.

Fever had now declared itself unmistakably. The fact was gently broken to the Queen, and she was warned that the illness must run its course, while the knowledge of its nature was to be kept from the Prince. She called to mind every thought that could give her courage; and Princess Alice, her father's true daughter, capable of rising to heights of duty and tenderness the moment she was put to the test, grew brave in her loving demotion, and already afforded the support which the husband and father was no longer fit to give.

Happily for her Majesty, the daily duties of her position as a sovereign, which she could not lay aside though they were no longer shared by the friend of more than twenty years, still occupied a considerable portion of her time. But she wrote in her diary that in fulfilling her task she seemed to live "in a dreadful dream." Do we not also know, many of us, this cruel double life in which the obligations which belong to our circumstances and to old habits contend for mastery with new misery? When she was not thus engaged the Queen sat by her husband, weeping when she could do so unseen.

On the 8th of December the Prince appeared to be going on well, though the desire for change continued strong in him, and he was removed at his earnest request to larger and brighter rooms, adjoining those he had hitherto occupied. According to Lady Bloomfield one of the rooms—certainly called "the Kings' rooms"—into which the Prince was carried, was that in which both William IV. and George IV. had died; and the fact was remembered and referred to by the new tenant, when he was placed where he too was destined to die. The Queen had only once slept there, when her own rooms were being painted, and as it happened, that single occasion was on the night before the day when the Duchess of Kent had her last fatal seizure.

The Prince was pleased with the greater space and light and with the winter sunshine. For the first time since his illness he asked for music, "a fine chorale." A piano was brought into the room, and his daughter played two hymns—one of them "Ein fester burg ist unser Gott" to which he listened with tears in his eyes.

It was Sunday, and Charles Kingsley preached at the Castle. The Queen was present, but she noted sadly that she did not hear a word.

The serious illness of the Prince Consort had become known and excited much alarm, especially among the Cabinet Ministers. They united in urging that fresh medical aid should be procured. Dr. Watson and Sir Henry Holland were called in. These gentlemen concurred with the other doctors in their opinion of the case as grave, but not presenting any very bad symptoms. The increased tendency of the Prince to wander in his mind was only what was to be expected. The listlessness and irritability characteristic of the disease gave way to pleasure at seeing the Queen and having her with him, to tender caresses, such as stroking her cheek, and simple loving words, fondly cherished, "Liebes frauchen, gutes weibchen." [Footnote: "Dear little wife, good little wife."] The changes rung on the relationship which had been so perfect and so satisfying.

On the 10th and the 11th the Prince was considered better. He was wheeled into the next room, when he called attention to a picture of the Madonna of which he was fond; he said that the sight of it helped him through half the day.

On the evening of the 11th a slight change in the Prince's breathing was perceptible and occasioned uneasiness. On the 12th it was too evident the fever and shortness of breathing had increased, and on the 13th Dr. Jenner had to tell the Queen the symptom was serious, and that there was a probability of congestion of the lungs. When the sick man was wheeled into the next room as before, he failed to notice his favourite picture, and in place of asking to be placed with his back to the light as he had hitherto done, sat with his hands clasped, gazing abstractedly out of the window. That night the Prince of Wales was summoned from Cambridge, it was said by his sister, Princess Alice, who took upon her the responsibility of bringing him to Windsor.

All through the night at hourly intervals reports were brought to the Queen that the Prince was doing well. At six in the morning Mr. Brown, the Windsor medical attendant of the family for upwards of twenty years, who was believed to be well acquainted with the Prince's constitution, came to the Queen with the glad tidings "that he had no hesitation in saying he thought the Prince was much better, and that there was ground to hope the crisis was over." There are few experiences more piteous than that last flash of life in the socket which throws a parting gleam of hope on the approaching darkness of death.

When the Queen entered the sick-room at seven o'clock on a fine winter morning, she was struck with the unearthly beauty—another not unfamiliar sign—of the face on which the rising sun shone. The eyes unusually bright, gazing as it were on an unseen object, took no notice of her entrance.

The doctors allowed they were "very, very anxious," but still they would not give up hope. The Queen asked if she might go out for a breath of air, and received an answer with a reservation— "Yes, just close by, for a quarter of an hour." She walked on one of the terraces with Princess Alice, but they heard a military band playing in the distance, and at that sound, recalling such different scenes, the poor Queen burst into tears, and returned to the Castle.

Sir James Clark said he had seen much worse cases from which there had been recovery. But both the Queen and the doctors remarked the dusky hue stealing over the hands and face, and there were acts which looked like strange involuntary preparations for departure—folding of the arms, arranging of the hair, &c.

The Queen was in great distress, and remained constantly either in the sick-room or in the apartment next to it, where the doctors tried still to speak words of hope to her, but could no longer conceal that the life which was as her life was ebbing away. In the course of the afternoon, when the Queen went up to the Prince, after he had been wheeled into the middle of the room, he said the last loving words, "Gutes frauchen," [Footnote: "Good little wife."] kissed her, and with a little moaning sigh laid his head on her shoulder. He dozed and wandered, speaking French sometimes. All his children who were in the country came into the room, and one after the other took his hand, Prince Arthur kissing it as he did so, but the Prince made no sign of knowing them. He roused himself and asked for his private secretary, but again slept. Three of the gentlemen of the household, who had been much about the Prince's person, came up to him and kissed his hand without attracting his attention. All of them were overcome; only she who sat in her place by his side was quiet and still.

So long as enough air passed through the labouring lungs, the doctors would not relinquish the last grain of hope. Even when the Queen found the Prince bathed in the death-sweat, so near do life and death still run, that the attendant medical men ventured to say it might be an effort of nature to throw off the fever.

The Queen bent over the Prince and whispered "Es ist kleins Frauchen." He recognised the voice and answered by bowing his head and kissing her. He was quite calm, only drowsy, and not caring to be disturbed, as he had been wont to be when weary and ill.

The Queen had gone into the next room to weep there when Sir James Clark sent Princess Alice to bring her back. The end had come. With his wife kneeling by his side and holding his hand, his children kneeling around, the Queen's nephew, Prince Ernest Leiningen, the gentlemen of the Prince's suite, General Bruce, General Grey, and Sir Charles Phipps, the Dean of Windsor, and the Prince's favourite German valet, Lohlein, reverently watching the scene, the true husband and tender father, the wise prince and liberal-hearted statesman, the noble Christian man, gently breathed his last. It was a quarter to eleven o'clock on the 14th of December, 1861. He was aged forty-two years.

CHAPTER XXXVI.THE WITHDRAWAL TO OSBORNE—THE PRINCE CONSORT'S FUNERAL.

The tolling of the great bell of St. Paul's, borne on the wintry midnight air, thrilled many a heart with grief and dismay, as London was roused to the melancholy fact of the terrible bereavement which had befallen the Queen and the country.

To the Prince indeed death had come without terror, even without recoil. Some time before he had told the Queen that he had not her clinging to life, that if he knew it was well with those he cared for, he would be quite ready to die to-morrow. He was perfectly convinced of the future reunion of those who had loved each other on earth, though he did not know under what circumstances it would take place. During one of the happy Highland excursions in 1861, the Prince had remarked to one of the keepers when talking over with him the choice and planting of a deer-forest for the Prince of Wales, "You and I may be dead and gone before that." "He was ever cheerful, but ever ready and prepared," was the Queen's comment on this remark.

But for the Queen, "a widow at forty-two!" was the lamenting cry of the nation which had been so proud of its young Queen, of her love- match, of her happiness as a wife. Now a subtler touch than any which had gone before won all hearts to her, and bowed them before her feet in a very passion of love and loyalty. It was her share in the common birthright of sorrow, with the knowledge that she in whose joy so many had rejoiced was now qualified by piteous human experience to weep with those who wept—that thenceforth throughout her wide dominions every mourner might feel that their Queen mourned with them as only a fellow-sufferer can mourn. [Footnote: "The Queen wrote my mother, Lady Normanby, such a beautiful letter after Normanby's death, saying that having drunk the dregs of her cup of grief herself, she knew how to sympathise with others."—LADY BLOOMFIELD.] All hearts went out to her in the day of her bitter sorrow. Prayers innumerable were put up for her, and she believed they sustained her when she would otherwise have sunk under the heavy burden.

On the Sunday which dawned on the first day of her Majesty's widowhood, when the news of her bereavement—announced in a similar fashion in many a city cathedral and country church, was conveyed to the people in a great northern city by Dr. Norman MacLeod's praying for the Queen as a widow, a pang of awe and pity smote every hearer; the minister and the congregation wept together.

The disastrous tidings had to travel far and wide: to the Princess Royal, the daughter in whom her father had taken such pride, who had so grieved to part from him when she left England a happy young bride, who had been so glad to greet him in his own old home only a few months before; to the sailor son on the other side of the globe; to the delicate little boy so lately sent in search of health, whose natural cry on the sorrowful tale being told to him was, "Take me to mamma."

Deprived in one year of both mother and husband, alone where family relations were concerned, save for her children; with her eldest son, the Prince of Wales, a lad of not more than twenty years, the devoted servants of the Queen rallied round her and strove to support and comfort her. In the absence of the Princess Royal and the Princess of Hohenlohe, the Duchess of Sutherland, one of the Queen's oldest friends, herself a widow, was sent for to be with her royal mistress. Lady Augusta Bruce watched day and night by the daughter as she had watched by the mother. The Queen's people did not know how sore was the struggle, how near they were to losing her. Princess Alice wrote years afterwards of that first dreadful night, of the next three terrible days, with a species of horror, and wondered again and again how she and her mother survived that time. The Queen's weakness was so great that her pulse could hardly be felt. "She spoke constantly about God's knowing best, but showed herself broken-hearted," Lady Bloomfield tells us. It was a sensible relief to the country when it was made public that the Queen had slept for some hours.

The doctors urgently advised that her Majesty should leave Windsor and go to Osborne, but she shrank unconquerably from thus quitting all that was mortal of the Prince till he had been laid to rest. The old King of the Belgians, her second father, afflicted in her affliction as he had gloried in her happiness, added his earnest entreaty to, the medical men's opinion, in vain, till the plea was brought forward that for her children's sake—that they might be removed from the fever-tainted atmosphere, the painful step ought to be taken. Even then it was mainly by the influence of the Princess Alice that the Queen, who had proved just and reasonable in all her acts, who had been confirmed by him who was gone in habits of self-control and self-denial, who was the best of mothers, gave up the last sad boon which the poorest might claim, and consented to go immediately with her daughters to Osborne.

But first her Majesty visited Frogmore, where the Duchess of Kent's mausoleum had been built, that she might choose the spot for another and larger mausoleum where the husband and wife would yet lie side by side. It was on the 18th of December that the Queen, accompanied by Princess Alice, drove from the Castle on her melancholy errand. They were received at Frogmore by the Prince of Wales, Prince Louis of Hesse, who had arrived in England, Sir Charles Phipps, and Sir James Clark. Her Majesty walked round the gardens leaning on her daughter's arm, and selected the place where the coffin of the Prince would be finally deposited. Shortly afterwards the sad party left for Osborne, where a veil must be drawn over the sorrow which, like the love that gave it birth, has had few parallels.

The funeral was at Windsor on the 23rd of December. Shortly before twelve o'clock the cortège assembled which was to conduct the remains of the late Prince Consort the short distance from the state entrance of Windsor Castle, through the Norman Tower Gate to St. George's Chapel. Nine mourning-coaches, each drawn by four horses, conveyed the valets, foresters, riders, librarian, and doctors; the equerries, ushers, grooms, gentlemen, and lords in waiting of his late Royal Highness; and the great officers of the Household. One of the Queen's carriages drawn by six horses contained the Prince's coronet borne by Earl Spencer, and his baton, sword, and hat by Lord George Lennox. The hearse, drawn by six horses, was escorted by a detachment of Life Guards.

The carriages of the Queen, the Prince of Wales, the Duke of Cambridge, and the Duchess of Cambridge followed. The company which had received commands to be present at the ceremony, including the foreign ambassadors, the Cabinet Ministers, the officers of the household, and many of the nobility and higher clergy, entered St. George's Chapel by the Wolsey door and were conducted to seats in the choir. The Knights of the Garter occupied their stalls. The royal family, with their guests, came privately from the Castle and assembled in the chapter-room. The members of the procession moved up the nave in the same order in which they had been driven to the South porch. Among them were the representatives of all the foreign states connected by blood or marriage with the late Prince, the choir, canons, and Dean of Windsor. After the baton, sword, and crown, carried on black velvet cushions, came the comptroller in the Chamberlain's department, Vice-Chamberlain, and Lord Chamberlain, then the crimson velvet coffin, the pall borne by the members of the late Prince's suite. Garter-King-at-Arms followed, walking before the chief mourner, the Prince of Wales, who was supported by Prince Arthur, a little lad of eleven, and the Duke of Saxe-Coburg, and attended by General Bruce. Behind came the son-in-law, the Crown Prince of Prussia, the cousins—the sons of the King of the Belgians—with the Duc de Nemours, Prince Louis of Hesse, Prince Edward of Saxe-Weimar, the Queen's nephew, Count Gleichen, and the Maharajah Dhuleep Singh. The gentlemen in waiting on the foreign princes wound up the procession.

When the coffin arrived within the choir, the crown, baton, sword, and hat were placed on it. That morning a messenger had come from Osborne with three wreaths and a bouquet. The wreaths were simple garlands of moss and violets woven by the three elder princesses; the bouquet of violets, with a white camellia in the centre, was from the Queen. These were laid between the heraldic insignia. The Prince of Wales with his brother and uncle stood at the head, the Lord Chamberlain at the foot, the other mourners and the pallbearers around. Minute-guns were fired at intervals by Horse Artillery in the Long Walk. A guard of honour of the Grenadier Guards, of which the Prince Consort had been colonel, presented arms on the coming of the body and when it was lowered into the grave. During the service the thirty-ninth Psalm, Luther's Hymn, and two chorales were sung.

The Prince of Wales bore up with a brave effort, now and then seeking to soothe his young brother, who, with swollen eyes and tear-stained face, when the long wail of the dirge smote upon his ear, sobbed as if his heart were breaking. At the words—

"To fall asleep in slumber deep,
Slumber that knows no waking,"

part of a favourite chant of the Prince Consort's, both his sons hid their faces and wept. The Duke of Coburg wept incessantly for the comrade of his youth, the friend of his mature years.

Garter-King-at-Arms proclaimed the style and title of the deceased. When he referred to her Majesty with the usual prayer, "Whom God bless and preserve with long life, health, and happiness," for the first time in her reign the word "happiness" was omitted and that of "honour" substituted, and the full significance of the change went to the hearts of the listeners with a woeful reminder of what had come and gone. The Prince of Wales advanced first to take his last look into the vault, stood for a moment with clasped hands and burst into tears. In the end Prince Arthur was the more composed of the two fatherless brothers.

As the company retired, the "Dead March in Saul" was pealed forth.

The whole ceremony was modelled on the precedent of other royal funerals, but surely rarely was mourning so keen or sorrow so deep.

CHAPTER XXXVII. THE FIRST MONTHS OF WIDOWHOOD— MARRIAGE OF THE PRINCE OF WALES, ETC., ETC.

The Princess of Hohenlohe arrived in England on the 20th of December, and immediately joined the Queen at Osborne before the funeral of the Prince. The old King of the Belgians came to Osborne on the 29th of

December—one can imagine his meeting with the widowed Queen.

On the 10th of January, 1862, occurred the terrible Hartley Colliery accident, by which upwards of two hundred miners perished. The Queen's grief for the Prince was not a month old when she telegraphed from Osborne her "tenderest sympathy for the poor widows and mothers."

The Prince of Wales left Osborne on the 6th of February in strict privacy to accomplish the tour in the East projected for him by his father. The Prince was accompanied by Dean Stanley, General Bruce, &c.

In the Queen's solitude at Osborne Princess Alice continued to be the great medium of communication between her Majesty and her Ministers. (Times.)

The opening of the second great Exhibition in the month of May must have been full of painful associations. At the State ceremony on the first day the royal carriages with mourning liveries were empty, but for the Crown Prince of Prussia, Prince Oscar of Sweden, and the Duchess of Cambridge with her daughters. Tennyson's ode was sung. It contained the pathetic lines—

"O silent father of our kings to be,
Mourned in this golden hour of jubilee,
For this, for all we weep our thanks to thee."

It was decided that the Queen's birthday should be spent at Balmoral, a practice which became habitual. Dr. Norman Macleod was summoned north to give what consolation he could to his sorrowing Queen. He has left an account of one of their interviews. "May 14th. After dinner I was summoned unexpectedly to the Queen's room; she was alone. She met me, and, with an unutterable expression which filled my eyes with tears, at once began to speak about the Prince…. She spoke of his excellences, his love, his cheerfulness, how he was everything to her; how all now on earth seemed dead to her…."

On the 4th of June the Prince of Wales arrived in England from his eastern tour. A melancholy incident occurred on his return—General Bruce, who had been labouring under fever, died soon after reaching England on the 24th of June. Another sad death happened four days later—that of Lord Canning, Governor-General of India. He had also just come back to England. He survived his wife only six months.

Princess Alice's marriage, which had been delayed by her father's death, took place at Osborne at one o'clock on the afternoon of the 1st of July, in strict privacy. The ceremony was performed by the Archbishop of York in room of the sick Archbishop of Canterbury. The Queen in deep mourning appeared only for the service. Near her was the Crown Princess of Prussia—already the mother of three children—and her Majesty's four sons.

The father and mother, brothers and sister of the bridegroom, and other relatives, were present. The Duke of Saxe-Coburg in the Prince Consort's place led in the bride. Her unmarried sisters, Princesses Helena, Louise, and Beatrice, and the bridegroom's only sister, Princess Anna of Hesse, were the bridesmaids. Prince Louis was supported by his brother, Prince Henry.

The guests were all gone by four o'clock. No contrast could be greater than that of the brilliant and glad festivities at the Princess Royal's wedding and the hush of sorrow in which her sister was married. The young couple went for three days to St. Clare, near Ryde, and left England in another week. The English people never forgot what Princess Alice had proved in the hour of need, and her departure was followed by prayers and blessings.

In August the Queen was at Balmoral with all her children who were in this country. On the 21st she drove in a pony carriage, accompanied by the elder Princes and Princesses on foot and on ponies, to the top of Craig Lowrigan, and each laid a stone on the foundation of the Prince Consort's cairn. On the late Prince's birthday another sad tender pilgrimage was made to the top of Craig Gowan to the earlier cairn celebrating the taking of the Malakoff.

Her Majesty, whose health was still shaken and weakened, sailed on the 1st of September for Germany. She was accompanied by the Prince of Wales, Prince Arthur, and Prince Leopold, Princesses Helena, Louise, and Beatrice, and the Princess Hohenlohe. During the Queen's stay with her uncle, King Leopold, at Laeken, in passing through Belgium, she had her first interview with her future daughter-in-law, Princess Alexandra of Denmark. The Princess with her father and mother drove from Brussels to pay a private visit to her Majesty.

The Queen's destination in Germany was Reinhardtsbrunn, the lovely little hunting-seat among the Thuringian woods and mountains, which had so taken her fancy on her first happy visit to Germany. There she was joined by the Crown Prince and Princess of Prussia and their children, Prince Louis and Princess Alice, and Prince Alfred.

Her Majesty could not quit Germany without revisiting Coburg, hard as the visit must have been to her. One of the chief inducements was to go to one who could no longer come to her, the aged Baron Stockmar, whose talk was still of "the dear good Prince," and of how soon the old man would rejoin the noble pupil cut off in the prime of his gifts and his usefulness.

Prince and Princess Louis of Hesse spent the winter with the Queen in England, and in the month of November Princess Alexandra of Denmark paid a short visit to her Majesty, when the Princess's youthful beauty and sweetness won all hearts.

Early in the morning on the 18th of December the Prince Consort's remains were removed from the entrance of the vault beneath St. George's Chapel to the mausoleum already prepared for them at Frogmore. The ceremony, which was attended by the Prince of Wales, Prince Arthur, Prince Leopold, and Prince Louis of Hesse, was quite private. Prince Alfred had a severe attack of fever in the Mediterranean.

The Duchess of Sutherland presented the Queen with a Bible from "many widows of England," and to "all those kind sister widows" her Majesty expressed the deep and heartfelt gratitude of "their widowed Queen."

As a consequence of the failure of the cotton crop in America, caused by the civil war rending the country asunder, the Lancashire operatives were in a state of enforced idleness and famine, calling for the most strenuous efforts to relieve them.

When Parliament was opened by commission on the 5th of February, 1863, the Queen's speech announced the approaching marriage of the Prince of Wales. On the 7th of March Princess Alexandra, accompanied by her father and mother, brother and sister, arrived at Gravesend, where the Prince of Wales met her. Bride and bridegroom drove, on the chill spring day which ended in rain, through decorated and festive London, where great crowds congregated to do the couple honour.

In the afternoon at Windsor the Queen was seen seated with her two younger daughters at a window of the castle which commanded the entrance drive. The little party waited there in patient expectation till it grew dark.

On Tuesday, the 10th of March, the marriage took place in St. George's Chapel. The Queen in her widow's weeds occupied the royal closet, from which she could look down on the actors in the ceremony. She was attended by the widow of General Bruce. Among the English royal family were Prince and Princess Louis of Hesse, and the Crown Princess of Prussia leading her little son, Prince William.

The Prince of Wales, who wore a general's uniform with the star of the Garter, was supported by the Duke of Saxe-Coburg and the Crown Prince of Prussia.

Princess Alexandra came in the last carriage with her father, Prince Christian of Denmark, and the Duke of Cambridge. The bride's dress was of white satin, and Honiton lace, with a silver moiré train. She had a wreath of orange-blossoms and myrtle. She wore a necklace, earrings, and brooch of pearls and diamonds, the gift of the Prince of Wales, rivières of diamonds, the City of London's gift, an opal and diamond bracelet, presented by the Queen, &c., &c. The bride's train was borne by eight unmarried daughters of English dukes, marquises, and earls.

Princess Alexandra was in her nineteenth, the Prince of Wales in his twenty-second year.

On reaching the haut pas, the bride made a deep reverence to the Queen. During the service her Majesty was visibly affected. Indeed an interested spectator, Dr. Norman Macleod, remarked as a characteristic feature of the marriage that all the English princesses wept behind their bouquets to see—not the Prince of Wales, not the future king, but their brother, their father's son, standing alone before the altar waiting for his bride.

The bride and bridegroom on leaving the chapel occupied the second of the twelve carriages, and were preceded by the Lord Chamberlain, &c., &c. Her Majesty received her son and new daughter at the grand entrance. The wedding breakfast for the royal guests was in the dining-room, for the others in St. George's Hall. At four the Prince and Princess of Wales left in an open carriage drawn by four cream- coloured horses for the station, where the Crown Princess of Prussia had already gone to bid her brother and his bride good-bye, as they started for Osborne to spend their honeymoon.

That night there were great illuminations in London and in all the towns large and small in the kingdom. Thousands of hearts echoed the poet-laureate's eloquent words—

Sea kings daughter from over the sea,
Alexandra.
Saxon and Norman and Dane are we,
But all of us Danes in our welcome to thee,
Alexandra.

Among the Princess of Wales's wedding presents was a parure of splendid opals and brilliants from a design by the late Prince Consort, given in his name as well as in the Queen's.

The town and country houses selected for the Prince and Princess of Wales were Marlborough House and Sandringham.

On the 4th of April Princess Alice's first child, a daughter, was born at Windsor.

On the 8th of May the Queen paid a visit to the military hospital at Netley, in which the Prince Consort had been much interested.

Her Majesty left England on the 11th of August for Belgium and Germany. She was accompanied by the Princes Alfred and Leopold and the Princesses Helena and Beatrice. Their destination was Rosenau, near Coburg, where the Queen was again joined by the Crown Prince and Princess of Prussia and Prince and Princess Louis of Hesse. In the house which was so dear and so sad, the late Prince's birthplace, his widow and children spent his birthday. During the Queen's stay in Coburg she went to see the widow of Baron Stockmar, and Mr. Florschütz, the late Prince's tutor. The venerable superintendent Meyer was still alive and able to preach to her. Her Majesty's health continued feeble, but she was able to receive visits at Rosenau from the King of Prussia and the Emperor of Austria. She quitted Coburg on the 7th of September, spending the 8th at Kranichstein, near Darmstadt, the country house of Princess Alice and her husband.

Later on in autumn the Queen with nearly the whole of her family was at Balmoral and Abergeldie. The cairn on Craig Lowrigan was finished. It formed a pyramid of granite thirty feet high, seen for many a mile.

The inscription was as follows:—
"TO THE BELOVED MEMORY
of
ALBERT, THE GREAT AND GOOD,
PRINCE CONSORT,
RAISED BY HIS BROKEN-HEARTED WIDOW,
VICTORIA B.,
AUGUST 21, 1862.

He being made perfect in a short time, fulfilled a
long time, for his soul pleased the Lord,
therefore hastened He to take him away
from among the wicked.

Wisdom of Solomon, iv. 13, 14.

The appropriate verse is said to have been suggested by the Princess Royal.

Immediately after her Majesty's arrival at Balmoral she went to Blair to see the Duke of Athole, who was hopelessly ill with cancer in the throat. The poor Duke bore up bravely. He had to receive the Queen in his own room, "full of his rifles and other implements and attributes of sport now for ever useless to him." But he was able to present the white rose, the old tribute from the Lords of Athole to their sovereign, and he was gratified by the gracious and kindly mark of attention shown in her Majesty's visit. He insisted on accompanying her to the station, where she gave him her hand, saying, "Dear Duke, God bless you." He had asked permission that the same men who had gone with the Queen and the Prince Consort through the glen two years before might give her a cheer. "Oh! it was so dreadfully sad," was the Queen's comment in her journal.

About three weeks afterwards, on the 7th of October, the Queen had an alarming accident. She was returning from Altnagiuthasach with two of her daughters in the darkness of an autumn evening, when the carriage was upset in the middle of the moorland. Her Majesty was thrown with her face on the ground, but escaped with some bruises and a hurt to one of her thumbs. No one else was injured. The ladies sat down in the overturned carriage after the traces had been cut and the coachman despatched for assistance. There was no water to be had, nothing but claret to bathe the Queen's hand and face. In about half an hour voices and horses' hoofs were heard. It was the ponies which had been sent away before the accident, but the servant who accompanied them, alarmed by the non-appearance of the Queen and by the sight of lights moving about, rode back to reconnoitre. Her Majesty and the Princesses mounted the ponies, which were led home. At Balmoral no one knew what had happened; the Queen herself told the accident to her two sons-in-law who were at the door awaiting her.

Six days afterwards the Queen made her first appearance in public since the Prince's death a year and nine months before, at the unveiling of his statue in Aberdeen. She was accompanied by the Crown Prince and Princess of Prussia, Prince and Princess Louis of Hesse, Princesses Helena and Louise, and Princes Arthur and Leopold. The day was one of pouring rain, and the long silent procession was sad and strange. The Queen was trembling; she had no one as on former occasions to direct and support her. She received the Provost's address, and returned a written reply. She conferred the honour of knighthood on the magistrate, the first time she had performed the ceremony "since all was ended."

On the 14th of December the Queen and her family visited the mausoleum, [Footnote: Dr. Norman Macleod describes an earlier visit in March, 1863 "I walked with Lady Augusta to the mausoleum to meet the Queen. She was accompanied by Princess Alice. She had the key, and opened it herself, undoing the bolts, and alone we entered and stood in silence beside Marochetti's beautiful statue of the Prince. I was very much overcome. She was calm and quiet."] to which she went constantly on every return to Windsor. Princess Alice in her published letters calls the sarcophagus—with the exquisite decorations which were in progress, and cost more than two hundred thousand pounds paid from her Majesty's private purse—"that wonderfully beautiful tomb" by which her mother prayed. It became the practice to have a religious service celebrated there in the presence of the Queen and the royal family on the anniversary of the Prince's death.

In December Lady Augusta Bruce left the Queen's service on her marriage with Dean Stanley. On the night of the 23rd of December Thackeray died.

Prince Albert Victor of Wales was born unexpectedly at Frogmore, where the Prince and Princess of Wales then resided occasionally, on the 8th of January, 1864. The child was baptised in the chapel at Buckingham Palace on the first anniversary of his parents' marriage, as the Princess Royal had been baptised there on the first anniversary of the Queen and Prince Albert's marriage. The Queen and the old King of the Belgians were present among the sponsors.

When the Queen went north this year she was accompanied by the Duke and Duchess of Saxe-Coburg.

On the 14th of March, 1865, her Majesty visited the Hospital for Consumption at Brompton, walking over the different wards and speaking to the patients.

The news of the assassination of President Lincoln reached England in April, when the Queen became, as she has so often been, the mouthpiece of her subjects, writing an autograph letter expressing her horror, pity, and sympathy to Mrs. Lincoln.

Prince Alfred on the 6th of August, his twenty-first birthday, was formally acknowledged heir to his childless uncle, the Duke of Saxe- Coburg.

Two days later the Queen embarked with Prince Leopold, the three younger Princesses, the Duchess of Roxburgh, Lady Churchill, &c., &c., at Woolwich for Germany. She arrived at Coburg on the 11th and went to Rosenau. On the 26th, the birthday of the Prince Consort, perhaps the most interesting of all the inaugurations of monuments to his memory took place at Coburg. A gilt-bronze statue ten feet high was unveiled with solemn ceremony in the square of the little town which Prince Albert had so often traversed in his boyhood. After the unveiling, the Queen walked across the square at the head of her children and handed to the Duke of Saxe-Coburg flowers which he laid on the pedestal. Each of her sons and daughters followed her example, till "the fragrant mass" rose to the feet of the statue. Princess Alice writes of "the terrible sufferings" of the first three years of the Queen's widowhood, but adds that after the long storm came rest, so that the daughter could tenderly remind the mother, without reopening the wound, of the happy silver wedding which might have been this year when the royal parents would have been surrounded by so many grandchildren in fresh young households.

While the Queen was in the Highlands during the autumn, her journal, in its published portions, records a few days spent with the widowed Duchess of Athole at her cottage at Dunkeld. This visit was something very different from the old royal progresses. It was a private token of friendship from the Queen to an old friend bereaved like herself. There was neither show, nor gaiety, nor publicity. The life was even quieter than at Balmoral. Her Majesty breakfasted with the daughter who accompanied her, lunched and dined with the Princess, the Duchess, and one or more ladies. There were long drives, rides, and rows on the lochs—sometimes in mist and rain, among beautiful scenery, like that which had been a solace in the days of deepest sorrow, tea among the bracken or the heather or in some wayside house, friendly chats, peaceful readings. This year Princess Helena was betrothed to Prince Christian of Schleswig-Holstein-Sonderburg, a brother of the husband of her cousin, Princess Adelaide of Hohenlohe. The family connection and the personal character of the bridegroom were high recommendations, while the marriage would permit the Princess to remain in England near her mother.

CHAPTER XXXVIII.DEATHS OF LORD PALMERSTON AND THE KING OF THE BELGIANS—THE QUEEN

AGAIN OPENS PARLIAMENT IN PERSON, &C., &C.

The Prime Minister so long connected with the Queen, Lord Palmerston, energetic to the last, died at Brockett Hall on the 18th of October.

A still greater loss befell her Majesty in the month of December—a marked month in her history. King Leopold died on the 9th at Laeken, within a few days of attaining his seventy-sixth year, the last of a family of nine sons and daughters. He had been cured of a deadly disease by a painful and dangerous operation two years before. He had suffered afterwards from a slight shock of paralysis, which had not prevented him from coming to England to be present at the baptism of Prince Victor of Wales, the fifth generation, counting that of George III., which King Leopold had known in connection with the English throne. In addition to his fine mental qualities, he was singularly active in his habits to the end. He walked thirty miles, and shot for six hours in winter snow, after he had entered his seventy-fifth year. Though the Queen must have been prepared for the event, and his death was peaceful, it was a blow to her—much of her early past perished with her life-long friend and counsellor.

In 1866 the Queen opened Parliament in person for the first time since the death of the Prince Consort, and there was a great assemblage to hail her reappearance when she entered, not by the State, but by the Peers' entrance. There were none of the flourishes of trumpets which had formerly announced her arrival—solemn silence prevailed. She did not wear the robes of state, they were merely laid upon the throne. Her Majesty was accompanied by the Princesses Helena and Louise. When the Queen was seated on the throne the Prince of Wales took his seat on her right, while the Princesses stood on her left. Behind the Queen was the Duchess of Wellington, as mistress of the robes, and a lady in waiting. Her Majesty's dress was dark purple velvet bordered with ermine; she wore a tiara of diamonds with a white gauze veil falling down behind. The speech, which in one passage announced the coming marriage of Princess Helena and Prince Christian (who sat near the end of one of the ambassadors' benches) was read by the Lord Chancellor. The Parliament granted to Prince Alfred an annuity of fifteen thousand pounds— voted in turn to each of his younger brothers on their coming of age—and to Princess Helena a dowry of thirty thousand and an annuity of six thousand pounds, similar to what had been granted to Princess Alice and was to be voted to Princess Louise.

In March the Queen instituted the "Albert Medal," as a decoration for those who had saved life from shipwreck and from peril at sea, and for the first time during five-years revisited the camp at Aldershot and reviewed the troops. She was accompanied by Princess Helena and the Princess Hohenlohe, who was on a visit to England.

Queen Amélie died at Claremont on the 24th of March, aged eighty-three years.

On the 25th of May Prince Alfred was created Earl of Ulster, Earl of Kent, and Duke of Edinburgh.

The Princess Mary of Cambridge was married to the Prince of Teck on the 12th of June, in the presence of the Queen, in the parish church of Kew, where the bride had been confirmed, "among her own people." Parliament granted her an annuity of five thousand pounds. Another marriage, that of Princess Helena, was celebrated in St. George's Chapel, Windsor, by the Archbishop of Canterbury and the Bishop of London, on the 7th of July. The bridegroom was supported by Prince Frederick of Schleswig-Holstein and Prince Edward of Saxe-Weimar. The bride entered between her Majesty and the Prince of Wales. The usual eight noble bridesmaids followed. Prince Christian was in his thirty-sixth, Princess Helena in her twenty-first year. Their home has been first at Frogmore and afterwards at Cumberland Lodge.

While the German war which had Schleswig-Holstein for a bone of contention was still only threatening, the Crown Princess of Prussia lost a fine child, Prince Sigismund. Afterwards the Queen had the pain of seeing her married children, with their unfailing family affection, inevitably ranged on different sides in the war. Princess Alice trembled before the fear of a widowhood like her mother's as the sound of the firing of the Prussian army, which lay between the wife at home and the husband in the field, was heard in Darmstadt. The quiet little town fell into the hands of the enemy, and was at once poverty and pestilence stricken, small-pox and cholera having broken out in the hospitals, where the Princess was labouring devotedly to succour the wounded. In such circumstances, while the standard of her husband's regiment lay hidden in her room, Princess Louis's third daughter was both. Happily peace was soon proclaimed. In honour of it the baby, Princess Irene, whose godfathers were the officers and men of her father's regiment, received her name.

This year Hanover ceased to be an independent state, and became annexed to Prussia.

Dr. Norman Macleod has a bright little picture of an evening at Balmoral in 1866. "The Queen sat down to spin at a nice Scotch wheel while I read Robert Burns to her, 'Tam o' Shanter,' and 'A man's a man for a' that'—her favourite."

Her Majesty sent her miniature with an autograph letter to the American citizen, Mr. Peabody, in acknowledgment of his magnificent gift of model lodging-houses to the Working people of London.

In 1867 the Queen again opened Parliament in person, her speech being read by the Lord Chancellor.

The grievous accident of the breaking of the ice in Regent's Park, when it was covered with skaters and spectators, took place on the 15th of January.

"The Early Tears of the Prince Consort," the first instalment of his "Life," brought out under the direction of General Grey, with much of the information supplied by the Queen, was published, and afforded a nobler memorial to the Prince than any work in stone or metal.

On the 20th of May her Majesty laid the foundation of the Albert Hall. She was accompanied by the Princesses Louise and Beatrice, Prince Leopold, and Prince Christian, and received by the Lord Steward, the Lord Chamberlain, and the Queen's elder sons. The latter presented her with a bouquet, which she took, kissing her sons. In reply to the Prince of Wales's speech her Majesty spoke in accents singularly inaudible for her. She mentioned the struggle she had undergone before she had brought herself to take part in that day's proceedings, but said she had been sustained by the thought that she was thus promoting her husband's designs.

In June and July the Queen of Prussia and the Sultan of Turkey came in turn to England. The latter was with her Majesty in her yacht at a great naval review held in most tempestuous weather off Spithead. In the end of July the Empress of the French paid a short private visit to her Majesty at Osborne.

On the 20th of August the Queen left for Balmoral. On her way north she spent a few days with the Duke and Duchess of Roxburgh at Fleurs, when her Majesty visited Melrose and Abbotsford. After inspecting with great interest the memorials of Sir Walter Scott, who had been presented to her when she was a little girl at Kensington Palace, she complied with a request that she should write her name in the great author's journal, adding the modest comment in her own journal that she felt it presumption in her to do so.

During the autumn the Queen paid an informal visit to the Duke of Richmond's shooting lodge in Glen Fiddich. On the first evening of her stay the break with the luggage failed to appear, and her Majesty had to suffer some of the half-comical inconveniences of ordinary travellers. She had to dine in her riding skirt, with a borrowed black lace veil arranged as a head-dress, and she had to go to bed without the necessary accompaniments to her toilette.

In 1867 the terrible news from Mexico that the Emperor Maximilian (Archduke of Austria and husband of the Queen's cousin, Princess Charlotte of Belgium) had been shot by his rebel subjects, while his wife was hopelessly insane, rendered it a mercy to all interested in the family that old King Leopold had not lived to see the wreck of so many hopes.

In 1868 the Queen gave to her people the first "Leaves" from her journal in the Highlands, which afforded most pleasant glimpses of the wonderfully happy family life, the chief holidays of which had been spent at Balmoral. Her Majesty sent a copy to Charles Dickens, with the graceful inscription that it was the gift of "one of the humblest of writers to one of the greatest."

On the 13th of May the Queen laid the foundation stone of St. Thomas's Hospital, and on the 20th she held a great review of twenty-seven thousand volunteers in Windsor Park. Instead of her mother or her little children, her daughter-in-law and grown-up daughters, the Princess of Wales, Princess Christian, and Princess Louise, were in the carriage with her, while in room of her husband and her brother or cousin, her two soldier sons rode one on each side of the carriage.

On the 5th of July her Majesty, whose health required change of air and scene, left for Switzerland, which must have possessed a great attraction to so ardent an admirer of mountain scenery. She went incognito as Countess of Kent. She was accompanied by Prince Leopold and the Princesses Louise and Beatrice. The Queen travelled in her yacht to Cherbourg, and thence by railway to Paris, where she stayed all day in seclusion in the house of the English Ambassador, receiving only a private visit from the Empress Eugénie—a different experience of Paris from the last. The Queen continued her journey in the evening to Basle, and from Basle to Lucerne, where for nearly two months she occupied the Pension Wallis, delightfully situated on the Hill Gibraltar above the lake. She made numerous enjoyable excursions on her pony "Sultan" to the top of the Rhigi, and in the little steamboat Winkelried on the lovely lake of the Four Cantons, under the shadow of Pilatus, to William Tell's country—she even ventured as far as the desolate, snow-crowned precipices of the Engelberg. Her Majesty returned by Paris, driving out to St. Cloud, and being much affected as she walked in the grounds, but not venturing to enter the house, where she had lived with the Prince during her happy fortnight's visit to her ally in the Crimean war.

Three days after her arrival in England the Queen proceeded as usual to Balmoral, where she took a lively interest in all the rural and domestic affairs which stood out prominently in the lives of her humbler neighbours. The passages from her journal in this and in subsequent years are full of graphic, appreciative descriptions of the stirring incidents of "sheep-juicing," "sheep-shearing," the torchlight procession on "Hallowe'en," a "house-warming;" of the grave solemnity of a Scotch communion, and the kindliness and pathos of more than one cottage "kirstenin," death-bed, and funeral, with the simple piteous tragedy of "a spate" in which two little brothers were drowned.

Considerable excitement was caused in the House of Commons during the debate on the disestablishment of the Irish Church, by the Premier, Mr. Disraeli, mentioning the Queen's name in connection with an interview he had with her on his resignation of office and on the dissolution of Parliament. The conduct of Mr. Disraeli was stigmatised as unconstitutional both in advising a dissolution of Parliament and in apparently attempting to shift the responsibility of the situation from the Government to the Crown.

The Queen lost by death this year her old Mistress of the Robes, one of the earliest and most attached of her friends, Harriet, Duchess of Sutherland.

In September, 1869, her Majesty, with the Princesses Louise and Beatrice, paid a ten days' visit to Invertrosachs, occupying Lady Emily Macnaghten's house, and learning to know by heart Loch Katrine, Loch Lomond, &c., &c.

In November the Queen was in the City after a long absence, for the double purpose of opening Blackfriars Bridge and the Holborn Viaduct. Happily for the cheering multitudes congregated on the occasion the day was bright and fair though cold, so that she could drive in an open carriage accompanied by her younger daughters and Prince Leopold. The Queen still wore deep mourning after eight years of widowhood, and her servants continued to have a band of crape on one arm. Her Majesty was received by the Lord Mayor, &c., &c. After Blackfriars Bridge had been declared open for traffic her carriage passed across it, followed by his. The same ceremony was performed at the Holborn Viaduct.

This season the Prince of Wales revisited the East, accompanied by the Princess.

In 1870 the Queen signed the order in council resigning the royal prerogative over the army.

On the 11th May her Majesty opened the University of London. She was received by Earl Granville and Mr. Grote. Baboo Keshub Shunder Sen was conspicuous among the company. The Queen received an address, said in a clear voice "I declare this building open," and the silver trumpets sounded.

Charles Dickens died on the 9th of June.

The Franco-German war, in which the Crown Prince of Prussia and Prince Louis of Hesse were both engaged with honour, happily this time on the same side, was filling the eyes of Europe; and before many months had passed since "Die Wacht am Rhein" had resounded through the length and breadth of Germany, the Empress of the French arrived in England as a fugitive, to be followed ere long by the Emperor.

In the autumn at Balmoral, Princess Louise, with the Queen's consent, became engaged to the Marquis of Lorne, eldest son of the Duke of Argyle. The proposal was made and accepted during a walk from the Glassalt Shiel to the Dhu Loch.

In November the Queen visited the Empress at Chislehurst.

During the war, while the number of the French wounded alone in Darmstadt amounted to twelve hundred, and Princess Alice was visiting the four hospitals daily, her second son was born.

The death of Sir James Clark, at Bagshot, was the snapping to the Queen of another of the links which connected the present with the past.

In 1871 the Queen again opened Parliament in person, with her speech read by the Lord

Chancellor. As described by an eye-witness, her Majesty sat "quite still, her eyes cast down, only a slight movement of the face." The approaching marriage of the Princess Louise was announced, and reference was made to the fact that the King of Prussia had become Emperor of Germany.

For the first time since the death of the Prince Consort, the Queen spent the anniversary of their marriage-day at Windsor.

On the 21st of March Princess Louise was married in St George's Chapel, Windsor, to the Marquis of Lorne. The bridegroom was supported by Earl Percy and Lord Ronald Leveson-Gower. The bride walked between the Queen and the Duke of Saxe-Coburg. Her Majesty by a gesture gave away her daughter. Princess Louise was twenty-three, Lord Lorne twenty-six years of age. The Princess has rooms in Kensington Palace for her London residence.

Eight days afterwards the Queen opened the Albert Hall.

On the 3rd of April her Majesty visited the Emperor of the French at Chislehurst—a trying interview.

On the 21st of June the Queen opened St. Thomas's Hospital, knighting the treasurer.

This summer the Emperor and Empress of Brazil visited London, while the Tichborne trial was running its long course.

On the Queen's return from Balmoral in November, she was met by the alarming tidings that the Prince of Wales lay ill of typhoid fever at Sandringham. The Queen went to her son on the 29th and remained for a few days. The disease seemed progressing favourably, and she returned to Windsor in the beginning of December, leaving the invalid devotedly nursed by the Princess of Wales and Princess Alice—who had been staying with her brother when the fever showed itself, and by the Duke of Edinburgh. On the 8th there was a relapse, when the Queen and the whole of the royal family were sent for to Sandringham. During many days the Prince hovered between life and death. The sympathy was deep and universal. The reading of the bulletins at the Mansion House was a sight to be remembered. A prayer was appointed by the Archbishop of Canterbury for "Albert Edward Prince of Wales, lying upon the bed of sickness," and for "Victoria our Queen and the Princess of Wales in this day of their great trouble." Supplications were sent up alike in Catholic churches and Jewish synagogues. On the night of Wednesday the 14th, a date which had been dreaded as that of the Prince Consort's death ten years before, a slight improvement took place, sleep at last was won, and gradual recovery established. The Queen returned to Windsor on the 19th, and wrote on the 26th of December to thank her people for their sympathy.

On the 8th of February, 1872, the Governor-General of India, Lord Mayo, was assassinated.

The 27th was the Thanksgiving Day for the Prince of Wales's recovery. No public sight throughout her Majesty's reign was more moving than her progress with the Prince and Princess of Wales and Princess Beatrice to and from St. Paul's. The departure from Buckingham Palace was witnessed by the Emperor and Empress of the French, who stood on a balcony. The decorated streets were packed with incredible masses of people, the cheering was continuous. The Queen wore white flowers in her bonnet and looked happy. The Prince insisted on lifting his hat in return for the people's cheers. The royal party were met at Temple Bar by the Lord Mayor and a deputation from the Common Council. The City sword was presented and received back again, when the chief magistrate of London remounted and rode before the Queen to St. Paul's. Thirteen thousand persons were in the City cathedral. The pew for the Queen and the Prince was enclosed by a brass railing. The Te Deum was sung by a picked choir. There was a special prayer, "We praise and magnify Thy glorious name for that Thou hast raised Thy servant Albert Edward Prince of Wales from the bed of sickness." The sermon was preached by the Archbishop of Canterbury. The return was led by the Lord Mayor and Aldermen to the bounds of the City. When Buckingham Palace was reached the Queen showed herself with the Prince for a moment on the central balcony. There was an illumination in the evening.

On the 29th of February, as the Queen was returning from a drive in the Park, having come down Constitution Hill and entered the courtyard, when about to alight, a lad with a paper in one hand and a pistol in the other rushed first to the left and then to the right side of the carriage, with arms extended to the Queen, who sat quite unmoved. Her Majesty's attendant, John Brown, seized the assailant. He was a half-witted Irish lad, named Arthur O'Connor, about seventeen years of age, who had been a clerk to an oil and colour merchant. He had climbed over the railings. There was no ball in the pistol, which was broken. The paper was a petition for the Fenians. The public indignation was great against the miserable culprit, who was dealt with as in former outrages of the kind, according to the nature of the offence and with reference to the mental condition of the offender. The Queen, who had been about to institute a medal as a reward for long and faithful service among her domestics, gave a gold medal and an annuity of twenty-five pounds to John Brown for his presence of mind and devotion on this occasion.

Her Majesty had gone to Balmoral for her birthday, and was still there on the 16th of June when she heard of the death of her valued friend, Dr. Norman Macleod. He had preached to her and dined with her so recently as the 26th of May. What his loss was to her she has expressed simply and forcibly in a passage in her journal.... "When I thought of my dear friend Dr. Macleod and all he had been to me—how in 1862, '63, '64, he had cheered and comforted and encouraged me—how he had ever sympathised with me … and that this too like so many other comforts and helps was for ever gone, I burst out crying."

On the 1st of July the Queen, accompanied by the Duke of Edinburgh and Prince Leopold and the two younger princesses, visited the Albert Memorial, Hyde Park, which was complete save for the statue.

Three days afterwards, in very hot weather, her Majesty was present at a great review at Aldershot.

CHAPTER XXXIX. STAY AT HOLYROOD—DEATHS OF PRINCESS HOHENLOHE AND OF PRINCE FREDERICK OF DARMSTADT— MARRIAGE OF THE DUKE OF EDINBURGH.

The Queen arrived at Holyrood on the 14th of August, and made a stay of a few days in Edinburgh for the first time during eleven years. A suite of rooms called the "Argyle rooms" had been freshly arranged for her occupation. She went over Queen Mary's rooms again for the gratification of Princess Beatrice, and with the Princess and Prince Leopold took the old drives to Dalkeith and Leith which her Majesty had first taken thirty years before.

A favourite project in the past had been that her Majesty should go so far north as to visit Dunrobin, and rooms had been prepared for her reception. When the visit was paid the castle was in the hands of another generation, and the Queen laid the foundation stone of a cross erected to the memory of the late Duchess.

Soon after her Majesty's return to Balmoral, on the 23rd September, she had the grief to receive a telegram announcing the death of her sister, Princess Hohenlohe. Though not more than sixty-five years of age the Princess had been for some time very infirm. She had received a great shock in the previous spring from the unexpected death by fever, at the age of thirty-three, of her younger surviving daughter, Princess Feodore, the second wife of the Duke of Saxe-Meiningen. The Emperor Napoleon III, who had long been labouring under sore disease, laid down his wearied and vanquished life at Chislehurst on the 9th of January, 1873.

The coming marriage of the Duke of Edinburgh to the Grand Duchess Marie of Russia was announced to Parliament.

On the 2nd of April the Queen was present at the opening of the Victoria Park. Prince Arthur was created Duke of Connaught.

A fatal accident to the younger son of Prince and Princess Louis of Hesse happened at Darmstadt on the 29th of May. The nurse had brought the children to see the Princess while she was in bed, and had left the two little boys playing beside her. The windows of the bedroom and of a dressing-room beyond were open. Princess Louis, hearing Prince Ernest, the elder brother, go into the dressing-room, leapt out of bed and hurried after him. In her momentary absence Prince Frederick, between two and three years of age, leant out of one of the bedroom windows, lost his balance, and fell on the pavement below, receiving terrible injuries, from which he died in a few hours, to the great sorrow of his parents.

In September the Queen and Princess Beatrice, with Lady Churchill and General Ponsonby, spent a week at Inverlochy, occupying the house of Lord Abinger at the foot of Ben Nevis, among the beautiful scenery which borders the Caledonian Canal, and is specially associated with Prince Charlie—in pity for whom her Majesty loved to recall the drops of Stewart blood in her veins.

This year more than one figure, well-known in different ways to the Queen in former years, passed out of mortal sight—Bishop Wilberforce, Landseer, Macready.

In January, 1874, the Duke of Edinburgh was married at the Winter Palace, St. Petersburg, to the Grand Duchess Marie of Russia. The Duke was in his thirtieth, the Grand Duchess in her twenty-first year. The royal couple arrived at Gravesend on March 7th, and entered London on March 12th in a heavy snowstorm. In spite of the weather the Queen and the Duchess, with the Duke of Edinburgh and Princess Beatrice seated opposite, drove slowly through the crowded streets in an open carriage drawn by six horses. The Prince and Princess of Wales, Princess Louise, &c., were at the windows of Buckingham Palace. The Queen went out with the Duke and Duchess on the balcony. The Duke and Duchess's town and country houses are Clarence House and Eastwell Park.

In March her Majesty, accompanied by all her family in England, reviewed the troops returned from the Ashantee War in Windsor Great Park, and gave the orders of St. Michael and St. George to Sir Garnet Wolseley and the Victoria Cross to Lord Gifford.

The first volume of the "Life of the Prince Consort," by Sir Theodore Martin, came out and made a deep impression on the general public.

Her Majesty had for many years honoured with her friendship M. and Madame Van de Weyer, who were the Queen's near neighbours at Windsor, the family living at the New Lodge. In addition they had come for several seasons to Abergeldie, when the Court was at Balmoral. M. Van de Weyer was not only the trusted representative of the King of the Belgians, he was a man highly gifted morally and intellectually. This year the friendship was broken by his death.

On the 15th of October the Duke and Duchess of Edinburgh's son—was born.

The news of Livingstone's death reached England.

Early in 1875 Prince Leopold, then twenty-two years of age, suffered from typhoid fever. So great were the fears entertained for his life that the Queen was prevented from opening Parliament in person. Already Princess Alice in her letters had referred to her youngest brother as having been three times given back to his family from the brink of the grave.

During the spring the Queen was deprived by death of her Clerk to the Council and literary adviser in her first book, Sir Arthur Helps.

Charles Kingsley, whose work was much admired by the Prince Consort, died also.

On the 18th of August, when the Queen was sitting on the deck of the royal yacht as it crossed from Osborne to Gosport, the yacht Mistletoe ran across its bows and a collision took place, the Mistletoe turning over and sinking. The sister-in-law of the owner of the yacht was drowned. The master, an old man, who was struck by a spar, died after he had been picked up. The rest of the crew were rescued. Her Majesty, who was greatly distressed, aided personally in the vain efforts to restore one of the sufferers to consciousness.

In September the Queen, in paying a week's visit to the Duke and Duchess of Argyle at Inverary, had the pleasure of seeing Princess Louise in her future home. It was twenty-eight years since her Majesty had been in the house of MacCallummore, and then her son-in-law of to- day had been a little fellow of two years, in black velvet and fair curls.

Towards the end of the year the Prince of Wales left for his lengthened progress through her Majesty's dominions in India, which was accomplished with much éclat and success.

In 1876 the Queen opened Parliament in person.

On the 25th of February her Majesty, accompanied by the Princess of Wales, Princess Beatrice, and Prince Leopold, and received by the Duke of Edinburgh, attended a state concert given in the morning at the Albert Hall. Since 1866 the Queen had been able gradually to hear and enjoy again the music in which she had formerly delighted, but she had taken the gratification in her domestic life. Her royal duties had been only intermitted for the briefest space. Every act of beneficence and gracious queenliness had been long ago resumed. But no place of public amusement had seen the face of the widowed Queen.

Lady Augusta Stanley died, after a lingering illness, on the 1st of March. It was the close—much lamented from the highest to the lowest— of a noble and beautiful life. The Queen afterwards erected a memorial cross to Lady Augusta Stanley's memory in the grounds at Frogmore.

On the 7th of March her Majesty, accompanied by Princess Beatrice, opened a new wing of the London Hospital.

Two days afterwards the statue of the Prince Consort in the Albert Memorial was unveiled without any ceremony. The whole memorial thus completed stood, as it stands to-day, one of the most splendid tokens —apart from its artistic merit—of a nation's gratitude and a Queen's love. Opinions may differ on the use of gilding and colours, as they have been rarely employed in this Country, upon the towering facades and pinnacles, and on the choice of the central gilt figure of the Prince, colossal, in robes of state. But there can hardly be a doubt as to the striking effect of the magnificent monument taken altogether, especially when it has the advantage of a blue sky and brilliant sunshine, and of the charm of the four white marble groups which surround the pedestal, seen in glimpses through the lavish green of Kensington Gardens. An engraving of the statue of the Prince is given in Vol. I., p. 172.

In the end of the month the Queen, travelling incognito as Countess of Kent, having crossed to Cherbourg, arrived at Baden-Baden accompanied by Princess Beatrice. Her Majesty visited the Princess Hohenlohe's grave. She continued her journey to Coburg. In passing through Paris on her return to England towards the end of April, her Majesty had an interview with the President of the French Republic.

On the 1st of May the Queen was proclaimed Empress of India.

In the season the Empress of Germany and the ex-royal family of Hanover visited England. On the 17th of August the Queen, with the Princes Arthur and Leopold and Princess Beatrice, stayed two nights at Holyrood for the purpose of unveiling the equestrian statue to the late Prince in Charlotte Square. Her Majesty recalled the coincidence that the last public appearances of both her husband and mother were in Edinburgh—the Prince Consort in laying the foundation stone of the new post-office in October, 1861, only six weeks before his death, the Duchess of Kent at the summer volunteer review in 1860. The town was gay and bright and crowded with company. In Charlotte Square the Duke of Buccleuch, chairman of the committee, read the address, to which the Queen read a reply. On her return to the palace she knighted the sculptor, Sir John Steel, and Professor Oakeley, the composer of the chorale which was sung on the occasion. In the evening there was once more a great dinner at Holyrood—Scotts, Kerrs, Bruces, Primroses, Murrays, &c., &c, being gathered round their Queen.

A month afterwards at Ballater, amidst pouring rain, her Majesty presented new colours to the 79th regiment, "Royal Scots," of which her father was colonel when she was born. She spoke a few kind words to the soldiers, and accepted from them the gift of the old colours, which are in her keeping.

On the 15th December the Queen and the Princess Beatrice paid a visit to Lord Beaconsfield at Hughenden, lunched, and remained two hours, during which the royal visitors planted trees on the lawn.

In consequence of fever in the Isle of Wight her Majesty held her
Christmas at Windsor for the first time since the death of the Prince
Consort.

On New Year's day, 1877, the Queen was proclaimed Empress of India at
Delhi. Her Majesty opened Parliament on the 8th of February.

In September, when the war between Russia and Turkey was raging, her Majesty, Princess Beatrice, the Duchess of Roxburgh, &c., spent a week at Loch Maree Hotel, enjoying the fine Ross-shire scenery, making daily peaceful excursions, to which such a telegram as told of the bombardment of Plevna must have been a curious accompaniment.

In February, 1878, the Queen's grandchild, Princess Charlotte of
Prussia, was married at Berlin to the hereditary Prince of Saxe-
Meiningen, at the same time that her cousin, Princess Elizabeth of
Prussia, was married to the hereditary Grand Duke of Oldenburg.

On the 12th June the Queen's cousin, who had been the blind King of Hanover, died in exile at Paris. His body was brought to England and was buried in the royal vault below St. George's Chapel, Windsor.

The Queen saw a naval review off Spithead in August. In the end of the month the Queen, with Princess Beatrice and Prince Leopold, stopped at Dunbar on the way north in order to pay a visit to the Duke and Duchess of Roxburgh at Broxmouth. During her Majesty's stay she heard of the death of Madame Van de Weyer at the New Lodge, and wrote in her journal, "Another link with the past gone! with my beloved one, with dearest Uncle Leopold, and with Belgium."

In September a terrible accident occurred in the Thames off Woolwich, when the Princess Alice steamboat on a pleasure trip was run down by the Bywell Castle, and about six hundred passengers perished.

In the end of the month the Queen had the misfortune to lose her old and faithful servant Sir Thomas Biddulph, who died at Abergeldie Mains. When she went to see him in his last illness and took his hand, he said, "You are very kind to me," to which she answered, pressing his hand, "You have always been very kind to me."

The Marquis of Lorne had been appointed Governor-General of Canada, for which he and Princess Louise sailed, arriving at Ottawa on the 23rd of November.

Already the Queen, who was still at Balmoral, had heard of the disastrous outbreak of diphtheria in the Darmstadt royal family. It attacked every member in succession, the youngest, Princess Marie, a child of four years of age, dying on the 16th of November. It was supposed that the Duchess had caught the infection from having once, in an abandonment of sorrow for the death of her little daughter, forgotten the necessary precautions, and rested her head on the Duke's pillow. Her case was dangerous from the first, and she gave orders lest she should die, but did not seem to expect death. In her sleep she was heard to murmur, "Four weeks—Marie—my father." On the morning before she died she read a letter from her mother. Her last words when waking from sleep, she took the refreshment offered her, were, "Now I will again sleep quietly for a longer time." Then she fell back into the slumber from which she never awoke. She died on the 14th December, exactly four weeks from the death of her child, and seventeen years from the death of her father. She was thirty-five years of age. Princess Alice was a woman of rare qualities and remarkable benevolence.

The Prince of Wales and Prince Leopold went to Darmstadt and followed the funeral from the church to the Rosenhöhe, where all that was mortal of Princess Alice rests beside the dust of her children. A fine figure in white marble of the Princess, recumbent, clasping her little daughter to her breast, has been placed close to the spot as a token of the loving remembrance of her brothers and sisters. The engraving represents this beautiful piece of monumental sculpture.

In 1879 the Zulu war broke out. On the 11th of March Princess Louise of Prussia arrived in England, and on the 13th she was married in St. George's Chapel, Windsor, in the presence of the Queen and all the members of the royal family and the bride's father and mother, Prince and Princess Frederick Charles of Prussia. The bridegroom was supported by his brothers, the Prince of Wales and the Duke of Edinburgh. The bride walked between her father and the Crown Prince of Germany, and was followed by eight noble bridesmaids. The Duke of Connaught was in his twenty-ninth and Princess Louise of Prussia in her nineteenth year. Their residence is Bagshot Park.

Twelve days later the Queen left with Princess Beatrice and, travelling by Cherbourg and Paris, reached Lake Maggiore on the 28th. Immediately after their arrival the news came of the death, from diphtheria of one of the Crown Princess of Germany's sons, Prince Waldemar of Prussia, a fine boy of eleven years of age.

Her Majesty left on the 23rd of April, and returned by Milan, Turin, Paris, and Cherbourg, to England.

CHAPTER XL.BIRTH OF THE FIRST GREAT-GRANDCHILD— MARRIAGE OF THE DUKE OF ALBANY— CONCLUSION.

The Queen's first great-grandchild, the child of the Princess of Saxe-Meiningen, was born on the 12th of May.

On her Majesty's arrival at Balmoral on the 22nd of May she went to see the granite cross erected to the "dear memory" of Alice, Duchess of Hesse, by her "sorrowing mother"

The Queen remained at Balmoral till after the 19th of June, when the melancholy tidings arrived that the Prince Imperial had been killed in the Zulu war. Her Majesty left on the 20th, and crossed over the Tay Bridge, which was destroyed in the terrible gale of the 29th December of the same year.

In 1880 the Queen opened Parliament in person. Her Majesty, accompanied by Princess Beatrice, left Windsor on the 25th of March for Baden-Baden and Darmstadt. The Queen was present at the confirmation of the Princesses Victoria and Elizabeth, and visited the Rosenhöhe, where their mother was buried.

About the same time the ex-Empress Eugénie embarked at Southampton for the Cape of Good Hope, that she might see the place where her son fell on the anniversary of his death.

On the 24th of April the Princess Frederica of Hanover, elder daughter of the late King, was married to Baron von Pawel-Rammingen, who had been equerry to her father, in St. George's Chapel, Windsor. The Queen and several members of the royal family witnessed the ceremony.

In September the Duke of Connaught and his bride were welcomed to Balmoral, and a visit paid to the cairn erected in their honour when their healths were drunk with "three times three" in the presence of the Queen, Princess Beatrice, and the ladies and gentlemen of the household. Later in the autumn the childless widow, the Empress Eugénie, stayed for a little time at Abergeldie.

At the close of 1880 Lord Beaconsfield published his last novel of "Endymion." George Eliot died on the 22nd December, and in 1881 Thomas Carlyle died, on the 5th of February, in the eighty-sixth year of his age.

Her Majesty's eldest grandson, Prince William of Prussia, was married at Berlin on the 27th of February to Princess Augusta Victoria of Schleswig-Holstein. The bride was the granddaughter of the Queen's sister, Princess Hohenlohe, and the niece of Prince Christian.

On March 13th the Emperor of Russia was assassinated.

Lord Beaconsfield died on the 19th of April at his house in Curzon Street. Ten days later the Queen and Princess Beatrice visited Hughenden while the vault was still open, and placed flowers on the coffin.

In June Prince Leopold took his seat in the House of Peers on his creation as Duke of Albany. On the 19th of September President Garfield died, after a long struggle, with the effects of his assassination, when the Queen wrote to Mrs. Garfield her indignation and pity as she had expressed them to the widow of President Lincoln.

In 1882 a monument was erected in Hughenden Church to Lord Beaconsfield "by his grateful and affectionate sovereign and friend,
"VICTORIA R. I.
Kings love him that speaketh right.
PROVERBS xvi 13."

The Queen's speech on the opening of Parliament in 1882 announced the approaching marriage of the Duke of Albany to Princess Helen of Waldeck.

On the 2nd of March, as her Majesty was entering her carriage at Windsor station, she was fired at by a man named Roderick Maclean, the ball passing between her Majesty and Princess Beatrice. The criminal, who proved to be of respectable antecedents, was arrested and committed for high treason. He was tried, found not guilty on the plea of insanity, and sentenced to be confined during her Majesty's pleasure. Much sympathy and indignation were felt, and addresses were voted by both Houses of Parliament.

The Queen left with Princess Beatrice, twelve days afterwards, by Portsmouth, Cherbourg, and

Paris for Mentone, where her Majesty stayed a fortnight.

Princess Helen of Waldeck, accompanied by her parents, arrived on the 25th of April. The King and Queen of the Netherlands, the bride's brother-in-law and sister, came next day, and the marriage was celebrated on the 27th of April in St. George's Chapel, Windsor, before the Queen and the royal family. The Duke of Albany was in his twenty-ninth, and Princess Helen in her twenty-first year. Claremont was assigned to the young couple as their future residence. Eight days after the marriage a sad event broke in on the marriage rejoicings; the bride's sister, Princess William of Wurtemberg, died in childbirth at the age of twenty-three.

On the 6th of May the Queen, with Princess Beatrice, went in state to Epping Forest, where they were received by the Lord Mayor, the Sheriffs, and the Duke of Connaught as ranger of the forest. After an address the Queen declared the forest dedicated to the people's use.

On the same day Lord Frederick Cavendish and Mr. Burke were assassinated in the Phoenix Park, Dublin.

Garibaldi died at Caprera on the 2nd of June.

The Egyptian war broke out, and among the officers who sailed with the troops under Sir Garnet Wolseley in August was the Duke of Connaught. The Duchess and her little daughter were with the Queen at Balmoral, where anxious days were spent as mother and wife waited for the news of battle. Successive telegrams announced that an attack was determined on, that the army had marched, that fighting was going on, and that the enemy had been routed with heavy loss at Tel-el-Kebir. The Queen wrote in her journal "How anxious we felt I need not say, but we tried not to give way…. I prayed earnestly for my darling child, and longed for to-morrow to arrive. Read Korner's beautiful, 'Gebet vor der Schlacht,' 'Vater ich rufe Dich,' ('Prayer before the Battle,' 'Father, I call on Thee'). My beloved husband used to sing it often…."

At last came the welcome telegram, "A great victory, Duke safe and well," and a further telegram with details and the concluding sentence, "Duke of Connaught is well and behaved admirably, leading his brigade to the attack," and great was the joy and thankfulness.

In the meantime the Duke and Duchess of Albany had been expected on their first visit after their marriage, and were met at Ballater. When their healths were drunk with Highland honours, the happy Queen asked her son to propose another toast "to the victorious army in Egypt" coupled with the Duke of Connaught's name, and the health was drunk in the hearing of his proud wife and his unconscious infant in her nurse's arms.

In November the Queen reviewed the troops returned from Egypt in St. James Park, and afterwards distributed war medals to the officers and men.

On the 4th December her Majesty opened the New Law Courts. She was received by the judges and the representatives of the Bar. Lord Chancellor Selborne was raised to the rank of an earl, and knighthood was conferred on the Governors of the Inns of Court.

The Duke of Connaught, accompanied by the Duchess, went to fill a military post in India.

We have seen that Prince Leopold, Duke of Albany, her Majesty's fourth and youngest son, who was born on the 7th of April, 1853, had a delicate childhood and boyhood. He suffered from a tendency to haemorrhage on the slightest provocation. Ailments in the joints are apt to accompany such constitutional weakness, and one of Prince Leopold's knees was affected. As he grew up he was again and again brought to the brink of the grave by sudden and violent fits of indisposition. It is hardly necessary to say that the precariousness of Prince Leopold's health, combined as it was with an amiable disposition and intellectual gifts, only served to endear him the more to his family and friends.

The bodily weakness which set the Duke of Albany apart from his elder brothers and from lads of his age, which prevented his being regularly trained either as a soldier or a sailor, in the two professions which have been long held fit for princes, made him peculiarly the home-son of the Queen, and caused him to be much longer associated with her than he might otherwise have been, in her daily life and in her public appearances during the later years of her reign.

It did not follow from this circumstance that Prince Leopold relinquished an independent career or led an idle life. In 1872, when he was in his twentieth year, he matriculated at Oxford, where he kept his terms with credit alike to his original abilities and his conscientious diligence. His honourable and pleasant connection with his university remained a strong tie to the end of his short life, and it was doubtless in relation to Oxford that he came sensibly under the influence of Mr. Buskin.

On leaving college Prince Leopold continued to lead the quiet yet busy life of a scholarly and somewhat artistic young man to whom robust health has been denied. In addition to the many dignities of his rank, including four orders of knighthood, belonging to the Garter, the Thistle, the Star of India, and the Order of St. Michael and St. George, he became a D.O.L. of Oxford in 1876, and in the following year a bencher of Lincoln's Inn. A less characteristic honour given him was the rank of a colonel in the army.

It was a marked feature in Prince Leopold's individuality, as it had been in that of the Prince Consort, that he sought to turn all his gifts and pursuits to practical use, not only in the interests of science and art, but in order to improve the condition and increase the happiness of the Queen his mother's people. His speeches on the increasing occasions when he took the chair at public meetings in aid of the objects he had at heart, were remarkable in so young a man, not only for good taste and for the amount of carefully acquired knowledge they displayed, but for the spirit of enlightened humanity and benevolence which breathed through them. Gradually but surely Prince Leopold's graceful, well-considered, kindly utterances, with which he was ready whenever his services were required, were making a most favourable and permanent impression on the public which was too soon to mourn his loss. The extension of education and of innocent amusements through all classes, the Kyrle Society for the fostering of Art among the homeliest surroundings, the higher and more general cultivation of music, the introduction of lessons in cookery into the poorest schools; were among the schemes which the Duke of Albany warmly advocated.

The Duke's marriage took place, as we have recorded, on the 27th of April, 1882, and in 1883 a daughter was born to him, who received the dear and hallowed name of "Alice."

In March, 1884, the Duke of Albany went to Cannes in order to escape the spring east winds, leaving the Duchess, who was in a delicate state of health, behind him at Claremont. He appeared to profit by his stay of a few weeks in the south of France, was unusually well in health and in excellent spirits, entering generally into the society of the place. But on the 27th of March, in ascending a stair at the Cercle Nautique, he slipped and fell, injuring his ailing knee in a manner in which he had hurt it several times before. He was conveyed in a carriage to the Villa Nevada, at which he was residing, and no danger was apprehended, the Duke writing with his own hand to the Duchess, making light of the accident. During the following night, however, he was observed to breathe heavily, was found to be in a fit, and in a few minutes afterwards, early on the morning of the 28th of March, 1884, he died in the arms of his equerry, Captain Perceval. The melancholy news was telegraphed to Windsor, and broken to the Queen by the Master of her Household, Sir Henry Ponsonby. Under the shock and grief, with which the whole country sympathised, her Majesty's first and constant thought seems to have been for the young widow at desolate Claremont.

The Prince of Wales started for Cannes, and accompanied the remains of his brother to England, the royal yacht Osborne landing them at Portsmouth. On the arrival of the melancholy cavalcade at Windsor, on Friday, the 4th of April, the Queen went with her daughters, Princess Christian and Princess Beatrice, to the railway station to meet the body of the beloved son who had been the namesake of King Leopold, her second father, and the living image in character of the husband she had adored. The coffin was carried by a detachment of the Seaforth Highlanders through the room in which her Majesty awaited the procession, and conveyed to the chapel, where a short service was afterwards held in the presence of the Queen and the near relatives of the dead, and where the nearest of all, the widowed Duchess, paid one brief last visit to the bier. On the following day, Saturday, the 5th of April, towards noon, the funeral took place, with all the pomp of the late Prince's rank, and all the sorrow which his untimely end and many virtues might well call forth. The Prince of Wales, as chief mourner, was supported by the Crown Prince of Germany, the Duke of Hesse-Darmstadt, Prince Christian of Schleswig-Holstein, Prince Albert Victor of Wales, and the Duke of Cambridge. The coffin, with its velvet pall nearly hidden by flowers, was again borne by a party of the Seaforth Highlanders to the solemn music of Chopin's "Funeral March" and the firing of the minute-guns, to the principal entrance of St. George's Chapel. Among the same company that had been assembled when the Duke of Albany had been married not two years before, were his father-in-law and sister-in- law, the Prince of Waldeck-Pyrmont, and the Queen of Holland.

While the dirge-like music and the booming of the cannon filled the air, the Queen in deep mourning entered, leaning on the arm of the Princess of Wales, and followed by Princess Christian, the Princesses Louise and Beatrice, and Princess Frederica of Hanover, the royal party being conducted by the Lord Chamberlain to seats near the choir steps. The Duchess of Albany and the Duchess of Edinburgh were unable, from the state of their health, to attend the funeral. As the coffin, every movement of which was regulated by the word of command spoken by the officer appointed for the duty, passed through the screen and entered the choir, the Queen and Princesses rose as if to greet him who came thus for the last time among them. The rest of the company had remained standing from the moment of the Queen's entrance. The Dean of Windsor read the Funeral Service. When the choir sang the anthem, "Blessed are the Departed," the Queen again rose. Lord Brooke, a young man like the Prince who was gone, who had been with him at Oxford, was one of the most intimate of his friends, and had been named one of the executors of his will, threw, with evident emotion, the handful of earth on the coffin while the Dean recited "Earth to earth, ashes to ashes, dust to dust."

After the singing of the hymn, "Lead kindly light," during which her Majesty stood, she and the Princesses quitted the chapel. Garter-King- at-Arms having proclaimed the style and titles of the deceased, the coffin was lowered into the vault below St. George's Chapel, the Prince of Wales gazing sadly on its descent. The Queen, with her long discipline of sorrow, had in the middle of her affliction preserved her coolness throughout the trying ceremony. Prince Leopold, Duke of Albany, had almost completed his thirty-first year. The anniversary of his birthday was on the second day after his funeral.

The Queen has left her mark on the palaces and humbler houses which have been her homes. In indicating it we have nothing to do with grey Windsor in its historical glories, or even in its more picturesque lights. We leave behind the Waterloo Gallery, the Garter-room and the quaint cottages of the Poor Knights in order to point out the touches which are the tokens of Queen Victoria's presence. Though she dwelt here principally in the bright days of her early reign, the chief signs which she will leave behind her are those of her widowhood and of the faithful heart which has never forgotten its kindred dead. The most conspicuous work of the Queen's is the restoration and rechristening of the Wolsey Chapel. As the Albert Chapel, the beautiful little building is fall of the thought of him who was once master here. Its rich mosaics, stained glass, "pictures for eternity" fretted in marble, scriptural allegories of all the virtues—the very medallions of his children which surmount these unfading pictures, are all in his honour. Specially so is the pure white marble figure of the Prince, represented as a knight in armour, lying sword in hand, his feet against the hound—the image of loyalty, while round the pedestal is carved his name and state, and the place of his burial, with the epitaph which fits him well, "I have fought the good fight, I have finished my course."

In St. George's Chapel her Majesty has erected five monuments. A recumbent marble figure on an alabaster sarcophagus is to her father, who was so fond of the infant daughter whom he left a helpless baby. A white marble statue, larger than life, in royal robes, is to the man who took the Duke of Kent's place, Leopold I., King of the Belgians, of whom his niece could cause to be written with perfect truth "who was as a father to her, and she was to him as a daughter." This statue is reared near the well-known monument to the dead King's never forgotten first wife, Princess Charlotte of Wales. [Footnote: Princess Alice mentions in one of her published letters that King Leopold had entertained a wish that he might be buried in England.] The third and fourth monuments are to the Queen's aunt and cousin, the good Duchess of Gloucester and the late King of Hanover. The last was executed by the Queen's nephew, Count Gleichen (Prince Victor Hohenlohe). The inscription has several pathetic allusions. "Here has come to rest among his kindred, the royal family of England, George V., the last King of Hanover." "Receiving a kingdom which cannot be moved." "In this light he shall see light." The fifth monument has been raised to a young eastern prince, son of Theodore, King of Abyssinia, who came to England as a lad and died here "I was a stranger and ye took me in" is the epitaph.

At the entrance to the fine corridor which runs round two sides of the quadrangle of the Castle, and forms a matchless in-door promenade, is Theed's beautiful group of the Queen and the Prince, conceived and worked out after his death, with the solemn parting of two hearts tenderly attached as the motive of the whole. The figures are not only ideally graceful while the likeness in each is carefully preserved, the expression is beyond praise. The wife clings, in devotion so perfect that impassioned hope contends with chill despair, to the arm of the husband who looks down on her whom he loves best, with fond encouragement and the peace of the blessed already settling on the stainless brow. The inscription is from Goldsmith's "Deserted Village"— "Allur'd to brighter worlds and led the way,"

It is part of an exquisite passage:—

"And as a bird each fond endearment tries
  To tempt its new-fledg'd offspring to the skies,
He tried each art, reprov'd each dull delay,
  Allur'd to brighter worlds, and led the way."

The corridor, among its innumerable vases, cabinets, and pictures of kings and great men— including a fine portrait of Sir Walter Scott— has a whole series of pictures illustrating, the leading events of her Majesty's life, from her "First Council," by Wilkie, through her marriage, the baptisms of the Princess Royal and the Prince of Wales, the first reception of Louis Philippe, &c., &c., to the Princess Royal's marriage.

The white drawing-room, said to be a favourite room of her Majesty's, is not far from her private sitting-room on the south-east side of the quadrangle which looks out on the Long Walk and

Windsor Forest, the white drawing-room commanding the Home Park.

Going down the stately double avenue of elms called the Long Walk, a lodge and side walk at no great distance lead to Frogmore, with its mausoleum half hidden in luxuriant foliage. In the octagonal building, which forms a cross, and is richly decorated with coloured marbles, is the famous recumbent figure of the Prince in white marble by Baron Marochetti. When the Queen's time comes, which her people pray may still be far distant, she will rest by her husband's side, and a similar statue to his will mark where she lies. Memorials of Princess Alice and of her Majesty's dead grandchildren are also here.

The late Duchess of Kent is buried in a separate vault beneath a dome supported by pillars of polished granite and surrounded by a parapet with balconies. In the upper chamber, lit from the top by stained glass, is a statue of the Duchess, by Theed.

40717789R00175

Made in the USA
Middletown, DE
20 February 2017